CONTENTS

GW00567298

Introduction

According to *Zōhyō Monogatari* (literally 'The Soldier's Tale'), 'When faced with an enemy on horseback the best course of action is to shoot the horse first and then the man. However, everything depends upon the timing; sometimes it is better to shoot the man and let the riderless horse run off into the enemy lines and create havoc' (Sasama 1968: 363). *Zōhyō Monogatari* is believed to have been compiled by a high-ranking samurai general during the peaceful Edo Period (1603–1868), probably sometime around 1649. The book is essentially a training manual for those officers who had command of the ashigaru (literally the 'light feet'), the foot soldiers in a contemporary Japanese army. The passage refers specifically to the deployment of organized ashigaru weapon squads against elite mounted samurai, the dramatic contrast in both weaponry and status that is the theme of this book.

Around 1640 the need for expert advice on how to deal with such a confrontation between troop types was taken for granted. In 1540, however, when wars were still being fought, providing such advice would have been seen as an insult to samurai pride, because the samurai regarded themselves not only as elite warriors but also as the only real warriors in Japan. The mounted samurai despised the foot soldiers against whom they were sometimes compelled to fight, and indeed many of the lower-class troops deployed at that time were still being casually recruited into an army by the prospect of loot and just as casually dismissed. They were contemptuously regarded as ill-disciplined mobs that could be dispersed as carelessly as they had once been recruited, so to a samurai the concept of 'mounted samurai versus ashigaru' in any serious confrontational sense would have been a ridiculous idea. It would require a military revolution to make the samurai change their minds, and this is the story of how that revolution happened when the unquestionable notion of samurai supremacy was seriously challenged.

OPPOSITE
The theme of this book is the contrast between the proud and magnificent mounted samurai and the lowly ashigaru, and the appearance of the former is summed up in this illustration of Naitō Ienaga (1546–1600), shown here posed on a general's camp stool in a painting in Nobeoka Museum. Naitō Ienaga served Tokugawa Ieyasu (1542–1616) and is depicted here as a samurai archer like his noble ancestors with an ornate fur-covered quiver and a lacquered bow. His armour is nevertheless a practical battledress of the Sengoku Period. He has a sword and dagger at his belt. This painting sums up the idea of the elite samurai.

The subsequent 'mounted samurai versus ashigaru' confrontations described in this book would become a collision of tactics, social attitudes and even Japanese culture itself. The three battles chosen as case studies took place against a backdrop of seemingly unending strife, because by the 1540s Japan had been a country at war with itself for almost 100 years. The central authority maintained for centuries by the Shogun – a position equivalent to that of a military dictator – had virtually collapsed, leaving the provinces of Japan as lawless places where rival warlords called daimyo (literally 'big names') engaged in a series of local civil wars. Later historians would call the era 'The Age of Warring States' (1467–1603). As time went by some daimyo inevitably prospered and grew stronger while others failed, a situation that became abundantly clear to the first European visitors to Japan who arrived from Portugal in 1543. The country may have been nominally united under the Shogun by the grace of the sacred emperor, a man who (the Portuguese quickly discovered) possessed even less political power than the Shogun, but in practical terms no one seemed able to control the leaders of the petty kingdoms with which the incoming merchants, missionaries and traders exclusively had to deal.

The other observation which the Portuguese would have made very early on in their relations with Japan was that the fighting between these rival daimyo seemed to be conducted by armies of elite warriors called samurai. Most samurai rode horses, carried long spears and wore elaborate armour that looked very strange to anyone accustomed to the smooth iron plates worn by Europe's own noble knights. The more astute Portuguese observers might also have noted that in addition to these splendid warriors a daimyo's army would

ABOVE RIGHT
The first ashigaru to be used in daimyo armies were casually recruited and poorly armed, as shown by this representative group in a detail from *Ehon Toyotomi Kunkoki*. Only one ashigaru has a proper spear. His companion has a spear made out of a piece of cut bamboo. A third ashigaru has an improvised weapon made by tying a sickle to a pole. All three ashigaru have swords at their belts but are otherwise without any defensive armour or weaponry.

MAP KEY

The three 'samurai versus ashigaru' conflicts described in this book were important milestones in the strategic ambitions of the Takeda family. Each of the three battles was the culmination of a particular military campaign conducted by the Takeda as part of a programme to extend their influence beyond their landlocked home province of Kai (modern-day Yamanashi Prefecture), which was looked down upon and defended by huge mountains including the famous Mount Fuji. The provinces through which the competing armies marched were dominated by these mountains, now known as the Japan Alps, which are separated from the Pacific Coast by a comparatively narrow strip of flat land. In 1540 the mountains could only be crossed in two ways: by a few long-established mountain passes or by taking more tortuous routes that followed the flow of a number of rivers. The location of the Takeda headquarters at Tsutsujigasaki

(modern-day Kōfu City) and the presence of hostile enemies to the east therefore required the Takeda armies to begin all three campaigns by marching north. In 1548 Takeda Shingen carried on northwards to confront Murakami Yoshikiyo, who was based at the castle of Katsurao, at Uedahara. In 1572 and 1575 the Takeda armies swung round to the south-west from the area of Lake Suwa to threaten the territories of Oda Nobunaga and Tokugawa Ieyasu. The 1572 advance eventually split into four separate movements. Nobunaga's key positions were Gifu in Mino Province and Kiyosu in Owari Province. The Tokugawa targets were Ieyasu's Hamamatsu Castle in Tōtōmi Province and his son Nobuyasu's Okazaki Castle in Mikawa Province. Other battles and castles indicated here, such as Takatenjin and Kawanakajima, played a role in separate conflicts involving the Takeda and are described in the text.

probably include many foot soldiers, although they were a very mixed bag. Some were lucky enough to serve on a long-term basis as servants, labourers, grooms and weapon-carriers for their betters. Others were the inadequately protected and poorly disciplined ashigaru. Some daimyo, however – the more successful ones, as future events would demonstrate – had begun to organize their ashigaru in disciplined fighting units, retaining them in their service beyond any immediate campaign and even entrusting them with the traditional samurai weapons of bows and spears with which to bring down enemy samurai from their horses.

This positive attitude towards ashigaru was a vision of the future for Japanese warfare in which the newly arrived Portuguese merchants would play an unexpected role, because in 1543 they had brought with them some matchlock muskets, a type of firearm also called an arquebus. The Shimazu daimyo of Satsuma Province (modern-day Kagoshima Prefecture) where the Portuguese first landed had immediately appreciated the implication of these weapons, which were far superior to the simple Chinese handguns then being used in Japan. Within a few years daimyo elsewhere in Japan would be deploying home-produced Japanese matchlock muskets on battlefields and during castle attacks and using them to good effect. This study traces how that important development came about and how it helped disciplined foot soldiers to confront mounted samurai.

Three key battles fought by the Takeda family – one of Japan's greatest samurai clans – illustrate the shift in thinking that brought about Japan's infantry revolution. The elite mounted warriors of the Takeda fought under their illustrious leader Takeda Shingen Harunobu and provide the best examples in Japanese history of classic mounted samurai warfare, although quite early on in his career Shingen (the Buddhist name by which he is commonly known) had begun to appreciate the potential of disciplined ashigaru. That realization was given shocking confirmation in the first case

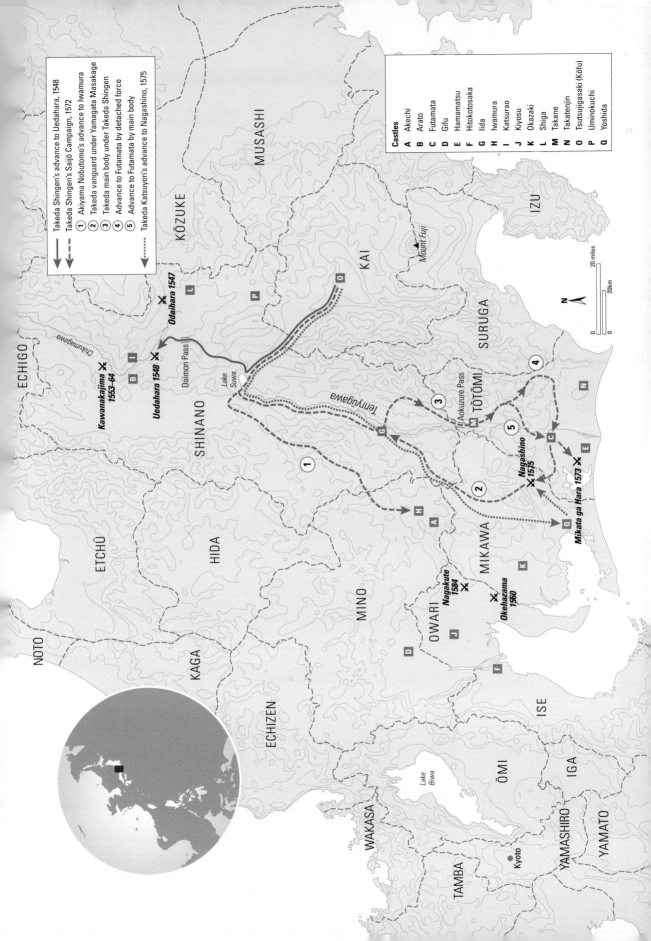

Takeda Shingen's advance to Uedahara, 1548

Takeda Shingen's Saijō Campaign, 1572

① Akiyama Nobutomo's advance to Iwamura
② Takeda vanguard under Yamagata Masakage
③ Takeda main body under Takeda Shingen
④ Advance to Futamata by detached force
⑤ Advance to Futamata by main body
⑥ Takeda Katsuyori's advance to Nagashino, 1575

Castles
A Akechi
B Arato
C Futamata
D Gifu
E Hamamatsu
F Hitokotosaka
G Iida
H Iwamura
I Katsurao
J Kiyosu
K Okazaki
L Shiga
M Takane
N Takatenjin
O Tsutsujigasaki (Kōfu)
P Uminokuchi
Q Yoshida

ECHIGO

KŌZUKE

MUSASHI

KAI

Mount Fuji

IZU

SURUGA

Chikumagawa

Kawanakajima 1553–64

Odaihara 1547

Uedahara 1548

Daimon Pass

Lake Suwa

SHINANO

Tenryugawa

Aokuzure Pass

TŌTŌMI

③

M

⑤

C

N

E

④

G

①

Nagashino 1575

Q

Mikata ga Hara 1573

H

A

②

MIKAWA

K

ECHIGO

ETCHŪ

HIDA

NOTO

KAGA

MINO

OWARI

Nagakute 1584

J

Okehazama 1560

ECHIZEN

D

F

ISE

WAKASA

Lake Biwa

ŌMI

IGA

Kyoto

TAMBA

YAMASHIRO

YAMATO

N

20 miles

20km

O

Mount Fuji

A beautiful example of an ornate *teppō* (matchlock musket or arquebus). Introduced into Japan by the Portuguese in 1543, matchlock muskets would revolutionize Japanese warfare when they were deployed correctly, and that required a sensible use of the lower-class ashigaru, who could be trained to fire them in massive and disciplined volleys.

study in this book: the battle of Uedahara in 1548, when mounted samurai from the Takeda suffered a reversal against the ashigaru spearmen and archers of the Murakami clan. All that either side had then in the way of firearms were a handful of simple Chinese handguns that may not even have been used. In the second case study, the battle of Mikata ga Hara in 1573, Shingen's horsemen faced squads of ashigaru armed with European-style firearms alongside archers and spearmen, although the battlefield environment prevented them from being used effectively. Instead, Mikata ga Hara became the last triumph of Shingen's mounted samurai against disordered ashigaru. The situation then changed dramatically in the year 1575 when, ironically, it would be the Takeda's greatest enemy – an up-and-coming young daimyo called Oda Nobunaga – who would show Japan how to deploy lower-class troops in the most effective manner. The mounted samurai of the Takeda under Shingen's son and heir Takeda Katsuyori were defeated at the ensuing battle of Nagashino where the disciplined firepower and defensive spears of lowly ashigaru played a key role.

Modern reproductions of the fences used by Oda Nobunaga's matchlock musketeers at Nagashino, looking from within them across the valley where the Takeda horsemen charged in 1575. The fields are full of young rice plants. The three battles examined in this book were fought on flat plains containing fertile paddy fields that would be used otherwise for producing rice, and the men who grew the food for the samurai were the same men who would fight for and against them as ashigaru. Rice is cultivated in carefully maintained paddy fields that require intensive work, so the usual campaigning season for Japanese warfare began once the harvest had been gathered and the cooler winds had allowed the fields to dry out and harden. This was the environment in which samurai fought ashigaru: their enemies on the battlefield but the producers of the food that everyone needed.

The Opposing Sides

STATUS, RECRUITMENT AND MOTIVATION

The samurai

In social terms the samurai cherished an ideal of themselves as a landowning military aristocracy who could leave the business of farming to others, although it would not be until around the 1590s that it became the norm for a member of the samurai class to be defined solely as someone who did nothing but fight. Otherwise they were mainly *jizamurai* (samurai of the land) who combined the roles of warrior and owner of a smallholding and would not be too proud to get their hands dirty in a paddy field. It would be personal opportunity or promotion gained by bravery on the battlefield that enabled a *jizamurai* to move closer to the ideal of the perfect mounted warrior who had the wealth and connections to live exclusively as a military gentleman: a status that was then really only enjoyed by a daimyo's family members or his long-standing hereditary retainers.

On the battlefield these proud elite samurai were the knights of Old Japan, and just like the European knights they placed a huge emphasis on tradition and precedence when it came to waging war. Their imaginations were fed by numerous heroic tales of their ancestors, whose exploits had grown considerably in the telling. These almost legendary figures had been noble mounted archers with close imperial connections, who – so the stories related – fought only with worthy opponents whom they would challenge to single combat in the midst of a battle. If victorious they would take their enemy's head; if defeated they would commit honourable suicide. It is true that instances of *ikki uchi* (single horseman fighting) still occurred during the Sengoku Period, but they now tended only to be curtain-raisers to a battle or a siege, where a successful challenge in view of everyone could greatly influence morale. When the armies actually clashed something approaching mass cavalry deployment was the norm for samurai warfare.

The ashigaru

The ultimate origins of the men who made up the ranks of the ashigaru foot soldiers were the rice fields on which everyone's survival depended. Most of Japan's agricultural workers were simple farmers who owned none of the lands on which they worked so hard, but in the chaos of the Sengoku Period an escape from that punishing life could be found by serving a daimyo in war. Some of these willing recruits provided simple yet vital support functions such as baggage carrying, and as many as 40 per cent of the total number of troops in a typical army performed similar non-combatant duties. Those whose origins lay in criminal activities such as mountain banditry or piracy tended to be employed for espionage and infiltration and other high-risk operations: tasks that would eventually give rise to the legends of the ninja. Those men were also given the sordid tasks of abducting other farmers from rival provinces to work a daimyo's fields or of scavenging a battlefield for discarded weapons once the fighting was over, leaving the serious business of warfare to the noble samurai and the trusted foot soldiers who supported them.

At this time in history a foot soldier could achieve glory, reward and even promotion to the samurai ranks by his conduct on the battlefield in the aforementioned roles or in the newly created weapon squads. One enlightened early daimyo from the Asakura family commented that if 1,000 spears could be purchased for the price of one superlative sword then it should be the spears for ashigaru that made their way into the shopping basket rather than the fine sword for a samurai (Sasama 1968: 289). Takeda Shingen fully appreciated that point, and when he took over Kai Province following the deposition of his father in 1541 he began a thorough review of the province's military strength. One realization that he came to was that too much reliance had been placed upon pedigree and ancestry, whereby the fighting strength of the Takeda (as it was

with most other clans) had depended upon a system called *korōtō*, which literally meant 'sons of vassal bands'. To create an army based almost exclusively on the sons of samurai, backed up by casually recruited ashigaru used for menial tasks or fairly disorganized weapon work, was inefficient and unnecessary, so Shingen cast his net wider and offered places in his army to sturdy sons of non-landowning farmers. Military skills and bravery, rather than family connections, allowed these men entry to the ashigaru weapon squads of bows (*yumi-gumi*), spears (*yari-gumi*) and firearms (*teppō-gumi*) and even promotion within the samurai ranks.

Ashigaru were first attracted to armies and fighting because of the prospect of loot, but mundane tasks such as raiding were still assigned to them after they formed weapon squads in a daimyo's army. In this painting we see 'regular' ashigaru doing some official looting on a grand scale on behalf of the Asakura daimyo in 1566. Their spoils even include a temple bell which they have loaded on to a cart.

It is unusual to find a print that shows a samurai charging forwards against a hail of bullets from ashigaru musketeers; the topic was less than flattering for a proud mounted warrior. The figure depicted here is Baba Nobuharu, one of Takeda Shingen's 'Twenty-Four Generals', who was killed during the battle of Nagashino in 1575. Here he rides to his death.

COMMAND, CONTROL AND ORGANIZATION

The samurai

Every samurai army in Sengoku Period Japan came under the supreme command of its daimyo. He was the head of the family and would certainly be present on the battlefield during a major campaign unless age or injury forced him to remain behind. The presence of two rival daimyo was a factor in each of the three battles described in this book. Very little is known about the command structure under Murakami Yoshikiyo (1501–73) at Uedahara, but, as the following pages will show, it proved to be very effective and probably differed little from the well-documented organization of his enemies the Takeda, whose tried-and-tested model is described in detail in the great Takeda chronicle called *Kōyō Gunkan*. At Uedahara and Mikata ga Hara the Takeda army fought under the great Takeda Shingen Harunobu (1521–73), whose influence would last beyond his death and whose brooding, ghostly presence may be discerned even at Nagashino. Shingen's military leadership was characterized by a strategic vision that went far beyond the immediate tactical needs of any current battle, of which there would be many. Shingen also inspired his men, receiving decades of loyalty from his chiefs of staff known popularly as the Takeda 'Twenty-Four Generals'.

The command structure immediately below the daimyo was fairly common whichever clan is under discussion; Murakami Yoshikiyo, Tokugawa Ieyasu and Oda Nobunaga each had their own equivalent (and number) of the Takeda's 'Twenty-Four Generals'. These *taishō* (generals) were the *crème de la crème* of the elite samurai who were closest to the daimyo and were called his *hatamoto* (those who stand beneath the flag), an expression that could be taken literally on the battlefield. As part of the daimyo's 'household division', the top generals occupied senior administrative and leadership roles, ranging

RIGHT
Takeda Shingen Harunobu (1521–73), the great leader of the much-feared mounted samurai of Kai Province, shown here on a painted scroll in the Nagashino Castle Preservation Hall. He wears his favourite helmet which was ornamented by a plume of white horsehair. Shingen likened himself to the god Fudō Myo-ō ('the immoveable wisdom king') who is usually depicted seated on a rock surrounded by flames, holding a sword in his right hand and a coiled rope in his left, and surviving portraits of Shingen show a strong if somewhat corpulent man who projected just such an intimidating image. Yet Shingen was also renowned for the successful way in which he governed his province, and his farmers were certainly not like many of their contemporaries who readily deserted one daimyo for another, but stayed under the protection of their fierce lord and his prosperous economy. Most tellingly, Shingen's headquarters building was not a castle. Instead he ruled from a *yashiki* (mansion) called Tsutsujigasaki, which is now the site of the Takeda Shrine in Kōfu City.

FAR RIGHT
Takeda Katsuyori (1546–82) was the son and heir of Takeda Shingen. Katsuyori was an accomplished general both in carrying out castle attacks and in leading mounted samurai, but he never gained the confidence of the 'Twenty-Four Generals' that Shingen had enjoyed during his lifetime. The campaign of 1575 that led to the battle of Nagashino was conducted against their recommendations and ended in disaster.

from strategic planning to communications, while hundreds more samurai and ashigaru stood 'under the flag' as the daimyo's personal bodyguard. If the account of a particular battle tells us that an attack has penetrated the ranks of a daimyo's *hatamoto* then it is clear that a very serious situation has developed.

The units in which the *hatamoto* served were usually called *ban* (guards), and their ranks included the elite *go umamawari-shū* (Horse Guards) whose role was not merely that of protecting the daimyo, because they led some of the fiercest recorded attacks in history. The *hatamoto* also included *kachi* (Foot Guards) and *koshō*, whose title can be suitably translated as 'squires' or 'pages'. The latter were often the sons of retainers, but the duties assigned to these young men were far from ceremonial because they fought within the *hatamoto* as part of their training for higher office.

Some of the most senior generals had commanding roles over the samurai on the battlefield, and most of the samurai serving under these *samurai-taishō* were assigned to groups varying in size from ten to 100 men, although it is often difficult to ascertain their exact numbers on any particular battlefield because they would always be accompanied by their own *kinju* (followers). These men were not assigned to other units but stayed to support their personal leaders. They appear on painted screens as little clusters of loyal samurai and foot soldiers standing around their masters as bodyguards and servants, and would have been provided by the retainer himself as part of his obligation to the daimyo. A samurai of even the most modest means would have had at least one armed servant. *Ki*, the counting suffix for horsemen, therefore referred to the *kiba musha-gumi* (man-and-horse samurai group), rather than just the individual mounted warrior.

To some extent the command-and-control structure of the fighting samurai was a very fragmented one when compared to the rigid discipline that had to be used for the ashigaru. A general in charge of elite samurai had

Tokugawa Ieyasu, daimyo of the Mikawa and Tōtōmi provinces, who was defeated by Takeda Shingen at the battle of Mikata ga Hara in 1573, is shown here on a painted hanging scroll in the Nagashino Castle Preservation Hall. The museum is built on the site of the Takeda's greatest defeat, a battle in which Ieyasu would participate.

A hanging scroll in the Nagashino Castle Preservation Hall showing the 'Twenty-Four Generals' of the Takeda under their leader Shingen. The term 'Twenty-Four Generals' is in fact a later invention, but the chain of command of the Takeda did indeed pass through this group of men between about 1540 and 1582. They were all leaders of mounted samurai apart from those who had special responsibility for the ashigaru, an honourable position nevertheless. The group's composition would change greatly over time (two early members were killed at Uedahara in 1548), but their devoted service never changed. On the battlefield they commanded the Takeda divisions of vanguard, main body, wings and rear guard where they excelled above everything else in the traditional samurai skills of mounted warfare.

to cope with supreme individualists who were more used to giving orders than receiving them. They may have been loyal to the point of death, but the demands of personal glory were always present, and a particular samurai's personal attendants would be more cognizant of their master's needs than their own place in any overall strategy. Orders flowed down from the daimyo using drums, conch shells, signalling flags and through the highly mobile mounted *tsukai-ban* (Courier Guards), but at the end of the chain of samurai command there were no packed ranks of European-style cavalry but mixed groups of proud warriors and their followers. As we shall see, the fate of Shingen's general Itagaki Nobukata at Uedahara bore a direct relationship to this very loose composition and command structure.

The ashigaru

As in the case of the aforementioned samurai organizations, the well-documented structure of the Takeda army's ashigaru corps was probably typical of any daimyo who properly appreciated the contribution his lower-class recruits could make. It was noted earlier that Takeda Shingen cast his net widely in seeking out military talent, but his innovative recruitment programme of local farmers did not mean that class distinction was abolished, because the new recruits from the villages were placed in appropriate units

Oda Nobunaga (1534–82) was the first of Japan's unifiers. He was ahead of his time in his appreciation of the potential of the use of firearms on the Japanese battlefield, and implemented his ideas in a very successful form at the battle of Nagashino in 1575, where his ashigaru musketeers broke the charge of the mounted samurai of the Takeda.

under the overall command of officers who were drawn from the samurai ranks under the overall *ashigaru-taishō* (general of ashigaru), in which role several of his 'Twenty-Four Generals' served proudly. Saigusa Moritomo, who was killed at the battle of Nagashino, was an *ashigaru-taishō*. Similar structures were found in other daimyo armies.

Under the *ashigaru-taishō* and his samurai assistants were two ranks of officers of ashigaru status who were broadly equivalent to NCOs. The *kashira* (senior officer) would normally have command of companies that were homogeneous in terms of weaponry, so they were therefore usually referred to as 'weapon'-*kumigashira* ('group leaders') using one of the three prefixes *yumi-* (bow), *yari-*(spear) or *teppō-*(musket). For much of the Sengoku Period matchlock muskets and bows were mixed up together, with the archers being required to keep up the fire while the musketeers were reloading, as is illustrated by *Kōyō Gunkan*, which notes a unit of 'ten *teppō* and five bows' at one stage in the Takeda army's development (Sasama 1969: 72).

Serving under the *kashira* were the *kogashira* (literally 'lesser leaders'). To give an example, in one particular section of *Kōyō Gunkan* one ashigaru *kumigashira* has five *kogashira* serving under him to command his company of 75 archers and 75 musketeers, so that each *kogashira* had responsibility for 30 men (Sasama 1969: 72). In the case of mixed squads of archers and musketeers the *teppō-kogashira* would work in close conjunction with the archers' own *yumi-kogashira*, whose responsibilities included judging the distance between

ABOVE LEFT
This illustration from the 17th-century *Zōhyō Monogatari* shows a *teppō-kogashira*, who would have had immediate command over a group of ashigaru musketeers. He is ready for his duties with a spare fuze cord wrapped around his left arm and a bamboo *mashaku* (ranging pole) with which to judge distance between his squad and the advancing enemy horsemen.

ABOVE RIGHT
In this detail from *Ehon Taikō ki* ashigaru musketeers, wearing headbands rather than helmets, discharge their weapons from a kneeling position. The musketeers who operated during the four decades after 1540 are likely to have been dressed as simply as these musketeers.

his archers and their target in order to give them the appropriate command. To help him predict the range the *yumi-kogashira* carried a bamboo *mashaku* (ranging pole). He also ensured that there was a steady supply of arrows from the storage boxes. Similarly, the *teppō-kogashira* also used a ranging pole to judge distance for the firearms and would oversee the distribution of bullets, which were stored in large bullet boxes carried by other ashigaru and then transferred to the bullet pouches worn at the musketeers' belts. He would also have around his left arm one or more spare smouldering fuzes in case any musketeer's fuze became extinguished.

The first exchange of fire on a battlefield was likely to be between the rival musket troops, firing at a maximum range of about 100m. As the *ashigaru-taishō* was probably in the most forward position of the samurai commanders, he would be able to judge when the initial firing had disorientated the enemy sufficiently for a charge to be ordered. At this point, according to theory, the ashigaru spearmen would advance and the samurai would attack on foot or from horseback. While this was going on the ashigaru missile troops would be reorganized by the *kashira* under the protection of other ashigaru spearmen. Throughout all of these operations the *ashigaru-taishō*'s judgement was crucial, and Sasama notes an interesting miscalculation involving the musket corps of Ōtomo Yoshimune (1558–1605) during the Korean Invasion of 1592–93. More than 1,200 musketeers discharged their weapons repeatedly at too great a range, leaving them vulnerable to an attack by advancing enemy archers. They were saved by Harada Iyo (a man probably of *kashira* rank), who had made sure that some bullets were kept back in reserve (Sasama 1968: 364).

TACTICS

The samurai

When charging into battle mounted samurai relied on terror, shock and the cutting power of their spears and other edged weapons. According to the writings of various contemporary schools of horsemanship, there were three basic techniques of mounted warfare to be found on a typical battlefield. The first was called *norikomi* ('ride and enter'), where horsemen acted essentially as *monomi* (scouts) to carry out a reconnaissance-in-force, riding into the enemy lines and fighting only briefly before rapidly withdrawing. The second was *norikiri* ('ride and cut'), where horsemen were sent into a breach created in the enemy lines by missile fire to exploit the disorder. Finally, *norikuzushi* ('ride and destroy') was the classic cavalry charge whereby mounted samurai assaulted the lines of enemy ashigaru to break and overrun them by their impact.

Norikuzushi was traditionally regarded as a tactic in which the Takeda excelled, a mode of warfare in which Shingen and his army enjoyed an enviable reputation that went far back into the wider history of Eastern Japan (Tanaka 1997: 108). The flat lands around the Kantō plain had always been famous for breeding horses and as early as the Nara Period (710–794) reference was being made to the speedy 'black horses of Kai Province' (Maruta 1988: 170). This

reputation continued into the Sengoku Period. Neither the sound of guns nor the smell of burning frightened the Takeda mounts, but it is important to note that Japanese horses at the time of Shingen were smaller than the ones we see today in samurai films. This was confirmed in 1989 when archaeologists excavated a horse's skeleton from the site of Takeda Shingen's mansion at Tsutsujigasaki in modern-day Kōfu City. Its height to the shoulder was just under 1.2m and its weight was estimated as 250kg, which compares to 1.6m and 500kg for a modern thoroughbred.

So of what did a 'cavalry charge' consist when it was delivered by these horses? First, they would gallop more slowly than the horses used in samurai films, and as the samurai steed had to carry an armoured rider the velocity and momentum of a charge would be that much less than that of a modern racehorse. Mounted samurai nevertheless had the ability to deliver a considerable shock, although Japanese cavalry actions would have produced nothing like the impact of European knights in full body armour and carrying stout lances. A further hindrance was the fact that each samurai horseman would also be accompanied by his personal attendants running as fast as they could, whom a samurai tried not to leave behind. The names such as 'spear carrier' that were given to these men were not honorary titles but descriptions of actual functions carried out as part of the small supportive fighting unit. Other warriors who fought dismounted would also be needed to exploit any breach created by a mounted charge, so mounted samurai operating in a *norikuzushi* manner would not wish to get too far in front of their troops following on foot. The distinction found during, say, the Napoleonic era between cavalry and infantry was

ABOVE LEFT
In this detail from *Ehon Toyotomi Kunkoki* a mounted samurai moves into battle supported by his personal attendants. He is particularly well supported by a squad of musketeers. In front one ashigaru carries a bale of rice. Another ashigaru is his personal standard bearer.

ABOVE RIGHT
On this painted screen of the battle of Sekigahara (1600) in the Watanabe Museum in Tottori a mounted samurai is shown with his typical band of personal followers of ashigaru rank. They would include weapon carriers, grooms, servants and bodyguards. The samurai, in a suitably fine suit of armour, is mounting his horse from the left side.

This haughty and magnificent figure is Sakakibara Yasumasa (1548–1606), one of Tokugawa Ieyasu's *shitennō* ('Four Guardian Kings'), the closest to their leader among Ieyasu's *hatamoto* (those who stand beneath the flag). Sakakibara Yasumasa fought at Anegawa (1570), Mikata ga Hara, Nagashino and Sekigahara (1600). His sneering expression makes him the epitome of the proud samurai who is ready and waiting to cut down enemy ashigaru using his weapon of choice: a *nodachi*.

Weapons, dress and equipment

Sakakibara Yasumasa is well-armed with a sword (**1**) slung blade-downwards (*tachi*-style) from his belt and a large *nodachi* (extra-long sword; **2**).

As befitted their elite status, mounted samurai such as Yasumasa had always tried to look suitably splendid, although the *yoroi* style of armour – highly elaborate, multi-laced and multi-coloured rigid box-like armour with leather breastplate – once favoured by the mounted archers of the 12th century had now usually been replaced by a simpler type termed *dō-maru* armour. The absence of knots and small plates of armour provided fewer opportunities for an ashigaru spearman to make contact using a weapon and pull the rider from his horse. Shoulder guards and leg armour were also contoured, while the samurai's arms were enclosed in mail and plate sleeves that were very similar to those of an ashigaru. Yasumasa has, however, gone one better in terms of wearing a smoothly contoured armour, because his suit is based on a converted Portuguese breastplate called a *namban-dō* ('Southern Barbarian body armour') to which have been attached protective tassets (**3**) in the Japanese style called *kusazuri* ('grass rubbing'). Yasumasa is known to have owned this actual suit of armour which is now in Tokyo National Museum. The breastplate is lacquered to give it a russet-iron finish, as is the *namban kabuto*

(European helmet; **4**). Both were probably bullet-proof, and in typically flamboyant Japanese fashion the very plain helmet is adorned with a white horsehair plume. The *sode* (shoulder guards; **5**) are very small. The *kote* (sleeves; **6**), *suneate* (shin guards; **7**) and *haidate* (thigh guards; **8**) are all of a very basic and practical design that would have been worn by hundreds of samurai at the time, not just a general.

It was customary for samurai to wear a *sashimono* (back flag; **9**) on the back of the armour. Normally this would bear a simple and common design that indicated the wearer's unit. The device on it was often modelled on the family *mon* (badge), but as Yasumasa is a high-ranking commander his *sashimono* is unique to him alone, so he would have been instantly recognizable on the battlefield. Its shaft lay within a holder attached to the rear of the armour.

From the knees downwards Yasumasa is wearing apparel that all samurai shared with the ashigaru, including the useful and comfortable straw sandals (**10**). His horse has quite simple trappings that are typical of the age. The silken tassels (**11**) are largely decorative, but hanging down on either side of the saddle are two stout panels of leather (**12**) ornamented with gilt fittings. Their purpose is to protect the horse from being struck by the rider's heavy iron *abumi* (stirrups; **13**), slung from adjustable leather straps.

therefore by no means so clear-cut on a Sengoku Period battlefield, nor were the operations of the Takeda *kiba gundan* (mounted war-band) anything like the cavalry tactics of Mongol horsemen. The other consideration that would reduce the impact of a cavalry charge was of course the fact that as the samurai galloped into action the enemy ashigaru would be launching volleys of arrows and bullets towards them.

Even if the charging horseman survived the initial onslaught of arrows and bullets to engage at close quarters with the enemy, his opponent would not necessarily be another samurai who wished to engage him in honourable single combat as the legends related. Instead he would be more likely to encounter a small group of ashigaru intent on dragging him off his horse and stabbing him to death. Such a tragic end was of course directly related to the other factor that a Japanese general had to contend with: the samurai love for personal glory and the means of achieving it that were directly linked to the ancestral accomplishments noted earlier. It was not unheard of for a samurai horseman to deviate from the overall attack plan and go his own way to take the head of a promising opponent. If he was unsuccessful in this the isolated horseman could fall prey to a counter-attack by small groups of enemy ashigaru, as would happen to Itagaki Nobukata at the battle of Uedahara.

The ashigaru

The oldest established ashigaru group technique was that of deploying archers, because for many centuries bows and arrows had been the sole missile weapons deployed on Japanese battlefields apart from a few isolated incidents of stone-throwing. Their importance hardly decreased when firearms were introduced, and in *Hōjō Godai ki* we read, 'At this time guns were few but bows were many … They took note of a ranging arrow and fired bundles of arrows into the enemy ranks and disordered them' (Sasama 1968: 288). In the 1575 Uesugi muster rolls 1,018 ashigaru archers are listed beside only 321 musketeers. Occasionally we hear of archers acting as skirmishers or even sharpshooters, but the daimyo who deployed the ashigaru bowmen squads knew that the Hōjō's 'bundles of arrows' delivered in a coordinated manner was the best way to use archers against a mounted samurai charge or even an isolated individual horseman. Ideally, the arrow fire from the archer groups only began when the enemy samurai were within 50m range, but fear could drive archers to loose their arrows at threatening ranks of horsemen when they were as far as 150m away, so discipline was essential, as was a good supply of arrows. Ammunition was stored in large boxes called *yabako* that each held 100 arrows and were carried on another ashigaru's back. Because an archer whose arrows were spent was a vulnerable target the arrows in an archer's personal quiver would be left unused until the last moment, when the ashigaru might well be within touching distance of a hostile samurai's spear blade.

From 1543 onwards a greater firepower could be provided by the musketeers. When Portuguese matchlock muskets were first introduced into Japan in 1543 they may have been seen as prestige weapons for individual samurai, but things would soon change and the matchlock musket became regarded as primarily an ashigaru weapon. Over the next half-century the

ashigaru *teppō-gumi* (musket squads) gradually replaced the *yumi-gumi* (archery squads) as the main ranged-combat squads in a daimyo's army. The matchlock muskets they used were mass-produced and improved Japanese copies of the Portuguese originals. They were slow to load and inaccurate, but once their correct deployment was understood they became a huge asset because of their long range and the absence of a need for the years of training required to produce good archers. As skills developed cartridges were introduced, thus speeding up the process of loading, but these had not been invented by the time of Nagashino.

The third category of weapon squad – the ashigaru *yari-gumi* (spear squads) – almost always outnumbered all the missile troops within an army. Oda Nobunaga's *yari-gumi* made up 27 per cent of his ashigaru fighting force, compared to 13.5 per cent for the musketeers. Discipline was every bit as essential for the *yari-gumi* as it was for the missile troops. They may never have employed the 'push of pike' that occurred in contemporary Europe – a technique whereby rival hedgehogs of men collided, stuck fast and tried to force their opponents back – but close-rank fighting techniques were used, even if accounts of Japanese warfare suggest they involved much more fluid movement than was the case in European infantry warfare.

The spearmen would make ready by removing the scabbards from their spear blades and placing them in their belts or down their armour. They would then stand shoulder to shoulder, trying to keep their spear points in line and awaiting the command 'Uteya!', which means 'thrust'. If their opponents were other ashigaru the aim was to break their ranks and disorder

ABOVE LEFT

An ashigaru carrying the bullet box to supply his comrades in the *teppō-gumi* (musket squad). As well as the ammunition, he has a spare ramrod in case that of a musketeer should break in action. The picture is from *Zōhyō Monogatari.*

ABOVE RIGHT

A small group of ashigaru from about the 1540s are shown in this detail from *Ehon Taikō ki.* It illustrates the changes in weaponry that happened when ashigaru began to be valued and disciplined. They are well armed: one has a matchlock musket and another a bow, and the others wave swords bravely. They are wearing simple armour, although only one has head protection in the form of the ashigaru's *jingasa* (war hat).

This plate shows a typical ashigaru musketeer from the Takeda weapon squads at about the time of Mikata ga Hara. Still somewhat despised by the elite samurai, the ashigaru's inferior status is noticeable even in the physical state of this former farmer, because he is shorter in stature than Sakakibara Yasumasa, and his prematurely aged face shows nothing of the fine breeding of the upper classes. Nevertheless, as a musketeer he is something of an elite figure among the ashigaru. He has prepared his equipment carefully for action, and on the front of his *jingasa* and breastplate appears the *mon* of the Takeda family in which he serves proudly

Weapons, dress and equipment

This musketeer ashigaru is lightly armed and highly mobile. He is equipped with a matchlock musket (**1**), its fuze (**2**), a bullet pouch (**3**) two swords (**4**) and a powder flask (**5**). Spare ramrods (**6**) are held in the musket's leather case which now protrudes from his belt.

He is protected by a very plain *okashi-gusoku* ('munitions armour') without *haidate* (thigh guards). The first ashigaru who turned up to join a daimyo's armies would either have supplied their own home-made armour or wore old suits pilfered from former battlefields and stored in the villages. The daimyo who offered ashigaru regular employment strove towards a more uniform appearance and a better form of protection, although no ashigaru armour was ever of the quality worn by the samurai. It would instead be just a simple *okashi gusoku* ('loan armour' or 'munitions armour') usually of the *okegawa-dō* (barrel-shaped) style of a plain breastplate (**7**) with short *kusazuri* (hanging tassets; **8**). Armoured sleeves might be included,

but the biggest difference in appearance and protection came with the helmet. The ashigaru wore only a simple iron *jingasa* (war hat; **9**), which was usually shaped like a lampshade and had a cloth neck guard hanging from the rear to shade his neck from the sun if not from sword strokes. The members of the ashigaru weapon squads were identifiable on the battlefield under a common *hata-jirushi* (unit banner) together with some form of personal identification device such as a company flag, although in this particular case the ashigaru bears the clan's *mon* (badge; **10**) stencilled with lacquer on his armour and helmet.

Underneath his armour are short trousers (**11**) and a shirt that provide a little padding. He wears straw sandals (**12**) just like the samurai. His other equipment includes a bamboo water bottle (**13**), spare sandals (**14**) and a 'necklace' of ration bags (**15**), each containing rice for one meal.

ABOVE LEFT
This illustration from *Zōhyō Monogatari* shows the ashigaru whose responsibility it was to carry the *yabako* (arrow box) which contained 100 arrows for the archery squads. The *yumi-gumi* archers would use these arrows first in battle, keeping the ones in their quivers for use only at the last moment.

ABOVE RIGHT
A member of the ashigaru *yumi-gumi* is shown here in an illustration from *Zōhyō Monogatari*. He is stringing his bow. Note his fur-covered quiver and the spare bowstring reel hanging from his belt. Archers were the only missile troops in Japanese armies until the introduction of matchlock muskets in 1543.

them by inflicting as many casualties as possible. The spearmen would then be ordered to the flanks to let samurai through. The ashigaru spearmen might be allowed to take part in a pursuit, but their long spears would have been clumsy weapons for such encounters so it was normal for them to be pulled back into a new formation. If the spearmen's opponents were mounted samurai and there was nothing in the way of field defences such as were built at Nagashino, the cavalry charge would be received by the spearmen from a kneeling position. At the right moment they would be ordered to stand and, just like the musketeers, they would direct their weapons at the riders' horses. The dismounted samurai would then be left to be finished off (and his prized head collected) by the samurai. *Zōhyō Monogatari* states:

> When facing an attack by horsemen line up in one rank on one knee, lie the spear down and wait. When contact is imminent lift up the spear head to a level with the area of the horse's breast. When the point pierces the skin hold on to it. Whether you are cutting at men and horses, it may be that you will feel you are being forced to pull out the spear, and it is a general rule to stand fast to the bitter end and not throw the cooperative operation into disorder. (Sasama 1969: 68)

Ashigaru spearmen had much more freedom of movement and action when pursuing a disordered enemy, and it is on occasions like these (of which all three selected battles provide good examples) that we read of isolated samurai being surrounded by ashigaru spearmen acting in small groups rather than in long organized ranks. *Zōhyō Monogatari* provides a particularly vivid instance:

> Believing that I would be hit if I attacked him from the left I came at him from the right, taking a firm grip on the shaft of my spear and aiming at the horse's

rump. I tried to judge the best place to strike where it would not hit one of the horse's bones. I tried to stab it around the base of the tail, but when the spear blade met the horse it bounced off and flew about five ken away, and I slipped and fell down. If I had still been holding on to the spear when I fell the horse would have run off, but luckily I had let go of it as I fell and it made the horse stumble and collapse. The enemy fell off facing upwards so I could cut his head off with ease. (Sasama 1968: 367)

WEAPONS AND EQUIPMENT

The samurai

The collision between mounted samurai and masses of ashigaru on most Sengoku Period battlefields meant that the ideal world of honourable single combat which the samurai had imbibed from legends could hardly ever be realized in the press of battle, and the 16th-century mounted samurai's weaponry reflected one aspect of that harsh reality. Sengoku Period samurai had been fed on tales of mounted archery, and there were still a few samurai whose preferred individual weapon was the traditional *yumi* (longbow). Mounted archery was, however, a skill that required constant practice, and the use of bows from horseback was not conducive to the success of *norikuzushi* tactics, so the vast majority of the Takeda samurai wielded a pole-arm of some sort. The usual samurai *yari* (spear) – normally called a *mochi yari* (held spear) to distinguish it from the longer

The use of a *nodachi*, an extra-long type of sword, is shown here in a modern painting on the site of the battle of Anegawa in 1570. Makara Jūrōzaemon was a man of exceptional strength, which allowed him to wield this very clumsy weapon from a horse's back. In the rear an ashigaru is flung backwards by the impact.

ashigaru weapon – was about 4m long, and an interesting and authentic example of one presented to Hattori Hanzō by Tokugawa Ieyasu is still preserved in Tokyo. Its original shaft length was 3.1m, and originally it had a long blade (now broken) of 1.27m. The total length of the weapon was therefore 4.38m, of which the blade made up just over one-quarter. The weight of the remaining parts is 7.5kg, indicating that the original weight was about 12kg.

Mochi-yari were highly versatile weapons when wielded by strong and well-practised samurai. Spears could be couched like European lances but were far more likely to be swung freely from the saddle. When attacking another mounted samurai the greatest level of spear control was achieved by having one's opponent on one's left. The spear would be held with the right hand across the body, while the left hand controlled the horse. Otherwise the spear was held out to the side of the horse in the right hand and swung either in huge slashing strokes or with more delicacy and precision as a thrusting weapon. When attacking ashigaru or other samurai on foot a stabbing spear could be used like the lance of a Napoleonic-era light cavalryman, and there are illustrations of mounted samurai 'pig-sticking' unfortunate ashigaru on the ends of their spear blades. The momentum of the thrust could well lift the unfortunate victim into the air.

Other horsemen preferred the heavier types of pole-arms that were primarily cutting weapons rather than thrusting ones. These included *naginata* (glaives), which had a spear shaft on which was mounted a short curved blade; a *nagamaki* (a *naginata* with blade and shaft of equal length); or a *nodachi*, a very long sword that only a strongly built expert could wield from the saddle. All these weapons needed two hands rather than one, so it is difficult to see how they could be used at full gallop. We may therefore envisage them being used when the mounted samurai was engaged in a mêlée after the initial charge. One of his weapon carriers would exchange his master's *yari* for, say, a *nodachi*. The samurai would then wield the *nodachi* while two grooms steadied his horse for him. A classic example of *nodachi* use is the devastation wrought at the battle of Anegawa in 1570 by the giant Makara Jūrōzaemon, who lopped off limbs and heads as he swung the monstrous weapon from his saddle. When fighting ashigaru with these weapons the samurai would cut down at their opponent, just as would be done with a horseman's very sharp *katana* (samurai sword): the normal weapon of choice if one's spear was lost or broken. The horseman's elevated position and the forward momentum of the swing would add greatly to the force and cutting power of the descending blade.

Turning to the armour worn by the samurai, contemporary chronicles give a good idea of the effects of arrows and bullets on a samurai's armoured body. A direct arrow-hit between the eyes that avoided the peak of a samurai's helmet and his face mask would probably be instantly fatal, as is related in *Zōhyō Monogatari* in an anecdote about an ashigaru who had exhausted all his arrows but one:

> At that moment an enemy approached him with his mouth wide open like a crocodile's, so the ashigaru waited until he was as close as a spear length, and when he was as near as the length of the shaft he loosed the arrow, which pierced the

enemy through his mouth to the back of his neck and into the back plate of his armour. At this the enemy fell to the ground face upwards and the archer beheaded him. (Sasama 1968: 365)

It was far more usual for a samurai to die after sustaining multiple arrow hits. This was largely due to the impressive stopping power of their layers of armour, and the popular image from both woodblock prints and modern movies of a dying samurai crawling along like a porcupine with multiple arrows protruding from him is not too much of an exaggeration. Ashigaru bullets had much the same impact but their effective range was about two-and-a-half times that of arrows, which could kill at up to 30m compared to 50m for a bullet. The extreme range for both weapons was approximately 380m and 500m respectively (Futaki 1989, 16). During the battle of Hataya in 1600, a mounted samurai called Iida Harima-no Kami was felled by a distant bullet that appeared to come from nowhere:

He removed his helmet and gave it to an attendant to hold. Stretching his legs in the stirrups and shading his eyes with one hand he raised himself up, but a bullet

ABOVE LEFT
This is an excellent example of a very practical battledress armour for a samurai of the Sengoku Period. It has small shoulder plates, a bullet-proof layered iron breastplate and a multi-plate helmet with no unnecessary ornamentation.

ABOVE RIGHT
The effects of musket fire on a simple suit of armour are shown dramatically by this specimen on display in Matsumoto City Museum. There are three massive bullet holes in the breastplate.

came from somewhere and struck him on the forehead. The shot made him fall headlong from his horse. His followers were greatly concerned and tried to hold him to make him stand, but he had already died and was now a lifeless corpse. (Imamura 2005: 317)

The ashigaru

Ashigaru bows were made from deciduous wood faced with bamboo and lacquered to weatherproof them. The bow was bent against its natural curve and the pull of a bow could be so strong that it needed more than one person to string it. A spare bowstring on a reel would be worn at the archer's belt along with a quiver and a sword. A later development gave the archers the option of 'fixing bayonets' by fastening a small knife to the bow's tip, making it into a rudimentary spear known as a *hazu yari*. There are no descriptions of its use in the war chronicles, however, so the *hazu yari* probably owes its origin to the peaceful Edo Period. An account (possibly fictional) of its use appears in *Zōhyō Monogatari*, when an archer whose arrows have run out stabs an enemy samurai with his *hazu yari* with such force that the blade passes through the victim's face and out of his ear (Sasama 1969: 365).

The matchlock muskets used by the ashigaru produced quite a recoil and a lot of smoke. Unlike the heavier type of firearms that required a rest, however, the matchlock firearms used by the Japanese could be fired from the shoulder. In preparation for firing the leather bag in which the weapon was carried was removed and stuck into the musketeer's belt along with a supply of spare ramrods. Loading a matchlock musket was a slow and precise process. First some priming powder was introduced followed by the main charge and the bullet, which were rammed down. The *hibuta* (touch-hole cover) was then opened and priming powder inserted into the touch hole. After closing the *hibuta* for safety the *hibasami* (serpentine) was cocked and the end of the glowing and smouldering *hinawa* (match) was inserted into its jaws and fixed in place using a peg. If the *hinawa* was dropped in quickly or fitted badly the fire might go out, so a number of spare lighted fuzes were kept on a twig stuck into the ground. The musketeer's own lighted fuze was worn round his left arm and supported by

The fine detail of the spring and trigger of a Japanese matchlock musket. This example is in the Kunitomo Village Gun Museum in Nagahama. The very short stock was held in the right hand. Note the touch-hole cover, which has been closed as it would have been just prior to aiming and firing.

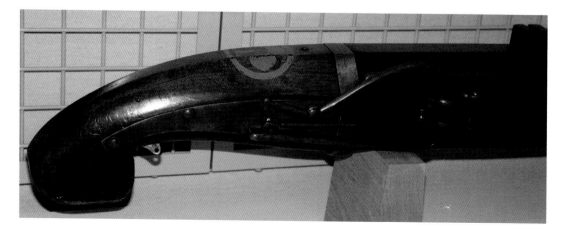

the fourth finger of the left hand. Aim was taken while the *hibuta* was still closed. At the given command it would be flicked open, followed by the order to fire. To save time between reloading the ramrod was not replaced in its hole beneath the barrel but was instead held in the left hand that supported the firearm.

The *yari-gumi* members were armed with *nagae-yari* (long-shafted spears) of three different standard lengths expressed in multiples of *ken*. At the beginning of the Sengoku Period one *ken* was equivalent to 1.6m (the dimensions changed later to 1.8m). A short *te-yari* (hand spear) was one *ken* long. A *niken-yari* (two *ken*) spear was therefore 3.2m long, while a *sangen-yari* (three *ken*) weapon was 4.8m long, similar to the length of a European pike. The longest spears of all were probably to be found in Oda Nobunaga's armies, because there is a reference in *Shinchō-kō ki* for April 1553 to '500 3½ *ken* [5.6m] long spears' (Kuwata 1965: 26), although these may have been a 'one-off' as this was the occasion when Nobunaga was trying to impress an ally by his military might. The spears' great length required them to be of composite construction of bamboo strips glued around a core of oak. The entire shaft was lacquered and bound with thread and cloth to provide a secure handgrip, and the almost-finished product was then lacquered one more time. The hilts of the steel blades (which were shorter than the samurai spear blades) were sunk deeply into the upper part of the spear shaft and secured with wooden pegs around a metal 'mouthpiece', with a similar metal butt at the other end. The spear blades might have had a side-blade to help pull a samurai from his horse.

This picture from *Ehon Toyotomi Kunkoki* shows an incident in the life of Toyotomi Hideyoshi (1537–98) when he carried out an experiment by matching ashigaru spearmen who were armed with normal-sized *nagae yari* (long-shafted spears) against a squad who had been given extra-long spears. The latter are shown triumphant in the mock battle.

Uedahara

23 March 1548

BACKGROUND TO BATTLE

The encounter between Takeda Shingen and Murakami Yoshikiyo which took place on the plain of Uedahara in 1548 provides an excellent example of a major clash between mounted samurai and ashigaru at a time when the deployment of the matchlock muskets that would become the ashigaru's most important weapon was still very rare. There are, however, a few tantalizing and somewhat confusing references to firearms of some sort, although they seem to have played no role in influencing the outcome of the battle. Instead the records describe several encounters between samurai and groups of enemy ashigaru whose principal weapon was still the bow or the long-shafted spear. One of the latter scenarios – a classic instance of a group ambush by ashigaru spearmen – led to the death of a Takeda general.

The battle of Uedahara was fought in Shinano Province (modern-day Nagano Prefecture) and was an important stage in Takeda Shingen's attempts to take over his immediate neighbours' territories. Shinano Province was originally a 'no man's land' between the Uesugi to the north and the Takeda to the south, and for years the two clans would fight over it, particularly at the famous five battles of Kawanakajima, which were fought between 1553 and 1564. The Takeda had invaded Shinano Province for the first time in 1536 under Shingen's father Nobutora (1494–1574). In 1547, by which time the Takeda had taken over much of southern Shinano Province around Lake Suwa, Shingen made an important gain in the province's Saku Valley when he took the castle of Shiga. The castle covered the mountain pass into western Kōzuke Province that is now the route of the modern Shinkansen ('Bullet Train') to Tokyo. This placed

Shingen very close to the territories of Murakami Yoshikiyo, a key ally of Uesugi Kenshin – the daimyo of Echigo Province and Shingen's deadliest rival.

Greatly alarmed by the Takeda advance, Murakami Yoshikiyo sent a relieving army from Kōzuke Province to aid Shiga, but Takeda Shingen responded with a picked force of 500 troops who ambushed them along the way on the flat plain of Odaihara. He then used psychological pressure by displaying in front of Shiga Castle the heads of about 15 senior samurai and 300 ashigaru that had been taken at the battle. This may have provoked a desperate act of treason among the garrison, because a mysterious fire started within the castle after which an assault began and the castle fell. The women and children from the castle were rounded up and sent to Kōfu where they were sold as slaves in one of the best-documented examples of the practice in Sengoku Period Japan. A samurai's wife apparently commanded five times the price of an ashigaru's wife.

Itagaki Nobukata, one of the Takeda 'Twenty-Four Generals'. Haughty and impetuous, he exemplified the attitude of the mounted samurai of the 1540s. He would be killed on the battlefield of Uedahara in 1548 at the hands of a group of socially inferior ashigaru. This portrait of him is in the Shingen-ko Museum in Enzan.

As winter moved towards its end, early in March 1548 Murakami Yoshikiyo mobilized his forces to recapture Shiga Castle and drive the Takeda out of Shinano Province forever. When the news reached Kōfu an army assembled under the personal command of Takeda Shingen. The Takeda advance to Uedahara began on the 1st day of the 2nd lunar month of the 17th Year of Temmon (10 March 1548) when Shingen left Kai Province at its north-western tip. From there his route followed the course of today's Chūō Railway Line towards Lake Suwa, an area that had been occupied by the Takeda since 1542. Shingen's main body of 5,000 men were joined en route by 2,000 more under his general Itagaki Nobukata from Uehara Castle to the east of Suwa. The combined Takeda army then crossed the Daimon Pass over the mountains to the Saku Valley to the north-east. Meanwhile the Murakami army left Yoshikiyo's headquarters at Katsurao and forded the Chikumagawa (Chikuma River) somewhere in the vicinity of today's Sakaki Railway Station. Their subsequent choice of route was dictated partly by caution and partly by geography, because they did not follow the course of the river (which may have been physically impossible along certain stretches) but swung round to the west, crossing the Mitsugashirayama range by the Muroga Pass and descending rapidly to the Chikumagawa again behind the mountain of Shiroyama. After little more than ten days of manoeuvring the rival armies were to be found facing each other on the flat land that was nearest to the Murakami's castles: the plain of Uedahara.

The Uedahara Campaign, March–April 1548

MAP KEY

1 Mid-March: Having left Kōfu on 10 March, Takeda Shingen advances over the Daimon Pass and into the Saku Valley.

2 c.20 March: Murakami Yoshikiyo leaves Katsurao Castle and fords the Chikumagawa.

3 21 March: Yoshikiyo crosses the Mitsugashirayama range by the Muroga Pass and heads for Uedahara.

4 0600hrs, 23 March: The battle of Uedahara begins with a charge by the Takeda vanguard under Itagaki Nobukata.

5 Midday, 23 March: Itagaki Nobukata is killed and the Murakami attack Takeda Shingen's *hatamoto* (guards).

6 Late afternoon, 23 March: Yoshikiyo disengages his forces.

7 Mid-April: Having remained in camp on the battlefield for 20 days, Shingen leaves and claims a victory.

Battlefield environment

The Murakami lands lay where the Chikumagawa broadened its flow around the modern city of Ueda. All three battles in this book were fought on flat lands such as these where the rivers had left their enclosing mountains and had spread out into flood plains. Here settlements and towns had been established, overlooked by a number of *yamashiro* (literally 'mountain castles') that provided the ultimate protection for the local daimyo's patch of land. In the case of Uedahara, Murakami Yoshikiyo's *yamashiro* of Katsurao was Shingen's target. It stood high above the Chikumagawa facing the smaller castle of Arato across the river on the hills to the west just north of Ueda. Another satellite castle called Toishi lay upriver, but Yoshikiyo chose to descend and engage Shingen on the fertile plain of Uedahara. The battlefield was hemmed in by mountains and the river, greatly restricting an army's movements and conducive to a rapid settlement by means of a fierce attack by mounted samurai who would drive the disordered ashigaru into the river. That was Shingen's plan, but Yoshikiyo had anticipated such a move precisely.

The battlefield of Uedahara looking westwards from the grave of Itagaki Nobukata (1489–1548) towards Shiroyama, the mountain that Murakami Yoshikiyo passed behind on his way to do battle on the plain of Uedahara.

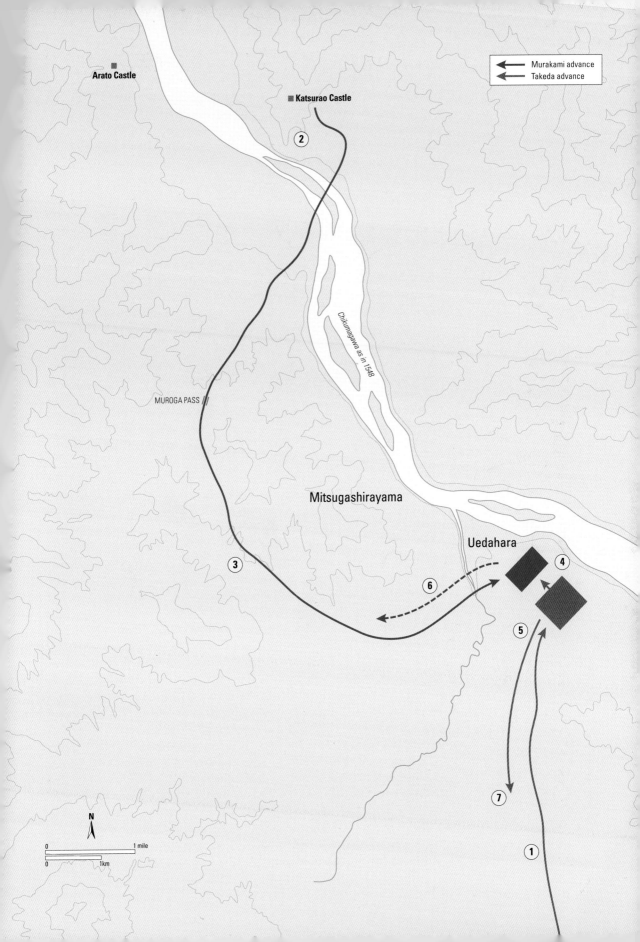

Arato Castle

■ Katsurao Castle

②

Chikumagawa as in 1548

MUROGA PASS

Mitsugashirayama

Uedahara

③

⑥

④

⑤

⑦

①

N

0   1 mile

0   1km

←— Murakami advance

←— Takeda advance

INTO COMBAT

A brief mention of the battle of Uedahara, which was fought on 2m 14d (23 March) is made in the contemporary chronicle *Katsuyama ki*, otherwise known as *Myōhōji ki* from the name of the temple where it was compiled. The account is very short and covers little more than an outline of the events and a list of the most prominent casualties. Much more detail would be provided later in *Kōyō Gunkan*, which contains important information about samurai/ashigaru combat at Uedahara, although like most similar works some of the material in *Kōyō Gunkan* is exaggerated (Nakamura 1965: 40–55). Chapter 27 describes the overall progress of the conflict and parallels *Myōhōji ki*, while the more interesting Chapter 28 consists of a supposed conversation about the battle between Murakami Yoshikiyo and Nagao Kagetora, the future Uesugi Kenshin. After a discussion of the long relationship between the two allies, Kenshin asks Yoshikiyo, 'How was it with the 'bows and arrows' [i.e. the military progress] of Takeda Harunobu?' Yoshikiyo replies that Takeda Shingen had enjoyed ten years of victories, but that it had now all come to an end. 'So how was it at the battle of Uedahara?' continues Kenshin. Yoshikiyo's reply to that question will shed important light on the theme of this book.

As far as the overall battle of Uedahara is concerned, there are slight discrepancies between the sources over the numbers engaged. In *Myōhōji ki*, Shingen is said to have left Kōfu with 5,000 men and been joined by 2,000 more, making 7,000 in total against the Murakami's 5,000 men. *Kōyō Gunkan* raises both figures somewhat, but it is fairly safe to say that the battle was fought between two sides that totalled at least 12,000 men of whom almost one-quarter – 2,900 men – would be killed. Crucial to Shingen's plans was the leader of his vanguard: Itagaki Nobukata (1489–1548), a veteran among the 'Twenty-Four Generals' who had been the young Shingen's mentor. Nobukata fought under a banner of a crescent moon and was above all a skilled leader of mounted samurai. Shingen's intention was that Nobukata should lead a dramatic charge and sweep the Murakami before them.

Murakami Yoshikiyo had, however, prepared for the battle by carrying out prior surveillance. 'Within our ranks was an *ashigaru-taishō*, a retainer of the Uesugi from Annaka in Kōzuke Province called Yagi Sōshichirō with his younger brother, who went as scouts (*monomi*) to investigate Itagaki Nobukata's Kai Province force' (Nakamura 1965: 54). Yoshikiyo also states that he was fully aware of the reputation of Takeda Shingen and his mounted samurai, because he says that 'at this battle we were up against Harunobu who was pre-eminent in military matters'; Yoshikiyo notes specifically that the Takeda had 'two hundred mounted samurai chosen for their skills at horsemanship under commanders of similar ability and holding in their hands two hundred spears' (Nakamura 1965: 53). So how did Murakami Yoshikiyo counter this threat? He replies, 'When we got to know of this, to counter the two hundred horsemen with spears we had two hundred spearmen with a horse apiece and also a hundred ashigaru, these men had one hundred long-shafted spears' (Nakamura 1965: 53). The

latter were clearly members of what was a trained ashigaru *yari-gumi*, but the most interesting information about the Murakami preparations follows immediately afterwards and reads as follows:

The view from the reconstructed Arato Castle, looking along the Chikumagawa (Chikuma River). Arato was a satellite castle of Katsurao, the headquarters of Murakami Yoshikiyo (1501–73), which was built on the hill in the left distance. The battle of Uedahara was fought on the flat plain further upstream where the valley in this picture starts to fade from view.

> To accompany our Horse Guards I chose two hundred skilled marksmen out of the army and to one hundred and fifty of these soldiers we gave five well-made arrows and a bow. To the remaining fifty ashigaru we gave *teppō* that were first imported in the Seventh Year of Eishō [1510] with three bullets per man. They were ordered to shoot when they were told and then to discard them and fight with their swords. I ordered the gunners to fire after the arrows had been shot, and placed an officer in charge of every five men. (Nakamura 1965: 53)

This important statement confirms that hand-picked ashigaru archers were deployed as a *yumi-gumi* in addition to the spearmen, but the most interesting reference is of course the mention of *teppō*. Taken at face value it appears to indicate that Murakami Yoshikiyo was deploying firearms for the first time on a Japanese battlefield, a year before their well-recorded use in 1549 by Ijūin Tadaaki, a vassal of the Shimazu, who used *teppō* during an attack on the castle of Kajiki in Ōsumi Province. There are, however, several very puzzling features about Yoshikiyo's account. The first concerns the firearms themselves. The reference to the year 1510 is quite precise and would appear to rule out any possibility that these firearms were based on the Portuguese matchlock muskets that had arrived only five years before Uedahara in 1543. Instead, the reference to the year reflects an entry in *Hōjō Godai ki*, the chronicle of the Hōjō family:

Long ago I heard of a yamabushi called Gyokuryūbo, who lived in Odawara. When he was young he used to climb Mount Ōmine every year. During the final year of the Kyōroku Era [1531], when he arrived at Sakai in Izumi Province he heard a large noise and wondered what it was. He later found out that it was a weapon called a *teppō* which had been introduced from China in the Seventh Year of Eishō [1510]. Realising how marvellous and precious it was, he brought one back for Lord Ujitsuna [i.e. Hōjō Ujitsuna, the second of the Hōjō dynasty, 1487–1541] who tried it out and treasured it. (Hagiwara 1966: 230)

If Yoshikiyo's account is to be taken literally it would mean that the *teppō* used at Uedahara were these primitive Chinese handguns rather than the Portuguese matchlock muskets. Judging by surviving examples, they would have consisted of a short barrel and chamber with a touch hole and a long wooden stock. Double-barrelled and triple-barrelled versions were also used. Although frequently dismissed as both primitive and ineffective, they had been in use for almost a century on the Ryūkyū Islands (modern-day Okinawa) and are likely to have been deployed in battle in Japan itself following their introduction from China in 1510. For example, in 1542, the year before the Portuguese arrived in Japan, 20 so-called *teppō* were deployed at Akana Castle in Izumo Province by the Amako family, so these must have been the Chinese handguns (Suzuki 2000: 40 & 63). I believe that Yoshikiyo's *teppō* were also of this earlier type and that we can go even further and identify them as three-barrelled handguns identical to the variety most commonly deployed on the Ryūkyū Islands. The proof lies in the *Kōyō Gunkan* description of how they were to be used, because Yoshikiyo gives each man three bullets. He orders them to fire and then not to reload but to discard the weapons for hand-to-hand fighting. This can only make sense if the handguns are three-barrelled, so the *Kōyō Gunkan* story is probably the best recorded use of the weapons on the Japanese mainland. The reference to these strange handguns at Uedahara is therefore not to the first use of the new Portuguese firearms but to what may be the final use in battle of the old Chinese ones.

The matter could have been cleared up if the author of *Kōyō Gunkan* had gone on to describe the firearms in action, but unfortunately the account does not say how they were used because they are not mentioned again. Murakami Yoshikiyo concentrates instead on the ashigaru's appearance, how they wore distinguishing heraldic devices of a *sashimono* (back flag) and a *sode-jirushi* (small shoulder flag) each bearing the character 'ichi' (the number 1) in black ink on a white background. As the battle of Uedahara began with a fierce charge by mounted samurai, neither the archers nor the mysterious handgunners may have managed to fire a single shot before the horsemen closed in on them.

The narrative in *Kōyō Gunkan* tallies with *Myōhōji ki* when it opens the battle with a classic mounted samurai advance led by Itagaki Nobukata of the Takeda force. As intended, his initial charge scattered the vanguard of the Murakami by its impact leaving the front ranks of ashigaru stunned and confused, but instead of cutting off the entire Murakami army at the

river it turned out that Itagaki Nobukata's fierce advance had only pierced the Murakami front line, leaving Nobukata's men vulnerable to a response. This could have been dealt with, but Nobukata paused to celebrate his achievement, a demonstration of over-confidence that was apparently one of his hallmarks. *Kōyō Gunkan* uses the phrase 'signs of carelessness' (Nakamura 1965: 48).

As noted earlier, Murakami Yoshikiyo had prepared for a Takeda cavalry assault and, if *Kōyō Gunkan* is to be believed, he had done it to such an extent that Itagaki Nobukata was a marked man at Uedahara. His personal contingent of bodyguards and servants were outnumbered by the Murakami ashigaru who were delegated to cover him at a ratio of 12:1, because Murakami Yoshikiyo mentions specifically 200 ashigaru in this role, who must have caught Nobukata and his team within a frightening hedge of spears. The main *Kōyō Gunkan* account says that Itagaki was 'pulled down from his horse' (Nakamura 1965: 48), an action that implies involvement by ashigaru who were ready with their spears, very probably somewhere near the spot that is now Itagaki Nobukata's grave, a place deep within the area that would have been occupied by the Murakami. We may therefore safely envisage a mass of Murakami ashigaru spearmen, some of whom had spears with short side-blades, surrounding Nobukata and neutralizing his immediate supporting followers before unhorsing him. This again showed Nobukata's carelessness in allowing such an event to occur. His head was soon taken, an action (naturally enough) that is not credited to any lowly ashigaru but to a samurai: a man called Kamijō

The battle of Uedahara from *Ehon Shingen Ichidai ki*. The Takeda army advances from the left rear against the Murakami. Uedahara provided several instances of conflict between mounted samurai and ashigaru fighting on foot. It proved to be a very fierce battle with a large number of casualties.

Itagaki Nobukata is surrounded at the battle of Uedahara

One of the most dramatic instances of fighting between an individual mounted samurai and ashigaru took place during the initial phase of the battle of Uedahara. Itagaki Nobukata, one of Takeda Shingen's 'Twenty-Four Generals', led a characteristically impetuous charge against the Murakami front line and broke through with ease. He then paused to reflect upon his achievement, at which point the Murakami counter-attacked. Here we see Nobukata separated from all his personal attendants apart from his standard bearer and being assaulted by a mass of enemy ashigaru. He is fighting back manfully, knocking his assailants to one side and impaling them upon his *mochi-yari* (spear) with such force that they are thrown into the air. Nobukata is shown wearing the suit of armour depicted in his portrait which hangs in the Shingen-ko Museum in Enzan. The armour is of somewhat old-fashioned design, a likely choice for a very superior samurai who despised the ashigaru rabble. It is laced in *kebiki-odoshi* (closely spaced cords), a style that was being rapidly abandoned because it offered so many places for an ashigaru's spearhead to make contact. Nobukata is fighting back, wielding his spear to good effect.

His standard bearer tries desperately to stay on his feet as he holds the crescent-moon banner high as a rallying point for other Takeda samurai to come to the aid of his master. He is of samurai rank and bears the Takeda *mon* (badge) as a *maedate* (helmet crest).

As clouds of arrows fly through the air towards approaching Takeda horsemen other Murakami ashigaru attack the now isolated Itagaki Nobukata. Their simple *okegawa-dō* body armour and *jingasa* (war hats) bear the character '*kami*' in the family name of Murakami. Those who belong to the specially selected force of spearmen wear an additional form of identification of a *sashimono* (back flag) and *sode-jirushi* (shoulder flag) bearing the character '*ichi*' (the number 1). The spearmen are all armed with long-shafted pike-like *nagae-yari* with which they are trying to dismount Nobukata. The ashigaru on the extreme left is holding a triple-barrelled Chinese-style handgun from which he has just discharged its three shots in one of the last such actions to be seen in Japanese history. He will now abandon the weapon and join in the assault on Nobukata with his sword as ordered by Murakami Yoshikiyo.

Oribe. At this a 'great shout' went up from the Itagaki ranks (Nakamura 1965: 54–55). In language characteristic of the genre, the *Kōyō Gunkan* notes that Murakami Yoshikiyo 'shed tears' at the loss of so noble a samurai leader, a gesture that was followed by Uesugi Kenshin when he was told the account (Nakamura 1965: 54).

Murakami Yoshikiyo then pressed on to confront Takeda Shingen's main body. 'One section of 600 men fought against Takeda Harunobu's *hatamoto* and drove them back two or three *chō* [200–300m] clashing swords with one man who looked like a general'; this unnamed samurai was unhorsed, but instead of committing honourable suicide 'as might be expected', notes Yoshikiyo, he fled (Nakamura 1965: 54). Amari Torayasu (1498–1548), another of the Takeda 'Twenty-Four Generals', was killed in action along with Zaima Kawachi-no-Kami and Hajikano Den'emon, the latter of whom is described as having been caught in a hail of arrows, another classic ashigaru weapon-squad tactic. Much more seriously, Takeda Shingen himself was also fully involved in the hand-to-hand spear fighting, 'attacking like flames from astride his horse' (Nakamura 1965: 55), and was wounded in his left arm as both sets of *hatamoto* fought hand to hand – evidence of how close the fighting was – leaving dead 145 mounted samurai of the Murakami and 450 of their ashigaru just in this phase of the action. On the Murakami side Yashiro Mototsuna, Kojima Ryōhei and Amemiya Gyōbu were the named senior casualties. In all there were 1,200 Takeda killed and 1,700 dead among the Murakami so that the waters of the Chikumagawa flowed red (Nakamura 1965: 47).

晴信

The two sides eventually disengaged, but instead of acknowledging his defeat Takeda Shingen is recorded as having stayed on the battlefield in a fortified camp for 20 days before withdrawing to Kōfu via Uehara Castle. This would appear to have been simply a political gesture by Shingen, who believed that the last to leave a battlefield must be regarded as the winner. This act of stubborn defiance drew no further response from Murakami Yoshikiyo, who had by now returned contemptuously to the safety of his castles. Shingen's untroubled withdrawal in style many days later allowed *Kōyō Gunkan* to record Uedahara as a victory when 'fortune favoured Lord Shingen' (Nakamura 1965: 50), and a remarkably precise figure of 2,919 enemy heads taken is included. *Myohōji ki* agrees, but records that there was dissension among the lower classes of Kai Province because the wars were going on for such a long time.

There is an amusing modern anecdote concerning the battle. Itagaki Nobukata is buried on the battlefield and among the offerings made to his shrine are cigarettes and tobacco. For some unknown reason Nobukata is believed by today's worshippers to have been a habitual smoker, hence the offerings. As tobacco was introduced to Japan by the Portuguese at about the same time as matchlock muskets, it is interesting to note a modern folk belief which would depend on the habit of smoking having travelled across Japan faster than the use of matchlock muskets!

A haughty and confident Takeda Shingen watches the Murakami depart from the battlefield of Uedahara in a spread from *Ehon Shingen Ichidai ki*. Believing that whoever left the battlefield last was the winner, Shingen stayed in a fortified camp for 20 days and then claimed victory, even though it was the first defeat of his career and had resulted in the loss of Itagaki Nobukata, one of his finest generals.

Mikata ga Hara

25–26 January 1573

BACKGROUND TO BATTLE

During the 25 years that passed between Uedahara and Mikata ga Hara, Takeda Shingen went from strength to strength. The mounted samurai of the Takeda distinguished themselves in several other encounters including the bloody fourth battle of Kawanakajima in 1561, and in 1573 Shingen gained a major victory at Mikata ga Hara, a battle that should never have happened. It was the unexpected bonus to a brilliant operation planned and executed by Shingen at the height of his powers and (unknown to him) the end of his career. Known as the Saijō Sakusen – 'the campaign to take Kyoto from the east' – it had the capital of Japan as its ultimate objective, although there is no evidence that in 1572 Shingen planned to go all the way to Kyoto. Nevertheless, any gains made along the Tōkaidō, the 'Eastern Sea Road' that led to Kyoto, would greatly facilitate such a scheme when it was eventually put into action. Sadly for the Takeda, no further moves would be made personally by their great leader because Shingen was to die just as the Saijō Campaign concluded, leaving his son Katsuyori to return to the fray two years later in 1574.

The seizure of Kyoto would have allowed the Takeda family to take control of the Shogun and achieve the reunification of Japan under their own rule but, needless to say, Takeda Shingen was not the only daimyo to cherish similar grandiose ambitions. Others were much better placed simply by geography alone to take over the Shogunate for themselves or at the very least to control the current holder of the post, which was still an institution that commanded unusual respect in spite of its military ineffectiveness. There are references throughout their history to Shoguns fleeing, being replaced, exiled or even assassinated, yet the honours and titles that could only be bestowed

The now reconstructed castle of Takane, which was the first prize for Takeda Shingen in the Saijō Campaign of 1572.

by a Shogun were still highly valued and often fought over. For example, in 1559 the incumbent Shogun would give the post of *shugo* (Shogun's deputy) of Owari Province to a minor local daimyo called Oda Nobunaga. The title meant little in military terms to Nobunaga; its value lay instead in giving Nobunaga official approval for the complete takeover of his home province that he would accomplish during that year.

Oda Nobunaga (1534–82) plays an important role in the story of Mikata ga Hara. As well as being highly skilled in military matters he cherished ambitious ideas of taking over the Shogunate for himself, although for many years he lacked the military and political resources to make any such move. All that changed in 1560 when he defeated an invasion of his home province by Imagawa Yoshimoto (1519–60), who controlled the provinces of Mikawa, Tōtōmi and Suruga. Ota Gyūichi, the author of *Shinchō-Kō ki*, Nobunaga's biography written in 1610, may be exaggerating somewhat when he states that Yoshimoto marched west with an army of 45,000 men ready to brush to one side Nobunaga's paltry force of 2,000 men, but the discrepancy was certainly a considerable one (Kuwata 1965: 54). After easily taking a few border forts Yoshimoto rested his army in a gorge called Okehazama while he performed the traditional ceremony of viewing the severed heads of the defeated. Nobunaga then launched a surprise attack. The death of Yoshimoto set in motion the rapid collapse of Imagawa influence and the consequent rise to power of Nobunaga, who marched on Kyoto in 1568 and set up his own nominee Ashikaga Yoshiaki (1537–97) as the fifteenth and (as it turned out) last Ashikaga Shogun, while the furious Takeda Shingen could only watch from his distant mountains.

Nobunaga's takeover of the Ashikaga Shogunate provides the background to Shingen's 1572–73 Saijō Campaign, when he moved against several key fortresses held by Nobunaga and his ally Tokugawa Ieyasu (1542–1616), a man who will also play a crucial role in this story. Ieyasu protected Nobunaga's eastern flank in Mikawa and Tōtōmi provinces, so the Saijō Campaign was a mighty showdown between the old power of the Takeda and the new Tokugawa/Oda alliance, which it tested almost to destruction. Overall, the cooperation between Nobunaga and Ieyasu would prove to be one of the best examples of a loyal partnership in the whole of Sengoku Period Japan and lasted successfully until the moment of Nobunaga's death in 1582. Throughout that period Ieyasu, who never entered into formal vassalage under Nobunaga, normally took direct orders as the lesser partner in the coalition and only once acted as commander-in-chief of their combined forces. That unfortunate instance happened on the plain of Mikata ga Hara in 1573 and was almost a total disaster because Ieyasu disobeyed Nobunaga's explicit instructions not to engage in battle. An unplanned clash that then took place would provide an excellent example of a conflict involving mounted samurai against ashigaru, for which the confused and unexpected conditions proved ideal.

Takeda Shingen's Saijō Campaign had become possible because the long-standing pattern of alliances and suspicion which had swirled around Kai Province had recently shifted from one of an almost traditional cooperation between the Uesugi and the neighbouring Hōjō against the Takeda to one of a new Takeda/Hōjō alliance. This new situation allowed Shingen to confront both Nobunaga and Ieyasu directly without any fear of danger at his rear, so he risked the campaign of a lifetime with an army that totalled 25,000 in all including 2,000 troops supplied by Hōjō Ujimasa (1538–90) as part of their new alliance. As no precise records of the composition of the army exist an estimate has to be made using figures from *Kōyō Gunkan* of about the same time. The total of *ki* in the Takeda army is 9,121, but as a *ki* included both the mounted individual samurai and his attendants the number of actual fighting horsemen was probably around 3,000, including those in the *hatamoto*. As for the ashigaru who served outside the *hatamoto* and were therefore presumably in the weapon squads, a precise number of 5,489 is given but there is no breakdown according to weaponry. If we use a similar proportion to the figures for Uesugi Kenshin in 1575 noted earlier, which was roughly 1,000 archers and 3,500 spearmen to 300 musketeers, there may have been about 500–600 musketeers in Shingen's army, so it was well-balanced in terms of the old power of the Takeda horsemen and the new potential of ashigaru. It is known that as early as 1555 Shingen had sent 300 matchlock muskets to help in the defence of Asahiyama Castle, so an estimate of 1,200 archers, 3,700 spearmen and 600 musketeers is perhaps not unreasonable for such an important campaign (Nakamura 1965: 305–29). Shingen was also under no doubt about the effectiveness of musket fire against horsemen, because there is an account in *Minowa Gunki* of their use in the siege of Minowa Castle in 1566: 'While over one hundred expert musketeers were firing from inside the castle about sixty horsemen attacked it, but the *teppō* ashigaru kept on firing and produced over 600–700 wounded and dead' (Sasama 1969: 64).

In 1572 Takeda Shingen was 52 years old and still projected his resolute image of the god Fudō despite having suffered from what is believed to have been pulmonary tuberculosis the previous year. Shingen was now master of

This statue of Takeda Shingen stands outside Kōfu Railway Station. The battle of Mikata ga Hara was one of his most convincing victories but in truth it should never have happened at all.

Shinano Province and had also taken a firm hold on a short section of the Pacific Coast by his capture of Suruga Province. That meant Tokugawa Ieyasu was now his immediate neighbour to the west in Hamamatsu Castle in Tōtōmi Province. The Tōkaidō Road ran through Suruga Province into Tōtōmi Province, an area which both the Takeda and the Tokugawa had fortified heavily, particularly in the environs of the provincial border. This made an advance by the Takeda against Ieyasu along the Tōkaidō Road an unlikely proposition, as was to prove to be the case when Shingen launched the Saijō Campaign, because he planned to attack Nobunaga and Ieyasu from the north-east in a three-pronged coordinated advance as shown on the map on page 7.

Takeda Shingen's initial moves cannot have attracted much suspicion because the geography of Kai and Shinano provinces required that he first head north from Kōfu towards Lake Suwa. The section that would move against Nobunaga's Mino Province would then swing round further north along the Nakasendō, the central mountain road that was an inland alternative to the Tōkaidō Road. The moves against Ieyasu also began in the region of Lake Suwa and headed down the Iida Valley along the general course of the long Tenryūgawa (Tenryū River), which enters the Pacific Ocean to the east of Hamamatsu.

The first move out of Kai Province was made by Shingen's vanguard under Yamagata Masakage, and Shingen's great confidence is shown by the fact

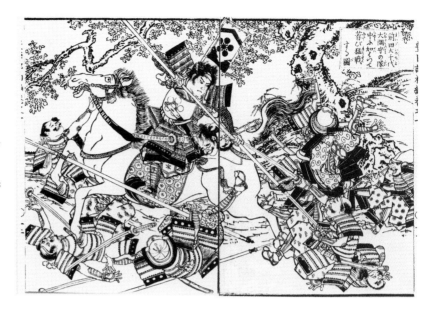

This is one of the best illustrations in *Ehon Taikō ki* to depict combat between samurai and ashigaru. The young Maeda Toshiie is shown using his spear to very good effect from horseback. He is already victorious, as shown by the two heads hanging from his saddle. Now he despatches no fewer than five more ashigaru who are knocked flying. Similar scenes must have occurred at the battle of Mikata ga Hara.

that his vanguard travelled by a totally separate route from the main body. Yamagata Masakage and the vanguard left Kōfu on the 29th day of the 9th lunar month of the Third Year of Genki 3 (2 November 1572), heading for eastern Mikawa. They were followed by the Takeda main body under Shingen on 10m 3d (8 November). To set off so late in the year may appear surprising, but Shingen was counting on moving on solid ground through the mountains while snowfalls to the north prevented Uesugi Kenshin from intervening. From Lake Suwa the main body headed straight for Tōtōmi Province along the general line of the Tenryūgawa. Meanwhile Akiyama Nobutomo, one of the 'Twenty-Four Generals', led 3,000 men in a separate advance against Nobunaga's Mino Province via the Nakasendō. Akiyama Nobutomo's army laid siege to the vital border fortress of Iwamura, an action which would continue for most of the Saijō Campaign until Toyama Kagetō, lord of Iwamura Castle, died of a sudden illness. The morale of the defending troops soon collapsed, so Toyama Kagetō's widow (an aunt of Oda Nobunaga) entered into negotiations with Akiyama Nobutomo. In mid-December they agreed terms whereby the castle would be surrendered without bloodshed if Lady Toyama agreed to marry Nobutomo, an unusual but successful peace deal.

On 10m 10d (15 November) Shingen's main body crossed the border between Shinano and Tōtōmi provinces over the Aokuzure Pass. The first Tokugawa outpost to fall was the castle of Takane that stood high above the Misakubogawa (Misakubo River), after which the Takeda forces occupied Inui Castle. Here the Takeda main body divided in two to approach Futamata Castle, Tokugawa Ieyasu's most important possession along the Tenryūgawa and the nearest major fortress to Hamamatsu. Needless to say, Ieyasu had been monitoring Shingen's movements closely. A scouting force sent out under Honda Tadakatsu encountered one of these two Takeda armies at Hitokotosaka and only managed to escape because of the adroit manner in which Honda Tadakatsu organized their withdrawal. Meanwhile, Yamagata Masakage's vanguard completed their march and joined Shingen at Futamata.

Futamata Castle was built on the edge of a cliff over the Tenryūgawa. A long siege of many weeks began under Shingen's son Takeda Katsuyori, but after many fruitless attacks he observed that the garrison depended upon a water supply obtained from the river by lowering buckets from a rather elaborate wooden water tower. Katsuyori conceived a plan of floating heavy wooden rafts down the river to smash against the water tower's supports. The tower eventually collapsed and the garrison finally surrendered on 12m 19d (22 January 1573). The Takeda army left Futamata shortly afterwards, but Shingen did not then head south to attack Hamamatsu. His objectives lay to the west across the nearby border with Mikawa Province. Shingen's strategy towards Hamamatsu was to ignore Ieyasu because the latter lacked the resources with which he could threaten the mighty Takeda army as it progressed.

Oda Nobunaga had sent reinforcements to Hamamatsu as soon as he heard about the attack on Futamata. Their leaders are named in *Shinchō-Kō ki* as Sakuma Nobumori, Hirate Jinzaemon Hirohide and Mizuno Shimotsuke-no-Kami (Kuwata 1965: 129). Nobunaga could not have known his enemy's precise objectives, but Shingen certainly appeared to be cutting a swathe through Tōtōmi and Mikawa provinces to coincide with the ongoing operation at Iwamura in Mino Province. Faced by these moves Nobunaga's strategy was to monitor the Takeda army's progress until they could be safely challenged on ground of his own choosing. Hamamatsu was clearly not the place to do so, so Nobunaga sent strict orders to Ieyasu to stay securely within the castle and await orders to move out and attack Takeda Shingen's rear when the time was opportune.

It was at that point that Ieyasu decided to disobey orders, and all the accounts of the subsequent events suggest that samurai honour was the sole motivation for him making a suicidal advance out of Hamamatsu Castle against the mighty army that had insulted Tokugawa pride by devastating his province. Revenge was not a dish that could be served cold. Ieyasu's decision to attack must have taken Shingen by surprise, although the latter had the luxury of being able to swing his army round to the north and make a tight loop to take up positions on the plateau of Mikata ga Hara where the battle would shortly be fought.

Elements of the Tokugawa army are shown here in action at the battle of Mikata ga Hara. They had already managed a successful withdrawal after being surprised by Takeda Shingen's advance and the loss of Futamata Castle. Tokugawa Ieyasu marched his army out for a pitched battle that proved to be a near-disaster.

1 Morning, 25 January: Tokugawa Ieyasu advances north from Hamamatsu and takes up position.

2 Morning, 25 January: Takeda Shingen advances from Futamata three days after it falls and wheels his army round when he learns of Ieyasu's movements.

3 Early afternoon, 25 January: Shingen sends stone-throwers towards the Tokugawa lines.

4 Early afternoon, 25 January: The Tokugawa musketeers respond, revealing their distance from the Takeda lines. A musket duel begins.

5 Mid-afternoon, 25 January: The Takeda left-flank vanguard under Baba Nobuharu advances against Nobunaga's troops.

6 Mid-afternoon, 25 January: A second-wave mounted attack by 50 horsemen and their supporters is led by Saigusa Moritomo.

7 Late afternoon, 25 January: Shingen launches a third-wave attack that reaches Ieyasu's *hatamoto*. The Tokugawa retreat begins.

8 Early evening, 25 January: Several samurai-versus-ashigaru encounters take place during the pursuit.

9 Night of 25/26 January: Ieyasu raids the Takeda camp at Saigagake.

10 26 January: Shingen holds a head-viewing ceremony and then withdraws to continue his campaign against Oda Nobunaga.

Battlefield environment

The initial troop disposition of the battle of Mikata ga Hara, which was contested during the afternoon and evening of 12m 22d (25 January 1573), is easier to envisage than many other similar encounters because *Mikawa Gofudo ki* states that each side took up a standard battle formation chosen from the *hachijin*, eight traditional Chinese battlefield formations associated with the second Tang Emperor Taizong (598–649). Shingen's formation was *gyorin* (*yu lin* – fish scales). This was a prudent decision on Shingen's part, because Taizong had originally recommended it as the formation to adopt if one's army was outnumbered. Shingen had numerical superiority, but *gyorin* allowed him to use the restricted area of the Mikata ga Hara plateau to its best advantage, keeping his army concentrated and ready for a decisive move outwards. Ieyasu's advancing army was heavily outnumbered by about three to one in a total army of 11,000, of which 8,000 were his own troops and 3,000 were reinforcements from Nobunaga. These he drew up in a *kakuyoku* (*he yi* – crane's wing). The choice showed Ieyasu's determination to defeat the Takeda in battle, because *kakuyoku* allowed the possibility of rapid conversion into an offensive movement to surround an attacking enemy. The vanguard would absorb the enemy advance using missile weapons and skirmishing while the outstretched and reverse-curved 'wings' that gave the formation its name spread out to envelop the enemy (Kuwata & Utagawa 1976: 25). The 3,000 men sent by Nobunaga were placed on Ieyasu's right wing while Sakai Tadatsugu of the Tokugawa force held the extreme right flank beyond them.

Neither of the two Chinese formations can have been kept in order for long, because the impression is given that once the fighting started there was huge confusion. This was partly due to the immediate battlefield environment. Mikata ga Hara was a flat and slightly elevated plateau that provided ideal conditions for bold mounted warfare, even though the Takeda samurai would be fighting with a river at their backs, but because of the time it took to dress their ranks no advance was made by either side until the afternoon. There were then only a few hours of fighting in a dull light of an overcast sky before darkness set in. The other contributing factor was the weather. Snow was looming and would fall before the battle was over, and to add to the visibility problem there seems to have been fog across the battlefield. By the time the Tokugawa army retreated to Hamamatsu Castle it was snowing and was so dark that they had to be guided back by burning torches and the beating of a drum.

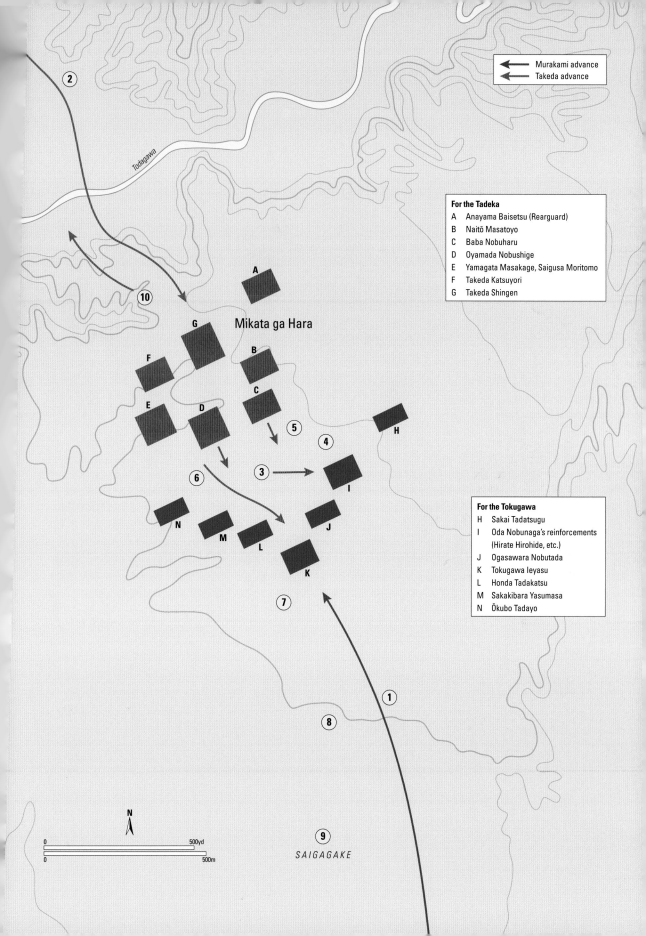

Murakami advance
Takeda advance

②

Todagawa

⑩

A

Mikata ga Hara

G

F

B

E

C

D

⑤

④

H

⑥

③

I

N

J

M

L

K

⑦

For the Tadeka

A   Anayama Baisetsu (Rearguard)
B   Naitō Masatoyo
C   Baba Nobuharu
D   Oyamada Nobushige
E   Yamagata Masakage, Saigusa Moritomo
F   Takeda Katsuyori
G   Takeda Shingen

For the Tokugawa

H   Sakai Tadatsugu
I   Oda Nobunaga's reinforcements
     (Hirate Hirohide, etc.)
J   Ogasawara Nobutada
K   Tokugawa Ieyasu
L   Honda Tadakatsu
M   Sakakibara Yasumasa
N   Ōkubo Tadayo

①

⑧

N

0   500yd
0   500m

⑨

SAIGAGAKE

INTO COMBAT

According to *Shinchō-Kō ki* the first shots of the battle of Mikata ga Hara were fired by Takeda Shingen's ashigaru, although they were 'shots' of a somewhat unusual kind. The account reads: '… ashigaru made contact at Mikata ga Hara. Sakuma, Hirate and other captains hurried there with horsemen, the two sides drew up their ranks and battle was joined. Shingen placed 300 men called *suiko no mono* into his front line and ordered them to throw stones' (Kuwata 1965: 129).

The use of stones is confirmed by *Mikawa Gofudo ki*, which states that Shingen had under his command 200–300 *zōnin* ('lower class fellows') who are not even dignified by giving them the title of ashigaru. 'They threw stones at Hirate's unit' (Kuwata & Utagawa 1976: 25). The word translated as 'stones' is *tsubute*, used elsewhere for the stone projectiles fired from Chinese handguns as at Uedahara, but as both sides now used European-type matchlock muskets in weapon squads it is very unlikely that these early weapons are indicated here. My conclusion is that the *zōnin* were nothing more than men press-ganged into service from the territories Shingen had captured from Ieyasu, a status also suggested by the literal meaning of 'water duty' for the expression *suiko no mono*. They were sent very close to the Tokugawa front line at great personal risk and told to use slingshots or even just hand-thrown stones picked up from the ground to intimidate the enemy vanguard into disclosing their position.

Mikawa Gofudo ki describes their action simply as 'weird' (Kuwata & Utagawa 1976: 25), although some of the stones fell with sufficient force to require the samurai to lean forward so that the neck guards of their helmets protected their heads and faces, and one or two suffered minor flesh wounds. The Tokugawa may have been somewhat surprised by the development, but they responded obligingly with gunfire from the ashigaru *teppō-gumi*, who fired blindly into the snow and gloom. Their actions may have achieved little more than cutting down the 'forlorn hope' stone-throwers, although this could be what Shingen had intended, because the ashigaru firing disclosed the Tokugawa positions and their likely distance away. Shingen therefore ordered a response from his own musketeers (Owada 1989: 181–182).

Takeda Shingen then took a great risk, because his musket barrage was followed by a mounted charge into the gloom by the Takeda vanguard horsemen to the beat of their war drums. Visibility must still have been a problem, but Shingen may have regarded that as an extra factor with which to intimidate the Tokugawa. An early success was registered on the Takeda left flank under Baba Nobuharu, and it was in this area that the first allied casualties occurred with the death of Hirate Hirohide from Nobunaga's force. Details of the hand-to-hand fighting appear in both *Shinchō-Kō ki* and *Mikawa Gofudo ki*, although most of the descriptions are concerned with the overall movements of the armies rather than any fine details. This is not surprising because of the visibility problems. The fighting continued while it grew steadily dark and the situation was always highly uncertain.

As for specific details of fighting between samurai and ashigaru, we know that two named senior samurai from Ieyasu's and Nobunaga's contingent

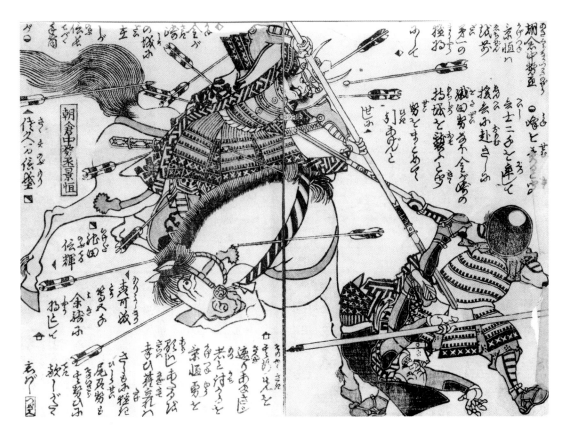

were killed during the first encounter. *Shinchō-Kō ki* notes: 'Shingen's men charged ahead. In the initial encounter Hirate Jinzaemon, some vassals from the Hirate house and Ieyasu's retainer Naruse Tōzō were killed' (Kuwata 1965: 129). These initial successes suggest that Shingen believed that the Tokugawa missile troops were so disordered that the battle could become a cavalry rout, so at that point Shingen calmly withdrew his forward units to rest and sent in fresh troops. The leader of the second wave was Saigusa Moritomo, who led 50 horsemen and their supporters in another fierce mounted assault against the disorganized Tokugawa. It was now getting dark, and seeing the Tokugawa troops reeling Shingen ordered a general attack by his main body, committing all his resources except those within his own *hatamoto*. Whatever firing there must have been from the Tokugawa ashigaru did nothing to stop the mounted advance, and their third wave even reached Ieyasu's *hatamoto*. There must have been considerable involvement by ashigaru at this stage of the battle, because *Mikawa Gofudo ki* uses the expression 'a hot fire of arrows and bullets from the right' in its description of what the Tokugawa suffered (Kuwata & Utagawa 1976: 28). This 'hot fire' can only have come from Shingen's weapon squads which were moved up quickly behind the charging horsemen, and it had the effect of further disorganizing Ieyasu's mounted samurai, most of whom must have realized that a retreat was inevitable.

One Tokugawa samurai who clearly appreciated the situation was Natsume Yoshinobu, the commander of Hamamatsu Castle. He had ridden out from the fortress to persuade his lord to withdraw, suggesting

This very fine book illustration shows a mounted samurai taking on two ashigaru spearmen with his own spear. His elevated position from horseback has served him well, and both his assailants are in peril. He is also under fire from ashigaru archers, however, and several arrows have hit both him and his unfortunate horse. This sort of situation happened frequently during the battles of Uedahara and Mikata ga Hara.

that he – Natsume – would hold back the enemy while Ieyasu retreated. Ieyasu seemed unwilling. He was clearly in a mood to die fighting so, with the future of the Tokugawa at stake and using the authority granted to him solely by his age, Natsume tugged on Ieyasu's bridle to bring his horse around, and struck it on the rump with his spear shaft. He called out to Ieyasu's personal attendants to ride with him for the castle.

The Tokugawa were now in full retreat, a situation that provided the perfect conditions for a further phase of ashigaru attacks on mounted samurai, who were now isolated and highly vulnerable. Tokugawa Ieyasu was of course the prime target, so Natsume performed the greatest act of service to a daimyo that any samurai could contemplate. He noticed that the Takeda troops were gaining on Ieyasu's party so he became Ieyasu's *kagemusha* (literally 'shadow warrior') – his body double. Hoping to mislead the Takeda, Natsume turned back into the mêlée shouting 'I am Ieyasu!' and plunged into the fight to be killed.

Natsume Yoshinobu's self-sacrifice distracted the Takeda for only a short while, however, and soon other Takeda samurai and ashigaru attacked Ieyasu and his attendants as they made their way out of the mêlée. One anonymous ashigaru archer was about to loose an arrow at Ieyasu at such close quarters that Amano Yasukage, who went on to survive the action, kicked the bow out of the man's hands. Surprisingly, Ieyasu appears also to have been armed with a bow (probably handed to him by his bow carrier) because he is recorded as having put an arrow through one Takeda ashigaru who ran at him with a long spear (Kuwata & Utagawa 1976: 28).

After these narrow escapes Ieyasu left the plain of Mikata ga Hara behind him and arrived at Hamamatsu Castle. His men were for barring the gates, but Ieyasu ordered them to leave them open and light fires to guide the retreating Tokugawa home. Sakai Tadatsugu went up into the gate tower and banged the war drum loudly to act as a further marker in the gathering darkness. This confident display had the further advantage of puzzling the pursuing Takeda, who stopped in front of the open gates, suspecting a trap. Had an assault been made at that point then Hamamatsu Castle could well have fallen, but Shingen held back. The castle was, after all, not his primary objective, and he noted that all the dead Tokugawa men, both samurai and ashigaru, had died facing the enemy. Those killed during the advance lay on their faces; those killed during the retreat were on their backs, so no night-time assault was made on the castle. Instead, the Takeda made bivouacs for the night just to the north of the castle in an area called Saigagake.

It was time for the Tokugawa ashigaru to hit back. Ōkubo Tadayō and Amano Yasukage assembled a squad of about 120 volunteers from among their surviving ashigaru including perhaps 16 musketeers, although a later source says there were 100 *teppō*. They were operating over familiar ground, so were able to get quite close to the Takeda camp. They then began pouring in bullets and arrows, and caused panic among the Takeda, some of whom were driven out of their lines in the darkness. Ōkubo Tadayō and Amano Yasukage had chosen their direction of attack well, because at Saigagake the lower slopes of the Mikata ga Hara plateau are split by a narrow and deep canyon about 30m deep in places. The surprise attack kept up the fiction of a strongly defended castle and was a further instance of how ashigaru could be used to harass a superior yet confused enemy. Scores of Takeda samurai and horses fell into this ravine, where the Tokugawa troops again fired on them and then cut them down as they lay helpless.

The following morning (12m 23d: 26 January), Takeda Shingen held a brief head-viewing ceremony before moving off. The head of Hirate Hirohide was sent to Nobunaga to show Shingen's disapproval of the latter's support for Ieyasu and to warn Nobunaga that, having defeated his ally Tokugawa Ieyasu, Shingen was on the move again and was heading for Mikawa Province. His army soon crossed the border for their next objective, Noda Castle, which the Takeda started besieging on Genki 4, 1m 11d (13 February 1573). Its commander held out for a month until lack of provisions made an honourable surrender likely. According to a lively local legend the garrison decided to dispose of their stocks of alcoholic drink in the most appropriate manner. One of their number contributed to the party by playing a tune on his flute. Takeda Shingen heard the sound and headed below the walls to listen more closely. He was recognized by a sharpshooting (and evidently still sober) ashigaru musketeer who put a bullet into him. An alternative version has Shingen succumb to illness during the siege, but whatever was the cause, he died during the subsequent retreat to Kai Province: the master of ashigaru organization felled by an ashigaru's bullet.

The mortal wounding of Takeda Shingen at the siege of Noda in 1573. Shingen is believed to have been hit by an ashigaru's bullet fired from the defended Noda Castle. He died on the way back to Kai Province. It was a sad end to a triumphant campaign from which the Takeda clan never really recovered.

Nagashino

28 June 1575

BACKGROUND TO BATTLE

In 1575 Takeda Shingen's heir, Takeda Katsuyori (1546–82), carried out an advance similar to his father's Saijō Campaign of 1572, but the 1575 operation bears no such grandiose title and will of course always be known as the Nagashino Campaign because of the battle by which it concluded, when Oda Nobunaga's ashigaru broke the charge of the legendary Takeda mounted samurai. Nobunaga's victory provides the most dramatic example in Japanese history of conflict between samurai and ashigaru. The deployment of musketeers and the strict control of their firing is the best-known factor of course, but Nobunaga's success depended most of all on good defensive tactics that took account of the terrain and the balance of manpower between the two sides.

Oda Nobunaga had shown an early appreciation of both spears and handguns, having received his first lessons in firearms technology at the age of 15. During a visit in 1553 to his father-in-law Saitō Dōsan, Nobunaga turned up at the head of an army carrying 800 spears and supposedly 500 *teppō*. This passage in *Shinchō-Kō ki* is regularly misquoted, however, because in Ōta Gyūichi's original text the 500 weapons cited consist of both firearms and bows, so Saitō Dōsan's positive impression of his ambitious son-in-law derived from Nobunaga's command of an army rather than any intimidating sight of long ranks of soldiers carrying innovative weapons (Kuwata 1965: 30).

The following year Nobunaga put his matchlock muskets into action during the short siege of Muraki Castle, and *Shinchō-Kō ki* tells us a revealing little anecdote about their use. Nobunaga's samurai had been vying with each other in crossing Muraki Castle's wide moat and scrambling up the castle walls, but suffered many casualties from shots fired from the castle's loopholes. Three apertures in particular were providing the fiercest fire, so Nobunaga resolved to silence them personally. Stationing himself on the edge of the moat, Nobunaga kept up a constant fire against the loopholes by exchanging one pre-loaded firearm for another (Kuwata 1965: 38–39). Oda Nobunaga's single-handed action shows that he appreciated how important it was for matchlock muskets to maintain a constant fire if they were to overcome the problem of their loading times, a challenge he would tackle on a grander scale at Nagashino.

The man who would be the loser at the battle of Nagashino was Takeda Katsuyori, the son of the great Takeda Shingen. He took over the clan in 1573, even though the Takeda tried to keep Shingen's death secret and did not hold his funeral until 1576. It was an unenviable task to inherit the reputation of a father who had become a legend in his own lifetime. The old generals had considerable respect for Katsuyori as a soldier, but little else, largely because Katsuyori proved unwilling to listen to their recommendations, preferring to make major policy decisions without first undertaking any consultation.

Nevertheless, prior to the actual battle of Nagashino Katsuyori's operations may be compared honourably to his late father's campaigns, because under their new lord the Takeda had continued to score wins against the Oda and Tokugawa alliance in Mino, Tōtōmi and Mikawa provinces throughout 1574. In March of that year Katsuyori led an army into Mino Province and surrounded Akechi Castle. Nobunaga hastily dispatched a relief force under his eldest son Nobutada and his follower Ikeda Nobuteru, but they arrived too late because the castle's commander had already surrendered. Later that year, Katsuyori would gain another notable victory by taking Tokugawa Ieyasu's Takatenjin Castle in Tōtōmi Province, and once again Nobunaga despatched a relief force which arrived too late.

The year 1575 therefore found Takeda Katsuyori continuing the aggressive policy which Takeda Shingen had set in motion years earlier and in which Katsuyori had participated with considerable honour and success. At that stage the ghost of Shingen would have been immensely proud of his son, and his pride would have swelled even more when he learned that Katsuyori now planned to take Ieyasu's provincial capital of Okazaki, a hugely symbolic prize and a considerable challenge to Oda Nobunaga. Okazaki lay at some distance from Katsuyori's previous gains because it was situated in western Mikawa Province. There was therefore a greater degree of risk in the operation, although Katsuyori's acquisition of Akechi Castle in Mino Province would help to cover the approach.

The projected capture of Okazaki, which was commanded by Ieyasu's son Nobuyasu, was therefore fully in line with all that Shingen had planned and achieved in his own lifetime. The idea, however, met with opposition from Katsuyori's senior generals, although the overall goals of the campaign did not worry them. They urged caution because of the timing. It was very late in the campaigning season so farm labour was already required, and they were also still in arms against Uesugi Kenshin to the north. What encouraged Katsuyori to override the generals' cautious advice was the existence of a traitor in Okazaki called Oga

Yashirō, who had offered to open the gates of the castle to an advance by the Takeda army. The Mikawa operation might, therefore, best be regarded as a planned surgical strike to capture a prize that was lying there for the taking. When Oga's treachery was explained to them the generals dropped their opposition to the campaign, but there was still the factor of manpower requirements, which probably accounts for the fact that Katsuyori departed with only 15,000 men rather than the 25,000 Shingen had taken on the Saijō Campaign. The missing ashigaru would have been working in the fields or serving in the contingent under Kosaka Danjō that had set off for Echigo against Uesugi Kenshin.

Takeda Katsuyori's army departed from Kōfu by the now well-established route via Lake Suwa on Tenshō 3, 4m 21d (8 June 1575). They followed the course of the Tenryūgawa as far as Iida Castle and then headed south-west in the general direction of Okazaki, but while they were somewhere near the border between Mino and Mikawa provinces news was brought to Katsuyori that Oga's plot had been discovered. The traitor had been captured and sentenced to the slow death of the bamboo saw, whereby the felon was buried up to his neck in the ground with his head protruding through a wooden board. Beside the board was a bamboo saw, which passers-by were invited to take to his neck. Oga died in agony a few days later.

An attack upon Okazaki could no longer be considered by Katsuyori with his small force, so he swung the army eastwards, determined to cause some destruction to the Tokugawa before he returned home. At Noda, the scene of his father's mortal wound, Katsuyori began to head downstream along the Toyokawa (Toyo River) towards a worthy secondary objective: the castle of Yoshida (modern-day Toyohashi) on the Pacific Coast. Their attack began on 5m 6d (14 June). The keeper of Yoshida Castle was Sakai Tadatsugu, commander of the eastern Mikawa division of the Tokugawa army and one of Ieyasu's most reliable generals, but when Katsuyori arrived outside its walls he discovered that its 7,000-man garrison had been augmented by Tokugawa Ieyasu himself, who was inside Yoshida Castle with a further 5,000 troops. Ieyasu had heard of Katsuyori's advance and had been following his movements, so he had speedily reinforced the base that he had judged correctly to be the Takeda's secondary target. Yoshida Castle therefore contained a large number of troops; but the one factor that may have encouraged Katsuyori was that the situation was very similar to that which had existed just prior to Mikata ga Hara, because Ieyasu was inside a castle and a large Takeda army was outside it. Could Ieyasu be persuaded to march his army out for a pitched battle once again?

The initial moves in the siege of Yoshida Castle looked promising for the Takeda, because small contingents of the Tokugawa garrison did indeed sally forth to do battle with the Takeda vanguard outside the castle walls. The purpose of these actions would appear to have been little more than the achievement of personal samurai glory, however, because the combatants were not followed by any larger Tokugawa force and were summoned back into the castle once their honourable encounters had finished. This fighting outside the walls of Yoshida Castle nevertheless adds usefully to our knowledge of samurai fighting ashigaru. The spear-and-musket fighting was pursued with

great ferocity by both sides, and one senior Tokugawa samurai at least fell victim to a musket ball, so Katsuyori must have deployed his *teppō-gumi* against the individual seekers of glory. In one such attack against a musket squad, Mizuno Tadashige from the Tokugawa force had his right elbow shattered by a bullet but continued to wield his spear in single combat using his left arm (Futaki 1989: 32).

Takeda Katsuyori eventually realized that the 12,000 men inside Yoshida Castle were not going to oblige him with a battle outside its walls, and that there was little point in carrying out a long siege against such a strong garrison. Katsuyori therefore decided to abandon the secondary objective of the campaign and turned his army in a northerly direction back up the Toyokawa, where lay a very suitable tertiary objective: the tiny Nagashino Castle. This castle was held for the Tokugawa by a small garrison under one of Katsuyori's most hated enemies: Okudaira Sadamasa, who had shifted his allegiance from the Tokugawa to the Takeda and then back again. It would be a good consolation prize with which to conclude the otherwise uninspiring Mikawa Campaign. Katsuyori held council with the 'Twenty-Four Generals' and received from them a considerable difference of opinion over what to do about Nagashino Castle. Shingen's veterans were for making an honourable withdrawal to Kai Province. The younger generals were for carrying on the fighting, however, and it was the latter course of action that appeared most attractive to Katsuyori, no doubt because he reckoned that his honour was at stake.

Showing obvious signs of distress, members of Takeda Katsuyori's senior staff (the so-called 'Twenty-Four Generals') prepare to face the coming battle of Nagashino. The scene is a council of war held the night before the battle, 20 June 1575. Takeda Katsuyori is in the upper left-hand corner. The scroll is now held in the Nagashino Castle Preservation Hall.

MAP KEY

1 **Evening, 27 June:** The Oda/Tokugawa army arrives. Takeda Katsuyori draws up his final plans.

2 **0500hrs, 28 June:** Oda Nobunaga takes up position behind a fence.

3 **0600hrs, 28 June:** The Takeda advance begins.

4 **0800hrs, 28 June:** The attack on the Tobigasuyama forts begins. The Takeda vanguard conducts its first charge.

5 *c.***0900hrs, 28 June:** A second Takeda charge is followed by a third and then a fourth charge. At *c.*1000hrs, the mêlée begins.

6 **1300hrs, 28 June:** The Takeda forces begin their withdrawal; Baba Nobuharu is killed.

Battlefield environment

The castle of Nagashino was situated on a bluff at the confluence of two rivers, both of which were deeper and faster-flowing than they are today. The Takeda siege lines included a number of forts on nearby mountains, which were raided at the same time that the battle of Nagashino began. The famous battle was fought somewhat to the west of the castle where Nobunaga arranged his lines as a temptation to the Takeda, to which Katsuyori responded by launching a series of charges against the Oda defences. A general mêlée then began which

lasted for several hours. The Takeda forces eventually retreated and were pursued, during which time several notable individual encounters took place.

The topography of the area meant that the action was confined to a narrow area of flat land between mountains and the river. The land was crossed by a narrow stream and the paddy fields are likely to have been in cultivation. There had been rain the night before, which Katsuyori hoped would cause problems for Nobunaga's musketeers.

The reconstructed fence at Shidarahara, the site of the battle of Nagashino. The photograph was taken at about the same time during the year that the battle took place. We are looking from the point of view of the attacking Takeda horsemen at about the distance from where the first bullets would have been fired by Oda Nobunaga's ashigaru.

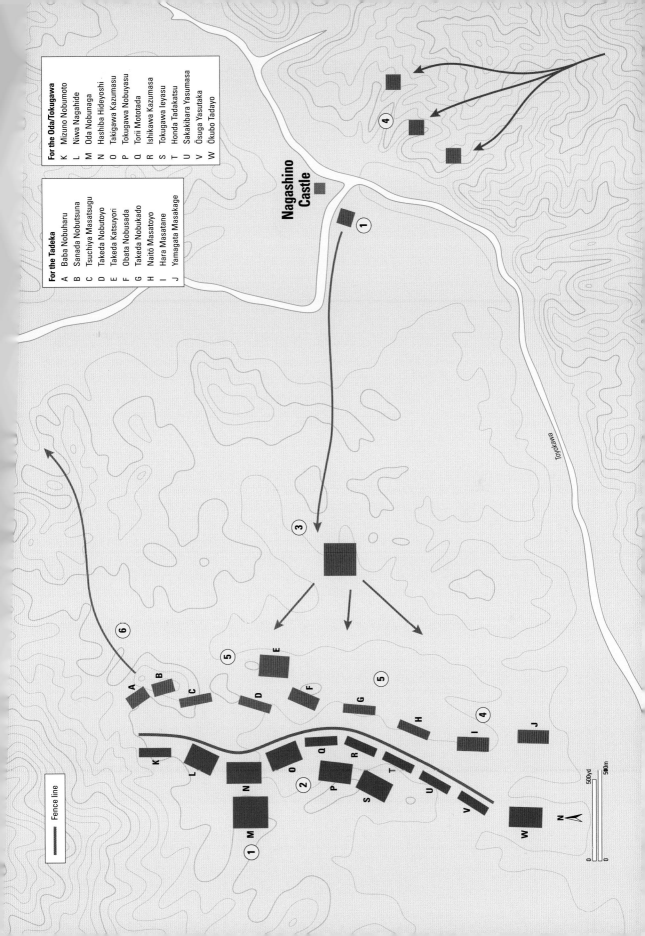

For the Tadeka

A Baba Nobuharu
B Sanada Nobutsuna
C Tsuchiya Masatsugu
D Takeda Nobutoyo
E Takeda Katsuyori
F Obata Nobusada
G Takeda Nobukado
H Naitō Masatoyo
I Hara Masatane
J Yamagata Masakage

For the Oda/Tokugawa

K Mizuno Nobumoto
L Niwa Nagahide
M Oda Nobunaga
N Hashiba Hideyoshi
O Takigawa Kazumasu
P Tokugawa Nobuyasu
Q Torii Mototada
R Ishikawa Kazumasa
S Tokugawa Ieyasu
T Honda Tadakatsu
U Sakakibara Yasumasa
V Ōsuga Yasutaka
W Ōkubo Tadayo

Nagashino Castle

Toyokawa

Fence line

500yd

500m

INTO COMBAT

Takeda Katsuyori began the assault on Nagashino Castle on 5m 11d (19 June). Over the next few days he appears to have tried everything to capture it: a waterborne attack from the rivers that flowed around it; tunnels from the land side, terrific assaults and night attacks. Nothing seemed to make any impression upon the castle, and Katsuyori knew that the longer he remained in his siege lines the more likely it was that Oda Nobunaga or Tokugawa Ieyasu would send a relieving army to the castle's aid. This was precisely what happened, because even though Nagashino was tightly sealed off from the outside world, one brave samurai from the garrison called Torii Sune'emon managed to slip out and contact Okazaki to urge immediate relief. Most heroically of all, Torii returned to the vicinity of the castle and lit a pre-arranged fire beacon to inform the garrison that help was on its way. When he attempted to swim the river back to Nagashino, however, he was captured, and was promised his life if he would send a false message to the besieged saying that no army was on its way and that surrender was inevitable. The Takeda clearly did not trust him because they bound him to a cross before letting him shout across the river. Torii told the defenders in a loud voice that Nobunaga was on his way to relieve them. Brave Torii was immediately put to death for his pains.

To the Takeda the situation at Nagashino was Mikata ga Hara in reverse. Oda Nobunaga arrived with 38,000 men and chose a position that was deliberately intended to entice the Takeda generals and their 15,000 men from within their secure siege lines. It was an uncomfortable comparison for the veterans of 1573, but soon even the old generals had to accept that Katsuyori was determined to meet Nobunaga in battle, so their attempts at persuasion changed from urging retreat to meeting Nobunaga on ground of their own choosing. Baba Nobuharu suggested that if there was to be a fight at all it should be conducted from within Nagashino Castle. The Takeda should therefore make a determined effort to take the fortress before the allied army arrived so that they could then face the Oda and Tokugawa from within its walls. This did not happen, and *Shinchō-Kō ki* comments that had Katsuyori even just occupied the high ground to the west as an alternative he would have been unassailable and the relieving army would have gone home (Kuwata 1965: 169). Instead he chose to meet Nobunaga in battle at Shidarahara – the ground of Nobunaga's own choosing. *Shinchō-Kō ki* describes this in detail, and the existence of the crucial fence is noted very precisely: 'The topography of Shidara [*sic*] was that of a large hollow into which Nobunaga carefully introduced his men in such a way that they would not be seen by the enemy. A palisade for repelling cavalry was erected in front of Ieyasu's and Takikawa's positions' (Kuwata 1965: 168–69).

Prior to the actual battle of Nagashino, Nobunaga arranged a little surprise for the Takeda in their siege lines similar to the raid delivered at Saigagake two years earlier. *Shinchō-Kō ki* puts Nobunaga's thoughts on the matter into very believable words:

'He has brought his troops so close that it must be a gift from heaven, and I shall kill them all,' thought Nobunaga. He considered how he could achieve this

without a single loss on his own side and made plans accordingly. He placed Sakai Saemonnojō in overall command of 2,000 skilled archers and musketeers from Ieyasu's army. He supplemented them with a unit of his own Horse Guards and 500 of his own musketeers, together with *metsuke* [observers]. (Kuwata 1965: 169)

Note how the raid is planned as a joint operation between ashigaru and Nobunaga's elite Horse Guards, evidence of the faith Nobunaga had in cooperation between arms. It also shows how confident he was of stopping the Takeda cavalry on the morrow at Shidarahara without the participation of these troops, even if their numbers seem somewhat exaggerated for what was only a raiding party. They left at midnight under the cover of a heavy rainstorm. Guided by local men, who were familiar with the territory even under conditions of darkness, the raiders covered the 8km distance safely. They swung widely out to the south, completely bypassing the Takeda lines, and approached the Tobigasuyama lines from the rear. At 0800hrs on 5m 13d (21 June), by which time the battle of Nagashino was already under way, this unit launched an attack on Takeda Nobuzane's lines on Tobigasuyama. The assault began with musket fire, followed by the loosing of fire arrows on to the temporary buildings, whose thatched roofs soon caught fire. Takeda Nobuzane was killed in the fierce hand-to-hand fighting that ensued. Soon smoke was seen rising from Tobigasuyama by the besiegers of Nagashino who were powerless to intervene, so all they could do was watch as one section of their army was annihilated. The chaos on Tobigasuyama had also been spotted by Okudaira Sadamasa and the garrison of Nagashino, and when Tobigasuyama went up in smoke Okudaira gave orders for the gate of Nagashino Castle to be opened, and he led a charge out and into the remaining besiegers.

The painted screen of the battle of Nagashino is a contemporary work in which stylized groups of figures convey the essence of the greatest encounter between samurai and ashigaru. In this section two separate units on the battlefield have been combined with artistic licence, so we see the Okubo brothers in charge with Honda Tadakatsu standing behind them. The musketeers are dressed more like samurai than ashigaru, but their armour is still of a simple nature as befits their lowly status. This is a modern copy of the original screen in Nakatsu Castle.

Yamagata Masakage

Few samurai match up to the notion of the ideal mounted warrior better than Yamagata Masakage (1529–75), who became one of the Takeda 'Twenty-Four Generals' and died from an ashigaru bullet at the battle of Nagashino. Masakage was a *samurai-taishō* (general of samurai) and was usually to be found in command of the vanguard of the Takeda army. Born in 1529, he was the son of Obu Dōetsu and the younger brother of Obu Toramasa. His first battle for the Takeda was an attack on Kannomine Castle during the Ina Valley Campaign of 1554. In 1557 he was sent into Shinano Province on a raiding mission in revenge for previous incursions by Uesugi Kenshin and captured Otari Castle. This led to the third battle of Kawanakajima (otherwise known as the battle of Uenohara) later in the same year, which was fought only between Shingen's vanguard under Masakage and Uesugi Kenshin's rearguard. In 1561 Masakage played an important part in the bloody fourth battle of Kawanakajima when his counter-attack against Uesugi Kenshin's vanguard helped save the day. Four years later Masakage had to deal with a family tragedy when his elder brother joined Takeda Yoshinobu in a rebellion against Shingen and was forced to commit suicide. Following his brother's death Masakage changed his family name to Yamagata and took over his brother's practice of dressing all his personal retainers in red armour, who 'exploded on the enemy like a ball of fire' according to *Kōyō Gunkan* (Nakamura 1965: 276), although it must be noted that other units in the Takeda army such as Obata Nobusada's also dressed in red. These *aka sonae* ('red regiments') were seen in action during the operations in Western Kōzuke and Suruga provinces, and in 1569 Masakage helped save the Takeda again at the battle of Mimasatoge (the pass of Mimasa). The plan was for the Hōjō army to ambush the Takeda as they made their way home through the pass after a raid against Odawara. This was carried out, and looked like succeeding until Masakage launched a devastating flank attack on the Hōjō left wing. The main body of the Takeda then broke through and escaped to Kōfu.

Masakage's boldest assignment was to lead the Takeda vanguard on an entirely separate route from the main body during the Saijō Campaign of 1572. He was also present when Takeda Shingen was shot

Yamagata Masakage was one of the finest among Takeda Shingen's so-called 'Twenty-Four Generals'. He led the vanguard during the Saijō Campaign of 1572 that ended in the battle of Mikata ga Hara, and was killed at Nagashino. Here he is seated on a camp stool with his general's *saihai* (baton of command) in his hand. This portrait of him is in the Shingen-ko Museum in Enzan.

and mortally wounded at the siege of Noda Castle in 1573. According to legend, when Shingen's palanquin stopped during the withdrawal to Kōfu the dying Shingen called out to Masakage to plant his banner on the bridge of Seta, the vital river crossing that has always acted as the outer defence of Kyoto, Shingen's ultimate goal. The loyal Masakage went on to serve Takeda Katsuyori, who ignored every attempt by the veteran warrior to dissuade him from a series of rash and unwise actions. As the devoted servant of the Takeda Yamagata Masakage accepted the orders that Katsuyori gave, and this consummate leader of mounted samurai paid for it by dying a suitable death during the charge at Nagashino when he was hit by a volley of ashigaru bullets.

Meanwhile the showdown at Shidarahara that history knows as the battle of Nagashino had already begun. The two armies were initially separated by 20 *chō* (2.18km), and the Oda army was drawn up behind the protection provided by a series of loose wooden fences augmented by large wooden

Toyotomi Hideyoshi

The ashigaru who served Japan's daimyo led a life that was divided between farming and fighting. With no family name and usually no land of their own, they fought and died almost anonymously, so little is known about any individual ashigaru. The battle of Nagashino, however, provides an example of one man at least who had had the experience of ashigaru life and had earned samurai status because of his conduct on the battlefield. This was Toyotomi Hideyoshi, the future unifier of Japan then known as Hashiba Hideyoshi, who was one of Oda Nobunaga's unit commanders. The *shiba* character in his family name was taken from the name of Shibata Katsuie, a general of Nobunaga whom Hideyoshi greatly admired, and the granting of a family name by Nobunaga in 1567 was an immense privilege that demonstrated how Hideyoshi had 'arrived' in the samurai class.

The future Hideyoshi had been born in very humble circumstances in the village of Nakamura (within modern Nagoya City) to a man who farmed land in this area of the Oda's Owari Province. His father Yaemon served when occasion demanded as an ashigaru in the army of Oda Nobuhide (Nobunaga's father), until an injury excluded Yaemon permanently from military service. There are no firm details about Yaemon's precise role, but he died in 1543 leaving a daughter and the seven-year-old Hideyoshi. His widow later remarried. In a popular tale of Hideyoshi's childhood we read of his being sent to a temple to be a monk but absconding to join Oda Nobunaga's army. He certainly served Nobunaga as an ashigaru and acted as a sandal bearer, a role equivalent to that of a batman. Hideyoshi would therefore have been found standing near Nobunaga as one of his personal attendants on the battlefield, and another popular story has him endearing himself to Nobunaga by his practice of warming his master's sandals inside his own shirt. At this time he assumed the family name of Kinoshita, but by 1567 Nobunaga gave him an official one – Hashima – following his conduct at the siege of Inabayama. By now Hideyoshi was a samurai, and he continued to serve at the battle of Anegawa in 1570, following which he received extensive grants of land. At Nagashino we see him at the height of his powers under Nobunaga.

Following Nobunaga's death in 1582 Hideyoshi carried out a coup, and after a series of massive military campaigns unified Japan in 1591. He then set in motion a series of measures that would eventually separate the samurai from the land, distinguishing the fighting samurai from the cultivating farmers, and ensuring along the way that no one else would follow in his footsteps from ashigaru to samurai.

This print by Yoshitoshi Tsukioka (1839–92) shows a mounted samurai using his two-handed sword to defend himself against the young Toyotomi Hideyoshi who is on foot and using a spear to bring him down. Hideyoshi is shown without a helmet to indicate his then lowly status as an ashigaru.

shields in which were left gaps to allow a counter-attack. *Shinchō-Kō ki* relates: 'The position at the front was the privilege accorded to a local warrior, and was therefore allotted to Ieyasu' (Kuwata 1965: 168–69). Unfortunately, the historical sources are in conflict over the number of firearms deployed behind the fence. *Mikawa Go Fudo-ki* says 3,000, but the earlier *Shinchō-Kō ki* notes only 1,000, which is a considerable discrepancy. The larger figure was well within Nobunaga's resources, but Nobunaga's enduring reputation depends on the use he made of his matchlock muskets, not the numbers of them he possessed. Indeed, his biographer Ōta Gyūichi had been surprised by the large number of firearms supplied to Nobunaga in 1570 by allies from the Negoroji temple, which greatly exceeded the number deployed by his master and 'made the heavens shake with their sound' (Kuwata 1965: 110).

Even though it uses the smaller number *Shinchō-Kō ki* portrays gunfire as the decisive element in the epic struggle, where the ashigaru musketeers were under the command of five *bugyō* ('commissioners', equivalent to the Takeda's *ashigaru-taishō*) named by *Shinchō-Kō ki* as Sassa Narimasa, Maeda Toshiie, Nonomura Masanari, Fukuzumi Heizaemon and Ban Kurōzaemon. The musketeers were protected as they reloaded by the ashigaru spearmen, whose contribution to the victory should not be underestimated; it is also more than likely that the musket fire would have been considerably augmented by the ashigaru *yumi-gumi*, who could put more arrows into the air compared to the number of bullets fired. To add to the defence provided by the palisade and the spears, a smoke screen must also have been expected to be produced by 1,000 matchlock muskets firing every few minutes.

Confident that the shock of the famous Takeda charge would sweep Oda Nobunaga's army to one side regardless of any casualties from bullets, Takeda Katsuyori ordered an advance along the line. The right wing of the Takeda was under the overall command of Anayama Nobukimi, and Baba Nobuharu led its vanguard with 120 mounted samurai. The brothers Sanada Nobutsuna and Sanada Masateru followed, while Tsuchiya Masatsugu and Ichijo Nobutatsu completed the assault. The centre companies were composed of about 3,000 men under the overall command of Takeda Nobukado, Katsuyori's cousin. Their vanguard was led by Naitō Masatoyo. Within the centre company was the largest single contingent of horsemen in the Takeda army: a 500-strong unit under Obata Nobusada. The left wing was composed of a further 3,000 men under the overall command of Takeda Nobutoyo, another cousin of Katsuyori's. Takeda Nobutoyo was the son of Takeda Nobushige, who had been killed at Kawanakajima in 1561. The vanguard of the left wing was in the most experienced hands of all, those of Yamagata Masakage, whose contingent attacked first.

These movements would be captured forever on the contemporary painted screen of the battle of Nagashino owned by the Tokugawa Art Museum in Nagoya. It is a highly stylized depiction because a few figures are used to represent what must have been large-scale and highly confusing encounters, but its major theme is the conflict between ashigaru musketeers and mounted samurai, who perish in a very dramatic fashion. Groups of musketeers discharge their weapons simultaneously under the watchful eyes of dismounted Oda and Tokugawa samurai, while the Takeda horses are shown falling dead and throwing their riders in classic images of a broken cavalry charge. *Shinchō-Kō ki* describes how the five waves of mounted attacks actually worked out, naming the Takeda generals who were met by the gunfire: 'Nobunaga gave orders for his ashigaru to take up forward positions

close to the enemy lines and watched them as they did so. The first wave of the attack was led by Yamagata Masakage. To the beat of their war drums the Takeda men came charging. Blasted by ferocious gunfire they pulled back ...' (Kuwata 1965: 170).

The more elaborate and romantic *Mikawa Go Fudoki* also describes Yamagata Masakage's advance against the right wing of the Oda army. The Oda commanders there were Ōkubo Tadayo and Ōkubo Tadasuke, who had fought the Takeda before at the battle of Mikata ga Hara and were under no illusions as to the task which was required of them (Kuwata & Uwagata 1976: 70–78). Their troops were not protected by a fence so Yamagata Masakage must have thought his opponents would be a pushover, and the clash is well illustrated on the Nagashino screen. Unhindered by any palisades, and with a wider ground over which to operate than their comrades along the line, the troops of the Takeda vanguard took casualties from the bullets and crashed into the Ōkubo body of troops. Here a fierce hand-to-hand fight developed, the first mêlée of the day.

Looking at the situation from the point of view of the horsemen who charged the palisades, it would be wrong to think of a cavalryman literally charging headlong into a fence, even if that fence was not blazing with gunfire. Under normal circumstances the horsemen relied on the infantry breaking as the cavalry approached, so that the foot soldiers could be cut down at will, just as had happened at Mikata ga Hara. A typical horseman at Nagashino might be expected to stop in front of the palisade to wield his spear to the best advantage against the defenders, who may well have loosed off one shot but should now be running in terror. As it turned out the actual scenario –

ABOVE LEFT
Two of the Takeda contingents (the Yamagata and Obata units) at Nagashino had samurai who dressed all in red. The colour would have resembled the face mask on this specimen of red armour in Kawagoe History Museum. It also shows one way by which a simple helmet bowl can be given an individual touch. In this case the crown is covered with horsehair to resemble a human scalp.

ABOVE RIGHT
A section from *Ehon Toyotomi Kunkoki* showing a small group of ashigaru spearmen in a daimyo's *yari-gumi*. The implication is that their spears are very long *nagae-yari*, as shown by the shafts disappearing out of the illustration. The ashigaru spearmen played a vital part at Nagashino even though their achievements have been overshadowed by the use of gunfire during that battle.

repeated along the line – was that the musket fire caused initial chaos but soon became sporadic and individual as the immediate area of the battlefield turned into one huge hacking mass of men and horses. The samurai may have sought single combat, but that would have been difficult amid the mêlée and the smoke. The personal attendants tried to protect their lords, while the ashigaru spearmen and musketeers lashed out at any they could see who were identified as enemy.

Returning to the individual case of Yamagata Masakage, here was a samurai skilled in single combat who had already demonstrated his prowess outside the walls of Yoshida Castle. He also still had the assistance of the three samurai who had attended him at that time. Yamagata Masakage therefore continued to fight as an individual and must have stayed on his horse, because we read of him breaking free from the mêlée and leading his men in another charge against the unit of Honda Tadakatsu. Here he was met by a further hail of bullets and was shot from off his horse's back. As he fell an Oda samurai ran up and cut off his head, which was taken back in triumph. *Shinchō-Kō ki* continues as follows to say that Yamagata Masakage was:

> … replaced by a second wave under Takeda Nobukado, whose men attacked, were repulsed and charged again even though the muskets had thinned their ranks, just as Nobunaga had ordered. When over half their number had been hit they retreated but were replaced by a third wave. These were Obata Nobusada's troops from Western Kōzuke Province, who were dressed all in red. Warriors from the Kantō like these are skilled horsemen. Their preferred tactic was always to charge straight into the enemy ranks on horseback, so they galloped forwards to the beat of their war drums. But Nobunaga's men, lined up behind shields, waited with their muskets at the ready. Over half of Obata Nobusada's samurai were shot down, so his tattered force quit the battlefield. The fourth wave of the attack was led by Takeda Nobotoyo, whose samurai were dressed in black. (Kuwata 1965: 170)

These dramatic events were only the first phase of the samurai-versus-ashigaru encounter that was developing across the battlefield, because the battle of Nagashino still had several hours to run. From this point onwards the spears and swords of the Oda samurai came into their own to add to the ashigaru's own bullets, arrows and blades along with the occurrence of hand-to-hand fighting between mounted Takeda samurai and ashigaru spearmen. The presence of the palisade and the covering archery fire by the well-organized ashigaru *yumi-gumi* would have provided the opportunity for the musketeers to reload, and while they were doing so the spears of the *yari-gumi* 'would meet horses' breasts', in the later words of *Zōhyō Monogatari* (Sasama 1969: 68). Some thrusts would have been delivered through the fences, although it is likely that more (and much fiercer) encounters would have taken place against Takeda cavalrymen who had passed through the deliberately designed openings. These gaps allowed the creation of a killing-ground for the separated horsemen, who became the prey both for ashigaru spears and samurai swords.

It is important to note that *Shinchō-kō ki* insists that none of Oda Nobunaga's troops were let out of the protection of the fence. The precise words are, 'Thus one enemy unit relieved another, but not even one of Nobunaga's

In this modern copy of the Nagashino Screen on display in the Matsuura Historical Museum in Hirado, we see war drummers running forward beside mounted Takeda samurai who are being shot down. In the upper left of the picture a samurai takes the head of Yamagata Masakage.

commanders made his troops go forward from their lines. Nobunaga simply put more *teppō* to work, letting his ashigaru deal with everything' (Kuwata 1965: 171). The musketeers themselves would of course have been totally preoccupied with the business of loading, firing and reloading, keeping up the rhythm that their officers forced upon them and protected by the long spears of the *yari-gumi* ashigaru, whose contribution to the battle was in no way inferior to that of their musketeer colleagues. Yet still the Takeda charges kept coming and still the Oda guns kept firing:

> Nobushige's men were shot down too and forced into a retreat. Baba Nobuharu led the fifth wave of the attack. They charged forward to the beat of the war drums, but Nobunaga's men stood firm in their positions and shot down Baba Nobuharu's followers, just as they had done for the others. The Takeda army continued with these repeated attacks in spite of the casualties. (Kuwata 1965: 171)

The next phase of the battle was a clash between Nobunaga's ashigaru and the now disordered and sometimes isolated Takeda mounted samurai, because not all of the senior casualties among the Takeda were killed during the charge. Two were killed during the retreat. The first prominent person to be caught was the commander of the vanguard of the centre squadron, the veteran Naitō Masatoyo, who was accompanied by the 100 men left out of his initial command of 1,000. Naitō Masatoyo was apprehended by Honda Tadakatsu, Ōsuga Yasutaka and Sakakibara Yasumasa, who had with

Shibata Katsuie (1522–83) was one of Oda Nobunaga's generals, and is shown in *Ehon Taikō ki* as a highly skilled mounted samurai. In this picture, his spearwork has sent four ashigaru flying into the air while four more are trampled underfoot. His loyal standard bearer runs along behind him holding Shibata's personal device of a golden *gohei* (a device used by Shinto priests to bestow blessings).

Samurai and ashigaru clash at Nagashino

Samurai view: This view shows the onslaught of the Takeda horsemen at the battle of Nagashino. The section depicted is the attack by the centre company's vanguard under Naitō Masatoyo, who leads his men against the fence. Masatoyo is dressed in prominent red armour. Even though this is a cavalry charge none of the horsemen are fighting alone, because each is accompanied by personal attendants on foot, although in nearly all the cases they have been left behind by the enthusiastic horsemen. Apart from Masatoyo they are all dressed fairly uniformly in practical battledress armour with an identical black *sashimono* (back flag) bearing the Takeda *mon* in white.

Ashigaru view: This picture shows the moment of firing by Oda Nobunaga's ashigaru who are stationed in the centre of the line behind the protection of the fence. This is the contingent who were under the command of Honda Tadakatsu, whose antler helmet is visible to the rear along with his personal banner depicting Shoki, the Queller of Demons from Chinese mythology. Their matchlock muskets blaze away, and soon the whole scene will be obscured by smoke. Because the musketeers have been drawn from different units in Nobunaga's army their ranks are far from uniform. The days of musket drill and rotating volley firing still lie in the future, but they stand and kneel shoulder to shoulder and fire on the command of the *teppō-kogashira*, who is seen lifting his bamboo *mashaku* (ranging pole). Behind the musketeers stand the rows of spearmen. Some of the musketeers have their weapons protruding already through the fence.

them a number of ashigaru archers. The archers fired at Naitō Masatoyo, hitting him many times. He fell from his horse, and, seeing him trying to lift his spear, a samurai called Asahina Yasukatsu thrust a spear at him and took his head. The most heroic death during the withdrawal was suffered by the other great veteran Baba Nobuharu, who took it upon himself to ensure Takeda Katsuyori's safety by covering his retreat. When the Oda forces caught up with the rearguard unit Baba Nobuharu announced his name in the manner of the samurai of old, stressing that only the greatest of samurai would take his head. The written account has him surrounded by a group of six spearmen in a classic ashigaru manoeuvre. On the painted screen the challenge is answered instead by two representative figures with spears, who attack him simultaneously.

Shattered by the carnage all around him, Takeda Katsuyori abandoned the battlefield and the hopeless struggle. Meanwhile swift messengers had conveyed the grim news back to Kōfu, so Katsuyori was met en route

Takeda samurai fall like flies on this painted screen of the battle of Nagashino. In a detail from the copy in Nakatsu Castle the units under the Takeda generals Mochizuki Nobumasa and Hara Masatane are shown being shot down, while in the lower right-hand corner Obata Norisada, the leader of the Western Kōzuke unit, rides on grimly; he would in fact survive the battle.

by Kosaka Danjō, who had abandoned his campaign against the Uesugi and hurried down to safeguard his lord's entry into Kai Province. The appearance of the Kosaka force on the border set a limit to Nobunaga's pursuit, so Katsuyori escaped. He finally withdrew into the safety of the mountains, accompanied at the last by only two samurai retainers, Tsuchiya Masatsune, brother of another Tsuchiya who was killed at Nagashino, and Hajikano Masatsugu. It would be several years before Nobunaga finally made an end of Katsuyori at the battle of Temmokuzan in 1582.

Takeda Katsuyori left behind on the battlefield of Nagashino 10,000 dead out of a total Takeda army of 15,000, a casualty rate of 67 per cent. As *Shinchō-Kō ki* puts it, 'About 10,000 Takeda troops, from high ranking warriors to common ashigaru, fell on the field of battle. Countless others either fled into the mountains to die of starvation, or were thrown from bridges into the water, or they drowned in the rivers' (Kuwata 1965: 171). The losses were particularly acute among the upper ranks of the Takeda retainers and family members. These were the men who had led from the front and had charged the Oda/Tokugawa lines at the head of their followers. Out of 97 named samurai leaders at Nagashino, 54 were killed and two badly wounded, 56 per cent of the total. No fewer than eight of the veteran Takeda 'Twenty-Four Generals', the men of Takeda Shingen's generation, lay dead. Losses on the allied side were also quite heavy, 6,000 killed out of 38,000, but this did not compare to the tragedy for the Takeda that bore the name of Nagashino, the greatest victory in Japanese history that can be credited in any way to ashigaru overcoming samurai.

Analysis

The three battles described above illustrate important milestones on the road towards Japan's military revolution which, just as in contemporary Europe, would be characterized by a new reliance on mass infantry tactics conducted by organized and highly valued foot soldiers. At Uedahara the process had only just begun, and the confusion on the battlefield also reflects Takeda Shingen's inexperience of open warfare. Up until then Shingen's personal involvement had only been in castle attacks, leaving the conduct of field battles to his trusted generals. Uedahara – a battle of movement fought on a wide plain – was a new situation and the first defeat of Shingen's career.

The experience of Uedahara showed that the discipline which would soon be needed for successful musketry was already being applied to archers and spearmen even if self-discipline was woefully lacking in the samurai leader of the Takeda vanguard, who let Shingen down very badly. The entire emphasis of the Murakami's ashigaru deployment in 1548 is on the actions of their archers, spearmen and a handful of musketeers wielding Chinese-style handguns, all of whom had been well prepared to face an attack by the famous Takeda mounted samurai. Japanese infantry tactics may still have been work in progress, but they were already proving effective, because at Uedahara samurai were felled by 'hails of arrows' and Itagaki Nobukata was surrounded by 'hundreds of spears' belonging to disciplined ashigaru, who brought down a major prize (Nakamura 1965: 54).

By the time of Mikata ga Hara matters had moved on considerably. Both sides now commanded organized ashigaru squads, an asset that Tokugawa Ieyasu was prepared to throw away by abandoning his strong defensive position inside Hamamatsu Castle. Takeda Shingen, who had his own musket squads too, teased out the Tokugawa firepower and their likely position by the simple expedient of forcing expendable recruits to throw stones at them from a close distance. He then risked a cavalry charge, followed by another, and by the time that his third wave reached the Tokugawa *hatamoto* a classic mounted

A re-enactor from the Marugame Group on Shikoku Island fires his matchlock musket in unison with his colleagues. The smoke from this small discharge is quite noticeable, and one can appreciate the dense clouds that must have accompanied the battle of Nagashino, when 1,000 guns were discharged in rapid succession. The Marugame Group recreate Sengoku Period musketry with great accuracy, even though they do it dressed as samurai rather than lowly ashigaru.

samurai victory was on the cards. The Tokugawa ashigaru who could have stopped his mounted advance were in retreat along with the samurai.

At the battle of Nagashino Shingen's heir Takeda Katsuyori would be decisively defeated by a skilled general who finally used a combination of arms to its best advantage, whereby organised bodies of musketeers, backed up by archers and protected by simple field defences and the long spears of their comrades, broke a mounted charge and allowed their own samurai to come to grips with their enemy. It is therefore tempting to see Nagashino as the decisive moment in history when ashigaru finally triumphed over mounted samurai, but such an analysis of the victory is somewhat exaggerated. As an example of this tendency, A.L. Sadler, in his *The Maker of Modern Japan* (1937), whose source for the battle was *Mikawa Gofudo ki*, credited Nobunaga with choosing 'three thousand specially selected marksmen' who would 'fire in volleys of a thousand men alternately … It was the machine gun and wire entanglement of those days' (Sadler 1937: 103–05). This has become the accepted view of Nagashino, and the notorious final scene depicting the battle in Kurosawa Akira's film *Kagemusha* (1980) makes the action look as though the bullets were indeed delivered by machine guns.

Oda Nobunaga did not possess the resources to mimic machine guns by keeping up a constant barrage of fire, because true volley firing by three alternating ranks – a tactic that would be first introduced to Europe many decades later – depended upon hours of drill and practice. Many of the musketeers Nobunaga arranged behind the palisades were not his own troops

This print by Utagawa Kuniyoshi (1798–1861) shows a remarkable fight between a mounted samurai and ashigaru. While defending his castle of Nagakubo against the Takeda army in 1543 Oi Sadataka (here called Odai Yorisada) is unhorsed and wounded by a hail of arrows from the Takeda ashigaru, yet he still manages to transfix three of them at once on the end of his spear.

but had been supplied by allies and subordinates just a few days before the battle took place. There was therefore no time to drill them in anything like the counter-march of Renaissance Europe. Alternate volleys of numerous bullets were certainly delivered, but these should be understood as a response to the successive waves of attack launched by the Takeda cavalry, not the rotating barrage in *Kagemusha*. The firing was nonetheless deadly and was delivered not in any sporadic or opportunistic manner but in organized volleys controlled by the iron discipline of the five senior samurai whom Nobunaga had placed in command of the hastily assembled musketeers.

So why did Takeda Katsuyori charge the guns? *Kagemusha* makes it look like an act of mass suicide, but the written accounts show that Katsuyori was well aware of the number of guns that Oda Nobunaga possessed and that two factors had encouraged him to proceed in spite of them. The first was the heavy rain of the night before, which was likely to have rendered the matchlock muskets unusable. The second was the great speed and impact of the Takeda mounted charge. Katsuyori was a cavalryman through and through and had led a charge at Mikata ga Hara against a disordered enemy. At Nagashino his mounted samurai had only 200m to cover. It was likely that there would be some casualties from bullets, but not enough to break the momentum of the charge which would then disorder the Oda troops. Logic then said that the Takeda horsemen would be upon the hopeless ashigaru as they tried to reload. There would be hand-to-hand fighting in which the Oda guns would be useless, and indeed an encumbrance. The renowned Takeda samurai would sweep the flimsy fences to one side, cut down the ashigaru with their swords and spears, engage the demoralized enemy samurai and pursue them down to the Toyokawa, where the river would cut off their retreat. The outcome, of course was the exact opposite.

The manner in which Katsuyori's defeat was accomplished was more than a personal disaster. It was also a challenge to samurai pride, because effective musket fire, much more than archery, required the ashigaru to be placed at the front of an army, and that was the position traditionally occupied by the most loyal and glorious samurai. For centuries there had been great honour attached to being the first to come to grips with an enemy, so to place the lowest-ranking troops in such a position ignored the demands of samurai glory. The successful daimyo of the future would learn how to cope with this, and would regularly use ashigaru fire to break down the enemy ranks ready for a spirited charge by samurai, at which point the samurai spear and sword would dominate the fighting, just as Oda Nobunaga had done at Nagashino.

By the 1590s these arrangements had become commonplace, reflecting a profound change in attitude by the daimyo, although not everyone approved. Some samurai still thought that ashigaru were contemptible and that the matchlock muskets they wielded so effectively should really be weapons for an individual samurai, so we read many years later in *Jōzan Kidan* (Chronicle of Armed Warfare, 1770): 'As a rule on the battlefield, it is the job of the ashigaru to face on to the enemy and fire *teppō* in volleys into the midst of the enemy. As for the *teppō* owned by samurai, they are for shooting and bringing down an enemy of importance' (Sasama 1969: 61). There also exists one scornful and snobbish comment in another chronicle which laments that, 'instead of ten or twenty horsemen riding out together from an army's ranks, there are now only ashigaru armies' (Sasama 1968: 289). These 'ashigaru armies' of course represented nothing less than the emergence in Japan of large-scale infantry tactics in an exact parallel to the similar trend that was happening in 16th-century Europe.

The fateful charge of the mounted samurai of the Takeda clan at Nagashino is brilliantly realized in this full-sized diorama at the Ise Sengoku Village, a historical theme park near Ise in Mie Prefecture. The samurai are carrying typical *mochi-yari* spears and have the Takeda badge on their back flags.

Aftermath

The events that occurred on the battlefield of Nagashino constituted a vital episode in the Japanese military revolution, and nothing better illustrated its political fallout than what was to happen when the smoke had cleared, because the victorious Oda Nobunaga went on to become the first daimyo to lay the foundations for a newly unified Japan. One of the ways he did this was by developing the concept towards which Takeda Shingen had been moving: that the different fighting skills and weaponry of the samurai and the ashigaru were complementary and could be brought together in an organized and disciplined manner. Indeed, not only could it be done, it *had* to be done, and so successful would the model prove that when Japan's reunification was finally achieved by Toyotomi Hideyoshi in 1591 the ashigaru were on the way to being integrated into daimyo armies as the lower ranks of the once-exclusive samurai class. Not only that, but Toyotomi Hideyoshi, the daimyo who brought Japan under one sword for the first time in over a century, had originally served as an ashigaru.

The three key battles described in this book had pointed the way in which Japanese warfare was moving, and from Nagashino onwards the battles of the Sengoku Period had to be approached as potential contests between the shock of a cavalry charge and the disciplined reaction from protected infantry. Thus it was that at the battle of Komaki in 1584 both sides took to the field under commanders who had fought at Nagashino, so both erected field fortifications. So firmly held was each line that one army went off on a raid elsewhere and the subsequent battle of Nagakute was fought on open fields far from the defences. Eight years later, musketry would become particularly effective during the very one-sided battles of the invasion of Korea in 1592, and even the effects of an initial volley of musket fire could make a tremendous difference to the outcome of a battle. At Tennōji in 1615, with which the siege of Osaka concluded, some of the Toyotomi troops were forced into a disastrously precipitate action by musket fire.

The overall lesson that Japan had learned by the time of the peaceful years of the Edo Period was that no unit within a daimyo's army could operate alone. There had to be cooperation between the ranks, and in time the nomenclature of the samurai class evolved to reflect this. In particular, the term *hatamoto* gradually changed from meaning the Tokugawa household troops who served literally beneath the flag on a battlefield to the senior tier of the samurai class who administered the Shogun's affairs in peacetime and, if ever it again became necessary, in war. Beneath the *hatamoto* ranked the samurai known as *yoriki*, otherwise known as *gokenin* (housemen), while below the *yoriki* ranks were the ashigaru, now both understood and appreciated as the lowest-ranking samurai, yet 'proper' samurai nevertheless. With this formal acknowledgement of the ashigaru as samurai came the further recognition provided by the remarkable *Zōhyō Monogatari*, written by a serving samurai who had command of ashigaru and wished to pass on to posterity his own tips on how to get the best out of them. The significance of *Zōhyō Monogatari* lies in the fact that it was written at all. The wars of the earlier centuries had produced a literature that concentrated almost exclusively on the individual heroic prowess of named samurai. *Zōhyō Monogatari* is a handbook for the commanders of ashigaru, a class of fighting man whom the earlier writers had preferred to regard almost as non-existent. By 1649 the ashigaru were recognized for the immense contribution they could make as real samurai. Their integration was complete.

This vivid book illustration is a graphic depiction of a group of ashigaru overcoming a samurai who has been pulled from his horse. Two attack him with spears; one has a sword and another has a dagger. The samurai looks on helplessly as the fifth ashigaru wrests his sword from his right hand.

BIBLIOGRAPHY

A note on sources

The researcher of Japanese warfare in the Sengoku Period is fortunate in that there are a large number of primary sources available. These include battle reports, often compiled by a commander on the field in order to claim rewards for his men from a higher authority; family histories, chronicles of wars and battles (sometimes composed while there were eyewitnesses still living); and the romantic versions of the latter which were the *gunkimono* or 'war tales'. The latter works tended to exaggerate the individual exploits of heroic samurai, but they contain many fascinating points of details regarding weapon use that help to expand on the overall narrative of a conflict. Three works in particular have been employed for this book. *Kōyō Gunkan* is the epic chronicle of the Takeda family attributed to Kōsaka Danjō, one of Shingen's 'Twenty-Four Generals', and finally completed by Obata Kagenori in 1616. It has many of the characteristics of a *gunkimono*, and some of its sections are outright works of fiction, but its account of the battle of Uedahara is backed up by other contemporary sources and is widely regarded as reliable. Much more reliable is *Shinchō-Kō ki*, the biography of Oda Nobunaga written by his follower Ōta Gyūichi, who was an eyewitness to many of the incidents he describes. *Shinchō-Kō ki* is therefore regarded as both accurate and factual so, for example, the figures Ōta Gyūichi presents for the number of matchlock muskets at Nagashino are more likely to be true than those found within *Mikawa Gofudo ki*. That work took its final form only in 1833 and although based on the huge amount of detail that was available about its subject, Tokugawa Ieyasu, the author's desire to please the Tokugawa shoguns may have led to a certain exaggeration. My treatment of Mikata ga Hara is drawn from *Mikawa Gofudo ki*, which presents an account of the battle so unflattering to Ieyasu that it has a considerable ring of truth!

Also quoted here are *Hōjō Godai ki* and *Ōu Eikei Gunki*, which deal with the Hōjō family of Odawara and the northern daimyo respectively, and have been used in this book for points of detail, as have a few minor snippets from elsewhere. Finally, we have the valuable *Zōhyō Monogatari*, which is attributed to one of Ieyasu's generals. He is describing weapons and modes of fighting of his day, which are based on the lessons learned during the Sengoku Period, so there are some traps for the unwary historian such as his description of the knife that makes a bow into a spear. Nevertheless his account of ashigaru life has the ring of truth, even if their organization during the time of Takeda Shingen and Oda Nobunaga was much less rigid.

All the quotations I have translated from Japanese sources are taken from printed versions of the originals as listed below under the names of their modern editors, except in the case of *Zōhyō Monogatari*, where I have used the extensive sets of excerpts in the two books listed by Sasama: *Buke Senjin Sakuhō Shūsei* (1968) and *Ashigaru no Seikatsu* (1969). Sasama's 1968 book is also the source of brief quotations from *Jōzan Kidan* and other documents as noted above. There are a few other original sources quoted in the two main secondary works for Mikata ga Hara and Nagashino by Owada (1989) and Futaki (1989) respectively.

In this print by Utagawa Kuniyoshi (1798–1861) a samurai on foot lowers his *mochi-yari* (spear) against an oncoming attack of what is likely to be a group of ashigaru spearmen, although all that we can see are the tips of numerous threatening spear blades.

Works cited

Brown, Delmer M. (1948). 'The Impact of Firearms on Japanese Warfare, 1543–98', in *Far Eastern Quarterly* Vol. 7: 236–53.

Elisonas, J.S.A. & Lamers, J.P., trans. and ed. (2011). *The Chronicle of Lord Nobunaga by Ōta Gyūichi.* Leiden: Brill.

Futaki Ken'ichi (1989). *Nagashino no tatakai.* Tokyo: Gakken Mook.

Hagiwara Toshio, ed. (1966). *Hōjō Godai ki*, in *Sengoku Shiryō Sōsho* Vol. 21. Tokyo: Jinbutsu Ōraisha.

Imamura Yoshio, ed. (2005). *Ōu Eikei Gunki.* Tokyo: Jinbutsu Ōraisha.

Kuwata Tadachika, ed. (1965). *Shinchō-Kō ki.* Tokyo: Jinbutsu Ōraisha.

Kuwata Tadachika & Utagawa Terao, eds (1976). *Kaisei Mikawa Gofudo ki.* Tokyo: Akita Shoten.

Lamers, J.P. (2000). *Japonius Tyrannus: The Japanese Warlord Oda Nobunaga Reconsidered.* Leiden: Hotei Publishing.

Lidin, Olof G. (2002). *Tanegashima: The Arrival of Europeans in Japan.* Guildford: Nias Press.

Maruta Junichi (1988). 'Sengoku saikyō – Takeda kibadai no shinsō', in various authors, eds, *Takeda Shingen* (Vol. 5. of the series *Rekishi Gunzō*) Tokyo: Gakken: pp. 170–75.

Nakamura Kōya et al., eds (1965). *Kōyō Gunkan* Vol. 2. Tokyo: Jinbutsu Ōraisha.

Owada Tetsuo (1989). *Mikata ga Hara no tatakai.* Tokyo: Gakken Mook.

Sadler, A.L. (1937). *The Maker of Modern Japan.* London: Allen & Unwin.

Sasama Yoshihiko (1968). *Buke Senjin Sakuhō Shūsei.* Tokyo: Yūzankaku.

Sasama Yoshihiko (1969). *Ashigaru no Seikatsu.* Tokyo: Yuzankaku Shuppan.

Suzuki Masaya (2000). *Teppō to Nihonjin.* Tokyo: Chikuma Shobō.

Tanaka Yoshiatsu (1997). 'Kiba gundan 'saikyō' densetsu no shinsō o ou', in various authors, eds, *Sengoku Kassen Taizen*, Rekishi Gunzō Series Vol. 50. Tokyo: Gakken: pp. 104–09.

Turnbull, Stephen (2017). *Ninja: Unmasking the Myth.* London: Frontline Books.

Varley, H. Paul (1994). *Warriors of Japan as portrayed in the war tales.* Honolulu: University of Hawaii Press.

A modern-day drawing from Ueda Castle showing a *teppō-gumi* (musket squad) in action. They are going through the various stages of ramming, preparing the pan and firing from a kneeling position. They are also using cartridge boxes, introduced sometime after Nagashino, which were very useful in speeding up the reloading process.

INDEX

References to illustrations are shown in **bold**.

Thrift, a spectacular coastal plant, is best seen along
the coast road between Bunmahon and Annestown

Coastal heath near Poll na gCapall, Ballynagaul More

A guide to...

The

Waterford Coast

Declan McGrath

2011

Published in 2011

ISBN 978-0-9541062-3-2

Printed by Intacta Print Ltd., Waterford Airport Business Park, Waterford,
www.intactaprint.ie, 051 306006.

Front cover: *Creadan Head*
Back cover: *Goat Island*

Contents

This publication has received support from

The Heritage Council

under the

2011 Heritage Education, Community and Outreach Grants Scheme

An Chomhairle Oidhreachta
The Heritage Council

This support is greatly appreciated.

A guide to...

The

Waterford Coast

ACKNOWLEDGEMENTS

I would like to thank the following people for their help
in various ways during the writing of the book:

Dominic Berridge, Albert Byrne, Ian Doyle, Colm Long, Paul Green, Pat Hayes,
Dr Martyn Linnie, Cliona O'Brien, Professor Mark Seaward and Dr Paul Walsh.

The following people read and considerably improved drafts of the book:
Dominic Berridge, Paul Green and Dr Paul Walsh.

A selection of the bird records were taken from **www.waterfordbirds.com**; I thank Paul Walsh
for permission to use these and the many observers who contribute these valuable
sightings. Similarly, most of the cetacean records are validated and available on **www.iwdg.ie**;
I thank the many contributors and The Irish Whale and Dolphin Group for making this
valuable resource available.

The maps are reproduced with permission:
© Ordnance Survey Ireland/Government of Ireland,
Copyright Permit No. MP 002111.

Christy O'Connor, as usual with this publication and previous publications,
added his considerable expertise to make this the attractive publication that it is.

Eamon Griffin of Intacta Print was also extremely supportive and helpful.

Finally, to my wife Muireann and two daughters Máire and Laoise, I owe a debt of
thanks for allowing me the time and absences to compile and write the book.

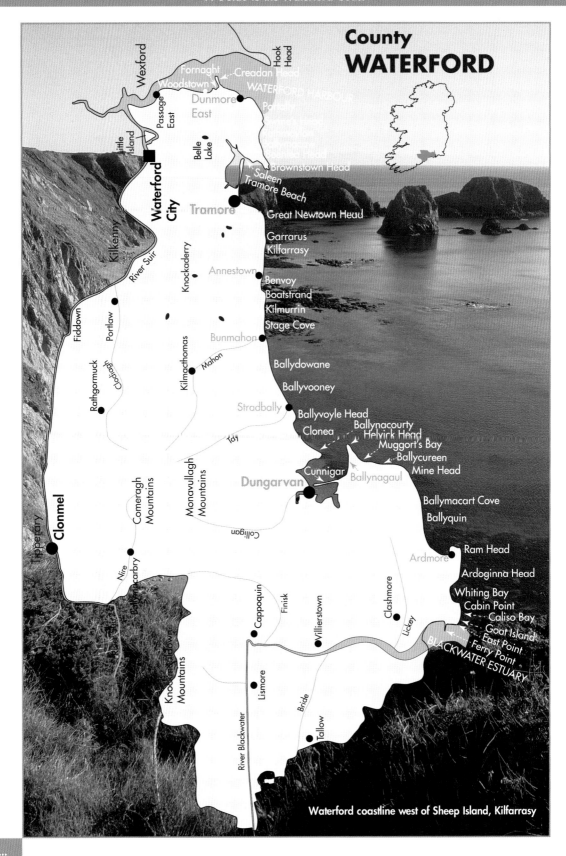

County WATERFORD

Wexford
Hook Head
Fornaght
Woodstown
Creadan Head
WATERFORD HARBOUR
Passage East
Dunmore East
Port
Little Island
Belle Lake
Saleen
Brownstown Head
Waterford City
Tramore Beach
Kilkenny
Tramore
Great Newtown Head
Knockaderry
Garrarus
Kilfarrasy
River Suir
Annestown
Benvoy
Boatstrand
Fiddown
Portlaw
Kilmurrin
Stage Cove
Kilmacthomas
Bunmahon
Rathgormuck
Clodiagh
Mahon
Ballydowane
Ballyvooney
Stradbally
Ballyvoyle Head
Clonea
Ballynacourty
Tay
Helvick Head
Muggort's Bay
Ballycureen
Cunnigar
Ballynagaul
Mine Head
Monavullagh Mountains
Dungarvan
Ballymacart Cove
Comeragh Mountains
Ballyquin
Colligan
Clonmel
Tipperary
Ram Head
Ardmore
Ardoginna Head
Nire
Ballymacarbry
Whiting Bay
Cabin Point
Cappoquin
Finisk
Villierstown
Clashmore
Lickey
Caliso Bay
Goat Island
East Point
Ferry Point
BLACKWATER ESTUARY
Knockmealdown Mountains
Lismore
Bride
Tallow
River Blackwater

Waterford coastline west of Sheep Island, Kilfarrasy

Introduction

The Irish coastline is long and indented and, at around 7,500 kilometres, it has a longer coastline than most of its European neighbours. It is a diverse coastline that has been spectacularly shaped by the sea over time, though certain areas have been subject to more intense activity. The western seaboard, for example, suffers most from the Atlantic storms that pound its coastline and, over time (lots of it), high rugged cliffs and spectacular beaches have formed. The more sheltered east coast is generally low-lying and sandy, but the south coast, although less exposed than the west coast, is also impacted by the relentless onslaught of the sea, and impressive coastal features have formed. All around the Irish coast there are high cliffs, indented bays, rocky headlands, impressive sand dune systems and highly productive estuaries where the land–and the runoff from it–meets the sea, allowing a distinctive flora and fauna to develop.

The Waterford coastline at around 170 kilometres long, is reasonably linear and has all the coastal features that typify the Irish coastline. There are high cliffs, small offshore stacks and islands, superb sandy beaches, two massive estuaries at either end of the county (Waterford Harbour and the Blackwater Estuary) and there are two other important wetlands in between, at Tramore and Dungarvan. All these features are reasonably close to the cities, towns and villages of the county and the wider region, and they form an important recreational asset and source of inspiration throughout the year, especially in summer, when the warming waters and spectacular coastal scenery attracts people from far and wide.

The first Mesolithic hunter-gatherers arrived on the Irish coastline around 10,000 years ago and they sustained themselves and their families by living off the fruits of the sea, mostly shellfish (cockles and mussels, mainly) and whatever fish they could catch. In doing so they left the remains of their foraging in kitchen middens, the most spectacular of which in Waterford can be seen in the Tramore dunes. However, since the ending of the last Ice Age, which allowed people to arrive and thrive here, much of the earlier coastal landscape is buried under the sea as the land readjusted to the removal of the massive ice sheets, causing southern areas to sink into the sea while more northern areas are now well above the level of the sea that prevailed during the Ice Age.

Later inhabitants left their mark on the coastal landscape by constructing promontory forts, which not alone had a defensive purpose, but their prominent coastal position provided excellent views of the sea offshore, allowing users to monitor and control sea movements. Many of these promontory forts

The impressive dune system at Tramore

I ndil cuimne
ar na hiascairi a cailleaó
ar an tarna lá bealtaine 1945
óá lá tar éis óeireaó an cogaió
nuair a cuaig mianac cogaió in
acrann ina lionta
7 gur séideaó a mbáó san aer.

maraíoó
Seán Ua Gríofa,
a mac, Seán,
7 nioclás Ua Cuidite (Cuoo).

Plaque at Helvick pier in memory of John Griffin, his son John and Nick Cuddihy, who died when their boat, *Naomh Garbhán*, struck a mine in 1945

are still visible on the landscape and there are some impressive examples on the Waterford coast, though there are relatively few extant tower houses and castles; some of these imposing structures disappeared into the sea in the face of relentless erosion.

The most notable and prominent of the visible coastal structures are the more recent towers and lighthouses that warn mariners of dangers close to shore. These have a dominating but pleasant visual impact on the coastal landscape, apart from the vital service they provide. The coastal towns and villages, where people live in sight of the coast are vibrant places, and enjoy the many natural facilities on offer. However, the coastal zone is under constant development pressure and there is an increasing demand for additional development along the coast. Some of this demand is to cater for the natural expansion of existing settlements but there is also pressure for one-off housing and other facilities close to the coast, which potentially could alter the physical appearance of the coast as people flock to it and thereby destroy the very resource they wish to enjoy.

Waterford, as a maritime county, has a rich seafaring tradition and, over the generations, many have lived in and off the sea, sometimes in cruel conditions, and the coastal communities of the county have developed and evolved from seafaring and the rich harvests of fishing activities locally and further afield. But many have left our shores too for employment opportunities elsewhere, usually related to fishing activities, and a good number never returned. The sea has exerted a heavy toll on the local fishing community, and there have been countless tragedies, when men (mostly) paid the ultimate price for plying the most dangerous workplace in the world, and have left grieving loved ones, whose loss is endured for generations, when their menfolk never come home from the sea.

The coastal zone is the natural interface between land and sea and it is inhabited by a range of wildlife species that is both diverse and spectacular. The waters just off the land are usually sheltered, shallow and productive, where a whole host of species live out their lives or even just part of it, in often turbulent but generally benign conditions. These species in turn attract a range of other life forms and it is probably true to say that the nearshore coastal zone has many more species than landward habitats. Many species have to come to land to breed and the caves and cliffs often abound with wildlife in the summer months, when throngs of breeding birds in particular enliven the coastal cliffs. Even in winter, other coastal areas such as the

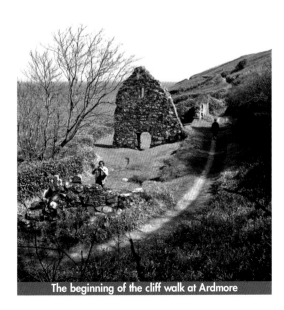

The beginning of the cliff walk at Ardmore

wetlands and the estuaries teem with wintering birds availing of the massive food resources available to them while escaping the harsher conditions elsewhere.

The coastal zone, for a coastal county like Waterford, is of inestimable value to the people of the county, who–probably without exception–visit the coast throughout the year. Consequently, coasts and seas enhance the overall quality of our lives and they are vital assets locally and nationally, with many benefits for the local and national economy, which are sustainable into the future for many communities, and particularly those closest to the sea. In this respect, viable, productive and sustainable fisheries are essential for the economic well-being of coastal communities but water quality, properly regulated coastal development and the overall quality of the coastal zone are equally important for the many, many people who visit and enjoy the coast.

However, the coastal zone–perhaps the most natural of the varied habitats we have in the county–is under further threat from the consequences of climate change, and valuable natural habitats such as mudflats, salt marsh and dune systems, and all their associated species are gradually being whittled away, and what remains will be increasingly constrained by man-made coastal defences, themselves under threat from rising sea-levels.

The Waterford coast is therefore of great interest to us and there is much to enjoy and appreciate there throughout the year.

The purpose of this book is to inform the interested visitor of what it is about the Waterford coast that is worthwhile and interesting. The complex and varied geology is outlined in a reasonably simple way and the forces that shape the cliffs, the sandy beaches and the wetlands are described. Some weather parameters, by comparison, have a relatively benign impact in coastal areas, though wind is a major formative agent, which often exerts a significant influence and occasionally causes destruction on a massive scale in vulnerable coastal areas when strong winds combine with high tides and strong currents. All these issues are discussed in some detail and the consequences outlined.

There are many facilities along the coast which provide important information for the seafaring communities that depend on the sea and for others who enjoy the sea in all its moods for recreation. Obvious archaeological features on the coastal landscape and the more important ones are highlighted so that the visitor may seek them out and learn about their function and former use. There is a comprehensive section on the flora and fauna to be seen along the coast and in the seas just offshore (records up to the end December 2010 are presented); thus any reasonably curious and observant visitor will know what to look out for and what might be seen during a day at the seaside.

Sculpture ("Ice, Fire & Water") just west of Dunabrattin

The picturesque Portally cove

offer superb walking in spectacular coastal surroundings. Walks to and around the coastal areas over time allows the visitor to observe and monitor the changes that inevitably occur, and all the recent and ongoing changes are mentioned to familiarise the reader with the agents of coastal change and the often profound implications these changes pose for the coastal zone. The Waterford coast is an important conservation area and the various designations that apply to it are outlined in some detail along with the site descriptions listed in local and national development plans. Any visitor to the Waterford coast needs to be prepared and there is a chapter giving details on weather, required equipment, safety, access information and what maps are available. There is also a comprehensive list of reading material to assist the reader wishing to acquire additional information.

For many people, the main attractions of any coastal area are the accessible beaches where uninterrupted walks may be enjoyed. All the Waterford beaches are described, including how to get to them, what may be seen there and particularly what to look out for. There are very few cliff walks in the county, but those that can be safely walked

The Waterford coast has charmed generations of people attracted to its many and varied features. The hope is that this book will foster an interest in, and an appreciation of, what is available to see and enjoy on the Waterford coast, and in doing so, may help to protect and preserve this spectacular coastline for those that follow.

Shore angling at Passage East

4

Geology, Climate & Coastal Processes

Waterford is well-endowed with scenic landscapes and physical features, due largely to the underlying rocks and the forces that formed and shaped them over geological time. The east-west trending valleys and ridges reflect the trend of folding; generally the ridges are anticlinal (the folds are convex up) while the valleys are synclinal (the folds curve downwards). The Comeraghs and the Knockmealdowns are formed from the sandstones and mudstones of the Devonian Period, while the river valleys comprise the poorly-exposed Carboniferous limestones. Drainage generally follows the trend of the synclines with tributaries and streams flowing at right angles off the ridges; at Cappoquin the river Blackwater flows east along a major valley before abruptly turning southwards to cut through a deep channel in an anticlinal ridge on its journey to the sea.

A GEOLOGICAL TIME SCALE			
Age (before present, in millions of years)	**Era**	**Period**	**Event**
1.6	CENOZOIC	Quaternary	Man arrives, vegetation spreads, Ice Ages
6.5		Tertiary	Opening of Atlantic Ocean, Volcanoes
135		Cretaceous	Erosion
205	MEZOZOIC	Jurassic	North Atlantic begins to open, Irish & Celtic Seas develop
250		Triassic	
290	UPPER PALAEOZOIC	Permian	Faulting, desert conditions
355		Carboniferous	Land submerged, limestone deposition in shallow seas
410	Rocks of this age are represented in Waterford	Devonian	Mountain building, massive erosion
438	LOWER PALAEOZOIC	Silurian	Closure of Iapetus Ocean
510		Ordovician	Volcanism
570		Cambrian	
ca. 1800 ca. 4000 4600	PRECAMBRIAN		Mountain building, metamorphism Oldest rocks in Ireland Oldest rocks on Earth Formation of Solar System

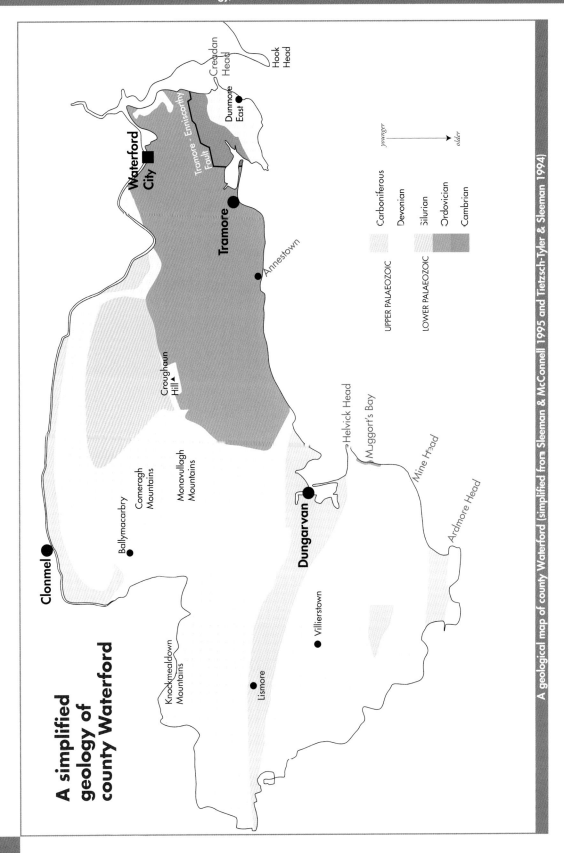

A simplified geology of county Waterford

Clonmel ●

Ballymacarbry ●

Comeragh Mountains

Monavullagh Mountains

Knockmealdown Mountains

Lismore ●

Villierstown ●

Dungarvan ●

Helvick Head

Muggort's Bay

Mine Head

Ardmore Head

Croughaun Hill ▲

Annestown ●

Tramore ●

Waterford City ■

Tramore - Enniscorthy Fault

Dunmore East ●

Credan Head

Hook Head

younger ← → older

UPPER PALAEOZOIC
- Carboniferous
- Devonian

LOWER PALAEOZOIC
- Silurian
- Ordovician
- Cambrian

A geological map of county Waterford (simplified from Sleeman & McConnell 1995 and Tietzsch-Tyler & Sleeman 1994)

Most of the underlying rock is hidden beneath a mantle of sediments laid down in the much more recent Quaternary Period and these in turn are covered with a distinctive vegetation which all but obscures what lies beneath. However, even if the mantle of vegetation and the Quaternary deposits were to be rolled back, the geological history of our scenic county would not be obvious; erosion on a massive scale has removed some of the geological succession, much of it is also buried deep beneath what is obvious and earth movements over time have removed some of the evidence and deposited it elsewhere. More recently, human developments have cloaked the landscape with above-ground structures which hide the layers of geological history. Paradoxically, some of these developments have increased our knowledge of geological events and activities in that they reveal the underlying rock which would not otherwise be exposed; sometimes too the exposed sediments are quarried to facilitate development.

Although only some of the geological succession is represented in Waterford, much of what is obvious is spectacular and is responsible for the dramatic landscapes of the county. This is especially true along the coast of Waterford, where the turbulent interface between land and sea has resulted in superb features and contorted cliffs, which, lacking in vegetation, reveals the varied geological history and events which formed them.

GEOLOGY

Geologists believe that the crust of the earth consists of rigid plates, perhaps up to 100 kilometres thick under the continents (though they are much thinner under the oceans), which are supported on less rigid material, the partly molten interior of the earth. These massive plates move slowly relative to one another, at rates of a few centimetres a year, but over millions of years they cover large distances. The edges of the plates may move apart, as new molten magma is squeezed up between them–as is happening today down the middle of the Atlantic Ocean–or they may jostle one another, converging, colliding, or sliding past one another (often causing earthquakes or tsunamis, like the one, for example, which caused so much damage in March 2011 in Japan). In coming together, one plate, usually an oceanic plate may be forced downward under the other, the continental plate.

Subduction is the term used to describe what happens when tectonic plates with different densities collide. The denser plate sinks beneath the other, which may happen when a plate carrying a continent rides over an oceanic plate, forming a trench that may be several miles deep and wide. As the lower plate is pushed down into the mantle it heats up, and water and other volatile chemicals are released from it, causing parts of the overlying mantle to melt. Some of the resulting melt rises up through the crust, forming chains of volcanoes (often these are referred to as island or volcanic arcs) subject to many earthquakes, as are seen today all down the western coasts of North and South America, or in the East Indies and Japan. Immense forces are involved when plates collide and, as a result, one plate or both can become crumpled on an immense scale leading to the formation of mountain ranges as one mass heaves against another. The Himalayas are the result of the Indian Plate crashing into the Eurasian plate but there is no trench here as both plates were carrying continents where the plates collided.

During the Lower Palaeozoic Era, over 500 million years ago, the northern and southern parts of Britain and Ireland were split wide apart and attached to two separate continents on different plates; the northern part was connected to a proto-American continent, and the southern part to a landmass attached

460 million year old rocks at Ballyvooney cove

Sediments, chiefly of sand, silt and clay, accumulated on the sea floor of the Iapetus Ocean, sometimes up to thousands of metres in thickness and volcanoes erupted huge quantities of lavas and ashes into the ocean and along the coasts of the continents. This was one of the greatest periods of volcanic activity the world has known. The Lower Ordovician rocks of the county (much of east Waterford and the inlier at Muggort's Bay) were deposited in a deep marine basin on the southern margin of the Iapetus Ocean. Subduction of the ocean floor under the continental margin around where the present landmass of the county is situated resulted in considerable volcanic activity on the continental plate creating the basaltic rocks found at Bunmahon, the shales around Dunabrattin and the Tramore Limestone Formation further east.

From Tramore to just east of Ballyvoyle Head, the rocks are middle to late Ordovician age (around 500 million years old) and are well exposed along the coast but poorly so inland. Collectively, they are known as the Duncannon Group of rocks as the sequences extends right into Wexford. They are largely volcanic rocks, shale-dominated sedimentary successions and near-surface intrusions and were formed along the volcanic arc at the continental margin above the subducting Iapetus Ocean. Within this Group, the Bunmahon Formation is best seen along the coast between Knockmahon and Stradbally. Further east, the Dunabrattin Formation is comprised of laminated shales, siltstones and fine sandstones, while the Tramore Limestone Formation has impure limestone bands with a rich shelly fauna within the calcareous sandstones, siltstones and shales. The acid volcanic rocks and shales of the base of the Campile Formation can just be seen at Great Newtown Head. The inlier of Lower Palaeozoic rocks at Muggort's Bay (near Helvick Head) cannot be dated precisely and they are dominated by shales, sandstones and

to proto-Africa. A vast sea, the Iapetus Ocean, enveloped much of the globe between the two continents, and formed a wide oceanic basin between Laurentia (present day Scotland, Greenland and North America) and Baltica to the south (which included most of Ireland, England, Wales and the rest of Europe); these two continents were further apart than the British Isles are today from North America. At the end of the Silurian Period (around 440-420 million years ago) the Iapetus Ocean had completely disappeared following subduction of the tectonic plates and the preceding continental collision brought together fossils that were once alive in separate seas. The collision of the continents united the two parts of Ireland and this line of collision can be traced right across the country. The two continents remained attached for 200 million years before moving apart again to form the Atlantic Ocean and the configuration of the continents that we see today.

siltstones with thin tuffs from volcanic eruptions and thinly bedded distal turbidites from deep water sedimentation.

When subduction was almost complete, and the Iapetus Ocean nearly closed, the sedimentary sequences of the Silurian Period were deposited. These sediments and the volcanic material were to form the Lower Palaeozoic rocks which were to be folded, buckled and intruded by huge masses of granite (some of which can be seen in the Wicklow Hills) to produce a great mountain chain when the two continents approached one another. The mountain chain known as the Caledonides, can be followed through the Appalachians on the east coast of North America, Newfoundland, parts of Greenland, northwest Ireland, Scotland and Scandinavia. The eroded stump of this vast mountain chain can be traced across Ireland with folds running east-northeast/west-southwest, giving a Caledonide 'grain' to the hills of southeastern Ireland.

By the early part of the Devonian Period (410 million years ago) the Caledonide mountain chain had reached its maximum height and for the next 50 million years or so they were subjected to prolonged erosion. The higher the mountains the more severe was the onslaught from frost and ice, and erosion by mountain torrents, which whittled down the Caledonides and spread the eroded material across the lower ground below them. Enormous quantities of sand and gravel were deposited from huge meandering rivers and laid down as gravel bars in braided streams and were then spread across the great flood plains; some of the debris also reached the sea to the south of Ireland. All these Devonian sandstones, siltstones and mudstones were laid down in low altitude, desert or arid conditions. During this time volcanoes continued to erupt, though much less frequently, and the ever-thickening layers of Caledonide debris, together with the ash and lavas, were gradually cemented under their own weight into Old Red Sandstone rocks in

Bedding planes and ledges in the conglomerate of the Old Red Sandstone cliffs at Dunmore East provide safe nesting ledges for kittiwakes

The big cliffs east of Annestown

a large trough which continued to subside, generating sequences up to six kilometres thick. Because of the hostile environment in which these sediments were deposited, no fossils were created, and hence Old Red Sandstone rocks are difficult to date precisely.

The name "Old Red Sandstone" is given because of the distinctive colour of the rock, produced by the oxidation of iron, one of the most abundant elements in the world, in this terrestrial, dry and warm environment. The red colour of the sedimentary rocks of east Waterford in particular is especially obvious and striking in the cliffs around Dunmore East though it is not as obvious in the cliffs of the Comeragh Mountains, largely because of weathering and the mantle of lichens covering the rocks. The Comeragh Mountain Old Red Sandstone is a more complete succession than the other outliers in the county, (northwest of Waterford City around Quarry Road and in the cliffs around Dunmore East) where only the uppermost layers of the Old Red Sandstone succession is obvious, and reflects the localised nature of sedimentation here along the edges and outside of the eastern section of the Munster Basin, which stretched from county Kerry to the Comeraghs in county Waterford.

The Comeragh succession is up to five kilometres thick but it thins out rapidly towards the coast and is only around 100 metres thick at Ballyvoyle Head and a little more (140 metres) at Helvick Head. The most obvious coastal outlier of the Comeragh Old Red Sandstone succession is on the east side of Ballydowane Bay, where the interbedded conglomerates, red and purple siltstones and sandstones can be seen in the cliff face. At Helvick and further west at Ballyquin (east of Ardmore), there are red mudstones with sandstones where considerable quantities of quartz pebble conglomerate line the bases of the sandstone, while at Mine Head there are greyish-red

mudtsones and sequences of sandstones, varying in colour from pale red to yellowish-green. At Ardmore, there are grey and pale red sandstones with grey red siltstones; the lowest Carboniferous beds occur near the boat slip where they are exposed at low tide. Further west at Whiting Bay, the lowest beds can be seen by walking south from the car-park; these are mostly pebbly sandstones.

During the Carboniferous Period, after the Old Red Sandstone was deposited, much of northwest Europe was again covered in a warm sea, which was inhabited by marine organisms. Ireland by now was around the equator and lapped by shallow, clear seas but then great thicknesses of plant and animal remains accumulated on the ocean floor and subsequently became consolidated into limestone. This Carboniferous limestone, despite all the subsequent upheavals, still forms part of the rock mantle of much of the country. The beginning of the Carboniferous Period in the Munster Basin is recorded in the rocks around Ardmore, and, although it is only five metres thick, it is a recognisable mudstone unit, indicating a deepening of the sea and the movement of the shoreline of the late Devonian-early Carboniferous sea northwards. It represents the deposition that occurred on the North Munster Shelf which succeeded the Munster Basin in the Carboniferous Period. To the north, a more extensive formation occurs along the Lismore syncline, which is about 300 metres thick but it is generally very poorly exposed except on the coast at Clonea.

Earth movements again affected Ireland, mainly in the south of the country. The sandstone beds or layers now forming the Comeraghs were then horizontal. The Old Red Sandstone and the younger limestone deposits were crumpled into mainly east-west folds, and faulted resulting in the typical east-west trending hill and valley topography of south Munster. The folds are gentle, and the dips of the beds are generally quite slight–20° to 30° at most–but some of the fault blocks have been tipped almost on end, giving near vertical beds, as can be seen on the coast at Bunmahon Head and Ballydowane Bay. Once again atmospheric erosion savaged the rocks and the easily weathered limestones were gradually eroded away, exposing the more resistant underlying sandstones. Only in the synclinal valleys of the rivers Blackwater and Suir did the limestone survive, between the sandstones of the anticlinal Knockmealdown and Comeragh Mountains.

The more recent sediments to be deposited have never been consolidated into rock. For most of the Quaternary Period (1.6 million to 10,000 years ago) the country was covered by vast ice sheets on a number of occasions. During this Pleistocene Epoch, the massive ice blocks scoured the bedrock, and deposited vast quantities of sediment to form prominent landscape features around the country. These glacial deposits are quite thin (usually no more than 3-4 metres thick) though up to 60 metre thickness has been recorded in the Blackwater valley. The county of Waterford was impacted by ice sheets from the midlands and from the Irish Sea basin, while smaller glaciers impacted locally from the higher mountain valleys where they gouged out the hollows or coums seen so spectacularly in the Comeragh Mountains. In the cliffs on the shore of Whiting Bay, shelly glacial deposits from the Irish Sea Basin can be seen. Usually the local glacial deposits reflect the geology of the underlying rock, though the limestone valley of the Blackwater is carpeted with sandstone till from the hills further north.

The Holocene Epoch of the Quaternary Period (10,000 years ago to the present) has been a warm postglacial period with little of the cataclysmic events that preceeded it. However, in Ireland at least, it has been wet and mild, which resulted in the formation of blanket bogs on the high mountains and fens in the valleys. Rivers developed extensive flood plains and coastal features such as beaches, mudflats and spits formed as sea level stabilised and land masses rebounded while the extensive sea cliffs around our coast became ever more prominent.

Quite apart from the significant and often impressive landscape features of geological activity, there are important mineral resources resulting from geological upheavals which have been, and continue to be, exploited for the common good. Currently, the two most important quarries in the county are at Grennan, on the main N25 at Carroll's Cross, where the volcanic rock rhyolite is quarried, and at Kilgreany, near Cappagh, where limestone is extracted. A major copper-bearing lode or vein near Bunmahon was mined from 1824 to 1878 and up to 800 people were employed in extracting the copper from the rock. Another brief period of extraction activity followed at nearby Tankardstown in 1906. Copper iron sulphide (or chalcopyrite) is the main copper ore to be found within the volcanic rocks along the coast here and the host rocks are well exposed in the friable cliffs. Other, smaller quarrying activities were undertaken inland from Bunmahon and some are now used as storage facilities by Waterford County Council. Off the Waterford coast, there are extensive deposits of sand and gravel on the seabed but there has been little or no exploitation of these other than exploration at the mouth of Waterford Harbour off Hook Head.

Of similar importance are the significant groundwater resources retained by the limestones and the volcanic rocks. Regionally important aquifers exist in the Carboniferous limestones along the synclinal valleys and the Devonian rocks that outcrop on some of the anticlinal ridges. In these aquifers, the permeability of the parent rock material depends on the widespread fracturing of the rock, and, in the case of the limestone areas, the rock fracturing has been enhanced by chemical dissolution. The sub-surface groundwater resources are quite significant and some of Ireland's most productive boreholes are available for exploitation in the area. Because groundwater is easily contaminated, the important aquifers are carefully guarded and development within or close to them is strictly controlled.

Soils

Generally the soil associations along the Waterford coast reflect the nature of the parent rock beneath. Ice played a part too in that it not alone ground down the underlying rock material but it also transported massive quantities of sediment which accumulated locally when the ice retreated. The Waterford area was impacted upon by massive glaciers from the north, and to a lesser extent by glaciers from the Irish sea, which impinged on the east and southeast coasts. Only parts of the Comeraghs remained unglaciated such was the extent of the ice cover. Once the ice retreated time, climate, topography and,

more lately, man's influence has formed and shaped the soils that are now covered in a green mantle of grass and other vegetation throughout the county.

The central coastal area of county Waterford is dominated by acid brown earths. This is a well-drained soil, with a coarse, sandy texture and a dark, greyish-brown colour. The coarse nature and friability of this earth type ensure that it is easily tilled and is ideal for most agricultural purposes. Associated with this acid brown earth is poorly drained gley soil, which forms a significant proportion (up to 25%) in places. The synclinal valleys in the county are dominated by acid brown earths formed from glacial drift of mixed Old Red Sandstone and Carboniferous limestone and this soil type is found around Dungarvan and Ardmore where the underlying rock is Carboniferous limestone. Grey brown podzolic soils can be found where there is a stronger limestone influence; gley soils also occur in this association. These are agriculturally rich soils that are easy to cultivate and suitable for all types of crops and livestock.

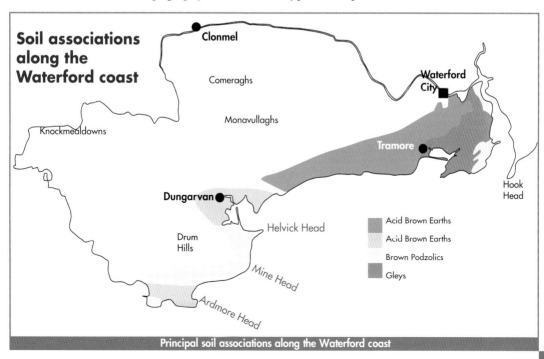

Soil associations along the Waterford coast

Clonmel

Comeraghs

Waterford City

Knockmealdowns

Monavullaghs

Tramore

Hook Head

Dungarvan

Acid Brown Earths

Acid Brown Earths

Brown Podzolics

Gleys

Drum Hills

Helvick Head

Mine Head

Ardmore Head

Principal soil associations along the Waterford coast

The coastal fringe at the extreme east of the county is dominated by brown podzolics, which comprises around 60% of the soil association (acid brown earths and gleys make up the remainder). These soils are formed mainly from glacial drift of Old Red Sandstone, shales and slates. The distinctive red colour is particularly obvious in ploughed fields and wherever development occurs (around Creadan Head, for example). Nearby, to the northeast of Tramore, a calcareous glacial till carried in from the Irish Sea and intermixed with limestone and shales, forms the predominant and poorly-drained gley soils with a high clay and silt content (grey brown podzolics are also present in the soil association here). While grassland is the main land use along the coast, the soils are also suitable for cultivation, because of favourable climatic conditions and good land management.

The topography of the land close to the Waterford coast is generally flat to slightly undulating and is usually no more than 150 metres above sea level. At this elevation, at the interface between land and sea, there are high and spectacular sea cliffs with a characteristic flora able to withstand the usually hostile and changing conditions; the cliffs are also home to a large number of breeding seabirds and some landbirds for whom cliffs are a favoured habitat. Other species also occur in winter and the rich agricultural land behind these cliffs offers feeding opportunities throughout the year for many of these breeding and visiting birds.

CLIMATE

The cliffs that are so spectacular all along the Waterford coast are primarily the result of geological activity and the ready availability of sediment whose supply was enhanced by varying sea levels. They are also subject to the erosive forces of the sea acting over millions of years, which continually shape and rework them. This constant attack releases large quantities of sediment that is then ground down and moved by the sea, usually in the direction of the prevailing winds, which are typically southwesterlies along the south coast of Ireland. This sediment load may eventually be deposited close inshore to form and

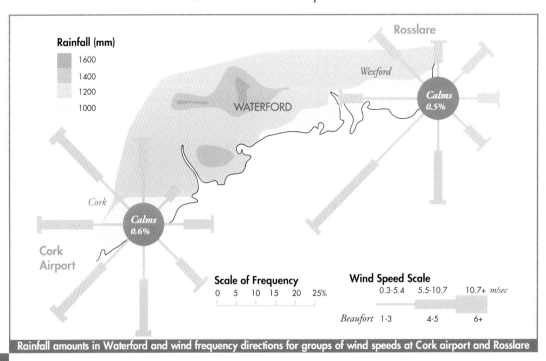

Rainfall amounts in Waterford and wind frequency directions for groups of wind speeds at Cork airport and Rosslare

CLIMATE VARIABLES FOR WEATHER STATIONS IN SOUTHEAST IRELAND IN 2007	Yearly Rainfall (mm)	Average Temperature (°C)	Sunshine (hrs)
Station			
Cork Airport	1,057	10.6	4.3
Kilkenny	880	10.6	4.3
Rosslare	757	11.4	4.85
Waterford City (1951-80)	1,008	10.0	n/a
Dungarvan (1951-80)	n/a	10.1	n/a

n/a = not available. Source: www.met.ie

supplement beaches and shingle areas. These 'soft' coasts (the beaches, dunes and salt marsh areas) are more susceptible to the erosive powers of the sea and change quickly and often more obviously in response to extreme weather events, particularly storms.

Hence, while the configuration of the coast, its aspect and slope in relation to the surrounding topography are important factors, meteorological conditions such as wind speed, its direction and the related wave regime, have had an important bearing on shaping the coastal features observable today.

Latitude, closeness to the sea (oceanicity), and topography are the main geographical factors which influence climate. The Waterford coast is around 52° N and at this middle latitude the atmospheric circulation is predominantly westerly.

Weather
Wind speed and direction are the main parameters influencing coastal areas; of less importance are rainfall and temperature as these are less extreme in their occurrence and effects. Snow falls infrequently and rarely lodges and ice formation along the coast is usually a rare occurrence, except during very severe cold conditions (in late November and December 2010, for example).

Sea area forecasts are broadcast regularly throughout the day at nominated times on national radio and more frequently on the Irish Coast Guard VHF Channels. Coastal reports are also issued from several stations around the coast (Roche's Point Automatic in Cork is the closest station to Waterford) and these coastal reports include information on wind direction (on a 16 point compass and speed in knots, or more lately in metres per second where one metre per second = 1.94 knots = 2.24 miles or 3.58 kilometres per hour), weather, visibility (in nautical miles), pressure (hectopascals) and pressure tendency (which gives a good indication of how weather might change). In coastal areas, visibility is an important consideration for mariners and this element of the forecast is described using standard terms: good (>5 nautical miles or 9 kilometres), moderate (2-5 nautical miles or 4-9 kilometres), poor (0.5-2 nautical miles or 4 kilometres) and fog (<0.5 nautical miles or 1000 metres). The forecasts may also be accompanied by swell warnings (if swells of greater than four metres

SUMMER RAINFALL IN MILLIMETRES AT WATERFORD COASTAL STATIONS IN 2008	Total	Max Daily	Rain Days
Station			
Fenor	434.6	44.9	54
Tramore	461.4	41.4	59
Dungarvan	388.6	31.4	51
Stradbally	497.4	53.0	60

Source: www.met.ie

BEAUFORT WIND SCALE				
Force				Wave
	Description		Speed	height
		knots	km/hr	m
0	Calm	<1	<1	0.1
1	Light air	1-3	1-5	0.1
2	Light breeze	4-6	6-11	0.2
3	Gentle breeze	7-10	12-19	0.6
4	Moderate breeze	11-16	20-28	1
5	Fresh breeze	17-21	29-38	2
6	Strong breeze	22-27	39-49	3
7	Near gale	28-33	50-61	4
8	Gale	34-40	62-74	5.5
9	Strong gale	41-47	75-88	7
10	Storm	48-55	89-102	9
11	Violent storm	56-63	103-117	11.5
12	Hurricane	64+	118+	14

are present) or small craft warnings (if winds of Force 6 or more are expected up to 10 nautical miles offshore).

Because of the rotation of the earth, the movement of air in the northern hemisphere is deflected to the right by a phenomenon known as the Coriolis effect. As winds are generated when air moves from areas of low pressure to areas of high pressure, they circulate largely in an anti-clockwise direction around the area of low pressure. These areas of low pressure form out in the Atlantic and track in an east to northeast direction over Ireland, generating winds that blow largely in one direction. The prevailing wind direction along the south coast of Ireland is between south and west with northwest, west, southwest and south winds blowing most often though southwesterlies are probably the most frequent and intense.

Winds have three main effects on coastal processes: they dry and then move large amounts of sediment and sand in inshore areas, particularly on beaches, sandflats and sand spits; they may raise (or lower) water levels, which may then impact severely on soft coastlines; and they generate waves which may move large amounts of sediment that may damage or even destroy man-made coastal protection structures or they may undermine soft cliffs.

There are no weather stations in Waterford and hence no direct data is available on the important weather variables along the Waterford coast. The nearest weather stations are at Rosslare, county Wexford, opened in 1956 and closed in 2008 (it was replaced by an automatic station at Johnstown Castle in county Wexford) and Cork Airport, opened in 1961. Data from both these stations can be used to infer weather patterns along the Waterford coast.

Winds speeds vary from occasional flat calm conditions to very infrequent storm force conditions when wind speeds may reach Force 10 on the Beaufort scale or even more. However, Force 1 to Force 6 wind speeds are more common. Strong winds are generally more prevalent from October through to April, although they can occur at any time of the year, and they may be much more frequent and relentless in some years, thereby increasing the potential for damage and erosion. Gusts during storms can be extremely damaging to physical structures but the mean wind speed is usually of more importance in the generation of waves, which may impact destructively on the shore. July and August are usually the months when wind speeds are least and the winter months of December and January are usually the months when wind speeds are at a maximum. The mean annual wind speed along the south coast is six metres per second or around 11.6 knots (Force 4) and usually gale force wind conditions (Force 8) are recorded around 16 days per year at Rosslare. Gusts of up to 90 knots or 46 metres per second have been recorded at this station in the past. Coastal areas are open and exposed and little shelter is available so strong winds may generate conditions locally that are both spectacular and dangerous, with considerable potential for damage to coastal features such as beaches and embankments and other man-made structures. However, the south coast of Ireland is moderately sheltered from the prevailing winds, compared to the west coast, for example, which is exposed to the full force of the Atlantic Ocean.

Rainfall tends to be highest in winter and least in summer but exceptions do occur. At Rosslare (Wexford) in the period 1961-90, the greatest daily total (79.1 mm) was recorded in July while some recent summers have tended to be wet. For example summer 2008 (June, July and August) was very wet all over Ireland, and rainfall amounts were more than twice the average in the east and southeast and up to 208% of normal at Waterford stations where data was available (Cappoquin 196%, Tycor 208%).

Currently mean air temperatures along the south coast range between around 10.6 °C at Cork Airport to around 11.4 °C at Rosslare, values that are over one degree above average values recorded for the period 1961-90 in most places and above mean temperatures recorded at Waterford and Dungarvan for an earlier period (hence mean air temperatures are likely to be higher now in Waterford than those recorded in 1951-80). These mean values mask a considerable variation in monthly or even daily temperatures. For example at Rosslare in 2008, the absolute maximum temperature recorded, 26.2 °C, was in July while the absolute minimum, -4.4 °C, was recorded in January. Air frosts occur from November through to March or April while ground frost may occur from late September even into May, but is usually more frequent in December and January.

Sea temperatures around Ireland are reasonably favourable, due to the warm

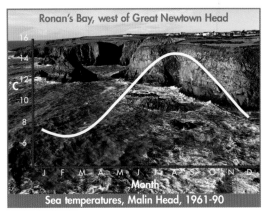

Ronan's Bay, west of Great Newtown Head

Sea temperatures, Malin Head, 1961-90

North Atlantic drift, which is also responsible for Ireland's temperate climate. The average monthly sea temperatures at Malin Head are lower by up to three degrees than those on the south Irish coast, so sea temperatures off the Waterford coast are even more favourable than at Malin Head, though sea temperatures may take some time to warm up (and cool down); sea temperatures are highest in August and September and are likely to be warmer in winter and cooler in summer than the ambient air temperature. There is little variation in water temperature with depth off the coast in winter and early spring but by mid-summer, surface temperatures may be up to 5 or 6 °C warmer than on the bottom.

The mean number of sunshine hours per day at Rosslare in the sunny southeast in the period 1961-90 was 4.85 hours, which masks quite an annual variation. Inevitably the greatest number of sunshine hours are available in summer (15.9 hours are possible in July at Rosslare) and are least in winter (up to 7.3 hours are possible at Rosslare in December, which is the darkest month of the year). It is unusual not to see the sun for some part of the day in spring and summer but December and January are the dullest months; up to 61 days without sun are possible annually at Rosslare.

Snow is rare in southeast Ireland (only 10.7 days had snow in the period 1961-90 at Rosslare) and is most likely in the winter

Wave-washed shore at Annestown: the offshore stacks are whittled away and the shingle is pushed in by the sea

months but rarely falls in sufficient quantities to cause disruption (except in late 2010). Hail and thunder are also infrequent (occurring on average on 11.8 and 6.7 days at Rosslare) but fog can be a hazard at times along the south coast, and while likely in any month, surprisingly, it is more prevalent in summer (on average Rosslare had 38.5 days of fog in the period 1961-90).

While weather variables along the Waterford coast are rarely extreme, some winters, for example, are more unfavourable than others. The early part of the winter of 2009/2010 was particularly wet, leading to damaging flooding, and was then followed by extremely cold conditions, which persisted for several weeks and caused further damage.

Tides

The rise and fall of rivers and oceans is caused by the variations in the relative positions of the earth, moon and sun and the gravitational attraction between planets of such size. The moon revolves around the earth and both together revolve around the much bigger, though more distant sun. This complex rotational system generates variable gravitational forces whose effects can be seen on the rivers and oceans of the world. Thus there are daily, fortnightly, monthly, seasonal and longer-term variations in the movement of water around the globe and these movements are known as tides. On average, around 30% of tidal motion is associated with the sun, and the remaining 70% fluctuates in phase with the moon. The relative and predictable movements of the planets may explain variations in tide levels, but less predictable are meteorological factors, which may profoundly influence the effects of extreme tides.

The moon revolves around the earth in an elliptical 27.55-day orbit and their distance apart during this orbit varies from 357,000 kilometres to 407,000 kilometres. This causes variation in the gravitational force between them, (since the attractive forces between planets is inversely proportional to the square of their distance apart) and hence a variation in the type of tide and the tidal range, which occurs twice in the lunar month. The closest approach at full and new moon yields a higher tidal range (e.g. spring tides) and these tides result in a greater height difference between high and low tide (the tidal range). The highest spring tides occurs a day or two after a full or new moon. When moon and earth are furthest apart, a lower tidal range or neap tides are generated.

Various terms are used to describe the various highs and lows reached by tides, the most useful of which is MHWS (Mean High Water Spring) or MLWS (Mean Low Water Spring) and the last letter is changed to N for corresponding terms describing neap tides.

Tidal height in Ireland is measured in metres, above a standard reference level, usually Chart Datum (CD) which may vary from port to port. In Waterford, tidal predictions are computed for Cheekpoint (52° 21N 7° 00W) and the tide levels refer to Chart Datum. Tide levels may be quoted relative to Ordnance Datum (OD) at Malin Head or mean sea level there between January 1960 and December 1969 and all heights on the National Grid mapping system are given in metres above this datum. Tides in Waterford are said to be meso-tidal because the vertical range of the tide is normally between two metres at neap tides to four metres at spring tides.

In Waterford tides are semi-diurnal as high and low tides occur twice each day. It takes usually slightly less than six hours for a rising tide to completely fill all intertidal areas and during some high tides the highest salt marsh areas are covered with seawater. The tide turns almost immediately, taking usually slightly more than six hours to drain completely, exposing mudflats, sandflats and beach to the air and to freshwater, either in the form of rain or runoff from the land. The tide does not rise and fall at the same rate and the maximum rate of fall is usually during the third and fourth hour of the cycle in either direction. Tide times vary from day to day, and are later each day from between 25 minutes to around 90 minutes, depending on the time of the month in the lunar cycle. As a general rule spring or strong tides tend to carry less and neap or weak tides carry more and, as the interval between successive low tides is more than 12 hours, tides are later each day.

Annual variations in tidal ranges also occur. When the sun and moon are in line on either side of the earth, the gravitational force on the oceans is at a maximum and the high tides arising from this alignment occur at the equinoxes in March and September. At the solstices in June and December, the moon, earth and sun are not so well aligned and hence spring tides are not as high. Conversely, when the sun and moon are at right angles relative to the earth, the gravitational pull, and hence the tidal range, is at a minimum. Seasonal variations are also linked to the closeness of the earth to the sun. In winter the earth is closer to the sun than at other times of the year; hence summer high tides are lower than winter high tides and the autumn equinoctial tides are highest of all. Variations in the tilt of the moon's orbit every 18.6 years are responsible for the lowest and highest astronomical tides and there are also even longer-term tidal cycles, related to the inclination of the sun and moon to the earth.

Onshore winds usually raise water levels as does low barometric pressure associated with Atlantic depressions (which are more common in winter). If high spring tides are accompanied by heavy rain, strong winds in a direction complimentary to the direction of flow of the tide, and low barometric pressure, severe flooding and harmful erosion may occur. Storm surges may raise water levels by up to one metre above predicted levels, which considerably increases the harmful effects of waves impacting on the shore. Even without these conditions high spring tides move massive quantities of debris higher up on the shore and they increase salinity levels further inland than any other tide.

The tide is the most significant physical influence along the coast. The twice-daily flow and ebb and the consequent submersion and exposure of the shore subjects living organisms to stresses that are unique to this environment. The southerly aspect of the Waterford coast increases the risks of living in inshore areas as strong sunlight may cause dessication, particularly if low tides occur in the middle of the day when the sun is at its warmest; conversely, shaded north-facing areas may remain permanently damp. The varying degrees of submersion and emersion through the lunar cycle also poses a significant risk for some species, who may be unable to withstand even the briefest of episodes. Low tides also expose large areas of sand to the drying effect of wind which is then easily moved by wind, leading to dune formation or depletion.

The interface between land and sea is often confused as there is seawater intrusion inland as well as freshwater discharging from the land. At high tide, freshwater floats on top of denser seawater and so can have little effect on living organisms. However at low tide freshwater may lower salinity levels across the shore and flows from streams and rivers may be supplemented by heavy rainfall and runoff from the land. Waves pounding constantly on the shore may have adverse physical affects on sand, shingle and cliff. Coastal breaches occur irregularly along the 'soft' parts of the Waterford coast, particularly during storms, when wave damage can be severe, but the undermining of friable cliff bases eventually leads to collapse. The cliffed coast of the county is very slowly being whittled away by the sea, as it relentlessly pounds the coastal areas.

Currents

Off the coast of Waterford, sea depth gradually increases from up to 10 metres within two kilometres of the shore to over 50 metres some 15 kilometres off. Tidal streams along the Waterford coast are generally weak (usually less than one knot) and are strongest off Waterford Harbour (1.5 knots). Sustained winds of any strength in the direction of the current may increase current speed by one knot or more. Current direction depends on the stage of the tidal cycle and both flows and direction can be complex around the prominent headlands, particularly where there is local discharges from rivers and estuaries. The combined catchments of the rivers Suir, Nore and Barrow (9,232 square kilometres) discharges an average of 150 cubic metres of freshwater per second through Waterford Harbour, a discharge rate which is exceeded in Ireland only by the river Shannon. The catchments of the river Colligan which discharge through Dungarvan (102 km^2) and the river Blackwater through Youghal (3,324 km^2) contribute rather less to freshwater flows off the Waterford coast.

The sea floor of the coastal bays at Tramore and Dungarvan are generally gently sloping and water depth decreases more or less uniformly towards the shore. Many factors, principally the type of tide and the time of the tidal cycle influence the strength of the rotational movements within the coastal bays. Strongest currents within the bays are generated on spring tides and peak current strengths are reached a few hours after the tide has turned. Notwithstanding the rotational movements in the bays and inlets, water currents are generally weak, though the often wind-assisted surface currents may be higher than the sea-floor currents that are retarded by friction. For recreation and amenity, such weak currents close inshore ensure that almost all of the coastal beaches in Waterford are safe for water-based leisure activities and swimming.

When the tide turns at low water, a large volume of seawater rushes into the coastal bays. This tidal prism generates the strongest tidal currents, regardless of wind conditions, though strong southerly winds can considerably increase water currents on a rising tide. Currents of 1.5 metres per second on spring tides are possible, though tidal currents are very much lower on neap tides, usually about 0.6 metres per second. Inevitably, with such strong currents, the channels in the bays fill rapidly and the incoming spring tide then rushes over the sandflats, very quickly filling the bays right up to, and sometimes even overtopping the salt marsh areas, long before high tide. The high flow rate usually results in good flushing of the bays, especially on spring tides, but the strong tidal currents ensure that some are very dangerous places for swimming (for example there are strong currents at Rinnashark, Tramore).

Within the bays at Tramore and Dungarvan, water depth is rarely more than one metre on spring tides, though this varies considerably, given the undulating nature of the sandflats; at high tide, water depth is greatest in the channels. Little water remains at low tide and it is possible to wander in many directions at that stage of the tide, though it is rarely possible to cross the bays because of deep channels in places or residual tidal flows. Low water on spring tides offer the best opportunities for walking the coasts and sandflats but they are also the most dangerous times as the tide turns quickly and rapidly fills the inshore areas. Unfortunately, there have been accidents and even fatalities, so great care is required when walking anywhere along the Waterford coast and an awareness of tide times is absolutely essential. The safest option is to stay close to the shore and know the safe exit routes. For example, the coastal shingle east of Annestown can only be safely walked when the tide is falling; never attempt this walk on a rising tide as the

tide fills rapidly cutting off access routes and the daunting vertical cliffs here are mostly sheer, loose and inaccessible.

On some Waterford beaches, weak longshore currents are often present in the surf zone due to the waves striking the beach at an angle; these currents can be important in moving sediment along the shoreline.

Most of the beaches offer excellent opportunities for walking and swimming. However, care is always required when swimming and the usual precautions should be taken (swim parallel to the shore, never alone or with alcohol taken or after heavy meals and be aware of local conditions). Ballydowane Bay may have rip currents under certain wave conditions so great care is needed if swimming here.

Waves

Waves are generated when energy is imparted to the sea by wind and the waves so formed then move in the direction of the wind. There is no horizontal movement of water as a result of the wave; rather there is circular movement within the wave as it passes. Generally waves form offshore and their energy is dissipated when they impact on the coastline. This energy dissipation is of great significance on 'soft' coasts and waves can

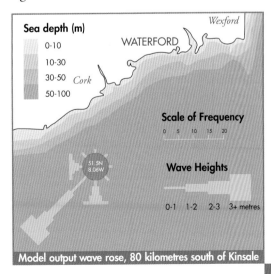

Model output wave rose, 80 kilometres south of Kinsale

The waves impacting on the beach at Curragh, near Ardmore, pose a threat to buildings built close to the shore

add or remove sediment from the shoreline. Severe waves can also cause significant erosion on beaches and dunes, and even man-made structures used for coastal protection can suffer damage from a succession of high waves impacting on them. Over time, the constant bombardment of coastal cliffs by high energy waves breaking at their base, eventually weakens the fabric of the cliff, often leading to spectacular collapses.

Most of the marine observations on sea conditions have been from ships in transit. Since 2000, however, a network of data buoys have been gathering data on wind, pressure, weather and waves from onboard sensors and they relay this information via satellite to the Irish Meteorological Service (Met Éireann). Buoy M5 was positioned in October 2004, approximately 50 nautical miles (around 93 kilometres) off Hook Head, and it is currently providing valuable data on sea conditions in the Celtic Sea. The British Met Office also has a network of Marine Automatic Weather Stations (MAWS) consisting of 11 moored buoys and seven systems on ships and islands. One of the Met Office buoys (K3) off the west coast of Ireland out in the Atlantic measured a significant wave height (the average wave

height from trough to crest of the highest one-third of the total number of waves) of 18.2 metres during winter 2007/08; the maximum wave height (crest to trough) may have been much higher than this.

Despite all the offshore technology there is little direct quantitative information available on wave heights off the Waterford coast. Off the south Irish coast, around 80% of the waves arrive from a west, southwest or south direction and the majority (around 75%) of these waves may be anything up to three metres in height. Wave heights above three metres are exceptional but, depending on the prevailing conditions, waves of up to and even above eight metres are possible. These are high seas indeed but waves of such heights rarely impact on the coast. The long southern coastline does have an attenuating effect on incoming waves as headlands, shallower water and bed friction all combine to decrease the energies of the incident waves. Nevertheless, high waves do occur, mainly in winter when frequent successive storms generate high seas offshore.

If strong winds blowing from any southerly direction, but particularly from the southeast, coincide with prolonged heavy rain, low barometric pressure and high spring tides, then storm surges may be experienced along the Waterford coast, resulting in raised sea levels of up to one metre above predicted levels and possible flooding of low-lying areas. Such episodes are expected to increase in frequency as a result of climate change. As the atmosphere warms, the oceans will absorb heat and expand, and the melting ice caps will increase ocean volumes. There may also be a relatively small natural raising of sea level due to geological uplifting on the south coast.

Wave height is a good measure of the energy contained in the wave (and its ability to cause erosion or accretion) and usually the higher the wave the greater the impact of the wave on the shoreline. In the marine environment offshore, waves are rarely simple, and they often interact in a complex, chaotic and unpredictable pattern, leading frequently to very turbulent sea conditions, especially during storms.

In generating wind waves, three factors are of importance: the distance over which the wind generating the wave is blowing (the fetch); the average wind speed; and the length of time that the wind is blowing. Obviously the greater any of these factors are, the greater

the wave generated, but only up to a point. Waves quite often become unstable as the weight of water rises vertically and they break into white crests. Wind waves may travel great distances across the oceans, beyond the influence of the generating winds and these swell waves gradually lose energy as the wave moves across the sea. Hence, superimposed on the wind waves generated locally are waves generated well offshore. They may combine constructively or destructively, thereby generating waves of varying heights which occasionally cause severe coastal damage and endanger swimmers, especially when a wave of great height arrives unexpectedly.

Out in deep water, the wave moves towards the shore without influencing the seabed. However as the wave approaches the shallower coastal areas, the behaviour of the wave changes and the now almost horizontal water movement within the wave disturbs the seabed and any sediment or other material there is liable to be carried along by subsequent water movement. Closer to the shore the speed of the wave decreases and the wave crests increase in height and steepness, sometimes leading to spectacular waves breaking on the shore, if the energy carried by the wave is high. Gradually this energy is

Waves impacting gently on the shore at Tramore

dissipated and is eventually lost completely when the wave breaks on the shore.

Waves breaking on the shoreline are primarily responsible for shaping beaches and profiling cliff faces. Waves usually break when they reach a water depth of around 1.3 times the wave height, so that low waves break closer inshore than high waves. Waves, when they break, are either constructive or destructive, depending on their profile. Constructive waves have an elliptical motion and they break gently on the shore with the resulting swash moving sand grains and pebbles up the shore. Destructive waves, on the other hand, break vertically downwards and their lost energy moves sediment down the shore, leaving a steep bank of sand or gravel up at the high tide mark. These plunging waves occasionally have a pronounced effect on beach profiles: they push shingle up the shore and steepen the upper parts of it but the backwash energy is diminished as the seawater percolates through the shingle. However, the lower, sandier parts of the beach are flattened by the retreating backwash, leaving a distinct boundary between the upper shingle and the beach.

The way in which the wave breaks is related to the slope of the shore and this parameter may vary closer to the shore; many Waterford beaches are shallow near the low water mark but become much steeper near high water level. Breakers are a great attraction for swimmers, and especially so for surfers who ride the waves with great ease and style all through the year but particularly so in winter when spectacular waves occur. The waves constantly crashing on our shores are usually a source of inspiration, wonder and even plain amusement to the countless thousands of people who walk the coastal beaches at all times of the day, and night; breakers crashing on the seawalls or other man-made structures frequently generate spectacular plumes of spray.

During storms the energy released by breaking waves causes seawater to rush up the beach and shingle or crash violently against the base of cliffs, and possibly to overflow at the tops of the beaches, spilling debris, sand and water everywhere, which may cause considerable damage if the storm is intense and prolonged. Waves are also reflected, especially from solid vertical seawalls and a reflected wave combining with an incoming wave may generate a wave with a height and energy that is greater than either of its constituent waves. These waves have the ability to undermine the base any defensive structure on which they break. Once undermined, the structure is weakened by further incoming waves and is likely to breach or collapse. Time takes its toll too and defensive structures, quite apart from the damage caused to them by the physical impact of high waves and the constant hurling of sand and gravel against them, are also prone to physical, chemical and biological weathering. There are several notable instances of man-made structures being damaged or washed away. In the winter of 1989/90, a particularly violent storm ravaged the Waterford coast and generated waves of such force that the dunes at Bunmahon and the seawall and slipway at Tramore were severely damaged necessitating extensive and costly remedial works.

Winter storm waves tend to remove beach material offshore where it forms bars in the inshore zone. Swell waves in summer moves the sediment in these offshore bars inshore to the beaches and sandflats. Consequently, levels may vary throughout the year. In general beach levels are lowest in spring and highest in autumn. Sand is more easily moved than shingle and may disappear offshore from beaches following storms. In winter beaches may look rocky and bare but are quickly replenished in summer, or between storms, when the blanket of sand is returned by the sea.

Flora of the Waterford Coast

Coasts are difficult places for plants to grow in and those that thrive have the ability to tolerate salt, which is the biggest threat. Few plants are able to tolerate high salinity levels and in areas exposed to seawater (for example at the interface between beach and dune or mudflat and salt marsh), only specialised plants may survive. Only about 20 plant species are able to use the coast exclusively for their usually short life cycles. Plants have to be able to retain water, which may seem surprising given that they are surrounded by water, but the high salt content in sea water causes the plant to dry out, unless it is able to regulate salt concentrations in its cells. Salt-laden winds are also harmful, even to plants that are never touched by seawater. Sand, shingle, mud and even the friable cliffs can move and may do so on a large scale under certain conditions so plants need to adapt to the occasionally severe changes that occur around them. For many an annual life cycle is appropriate in the hostile environments that may prevail at times on certain parts of the coast.

Pockets of earth on cliff cracks and ledges, mud on salt marshes and sand on the upper parts of beaches and in dunes provides the ground necessary for plants to germinate, grow and mature. This ground is invaded by colonists, usually in the form of seeds brought in by wind, animals or even the sea, but plant fragments can also suffice for some species for which the sea is an agent of dispersal. Conditions such as favourable temperatures, an available water supply (usually in the form of rainfall, though percolation from the land above, in the case of cliffs, may also be important), nutrients and an absence of predators, must be suitable for these seeds to germinate and for successful growth to maturity. Given prolonged suitable conditions, most plants will flower and themselves set seed, thereby perpetuating the process. But this is only part of the process; when plants arrive, they add organic matter to the soil and they affect the nutrient status and water supply in the soil. In the case of salt marshes, the organic matter may lead to an increase in siltation and, for dunes, the plants help to bind the sand and so are effective in consolidating the dune system. The tides too exert a powerful influence and are often a determining factor in what plants grow where and in what abundance.

Sometimes plants, especially large ones, may influence the type of other plants that may colonise by changing such microclimate parameters as surface evaporation and relative humidity in their vicinity. The presence of all these plants usually results in competition for

Cliff vegetation

Yellow-horned poppy on the cliffs at Garrarus

established on cliffs and offer a blaze of colour in summer and an overall mantle of vegetation throughout the year.

Although cliff plants are generally not subject to inundation by the sea or grazing by birds, they are prone to sea spray, and strong winds rushing up the cliff face are often damaging. Wave action may be an inhibiting factor for those plants growing lower down and the more exposed the cliff is the higher the level at which the vegetation begins. Exposed cliffs, where the soil cover may be particularly thin, quickly dry out in summer but freshwater run-off from above may help, at least in places, and a green flush of vegetation may be particularly dense. Seabird colonies may exert an influence and, for example, where cormorants nest on offshore stacks anywhere along the coast, vegetation may be very much altered, or even absent.

Cliffs are dangerous places at which to observe and examine plants and the generally high cliffs are particularly exposed and dangerous, so great care is needed. On some parts of the Waterford coast, it is possible at low tide to look up at some cliffs from the base, where conditions, although slippery underfoot, are more suitable for botanising.

available resources and plants may flower at different times to maximise their chances of successful reproduction. Eventually some form of balance is reached in how the various plants use the available resources and the plant communities gradually become stabilised. What species survive and which become dominant depends very much on what resources are available and how well they compete for them.

Cliff vegetation

The high cliffs of the Waterford coast are lashed by wind and rain and are battered by seawater during storm events. Though they are seldom afflicted by frost or snow, in summer they are baked by the searing action of the sun and are constantly exposed to undercutting by the sea and rockfalls from above. Nevertheless, almost all the Waterford cliffs have a thin soil covering somewhere which allows plants to take hold and flourish. They usually do so in the absence of grazing and, consequently, many plants become well

Sea pink or **thrift** is probably the most conspicuous plant of the cliff top and occurs on almost all the cliffs from low down to high up. In season (early summer), thrift forms dense carpets of rose-pink, honey-scented flowers. A long-lasting perennial, it has long roots which penetrate deep into the ground, ensuring a constant water supply for a plant that is quite tolerant of saline conditions. However, it dislikes waterlogged ground or too frequent inundation by seawater. At ground level there is a rosette of distinctive and narrow fleshy leaves, obvious even when the plant is not in flower. The dense hemispherical flower heads are borne on aerial stems and up to 20 individual

Thrift or sea-pink on the cliff top at Creadan Head

flowers occur on each head. The flowers on each plant are usually the same shade of pink, though there can be very obvious differences between plants. Although the vast majority of flowers are light pink in colour, an occasional flower is a very much deeper shade of pink and such flowers stand out among the rest. Thrift growing on elevated mounds appear to have a competitive advantage as they usually have longer stems and bigger petals than their lowly colleagues nearby. The occasional thrift plant may be in flower in late March but these are the early ones, as most wait until the warmer days of May.

Associated with sea pink is **sea campion**, a very distinctive coastal plant with a barrel shape and white flowers. It thrives on the sea cliffs, especially those enriched by bird droppings, and it adds significantly to the summer mass of colour flittering in

the updraughts. It is a plant that is most characteristic of the coastal cliffs but it grows inland on the walls of Dunhill Castle, and in some of the coums of the Comeragh Mountains, where the leaves are longer but not as wide compared with those found on the coast. **Tree-mallow** is a conspicuous plant of some of the coastal cliffs in Waterford, where it is undoubtedly native. It is an upright plant, with long woody stems and very attractive mauve and black flowers in summer. Look for it at the base of the kittiwake cliffs at Inner Harbour, Dunmore East, or less easily on Gull Island and other sea stacks, just west of Bunmahon, where it provides shade for nesting cormorants in some years.

Rock samphire can usually be found low down on any of the coastal cliffs where it grows in some abundance among the thrifts, campions and lichens. Individual plants may also

Sea campion flower

Rock samphire

dock, Yorkshire fog and other grasses, clovers, mayweed, ladies bedstraw, tufted vetch, bracken, kidney vetch, scarlet pimpernel, golden samphire, bird's-foot-trefoil and occasionally common centaury. In late April or early May the attractive **primrose** may be seen, and in certain places large clumps of them grow together, often with common and Danish scurvygrass and even sea beet nearby. **Lesser celandine** is more at home in woodland and along roadside verges than on coastal cliffs but its brilliant yellow flowers shine brightly in spring in places along the tops along with bluebells, **common dog-violet**, and dandelion.

Common spotted orchid, pyramidal orchid and **lousewort** may grow in some numbers in damp ground above the cliffs in some areas (west of Great Newtown Head near the cliff edge, for example). Less spectacular species may also be found growing on the cliffs too though these are usually less obvious plants like grasses, sea plantain and sea spleenwort, while **wild madder** finds a useful niche at some sites. The pearlworts are persistent weeds around paths and patios and are difficult to eradicate, especially annual pearlwort and procumbent pearlwort, which are common around the county. **Sea pearlwort** is confined to bare areas along the coast, especially on the tops of walls and open areas on the cliff tops, where it is not swamped by other vegetation. Hawthorn is the only tree species to survive the severe conditions that prevail on the cliffs but it is more shrub-like on some vegetated slopes, and is formed and shaped in the direction of the updraught.

English stonecrop is common on the coast, especially on field banks but not in the main dune systems (it doesn't grow either in the Tramore dunes or on the Cunnigar). This low-growing perennial is a very attractive species with red-tinged leaves, which stand out among the coastal swards.

grow quite large and it is well adapted for survival in such adverse conditions. Exposed to constant lashing by sea spray and wind, it has fleshy, thick-skinned leaves to store water and withstand desiccation. These leaves are often red-tipped and there is quite a distinctive bituminous smell when the samphire leaves are rubbed together (though some would say it smells like furniture polish or even citrus). A perennial, it has narrowly ridged, branched stems and the flower head has up to 20 branches, bearing tiny yellowish-green flowers. **Golden samphire** is a beautiful plant of rocky sea cliffs and other coastal areas. Unusually too, it grows along the edges of the salt marsh areas at Tramore. It has attractive yellow flowers and succulent leaves and is unmistakable where it occurs. It has a restricted distribution in Ireland, occurring on the south and east coast only, and its stronghold in Ireland is in Waterford, though it is not as common in all coastal habitats as it is at Tramore.

Flowering plants more typical of lowland areas behind the coast also brighten a walk around any of the coastal headlands or cliffs and these include silverweed, **common sorrel**, wild carrot, burnet rose, plantains,

Given the influence of sea spray, it is not surprising that plants more associated with salt marshes also grow on cliffs. Sea purslane grows in abundance some eight metres above the base of some cliffs (near Lady Doneraile's cove at Tramore, for example). Rare species include **hare's-foot clover**, which is probably more common in the west of the county; it has been seen near Helvick Head and Ballymacart cove, for example.

Coastal heath is an important habitat type, which is declining nationally, probably because of land clearance, grazing and recreational pressure. The main areas of dry coastal heath in Waterford are at Creadan Head and Helvick Head west to Muggort's Bay, where the shallow soils support a distinctive flora. The main components are autumn gorse, **bell heather** and **ling**, which cover the sloping cliff tops in a blanket of vegetation, that is visually appealing, especially in summer, and attractive to a range of other fauna. There are a number of associated plant species which include **wood sage**, **sheep's-bit**, devil's-bit scabious, **tormentil**, heath bedstraw, English stonecrop, common dog-violet, **goldenrod**, burnet rose and several lichen species on the exposed rocks. Common grass species include common and creeping bent, sweet vernal-grass and red fescue. In places common gorse, bracken and bramble take over, which make parts of the headlands very difficult to walk through and even impenetrable in places.

Flora of the upper beaches and embankments
Beaches are inhospitable places for plants and no plants are able to grow on the beaches themselves where conditions are just too severe; there is daily inundation by the sea and strong waves and recreational activities constantly rework the highly mobile sands. The interface between land and sea is, however, less disturbed and just above the tideline there is an available niche, which a small number of plants can exploit, despite

English stonecrop

lack of protection from the sun and the occasional inundation by very high tides. Consequently this atypical habitat is available to very specialised plants with the necessary adaptations to survive in the saline and exposed conditions. Wind is an important factor here as there is usually no surrounding vegetation to dissipate its flow. Nutrients are also scarce in the relatively porous sediments, which have only a very limited ability to retain water, while temperature variation may also be high and it may be very hot in warm summer weather so plants need to be able to store water to survive. Plants colonising this habitat may have to wait some time before conditions are suitable for germination; seeds tend to be large to sustain the plants, as they may have to grow from deep beneath the sand. Once these plants begin to grow they then have to contend with being trampled on by walkers and the constant battering by sand grains and even shingle moved by pounding waves and strong winds.

Sea sandwort is a small, low-growing perennial plant that can be seen among shingle and sand on the upper beach areas of the county, where few humans are keen to walk, and along embankments where it may

Sea sandwort

suffer damage from constant trampling. Its fleshy stolons are able to survive the winter and its triangular, fleshy leaves (apparently edible) appear in spring, usually from mid-March on. The small, almost inconspicuous but attractive flowers add some colour to this otherwise grey environment, but the bulbous seed heads become more grotesque as the summer progresses, almost dwarfing the leaves. On the mobile shingle it is usually the only plant species present, as colonisation by annuals is difficult, if not impossible, in the harsh environment. On the sandier areas of the upper beach, sea sandwort may be accompanied by **sea rocket**, a deep-rooted annual, dependent on the sea for dispersal of its seed. A gangly plant, sea rocket may occur in isolation or in aggregations; it may raise sand levels by up to one metre in summer, though plants are usually too scattered to generate any significant sand accumulation. Nevertheless, the plant contributes to embryo dune formation near dunes, and many conspicuous circular mounds of this attractive plant flourish in summer, where it may be surrounded by oraches. **Thyme-leaved sandwort** is a small, gangly plant, whose distribution in the county is mainly coastal; it is common only around Dungarvan.

Sand couch, one of the main instigators of dune growth on the upper parts of beaches, is a perennial grass and it grows in abundance along the sandy shorelines of the county. Its bright green colour in April is very obvious while the numerous dark spikelets on

its stem become more open as the season progresses. It flowers in the late summer when the heavy flower heads then bend over precariously. Sand couch is tolerant of seawater, both on the leaves and in the ground where it grows, provided inundations are brief. The leaves are very effective as a wind barrier to moving sand and they also provide shelter for sand that has already been deposited. Sand couch grows readily from seed, and it also grows vegetatively by sending out underground stems or rhizomes, which regularly send up new shoots. The earliest tillers it sends out are prostrate, and these give rise to a rosette of shoots, which fall flat on the sand. As the plant ages and the density increases, the plant grows more erectly. The horizontal rhizomes grow out to a distance of 60-90 centimetres and in the following season they produce a new crop of tillers which begin the process of sand accumulation again, while the growing underground root system assists in retaining the accumulated sand.

Sand couch and sea rocket are the two plant species most likely to initiate embryo dune growth on coastal beaches (the oraches may also play a part, but to a much lesser extent) and eventually a whole series of embryo dunes begin to form. Although these plants actively grow in response to sand gathering around them, they cannot outgrow burial by sand of more than 60 centimetres per year. The ability of sand couch to withstand inundation by seawater and accumulate sand, thereby generating sand hillocks, is crucial for the growth of the other dune building plant–marram grass.

Scattered among the sand couch on the upper areas of beaches are the oraches, the low-growing annuals that thrive on the relatively stable conditions prevailing in these areas between spring and autumn. **Frosted orache** (easily recognised by its frosted appearance) is generally confined to the

Prickly saltwort

and despite being a very striking maritime plant when in full bloom, it only rarely seems to reach such proportions in Waterford. With fleshy blue-green and cabbage-like leaves up to 45 centimetres long beneath a massive array of white flowers, it is truly a majestic plant that was once prized as a delicacy when eaten in spring. It is a long-lived perennial and favours maritime shingle that has been stable for at least five years. It is not surprising therefore, given the changeable conditions along many parts of the coast that this plant is scarce, though it was apparently more abundant in the 1970s at Tramore than in the 1950s and 1960s, when it was rarely recorded. It has been recently recorded at Ferry Point (1990, 1995 & 2009), Tramore and Saleen (1995), Monatray West (2002) and Whiting Bay (2009).

Sea bindweed is only a common plant in Waterford on the embankment leading to the dunes at Tramore, in the dunes themselves and at Saleen. It frequently invades the shoreline from the dunes, where it is more abundant. Sea bindweed has sprawling stems but fortunately these do not climb. Its kidney-shaped leaves are different to its garden relative but the flowers are much the same. And what beautiful flowers they are: bell-shaped with petals that fan out, the sea bindweed flower is big and obvious, even

beaches while **Babington's orache** is more common along the Waterford coast at the base of sea cliffs, the edges of salt marshes as well as on the beaches. **Common orache** and **spear-leaved orache**, which, apart from occurring in abundance throughout dune systems as well as close to growing embryo dunes, are also common inland on waste ground. The coastal oraches use special hairs on the leaves to store water as an adaptation to the roots growing in salty conditions.

Prickly saltwort, a strandline annual, is a very bushy plant, with many branches and small fleshy leaves ending in a sharp point. Never common on the coast, it has been seen near Bass Point on the Saleen side of Tramore Bay as well as on the strand near the tip of the Tramore dunes, the beach at Bunmahon, Ballynacourty, the Cunnigar and the beach at Ballynagaul. An occasional **sea-kale** plant grows along the strandlines in the county,

Sea bindweed

spectacular when it protrudes from the sand. It grows best, and is more obvious where other plants do not dominate. It has also been recorded on the dunes at Woodstown, Bunmahon and the Cunnigar.

The seeds of the **sea pea**, a coastal plant found on sand and shingle shores, have been seen on Tramore beach and at Whiting Bay. It is a common plant in North America, from where the seeds presumably drift. **Little-Robin** is only found around Dungarvan and is easily missed because of its small size. Look for it on the harbour walls and on the tops of the shingle beaches around the town. **Yellow-horned poppy** can be transitory in occurrence; it is seen annually on the cliffs at Garrarus but it is usually more obvious on the beaches, just above the tideline. It is very distinctive, with light green foliage and big yellow flowers. Several plants were in flower on the Cunnigar in 2008 and 2009 but it is probably most abundant on the shingle at Ferry Point, in the extreme west of the

Opium poppy on the Cunnigar

county. The **opium poppy** may also be seen occasionally on the edges of dunes.

Three scurvygrass species occur in coastal areas of the county. **Danish scurvygrass** and **common scurvygrass** are plants of sea cliffs, the edges of salt marshes, along the tops of sandy embankments and pebbly shores and on coastal walls. **English scurvygrass** is probably more common along the muddy shores of tidal rivers and estuaries though it also occurs at the tops of beaches and on coastal walls. Danish scurvygrass, the smaller of the three, is the first to appear in spring, usually on the sandy/rocky areas without tall vegetation. Its mauve or light purple flowers are smaller than those of common scurvygrass and there are around 25 individual flowers in an inflorescence whereas there are usually less than 20 white flowers in an inflorescence of common scurvygrass. To further distinguish between the species, examine the stems and notice that the leaves of Danish scurvygrass have petioles (leaf stalks) whereas common scurvygrass has none, at least on the upper stem. Common scurvygrass leaves are cordate (arrow shaped) and they clasp the stem tightly at the base. Perhaps the most distinguishing feature apart from colour is that the flowers of common scurvygrass are much larger. Danish scurvygrass usually forms large carpets in areas where there is little or no other vegetation, probably because they grow early in the year giving them a competitive advantage.

Sea-milkwort is a small but beautiful plant when in flower. With creeping, rooting stems and pairs of stalkless leaves, it bears attractive pink flowers in summer at the junction between stem and leaves; these flowers lack petals and it is the pale pink sepals that gives the flower its colour. It has small fleshy leaves like sea sandwort, which store fresh water, and it has a low growth form to reduce water loss by evaporation. It may be found growing on the edges of salt marshes, among other vegetation at the top of beaches and sometimes even at the base of sea cliffs. At Tramore, for example, it is more abundant on the salt marsh at Lisselan on the north side of the Backstrand, but it may also be found growing around Dungarvan and along the banks of the estuaries of the Suir and Blackwater. **Sea mayweed** has a rather attractive flower head with an array of white leaflets around a yellow disc (later to bear the seeds) and, although a somewhat gangly plant, it grows from spring through to autumn and is one of the last plants to lose its flowers. It may be found anywhere along the coast from the tops of beaches to the dune systems and even on the sea cliffs.

Sea beet is widespread along the coast and is a big and robust plant that is easily identified. It has thick, dark-green leathery leaves but unlike its relatives, sugar beet and beetroot, its root does not become swollen where it joins the stem. It is a conspicuous plant and has an obvious presence, especially when the many flower-bearing spikes appear in summer. The seeds of sea beet are able to withstand long-term immersion in seawater and successful germination is possible even after long-distance transportation by tides. **Sea radish** seeds are also transported by the sea and unaffected by it, even after floating for several days. It is a large plant whose leaves are covered in hairs; it has yellow flowers, which give way to globular seed pods that occur in clusters on the stems. It occurs sparingly on embankments, in dunes and in the coastal ditches.

Yarrow is a very persistent roadside plant but its ability to thrive on coastal sand is due in part to its deep water-gathering taproots. It flowers rather late in the season but its white, pink or rose-coloured flower heads are quite attractive, as indeed are the strongly divided and aromatic leaves. Renowned for its medicinal properties, at least in the past, it is reputed to be useful in the treatment of a

Sea beet

range of human ailments and to have anti-inflammatory properties.

The sandy nature of some coastal areas and the ever-present influence of the sea ensure that many plants that are more abundant elsewhere on the coast (in dunes, for example) also occur anywhere, though usually in much smaller numbers. Where these plants grow they add considerably to the floral diversity and colour scheme of the coastal areas when they flower in spring and summer. Species occurring include kidney vetch, sea plantain, sea spurge, sea rocket, bird's-foot trefoil, sand sedge, bindweed, rough hawkbit, marram, sea-holly, restharrow, **common stork's-bill**, and common centaury. **Autumn hawkbit** is quite abundant late in the summer and it may be the only flowering plant to be seen in September and October. The hawkbits have dandelion-like flowers and to distinguish between autumn and **rough hawkbit**, look at the leaves and the stems; autumn hawkbit usually has branched stems and hairless leaves while rough hawkbit has simple stems and hairy leaves.

Dune flora
Dunes are an inhospitable environment for plants. Sand is a very mobile entity and it

occurs in areas where winds are usually severe; it also has a limited water-holding capacity, a high rate of evaporation and a high surface temperature (occasionally around 50 °C) in summer. Sand is a poor heat conductor and while surface temperatures may be high, the temperature drops off rapidly with depth. Surface temperatures at night can very quickly fall below dew point and the air temperature may also fall allowing dew to form on the sand grains and then percolate down into the sand. Dew is a vital source–perhaps the only source of water–for plants in summer. In addition, nutrients and organic matter are often in short supply. Nevertheless, dunes are favoured by some plants, and one or two of these are dune specialists that contribute to dune formation and stabilisation (especially marram).

Most plants require special adaptations to survive in the difficult conditions that prevail in sand dunes. Many dune plants have long root systems, sometimes extending to over one metre in order to maintain a constant water supply. A low-growing form is an adaptation to constant abrasion by sand particles and desiccation by wind. Rolled leaves also help to reduce water loss by transpiration, the process by which water is moved from the roots to the leaves and eventually to the atmosphere through openings (called stomata) in the leaf surface.

Marram on the Cunnigar

Thick cuticles (the outside layer of plant cells) also help to reduce evapotranspiration as well as offering protection from sand blasting by strong winds.

The most conspicuous, widespread and ever-present plant growing in dune systems is **marram**. Superbly adapted for survival in sandy coastal environments, it grows best when blown sand accumulates around it, and usually the more sand that gathers the better the plant grows. Very flexible leaves allow it to withstand gales in all seasons, and these long and narrow leaves can curl up in dry weather; this habit along with ridges, furrows and hairs on the leaf surface help the plant to reduce water loss. The leaves are also covered with glossy cuticles that protect the plant from wind-blown damage by sand grains. Marram is a large tussock plant and is most impressive in the summer months when the flower heads sprout high above the stems. The long panicles, containing many spikelets, blow in unison when combed by wind in summer and then the whole dune system is a wavering mass of marram. It is extremely efficient at stabilising sand dunes, by means of rapidly spreading horizontal underground roots (rhizomes) and by sending up vertical shoots at regular intervals. These very rhizomes are displaced in vast quantities during storms when big breakers eat away at the dunes. The tattered fragments are then deposited elsewhere and if conditions are right–among them sand accumulation–the rhizomes will sprout and begin again the process of dune regeneration. Marram is sometimes planted by hand to regenerate blowouts when they persist in dunes.

Although relatively intolerant of saline conditions, marram is the main dune-building grass in Ireland. The leafy shoots of marram substantially slow the wind speed just above ground level and the moving sand grains drop in huge numbers, as the marram, growing rapidly in response to the accumulating sand, moves vertically through the fresh sand. In Ireland, marram is able to withstand rates of sand accumulation of around 60 centimetres per year, and sometimes more, and is most vigorous when sand is being actively deposited. Under such conditions, dense leafy growth may occur. With underground rhizomes growing horizontally through the sand and a root system extending vertically downwards by up to two metres or even more, marram is a very powerful agent of dune formation. Several other plant species grow in association with marram and these also help to stabilise the surface. However, once sand supply is diminished, marram loses its vigour and it may even decline, with its root system failing. Visually, marram growth is most obvious on the foredunes, just above the tideline and in the lee of blowouts, where a more pronounced growth much greener than the surrounding marram is especially obvious. Conversely, deep in the dunes, marram is often very sparse indeed, with little vigour, and in places large areas are practically bare, indicating a very much reduced sand supply.

Marram is such a prodigious agent of dune growth that dunes of over 30 metres can occur and it may take 20 years for one metre to be added to the dunes if there is a five centimetre gain in height per annum. A growth rate of one cubic metre of sand per metre of dune length will therefore require at least 400 years to reach 20 metres. The highest dunes in Waterford are at Tramore and it follows that many of the high dunes there are quite old and the cumulative age of the entire system is large.

While no other plant can surpass marram in terms of growth, abundance and extent **kidney vetch** is almost as abundant in summer and is much more colourful. The flower head is an inflorescence of about 18 individual flowers. Kidney vetch flowers are largely yellow when they first appear, but

Kidney vetch

occasionally other colour types are seen. In late summer, when the plant begins to wither and fade, the flowers gradually go brown adding another degree of contrast to a system gradually slowing down. Some years are much better for kidney vetch than others. This is related to conditions prevailing in the previous autumn. Seed dispersal is by wind and the dried, detached inflorescence is blown about, usually from late July, with each pod containing one seed. Germination begins almost immediately after dispersal. This late summer germination is dependent on moisture conditions and the openness of the ground, and both these essential requirements for a good flower show are sometimes difficult to achieve in August and September. In good years the Waterford dunes will be covered in a dense growth of this variable but very attractive plant. Kidney vetch flowers are a rich source of nectar but not all insects can open the large and often stiff petals to extract it. Bumblebees can, though some do so deviously through an incision made at the base of each flower. Kidney vetch is also the principal larval food plant of the six-spot burnet moth and the common blue butterfly is also a regular visitor to it.

Somewhat similar to kidney vetch, certainly in the colour of its flowers, is **bird's-foot-trefoil**, which may have roots of up to one metre in length, a useful adaptation to life in an environment where water is often in short supply. It, along with kidney vetch and some other dune plants, is very important in raising the nitrogen status of dunes, usually in a symbiotic relationship with nitrogen-fixing bacteria like *Rhizobium*. Sporting dazzling golden-yellow flowers, occasionally tinged with red, bird's-foot-trefoil grows throughout all of the dune systems in the county and is one of the most attractive plants of the coast. The lower petals are joined so insects often have a difficult job gaining access in search of nectar; the flower is curiously shaped as a result and has a bulbous appearance. Once pollinated, the petals fade away and the ovaries enlarge and elongate. These seedpods resemble a bird's claw, and it is from this characteristic that the plant derives its name. As the pods twist and split, several seeds are released and scattered. Although usually low-growing, the flowers are carried on stalked heads and while the leaves appear to have only three leaflets (and so the use of 'trefoil'), another pair are present close to the main stem.

The **bluebell** is usually associated with the woodland floor, where it forms large, dense carpets in spring but it also grows abundantly in dunes and on sea cliffs. With strap-shaped leaves, and pendulous flower spikes with anything from eight to 20 blooms, usually hanging to one side, the bluebell is unmistakable, even before the beautiful bell-shaped flowers appear. The first few leaves to appear in spring are usually flat to the ground with the young spike rising vertically among them. Soft and succulent, these early leaves are very prone to damage by passing walkers. Growing early in the season (though the

Eyebright flower

flower heads rarely appear before the end of April), the plant has a head start over others and it usually has the bare ground it favours to itself, at least for a while. However, the bare places are easily walked over, so the plant suffers when improving weather conditions in spring cause an increase in the number of human visitors, to the detriment of the vulnerable leaves of the bluebell. Crushed leaves are unable to supply the food requirements of this upright flower and frequently the plant dies. Nevertheless, the bluebell inevitably succeeds in many other places or on the fringes of the walkways, where a glorious display is often evident, especially on the higher dunes. Be on the lookout for the odd colour variant as the flowers are not always blue; occasionally, an all-white specimen may be found.

Germander speedwell is a creeping perennial found in all habitats throughout the county and it occurs sparingly in dunes, usually in isolated congregations here and there. Sand dunes are hardly its preferred habitat so its presence there may be ephemeral. Nevertheless it is a welcome addition when it does occur as the small but attractive blue flowers with a central white ring usually stand out among the surrounding vegetation.

Milkwort

Biting stonecrop is a diminutive plant that is particularly well adapted to life on the sand. Though small, it has a particularly attractive star-shaped yellow flower, which grows in clusters on short stalks festooned with alternating fleshy leaves, whose acid, peppery taste gives the plant its name. It has quite an array of creeping stems from whence the flowering and non-flowering stems grow.

This simple form ensures that the plant intercepts minimal heat radiation. It also closes its stomata during the day, which depresses the rate of transpiration (the process used in regulating water movement through the plant). For this strategy to be successful, it needs to be able to and can withstand the high temperatures that are possible in the dunes in summer. Favouring open areas with little vegetation, this short-lived perennial prefers a relatively stable sandy substrate but it is never common on the Cunnigar or in the Tramore dunes and, because of its size, it may take some time to find.

Eyebright species are small and they can be hard to spot among taller vegetation. They are very variable and they readily hybridise, so the individual species can be difficult to identify. The flowers of all eyebrights are small and colourful, and the two-lipped flower is blotched with yellow and purple. Eyebrights are semi-parasites; while they do have leaves, allowing them to manufacture at least some of their own food, their roots attach themselves to other plants such as plantains and clover, from whom they obtain some sustenance. Only two species are likely to be seen in any numbers along the coast *Euphrasia officinalis* agg. and *E. tetraquetra*, the latter being confined to the coastal grassland, dunes and sea cliffs. **Red bartsia** has purple leaves and whitish flowers and occurs in some abundance on unimproved grassland, as at Muggort's Bay, for example.

Dodder is a true plant parasite but it has only been recorded from three coastal sites in the county, largely in the nineteenth century so it is probably extinct now in the county; the most recent record is for the dunes at Tramore in 1967, where it was also found in some abundance between 1886 and 1892.

Although it shares the same name as sea-milkwort, **common milkwort** is no relation and it may be common in the dunes at

Thyme

Tramore (but not on the Cunnigar) or on the cliff tops. It is a small plant and there are many branches on the stems. All the oval-shaped leaves alternate up along the stem and the flowers form at the tips. The flowers themselves are quite small and unusual. There are five sepals, three of which are green and tiny; the other two are much bigger, bluish in colour and they almost hide the petals. The petals are blue in colour and are usually longer than the sepals so they protrude between the sepals. Within the petals, the stamens are joined together to form a tube surrounded by the petals. You need to get close to the flowers to see these unusual features and the trouble involved is definitely worth it. The flowers can vary quite a bit in colour and occasionally a pure white flower may be seen. **Heath milkwort** also occurs on the coast, generally in areas where there is heath, and it can be quite challenging to distinguish between the two milkwort species. The main difference is that the lower leaves in heath milkwort are opposite, whereas in common milkwort they are alternate right down to ground level. Unfortunately this character is not always obvious. Common milkwort is more likely on the coast. The name milkwort, apparently, refers to the belief that the plant could increase milk yields in farm animals.

Ladies bedstraw near Swine's Head

Wild thyme is never hard to find when in flower and is arguably one of the nicest herbs to be seen on the coast. It is a plant with low-growing but sprawling stems and it is the small, pale-purple flowers that are so appealing in summer. Underground it has deep root systems (longer than half a metre), which helps the plant to draw water in the dry months of summer. It also favours areas where it is not at a disadvantage from other more competitive species so it is best searched for in dunes or on the cliff tops where the vegetation is not high; when found, it often occurs in some abundance. The characteristic but unmistakable smell of thyme usually identifies the plant.

Masses of **lady's bedstraw** flowers carpet dune areas in summer. The striking bright yellow flowers are the most obvious feature of this perennial herb. The flowers are tiny but there is usually such a preponderance of them that all other parts of the plants are obscured. Look closer at an individual plant and you will notice the many-branched stems with single-veined leaves arranged in a whorl of

eight or more up the stem. The contrast in colour between the flowers of thyme, scarlet pimpernel and lady's bedstraw is quite pronounced and what a remarkable palette of colour they provide wherever they occur, especially when they are seen close together.

Asparagus cannot be described as a beautiful plant, but it does have presence and its stately form is enhanced when the red berries appear in autumn. It is of significant conservation importance as it is a declining species in Ireland, mainly due to human influences, especially the impacts of recreation and other activities on its main Irish habitat–sand dunes. Confined now to just a handful of sites on the east and southeast coasts of Ireland, this herbaceous perennial is largely confined to the eastern end of the Tramore dunes, where human impact is least. Its dark green leaves stand out among the marram and it is especially conspicuous when covered with the red berries in August. This is a threatened species whose continuing status in the Tramore dunes is very much dependent on it being left alone. If one plant is encountered, then a search nearby may also reveal others in the immediate area (57 individual plants were found in the dunes in 2000, considerably more than the four that were known in the late 1950s/early 1960s). There is also one **garden asparagus** plant between the two areas of wild asparagus, which is a rare garden escape in Ireland. It was first seen here in 1864 and was still present in 2003.

Common centaury is widespread in small numbers throughout the coastal dunes and more sparingly along the cliffs. Small as it is, this annual, a member of the gentian family, is quite beautiful with many coral-pink flowers on long and erect stalks. The oval or elliptical leaves have several prominent veins and paired leaves clasp the stem on either side and notice also the basal rosette of leaves. The petals are arranged in a long tube, which extends beyond the long-toothed sepals and so also does the fruit when ripe. **Lesser centaury**, a rare species now in Ireland, was found at Tramore Backstrand in 1899 and at Clonea in 1998; it can usually be confirmed by the absence of the basal rosette of leaves. It is smaller than common centaury, but some common centaury plants are also dwarfed, so this is not a distinguishing feature. Lesser centaury is known now from just a few sites on the south and east coasts.

Heath dog-violet is only known from the dunes at Tramore and Saleen, where the hybrid between it and common dog-violet also occurs. Much more common, and also a member of the gentian family is **yellow wort**. Its most distinguishing feature is the way the leaves, especially the upper ones, are fused around the stem like cups, so much so in fact that it appears that the stem passes through a single leaf, and this feature is obvious long after the flowers have withered. The yellow-petalled flower, like those of common centaury, usually close in the afternoon, and the flowers are borne on unbranched stems. It is only common in the dunes at Tramore, and sporadically elsewhere along the coast.

Whitlowgrass is a plant of early spring and a hands-and-knees approach is required to examine it closely. Although it was very rare in the Tramore dunes in the early 1960s, it now grows in some abundance but it is tiny and is easily missed. It also grows on the Cunnigar, and very occasionally on rocky outcrops and inland. It is a winter annual and grows best when evapotranspiration is low (usually in spring). Seeds lying near the surface of the dunes may germinate rapidly in autumn and so whitlowgrass may flower in winter, but only if weather conditions are suitable (on relatively warm days). Although not a grass at all, whitlowgrass has four diminutive white petals, each no more than a few millimeters across, and its low growth form may be attributable to the limited light

Common centaury

and low temperature it is exposed to for most of its life cycle low down on the coastal turf.

Sea mouse-ear, another winter annual, is similarly affected by low light levels and temperature. All mouse-ear species are small but they are often hairy (which may account for the 'mouse-ear' in the name) and the flowers, like those of whitlowgrass, are white and there are usually four petals. It can be found all along the coast, in dunes, on walls and in grassland. **Little mouse-ear** is somewhat similar to sea mouse-ear, and requires careful examination of the sepal hairs and the leaves around the flowers to distinguish between them; little mouse-ear is also much rarer and is most likely at Tramore, Bunmahon, the Cunnigar and sparingly on some of the cliff tops.

Wild angelica, wild carrot and hogweed are somewhat similar plants, at least from a distance. All are members of the parsley family and they are recognisable by their umbrella-like heads of small flowers. Their

Sea spurge

leaves are also divided into several distinct leaflets and, of the three, **hogweed** is the largest and most conspicuous. The flower heads or umbels of this species has up to 20 branches with many small leaves or bracts directly underneath. The flowers have a rather unpleasant smell but they are attractive to a number of insects for feeding and they are also large enough to serve as platforms for insect mating rituals. Hogweed grows throughout the summer and, although a big and ugly plant, it is not quite as obnoxious as its near relative, **giant hogweed**, which thankfully does not grow on the coast and is still a rare plant in Waterford, confined to around Dungarvan and the banks of the Suir. All umbellifers produce rising sap if the stems are cut but none are as damaging as that of giant hogweed (the sap of this species irritates

skin, making it hypersensitive to sunlight, causing blistering and reddening, though some people are also sensitive to common hogweed which may cause similar reactions).

By comparison, **wild angelica** is a handsome species, with a froth of white flowers often tinged with pink. Although not unlike hogweed, angelica is smooth with stout, lined stems whereas hogweed is roughly hairy. It has a mass of almost triangular leaves and the flower heads are at the end of a stalk arising from the angle between stem and leaf. **Wild carrot** has very divided leaves with a carroty smell, but, unlike the edible carrot, its roots are thin and wiry. The dome-shaped flower heads are generally white but are occasionally tinged claret or pink. They are very attractive to insects and, in July, the heads may be covered with ants and soldier beetles.

Sea-holly is restricted to dunes and sandy coastal areas. It may be more common around the edges of dunes where it is certainly more obvious and where it may be touched by extreme tides. It is a beautiful, rigid plant with metallic-blue flowers, pale-green holly-like leaves with a frosty blue tinge and the deeply toothed spiny leaves have a thickened white edge. Like many other plants growing in sandy environments open to sea-spray, the leaves are coated with a waxy cuticle, which reduces water loss, and it is deep-rooted. The rounded flower head has many tiny blue flowers, each surrounded by spiny leaves or bracts. The fruits, when formed, are covered in tiny hooks that assist in seed dispersal by animals. A hardy perennial, it grows slowly and in its prime it is one of the most striking and alluring of the flowering plants of the dunes. Growth begins in April and the initial wavy leaves above the sand are diminutive and uninspiring among the sea sandwort, with which it can often be found at the seaward edge of the dunes. Some of these early holly leaves have tiny

Sea-holly

fibrous fawn caps which, when removed, reveal the darkened leaf surface with the characteristic jagged edges.

Rather more ordinary than sea-holly and not particularly attractive, but just as widespread, are the spurges and three species are likely along the coast. **Sea spurge** is confined to coastal areas where succulent leaves, thick cuticles and a specialised root system allow it to thrive. Within three or four days after germinating, the roots reach a depth of five or six centimetres and after two weeks the 10-15 centimetre roots are well down into permanently moist sand. Early in the season, bright green new growth is very obvious at the tips and the red stems provide a good colour contrast on the individual plants. **Petty spurge** is common throughout the county while **portland spurge**, like sea spurge, is confined to the coast and rarely occurs in large numbers.

Wild pansy is only found in the Tramore dunes and the normally three-coloured flowers–most commonly yellow, violet and blue–are not hard to spot among the vegetation. The leaves are oval and toothed but there are deeply-lobed minor leaves (called stipules) at the base of the leaf stalk. But it is the flowers that really draw the eye and not just to the dazzling colour scheme but also to the petals of the flat-faced flower and their relative arrangement that forms a good platform for insects to land on. The much more common **field pansy** also occurs on the coast (it is a weed of cultivated areas and waste ground) and it may be abundant wherever it is found.

Gorse is a hardy and an adaptable plant that grows throughout the county and dense thickets of it are painful to walk through, such as on Helvick Head (though burning here in 2008 removed much of it). **Western** (or **autumn**) **gorse** is equally widespread, but it has a special significance in coastal areas in that it contributes to an important habitat type–coastal heath. It can be just as dense as gorse, but is never as tall. In areas where both occur together, there may be an attractive floral display throughout the year, as western

Ferns on a coastal lane at Ballycurreen

Restharrow

though not as abundantly as in the Comeraghs where dense stands carpet the slopes in summer. Bracken is not an attractive species and it can be poisonous to animals that eat it. Like its upland counterpart, the emerging fronds unfurl almost appealingly in spring and a vigorous summer growth is matched by a rapid but colourful decay in autumn. The golden fronds in that season add another layer of colour to the coastal areas where it occurs but these very fronds, wiry and sharp as they are, can be very difficult, even painful to walk through later in the year when the plant itself is dormant.

The smaller ferns find a suitable niche on the walls and coastal ditches and these species include **Hart's tongue, maidenhair spleenwort, wall rue** and **rustyback**, though none are exclusively coastal and are probably more common inland. They do, however, add interest to mortared coastal structures and are as visually attractive as the structures themselves. By comparison, **sea spleenwort** is almost exclusively coastal and can be seen, with difficulty, in damp crevices in the sea cliffs; otherwise, and more rarely, it may be seen on walls and bridges but never too far inland. **Black spleenwort** is widespread throughout the county and is also found along the coast. The rare **Irish spleenwort** has only been found at one site in the west of the county, on a damp sea cliff at Muggort's Bay, just west of Helvick Head.

gorse flowers mainly in summer, while gorse does so from winter through to spring; the hybrid between the two species has also been seen at Helvick Head.

Ferns are not particularly alluring plants in that there are no attractive floral displays at any time of year, but these primitive plants have interesting life cycles and several species occur in the county, many of which can be seen on the coast. **Royal fern** is perhaps one of the more stately of the large ferns. Though not common on the coast (it prefers damp conditions) it grows, for example, on the west side of Stradbally cove, where exposure to salt-laden winds ensures that the plant never reaches the proportions that are possible in more sheltered locations. **Polypody** is a small but attractive fern that finds life difficult in the coastal areas and wherever it is found there it is usually stunted; it occurs on walls and rocky outcrops, usually on the landward side where exposure isn't as severe. **Bracken** is a successful plant worldwide and it is no surprise that it occurs on the Waterford coast,

Restharrow grows abundantly on dunes of the county in summer and may also be found on coastal grassland and on the sea cliffs; it does occur inland but is less likely. A low-growing perennial, it has beautiful mauve flowers on a mass of trailing stems. Consequently, where it occurs, the dense aggregations of flowers provide a beautiful spectacle and exude a powerful, almost resinous smell. It is an important plant in sand dunes, as it, along with other leguminous plants like kidney vetch, it enhances the nitrogen status and its abundance in the more open areas helps to stabilise the dunes. It has to work hard to survive in coastal areas and its root system can grow to depths of two metres or even more; its common name is derived, apparently, from its ability to stop a horse-drawn harrow ploughing arable land.

Common vetch is very plentiful in some years along the coast but is particularly noticeable in late June and early July, when the black seedpods are conspicuous among the vegetation. Early in the year, the purple flowers and the tendrils, while not as conspicuous as the seedpods that arise later, are obvious in the vegetation. Other vetches also grow along the coast including **tufted vetch** and **bush vetch** while the rare **spring vetch** only grows in the dunes at Tramore, where 30 plants were seen in 2006. On warm days, the pods of vetches rapidly dry out and they pop audibly, so in certain coastal areas there is extra element to the cacophony of sounds to be heard in warm summer weather.

Sharp-leaved fluellen, a Red Data species in Ireland, and now listed as Endangered, is a hairy annual of arable land, that was quite common in the fields around Brownstown Head in the 1960s, though it hasn't been seen there recently; otherwise there are only mostly inland records in recent years for this rare but attractive weed.

Visit parts of the coast, especially the dunes, at the right time of year and the **pyramidal orchid** should be obvious. Although it is widely scattered, it may grow in some abundance where it occurs. The flowers are pure pink and July is the

Pyramidal orchid

month to see this attractive orchid (though individuals may appear in early June). Its name is very obviously derived from the pyramidal-shaped spike of flowers that ensures this particular orchid is unmistakable, especially when young. As with other orchids, the pyramidal orchid has an elaborate pollination mechanism. There is an abundant supply of nectar, which attracts many insects, especially butterflies and moths. When these land on the flower spike to feed, a modified stamen (called a pollinia) sticks to the tongue of the insect and when it visits the next flower, this stamen is forced directly on to its stigma ensuring pollination. The seed produced as a result of this pollination then depends on an intimate association with a fungus for its survival; its first leaves will not appear for four years, and, all going well subsequently, another three years must pass before the flower spike appears.

The **bee orchid** is much rarer than the pyramidal orchid and is only likely along the coast in the dunes at Tramore and on the Cunnigar. It may require patience before one is found but the effort involved

Common spotted-orchid

over a number of years is usually worth it when this beautiful orchid is eventually seen. As its name suggests, the lip of the flower head resembles a bumble bee, presumably to attract a bee to assist in pollination, though this purpose is redundant as the bee orchid reproduces by self-pollination. Other orchid species that have been recorded along the Waterford coast are **autumn lady's-tresses**, **frog orchid**, **heath** and **common spotted-orchid** and **marsh orchids** but some of these are rare, with only one or two records.

Late summer is also the time to look for **devil's-bit scabious** when it grows abundantly along the coast. There are numerous violet flowers or florets on each of the individual rounded flower heads. A closer examination of a floret reveals an inverted cup shape with four almost red anthers on the tip of the stamens. The tall, gangly stems help the plant to rise above other vegetation and the constant motion of these stems as they respond to the wind is a visually attractive spectacle in late summer when many other plants are already decaying. Devil's-bit scabious can suffer along the coast, especially in dune systems, because of

drought conditions and in particularly dry years the stems stay short and stunted. **Field scabious** also occurs on coastal road banks but is much less widespread.

Blackberries collected from **bramble** in hedgerows in autumn are usually tasty and they are to be savoured along the coast, though in places, especially on ungrazed coastal slopes, the plant is a nuisance and can be both difficult and painful to walk through. Several species are known in the county, many of them rare, but it requires a specialised knowledge before they can be identified to species level. **Dewberry**, however, is easy to identify, especially when the edible fruits appear, which they do in abundance in some years. These fruits are easy to distinguish from those of blackberry; there are fewer and consequently larger segments and the entire fruit is covered in a greyish/blue bloom. When ripe they can be quite difficult to pick, spilling a colourful and delicious juice, which stains strongly. Dewberry has a defensive covering of thorns on its stems though they are not nearly as damaging to skin as those of brambles. Surprisingly it is only common in the Tramore dunes where its abundance may be due to the absence of rabbits, as it invades readily once grazing is relaxed.

The **burnet rose** has a quite extensive covering of thorns and bristles on its stem (a distinctive feature), but unfortunately there are no edible fruits to savour after flowering. Its large flowers are much bigger than those of either dewberry or bramble and quite beautiful. The petals are white and frequently tinged with cream or even pink. Prominent golden stamens encircle the centre of the flower and the attractiveness of the flower is enhanced by its sweet aromatic smell. Once flowering is over, large round fruits remain, with a crown of long, withered sepals. Characteristically for this rose species is that the fruits are purplish black; usually rose hips

Burnet rose

are red or scarlet. The burnet rose is probably the most common rose species to be seen on the coast; interestingly, the hybrid between burnet rose and Japanese rose has only two stations in Ireland, both in Waterford, one of which is near Saint. Declan's Church at Ardmore.

Sea knotgrass is one of the rarest coastal plants in Ireland. Lorna Ferguson, while accompanying her husband Keith (from Tramore), found this species growing and in flower on sandy shingle on the beach at Tramore in July 1973. The plant more closely resembled Mediterranean plants than those from Britain, where it appears and disappears in Cornwall and in the Channel Islands. It is definitely a species that is washed in by the sea, and it may or may not become established; it has occurred at least once since at Tramore (the following year, in 1974). **Ray's knotgrass**, a prostrate species, may be found on sandy embankments, the tops of beaches and around the edges of dunes. It has been found sparingly on the Cunnigar, Tramore, Garrarus, Clonea, Dungarvan and Saleen. **Knotgrass** is by far the commonest species, found in all habitats throughout the county, which includes the tops of beaches.

Cottonweed was found in the dunes at Tramore in 1850 and it was last found there in 1883 (it was first recorded in Ireland in 1840 at Dungarvan), but it hasn't been seen at either site since. H. C. Hart mentions cottonweed in his report on the flora of the Wexford and Waterford coasts, though he didn't search specifically for it in the dunes. It was more widespread at the end of the nineteenth century and was known from six coastal counties, including the Waterford sites. Now known from just one site in Wexford, its most northerly station in Europe, where two adjacent colonies exist,

cottonweed is an endangered species in Ireland and is subject to close monitoring by conservationists.

H. C. Hart failed to find **purple spurge,** first found near Garrarus cove in 1839 by a Miss Trench, who deposited a voucher specimen in Trinity College Dublin. Several searches since have also failed to find it and it is almost certainly extinct now in the British Isles. Hart also mentioned that **Cornish heath** was said to be growing on the cliffs at Islandikane, west of Tramore (it was originally found by Richard Burkitt, a medical doctor based in Waterford City in 1836) though he didn't actually say that he located it. It too hasn't been seen since, despite repeated searches though there is some evidence that Burkitt simply got his specimens muddled. Praeger also mentioned **heath false-brome** (or **tor-grass**) growing at Tramore, where it grew in abundance, but he was more cautious about **squinancywort**, which was seen, apparently, in the Tramore dunes in 1866, the only record for the county; it hasn't been recorded since.

Wherever plants occur, grasses and sedges are sure to be found. Like other plants, grasses and sedges are best identified in summer when the flower heads appear, but unlike the flowering plants, the flower heads of grasses and sedges are often drab, colourless and even monotonous to look at and examine. Grasses have long, narrow and parallel-veined leaves with hollow, rounded stems whereas sedges have solid three-sided stems. The leaves of each are probably most useful in distinguishing between them; grass leaves form a sheath around the stem whereas for a sedge, a continuous cylinder of leaves is formed. A careful examination of the flower head is then necessary to identify the grass or sedge species found. Access to a good identification book, an understanding of the

Sand sedge

botanical terms (which can be technical) and time are essential for critical identification.

Only a handful of sedges are widespread along the Waterford coast and **sand sedge** is the most likely to be seen in the dune systems, where it may often be seen with lichens and red fescue. This sedge is usually low-growing and, although the leaves can be up to 60 centimetres in length, they are always narrow (no more than two or three millimetres). When in flower there may be anything from five to 15 spikes on the dense head or inflorescence. The top or terminal spike is usually male, as indeed are some of the middle spikes, while the lower middle spikes and the bottom spikes are almost always female. Sand sedge is more typical of open areas that may be revegetating after disturbance (rather than in dense marram, for example) and several plants may be found growing together. Unusually for sedges each sand sedge plant arises from the underground rhizome at regular intervals along its length allowing the apical bud of the underground stem to continue through the sand.

Glaucous sedge is different in appearance than sand sedge, especially the spikes on the inflorescence. There are usually two or three male spikes and below these are two or occasionally three female spikes. These spikes are well spaced and often droop on thin stalks. The stems and leaves of glaucous sedge are bluish-green in colour, another characteristic feature. Other sedges of coastal cliffs and streams and salt marshes are **distant sedge**, **long-bracted sedge**, **common sedge** and **dotted sedge**. Wood-rushes, although not sedges, are tufted perennials and are easily recognised by the presence of long white hairs that occur on the grass-like leaves. **Field wood-rush** occurs sparingly in coastal grassland and dunes, where it may be hard to find; the distinctive flower head has one unstalked cluster and some stalked clusters of chestnut-brown flowers.

Several grass species, apart from marram grass in dunes, flourish along the coast and their flower heads, dancing in the ever-present sea breezes in summer, are once again the key to their identification, though size

Coastal grasses on Fornaght beach

too may be of some help, at least for one or two species. The most widespread grass is undoubtedly **red fescue**. It is aptly named, as the panicles are reddish as are the leaf sheaths lower down on the plant. It is often used in lawn seeds mixes, but constant cutting rarely allows it to seed, although when not subject to cutting or grazing (as in dunes or other coastal areas, for example) it flowers profusely and prolific seed output results, which is vital for subsequent years flowering. It is typical of dry sandy areas and it grows in such abundance that it is not hard to find at flowering. Superficially similar to red fescue is **creeping bent**, a tufted plant which spreads by means of creeping stems which root and then form a dense tuft. It is more tolerant of wet conditions than red fescue, and, while both can occur together, red fescue is more likely to be found on the highest part of a mound with creeping bent around the edges. Creeping bent has long panicles, which are loose when the grass is in flower but are tight against the stem thereafter.

Dune fescue is much rarer, and is confined to the dunes at Tramore, Fornaght and Woodstown; it can be very difficult to locate in some years. The flower head of **sweet vernal-grass** is short and spike-like which fades to yellow as it ages. As its name suggests, it exudes a pleasant smell when in flower. **Yorkshire fog** is common on the coast (and elsewhere) and is at home as much on the sand dunes of the county as it is on the slopes of the Comeraghs or in the meadows. It is an attractive grass whose bushy flower heads vary in colour from delicate pinkish green in early summer to greyish-white in autumn.

Cock's-foot is so named because of a resemblance of the dense flower head to the foot of a cockerel. It is a tufted grass found growing in all sorts of wild places, where it is usually unmistakable. The flowering head consists of a number of short branches each with further branches supporting bunches of spikelets all on one side of the stem. A perennial, it is one of the few grasses that can be identified with some confidence before it flowers. There are two types of shoot, one of which is sterile and consists only of leaves that flower the following year; these shoots are flattened on one side. The fertile shoots are tall and cylindrical and these soon flower, revealing the characteristic cock's-foot arrangement that is so distinctive.

Early hair-grass, as the name suggests, is one of the earliest grasses to flower. As a winter annual, by early summer it will have almost completely died out. It is probably more common in dry years but regardless of that, winter annuals are usually restricted in terms of growth because of their life cycle. They germinate in the autumn and flower in spring and are never big and dominant like other grasses; this is especially true in dunes where nutrients may be scarce. Nevertheless, early hair-grass is most conspicuous just before flowering and since most other grasses are not yet in their prime, this attractive grass is usually relatively easy to find.

Downy oat-grass is much more vigorous and taller. It is a loosely-tufted perennial with hairy sheaths, which accounts for its common name. It is plentiful in the Tramore dunes, but sparse elsewhere. **Annual meadow-grass** can thrive in a wide variety of habitats, including sandy areas like dunes and hence it is common in the county. An annual, it can flower throughout the year and it may continue growing in winter; it may be no more than five or six centimetres high.

Sand cat's-tail is one of the smaller of the dune grasses and arguably one of the nicest. An annual, each plant usually has several long and narrow flower heads or panicles on relatively short stems or culms. The spike-like panicles are probably at their best when the plant has just finished flowering; straw-like and almost translucent then, sand cat's-tail is only a pale shadow of its former self but it still stands out, especially on less vegetated areas. It is only found in two areas on the coast: commonly in the Tramore dunes (known here since at least 1850) and more recently (1998) at in the dunes at Saleen.

Sea fern-grass, as the name suggests, is only found by the sea on walls, in dunes, occasionally on the sea cliffs and on some of the sandy embankments.

Flora of salt marshes

Salt marshes are subject to periodic flooding by the sea, which deposits mud, silt and other particles as the movement of the water slows down near high tide. Because of ongoing siltation, the profile of a salt marsh slowly changes and the upper marsh is only reached by the sea during exceptional storm surges, allowing a distinctive plant community to develop there. The frequent and varying tidal inundation causes rapid changes in the salinity levels of a salt marsh. Seasonally too there are wide variations in salinity levels with high evaporation rates in summer causing considerable increases in levels; conversely, during prolonged heavy rain, at any time of year but especially in winter, salt concentrations are very much reduced. Waterlogging is an obvious danger during high tides and especially during storm surges. The occasional severe storm may cause mechanical damage, especially to the pioneer plants low down on the marsh that are very susceptible to aggressive wave action.

Salt marsh plants need to withstand these tidally disturbed conditions and varying salinity levels; many are annuals and all are succulents, and pioneer species like the much-branched *Salicornia* offer a low frictional resistance to seawater flowing around them. There are a small number of salt-tolerant plants that can withstand periodic immersion by the tides and there is a clear zonation according to the frequency and duration of the inundation. Salt marsh vegetation is generally confined to the area between the mean high water level of neap tides and the extreme high water of spring tides. The lower salt marsh is subject to constant inundation by the sea and very few species are present there, and even these maintain a tenuous foothold. The pioneer communities here are dominated by glasswort and common cord-grass, while the muddy sediments nearby may support beds of eelgrasses. The greatest diversity of species is found in the upper salt marsh, especially where is merges with sandy areas.

Out on the mudflats proper, conditions are usually much too demanding for most plants but, because of this, one particular plant can flourish in the absence of competition. **Eelgrass** or *Zostera* is a seagrass and two species, **dwarf eelgrass** and **narrow-leaved eelgrass**, are now known in the county (a third species has recently been merged with narrow-leaved eelgrass and both together are now known simply as eelgrass). Both species may occur together, mainly at Tramore Backstrand and at Dungarvan, and are most obvious close to the landward limit of high tides. Both species seem to prefer areas that never completely dry out at low tide and yet are never deeply submerged at high tide. The undulating topography of mudflats and sandflats offers ideal conditions with many hollows holding seawater once the tide ebbs; consequently, the best time to see the eelgrasses is after high tide. Dwarf eelgrass is the smaller and more common of the two but narrow-leaved eelgrass may be dominant in one or two places, probably because of location and on the type of substrate where it grows (it prefers muds and muddy sands that may be difficult to walk on).

Both eelgrass species may occur together in the presence of the alga *Enteromorpha* and cord-grass, whose expansion on the edges of salt marshes may be to the detriment of *Zostera*. Wherever cord-grass grows, sedimentation increases, raising the level of the mudflat so that when the tide retreats no pools or standing water remains. Eelgrasses very quickly die out and little or no eelgrass grows on these raised hummocks, though they may persist in the wet mudflats between cord-grass hummocks. Eelgrasses are an important food source for brent geese in particular, who preferentially graze the highly nutritious leaves and shoots in September/October. Although the geese

Cord-grass is no longer used for stabilising salt marshes due to its impact on native habitats and species

consume most of the standing crop (and they occasionally damage the roots), when the geese are not around in summer the beds very quickly recover from the heavy grazing of the previous autumn. Winkles also graze on the eelgrass and thousands of the tiny snail *Hydrobia* may be seen clinging to the leaves in the many wet pools.

Cord-grass, or *Spartina,* dominates the lower levels of the salt marshes in the county. It is both obvious and invasive, and it often takes over completely, as it outcompetes other more attractive and less destructive plants for the available resources. It has many special adaptations allowing it to survive and thrive at the seaward limit of the salt marsh, where few other plants can exist, but in establishing here it dramatically influences the limited flora of the lower salt marsh areas. It is a perennial and is obvious at any time of the year but its normally unkempt appearance improves considerably from July onwards when the diminutive flowers or inflorescences appear on the growing spikes.

Spartina anglica has an interesting history and is a relative newcomer to the flora of Britain, where it was first introduced and from there then to Ireland. *Spartina alterniflora* is a widespread species on the Atlantic side of America and it arrived in Southampton in shipping ballast in the

Glasswort

It was planted in county Cork in 1925 and then to many other estuaries around the coast. J. P. Quigley planted a number of clumps in selected areas of the Backstrand at Tramore in 1944. He reasoned that:

if this Tramore area were successfully meadowed, the unhealthy and unsightly slob land would be eliminated and replaced by firm productive land over which passage would be possible,

and, according to himself:

these clumps flourished, flowered, bore seed and propagated vegetatively, thus proving the suitability of this plant to local conditions.

He was obviously influenced by F. W. Oliver (Professor of Botany at the University of London at that time) who in a letter to him (as to the suitability of *Spartina* for meadowing), stated:

the change in scenic effect is profound; to what had been a boundless mire, there has succeeded a covering of tender green taking wonderful tints from sun and sky.

Spartina grows extensively on the salt marsh areas of Dungarvan and Tramore and in the lower reaches of the tidal estuaries of Waterford Harbour and the Blackwater.

1820s. Also present on the south coast of England at that time was *Spartina maritima*, a species which existed there at the northern limit of its natural distribution. Both of these species rarely set seed but, following a brief encounter between the introduced species and the native species, they hybridised to produce a sterile hybrid called *Spartina x townsendii*, which was first recognised in 1878. Initially the spread of this hybrid was slow but then a remarkable event occurred. As a result of chromosome doubling in the sterile hybrid, a fertile form *Spartina anglica*, appeared around 1892 but this form wasn't properly distinguished as a separate species until around 1940. Around 1890, *Spartina* spread rapidly on British estuaries and this has been explained by the ability of the fertile form to move to new sites by means of seed dispersal. *Spartina anglica* was widely planted, initially in England, in an attempt to stabilise salt marshes and mudflats because of its ability to enhance the accumulation of sediment and to reduce wave energy.

The various *Salicornia* species, compared with *Spartina*, are much more appealing with few of the aggressive tendencies of the more vigorous neighbour, with whom they share the lower salt marsh areas (though *Salicornia* is often displaced eventually by the rampant cord-grass). The glasswarts, as they are more popularly known (because, dried and burned, the ash was once used in the making of poor quality glass), are succulents, and the fleshy, jointed leaves, resemble miniature cacti. The fleshy leaves are an adaptation to regular immersion by seawater and the much-branched form also offers low resistance to water currents, allowing the plant to grow where it otherwise might not.

All *Salicornia* species are annuals so they have only a couple of months in summer to complete their life cycle. Six *Salicornia* species grow on the Waterford coastal salt marshes. **One-flowered glasswort** is distinctive as it has a single flower and doesn't colour. It has a mainly southeastern distribution and can be seen on or around the drift line. **Purple glasswort** and **common glasswort** are very similar and are difficult to separate; the easiest way is to assume that common is the one lower down on the salt marsh and purple is higher up. Purple glasswort colours well in the autumn, going purplish red. Also found on the local salt marshes are **yellow glasswort** and **long-spiked glasswort** while **shiny glasswort**, the rarest species, only grows in the Backstrand at Tramore. By October the entire salt marsh will be endowed with a characteristic red hue as the multitude of *Salicornia* plants change colour and wither away but, even where there are no glassworts, decaying sea-lavender also contributes to the colour change. Some glassworts are off-yellow in colour and what a contrast these provide against their red and green neighbours nearby. Seawater entering the many channels on the salt marsh strip the *Salicornia* plants of their fleshy leaves, leaving just the plant frame, which then looks so bare and desolate, but even these stalks will be obliterated by late November or early December.

Lax-flowered sea-lavender is visually stunning, especially when it occurs in some numbers from June to late July, as the pale mauve flowers bloom (which they do in huge numbers at Tramore Backstrand). A very variable species, in some ways it is like thrift in that some plants on drier ground grow more vigorously and with larger flowers. It is more prevalent on the middle areas of the salt

Lax-flowered sea-lavender

marsh and is therefore more or less spared the constant trampling endured by plants on the upper salt marsh. Sea-lavender is low-growing and the spear-shaped leaves are quite obvious in May though it may be some weeks later before the flowers appear. The **rock sea-lavenders** are a group of somewhat similar species found on the coastal cliffs but they are difficult to separate to species level. They may even be inaccessible on some of the sheer cliff faces where they occur on the coast.

Sea aster bears purple flowers though yellow disk florets are almost always present and this feature is useful in separating this

Annual sea-blite

Buck's-horn plantain

the glassworts, it has fleshy leaves which contain cell sap with a high concentration of sodium salts in solution; this adaptation opposes, and indeed balances, the natural tendency of the surrounding seawater to suck the plant dry. Annual sea-blite is an unremarkable species in early summer, but by autumn it reveals its true colours–a fiery but beautiful red. The small flowers are found at the junction of the stem and leaf.

The shrubby **sea purslane** is not a particularly attractive plant of the salt marsh and nor does it provide beautiful floral arrangements in summer. It is dull and drab at any time of the year but it grows in abundance in most areas of the salt marsh. It is also found in or mainly along creeks and channels that cut through the coastal salt marshes and is therefore exposed to regular tidal inundation. An obvious silver sheen covers the leaves; these tiny air-filled scales on the leaf surface retain a layer of moisture. This feature helps to protect the leaf from the drying effect of salt water while also offering some protection against the drying effect of the sun, particularly when the tide is low. These very same leaves are shed in considerable abundance in autumn and early winter when the parent plants are settling down for the long months ahead. Late in the year, accumulations of these jelly-like leaves along tidelines can be very slippery to walk on. Well before that in high summer, the flowers are borne in clusters on the erect stems. Sea purslane is probably near its northern limit in Ireland. It is relatively scarce along the west coast of Ireland, suggesting a climatic influence on its distribution, given its abundance on Waterford salt marshes.

species from sea-lavender. Sea aster is a robust plant but it too is highly variable in form. Salt marsh plants like this species growing in exposed situations and subject to high levels of salinity are often low-growing and occasionally do not flower. Sea aster growing on the banks of the Suir, where salinity levels are much lower and soils are richer, can be well over a metre high, with many flowers. But it does depend on saline conditions and is usually absent when salt leaches away. Regardless of location it is an upright plant with stout stems and fleshy leaves and is at its best in late summer, when many other plants have withered. It doesn't like shade and is an opportunist species which finds a niche in gaps on the salt marsh created by drought conditions or the smothering of existing vegetation by tidal litter. It is widespread along the Waterford coast, from the upper reaches of the estuaries to the coastal walls but is most easily seen on the salt marshes.

Annual sea-blite is found only at Tramore, Dungarvan and around Kinsalebeg. High tides regularly cover the salt marsh areas where it grows, creating the very conditions that sea-blite is adapted to. A true halophyte (it thrives in high salt concentrations), like

The sea-spurreys are scruffy, low-growing plants that occur along the Waterford coast. There are three species: **greater** and **lesser sea-spurrey** can be found on the salt marshes (they also grow on the cliffs but are less likely in that habitat) while **rock sea-spurrey**, the commonest of the three, can be seen on rocks, cliffs and in the short turf among the vegetation of the cliff top.

The plantain family is a group of common perennials found on lawns and along paths, tracks, and waste ground and even along cracks in concrete and pavements. **Sea plantain** is one of the more obvious of the less conspicuous salt marsh plants and is probably the most familiar. A walk along any of the tracks on the upper salt marsh areas will confirm that the veined leaves of this common plant grow close to the ground. The flowering spike is prominent in summer, and each is adorned with several flowers. The flower heads tower well above the leaves and are normally apparent well into autumn. **Buck's-horn plantain** is smaller and definitely more stately than the other plantains. It grows out from the centre and then up so the plant is bowl shaped. The leaves are divided and the hairy stem bears a single dense flower head containing many flowers. Sea plantain and buck's-horn plantain are restricted to coastal areas, where they often grow together and in some abundance, especially in sparsely vegetated or trampled areas. The other common plantains in the county are **greater** and **ribwort plantain** (ribwort plantain usually grows taller than normal in places in coastal dune systems, where it has to compete with other vegetation, especially marram, for light).

Common saltmarsh-grass is a grass of coastal marshes where it occurs in some abundance, especially lower down. Its favoured growth form is radial rather than vertical. It is taller, wider and has longer leaves in the more open or pioneer areas of the salt marsh. **Reflexed saltmarsh-grass**, also grows on the margins of the salt marshes. It was only discovered recently (in 1997) in Dungarvan and is currently increasing in the county. **Sea arrowgrass** has long and distinctive flower spikes in summer, which contain numerous flowers, each with six fertile segments tinged with purple and these segments fall off when the fruit has matured. A hand lens is usually required to closely examine the individual flowers of sea arrowgrass. It is common on the salt marshes of the county and in the tidal areas of the estuaries. **Hard-grass** is entirely a coastal species where it may be found on the upper reaches of salt marshes at Tramore and Dungarvan. Easily overlooked, coastal populations are usually small and susceptible to dumping in certain areas where it occurs (at Tramore, for example).

Strawberry clover has a very local and mainly coastal distribution in Ireland. Apart from damp grassy areas, it also grows in heavy, brackish soils. It is only known in Waterford at Tramore, and now only at one site there–the salt marsh area to the north of the 'neck' of the Tramore dunes. The raising of the protective embankment at Lisselan in 2007 to protect the new racecourse probably obliterated it at the other site.

Weedy and other species
Other plants, although not restricted to coastal areas, also grow alongside the more salt-tolerant species, either on the salt marshes, the cliffs, the dunes or other areas nearby where the sea still has an influence.

Dandelion flower head

Groundsel is an annual plant of rough ground and grows anywhere from urban gardens to coastal dunes. The disturbed nature of some coastal embankments suits the plant, though it is never common.

Dandelion is a widespread perennial with a solitary yellow flower head on a hollow stem, which weeps a milky liquid when cut. There are many florets on the flower head and the leaves at ground level are green and ragged. Although an attractive plant, it is usually ignored because of its abundance but its circular dome of seeds is both characteristic and unmistakable. Clouds of these featherweight seeds are released by even light winds and they disperse widely ensuring the survival of the plant in subsequent years. Dandelion may be the only flowering plant to be seen in early February but it is perhaps more common on coastal embankments and cliff tops later in spring (even in early April, many will have gone to seed), probably because it is overshadowed later in the year by more aggressive species.

Equally well known are thistles; **creeping thistle** and **spear thistle** occur on less exposed and more fertile coastal areas, and in dense aggregations in some areas (usually of creeping thistle). They are despised because the mass of green leaves are dotted with

prickly tips which are uncomfortable, even painful when touched or brushed against. Attractive as the purple flower heads are, and to insects, these species are very ragged and unkempt following flowering, and when large numbers grow together, the scene is very untidy. **Prickly sow-thistle** and **smooth sow-thistle**, although somewhat similar to other thistle species, are also found in coastal areas though rarely in large numbers. **Knapweed** flowers are very similar to those of the thistle but the similarity ends there. Without the prickly thorns of the various thistle species, knapweed is altogether more appealing. A large and common perennial, its beauty lies in the many flower heads, each containing numerous identical reddish-purple florets.

Silverweed is so called because of the presence of fine silky hairs on its silvery green leaves, which hug the ground, and it has attractive five-petalled yellow flowers. It sends out stolons, which root at the tips, allowing the plant to spread without ever setting seed. **Daisies** are very intolerant of competition from other species but they are very tolerant of trampling. Consequently they thrive where constant walking eliminates other species, especially in short grass, and they are common on some coastal embankments in the county. Although regarded as a pernicious weed, especially on lawns, it is an attractive plant and the rounded leaves that are broader above the base, are dull by comparison with the flower heads, which have small yellow discs surrounded by a ring of white rays. The solitary flower heads are occasionally tinged with red, which adds to their attractiveness, at least on dune swards. Daisies like to begin their life cycle before other more aggressive plants outgrow them; consequently, many are in flower in early summer, which is a good time to see them along well-used walkways.

Ragwort is tolerant of a wide range of conditions and grows abundantly in coastal areas. Sporting beautiful golden flowers on

Ragwort flower heads

tall, upright stems, and with noticeably divided leaves, it is, unfortunately, a poisonous plant, at least to farm animals. Toxic alkaloids are present in all parts of the plant, and if eaten by livestock in hay or silage, death may result as the alkaloids are broken down in the liver of the animal. Several species of insect favour ragwort (almost 200 have been recorded), and one particular insect, the cinnabar moth, is dependent on it. The caterpillars of the cinnabar moth defoliate the plant in June and July and these are eaten by birds and parasitised by other insects. Seed of two types are produced in very large quantities. Seeds from the edge of the flower head are heavier than those in the centre and they stay on the plant longer; moreover, they are not carried far and they usually remain nearby or fall onto the bare patch vacated by the parent plant when it dies after seeding. The lighter seeds from the centre are covered with fine hairs, and they retain their long hairs so they are carried far by the wind, aiding colonisation of new sites far from their source. Ragwort is a very successful and a rampant plant, and is difficult to control in agricultural areas but control is not an issue in dunes, where, arguably, it enhances the biological diversity of the system.

One or two **buttercup** species occur along the coast and **white clover** is always to be seen, while **red clover** may be seen in the fields above the cliffs.

Scarlet pimpernel is an attractive plant and the bright and starry flowers are conspicuous in the dunes or on coastal grassland. A sprawling plant, with many branches hugging the ground, it is an opportunistic species, a weed really, but it finds a suitable niche on bare ground on the coast.

Red clover

The leaves are oval with a pointed tip and the plant is very well named, as the scarlet flowers are quite stunning (though various other hues are usually present).

Colt's-foot is pioneer species of open ground and, although it is not confined to the coast, it is particularly obvious on dunes, coastal cliffs and the tops of beaches. It flowers early, usually in March or even in February, and the flowers appear and disappear before the leaves. It is a beautiful plant that will always enthrall on bleak days in spring. The dazzling yellow flowers are borne on upright stems where the scale leaves lie dormant, awaiting their turn to appear long after the flowers have withered and died. Come back a couple of weeks later and the downy, seed-bearing parachutes will be obvious on the top of the stems. These are easily dispersed and the faintest breeze will send them airborne. The hoof-shaped leaves (which is probably why the plant is so named) are the last to appear by which time the fruiting heads, and certainly the flowers, are beginning to fade.

Also possible anywhere along the coast are ladies bedstraw and the very occasional **black medick** and **rough hawk's-beard**. The tall **common fleabane** is such an imposing plant with its yellow flower

Herb-Robert flower

55

heads that it is very obvious among the marram of the dunes or on the coastal cliffs. Other species like **agrimony** and **weld** may be found in the sandy grassland, while **meadowsweet, purple-loosestrife, curled dock** and **water mint** grow close to and on adjoining farmland. **Hairy bitter-cress** may occur too and, later, the relatively long seedpods are distinctive.

Disturbed ground near the former county dumps at Dungarvan and Tramore (both now closed) offers ideal conditions for two or three thistle species, **nettles,** ribwort plantain, **ivy-leaved toadflax, great mullein, common ramping-fumitory, water figwort, herb-Robert, winter heliotrope, oxeye daisy** and **honeysuckle**, and grass species like **couch grass**, creeping bent and cock's-foot. Typical weed species include white and red clover, **wild turnip, cleavers, broad-leaved dock, hedge bindweed**, one or two **cress** species and **fat-hen**. Tree-mallow may also occur sparingly. Growth of many of these species is dense and prolific and seed-eating birds feast on the bumper harvest in late summer. No doubt other species also grow and regular monitoring might reveal a few surprises.

Yellow iris

In the wetter areas, channels or small ponds that develop around salt marshes or between the dumps and the salt marshes there are opportunities for certain plant species that have a restricted coastal distribution. The dominant **bulrush** is most obvious as it outgrows everything else and the flowering spike is very characteristic. **Common reed**, a very distinctive plant, is tall and stately and it defines the edges of the tidal estuaries and many of the lakes in the county. It also grows near salt marshes, in pasture land behind salt marshes and even along the edges of streams flowing into the sea. Around the fringes of these water bodies, **sea club-rush, slender club-rush, jointed rush, toad rush, saltmarsh rush**, water mint (whose leaves are very aromatic), **marsh thistle, marsh lousewort, yellow iris**, and **great willowherb** grow in considerable abundance. **Field** and **great horsetails** grow in some numbers in damp areas near the coast and are unmistakable on poorly drained ground. Of interest too in summer in the larger pools and channels are the damselflies and dragonflies flitting and frolicking about the dense vegetation especially in warm sunny weather. Plants growing nearby on the drier areas include meadowsweet, **square-stalked St. John's-wort**, oraches, sea beet and the pinky-purple flowered **cuckooflower**.

The attractive **meadow foam** (or poached egg plant), a north American species, is widely available in garden centers, and may become rampant as it seeds readily. It is known from Newtown cove (where it occurs annually) and the dunes at Woodstown.

Trees and woodland

Most tree species usually like good fertile soil in which to grow an elaborate root system. In such situations they may grow tall and stately. Coastal areas are, however, generally unsuitable for tree growth and they offer little in the way of favourable conditions. Exposure and constant bombardment by salt-laden winds and sand are the most serious and ongoing threats. Many species simply cannot grow in hostile coastal environments, though some try, and suffer for it.

Sycamore is an introduced tree in Ireland, probably appearing sometime in the fifteenth or sixteenth century, and has since become naturalised, growing in all counties. It was extensively planted in the late eighteenth century and some of the best examples of this majestic tree date from this period. A mature sycamore can be exceptionally beautiful, with many fine branches bedecked with an abundance of leaves in summer. It is considered a weed species, partly because, when mature, it produces seed at a prolific rate and these winged, aerodynamically efficient fruits spread far and wide. It will grow almost anywhere and is tolerant of a wide range of soil conditions.

Quite a few sycamores grow along the coast, and even in the sand dune systems, though a closer look is often necessary to confirm the identity of the tree. Usually these coastal sycamores are not the typical sycamores that are instantly recognisable in parkland situations. Rather they are almost always stunted and low-growing, and the severity of these features depends on the degree of exposure. Growth is more lateral than vertical and several branches may grow side by side together in an uncharacteristic sprawl, often on the lee side of sand ridges. Even sheltered locations offer little protection from strong summer winds and it is not unusual to see a leafless sycamore in summer. Nevertheless tight groves of trees may prevail in some sheltered spots (on a northeast-facing slope on the Backstrand side of the Tramore dunes, for example). Often too, sycamore is planted around coastal homesteads, because it is one of the few tree species that will grow; if planted in sheltered areas, they may thrive, though they will always struggle to reach their mature stature.

Monterey cypress in the grounds of Ardoginna house

Monterey cypress is a hardy tree, well capable of surviving in coastal areas and is widely planted. It does, however, become straggly as it grows older, and this form may be exaggerated if subject to coastal exposure (such as the two large specimens planted at Ardoginna House). Surprisingly, there is only one site in the county where the tree is self-sown and that is in the Tramore dunes where a single tree grows poorly on the sheltered northern side, east of the 'neck'.

Hawthorn is a hardy species but it too suffers along the coastal cliff tops and in the inland ditches where it is usually stunted and shaped by the wind. In all coastal sites, hawthorns are low-growing, and usually point in a northerly direction, especially if growing on exposed slopes, and, without exception, they are poorly formed and unkempt. **Elder** grows throughout county Waterford and may be found in the coastal dunes where its general low growth form gives it some protection from prevailing winds, particularly if sited in relatively sheltered locations. It often reaches a more natural height than the stunted sycamore and it does offer feeding opportunities for birds like chiffchaff and blackbird, that are usually scarce in sand dunes, and as a substrate on which lichens like *Evernia prunastri* grow. Elder favours disturbed ground rich in nitrates and while it

Coastal crustose lichens

is an unimpressive tree for most of the year, it brightens up somewhat when laden with scented white flowers in spring or when drooping with berries in late summer and autumn. A single **sitka spruce**, self sown in a relatively sheltered part of the Tramore dunes in the 1990s, eventually succumbed to exposure and the dry summer of 2006.

Wild privet, a relative of garden privet, was once widely planted for hedging in suburban gardens. It is a semi-evergreen shrub and it grows throughout the county, but is probably only native along the sea cliffs and in the dune areas. It is known since at least 1866 from dunes at Tramore. Wind exposure and sand movement is reduced in the remote and sheltered parts of dunes and the calcareous ground provides good conditions for growth and survival. It is at its best in spring and early summer when the sweet-smelling white flowers appear in large numbers on the stems. The invasive **sea-buckthorn** no longer occurs in the Tramore area. It was planted on top of the shingle bank there in 1910 by W. E. Duffin, county surveyor, but the plants were vandalised ruining the experiment set up to investigate the ability of this thorny shrub to consolidate the beach. One plant grows in the dunes at Woodstown, where it was probably planted.

Scrub woodland grows on parts of the Waterford coast, in the stream valleys and along the ditches of the fringing farmland. Here species like bramble, gorse and bracken grow among the **blackthorn**, hawthorn, **ash**, **alder** and **spindle**, and in places there is a well-developed woodland canopy often with **hazel** as an additional species.

Lichens, mosses & fungi
Lichens are an association between a fungus and an alga and the association is very much different than either of its component parts. Lichens are widely distributed, are found in almost all habitats, and they can be examined and admired throughout the year, as there is little seasonal variation. They are usually very slow-growing and an extensive lichen cover is likely to be several years old.

Coastal areas are, by and large, inhospitable places for most lichen species and, as for flowering plants, only lichens adapted to exposure, tidal immersion and the influence of salt water occur. However, this very coastal exposure, which prevents other more competitive species from establishing, allows extensive bare areas to develop where specialised lichens grow, and in considerable abundance when conditions are suitable. The coastal zone is an important habitat for some lichens and for several species it is the only habitat where they may be found.

Sea ivory (grey) and *Xanthoria parietina*

Along the coast the three main habitats where lichens can be found are the coastal cliffs and rocks, within the sand dunes, and on trees and timber fence posts. Viewed from a distance, three distinct colour bands are usually present on the cliffs and rocks (because of the colour of the lichens that occur) and there is very obvious zonation of species, which is best seen at low tide. This is related to the ability of each species to withstand the varying levels of immersion in seawater, and the influence of sea spray on those further up on the shore. The lowest band is black and around the high tide mark there may be several *Verrucaria* species, which gives the zone its distinctive black colour; the most common species is probably *V. maura*. The black and shrubby *Lichina* species also occur in this zone and these are attached to the rocks by a holdfast. There are two species, one of which, *L. pygmaea*, usually occurs lower down and is frequently covered by the tide whereas *L. confinis* favours sunny, sheltered rocks. These might be confused with some of the smaller black seaweeds but *Lichina* species have terminal globular fruiting bodies, which, although small, are distinctive. A common species in this zone, but quite unlike a lichen, is *Collemopsidium foveolatum*. Look for it on limpets and barnacles, as well as on surrounding rocks; the black fruiting bodies should be visible on the shells when the tide is out.

The orange zone, as expected, is dominated by orange species though some of the black species, notably *Verrucaria maura*, may also occur. Further up on the shore the yellow/orange *Caloplaca* species flourish away from tidal immersion but are nevertheless exposed to considerable amounts of sea spray. There are several species, but they require detailed examination, including chemical tests to determine the exact species, but nearly all of them hug the rock surface and many have lobed margins. Expect to see *C. marina*, *C. thallincola* and *C. verruculifera*. At

Tephromela atra

the upper parts of this zone the leafy lichens appear, which would not survive the impacts of waves lower down. The most common of these is *Xanthoria parietina*, a yellow-orange lichen that grows abundantly around human settlements, on roofs, trees and fence posts and of course, near the coast. In areas, a brilliant yellow carpet of this leafy species may cover the coastal rocks or any other substrates that are available nearby.

The uppermost zone is grey, which is usually well above the sea spray and is comparatively dry. Here less specialised crustose species grow and are able to thrive in the lower salt conditions. Crustose lichens are those where the plant body forms a crust over the surface and two species are quite common on any of the larger rocks or on the

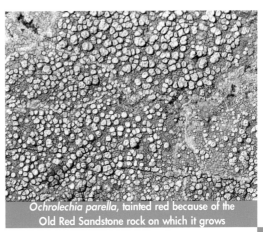

Ochrolechia parella, tainted red because of the Old Red Sandstone rock on which it grows

Xanthoria parietina on a discarded tyre

Dunmore East or further east at Creadan). Rare lichens include *Diploschistes caesioplumbeus*, a crustose lichen of the sun-lit cliffs at the Guillamene. *Teloschistes flavicans*, a declining species and now probably confined to southwest Ireland, grew on a headland near Beenlea Head in the 1980s but recent searches have failed to find it.

Shifting sands around the edges of dunes do not favour slow-growing lichens and those that occur on rocks and stones, are constantly buffeted by wind, sand grains and even the sea. Within the dunes themselves, conditions are more stable and hence suitable for some lichens, especially on open ground where they are not swamped by other vegetation, and on bushes where they grow undisturbed on stems and branches. Where privet is vigorous and woody, dense growths of *Xanthoria parietina* and *Physcia adscendens* may cover the stems and elder may have these species as well as *Evernia prunastri*, *Parmotrema perlata* and *Lepraria incana*, lichens that are more typical of less-exposed and non-marine situations. In the sandy areas within dune systems a few foliose (leafy) species may be found. *Collema tenax* (var. *ceranoides*) is one such lichen but some of the *Peltigera* lichens also occur. *Cladonia* lichens are usually light green with erect but hollow stems, though some are small with abundant 'leaves' (called squamules). Look for them within the dunes or beside paths in coastal heath, where a few species occur, and in great abundance, even covering the ground in certain areas (as, for example, beside the coastal path at Portally).

cliffs in the county. Both are similar but the fruiting bodies, usually in the centre of the lichen, may be of use in separating them. *Tephromela atra* has black apothecia (a spore-bearing structure) with a light grey rim whereas those of *Ochrolechia parella* have cream, almost doughnut-shaped apothecia. *O. parella* is by far the more common of the two; it is a conspicuous and widespread lichen and usually covers all the uppermost rocks in a long line (from a distance these rocks look whitewashed). Confusing their identification here and elsewhere may be other *Buellia*, *Lecanora*, *Lecidella*, *Porpidia* and *Pertusaria* species. *Rhizocarpon geographicum*, though, if present, is usually distinctive; a bright yellow-green lichen, it thrives in exposed sunny situations from the coastal rocks to the craggy conglomerate cliffs of the Comeragh Mountains. *Ramalina siliquosa* (or **sea ivory**) is stiff and tufted and is particularly abundant on the cliffs where it forms dense mats well above the tideline but it also grows along the rocky embankments.

Brown leafy lichens may also be seen and these include *Anaptychia runcinata* and some of the *Parmelias* while the leafy but stiff *Dermatocarpon miniatum* may be seen on some cliffs (such as the kittiwake cliffs at

Mosses require damp conditions in which to survive and most species are usually salt-intolerant so that coastal areas aren't really suitable for them. Moreover, they may not survive prolonged desiccation, which is a constant threat in sandy areas and in dunes, where they are most likely to occur, though a few specialised species are found on coastal cliffs and rocks. Because of their low-growth form they are usually confined to the open areas in dunes, where other vegetation is scarce or absent and they assist in stabilising the dune surface in these areas. Here, among the occasional marram or grass stem, the sand is loose but relatively immobile and some mosses in particular find a useful foothold.

Sand-hill screw-moss may be common and is quite a distinctive species; there are many shoots in a tuft with rosettes of hairy green-brown leaves. It may grow to three or four centimetres which helps it to avoid burial by sand. After a dry spell, the leaves, following rewetting, straighten instantly, flicking off sand grains in the process. **Neat feather-moss** is a big bryophyte (moss) and some of its individual shoots may be up to 13 centimetres long. It is quite an obvious moss and it grows extensively in some dune areas. **Yellow feather-moss** grows on sunny slopes in the dunes; the red fruiting capsules are quite distinctive with claw-like bristles at the apex, while **cypress-leaved plait-moss** is a common mat-forming moss. It grows horizontally while **big shaggy-moss** may be found in the older, established parts of the dunes. Other mosses may also occur such as **beard-mosses**, other **feather-mosses** (**whitish feather-moss** is most likely) and **thread-mosses** (**Bryums**), which might require patience in their identification.

Yellow crisp-moss is one of the few exclusively coastal mosses and, apart from growing in stable sand dunes, it is also found in rock crevices, a habitat it shares with **seaside grimmia**, that is most likely if there is freshwater percolation from above. Two *Tortula* species are also likely on coastal cliffs and rocks (**rib-leaf moss** and **bristly potia**) but only two liverworts are likely in the coastal zone: **dilated scalewort** (on cliff top turf) and **sea scalewort** (on rocks).

Fungi usually appear in the autumn, and this is the best time to see them. They do not

Fungi on the Cunnigar dunes

have chlorophyll, the pigment green plants use to manufacture energy from the sun using carbon dioxide and water. Hence they must obtain nourishment from other sources such as living or dead animal or plant tissues. Saprophytic fungi obtain their energy from dead and decaying matter so they are very effective disposers of natural plant detritus which would otherwise accumulate in vast quantities, especially in the autumn. Fungi come in all shapes and sizes and there are large colour variations. However, coastal areas are not particularly good for fungi and they are probably only likely to be seen in sand dunes, where there is less exposure and impacts from the sea. One or two *Lycoperdon* species occur; these are the puffballs, small round-headed mushrooms that darken with age and eventually release powdery clouds of spores, especially if stood on. There are at least 10 fungi associated with marram grass and *Psathyrella ammophila* is probably the most common; it is small and with a clay-brown cap that may be seen from early summer on, though it is never abundant. Inevitably, with so many people, dogs and horses passing along the trampled paths around beaches and dunes, spores of common species are introduced. The *Hygrocybe* fungi are characteristic of short

Knotted or egg wrack, *Ascophyllum nodosum*

air spaces or bladders in the leaves and this specialism increases their buoyancy when the tide is in. Other seaweeds without these buoyancy aids cannot survive in turbid waters and are restricted to the clear blue sea and to shallow areas where sunlight penetration at low tide may be high. Seaweeds are also very supple and much more so than flowering plants, allowing them not just to move about in the sea but also to survive in strong currents and stormy conditions. Some seaweeds are better adapted to the prevailing conditions leading to a marked zonation on the shore. This means that some species dominate certain areas to the detriment usually of all others that may dominate elsewhere and cover large areas.

Colour is an important characteristic. Seaweeds are green, red or brown, which is an adaptation to the quality of the light available to them in their respective positions on the shore. Seaweed colour is, therefore, a good indicator of the position of the seaweed in the marine environment. Green algae are probably most common in the intertidal areas and they can be particularly abundant on intertidal sand and mud. Brown algae are also found in the intertidal region but are more prevalent on rocky shores and cliffs where their large holdfast are better able to grip than on loose sand and they are also common in underwater shallow areas where there are suitable anchors. Red algae favour shallow areas and are usually dominant in pools or in inshore sub-tidal areas. In terms of conspicuousness, the brown algae feature prominently and, where conditions are suitable (such as rocky shorelines), they are very dominant and may outcompete all other algae. However, when the tide goes out and large areas of inter-tidal sandflats are exposed, the green algae are equally if not more obvious, covering large areas of the shore.

grass and they are either yellow or orange-red in colour. Look for them along the edges of the paths in the dunes, where the red ones in particular stand out; *Hygrocybe conicoides* is very likely in this habitat within dunes.

Algae

Seaweeds are robust and hardy. They have to be as, occasionally, they must survive very severe conditions such as storms, and there is regular or even constant inundation by seawater. They need to remain fixed, usually to rocks or to the base of coastal cliffs and this they do by means of a holdfast, which has no function other than to anchor the plant firmly in place. Unlike flowering plants, whose roots serve as both an anchor and provider of nutrients from the soil, seaweeds are entirely dependent on their 'leaves' (more usually called fronds) for the generation of food using energy from the sun in a process known as photosynthesis. Many species maximise their exposure to the sun by having

The most abundant green algae are the *Enteromorpha* species or **gutweeds**. They cover large areas of the sand flats throughout the year but especially in summer when growth is more prolific and obvious. In July, vast carpets grow at Woodstown, Tramore Backstrand and inner Dungarvan Bay and, later, massive quantities are washed up along all shores after storms and as much more may be buried under the sediments. Some of the green algae are difficult to identify and characters such as the degree of branching and whether they are filamentous or tubular may be of some help though a microscope may be required to confirm identification. The presence of vast carpets of some of these algae is indicative of some organic enrichment or pollution but they are also an important food item for wintering wildfowl, including brent geese, at certain times of the year, notably in spring when other food items have declined. **Sea lettuce**, by comparison, is usually much less extensive, and the quite massive leaves of this species may be seen in the sheltered channels. It is a low-shore opportunist and it may be hard to find, but once located it is quite distinctive and aptly named. In summer during long dry spells, all these green algae may be bleached white.

The brown seaweeds, because they are big and robust, may cover large areas of suitable shore, so that little else is visible, even the stones or rocks on which they are attached. Their colour immediately identifies them but a close examination of the wracks, kelps and other seaweeds reveals strikingly obvious, though occasionally subtle differences between them; be careful of variations in identification features due to exposure, as for example in bladder wrack. Their position on the shore may also be important and whether or not they are fixed in position or freestanding (in which

Serrated wrack, *Fucus serratus*

Carrageen moss

case they are likely to have been deposited by the tide). But all the brown seaweeds need something to anchor to and the coastal cliffs and platforms, the embankments and shingle undisturbed by wave action are the places to look for them. Any of the rocky shorelines of the county are good places to look for seaweeds, particularly when the tide is out around the pier at Tramore, off Garrarus beach, east of Annestown and around Ballyquin beach.

Bladder wrack is the dominant species low down on the shore close to the mud. **Egg** or **knotted wrack** is dominant mid-way further up while **channelled wrack** is dominant at the top (elsewhere this zonation may be reversed, at least for bladder and knotted wrack which may be related to the degree of exposure). Where conditions are severe the bladderless form of bladder wrack

Bootlace weed among the green and brown seaweeds

carrageen moss and the similar but warty *Mastocarpus stellatus*.

The rock pools are probably the best places to check for a wide variety of plant and animal species that may be present. Hours can be passed checking the various species and there is always something unusual to be seen. The dazzling array of colours on offer is also appealing, from the furry brown tongs of **bootlace weed** in the deeper pools, the pink **coral weed** and the reddish-pink **Lithothamnias** on the lower shore; in exposed, sunlit situations, carrageen moss, if present, should be an attractive pale yellow.

In some years, following certain weather conditions, vast quantities of brown seaweeds are washed up on the beaches of the county (as often happens at Woodstown beach, for example). Vast swarms of flies are attracted to the decaying masses of seaweed and the smell may be unbearable. In the peak summer months, these vast accumulations of seaweed are undesirable and unwelcome, and messy to walk through. However, in the autumn, swimmers usually enjoy seaweed in the water, and the iodine it provides.

is usually found and stunted knotted wrack may also occur. **Serrated wrack** also occurs and is easily identified by the jagged edges of the fronds. The **kelps** are usually less obvious as they are covered by the tide and, at low water during spring tides, they flop unimpressively about the sand or in the rock pools. They usually grow so large and so densely that few other seaweeds occur, though occasionally some of the red species may be found among them. Any of the rockier areas of beaches at low tide are safe places to look for them. *Bostrychia scorpoides* is a small brown seaweed quite unlike the larger browns. It grows in abundance on the roots of the sea purslane on salt marshes. The edible dilisk (from the Irish word *duileasc*) or **dulse** may be seen on the low rocks around some of the rocky coves and elsewhere in similar (though usually dangerous) situations. It grows in abundance on the rocks at Garrarus where it can be collected in relative safety at low tide. Many other brown and red seaweeds also grow here, among them

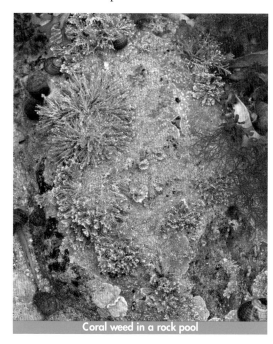

Coral weed in a rock pool

Fauna of the Waterford Coast

*U*nlike plants (that can manufacture their own food), animals depend on the local environment for food and shelter and the quantity and quality of these variables determine how successful the species is and how long they stay. The Waterford coast offers a wide variety of habitats, where the various species–some of them of high conservation importance–can rest, feed and linger, and where they can be observed, admired and enjoyed in their natural surroundings. Over time a regular visitor may eventually see most of the birds and other vertebrates that frequent the coastal zone but the insects and other invertebrates are a more difficult group and may require more careful and sustained examination for complete familiarity, though the more colourful species, like the butterflies, are usually easier to see and identify.

VERTEBRATES

More is known about terrestrial vertebrates (birds and land mammals) on the Waterford coast than any other group, as they are easily seen and recorded. Data has been collected by a committed group of naturalists over many years, which is readily available locally, and there is some very relevant and detailed historical information.

MEAN WINTER PEAK NUMBERS OF BIRDS AT WATERFORD WETLANDS, 2002-2007		
Site		*status*
Dungarvan	19,269	*Int*
Tramore Bay & Backstrand	10,336	*Int*
Blackwater Estuary	8,583	*Int*
Waterford Harbour	2,135	*Nat*

Int/Nat = International/National Importance

Birds

The Waterford coast is important for waders and wildfowl (mainly in winter), seabirds (largely in summer) and landbirds (throughout the year). Bird numbers in the county gradually increase in autumn and slowly decrease in spring. Numbers of wintering birds can be high, particularly on the Blackwater estuary, at Dungarvan and Tramore, and these wetlands are of international importance for wintering birds. While many of these birds remain here for the winter, there is also a considerable passage of birds, mainly through the coastal wetlands, especially in spring and late summer/autumn. However, the vast majority of the wintering birds on the coastal wetlands move elsewhere to breed, allowing the wetland flora and the invertebrates to recover. Breeding birds are far fewer in number and are widely dispersed along the coast; it is only at the seabird colonies that large numbers of birds are seen, sometimes with difficulty because of the sheer cliffs on which they nest.

Swans, geese & ducks

The most likely swan to be seen on the Waterford coast is the **mute swan**, but the species is confined to a few sheltered areas, usually well away from the coastal cliffs and sea. Even at well watched sites, such as Brownstown Head, mute swans have only rarely been recorded, usually flying by on their way to feeding areas nearby. One or two birds have been seen on the sea at Dunmore East but, again, this is an exception, rather than a regular occurrence. Mute swans are frequently seen at Tramore, either inside the embankments at the new racecourse, in the fields near Clohernagh or on the boating lake opposite the Majestic Hotel, where they breed (up to 59 birds have been seen there, in November 1993). They may be also be seen

Mute swans on the boating lake at Tramore

occasionally in the channel between the breached Malcomson embankments in the Backstrand. They are recorded less often around the Dungarvan wetlands or on the Blackwater estuary.

There have only been a handful of coastal sightings of **Bewick's swan** in Waterford, where it is now a rare species, most recently in December 1981 when two were seen on reclaimed land adjoining the Backstrand at Tramore. Small numbers of **whooper swans** have been seen in winter at Tramore, in the fields on the north side of the Backstrand for brief periods, sometimes along with the mute swans. Forty were present, albeit briefly, in November 1982 and, more recently, three stayed in the fields on the northern side of the Backstrand at Lisselan for a few months in early 2000, while four were there in late December 2000 and into February 2001. They have also been seen recently at Clonea (October 2004), at Ballyneety (November 2007 and February 2010), on the boating lake at Tramore (April 2010) and at Lisselan

(in early November 2010). Four were seen flying east past Ram Head in October 2007 and were tracked passing Mine Head; they may have been arriving or commuting between feeding areas.

The **brent goose** is the only goose species to be seen annually, at a number of regular haunts, along the Waterford coast. The pale-bellied form is the most numerous and this sub-species, that winters almost exclusively in Ireland, breeds in the high Arctic area of eastern Canada. This population leaves the breeding grounds from August onwards, and, having passed through Greenland and then Iceland, they arrive in Ireland. The vast majority congregate initially at Strangford Lough and Lough Foyle in Northern Ireland, though a small number arrive in Kerry around the same time, suggesting that they fly across the Atlantic directly from Greenland. Brent usually disperse from the Northern Ireland haunts to other wintering areas around Ireland from mid-October, though small numbers are usually present at

Dungarvan and Tramore from late August. These early birds might be either failed or non-breeding birds who, without reason to linger on their breeding areas, move south to Ireland in advance of the main flocks; young birds have, however, been seen at Tramore in early September in some years.

The two main wintering areas in Waterford are at Dungarvan and Tramore, where numbers have been increasing in recent years. More brent geese are now wintering in the county than at any time in the recent past as numbers nationally are increasing. The population of the light-bellied form of brent goose is between 35,000 and 40,000 birds (2007 estimate) and the majority of these winter in Ireland. The peak count at Dungarvan was recorded in November 2008 when 1,767 birds were seen, while at Tramore the peak count of 906 birds was made in December 2007. Brent geese can be seen anywhere around Dungarvan Bay, from Clonea strand or even Ballyvoyle to Ballyneety and off the Cunnigar; off the sports centre is also a favoured area for them in winter and good views can usually be had here. At Tramore they may be seen at the Backstrand, in the fields north of the Backstrand and up to 120 birds have been seen at the boating lake in the town.

Brent geese are grazing birds and they will preferentially eat eelgrass (or *Zostera*) when available, usually in autumn and early winter, before this resource is depleted by them, especially now that brent numbers in Waterford are so high. The *Zostera* beds at both Dungarvan and Tramore are the places to look for brent when they arrive from September onwards. The tight flocks that gather to feed are often easy to count as they spread out on either side of high tide, when the floating eelgrass is easier to graze. However, once the beds are exhausted the geese then disperse into smaller flocks and forage all over the mudflats on green algae (*Enteromorpha* and *Ulva*) and other estuarine plants. Geese also graze on grass and they are regularly recorded on fields around Dungarvan and Tramore. In recent years birds have taken to foraging at other sites along the coast and small numbers of brent geese may be seen in Waterford Harbour (anywhere between Passage East and Creadan Head, though Woodstown, where up to 140 have been recorded, is where they are more likely to be seen), Annestown, Ballyvooney and Whiting Bay. At Woodstown and off the Cunnigar, they may be seen feeding along the tideline around the shellfish trestles. Small flocks are occasionally recorded flying past the headlands or along the coast as they move between the main sites at Dungarvan and Tramore Backstrand.

Brent geese usually depart from March onwards. Small numbers of birds have been seen in late May at Dungarvan but these may have been either first year birds and in no hurry to breed, or injured birds, perhaps unable to undertake the long journey to their Arctic breeding grounds.

The flocks are worth checking for colour-ringed birds as a major research project on

Brent geese near the Tramore dunes

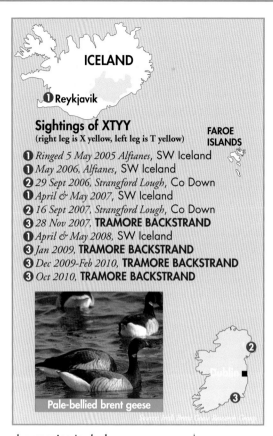

ICELAND

① Reykjavik

Sightings of XTYY
(right leg is X yellow, left leg is T yellow)

FAROE ISLANDS

① *Ringed 5 May 2005 Alftanes,* SW Iceland
① *May 2006, Alftanes,* SW Iceland
② *29 Sept 2006, Strangford Lough,* Co Down
① *April & May 2007,* SW Iceland
② *16 Sept 2007, Strangford Lough,* Co Down
③ *28 Nov 2007,* **TRAMORE BACKSTRAND**
① *April & May 2008,* SW Iceland
③ *Jan 2009,* **TRAMORE BACKSTRAND**
③ *Dec 2009-Feb 2010,* **TRAMORE BACKSTRAND**
③ *Oct 2010,* **TRAMORE BACKSTRAND**

Pale-bellied brent geese

The brent geese flocks are also worth checking for two other sub-species, the **black brant** and the **dark-bellied brent goose**. Both sub-species have been seen in recent years at Dungarvan and at Tramore. The black brant is a Pacific race and usually only one is present but up to three of the dark-bellied form have been seen. It breeds on the Russian tundras and winters in western Europe (Denmark, Finland, France and southeast England mainly). The first county record for the black brant was at Tramore in the winter of 1978/79, only the second Irish record, while the first county record of the dark-bellied form was at Dungarvan in November 1983. Sometimes all three can be seen together, which makes for interesting comparisons between plumage variations among the three forms. Keep an eye out too for young birds and family parties; the young birds have distinctive white wing bars which makes them instantly recognisable. The number of these birds in a flock and the size of family parties is always a good indication of how successful the previous breeding season was for the species.

the species includes monitoring the movement of marked birds, some of which were banded at Dungarvan. For example, DIWB (D White on the right leg and I Blue on the left leg) was ringed on the pitch & putt course, near Western Bay in December 2008. It was resighted in Dungarvan in January 2009 (again on or near the pitch & putt course), between February and May 2010 around Clonea strand and in October 2010 it was seen at Tramore Backstrand. There were no other sightings of this bird. However XTYY, ringed in Iceland in May 2005, has been seen since several times at various locations in southwest Iceland following migration from Ireland. It seems to spend the winter at Tramore, having touched down in Strangford Lough in the early autumn. The Waterford flocks always have a share of ringed birds, and, given close views (around the grotto at Saleen, for example), the coded colour-rings, which are mostly yellow, can be easily read.

Sites where 260 birds or more winter are considered to be of international importance for the species. Dungarvan and Tramore are of international importance, because of the numbers of brent that overwinter at these coastal sites over many winters. These counts show a general increase in wintering numbers over the last thirty years or so at both sites.

The **barnacle goose** and the **Greenland white-fronted goose** are occasionally seen near the Waterford coast. White-fronted geese winter annually on the Wexford Slobs and, not surprisingly, some of these occasionally touch down, usually in Tramore, for a rest or to feed on the vegetation; when they do their stay is likely to be short and may go unrecorded. Up to 40 have been counted, usually in the fields surrounding the Backstrand (most recently, five were at

Lisselan in late December 2010). All the Irish birds arrive from Greenland and the vast majority of the world population winters in Ireland. To be sure to see one, visit the Wexford Slobs at any time during the winter. The barnacle goose is very similar in appearance to the brent goose. It has a very distinctive white face with a black crown and, if present, it will stand out conspicuously among a group of brent. It winters on offshore islands off the northwest Irish coast so, unsurprisingly, it is only very occasionally recorded in Waterford. At Tramore one bird was seen with the brent in October 1994 while three were with brent geese near Barnawee Bridge, Dungarvan in late December 2009 and up to three were seen around Dungarvan in 2010. Like the white-fronted goose, it breeds on the east coast of Greenland and winters exclusively in Scotland and Ireland.

Rather surprisingly for a bird that winters annually in Waterford at Coolfin, the **greylag goose** is rarely recorded elsewhere in the county. A flock of 49 in the fields west of Clohernagh at Tramore at the end of December 2000 were still present in January and up to 79 were there in February 2001. There have also been occasional sightings at Dungarvan, usually in the fields around Western Bay. A **pink-footed goose** at Whiting Bay in October 1981 was the first county record of the species. One was present on the Backstrand in Tramore (at Lisselan) in September and October 2010, and one was also there in late December. Two **snow geese** seen at Tramore in October 1972 might have been escaped birds.

The **shelduck** is a colourful bird with white and brownish-red or sepia plumage that winters in the estuaries of the county and breeds in small numbers all along the coast. It is a bird with a physical presence because of its elegant profile in the water, a relatively long and graceful neck and that vivid plumage. Consequently it is instantly recognisable on the mudflats and cannot be mistaken for any other species. Wintering numbers are small enough at the three main haunts: Waterford Harbour (up to 50 birds), Tramore Backstrand (around 50 birds) and Dungarvan (up to 330 have been recorded).

Breeding has been confirmed at Tramore Backstrand, Dungarvan and Ballyquin beach and has been suspected at several other coastal sites (non-breeders may also swell summering numbers). Pairs are most vocal in March when they cackle and whistle in their search for nest sites. There are also breeding displays to enjoy with robust aerial chases and spectacular exhibitions by courting males. Nests are often in rabbit holes or more likely under bushes and brambles and up to 16 eggs may be laid, sometimes by more than one female. These are incubated for four weeks and, like all ducklings, the young assiduously follow the female as she patrols her territory, calling frequently and incessantly whenever danger threatens. Family parties can be seen along the creeks of the mudflats, where the fluffy, greyish-white young dabble in the mud in search of food. Shelduck prefer liquid mud, which they sieve through their bills by moving their long necks from side to side as they walk forwards, extracting whatever is present, usually small snails and crustaceans and particularly the snail *Hydrobia ulva*. Shelduck moult in July and most adults leave Ireland and congregate on the sand flats in Heligoland Bight in Germany, leaving the young in the care of a handful of adults. Birds can often be seen leaving and entering the main haunts in small numbers at any time of year, and there is also a small but regular passage off the main headlands and along the coast of the county as the birds move between sites. A hybrid **ruddy shelduck x shelduck** was present around the Cunnigar in late November 2008.

A range of duck species can be found either in open water at high tide, in the bays outside the main haunts at Tramore and Dungarvan or along the channels, creeks and waters edge of the mudflats at low tide. They are usually easily separable from the waders that are scattered all over the mud when the tide is out as the ducks tend to flock together. Relatively few duck species gather in the coastal areas of county Waterford in winter and flocks are usually small.

The **wigeon** is an attractive duck, the drake easily distinguished from other ducks by its white flanks, cream crown and evocative whistling. Wintering numbers of wigeon along the coast since 2000 have been low, with up to 274 at Dungarvan, up to 109 at Tramore and up to 99 at Waterford Harbour; birds have also been seen at Clonea in autumn. Wintering numbers are much smaller now than in the early 1970s when up to 2,000 occurred at Tramore. In the 1990s, no more than 303 were recorded at Tramore (in December 1991), which was exceptional for the period.

The reasons why wigeon numbers have declined at Waterford coastal sites are not known. Their diet is very similar to brent geese and both species feed on eelgrass and other algae along the coast. Brent geese numbers have increased at Dungarvan and Tramore since the 1980s, and wigeon numbers have declined, possibly because of inter-specific competition for the same food resources. Once the coastal food supplies have been depleted, the brent geese readily move to the grassy fields fringing the coastal wetlands but wigeon do not and they have yet to be found on grassland near the Waterford coast. Wigeon occur in greater numbers inland in Waterford at Knockaderry reservoir, Coolfin and Little Island but particularly on the Blackwater callows where around 1,600 birds wintered between 1996 and 2000 (though up to 3,000 have been

counted there). The majority of the Irish wintering population (around 90,000 birds) move to Iceland to breed, with the remainder breeding in Scandinavia and Siberia.

Relatively small numbers of **gadwall** (around 700 birds) winter in Ireland at a small number of sites, so, unsurprisingly, they are rarely recorded in Waterford, but sightings of them have increased in the last few years. Up to seven birds have been seen at Tramore (at the boating lake), Ballyneety, Killongford and Clonea but a total of 45 birds were counted at Tramore in late December 2010, probably the highest number ever recorded in Waterford.

The **teal** is the smallest duck to be seen at the coastal wetlands. Wintering numbers are low, but up to 343 have been counted at Dungarvan (February 2005), and 237 were at Tramore in January 1996. Teal are shy and secretive and can be hard to see and count when in the creeks and channels. The male is more colourful than the female, but because of their size and appearance, teal are almost inconspicuous. They are fast fliers and a small flock disturbed from the coastal wetlands or along the edges of waterbodies disappears very quickly. They probably do not breed along the coast as there are no confirmed records though they may do so, sparingly, along the banks of the main rivers of the county. **Green-winged teal** occasionally occur, most recently at Dungarvan when one was seen off the pitch & putt course in January 2006 and another was at Killongford in March 2007. **Garganey** has occurred at Kinsalebeg (September 1996 and May 2010) and Dungarvan (September 1999).

Of all the ducks, the **mallard** is probably the best known, especially the male, with its long green neck and distinctive white collar. They breed on many inland lakes, rivers and ornamental ponds, becoming semi-tame, so they are familiar and the 'quack quack' they

Young mallard on the Tramore boating lake

issue is a very familiar call sign which readily identifies the species. They probably breed at the boating lake in Tramore or around the lagoon inside the seawall on the northwestern corner of the Backstrand. Records of mallard pairs along the coast suggest that they breed in and around streams and wet areas draining into the sea and nests with eggs or young have been found on coastal heath near cliff tops. They rear young close to inland waterways elsewhere in the county and pairs with eggs or young have been found in upland areas and near bogs. These breeding birds are probably sedentary and they may remain in their breeding areas all year round. Wintering numbers at Tramore and Dungarvan are small, normally fewer than 100, though 270 were present at Tramore in late September 2010. Wintering numbers have declined, apparently, since the 1970s.

The male **pintail** is very striking with its long pointed tail and beautiful head pattern. There are just occasional records from Tramore (nine were seen in March 1975, one in November 1985, two in January 1995 and two were in the Backstrand in January 2005) and Dungarvan (a female was seen off the sports centre in January 2006 and again in November and December 2010 but, surprisingly, seven were off the Cunnigar in early December 2010).

The male **shoveler** is a striking bird and its most prominent feature is the long spatulate bill. Again, this is a scarce bird along the Waterford coast. A flock of 17 were seen at Tramore in December 1995 (four

were there in January 2010), while at Dungarvan single birds were seen in January, April and August 2006 with 12 off the pitch & putt course in January 2010 (up to five birds were also seen there in December 2010) and a single bird was at Annestown in late December 2010.

Pochards are more characteristic of fresh water habitats such as Ballyshunnock and Knockaderry reservoirs where they feed on vegetation by diving in relatively shallow water but one was seen at the Tramore boating lake in November 2005 and one was at Dungarvan in January 2010. **Tufted ducks** share similar habitats to pochards and they have bred in the county at Ballyshunnock and Knockaderry. They were seen at the Tramore boating lake in January 1996; they are equally rare at Dungarvan with just a few recent records (in 2010 four were off Abbeyside Church in January and two were seen at Ballyneety in December). The wintering distribution of the **scaup** is largely coastal in Ireland, and around 7,000 were recorded wintering here annually in the 1990s, a substantial increase on the previous decade. However, the bird is usually very scarce in Waterford and there are only a few records since 1970; the most recent records are: three birds at the Tramore boating lake in winter 2008/2009; and one at Lisselan in late October and November 2010.

The **eider duck** is a big and handsome sea duck, especially the black and white drake. It was first recorded in Waterford in 1970; there were four records in the 1980s and in the

BIRDS OCCURRING IN SIGNIFICANT CONCENTRATIONS
AT WATERFORD COASTAL SITES, 1996-2000*

Species	site •• Dungarvan Harbour	Blackwater Estuary	Tramore Bay & Backstrand	Waterford Harbour
Red-throated diver			40	
Brent geese	**521•**		**344**	
Wigeon	834			
Shelduck	497			
Red-breasted merganser	54			
Oystercatcher	784			784
Golden plover	4,700	3,098	2,755	
Grey plover	433		309	
Lapwing	3,097	2,663	3,208	
Knot	624			
Dunlin	4,567	1,430	1,474	
Black-tailed godwit	**736**	**634**	293	
Bar-tailed godwit	936		315	166
Curlew	841	1,041	698	
Redshank	687	489		
Greenshank	25			
Turnstone	169			

•• Data refer to the mean of peak counts over the 5-year period.
• Numbers in bold are of international importance for the species, other values are of national importance.

*Source: *Ireland's Wetlands and their Waterbirds: Status and Distribution.* O. Crowe, Birdwatch Ireland, Wicklow, 2005.

1990s there were at least two records: one in December 1993 when a male first-winter bird stayed in Tramore Backstrand for a couple of days; and the other in January 1994 when a male flew across the Bay. There have been more records since, mostly from the Dungarvan area: two were in the outer Bay in January 2008; two were off Ballynacourty in January and February 2008 and one was there in December 2010; one was off Ballynagaul and at Whiting Bay in November 2008; and one was off Helvick Head on a couple of occasions in early 2009. A male bird flew east past Mine Head a kilometre or so offshore in December 2010. Eiders breed on the north coast of Great Britain and Ireland (over 100 pairs breed in Ireland) and it is likely that the birds seen in Waterford are from these breeding populations.

The male **long-tailed duck** is a very handsome bird with its long tail and black and white head and is a welcome attraction when it is seen off the Waterford coast. There is a good chance of seeing one each winter somewhere in the county. Up to three birds were seen in Dungarvan in early 2009 (off the Gold Coast, the Cunnigar and Ballynacourty are most likely sites) and they are, if anything, more frequent at Tramore. A regular check of the Backstrand at low tide, especially the channel between the two Malcomson embankments, might be fruitful for a bird or two. They have been seen in the Bay, though they are more difficult to find there, especially in rough weather, and the views are likely to be distant. Up to five have been counted in the Backstrand but single birds are more likely. Single birds have also been seen off Bunmahon (November 2004) and at Whiting Bay (March 2009). No more than two or three hundred occur in Ireland, so that a sighting anywhere in the county in winter is a welcome treat.

Three scoter species are seen more or less annually in Ireland and, of these, the **common scoter** is the most numerous with around 12,000 wintering here. Unsurprisingly, they are also the most likely of the three scoter species to be seen in Waterford and there are sightings from several coastal areas of the county from Ardmore in the west (eight were seen there in November 2005) to Tramore Bay in the east (22 were there in January 2006, and there have also been a couple of records from the Backstrand). There are records too for Boatstrand, Bunmahon, Ballydowane, Ballyvooney, Clonea and Ballynagaul. It is also seen on passage in all months off the coastal headlands (143 off Helvick Head in July 2005 and 52 flying west off Ram Head were high counts).

The other two scoter species to be seen in Ireland overwinter in much smaller numbers. **Velvet scoters** have conspicuous white wing patches and are easily distinguished from common scoters; they have been recorded at several sites around Ireland, usually in single-figure numbers, but they are very rare in Waterford and most recent records are from Tramore. Up to five birds were seen at either Saleen or in the outer Bay in December and January/February of the 1991/92 winter and eight were recorded in the Bay in December 1992. None have been seen there since and there were just one or two records for Tramore prior to that. There is only one recent record for Dungarvan: one was off Ballynacourty pier on the 31st December 2010. The **surf scoter** is even rarer and usually only one or two birds are seen at a handful of Irish sites. It was first recorded in Waterford in April 1999 at Ballyvooney cove

and a single male was seen there again in November 2004 and 2005 (presumably a returning individual), while a pair were present there from January through to March in 2004. Up to two were seen in Bunmahon bay from January to March 2000.

Goldeneye are widely distributed in Ireland in winter at inland lakes and on the coastal estuaries. The male is especially attractive, and like many of the ducks, it is the head pattern that appeals and is the most useful identification feature. They are probably present every winter on the Waterford coastal estuaries, but always in small numbers. Dungarvan is the main haunt in the west of the county and 17 were there in February 2005, while in east they are most often recorded in Tramore Backstrand where up to five have been seen.

Three sawbill species have been recorded in Waterford. They are primarily fish eaters and much more so than most other ducks overwintering in Waterford that largely feed on vegetation. The **red-breasted merganser** is the commonest of the sawbills and is seen in almost every month, at Tramore Backstrand and at Dungarvan, though birds are also recorded occasionally in the Blackwater estuary in the west of the county and in Waterford Harbour to the east. It is primarily a winter visitor and there are no breeding records for Waterford (its breeding distribution in Ireland is largely western, though a few pairs breed in nearby Wexford). Wintering numbers are never high; groups of up to 15, sometimes even more, are regularly recorded at Tramore and over 50 have been recorded at Dungarvan. A visit to either area in winter will almost always result in a sighting of at least one merganser, though more (both males and females) are equally likely. They may be some distance away, and they may constantly disappear under the water as they dive in search of small fish and crustaceans. Very occasionally they may be close inshore and the long bill and mop of unkempt feathers on the head are very obvious features when such close views are obtained. There is also some sea passage off the coastal headlands, though numbers are usually very small.

The **goosander** is seen more rarely in Waterford. It is a somewhat bigger bird than the closely related red-breasted merganser. It has bred on a few occasions in Ireland; breeding was first confirmed in Donegal in 1969 and, more recently, they have been proved to breed in Wicklow and it seems likely that they breed annually in Ireland somewhere. There were only four county records for Waterford up to December 1983 (when a female was seen inside the seawall at Lisselan) but there were several coastal sightings from 2000 on, all at Dungarvan, when up to four were seen, usually opposite the mart at Ballyneety. The most recent coastal record was of one seen flying up the Colligan in March 2009. Rarer still is the smew, which prefers freshwater areas in winter. One was present on the Tramore boating lake from late 2009 to February 2010 and again in winter 2010/2011.

Divers & grebes
Although four species of diver have been recorded in Ireland, only two are regularly seen in Waterford. As their names suggest, these are diving birds that feed on fish and marine invertebrates like shore crabs. When feeding they dive repeatedly and often struggle with crabs when they surface. They are big, bulky birds but graceful in the water. With legs set well back on their bodies they are awkward on land and usually only come ashore when breeding; they are rarely, if ever, seen on land in Waterford.

Two diver species, the **great northern diver** and the **red-throated diver**, are recorded annually on the Waterford coast but neither breed (a few pairs of red-throated

diver breed annually in Donegal). The great northern diver is the bigger of the two and more bulky and is probably the more likely of the two species to be seen at Dungarvan (where the best place to see them is off Clonea strand, Ballynacourty or Ballynagaul) and at Tramore (the best place there is in Rinnashark channel off Saleen). Usually only small numbers of birds are present though more are occasionally possible (24 were off Clonea strand in March 2004 and up to 29 were counted between Tramore Bay and the Backstrand in April 1979). One seen in June 1990 at Ardmore was unusual in that it was a summer sighting; most occurrences have been in the winter months.

The red-throated diver is a smaller species and harder to see in choppy conditions but, occasionally, large numbers of this species may be seen, especially in Tramore Bay (102 were counted there in December 1995) or off Clonea strand (69 were there in December 2005). However, both diver species have been seen off many of the coves of the county in winter, suggesting that the Waterford coast is an important wintering area for these attractive birds. There is some sea passage off the coastal headlands in autumn and spring, usually one or two birds at most (though 48 flew west in a couple of hours off Helvick Head in January 2010).

The **black-throated diver** occurs infrequently (the second county record for the species was in Dungarvan Bay in December 1978). Some recent sightings are: Clonea (January 1985, December 1994 and February 2007); in Dungarvan Bay (May 1994 and January 2006); on the Colligan (April 2005); at Helvick (April 1998, December 2004 and January 2005); and two were out in Tramore Bay in March 1982.

Five grebe species have been recorded in Waterford. Although the **little grebe** breeds in the county on many of the lakes and reservoirs and along parts of the rivers Suir and Blackwater, it is rarely seen on the coast and only on a handful of occasions, when severe weather forces them to leave freezing inland waters. At Tramore, 22 were seen in the lagoon behind the seawall at Ballinatin in December 2007 (smaller numbers have been seen there since) while ten birds were at Ballyneety, Dungarvan in early December 2010. It is the smallest of the grebes and rather difficult to see, especially as it prefers to keep close to vegetation, and is rarely seen on open water in winter.

The **great crested grebe** breeds in Waterford and up to two or even three pairs can be found in the summer months at Ballyshunnock reservoir, when, in their much nicer summer plumage, they are a joy to watch, especially if they have young. They have also been seen at Monaneea Lake and summering birds are occasionally seen at Dungarvan and Tramore. The great crested grebe has a long, thin neck and is relatively easy to spot in the coastal areas in winter, though it may take some searching for, especially in choppy waters. Dungarvan is the best area for the species and 84 were counted there in winter (in January 2006), mostly in the outer bay. They have also been recorded in Waterford Harbour and off Woodstown (up to 69, in February 2010), in Tramore Backstrand, Annestown, off Helvick Head and in Ardmore Bay.

Slavonian, red-necked and black-necked grebes are rare winter visitors to Ireland and they are always worth looking out for, especially at Dungarvan, where they are mostly seen. Like the divers, grebes are diving birds and, with legs well back on their bodies, they are fast and efficient swimmers underwater; they usually have no difficulty in finding small fish. The slavonian grebe has been recorded infrequently at Tramore (October 1993 and November 1995 are the most recent sightings there). The species

occurs more often in Dungarvan Bay and up to 13 have been found wintering there (in winter 1979/80), though they have been scarce there in recent winters with three in December 2008 a highlight. They have also been seen at Kinsalebeg (in 1997 and 1999, both January records).

The black-necked grebe is a rare bird in Ireland, even in winter, and is seen at only a few coastal sites. In Waterford, all recent records have been from Dungarvan, usually single birds, though three at Ballynacourty in February and March 2009 and again in December 2010 was noteworthy. The red-necked grebe is even rarer and there are only four coastal sightings since 2000: one was off Clonea in October 2001 and December 2004; one was seen in Dungarvan Bay in February 2006; and probably the same bird was around Ballynacourty in March 2006.

Seabirds

Coastal cliffs and offshore waters are exploited by a specialised group of birds, collectively called seabirds, some of whom roam the oceans, covering vast distances as they forage. However, all seabirds must come to land to breed, and they do so in numbers dictated by the availability of safe nesting places and a good, dependable food supply nearby with which to feed their young. They nest in a variety of habitats, from urban rooftops (herring gulls at Dunmore East, for example) to windswept offshore stacks, rocks and islands, but mainly on precarious ledges on sheer cliff faces, where they safely raise their young, generally free of predation. Sometimes seabirds are widely dispersed along the coast but the really exciting places to see them are at the seabird colonies, where large numbers of birds gather in dense aggregations that are noisy and spectacular as the birds vie for space and constantly cackle and fight over and around the sheer faces. They may rest just offshore in large numbers at the colonies and the visual spectacle of

Seabird Censuses

Many seabirds use the coastal waters off Waterford and, although some species are resident throughout the year, most seabirds leave our shores in winter only to return to the coastal cliffs to breed, often in large colonies such as those at Dunmore East, Helvick Head and Ram Head near Ardmore. However, the other cliffed areas of the Waterford coast are equally attractive to certain non-colonial species, and, cumulatively, the Waterford coast supports important numbers of breeding seabirds in summer.

The entire coast of Waterford has been censused twice in recent years: around 2000 as part of a major project, *Seabird 2000*, aimed at establishing the breeding seabird population of the entire coastal area of Ireland and Great Britain; and more recently, in 2008, the Waterford coast was resurveyed, to complement *The Tetrad Atlas of the Breeding Birds of Waterford 2006-2011*, the object of which is to accurately map, at tetrad level (2 km x 2 km), the breeding distribution of all birds in the county. For fulmar, cormorant, shag, herring gull, great black-backed gull, guillemot and razorbill, late May to mid-June is the optimum time to census these species. However for the more elusive black guillemot, which breeds in crevices in the cliffs, early morning visits (before nine o'clock) in April are recommended, but the species tends to breed at traditional cliffs, which are well known and hence easily checked. The later visits for the other breeding seabirds allow the non-traditional cliffs to be checked for the presence of black guillemots for subsequent checking the following year (though none were found outside the known sites).

Counts of breeding seabirds on the Waterford coast in 2000 & 2008

	••Ful	Corm	Shag	Hg	Gbbg	Kit	Gui	Raz	Blg
East•									
2000	80	0	0	60	0	998	25	9	0
2008	121	0	5	75	0	485	22	10	6
Mid									
2000	276	167	20	180	52	0	40	6	24
2008	209	172	24	188	47	0	49	17	29
West									
2000	220	83	6	125	9	1,037	990	41	6
2008	89	83	2	111	6	472	808	30	6
Totals									
2000	576	250	26	365	61	2,035	1,055	56	30
2008	419	255	31	374	53	957	879	57	41
% change	*-27*	*+2*	*+19*	*-2*	*-13*	*-53*	*-17*	*+2*	*+37*

•• Ful = fulmar (AOS), shag (AON), Corm = cormorant (AON), Hg = herring gull (AON), Gbbg = great black-backed gull (AON), Kit = kittiwake (AON), Gui = guillemot (individual birds on land), Raz = razorbill (individual birds on land), Blg = black guillemot (individual birds in early April, before 0900 BST). [AOS = apparently occupied site, AON = apparently occupied nest].

• **East** is from Creadan Head to Rinnashark, **Mid** is from Tramore (Ladies cove) to Ballyvoyle bridge and **West** is from Helvick Head to Ferry Point.

such concentrations of birds on our coast is best appreciated in good summer weather. While most of the Waterford seabird colonies are on sheer, often daunting and relatively inaccessible cliffs (unlike the larger seabird colonies at Great Saltee in nearby Wexford), they are special places indeed. A flavour of the hustle and bustle of seabird colonies can be appreciated at the very accessible kittiwake colonies at Dunmore East, which are unique, at least in Ireland, for their proximity to man.

Nine seabird species currently breed on the Waterford coast (fulmar, cormorant, shag, herring gull, great black-backed gull, kittiwake, guillemot, razorbill and black guillemot). Other species can be seen at certain times of the year as they move between wintering sites and breeding sites elsewhere in Ireland (terns, for example), or they pass offshore (petrels, shearwaters and skuas, for example) on their movements around the oceans. Consequently seabirds can be seen off and on the coast of Waterford throughout the year and there is never a need to actively look for them, though seawatches off the headlands by the dedicated birdwatcher may prove very fruitful.

Fulmars are present all year round on the Waterford coast, though numbers are always highest during the breeding season. They breed on the coastal cliffs from Waterford Harbour to East Point and they forage in the surrounding waters. Fulmars rarely venture inland and it is most unusual to see them in the estuaries and wetland areas, but the cliffs and waters offshore may have many passing by or simply gliding effortlessly over the waves or along the cliff tops, where they are a joy to observe as they weave and soar.

Fulmars are plankton feeders though they exploit sandeels and other fish near the surface and they also take fish offal discarded by passing trawlers. They are distinctive birds that fly with rapid wing beats interspersed

with long gliding flights and they are usually inquisitive towards an observer walking along the Waterford cliffs, frequently flying close by to get a better view. Consequently they are ideal seabirds to observe and even photograph, as they are not easily disturbed, and they pose less of a challenge than other seabird species that usually remain far distant.

Fulmars are noisy birds on their nesting ledges, cackling raucously and remonstrating with each other. They may flush easily from the cliff ledges but they are less inclined to depart in the breeding season, especially if they have eggs or young. Most nesting ledges are inaccessible but occasionally the odd bird nests close to the cliff top, allowing for a closer view. They will, however vomit a foul-smelling fishy soup if approached too closely, which isn't advised because of the obvious dangers of friable cliff tops. The young, when well-grown, are big and fluffy and easy to see, especially later in the season when the adult birds may be away feeding.

The safest places to see fulmars at close quarters and safely is at Dunmore East (under the Strand Hotel or at outer harbour), where they nest in the Red Sandstone cliffs. Elsewhere, they usually nest on the cliffs close to or around many of the coastal beaches, where their comings and goings can be watched from a safe distance. June is the best

Fulmar and chick on Old Red Sandstone cliffs

month to census breeding fulmars but visiting birds may occupy ledges as may non-breeding individuals, leading to unreliable counts of breeding pairs, unless account is taken of these birds, which tend to be less attached to the cliffs and are easily flushed. Regular counts show that breeding numbers of fulmar vary. For example, the cliff ledges on the west side of Tramore Bay from the beach south to Great Newtown Head had 42 pairs of breeding fulmars in June 1986. Ten years later in 1996 a May count found 35 pairs breeding along this stretch but only 22 pairs were found along the same coastline in June 1999, and there were only seven breeding pairs in 2008. Seawatches may also prove rewarding, and while it may not be a target species, up to 900 birds may be seen passing per hour off the coastal headlands.

Fulmars are predominantly white but occasionally a bird with grey body plumage may be seen. These 'blue' fulmars are much darker than the light birds that are more usually encountered and they have been seen a number of times along the Waterford coast: one was on the sea off Great Newtown Head in March 1978; there were three records of birds off Brownstown Head in 1980 (two were seen passing east-west there in 1990); while there were five sightings at Helvick Head between 1983 and 1994 including one seen on the cliffs there in 1985 and 1986.

Shearwaters do not breed in Waterford but they can be seen offshore as passage migrants, usually in spring and summer. The most common species, the **Manx shearwater**, is the most likely to be seen along the Waterford coast and in some numbers at times (they breed on the Saltee Islands in Wexford, and more numerously on offshore islands on the west and southwest coast of Ireland and Wales where they come ashore at night to visit breeding burrows in the summer months). During the day and in

other seasons they roam the oceans in search of food. Shearwaters are so named because of their habit of gliding, usually at an angle close to the surface of the sea.

Fulmar

The best chance of seeing Manx shearwaters is between March and September from either Brownstown Head, Great Newtown Head or Helvick Head. Impressive numbers are recorded passing these headlands at times, though the birds may be far offshore. For example, over 9,000 were seen passing Helvick Head heading westward in around 30 minutes in August 2009 (and around 500 were on the sea there as well) and 6,400 passed westward off Brownstown Head in an hour a few days earlier. In August 2010 up to 3,500 were seen off Helvick during seawatches and more were usually passing west offshore. Numbers are not always as high as this but significant movements of Manx shearwaters are always possible on the Waterford coast. In June 2009 large numbers were present all along the coast (over 2,500 were off Dunabrattin Head, 2,000 were off Ballyvoyle and hundreds were circling and feeding off Garrarus strand) probably in response to a readily available food supply at the time. Occasionally large numbers may be seen even closer inshore, in the bays and inlets (for example, 1,500 were present in Tramore Bay in August 1974 and 1,900 were there in August 1979 with smaller numbers on occasions since then). There are occasional winter records (off Brownstown Head mainly) but the paucity of records in winter isn't wholly related to the lack of observers willing to sit for hours in poor light and bad weather checking for passing seabirds.

Seawatching from the main headlands (Brownstown and Helvick) might also result in **Balearic**, **sooty**, **Cory's** or **great shearwaters** on passage but all are relatively rare and usually only small numbers of birds are seen. The chances of seeing one of these species, while slim, are more than compensated for by the thrill experienced when one is seen. They require good identification skills, and not just to identify them as shearwaters but to separate them to species level. The sooty shearwater is probably the easiest to identify as they are completely dark, even black (apart from pale flashes on the underwing) and they are likely to occur in greater numbers than the other species. 26 were off Helvick in September 2009, but this was a high count; usually no more than a few birds are seen and the same can be said for Balearic shearwaters (though 15 were seen off Helvick in September 1999 and up to five were seen off Clonea in September 2009). Cory's and great shearwaters are rarely seen, and usually only one at a time, though up to 54 great shearwaters have been seen (off Helvick in September 1999). There is only one record for **Fea's** (or **Zino's**) **petrel** seen off Helvick in September 1998 (the first county record of this species) and a potential **Yelkouan-type shearwater** off Brownstown in August 2010, would be the first Irish record of the species, if confirmed.

The **storm-petrel** is a dainty seabird with shorter wings than the shearwaters and is the smallest of the seabirds that we have in Ireland. They have a conspicuous white rump, which makes them easy enough to identify if good views are possible. They have a slow but fluttering flight and they may even appear to walk on water as they hover over the sea and dip their feet into it. This distinctive habit allows the bird to search the water below carefully for food in the form of plankton, which they scoop up in their bills when found. They are very much at risk from attack by large gulls so they usually stay well offshore during the day. At night they come closer to shore and they can be attracted to land by playing tapes of their calls; many have been ringed near

Brownstown Head using this technique. The headlands are the best place to see them but numbers are usually small. Higher numbers have been recorded at seawatches (up to 68 at Brownstown Head in August 2004, over 100 at Helvick Head in July 2005, up to 50 off Ram Head in July 2005 and up to 20 off Mine Head in September 2009, while up to 3 have been seen in Tramore Bay). Passage offshore is greatest in the summer months, mainly from March to October.

Leach's storm-petrel is much rarer and can be distinguished from the storm-petrel by its forked tail and the pale grey panels on the upperwings (it also has a U-shaped white rump compared to the square white rump of the storm petrel, but this feature may be less easy to make out). There are only a few recent records: including one off Brownstown in December 1989; an unfortunate bird killed by a peregrine at Helvick Head in September 2004 (three were off the Head earlier in the same month); and one off the pitch & putt course at Dungarvan in December 2005. Twelve off Helvick Head in September 1999 was the greatest number of birds recorded at any one time in the county.

The **gannet** doesn't breed in Waterford but it is a big and obvious bird and is a regular visitor throughout the year to the Waterford coast. There are three gannet colonies on the south Irish coast; Great Saltee Island (Wexford), Bull Rock (Cork) and Little Skellig (Kerry). The Kerry colony has almost 30,000 breeding pairs on this windswept and inaccessible stack in summer and is a truly incredible sight. It is likely that the gannets seen flying by off the Waterford coast are foraging birds from these breeding colonies, as they may travel huge distances in search of food when feeding young.

Gannet

Apart from the black wing tips the gannet is an all-white seabird and, with a wing span of around two metres, it is very easy to see and identify, even in rough conditions. It is a strong flier with slow wing beats and it plunge dives, usually from a height when it encounters shoals of herring or mackerel. When such shoals appear in coastal waters, several gannets may arrive to feed on them in a spectacular display of dive-bombing which is delightful to watch. The wings are drawn well back into the body just before the bird enters the water (gannets have specially adapted wings, nostrils and heads to withstand the forces impacting on them when they hit the water). Over two thousand pairs of gannets breed on the western end of the nearby Great Saltee Island in Wexford and that colony is definitely worth a visit in summer. The pleasure of seeing such an accumulation of noisy seabirds is immense and there is also the likelihood that many of these same birds will be seen later foraging off the Waterford coast.

Summer is probably the best time to see gannets as the adults are constantly on the wing in search of food. Birds with a darkened plumage are immature birds (full adult plumage is not attained until the bird is five years old) and while these can be seen in summer, very few such birds are seen in winter as they disperse far from the colonies. Gannets seen in winter are more likely to be adult birds, the majority of whom tend to remain relatively close to the breeding sites.

The gannet is also a passage migrant and from the headlands at Great Newtown Head, Brownstown and Helvick up to 500 birds per hour may be seen, though numbers are usually less than this. Passing birds have been recorded in every month but the greatest numbers are seen in September and October. Occasionally big flocks come inshore in winter (over 1,000 birds were in Dungarvan Bay in December 1989 and 500 were in Tramore Bay in

December 2004). Roosting flocks of gannets could be seen on exposed sandbanks in Tramore Bay in the 1970s, and in some numbers at times.

Oiled and dead birds are occasionally washed up on the beaches of the county; these are worth checking for metal rings which, once posted off to the BTO (British Trust for Ornithology), will eventually give the age and birth place of the unfortunate bird, which, for gannets, is likely to be Great Saltee Island, Wexford where many were ringed over several years.

Cormorants and **shags** are predominantly black-plumaged birds and both breed annually on the Waterford coast. Although somewhat similar in appearance, with practice it is possible to distinguish between them. The cormorant is the bigger of the two birds, and this is an obvious feature when the birds are seen together. In breeding plumage, the cormorant has distinctive white flanks and is also white below the eyes. In contrast, the shag remains entirely black with a light green tinge to the feathers but a close view is essential to observe this characteristic; sometimes a head crest is also obvious. Both birds are diving birds but the shag jumps clear of the water as it dives whereas the cormorant does so with a less pronounced half-leap. Cormorants occur inland and can be seen on the rivers and lakes of the county but shags are entirely maritime and are rarely, if ever, seen inland.

Both birds also need to dry their feathers after feeding bouts and they do so by standing with outstretched wings facing the breeze. The bigger cormorant is more likely to be seen like this and several together on sandbanks or mudflats can be an impressive sight. Sometimes both shags and cormorants can be seen together close inshore feeding but, further out, they are not as conspicuous and the shag in particular may be hard to see

Shag

Cormorants nesting on Illaunglas, west of Great Newtown Head

in poor weather, especially when it is windy and the sea is choppy. Up to 146 cormorants have been counted in winter in Waterford Harbour and up to 30 cormorants and 50 shags may be seen at Saleen with as many more of both species out in Tramore Bay, where, at either site, conditions are likely to be more sheltered than along the open coast. Sometimes large flocks of roosting birds can be seen on the low ledges west of Creadan Head, where the sandstone platforms offer ideal roosting sites, close to good fishing just offshore. Both species are likely in Dungarvan Bay and in some numbers at times, but here, because of the sheer expanse of open water, they are more scattered and views of them are likely to be distant.

The breeding ledges are almost always inaccessible but from late March onwards is the best time to get good, close views from nearby headlands. Cormorants and shags are colonial nesters, especially cormorants, who are more conspicuous in the breeding season. The shag is much more discrete, favouring lower ledges and it can be difficult to see, especially the solitary pairs that use awkward ledges, though groups of seven pairs or more arc also likely. In any year it is not possible to predict where either species will breed as they move around various nesting sites west of Great Newtown Head in the case of the cormorant, and, for shags, all along the coast. This is particularly true for the cormorant

that moves from one stack to the next and then on to mainland cliffs in successive years.

Both species lay white eggs in a nest of seaweed gathered by the parent birds and the young hatch after about four weeks. Colonies are then much easier to find as the nests and surrounding cliffs are conspicuously whitewashed, even from a distance. Breeding colonies are noisy places (and the smell may be overpowering), as the non-stop movements of adult birds elicits constant squabbling between pairs and, later, between young birds. From the adjacent cliff tops the antics of these gregarious birds can only be admired as they struggle to rear their young in what may seem like chaotic conditions.

Herons & egrets
Two notable first county records were seen near the Waterford coast in 2007. In May a **great white egret** was seen on the Blackwater estuary. It breeds sparingly in eastern Europe and, although it is a partial migrant, it was a surprise to see one in Waterford. A **cattle egret** stayed around Garrarus from December 2007 into January 2008, which was an exciting find at the time. However there were further records, both inland in the county and on the coast, in 2008 and again in 2009, with up to six seen near Clohernagh in April 2008 and up to four were seen around Dungarvan earlier in 2008. It breeds in some numbers from April onwards in Europe,

Little egret

middle-Eastern countries and north Africa, where it is increasing. Hopes are high that if it continues to occur in the county in numbers it might soon begin breeding (up to eight were seen on the Tourig estuary, river Blackwater right into June 2009).

The first county record of the **little egret** was in 1970 when they were seen at Dungarvan, at Fornaght and on the Backstrand. The next didn't occur until 1981 but, from 1986 onwards, little egrets were recorded almost annually at Tramore with one or more birds present, usually around Clohernagh and along the north side of the Backstrand; up to six or seven were recorded at Tramore between 1996 and 2000, and some of these were probably the young of birds that bred elsewhere. They were recorded breeding in Ireland for the first time on the river Blackwater in 1997, having been present along many south coast estuaries for several previous winters. Given the increase in wintering numbers at Tramore it was inevitable that breeding would occur. While young birds were seen around the Backstrand in both 1998 and 1999, no other proof of breeding was obtained, perhaps because no one looked for them. The presence of 13 birds at Clohernagh in late March 2000, and four or five in May suggested that breeding was imminent. Finally, in early June 2000, proof of breeding was established when two or possibly three nests were found, and at least seven pairs bred in 2001. Breeding

around Dungarvan was confirmed soon after and 35 nests were counted at one colony in 2009. The little egret is now firmly established as a breeding species and they can be seen at all the coastal wetlands and along rivers and streams close to the sea.

They breed in trees, and groups of trees close to estuaries are favoured where they lay their single clutch of four or five eggs, which take around three weeks to hatch. As with any bird colony, their breeding places are a hive of activity once the young hatch and the parents have to forage incessantly in search of food for them. They are noisy places too as the birds come and go, squabbling and fighting as they pass between nests. Once the young fledge, after around 40-45 days, they disperse, initially to areas nearby and, as the summer progresses, the young venture farther afield. Late summer and early autumn is the best time to see large numbers of birds around Dungarvan and Tramore and elsewhere along the coast. They are big, white and obvious birds and are not easy to miss as they forage along the tideline or fly between sites or roost precariously in bushes and hawthorns along the edges of many of the coastal wetland sites.

The **grey heron** is a conspicuous and familiar bird of our rivers, lakes and coasts. It is a big stately bird and, with long legs, grey plumage and a dagger-shaped bill, it stands out as it forages along the edges of the channels and in the creeks. In flight they have a slow and measured wing beat and the characteristic kinked neck drawn back into the body is especially obvious. Herons have an elongated sixth neck vertebra, which allows the heron to lunge at fish it locates along the waterline and also allows the bird to fly more easily, as it can draw its neck back into the body. They feed on fish in the pools and streams but they will also avail of invertebrates, small mammals, frogs and even birds unlucky enough to come within

Grey heron

striking range. They mostly breed at inland locations in Waterford but there are a few small breeding colonies near the coast.

Herons are colonial breeders and early nesters. The female may be sitting on the four or five eggs in early February (or even earlier) high in the tree canopy, and usually out of sight, though as the young grow, the nests and contents are more easily seen. Herons display a lot at the nest before laying and once nesting is underway, they indulge in greeting rituals on arrival of one or other of the pair. The young, when they hatch, are ungainly looking and awkward but they constantly call and squeel, sounds which carry far, so that active heron colonies are usually easily pinpointed, though counting the number of nests is never easy.

Herons are present along the coast throughout the year and are usually seen when the tide is out as they forage along rocky shorelines, where pools provide an ample source of food for them. As with egrets numbers are highest immediately following the breeding season when the young of the year converge on the coast.

There are only a handful of records of the **spoonbill**, a rare vagrant from Europe,

mostly from the Tramore area. The first one seen in the county didn't last long as it was shot on the Backstrand in November 1891. Other recent Backstrand records include February 1974, May-June 2002 and August 2004 (at Ballinatin on the west side of Tramore Backstrand). The most recent record for the county is of up to four birds (one of which was colour-ringed) that were around Killongford Bridge, Dungarvan and the Cunnigar from July to December 2010. The first, and only county record, of the **night heron**, was from Dungarvan in July 2000, while the **squacco heron** has been seen in Waterford on four occasions, most recently in May 1994 when two were seen in Dungarvan Harbour (the first time more than one was seen in Ireland), one of which lingered at Dungarvan until August 1994.

Birds of prey
With such an abundance of birds available at all times of the year, but particularly in winter, it is no surprise that raptors are regularly recorded in the coastal areas of county Waterford. Some of these breed on the cliffs and, as they tend to stay on or close to their breeding territories throughout the year, they are very dependent on birds wintering along the coast. In summer, although all the wintering birds have

departed, the breeding passerines on the cliff tops, in dunes and around the field ditches provide good feeding opportunities for the smaller birds of prey, who themselves have young to feed in that season. Almost all of raptors seen along the coast are fast, agile and solitary and their visits are often brief and focused. Once a kill has been made, the bird quickly departs, usually to a safe location or to the breeding site where its meal can be eaten in safety or fed to young, and free from harassment from other birds.

The first county record of the **red kite** was in 1981, when one was seen at Waterford City dump at Kilbarry. There were two more inland records up to 1990 (one of which involved a wing-tagged bird found dead in the foothills of the Comeraghs). A tagged bird was spotted at Tramore dump in January/ February 1998, and another tagged bird was at Pickardstown in January 2006. These may have arrived from Wales, where a population of around 380 pairs breed (in 2005). Birds have also been introduced to England, Scotland and Northern Ireland and 30 young birds from Wales were reintroduced to Wicklow in July 2005, in an ongoing programme aimed at establishing a breeding population here in Ireland. Juvenile kites tend to wander away from their place of birth, so it is likely that young birds will be increasingly seen in Waterford in future years.

Sparrowhawk

Approximately 20,000 pairs of **buzzards** breed in Britain, mostly in Scotland and Wales. The main stronghold of the species here is in northern Ireland where in excess of 100 pairs breed. The breeding population of buzzards in the south is increasing and there are now annual sightings of the species in Waterford and they almost certainly breed. Although not particularly coastal, many of the earlier records are from Dungarvan, Tramore and Stradbally and in 2009 alone they were recorded at Whiting

Bay, Ram Head, Ardmore, Ballymacart, Dungarvan, Tramore, west of Garrarus and Woodstown, mainly in spring but some of the records involve birds seen in winter near the coast. They breed in trees and, once established in Waterford, are more likely to be seen over farmland and forestry but they will hunt over coastal farmland in search of small mammals, birds and frogs.

The **hen harrier** usually breeds in upland areas in Ireland, where its slow but measured flight is a joy to watch as it hunts over the heathery mountain slopes in search of meadow pipits and other small birds. It is rarely seen along the coast in the breeding season but harsh winter conditions in the uplands prompt the smaller passerines to move to the lowlands in search of food so there may be little to sustain the larger birds of prey that feed on them and they too must move to the lowlands; hence hen harriers are frequently seen along the coast in winter. Almost all coastal records of harriers have been from September to April, and most recently (since 2005) at Whiting Bay, Ram Head, Mine Head, Helvick Head, the Colligan river, Ballyvoyle, Ballyvooney, Annestown, Tramore Backstrand, Rathmoylan and near Ballymacaw.

Although it is a common bird of prey in Waterford, especially in woodland areas, the **sparrowhawk** is surprisingly elusive and only fleeting glimpses of this dashing bird are usually obtained. It hunts close to the ground and is a fast flier, hugging ditches and hedges as it weaves its way over the ground. It usually departs as quickly as it appears, especially if hunting with intent, when speed is of the essence. At other times, when it hasn't food on its mind, it flies higher than usual and much more slowly, and is often accompanied by a number of small birds flitting about around it, and they remain in attendance until the 'hawk' departs.

Sparrowhawks tend to be more obvious in the breeding season when courting birds display high over their nesting areas, usually in forests (broad-leaved and coniferous), clumps of trees or tall scrub. Moreover, when young are in the nest, the adults are more active and more likely to be seen. Sparrowhawks breed close to the coast in trees and are often seen flying fast over the cliff tops and field ditches but their preference is for the cover of woodland areas where they are adept at catching small birds (though the larger female can take prey as big as a woodpigeon).

The **kestrel** is perhaps the commonest bird of prey in Ireland and is probably the most conspicuous because of its habit of hovering over fields and roadside verges for long periods, ensuring that many people are aware of this attractive 'hawk'. It is seen in all months along the coast, especially over the cliffs, where the vegetated slopes offer feeding opportunities, more so perhaps than the farmland nearby. It may also be very obvious over the sand dune areas where small mammal prey and birds are often plentiful. Wherever it is seen, it hovers high over the land with its tail fanned, helping to maintain lift. Frequently it will break off only to repeat its hovering nearby with deadly intent or it may fly to a prominent knoll nearby. Once a prey item has been located though, it instantly swoops onto the unsuspecting victim, which is then quickly dispatched.

Male and female kestrels are predominantly brown in colour but the male has a bluish-grey tail that distinguishes the sexes. The kestrel, like all falcons, does not build a nest. Instead it uses either the stick nests of other species or it lays on ledges in sea cliffs where up to five eggs are incubated mainly by the female for around a month. A favoured nest site on the coast is in behind rock projections or boulders, which may offer some protection from weather conditions,

especially harsh winds. Once the young are born, the parent birds become much more active and alert. They are also more vocal, especially near the nest and the shrill, high-pitched 'kee kee kee' of the adult birds as they arrive or land with food can be heard from a long distance off. Once the breeding season is over the adult birds become less active but there are then many young birds about who are often more approachable, at least for a while. They may be seen all along the Waterford coast, usually singly, and the best sites are occupied year after year.

The **peregrine falcon** is a big, impressive bird with a fearless reputation and a long association with man for many reasons, good and bad. Seen at close range the peregrine is a fierce-looking bird with a very dark moustachial stripe on either side of the head, large talons and a menacing curved beak. Both adult birds have bluish-grey upperparts and pale or cream underparts with variable amounts of black barring. However the plumage differences between the sexes are slight and are not useful in distinguishing between male and female. The female peregrine is the bigger bird, a helpful feature to note if a pair is seen together.

Peregrines feeds on a wide variety of bird species and, because of the abundance of birds along the coast in winter (especially waders), they are regularly seen on all the wetlands of the county or in the adjoining farmland, where the large wader flocks often feed. Once a peregrine falcon appears the wader flocks usually lift off in a tight mass in the hope that sheer numbers might confuse this capable predator. The peregrine is not easily deterred and it singles out one bird, which it usually takes effortlessly. Territorial pairs usually stay close to the breeding ledges in winter and they never have far to travel for their next meal. The wintering birds of the coast offer a sustained food resource for the peregrine, which maintains the birds in good condition throughout the winter in preparation for the following breeding season when almost all of the wintering birds have departed to breed elsewhere.

Peregrines are cliff-nesters and occupy wide but sheltered ledges on coastal and inland crags. March is probably the best month to see them as they cavort high over their breeding ledges. The eggs are laid in April, incubated for a month and the young, up to four in number, fledge after about six weeks. Peregrines are aggressive birds and are constantly on the lookout for danger when they have young in the nest. It is rarely possible to approach an active eyrie without being spotted. The constant 'kek-kekking' can be heard from a long way off and, once issued, the young lie low in the eyrie until the danger has passed. In summer peregrines take a wide variety of bird species such as rooks, jackdaws, pigeons, seabirds and even the smaller passerines.

The **merlin** is the smallest of our raptors, and is a regular visitor to coastal areas in winter, though usually only single birds are recorded. It breeds very sparingly in upland areas, where it can be surprisingly difficult to find. Once weather conditions in the uplands deteriorate in the autumn, merlins probably disperse to the low-lying areas where small birds and waders are more plentiful in winter. However the frequency of winter records along the Waterford coast, suggest that birds move here from other areas of the country or even from outside Ireland where weather conditions in winter may be much more severe. Many of the winter records are from Tramore Backstrand (Lisselan and Clohernagh) and Dungarvan (Clonea, Killongford, Ballyneety, Ballynacourty, Kilminnin and the Cunnigar), especially from farmland close to the coast where the large wader flocks offer ample opportunities for hunting merlins. They are also regularly recorded at the headlands especially Helvick,

Great Newtown Head and Brownstown, usually in the autumn and they have also been seen elsewhere at Whiting Bay, Ardoginna, Ram Head, Ardmore, Mine Head, Ballydowane, near Bunmahon, Ballymacaw and Dunmore East.

Over 400 pairs of **ospreys** now breed in Britain (mostly in Scotland) and are increasing in numbers due to a concerted effort at protecting the species following its extinction there during the 1800s because of persecution. They are a migratory species and spend the winters in southern Europe and Africa so they move between breeding and wintering areas twice a year; these are the times they are most likely to be seen on passage. Most birds move through England but a small number of birds do so through Ireland and there are annual sightings in spring and autumn. Ospreys are fish eaters and clear but relatively shallow coastal waters are where they are more likely to be seen at migration times. Most recent records have been from Saleen, Tramore (in autumn 1999, August 2000 and 2009 and September 2005), Brownstown (in August 2010), Dungarvan (September 2001, October 2008 and April 2010), one flew west past Helvick Head in May 2008 and another flew west off the Cunnigar in October 2008 (a late bird). There are earlier September records for Dungarvan (1959 and 1986). Most recently, one stayed around for a few days at Ballyscanlon lake and Carrigavrantry reservoir in early summer 2010, close to the coast.

The **hobby** is a slight, long-winged falcon about the size of a kestrel, that can perform remarkable aerial manoeuvers in pursuit of prey. It isn't confirmed breeding in Ireland but does so increasingly in Britain (over 2,000 pairs is the most recent estimate) to where it migrates from Africa. Migrant birds rarely fly direct between their wintering grounds and breeding areas and some veer off course; moreover, following the breeding season, young of the year may not have the navigational skill of the adult birds and some inevitably get lost and turn up in Ireland.

The first county record of the species in Waterford was in September 1958 but there have been relatively few records since. One was seen at Helvick Head in May 1994, one was at Abbeyside, Dungarvan in September 2006, while one was at Ballynagaul at the end of June 2007 and another was chasing swallows at Cheekpoint in August 2007. There were three further coastal sightings in 2008 (in May at Bunmahon, Dunabrattin in summer and at Kilfarrasy in November). Surprisingly, three were around Ballyscanlon in early summer 2010 and one was at Seafield near Bunmahon in October 2010. With the increasing breeding population of this dashing falcon in Britain, it is likely that the species will be recorded more frequently here in Ireland, especially along the south coast, and who knows but they may soon start to breed here. They would be a welcome addition to our breeding bird population.

Rarer raptors seen infrequently along the coast include the massive **white-tailed eagle** (a possible bird was seen off Ram Head in April 2008 heading towards the Blackwater estuary, perhaps from the Kerry reintroduction programme) and a **red-footed falcon** seen off Helvick Head in May 1994, the first county record of this species.

Quail, corncrakes and rails

Quail are migratory game birds that arrive mainly from Africa to breed in small numbers in Ireland and some of these arrive on the Waterford coast where they are occasionally seen or heard. Almost all the records since the early 1950s have been from the coast from Mine Head to Ballymacaw, usually involving single birds, though up to three were at Portally in June 1989. More recently, in June 2006, one was heard at Brownstown Head (attracted, apparently, to a moth light trap).

Male pheasant

Pheasants are land birds but this tall and stately game bird is widely distributed in Waterford and is regularly seen and heard in the coastal fields, where it breeds. Much rarer is the **corncrake**, a migratory species from Africa, that breeds largely in the northwest, though the breeding population is small and the species is currently at risk of extinction in Ireland despite a massive conservation effort. There are infrequent reports of the species at migration time (spring and autumn) along the Waterford coast but birds rarely linger. One was heard calling at Creadan Head in early summer 1994 and another stayed at a coastal site near Tramore in 2009 and continued to call for a month or more, raising hopes that it might attract a mate and breed, though this wasn't confirmed.

The secretive **moorhen** is a bird that is heard rather than seen–unless they are disturbed–and they occur in all the wetland areas of the county including coastal waterbodies where they breed, usually unseen in the dense vegetation in the pools and along riverbank reedbeds. Numbers are never high and they are rarely seen but they may be heard, for example, in the pools on the Cunnigar not far from the carpark there, near the lagoon at Ballinatin inside the seawall on the north side of Tramore Backstrand, and in the dense vegetation on the Creadan side of Fornaght bog. Even more secretive, and hardly ever seen, is the **water rail**, a bird of dense reedbeds, where its pig-like squealing is the only way of confirming its presence in the breeding season. It can be heard in the reedbeds behind Woodstown strand, at Fornaght bog, Annestown, Killongford and in the reedbeds flanking the Blackwater.

Waders

Large numbers of waders gather on wetland areas in winter to avail of an abundant food supply in the form of invertebrates that are readily available and easily exploited. Most coastal wetlands are large and open so they offer good protection against predators and they are less likely to freeze over during hard weather conditions, ensuring that the birds can continue to feed. They are also relatively easy to count if the preferred areas where the birds gather are known. Most of the Waterford wetlands are counted at least once annually, to provide up-to-date information on the numbers of all species of birds present.

Estuaries and mudflats are, however, harsh environments, and fluctuating saline conditions allows only species with special adaptations to survive and thrive. Relatively few animals can withstand such conditions, so those that do may dominate and consequently vast numbers of invertebrates may occur, to the benefit of the wintering

Oystercatcher

birds. Waders have varying bill lengths which ensures that different species select different prey items, depending on their depth in the mud or sand column. The smaller waders with the shortest bills (plovers and dunlin) forage close to the surface while the largest waders (curlews and godwits), with the largest bills, can take the biggest prey that occur deep in the muds and sands. The bills of all waders are usually flexible, often with a special moveable connection to the skull allowing the bird to extract prey deep in the mud or sand. The bill tip is also especially sensitive to enable the bird to locate prey. Finally, all waders have relatively long legs and this allows them to forage along an incoming or outgoing tide, when many invertebrates are active, while long and slender toes ensure they can cope with walking in soft sediment.

Oystercatchers are big and obvious birds and this black and white wader with the long orange bill is found in almost all months of the year at Tramore and Dungarvan, as well as all of the smaller wetlands, the nearby fields and the rocky platforms at the base of the coastal cliffs. They feed on bivalve molluscs and they have powerful jaws and neck muscles, and a stout, fast-growing bill to allow them to cope with opening cockles and mussels (they also feed on crabs, worms and limpets). They bred in Dungarvan Bay in the mid-1950s and at Beenlea Head in east Waterford in the early 1970s but they no longer seem to breed here now. They are surprisingly absent as breeders from most of the south coast, though they breed at other coastal areas throughout Ireland and even at some inland locations in the west. Some summer here but it is mainly a wintering bird in Waterford and two or three thousand birds or even more occur annually. Some of the Irish breeding birds probably arrive in Waterford though the bulk of the birds wintering in Ireland (around 70,000) come from Scotland, Iceland and the Faroes. One colour-ringed bird seen at Knockanpower, Ring on the first of January 2010 had been ringed as a chick on the roof of the Aberdeen Cricket Club (Scotland) in May 2007.

An adult male and female **black-winged stilt** were recorded for the first time in Waterford at Tramore in May 1995. Almost as rare is the **avocet**, one of which was seen in Tramore Backstrand at the end of March 1997; it was presumed at the time that it was the same bird that was seen a week previously on the nearby North Slobs in county Wexford, and was only the second or third county record of this handsome wader.

The **ringed plover** is one of the smallest and indeed one of the daintiest of the waders found on the Waterford coast. It can be seen throughout the year as, apart from wintering here in greater numbers, a few pairs breed, mainly on shingle and sand near the tops of beaches and near dunes. The ringed plover is a master at camouflage at any time of the year and they can be surprisingly hard to see, as the distinctive head markings make them difficult to detect against the sandy background. Once on eggs in summer, they blend in well with their surroundings and when the nest is approached they move off and feign injury in an attempt to lead the intruder or potential predator away from the nest. They drag themselves along the ground away from the nest, calling incessantly, an approach that usually works well with predators like foxes and mink and they do not return to the eggs until the threat to them is gone. The four eggs are laid in a small depression in the sand and are exceedingly difficult to locate, as the appropriately spotted eggs merge imperceptibly with the surrounding matrix of pebbles, sand and shells. When the eggs hatch, the young are equally difficult to find and they disappear into nearby vegetation or they lie motionless, relying on their cryptic colouring for protection against predators.

The total number of breeding pairs in the county probably varies from year to year but most of the sandy beaches have a pair or two, sometimes more on the larger beaches at Tramore and the Cunnigar. Many are, however, unsuccessful, as beaches are popular places in summer and there is constant disturbance from the many people and their dogs who walk through their favoured breeding areas. Eggs may chill if the adult remains away too long or is repeatedly put off the nest and some clutches, inevitably, are predated. If the young hatch they have a reasonable chance of survival, as the adult birds are careful and attentive parents.

Juvenile ringed plover

It is estimated that around 15,000 ringed plover winter in Ireland annually on coastal wetlands mainly, though numbers at all the Waterford sites are small. Wintering birds congregate from August onwards, usually around mudflats at Tramore (on the north side of the Backstrand mainly, though there are always some birds on the mudflat area just north of the 'neck' of the main dunes) and Dungarvan (off the Cunnigar is a good place to see them there) but they can also be seen at Clonea and Whiting Bay.

A **little ringed plover** was seen at the Cunnigar in 1999, the only occurrence to date of the species in Waterford.

Golden plovers winter in much greater numbers than ringed plovers, but they do not currently breed here in Waterford (a pair bred in the early 1990s, the first nesting of the species in recent times but the nest was

TYPICAL WETLAND COUNTS	Tramore	Dungarvan
	19.02.2009	22.01.2009
Species		
Little grebe	2	6
Black-necked grebe	0	3
Great crested grebe	0	19
Great northern diver	0	8
Cormorant	15	15
Little egret	12	6
Heron	1	0
Mute swan	25	2
Brent goose	698	1,497
Shelduck	50	314
Wigeon	40	296
Teal	40	122
Mallard	115	30
Pintail	0	2
Goldeneye	0	4
Long-tailed duck	3	0
Red-breasted merganser	14	38
Oystercatcher	396	777
Ringed plover	37	63
Golden plover	70	2,020
Grey plover	233	360
Lapwing	147	2,345
Knot	184	837
Sanderling	4	48
Dunlin	620	3,224
Snipe	8	8
Black-tailed godwit	176	1,248
Bar-tailed godwit	205	621
Curlew	397	502
Redshank	165	801
Greenshank	16	20
Turnstone	3	272
Merlin	1	0
Hen harrier	1	0
Dark-bellied brent	1	2
Kestrel	1	0
Gadwall	2	0
Shag	3	17
Kingfisher	0	1

Counts were taken by experienced observers at known roosts and other locations around the wetland.

abandoned) and are rarely present in summer. In winter they form large flocks, which are truly spectacular when they wheel and turn over the wetland areas and the adjoining fields. Their breeding areas are Siberia, Russia and northwest Europe though there is a small breeding population in upland areas of the northwest of Ireland (400-600 pairs). The vast majority of the birds wintering in Ireland are immigrants, mainly from the breeding population of the Faroe Islands and Iceland.

Golden plover are difficult birds to count: they are small and usually very numerous, and it is never easy counting them in the fields where they are mainly found in Waterford in winter. Obtaining an exact count is even more difficult as birds can be anywhere and the flocks merge, separate and disperse, especially if disturbed or spooked by a hunting peregrine. Up to 150,000 golden plovers winter annually in Ireland and several thousand stay in Waterford, mainly at Tramore and Dungarvan (they also occur in Waterford Harbour and around the Blackwater estuary) where they feed on earthworms, beetles and sometimes plant material. During bad weather, there are mass movements of golden plover from the frozen inland wintering areas to the milder coastal areas, and it is during these episodes, usually in December or January, that maximum numbers occur in the county.

There have been three records of the **American golden plover** in Waterford, the first as recently as 1996. The second, a juvenile bird, was seen on the east side of the Cunnigar in November 2008 and the third, a moulting adult, was on Clonea strand in September 2009.

Grey plovers are much less gregarious than golden plovers, they occur in much smaller numbers, are almost entirely coastal and they feed in widely scattered flocks, usually at Dungarvan and Tramore, with lesser numbers at Waterford Harbour and the Blackwater estuary. Most of the grey plovers that occur in Ireland are on passage and originate in Siberia. Many of them move on to spend the winter in southern Europe or Africa but around 7,500 birds winter here. They do not breed in Ireland. Usually less than 1,000 birds occur in Waterford, with no more than 200 at Tramore and up to 610 at Dungarvan, but numbers vary depending on the severity of winter conditions elsewhere.

The **lapwing** is one of the better known of the wading birds; it has colourful plumage and a slow wingbeat, features that are most easily seen as it flies along river systems or over mudflats. The long thin crest arising from the rear of the head is also distinctive, and an appealing feature if the bird is seen at close range or through binoculars in good light. Around 20,000 pairs breed nationally but they may be seen in much larger numbers at all the county wetland sites in winter, when birds, largely from northern Britain, arrive on our shores. They feed mainly on soil invertebrates and are therefore more likely to be found in the fields surrounding the coastal wetlands. They are very mobile birds and, while they have some tendency to use the same fields each year, they can be found anywhere. For this reason, lapwings are difficult to count with any certainty but birds are always present around the two main wetlands, as well as up along the river estuaries. Around 200,000 birds overwinter in Ireland and around 3,000 birds are annually recorded at the Blackwater estuary, at Dungarvan and at Tramore, with smaller numbers elsewhere in the county. There is, however, some movement between sites, even on a daily basis, as birds respond to varying tide levels on the shore.

Knots are medium-sized waders that are always present in small numbers at the wetlands of the county in winter. Almost 35,000 birds overwinter in Ireland (almost

Roosting lapwing

half of which do so in Dundalk Bay and Strangford Lough) but much fewer do so in Waterford, with around 600 or so at Dungarvan and no more than 200 at Tramore. There is some evidence of a decline in wintering numbers at both Tramore and Dungarvan since the early 1970s (in 1971, for example, 1,600 of the total county estimate of 2,258 birds were at Dungarvan and around 450 were at Tramore). The majority usually arrive late from their breeding grounds in Greenland, as they stop off in Iceland before touching down here in November and most have left by March.

Sanderlings are small, almost white waders that anyone visiting the bigger coastal beaches in winter should know. They are usually seen along the tideline at Whiting Bay, the Cunnigar and the main beach at Tramore where they rush along in search of small food items, often running after the retreating waves only to be disturbed by the next incoming wave. They constantly move in, out and along the waters edge, scurrying backwards and forwards and occasionally flying off to a new section of beach, especially if disturbed by dogs or walkers. Wintering numbers are small, usually less than 100 birds at any of the coastal sites (around 7,000 birds winter in Ireland), and they breed further north from Canada to Siberia. One seen at Ballinclamper, Clonea in May 2010 had been ringed in Mauritania, west Africa in December 2005 (and resighted there in 2006 and 2007, also in December).

The **little stint** is a scarce passage migrant (rarely wintering), often seen with dunlin.

Sanderling and ringed plover

county record, was at Tramore Backstrand, one was seen at Dungarvan in August 1986 and the most recent sighting was at Whiting Bay in September 2010). The only record of **spotted sandpiper** was at Ballynatray on the Blackwater in November 1982.

Curlew sandpipers are scarce autumn passage migrants (they breed in Arctic Siberia and winter largely in Africa). Many records are of single birds though 20 were at the Cunnigar in late October 2007, six were seen on the mudflats off the Park Hotel, Dungarvan earlier in October 2007 and up to nine have been seen at Clonea, again in October. At Tramore up to 15 were seen in October 1972 and 32 in autumn 1998; larger flocks are possible occasionally, especially in some autumns (for example, up to 95 were at Ballyneety, Dungarvan in autumn 1999). Apart from various sites around Dungarvan Bay and Tramore Backstrand, birds have also been seen at Whiting Bay and Ardmore.

There have been several records since the mid-1970s, generally of single birds and usually in the autumn, from Fornaght strand, Waterford Harbour, Tramore, Clonea, Dungarvan, and Ardmore beach. Six together were seen at Tramore Backstrand in September 1998, though one record relates to a single bird seen in January, also at Tramore.

A number of other sandpiper species (some from North America) have been recorded occasionally along the coast: a **white-rumped sandpiper** was seen for the first time in September 2006 at Kinsalebeg and the second county record was at Clonea in October 2010 (and the bird obligingly stayed into November). A **semipalmated sandpiper** was seen on the Cunnigar in September 1998, the first county record of this small wader species. One was seen on Clonea in the same month the following year and there has been just one record since, a juvenile at the Cunnigar in September 2006. There have been two records of **Baird's sandpiper**: the first, from the coast at Kinsalebeg was in September 1982 (the second record was inland at Knockaderry reservoir in September 1984). The third county record of **pectoral sandpiper** was at Whiting Bay in September 2010, (the first was from Knockaderry in September 1984 and the second from the Cunnigar in July 2004). The **buff-breasted sandpiper** has been seen just once, in October 1986 at the Cunnigar. **Wood sandpiper** is also rare with only a handful of records, some of which were from the coast (one in 1960, the second

Purple sandpipers arrive in Ireland from Canada, Greenland and northern Europe and they are entirely coastal here in winter, where they forage and feed around rocky shorelines along the inter-tidal zone and coastal structures such as breakwaters and piers overgrown with seaweed. Less than 4,000 birds overwinter in Ireland and since they are widely scattered on the rockier part of the coast–areas that are rarely fully censused for wintering shorebirds–this figure probably grossly underestimates the number of birds here in winter. However purple sandpipers are very site-faithful and they tend to stay at the same haunts each year. They are a beautiful bird and are probably one of the easiest of the sandpipers to identify; they are much darker than any of the other sandpipers and they have an obvious white eye-ring. In the east of the county, the best place to see them is off the pier wall at Dunmore East where up to 30 have been seen. At Dungarvan, up to 11 have been seen at

Ballinclamper, Clonea strand and Ballynacourty point and birds have also been seen at Ballyvooney.

The **dunlin** is one of the smallest of the shorebirds wintering at the Waterford wetlands, though it occurs in much greater numbers than the plovers, sanderlings or other small sandpipers. The vast majority of the birds winter in the mudflat areas of Dungarvan Bay and Tramore Backstrand, where small invertebrates are probed for in the wet mud. There are always a few birds foraging with sanderlings on the main beaches but generally they maintain tight flocks, which can be large in winter. They are a busy little bird constantly probing the mud and moving along the tideline as the waters lap around their feet. It is only when the tide is in full that the dunlin flocks rest, but even then they are restless, and the airborne flocks weave and gyrate, moving from one roost to the next around the wetland.

Almost 150,000 dunlin overwinter in Ireland and, of these, less than 200 pairs stay and breed, mostly in the northwest of the country. The rest move off to northern Scandinavia and western Siberia to raise their young in the summer months. Dunlins have been seen in all months of the year in Waterford, though numbers peak in December, January and February each winter in the county. Numbers tend to be highest at Dungarvan and counts of over 5,000 birds have been made there (the Cunnigar, Barnawee and Clonea are good places to see them) and, while up to 3,170 have been recorded at Tramore Backstrand, numbers lately are usually much lower than this at around 600-700 birds.

Small numbers of **ruff** are seen annually in Ireland, usually in the autumn when the bird is on passage between its breeding grounds in northern and central Europe and its wintering areas in west Africa. Up to six

Dunlin feeding on the tideline

have been recorded in Waterford (at Tramore in September 1973, four males and two females), though usually only single birds are seen. Most recent records have been from Dungarvan (Ballyneety mostly, though they have also been seen at Clonea, the Cunnigar, Ballinclamper, Killongford and Abbeyside). This somewhat secretive wader is only occasionally recorded at Tramore, most recently in December 1992 when one was with the godwits at the boating lake.

The **snipe** is rarely seen on open mud or sand, preferring instead the vegetated marshy areas fringing the wetland areas of the county, though they can be seen anywhere in the county on wet ground. They are almost impossible to count accurately and usually only a rough estimate of the numbers present at Waterford wetlands is possible, and even then many birds are missed. They are usually widely scattered and a walk across the salt marsh areas is the only way to determine if birds are present and even then it is only those birds that are close to the observer that will fly. Once disturbed, the bird flies erratically issuing the characteristic 'scaap' call; the long bill should also be obvious. At least 10,000 pairs currently breed in Ireland (a big decline on estimates made in the 1970s) but the size of the wintering population is unknown such is the difficulty of counting this small and elusive wader.

Black-tailed godwits, still in summer plumage, on passage in September at Ballyneety

The **jack snipe** is much rarer and there are only occasional records from the coast (Whiting Bay, Dungarvan, Tramore and Brownstown most recently); there are more records from inland areas of the county for this elusive species, which is probably more numerous than the few records suggest. There has only been one record of the **long-billed dowitcher** in the county; a juvenile was on the Cunnigar in October 2010.

Two godwit species overwinter in Waterford, mainly at three sites, Dungarvan Bay, Tramore Backstrand and Waterford Harbour. The birds usually need to be seen in flight to distinguish between them, especially for an inexperienced observer. The **black-tailed godwit** has a black bar along the tip of the tail and the broad white wing-bar is also distinctive, while the **bar-tailed godwit** has no wing bar. Both species are tall and elegant and are easily separated from the somewhat similar curlew and whimbrel by their slightly upturned bills and less bulky appearance.

Up to 1,500 black-tails have been counted at Dungarvan, 462 at Waterford Harbour and 355 at Tramore (the black-tailed godwit is frequently seen at the boating lake where up to 260 have been counted). Up to 1,370 bar-tails have been counted at Dungarvan and 247 at Tramore; this species is only rarely recorded at Waterford Harbour where usually less than 100 birds are seen. Around 18,000 of each species overwinter in Ireland and numbers peak here in January. The black-tailed godwits are worth checking for colour-ringed birds: among the flock at the Tramore boating lake in December 2000 was a bird

colour-ringed in Iceland, while one ringed as an adult male in Portugal in February 2007, and seen in Kent in England in early April, was at Ballyneety in August 2007. Most recently, the ringed bird on the Gold Coast in early January 2010, was ringed at De Richel, the Netherlands in July 2003.

Both godwit species feed by sight as they forage along the tideline for lugworms or ragworms but they also feed on other worms, *Hydrobia*, small bivalves and earthworms in the grassy areas. Only the black-tailed godwit breeds in Ireland, though in very small numbers (two or three pairs at most) and the wintering birds leave the estuaries early in the year to breed in Iceland (black-tails) and northern Europe (bar-tails).

Whimbrel and **curlew**, like the two godwit species, are similar birds and can be difficult to separate unless they occur together. The whimbrel is smaller than the curlew and its shorter bill is more steeply curved. While both birds emit a plaintive and an evocative call, that of the whimbrel is more musical, a rippling 'whinny' made up of seven whistling notes. This distinctive call is often the initial identifying feature indicating the presence of the bird in an area, and is characteristic if heard at night when the bird is often on the move. The whimbrel is largely a passage migrant in spring (primarily) and autumn whereas curlew are largely present in winter and can be even scarce in spring.

Passage numbers of whimbrel vary but up to 400 have been recorded (at Clonea), though some flocks overfly the county without stopping, doing so along the coast or the main river systems, and they may do so in some numbers at night, when counting them is more difficult. They have been seen at many coastal locations including Fornaght, Dunmore East, Portally, Brownstown Head, Tramore, Kilfarrasy, Bunmahon, Ballyvooney, Island, Paulswort, Ardmore, Whiting Bay and Ferry Point, though they occur more often at Dungarvan and Tramore than anywhere else. In west Waterford, the largest numbers are recorded at Clonea (up to 615 in April 2003), but numbers are usually much smaller than this (up to 20 birds). There is some sea passage off the headlands, usually in spring but numbers are small, often less than 20, though up to 135 have been seen at Brownstown Head. Occasionally a bird or two may winter here.

Curlews are more numerous than whimbrel, especially in December and January, when peak numbers occur. Curlews probe the mud in search of worms and, with their long curved bills, they are obviously at an advantage in taking the large lugworms and ragworms that many other birds would find too difficult to locate and extract. They also forage in the surrounding fields where earthworms and larva are sought. It is a scarce breeder in upland areas of Waterford (around 12,000 pairs bred in Ireland in 1988-91, though there has been a big decline since). Of the non-Irish birds wintering in Waterford, many leave the mudflats early in the year to breed in Scotland, Norway and Sweden. Around 65,000 curlew winter in Ireland (down from 100,000 in the 1970s and 1980s) and of these up to 1,000, 800 and 700 are counted on the Blackwater, Dungarvan and Tramore, respectively, with smaller numbers at Waterford Harbour, but many more may be found on inland fields and on the Blackwater callows.

The **redshank** breeds in Iceland, across central Europe and Siberia and winters in

Curlew

Ireland, Britain and France. Around 5,000 pairs breed in Ireland, mostly in the mid-west of the country. The bright red legs and partly red bill are obvious features of the redshank if seen at close quarters. It has a white back and rump and always emits a raucous alarm call when disturbed. It is a medium-sized wader that is only likely to be confused with the spotted redshank or the greenshank, both of which winter in much smaller numbers in Waterford. Redshanks feed on small snails and worms and occur literally anywhere there is soft mud so they may be found on the mudflats, along creeks in the salt marsh areas and even on the drainage channels in the surrounding fields. They also occur on the river estuaries where single birds are more likely than larger flocks. There are few summer records (usually isolated records of individual birds), most birds having left for breeding grounds elsewhere. Around 32,000 birds winter in Ireland, and of these up to 950 have been seen at Dungarvan and up to 411 at Tramore Backstrand.

The **spotted redshank** is occasionally recorded in Waterford, mostly single birds, though 22 were seen at Tramore in September 1973 and 16 were at Kinsalebeg in November 1975. Most sightings are in autumn or early winter, though two were seen at Kilminnin (Dungarvan) in July (2004) and one was at Killongford in August 2010. Its paler upperparts and whiter underparts are obvious differences compared with the more numerous redshank.

Redshank

Wintering numbers of **greenshank** are always small but they are around every winter on the coastal wetlands and on the river systems. It is probably more numerous from July to October when the bird is on passage from its breeding grounds in Scotland, northern Europe and central Asia to wintering areas further south. August is probably the best month to look for them as both adult and juvenile birds from the Scottish breeding population (where up to 1,600 pairs nest in remote upland areas) are on the move southwards. It is larger than the redshank but it lacks any red on its body parts (its plumage is a drab grey and white), a feature which should allow it to be separated from the similar-sized and more numerous redshank and the much rarer spotted redshank. Around 1,700 birds winter in Ireland and, in Waterford, birds are more or less guaranteed on the Blackwater estuary (up to 25 have been recorded here), Dungarvan (up to 33) and Tramore (up to 29), with a scattering of birds elsewhere. Interestingly, a colour-ringed juvenile seen at Ballinclamper, Dungarvan on the 18th September 2009, was ringed in northeast Scotland on the 22nd August, a few weeks earlier.

The first county record of **lesser yellowlegs** was as recent as April 1999, when one stayed at Clonea strand for a few days. The third county record, a first-winter bird, was seen opposite the mart near the Park Hotel in Dungarvan in late September/early October 2005. The most recent record was a bird which spent a few days around the pools near the Cunnigar carpark in November 2009, and allowed close views. It breeds in Alaska and Canada but occurs more or less annually in Britain and Ireland, though most birds winter in South America.

The **green sandpiper** is an annual visitor to the county but never in any numbers. It is probably more likely to be seen inland (Blackwater callows, Dromana, Portlaw, Ballyshunnock, Kilmeaden pools and Knockaderry reservoir) though it also occurs on the coast, mainly at Dungarvan and Tramore (one was seen in December 2006 and September 2010 near Bunmahon, and, unusually, three were there in October 2010, while one was present at Ardmore in September 2010). Ballyneety and the Brickey river are probably the best places to see one at Dungarvan (it has also been seen at Helvick Head and on the Cunnigar). At Tramore, the majority of records are from around Clohernagh inlet (opposite the thatched pub), an easy place to view from the road, but a careful check of other areas might be fruitful (it has also been seen at Kilmacleague). Most of the records are from late summer and autumn, but it is recorded almost all year round on the Brickey. Usually only single birds occur but up to four have been seen at Dungarvan.

The **common sandpiper** is confined to the estuaries, river edges, lakes and reservoirs when breeding, which it does mostly in the west of Ireland. It is normally only recorded from April to September and coastal records invariably relate to birds on passage. Flocks of up to 27 have been recorded, though ones or twos are more likely along the coast, where the bird can be seen anywhere from the mudflats to the base of the cliffs and around the beaches and coves. It is an exciting bird to watch as it bobs up and down very characteristically when foraging along the mud or at the waters edge. When disturbed it flies low over the surface of the water with short bursts of rapid wingbeats, calling in alarm. There are now regular records of birds wintering in the wetlands of the county but the vast majority of the birds leave for the wintering areas south of the Sahara in Africa and the Mediterranean.

Turnstones are almost entirely coastal in their wintering distribution in Ireland and are often seen in small flocks at Tramore and Dungarvan. Numbers are greatest at Dungarvan (up to 284 have been counted there). Rocky habitats are the best place to look for them, where they turn over stones and seaweed in search of hidden food. The Ballinclamper end of Clonea strand or opposite the Gold Coast Hotel is worth watching for this mottled species and there are always a few birds with the purple sandpipers off the wall at Dunmore East. They do not breed in Ireland and summer records are very rare; most leave by May, returning to Canada and Greenland to breed.

Of the three species of phalarope recorded in Ireland, two have been seen occasionally in Waterford. The **red-necked phalarope** is very rare and there is just one record: a single bird was seen at Ardmore in summer 1969. The **grey phalarope** is more frequent and they have been seen at Tramore (one, September 1981), Mine Head (one, September 2009), Ballynagaul (one, November 2009), Helvick Head (two on each occasion in October 2005, September 2008 and November 2009 and six in October 2010), and at Ballyneety, Dungarvan (one, October 2005).

Skuas & gulls
Four skua species have been recorded off the Waterford coast. They are generally dark plumaged birds that are mainly predatory and piratical, obtaining fish from other birds such as auks and kittiwakes, though they also scavenge around trawlers and will fish themselves when required. The **pomarine**

skua is often the most common species in spring and is recorded off the headlands during seawatches, mainly at Brownstown Head and Helvick Head. They have also been seen off Ram Head, Ballynacourty, Ballinclamper, Ballyvoyle, Bunmahon and Great Newtown Head. They are passage birds that are usually recorded in April-May, though there are summer and autumn records and a few winter records. Passage numbers are usually small (less than five) though up to 29 have been recorded at Brownstown Head in a day (May 1980) and up to 22 at Ballynacourty point (May 2009).

The **arctic skua** is recorded mainly between April and October off the coastal headlands; 64 flew west in three hours off Brownstown Head in October 1977 and up to 48 have been counted at Helvick Head (in September 1999), though numbers are usually much smaller than this. They have also been recorded in Tramore Bay, and off Clonea, Ballynacourty, Mine Head, Ram Head, Ardmore Bay and Whiting Bay. None of the skuas breed in Ireland though the arctic skua and great skua do so in Scotland. The **great skua** usually occurs singly on passage off the headlands in spring, late summer and autumn (birds have been recorded off Brownstown and other locations in winter) and they have also been seen at Clonea, Ballyvooney and in Tramore Bay. Forty three birds passed Brownstown Head on one date in September 1978 but numbers recently are rarely as high as this, though 32 were recorded off Helvick Head in September 2010. There is also a record of a single bird with the gulls at Tramore dump in September 1973. The **long-tailed skua** is rare and there have been only a few recent records, all off Helvick Head: 3 juveniles in October 2005; two and one respectively on separate days in September 2006; and one in June 2010.

Gull plumage is largely grey and white and sometimes black though the immature

HERRING GULL NESTS AT DUNMORE EAST		
	1994	**2008**
no of nests	41	42-48

gulls are very variable, even as they age towards adulthood. Gulls are fascinating birds to watch and endless hours of enjoyment can be had in trying to distinguish between the different species or in ageing immature birds. Once the birds are breeding, there are opportunities in watching them going about the business of reproduction and seeing the young birds fledge. And they are present in Waterford throughout the year.

Sixteen gull species have been recorded along the Waterford coast but only three or four species breed. The others are mainly winter visitors and some of these are rare. They can be seen all along the coast, in the coves, bays and on the beaches and formerly in some numbers at the town dumps at Tramore and Dungarvan and during fish processing activities at Dunmore East and Helvick Head, where the odd rare gull that appeared were eagerly sought out by avid birdwatchers. With the closure of both dumps and a reduction in fish processing, large gull flocks are no longer seen in Waterford, though good numbers can be seen following boats off the coast, when fish offal is being discarded overboard.

Dumps, despite the increased food supply they offered, were extremely dangerous places for foraging gulls as botulism, caused by the bacterium *Clostridium botulinum* multiplying in the anaerobic conditions in rotting food, caused much morbidity and mortality. Most affected birds died from dehydration rather than from the toxin itself. Mortality of gulls infected with botulism is high and

birds have only a very slim chance of survival, regardless of attempts at rehabilitation. The observed decline in recent years in the breeding numbers of herring gulls all around the Irish coast, including Waterford, is thought to be associated with botulism.

The **herring gull** is probably the commonest gull in the county. It is to be found almost everywhere, from the mudflats at Tramore to the bigger lakes in the Comeraghs, though it is commonest along the coast. It is present all the year round, breeding on coastal cliffs, stacks and offshore rocks and even on roof tops at Dunmore East. It forages inland, along the shore, at sewage works and can be seen over the cities and towns and along the quay of Waterford and in and around Dungarvan. But it is a noisy and aggressive bird, constantly harassing and chasing its neighbours. At Dunmore East where it nests on flat roofs, hipped roofs and between chimney pots, it can be quite aggressive towards the people living in the houses where it nests, dumping excrement as it flies past repeatedly. Many an unwary visitor to that village has been upset by the unwanted attentions of the herring gull. Look up at some of the chimneys in Dunmore East and you will see the valiant efforts that have been undertaken to deter them from nesting. Sometimes these deterrents work and sometimes they don't; the gulls often nest on the tops of the cages used around the chimneys, for example.

Complete counts of roof-nesting herring gulls were achieved in 1994 and again in 2008. There was a small increase in the number of pairs between the two census years. The gulls were opportunistic as to where the nests were constructed. They chose stable positions on roofs but the nests weren't rechecked to see which roof situation was more successful in terms of fledging young. Usually only one nest was constructed on any

Herring gull

roof, though a very gently sloping roof in the harbour area had nine nests in 2008 (one on the east side and eight on the west side). The gulls didn't confine themselves to roofs and a nest was constructed on top of a large vertical tank beside the adventure centre shop while two more nested on the wall plate of a derelict factory near the ice factory in the inner harbour. The Haven Hotel had a pair, as had the Garda station and there were three pairs on the old convent building overlooking the harbour (now converted to apartments). There was some uncertainty in 2008 about the exact number of pairs as some of the birds may have had nests out of sight on flat roofs at the back of buildings (the Ocean Hotel, for example). One great black-backed gull nest was also seen in 2008.

The herring gull usually constructs a grass-lined nest on coastal cliff ledges and on Dunmore roofs where two or three eggs are laid, which are incubated for a month or so. When the young hatch they can be difficult to see as they lie low among the vegetation or hide under ledges when alarmed, while the

Roof-nesting herring gull at Dunmore East

adults call continuously ('ag ag ag') and fly by repeatedly overhead. At Dunmore East, the constant movements of adults and young, from dawn to dusk, is disconcerting for some residents for the five or six week period in summer when the birds are clattering about roof tops. Breeding numbers declined markedly on the Waterford coast in recent decades from a peak in the 1970s.

The **yellow-legged (herring) gull** has been recorded on a number of occasions since first seen at Tramore in January 1996: a third-winter bird was seen on the 27th February 1999 and another, also a third-winter bird, was seen on the 28th February, both at Dungarvan; an adult was at Dungarvan on Christmas Day 2001; and there have been several more sightings since of single birds at Whiting Bay, Curragh beach, Rincrew (on the Blackwater estuary), Gull Island (near Stradbally), Ballyneety, the Cunnigar, Cheekpoint (where two adults were seen), Stradbally, Helvick Head, Ballynacourty and Tramore.

The **great black-backed gull** is the largest of the gulls to be seen in Waterford. It is also the most notorious as it is capable of taking other seabirds as food and can be quite a menace around seabird colonies. Around 60 pairs breed on the Waterford coast, mostly between Great Newtown Head and Ballyvoyle. They usually do so singly on the

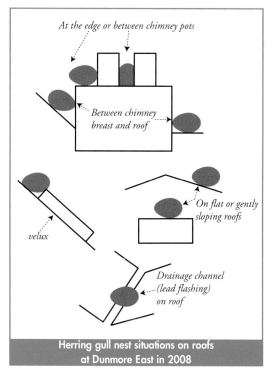

At the edge or between chimney pots

Between chimney breast and roof

velux

On flat or gently sloping roofs

Drainage channel (lead flashing) on roof

Herring gull nest situations on roofs at Dunmore East in 2008

COUNTS OF KITTIWAKES AT EAST WATERFORD COLONIES, 1964-2010

Counts in 1964 and 1974 refer to counts of nests with young ('pairs') around mid-July, while counts thereafter refer to counts of apparently occupied nests (AONs) in early June. Counts in July usually underestimate the peak breeding population.

	1964 'pairs'	1974 'pairs'	1984 AONs	1994 AONs	2004 AONs	2010 AONs
Beenlea Head	0	55	0	0	0	0
Ballymacaw	nc	nc	nc	6	0	0
Portally	164	802	87	114	51	55
Black Knob	408	387	185	364	111	101
Inner Harbour	138	102	201	127	126	153
Outer Harbour	300	769	576	526	518	281
Foilakipeen	0	369	6	0	0	0
Ardnamult	nc	500	29	72	15	10

tops of offshore stacks but more pairs breed at Gull Island, just west of Ballyvooney (22 pairs in 2008) than anywhere else. Both birds construct the grassy nest where two or three eggs are incubated for around 30 days, after which both parents are busy feeding the young, who fly after about seven weeks. In winter, many more birds can be seen all along the coast and, given their size, they are easy to spot roosting on sand banks or wandering around the rocky beaches.

Kittiwakes are the most oceanic of the gulls and they rarely occur inland. Large numbers are present at the Waterford breeding colonies in summer, mainly at Dunmore East, Portally, Helvick Head and Ardmore/Ram Head. The colony on the Old Red Sandstone cliffs at inner harbour, Dunmore East is unique in Ireland as the birds breed so close to humans and can be observed so easily from the pier.

William Thompson writing in the *Natural History of Ireland* (1851) makes no mention of kittiwakes nesting at Dunmore East but he stated that:

about Helvick Head, they were observed in profusion in the summer of 1838.

There are several photographs in the Lawrence collection in the National Library of the harbour area in Dunmore East taken between 1880-1914, but none of these photographs show kittiwakes or signs of them either on the cliffs or in flight at the inner harbour cliffs. Richard Ussher, who lived in Waterford (at Cappagh) and who knew the coast well, writing in *The Birds of Ireland* (published in 1900), stated that:

in Waterford the kittiwake has no considerable colonies.

In his notes (held in the Royal Irish Academy Dawson Street, Dublin) he records that they bred at Dunmore East since at least 1910 and there were "*a dozen*" nests there in 1911. There is surprisingly little information on the subsequent growth in breeding numbers at Dunmore East and counts up to 1964 are incomplete and infrequent. More systematic counts between 1964 and 1974 indicated that numbers were increasing at Dunmore East, as they were elsewhere in Britain and Ireland. By 1984, when the next complete survey of breeding numbers were conducted, it was obvious that there had been a considerable decline in numbers, though it wasn't possible to say with any certainty when the decline occurred; different methodologies also complicated the interpretation of the observed changes in the breeding population between survey years.

Kittiwakes breed in the northern hemisphere from Portugal to the low Arctic zones and they are so named because of the distinctive sounding call 'kit-ee-wayke', which echoes around breeding colonies in summer. Kittiwakes construct compact nests of grass and seaweed on tiny ledges on sheer cliffs of solid rock, where few other birds can breed so they can occur in large numbers at colonies. At Dunmore East, and especially at the inner harbour colony, discarded fishing material is used extensively in nest building and from one to three kittiwakes (young, juveniles or adults) die each year, through becoming trapped in this nylon netting material used in the construction of nests, though occasionally birds are also snared in overhead branches. Because of its persistence, layer upon layer of this synthetic material and other debris has accumulated over the years, resulting in stable nest platforms and probably allowing for more nests than would be the case if it wasn't used or it was all removed.

From one to three eggs (usually two) are laid in the cup-shaped nests from early to mid-May onwards, which the parent birds incubate for up to four weeks. The young hatch in early June, but the small downy chicks may be difficult to see in the deep nests, especially as the parent birds continuously brood for the first couple of weeks. When the young hatch, the colony literally comes alive with the constant movements of the parent birds attending to the growing needs of the young birds. During the breeding season kittiwakes feed mainly on small pelagic shoaling fish such as sandeels, sprats and young herring and the adult birds often fly up to 50 kilometres out to sea in search of food and will fish both by day and night; they feed their young by regurgitating

food when they return to the nest and the young 'encourage' their parents by continuously pecking at their beaks.

Kittiwakes call and cackle continuously at the colony and they fight like dogs with their neighbours if they accidentally intrude on each others 'space'. They often come to blows, especially if a landing bird does so on the wrong nest, and both birds will peck the hell out of each other. If they lock bills, both may tumble downward only to separate before they hit the ground, unless they land in water and the aggression will continue. Kittiwake colonies are therefore noisy places in summer, which isn't an issue on the coastal cliffs at Ram Head (Ardmore) and Helvick Head, where few people venture but it can be disconcerting for visitors to Dunmore until they realise the birds are harmless. The inner harbour colony is a fantastic place to visit in summer; where else in Ireland can a raucous seabird colony be seen and admired with such ease. Children, in particular, are usually mesmerised by the antics of the adults and the presence of young in the nests.

The young birds grow quickly and they fledge after 35-42 days; most have left the colony by mid-August. By September the nests are deserted and both adults and young move offshore; the immature birds wander far from Dunmore and can be found anywhere over the North Atlantic during their first couple of years of life but the adult birds

Kittiwake adult and young, Dunmore East

usually do not venture as far. In the 1980s, the adult birds returned to the Dunmore colonies from late November onwards where they availed of fish offal and discards around fishing boats and in the harbour. More lately, because of the decline in fish processing in the local factories, the birds return later and later and it is now well into the New Year before birds are seen on their old nests.

Kittiwakes at Dunmore East are the most studied kittiwakes in Ireland, not surprising really given the ease with which the birds can be seen and counted, even from a car at inner

harbour, if the weather is unfavourable. Most kittiwake colonies are on sheer and usually high cliffs, which can be difficult to reach safely let alone count (at Helvick, for example). Consequently the Dunmore kittiwakes are important indicators of the overall status of the Irish kittiwake population and the conclusions of ongoing studies can be broadly applied to other colonies, which are far more difficult to monitor. Accurate annual counts of the kittiwakes at Dunmore are available since 1984, taken using standard and repeatable methods, and which can be reliably compared with counts taken at other colonies in Britain and Ireland as part of the Seabird Monitoring Programme coordinated by the Joint Nature Conservation Committee in Scotland to whom the annual counts from the Dunmore colonies are sent. The recommended method of counting kittiwakes is to count all nests that can hold eggs, young or an incubating adult in early to mid-June and then to repeat the count around mid-July when nests with young only are recorded. This minimum of two visits gives a reasonably accurate population estimate and this method is used at all Waterford colonies, except at the inner harbour colony where a more intensive method of weekly visits to the colony from mid-May to mid-August has been used between 1984 and 2010.

The total breeding population in Britain and Ireland in the period 1998-2002 was around 416,000 pairs, of which 49,000 pairs were in Ireland (representing an overall decline of 23% since the previous census in 1985-88). About 1,800 pairs of kittiwakes bred at seven Waterford colonies in 2005 and between 105 (in 2000) and 224 pairs (in 1987) breed annually at the inner harbour colony at Dunmore East. The Dunmore kittiwake colonies regularly exceeds 1% of the estimated national breeding total and the area is considered to be of national conservation importance for the species.

DUNMORE EAST
Kittiwake colonies

Outer Harbour

N

0   100m

Inner Harbour

Black Knob

Kittiwake breeding cliffs

The location of the kittiwake colonies and the breeding cliffs at Dunmore East, Co. Waterford

There are five kittiwake colonies in East Waterford, all on coastal cliffs varying in height from 15 to 40 metres, at Portally and Ardnamult and the three Dunmore East colonies at Shanooan (or Black Knob), inner harbour and outer harbour. Three other cliffs at Beenlea Head, Ballymacaw and Foilakipeen haven't been used for several years (they are only used when the population is high and the other, more attractive colonies are 'full'). The inner harbour colony is the most accessible of the three colonies at Dunmore East and the most studied, though all three can be safely visited. It is at this colony that the most intensive studies have taken place, including the ringing of birds; 671 birds (96 adults and 575 young birds) were ringed here between 1987 and 1990, the majority of them using coded yellow plastic rings, which can be easily read, especially at inner harbour, allowing the fascinating lives of these seabirds to be monitored and followed as they move around and between colonies.

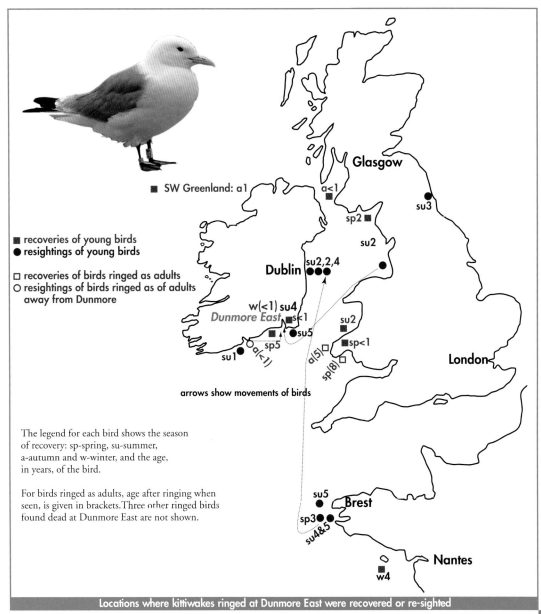

Locations where kittiwakes ringed at Dunmore East were recovered or re-sighted

Oceanic birds like kittiwakes usually have a low rate of ring recovery (around 1.7%), as birds that die far offshore are seldom encountered. There were 10 recoveries and 12 resightings of 10 birds away from Dunmore East. Birds were mainly seen or found dead on the east and south coast of Ireland (Rockabill, Great Saltee Island and Old Head of Kinsale), the east and west coast of Britain (Gateshead, Newcastle and Liverpool) and in France (Brittany) and one was shot in west Greenland within 15 months of ringing. Only one of the resightings involved an adult bird (it was seen in early September at Ballycotton, county Cork and was back on its own nest in December). There was also some movement between colonies: one bird moved from Cap Sizun in Brittany to Rockabill, off the Dublin coast, and another seen at Liverpool later returned to the outer harbour colony at Dunmore East. These were young birds prospecting for places in which to nest. Four birds ringed elsewhere were seen at Dunmore: three of these were colour-ringed at Great Saltee Island, Wexford and the fourth bird was ringed at Dunbar harbour in Scotland 11 years previously. The metal codes on 14 ringed adult birds from 311 chicks ringed at inner harbour in July 1974 were also read between 1979 and 1987.

The ringing studies estimated adult survival at 80% per annum, which was similar to survival rates measured at other colonies elsewhere (mostly in the UK). Surprisingly only around 16% of the young birds reared at inner harbour returned to breed at Dunmore East, which is a low rate of recruitment, and could explain why the population was declining. Two thirds of the returning birds bred at the inner harbour colony, with 27% and 6% breeding at outer harbour and Black Knob, respectively.

Colour-ringing allows the lives of individual birds to be monitored and provides a fascinating insight into the behaviour of the birds, at least while they are at the breeding colony. The oldest known bird at the inner harbour colony in 2010 (at 22 years old) was ringed as a chick on the 30th June 1988. This bird, H84, was first seen back at the colony in 1991 but it didn't breed successfully until 1994 and even though it produced young that year, none fledged. However, it has remained faithful to the same nest in all subsequent years that it was seen at the colony (it wasn't recorded in either 1997 or 2006, though it could have been present unseen in these years), and only a few metres from the nest in which it was born. It successfully reared young in most years that it bred at the colony and it had two young in 2010. There are no sightings of H84 when it is away from the colony, which is typical for seabirds that venture offshore following breeding. An even older bird, C75, ringed as a breeding adult in 1988 was last seen in 2009 so, by then, it was at least 24 years old and possibly older.

The overall trend in breeding numbers at Dunmore East was one of decline between 1984 and 2010. This decline could be linked to climate change and oceanic plankton production perhaps leading to increased mortality of young kittiwakes outside of breeding season. At Dunmore East, it is almost certain that the cessation of the herring fishery and the associated onshore fish-processing activities, have also impacted

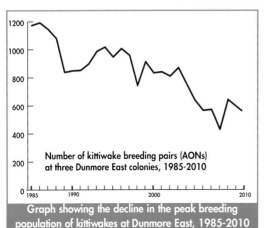

Number of kittiwake breeding pairs (AONs) at three Dunmore East colonies, 1985-2010

Graph showing the decline in the peak breeding population of kittiwakes at Dunmore East, 1985-2010

on the breeding population as the birds must wander farther over the ocean in winter in search of food. The studies have also shown that the inner harbour colony is consistently the most productive of all the east Waterford colonies and fledges more young per nest than either of the other two Dunmore colonies, regardless of weather conditions. In this respect, Black Knob often fares worse, possibly because in bad summers low nests there are lashed by high waves and strong winds crashing against the cliffs. Kittiwake eggs (one per nest), taken for analysis for pollutants, indicated that the low levels of contaminants found were unlikely to have had any impact on breeding performance and that the levels of pollutants were much lower in eggs taken in 1998 compared with levels found in 1987/1989. In all samples, the industrial polychlorinated biphenyls (PCBs) occurred at greater concentrations than any of the other contaminants.

Other problems can impact on birds nesting in urban situations, such as those at the two main Dunmore East colonies (inner harbour and outer harbour). Based on detailed mapping of individual nests at the inner harbour colony each year, 57 nests were lost between 1987 and 2003 due to encroaching vegetation, mainly from the upper sections of the cliffs. An additional 46 nests were, however, created in the period 1988-2003 that were not in use in 1987. This suggests that birds displaced because of the encroaching vegetation and/or the effects of predation built nests elsewhere on the cliff. Some vegetation was removed in December 2004 though the relatively low population at the time ensured that the new areas weren't used for nesting by prospecting birds.

Significant predation incidents occurred at inner harbour in 1988 and 1991, mainly on the lower cliffs nearer the RNLI building, leading to the deaths of young and poor breeding performance on the cliffs concerned.

Anti-gull device on the RNLI building, Dunmore East

The main predators were cats and foxes, and rats were seen in some nests in some years; mink have also been seen (rarely) in the harbour area and these could also cause predation. On rare occasions, ravens were seen landing on breeding ledges and taking eggs at the outer harbour colony. Some of these predators gained access from below and some from above, so excessive trimming of vegetation may increase the risk of predators gaining access to the cliffs. Over the years, stones and, exceptionally, a large bottle of Guinness, were seen in nests and it is almost certain that these arrived, either accidentally or intentionally, from the cliff top or path above. The largely impenetrable cliff top vegetation at the inner and outer harbour cliffs offers protection to the nesting kittiwakes in that it forms a natural barrier to mammalian predators (though it may also provide a refuge for the smaller or more determined predators) and is an effective screen against casual, accidental or deliberate disturbance by passing people on the cliff top path above. Very occasionally someone will throw stones at the birds from below at inner harbour but the people of Dunmore cherish the kittiwakes dearly and such incidents are quickly seen and dealt with appropriately.

About 30 pairs nested in the harbour area in 1935 and, by 1959, 977 pairs were counted at Dunmore East at the three colonies, quite a dramatic increase in a little over 20 years. Major development works took place in the harbour between 1963 and 1969 which included the removal of cliff faces used by the kittiwakes, the building of the roadway at the base of the inner harbour cliff and the extension of piers and jetties. Inevitably, the disturbance resulted in the kittiwakes leaving the inner and outer harbour cliffs to breed at the nearby cliffs of Portally, Black Knob, Foilakipeen and Ardnamult. The birds returned to inner harbour in 1966 with around 65 pairs breeding there until 1970 when numbers increased. Fifty four pairs returned to outer harbour in 1966 and numbers steadily increased thereafter; by 1970, 903 pairs were present, probably the highest number ever to breed there. Numbers nesting at Beenlea Head were always small, and probably peaked at 55 pairs in 1974, though none breed there now. It isn't known when kittiwakes first bred near Ballymacaw but numbers there too were always small, at no more than 30 pairs, and they were only present for a few years in the early 1990s. Kittiwakes were first recorded breeding at Portally in 1952 (162 pairs were counted) though, given the numbers recorded, they were probably breeding there long before this. Numbers increased substantially in 1965 to 518 pairs, and many of these probably moved from the Dunmore East colonies due to disturbance from the construction works in the harbour. Kittiwakes didn't, apparently, breed at Foilakipeen until 1971, when 34 pairs nested, and the colony increased in size to 369 pairs by 1974. At Ardnamult around 500 pairs were breeding on the sandstone ledges there in 1974.

In some winters, large concentrations of kittiwakes may occur just off the Waterford coast, probably because of high food availability locally. For example, in the winter of 1985/86, around 20,000 kittiwakes were seen offshore between Waterford Harbour and Dungarvan Bay and 9,000 of these were recorded in Tramore Bay in December.

There is some passage past the headlands and several hundred birds may fly by in either direction, with the greatest numbers passing in December and January, though a small spring passage has been noticed in some years. These passing birds could be from anywhere and going anywhere; a bird ringed as an adult in Rost, Norway in June 1983 was found dead at Tramore in January 1984.

The **lesser black-backed gull** is a rare breeder in Waterford. The last known breeding record was on Gull Island in 1983, but it winters or passes through in considerable numbers. Up to 1985/86 very few birds were recorded in winter suggesting a change in status, in line with its migratory patterns elsewhere in the British Isles. Up to 1,060 birds have been seen at Tramore (in January 1986) with 1,140 at Dungarvan (in December 1988). High numbers have been seen roosting at dusk off the Waterford coast (163 at Dunabrattin in November 2007 and 750 in Bunmahon Bay in November 2006) and in the estuaries (1,150 in Waterford Harbour in January 2005 and 560 at Rincrew on the Blackwater in November 2007) and bays (510 in Tramore Bay in November 2004). One seen at Rincrew on the river Blackwater in August 2010 was ringed in southwest Iceland in August 2008.

The **common gull** is one of the least common of the breeding gulls we have in Ireland. It is a slightly smaller version of the herring gull and it breeds on islands in the lakes and offshore islands on the west coast of Ireland. In winter, these native birds are supplemented by others arriving from breeding colonies in Europe, Iceland and Russia. Up to 18,000 birds spend the winter months on inland areas and along the coasts of Ireland. Numbers have been increasing in Waterford since about 1975 but coverage has also improved due mainly to careful counts of birds flying to roost at dusk having spent the day at inland locations. Late in the evening

Black-headed gulls

large flocks of birds can often be seen flying down along Waterford Harbour to roost off Passage, Geneva strand or Woodstown. Highest numbers are always recorded in December, possibly because of adverse weather conditions further north. For example, 2,700 birds were off Woodstown in December 1985 while 1,300 were in Ardmore Bay in February 2006.

The **black-headed gull** is a familiar bird around the rivers, estuaries, mudflats and coastal areas and even following the plough in the surrounding fields. It can be seen in all months of the year and it may even be the commonest gull species in Ireland; it doesn't, however, breed in Waterford (the nearest breeding colony is in Wexford). Almost 14,000 pairs breed here in Ireland, mostly in the northwest (a bird seen at Dungarvan in July 2009 and again in January 2010 was ringed as a chick on Lough Mask, Mayo in June 2007). Large numbers of black-headed gulls are widely scattered in the county in winter and they can be anywhere, even on playing fields in towns and Waterford City, especially after heavy rains. The greatest numbers are on the coast and the maximum number counted was over 3,000 birds at Tramore in December 1989; large numbers have been counted elsewhere (1000+ at Clonea strand in September 2010 and 900 in Ardmore Bay in November 2008).

The **Iceland gull** and the **glaucous gull** are scarce winter visitors from the Arctic. The Iceland gull was first recorded here in July

1959 and there have been many records since at various sites including Woodstown, Dunmore East, Bunmahon, Ballyvooney, Stradbally, Dungarvan, Helvick Head, Mine Head, Whiting Bay, Ferry Point and Rincrew. Most of the records in the 1980s were from Dunmore East when fish processing was at its peak. Most recent records have been from Helvick Head and the majority of records are from the period January to March. There have been many more records of the glaucous gull from several coastal sites, mostly one to three birds, though 17 were seen at Tramore in January 1979. Many of the recent records relate to immature birds but adult birds have also been seen. A **glaucous x great black-backed** hybrid was seen at Rincrew on the Blackwater in February 2008.

The **Mediterranean gull** is not unlike the black-headed gull but the adult birds are unmistakable with all white flight feathers (apart from the black head of summer adults, a feature shared with black-headed gull). It was first recorded in Waterford at Ballymacaw in July 1974 and sightings have increased substantially since. In 2009 alone there were many records of birds seen mostly around Dungarvan (at Ballyneety, Barnawee, Clonea strand, Ballinard, the Cunnigar, Killongford and Ballynacourty) but also at Rincrew, Ardmore, Whiting Bay and Tramore boating lake. Some of these birds were colour-ringed, which showed that one was ringed in Denmark and the other in Belgium (and was nine years old when seen at Dungarvan in July 2009). Up to five birds

The waters around the Sandhills at Tramore are always good for migrating terns in spring and autumn

were seen at some sites (eight were seen on Ardmore beach in September 2008) and numbers are likely to increase here given that the bird is breeding now in Ireland, albeit still in small numbers (it was first proved to breed here, in Wexford, in 1995).

The **little gull** is the smallest gull to be found on the Waterford coast and it is never plentiful. It is almost entirely pelagic in winter and it is only following storms that it may be driven close inshore. The majority of the records are from the east coast and inner Galway Bay. It was a great rarity in Ireland before 1950 and it is only since then that numbers have increased. Since 1971 it has been seen on the Waterford coast at Passage East, Woodstown, Dunmore East, Brownstown Head, Dungarvan (Helvick Head, Ballynagaul, the Cunnigar, Ballynacourty, Ballinard, Ballyneety and Clonea strand), Ardmore and Whiting Bay. While single birds are seen most often, there are records of up to 14 birds and it has been seen in all months, though it is more frequent from August to March.

The **ring-billed gull** was first recorded in the county at Kinsalebeg in January 1985 (the first Irish record of this North American gull was in 1979). It has probably been seen more often at Tramore than anywhere else and most records have been of single birds. From 1991 on a single bird was present for at least 10 successive winters at the boating lake, probably still the best place to see one,

though they have also been seen at Rincrew, Whiting Bay, Ballynagaul, the Cunnigar, Barnawee, Ballyneety and Clonea strand. The species is difficult enough to separate from commoner herring gulls unless seen together, when the differences between them should be obvious. Gull flocks are always worth checking for the presence of this gull, especially in the winter months when sightings are more likely.

Rarer gulls seen in Waterford include an **ivory gull** in Dungarvan Harbour in January 1988 for the first and only time and a **Sabine's gull**, seen for the first time at Dunmore East in September 1980 and on a number of occasions since, mostly at Helvick Head but also at Dunmore East, Rathmoylan cove, Brownstown Head, Tramore, Dungarvan and Clonea strand. **Bonaparte's gull** has been seen three times, the first in April 2004 at Ballyneety, Dungarvan and since then at Ardmore Bay in October 2007 and again there in September 2008. The rarest gull seen in the county is the **Caspian gull**, seen just once at Kinsalebeg/Rincrew on the Blackwater estuary in February 2007.

Terns

Terns arrive in spring and spend time feeding off our coast before heading off to breeding colonies elsewhere in Ireland (no tern species currently breeds in Waterford). They are generally smaller than gulls and with their long, pointed wings and forked tails, they are very elegant and graceful in flight and are a joy to watch offshore as they dive in pursuit of small fish and other marine life. They return to the Waterford coast in autumn when large numbers, swelled by the young of the year, gather off many of the coastal beaches to feed before heading off to west Africa for the winter months.

The **Sandwich tern** probably occurs in greater numbers than any of the other tern species, and their distinctive call usually confirms their presence. They arrive from March onwards (most arrive in early April) and they can be found all along the Waterford coast, daintily flying along and diving spectacularly when they see fish under the water. Much greater numbers occur in August and September when gatherings of up to 100, and sometimes more, can be found in the coastal bays, especially Tramore Bay and off Clonea strand, when they prey on sandeels that appear inshore at this time. These flocks often roost in some numbers on the sandbars, and the darker-plumaged juvenile birds are easily distinguished from the adult birds if close views are possible. Occasionally large numbers are recorded on passage off the headlands (around 1,500 were off Helvick Head in August 2009).

Roseate terns are much rarer and only small numbers are seen off the coast, mainly in autumn. Up to 12 birds have been seen on Clonea strand and birds have been seen on passage at the headlands during seawatches (49 were off Helvick Head during a two hour seawatch in September 2009). At Lady's Island in Wexford 89 pairs bred in 2007 but the bulk of the European population (excluding the Azores) breeds on Rockabill, off the Dublin coast, where 1,093 pairs were found in 2010; special conservation measures and an annual monitoring programme are in place there for this endangered species.

Common and **arctic terns** are difficult to separate unless they are seen at close range so when birds of either species are seen offshore they are referred to simply as "commic" terns. They occur in small numbers off our coast in April and May and again in the early autumn. Birds of either species have been seen off the Cunnigar, Clonea strand and in Tramore Bay but rarely in any numbers (40+ common terns on Clonea strand in August 2009 was a high count). They have also been seen on passage off the headlands when small numbers pass in either direction in spring and autumn.

Little terns breed on sand and shingle beaches along the coast but the species is very susceptible to disturbance and is easily predated at mainland sites. For these reasons the little terns that bred at a colony at Saleen on the east side of Tramore Bay were enclosed during the 1973 breeding season and they continued to breed successfully for a number of years thereafter. However, the colony never returned after the 1982 breeding season. There have only been a few casual records since, of up to three birds in spring on Clonea strand, but a small passage is probably annual along the coast. They did, apparently, breed at Caliso Bay, in the far west of the county, in 1976 (around 20 pairs) and they also attempted to breed at Bunmahon in the 1970s. The main breeding colonies are off the east and west coasts of Ireland so incoming birds rarely stay too long on the Waterford coast.

There have been occasional records of rare terns in the county. **Forster's tern** was first recorded here in January 1985 in Dungarvan Harbour and there are three further records, all from Dungarvan: in March 1987; from late October to early December 1995 (both were adult birds); and a first winter bird was at Barnawee in March 2006. There is only one record of the **whiskered tern**, seen at Dungarvan in April 1994, but the **black tern** has been seen on several occasions at Whiting Bay, Dungarvan Bay, Clonea strand,

Guillemots on the breeding ledges at Helvick Head

Ballyvoyle, Bunmahon, Tramore and Dunmore East. There is some passage off Brownstown Head (four were seen there in May 1988) and Helvick Head (six were sighted from there in September 1979).

Auks

The auks are almost exclusively maritime birds and they only come ashore to breed. They are hardy birds and can survive severe weather conditions at any time of year in the offshore coastal zone. They have small, pointed wings which, with rapid wing beats, results in fast aerial flight. The wings are also used to propel the birds along underwater when in search of fish. In winter they forage far from land but, occasionally, birds are driven inshore by stormy conditions. They are also susceptible to drowning in synthetic nets and to oiling, and following oil pollution incidents offshore they are occasionally washed up on the beaches of the county. Other beached birds may have succumbed to bad weather offshore, starvation or entanglement in various plastic materials.

Razorbills and **guillemots** are colonial breeders, and both species nest along the Waterford coast at Ardnamult, Beenlea Head, Island, Helvick Head and Ram/Ardmore Head. Tightly packed groups of guillemots lay their single eggs precariously on narrow cliff ledges but razorbills tend to do so in crevices or behind boulders in less exposed situations and in less numbers. Although the young are not capable of flight until six or seven weeks old they leave the nest after about 20 days and swim far out to sea where they are cared for by the parent birds. Guillemots and razorbills are similar in appearance but they usually occur together on breeding cliffs allowing the obvious differences between them to be seen.

There is a good sea passage of both species off the headlands throughout the year; otherwise an odd bird or two may be seen inshore in winter and occasionally large flocks occur off the coast. For example, in November 2005, 2,700 auks passed per hour off Ballyvooney and, in February 2007, there were 'huge numbers' of razorbills (mainly) between Helvick Head and Ballynacourty. Both species nest in noisy and spectacular colonies on Great Saltee Island in Wexford, where they can be more easily seen and in much greater numbers. Keep an eye out too when walking on the coastal beaches for beached auks, some of whom might be ringed; one such guillemot found on the Cunnigar in July 2007 was ringed on Great Saltee in June 1993.

The **black guillemot** nests in holes and crevices in the cliffs and are almost impossible to reach, let alone find, at least in Waterford. They breed along the coast in small numbers at traditional sites, which tend to be occupied year after year, though no more than a few pairs may be seen at any particular site. In the breeding season, they can be difficult to locate and the best time to find them is early in the morning in early April (which is the recommended time to undertake a breeding census). They are a distinctive bird in the breeding season and are rarely confused with the other auks; the white upper wing patches on an otherwise black plumage (and the red bill, if close views are possible) are usually obvious as the bird bobs about on the sea. In winter they lose their black coats and are whitish-grey in that season, though usually no more than one or two birds are seen. They

Razorbill

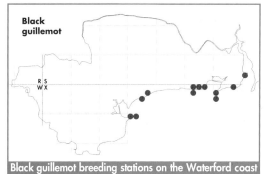

Black guillemot

R S
W X

Black guillemot breeding stations on the Waterford coast

may then be difficult to see in rough conditions among the waves, or on dull days, unless they are close inshore or are washed up exhausted after storms.

There are relatively few sightings of the **little auk** in Waterford (a few dozen since 1979), usually involving one or two individuals, and some of the records have been storm-bound birds, washed up on the coast either dead or exhausted from constant buffeting by strong winds offshore. The most recent record was of an adult bird in summer plumage off Helvick Head in April 2007.

The **puffin** is the most attractive and photogenic of the auks. It has a colourful beak and an unusual appearance and what a pity it is that the bird is rarely seen in Waterford, at least at a distance where good views are possible. They may have bred once in the county as R. J. Ussher, the noted Waterford ornithologist, was told by Patrick Roache of Bunmahon that puffins ('sea parrots') bred on the point at Kilfarrasy and by James Graves of Helvick in 1882 that an old man told him that he remembered sea parrots breeding at Helvick. In July 2010, several were off the cove at Helvick, and birds were seen flying down off the cliff slopes into the sea, suggesting that birds were at least prospecting at the Head. Around 1,000 pairs breed on the nearby Saltee Islands, which is the best place to get good views of them, especially in the breeding season when the bird

is at its best. They are regularly recorded on passage past the headlands, mainly Helvick Head and Brownstown Head, but they have also been seen off Ram Head, Mine Head and Ballyvooney, usually in ones or twos but up to 38 have been recorded at Helvick Head. In winter, the puffin loses all its colour, but there are few sightings in this season, suggesting that they overwinter far offshore, and well out of view.

The **great auk** is an extinct flightless bird whose remains were found in kitchen middens in the sand dunes at Tramore by Richard Ussher. In *The Birds of Ireland* he describes what he found:

among the sand-hills on Tramore Bay are extensive kitchen middens, containing layers of shells of oysters and cockles with limpets, mussels and other shells, charcoal, burned stones (split from use as pot boilers), and bones of domestic animals and fowls, with bones and horns of red deer. Among these objects, which were on the surface, my companions and I found in different places, seventeen bones of great auk, comprising eight coracoids, five humeri, one tibia, two metatarsels and one pelvic bone. In one case a right and left humerus were found together. The coracoids, according to Dr. Gadow, who kindly determined the remains, represent at least six individual birds.

The great auk may have been common in Waterford, and almost certainly bred here, but firm evidence is lacking. The last known bird in Ireland was captured alive close to the cliffs between Ballymacaw and Brownstown Head in the east of the county in May 1834 by a fisherman named Kirby on the instructions of David Hardy of Kilmacleague. It was then sold to

The last Irish great auk (preserved in the Zoological Museum, Department of Zoology, Trinity College Dublin)

Francis Davis of Waterford City who sent it to Jacob Goff in Horetown, county Wexford where it was kept alive for around four months. When it eventually died it was kindly presented to Trinity College Museum in Dublin by Dr. Robert Burkitt who lived in Lady Lane in Waterford City. He was subsequently presented with a 'great auk pension' of £50 as a token of gratitude by Trinity College. It was subject to necessary conservation treatment and repairs in August 2009 by the Museum (there are very few great auk exhibits left in the world, hence the importance of the Trinity bird).

Landbirds

Landbirds have a much greater choice of habitats in which to live and breed, and, while relatively few species live exclusively in coastal environments, many either pass through on their way elsewhere or they avail of feeding opportunities in the form of other birds, small mammals, invertebrates, fish and vegetable matter that is available to them near the coast. Moreover, some of those species that frequent the coastal habitats are bright, attractive and flighty so they add interest and variety to the cliff tops and the coast.

Pigeons are drab birds that occur all over Waterford, but one species in particular finds a niche in the coastal cliffs. **Rock doves** or their feral equivalents breed in crevices and holes, usually out of sight, but they are about the sea cliffs all year round. It is hard to know if there are any truly wild rock doves left in the county given the contamination of the wild strains by feral or domesticated birds. Regardless of this, the birds can live out their lives, rearing their one or two young twice or three times each breeding season, in the relative safety of the cliff ledges where they are safe from most predators, except perhaps the peregrine falcon, that can often be seen at the very same cliffs. Small flocks are occasionally seen in the fields above the cliffs where they may be confused with the

seed-eating **stock doves**, a bird that favours lowland woods and farmland and is relatively rare along the coast.

The **woodpigeon** is the largest of the pigeons, and is the more obvious and the best known pigeon species, given the characteristic display flight, the sonorous territorial song and the wide variety of habitats where it can be found, including cities, towns and villages. They breed almost throughout the year wherever there are trees or bushes so there are areas of the Waterford coast, including the wooded glens and valleys, where they lay their eggs (two usually) and rear their young. They are also regularly encountered in stubble fields adjoining the coast or on nearby farmland at any time of year.

The **collared dove** is a relative newcomer to Ireland (it probably bred for the first time in Waterford in 1963 or 1964 at Dunmore East and Dungarvan), and is arguably the most attractive member of the pigeon family. It favours urban areas and is thus more likely to be seen in the coastal towns and villages rather than the surrounding areas and it is generally rare around the cliffs.

The **turtle dove** is a passage migrant from Africa that arrives in small numbers on our shores in spring. Single birds usually occur but up to four have been recorded and they are seen almost annually at either Brownstown Head, Helvick Head, Mine Head or Ardmore in spring and autumn. The turtle dove breeds very occasionally in Ireland (one or two pairs at most in any one year) so it is likely that birds seen in Waterford either missed or are on their way to England, Wales and lately southeast Scotland where there is a thriving breeding population.

The **cuckoo** is a spring migrant from Africa and breeds here in small numbers, usually in upland areas. It has a very characteristic song, which it loudly issues on

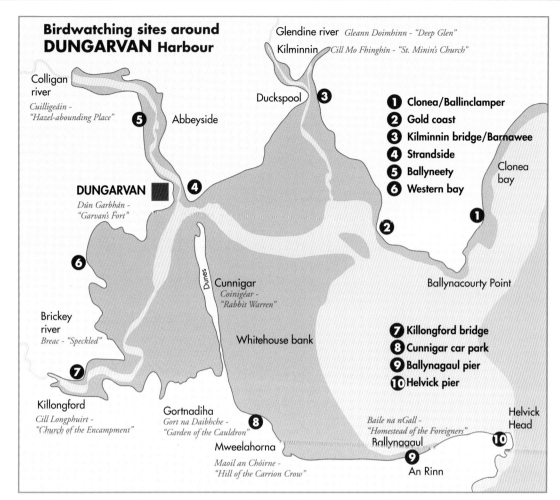

Birdwatching sites around DUNGARVAN Harbour

Glendine river *Gleann Doimhinn - "Deep Glen"*
Kilminnin *Cill Mo Fhinghín - "St. Minin's Church"*

Colligan river
Cuilligeáin - "Hazel-abounding Place" ⑤
Abbeyside

Duckspool ③

DUNGARVAN ■
Dún Garbhán - "Garvan's Fort" ④

① Clonea/Ballinclamper
② Gold coast
③ Kilminnin bridge/Barnawee
④ Strandside
⑤ Ballyneety
⑥ Western bay

Clonea bay

①
②

⑥

Dunes Cunnigar
Coinigéar - "Rabbit Warren"

Ballynacourty Point

Brickey river
Breac - "Speckled"

Whitehouse bank

⑦ Killongford bridge
⑧ Cunnigar car park
⑨ Ballynagaul pier
⑩ Helvick pier

⑦

Killongford
Cill Longphuirt - "Church of the Encampment"

Gortnadiha
Gort na Daibhche - "Garden of the Cauldron" ⑧

Baile na nGall - "Homestead of the Foreigners"
Ballynagaul

Helvick Head

⑩

Mweelahorna
Maoil an Chóirne - "Hill of the Carrion Crow"

⑨
An Rinn

---

arrival, and is very definitely a harbinger of spring. In flight it is reminiscent of a hunting sparrowhawk as it skims low and fast over the ground. While most records of the species in Waterford are from the inland breeding areas it has also been recorded at Helvick Head, Beenlea Head, Ballynacourty, Clonea strand, Ballyvoyle glen and Ballymacaw cove, where it is usually seen rather than heard, though occasionally a bird issues its characteristic and evocative call along the coast.

Owls are primarily nocturnal and are out and about in search of food when few people are around to see or hear them. They are under-recorded as a result so it is difficult to state with any certainty their precise status, and too many records relate to birds found dead on the roads. The two breeding species,

the **barn owl** and the **long-eared owl**, prey mostly on small mammals, though birds and even bats may also be taken. There are few records of either species along the coast, probably because so few people are about the coastal habitats where these owls are likely to be foraging in search of prey. In 2009 a barn owl was seen on two occasions in June at Tramore Backstrand, and another was seen in July at Great Newtown Head. The long-eared owl is a woodland specialist and it would be surprising if a pair or two wasn't present in the wooded valleys and glens along the coast; the species has also been recorded at Brownstown Head on a number of occasions.

The **short-eared owl** breeds very occasionally in Ireland but it is primarily a winter visitor, probably from Scotland and northern England, where several hundred pairs breed, mostly on heather moorland, and here the short-tailed vole (which is not found in Ireland) is the favoured prey. The short-eared owl is the more likely of any of the owls to be seen in daylight. It has been seen at Tramore (mainly in the dunes, but also on the beach and on the salt marsh), Brownstown Head, Clonea strand, the Cunnigar, Helvick Head and Ram Head. The **scops owl** has been recorded just once in the county, at Brownstown Head in April 1998, but unfortunately it was freshly dead, a presumed overshoot from southern Europe.

Swifts arrive in Ireland from late April on but it is in May that this fast-flying bird arrives in numbers. It nests in towns and cities in the eaves of buildings and churches and in whatever other suitable holes it can find. It is constantly in flight in the urban areas around the coast in summer but, as it feeds almost exclusively on the wing, it is very dependent on good weather to reproduce successfully. They can be heard screaming loudly as they zip through the air, particularly on warm evenings. They leave early and most have gone by August to their African wintering grounds. The **Alpine swift** has been recorded five times in the county but amazingly the third, fourth and fifth occurrences of the species were over Dungarvan town on more or less the same date in April 2005, 2006 and 2008, respectively. The **chimney swift** has been seen just once, again in Dungarvan, in November 2005.

The **kingfisher** is a dazzling blue bird and is arguably one of the more beautiful of our native birds. It requires still or slow-moving, clear and shallow water over which to fish and vertical mud banks in which to breed. It isn't common on the Waterford coast and is more likely to be seen along the rivers and streams discharging into the bays and coves. It is, however, regularly seen at Clohernagh inlet at Tramore, opposite the thatched pub where it is often perched in an overhead branch near the head of the inlet, waiting to pounce on any unwary fish that appears in the stream below. They have also been seen, especially in the winter months, at Ballyquin, the Cunnigar, on the Brickey river, opposite the Park Hotel in Dungarvan, at Bunmahon and on the Anne river at Annestown.

The **hoopoe** is a scarce but annual spring migrant in Ireland and the bird is regularly recorded in Waterford. It is a striking bird with a prominent crest, orange and white plumage and an undulating flight. Usually only one bird is seen but occasionally two are seen together. Most of the Waterford records are from the coast, and most recently at Whiting Bay (March 2009), near Clonea strand (April 2008), the Cunnigar,

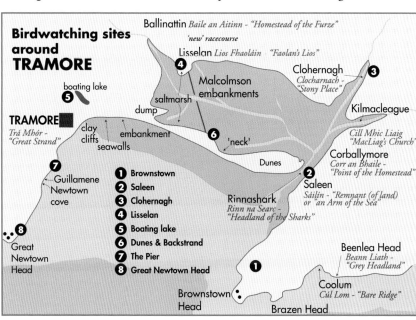

Birdwatching sites around TRAMORE

Ballinattin *Baile an Aitinn* - "Homestead of the Furze"

'new' racecourse

Lisselan *Lios Fhaoláin* "Faolan's Lios"

Clohernagh *Clocharnach* - "Stony Place"

Malcolmson embankments

boating lake

saltmarsh

dump

Kilmacleague

TRAMORE *Trá Mhór* - "Great Strand"

clay cliffs

embankment

seawalls

'neck'

Cill Mhic Liaig "MacLiag's Church"

Dunes

Corballymore *Corr an Bhaile* - "Point of the Homestead"

Guillamene Newtown cove

① Brownstown
② Saleen
③ Clohernagh
④ Lisselan
⑤ Boating lake
⑥ Dunes & Backstrand
⑦ The Pier
⑧ Great Newtown Head

Rinnashark *Rinn na Searc* - "Headland of the Sharks"

Saleen *Sáilín* - "Remnant (of land) or "an Arm of the Sea"

Great Newtown Head

Beenlea Head *Beann Liath* - "Grey Headland"

Brownstown Head

Coolum *Cúl Lom* - "Bare Ridge"

Brazen Head

Ballyvoyle, Dunmore East (2006) and Ballynagaul (April 2004). The hoopoe likes warmth and sun so they rarely hang around for long, though there is occasional breeding in the warmer parts of the south of England.

The **wryneck** is drab coloured but it can rotate its head in a most unusual snake-like manner, quite unlike any other bird. It is a rare bird in Waterford, and is a treat when it appears. Recent sightings are from Brownstown Head in September 2005 and October 2006, from Clonea in April 2007 and Whiting Bay in October 2010.

Sand martins arrive in March and April from their wintering grounds in Africa and they seek out elevated sand or mud banks where nesting holes can easily be formed, a habitat that is frequently found on the coast. However ongoing erosion and slumping of sandy cliffs from one year to the next both creates suitable nesting habitat and destroys it so some colonies are ephemeral, present one year and gone the next.

In recent years (2006-2010) sand martins were known to nest on the coast at Woodstown, Saleen, Kilfarrasy, Annestown, Bunmahon, Kilmurrin, Ballyvooney, Clonea strand, Ballyquin, Curragh beach and

House martins nesting on the RNLI building, Helvick

Whiting Bay. Occasionally the eroding dunes on the north side of the Tramore dunes has provided nesting opportunities (at least 6 pairs were present in 1996 and 1997 but birds were absent again in 1998). A handful of pairs dug holes in the cliff top turf at Newtown cove, south of Tramore, between 1999-2001, while in early May 2001 a few birds were prospecting north of the pier at Tramore, where subsidence had exposed vertical earthen banks near the cliff tops. The adults line the nest chamber they scrape out in the sand, which can be up to 120 centimetres deep, with feathers and plant material, where they lay up to seven eggs. They are normally double-brooded and the young fledge around 35 days after the first egg is laid, so that the adult birds can begin the breeding process again.

The real sign of spring is the arrival of the first **swallow** from South Africa, usually from late March onwards. The preferred breeding habitat is farm outhouses and old buildings anywhere, which includes the coast, where they can be watched flying in and out feeding young in mud nests up in the roof. Here they lay their clutches of up to eight eggs, which hatch two week later. Then the parent birds are kept busy feeding the young for the next three weeks or so. Swallows are double-brooded or even treble-brooded so when breeding is over quite large numbers of birds may be seen along the coast and elsewhere. They frequently gather in lines along overhead wires or on roof tops, perhaps waiting for conditions to improve before they undertake their long journey south. There are occasional winter records of single birds (in November and December mainly).

House martins breed in cliffs along the Waterford coast (they also nest under the eaves of buildings), and often colonially, where they are seldom seen. They have obvious white rumps, which helps to distinguish them from sand martins and swallows (the long tail streamers of swallows are distinctive too). They build mud nests, which are completely enclosed apart from a narrow opening near the top, where the female lays her eggs (up to six in number) from April on. She may re-lay two or even three times, with each attempt taking up to 43 or 44 days from laying to fledging. Luckily the young of earlier broods may hang around and care for later broods. Most house martins leave in September but occasionally birds linger into October.

The most common landbird in the dune areas of the county is the **skylark** where it delivers its distinctive song with gusto, which is usually delivered in flight as it ascends high overhead. It also occurs on farmland and on the cliff top turf. Nests are usually in dense marram or other ground vegetation but they can be surprisingly difficult to locate. Although the birds themselves are very conspicuous when their display flight takes them high into the air, the area below does not necessarily contain the nest. Once on the ground, skylarks are very inconspicuous and wary of observers nearby. The three or four eggs take 10 or 12 days to hatch and the young leave the nest after another nine or 10 days. It is at this time that the adults are most conspicuous as they forage incessantly, returning with beaks full of insects for the ravenous young. Once the breeding season is over, the birds are less active and are likely to be more dispersed anywhere along the coast and the surrounding farmland, where flocks of up to 500, or even more, are possible. Similar sized flocks have occasionally been recorded in autumn at Brownstown Head.

Another bird that is relatively common along the coast is the **meadow pipit**, especially in the dune and rough grassland areas, and, although not quite as demonstrative as the skylark, it is equally at home in coastal vegetation. It lays four to six eggs in tussocks on the ground and these are

Rock pipit

also hard to find. The young hatch within two weeks and are out of the nest a fortnight later. The young of the year swell the autumn flocks gathering anywhere along the coast or inland and several hundred have been recorded at Brownstown Head, though numbers elsewhere may not always be this large. Smaller numbers gather for the feast of insects feeding on the decaying seaweed along the beaches but birds are likely to appear anywhere from autumn onwards as upland birds move to the lowlands for the winter.

The **rock pipit** may be found on rocky headlands and at the base of cliffs. It is more solitary than either skylark or meadow pipit, and, unlike either of these two species, it is exclusively coastal. The bird can be seen on the beaches in the autumn chasing flies over rotting seaweed, when numbers are swelled by young of the year. At other times they are less visible as they prefer the rockier parts of the coast. Nests are usually inaccessible as they are constructed in holes and crevices in

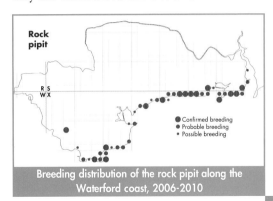

Rock pipit

R S
W X

● Confirmed breeding
● Probable breeding
• Possible breeding

Breeding distribution of the rock pipit along the Waterford coast, 2006-2010

Pied wagtail

the cliffs or depressions in the ground under vegetation. They are normally double-brooded, and the four to six fledglings leave the nest after around two weeks or so, though it may be another month before they are fully independent of their parents. The bird showing characters of **Scandinavian rock pipit** (*littoralis* sub-species) has been seen on a number of occasions since 2006, at Annestown, Clonea strand, Goat Island and Whiting Bay, and was, apparently, paired with a rock pipit on one occasion and presumed to be breeding.

Rarer pipits seen along the coast include **Richard's pipit**, seen for the first time in the county at Whiting Bay in October 1983, a **tawny pipit** at Brownstown Head in April 2008 (an indeterminate Richard's or tawny was there in October 2008) and **tree pipit**, seen on a number of occasions at Brownstown Head and also at Helvick Head and the Cunnigar. A North American **buff-bellied pipit** was seen for the first time in Waterford at Ballinclamper (Clonea strand) in October 2010 and remained there for a number of weeks. Rather surprisingly, another different bird, and the second county record of the species, was found on the 12th November 2010, also at Ballinclamper.

The **pied wagtail** is a familiar bird of villages, towns and cities and it breeds in close proximity to man, feeding on the masses of flies that occur in summer. It also occurs along the coast, where it may be particularly noticeable in the autumn on the beaches among the rotting seaweed; flies are the main attraction for them at this time. The less common **grey wagtail** is more frequent around streams or rivers entering the coves and beaches, so places like Ballymacart, Ballyvoyle and Stradbally are likely haunts for this attractive species. It breeds in hollows in river banks or cliffs, and occasionally high in the roots of a streamside tree. **White wagtails** are now regularly recorded as passage migrants at Clonea and Whiting Bay, and up to 60 have been counted. The **yellow wagtail** doesn't breed in Ireland but it has been seen occasionally in Waterford at Helvick Head, Ballynacourty and Brownstown Head. The **citrine wagtail** has been seen just once in the county, in a flooded field near Abbeyside Prom, Dungarvan in September 2009.

The **dipper** is a riparian species, found almost exclusively along rivers, so, as with the grey wagtail, wherever streams discharge on the coast there is a good likelihood that dippers may be seen. Stradbally cove is probably the best place on the coast where dippers are regularly seen (around the bridge) but they also occur at Ballyvoyle (check upstream of the bridge here), Ballyvooney, Ballymacart and Ardmore. It is always worth checking rocks and boulders midstream where the presence of bird droppings are usually an indication that either dipper or grey wagtail are present. If a stream is checked often enough, the quick flash of this largely brown bird with the white throat may be seen as it flies strongly upstream. From a distance they are a delight to watch as they disappear underwater in search of food only to reappear suddenly on a favourite boulder with their waterproof plumage instantly drying out, as they bob up and down, watching for the next food item. They may raise two or three broods in the breeding season but the nests can be difficult to find.

Farmland and scrub along the coast is host to many of the more common passerines and many of these may be seen on the cliff top vegetation or on heathy headlands. **Wrens**, **dunnocks**, **robins, song thrushes**, **mistle thrushes**, **chaffinches** and **blackbirds** are common everywhere, and of these the diminutive wren is probably the most common around the cliffs. The shy and retiring dunnock, common though it is, is seldom seen, as it lurks in coastal hedges and scrub. Also to be seen in the wooded glens and valleys of the coast are **greenfinches**, the three tit species (**blue, great** and **coal**), **blackcaps, goldfinches** and, more rarely, **long-tailed tits** and **goldcrests** in the shrubs, bushes and trees around towns and villages. The winter thrushes, **redwing** and **fieldfare**, can occur in large numbers on farmland long the coast if weather conditions are severe elsewhere (a mixed flock of up to 400 birds came in off the sea at Whiting Bay in early November 2010), while breeding birds of such habitats include **bullfinch**, **linnet**, and **yellowhammer** who are also resident there at other times of the year.

Summer visitors that breed in farmland ditches and scrub, are **sedge warblers**, **grasshopper warblers**, **whitethroats** and **willow warblers** with **chiffchaffs** in taller trees. The whitethroat in particular seems to be at home along the coast, and wherever there is scrub they are sure to be seen or more likely heard (they issue a brisk and lively warble which is unmistakable once known). The constant rattle of sedge warblers, chiffchaffs and willow warblers as they sing from bushes and coastal vegetation is a pure delight in spring and is always something to look forward to after long winters, when these appealing species are elsewhere. Chiffchaffs are occasionally seen in the county in winter, usually at coastal locations.

The **reed warbler** is a relatively new breeding bird in the county (breeding was confirmed at Belle Lake in 2000) though there were a long series of records of the species up to that (and since), many of which were juveniles or first-year birds, at Brownstown Head in the early autumn with one or two at Helvick Head. It has also been seen or heard recently at Caliso Bay and the reedbeds at Woodstown.

Treecreepers are found wherever there are trees, and while they are unlikely to be seen too close to the coast, they have been noticed at Corballymore wood and Cove cross (both near Tramore) and very rarely at Brownstown.

The **spotted flycatcher** is a relatively drab dull brown bird, that arrives on our shores from Africa. It may be more of a woodland bird but it is seen in some numbers on the coast, especially at Helvick Head, when it arrives from late April onwards. **The red-breasted flycatcher**, which doesn't breed in the county, was first seen at Helvick Head in October 1996 and again at Brownstown Head in October 2005. The **pied flycatcher** is a more regular migrant and has been seen at Ardmore Head, Crobally Lower, near Mine Head, Helvick, Knockanpower, Ballynacourty, Brownstown and Ballymacaw. It doesn't breed either in the county though it has bred in county Wicklow.

Tree sparrows are declining nationally but there are regular records in Waterford; 10 were seen at Brownstown Head in September 1990 and it has been seen there many times

Chiffchaff

since; breeding was confirmed there in 2008 and 2010. They have also been seen near Corballybeg (near Ballymacaw), Rathmoylan, Mine Head, Ardoginna, Ardmore Head, Whiting Bay (Ballysallagh) and Goat Island. At the Ballysallagh site over 20 birds are counted on occasions. **House sparrows** occur in the towns and villages but they may also be seen close to coastal dwellings, where they breed in roofs and under gutters.

Starlings are widely distributed in Waterford and they occur along the coast, in the fields and nearby homesteads but the **rose-coloured starling** has been seen just once in the county, at Brownstown Head, in October 2006.

Reed buntings are often seen in scrub around the headlands and even in privet bushes in the dunes where they probably breed. Sadly **corn buntings** are no longer found in Waterford.

Redstarts and **black redstarts** are passage migrants that are occasionally seen in autumn though the black redstart is also a winter visitor likely to be seen from September through to May and it is also more common in the county than the redstart. Sites with black redstart records include Ferry Point, Whiting Bay, Ardmore, Ballymacart, Helvick Head, Ballynagaul, Dungarvan, Clonea, Ballyvooney, Ballydowane, Kilmurrin cove, Tramore (pier, boating lake and beach), Brownstown Head and Dunmore East.

Stonechats are probably the most conspicuous of the coastal landbirds, though they can be found in all habitats in Waterford. They are very approachable birds that are most often seen on cliff top gorse, which is probably their favourite breeding habitat. The male is especially obvious as he perches on the highest branches and calls in alarm ('whit whit whit'). They are delightful birds, especially in the breeding season, and

the more brightly coloured male is especially attractive with its black head and white collar; both birds nervously flick both wings and tail if a human observer is nearby.

Eggs are laid in nests that are constructed deep in gorse or other vegetation on the cliff tops or in dunes. Once incubating (for around two weeks), the birds are less conspicuous but when the young fledge, the entire family will perch high and remonstrate at the intruder. But the parent birds usually breed again and even perhaps for a third time in good summers so by early autumn there may be many stonechats around the coastal vegetation. In winter stonechats are much less conspicuous, but they are very susceptible to cold winters. Numbers were increasing in Waterford in recent years, but the unusually cold winters in 2008/09 and especially 2009/10 and December 2010 probably exacted a heavy toll on the population.

Not too unlike the stonechat is the **whinchat** which is much rarer and doesn't breed in Waterford (around 2,000 pairs breed elsewhere in Ireland); it is seen mainly in the autumn (though there is one November record) at Helvick Head and Brownstown Head but it has also been seen at Caliso Bay, Whiting Bay, Ardmore, Clonea, Ballyvooney and Bunmahon.

Wheatears are migrant birds from Africa that come to Ireland to breed and they do so largely in upland areas like the Comeraghs and Knockmealdowns with a lesser number breeding on the coast. They arrive in small numbers in March but most appear in April and they may linger around the dunes and cliff tops before moving inland, with some remaining to breed along the coast. The male is a handsome bird and the black wings, black eye stripe and the white rump are distinctive; they also perch quite prominently and even inquisitively as they are approached only to fly off to the next perch. Numbers increase considerably in late summer and several may be seen together on the shingle, the beaches and the cliff tops.

Rarer birds which have been seen recently but infrequently along the coast include a **bluethroat** first seen at Brownstown in October 2006 followed by another at Saleen (Tramore) in April 2008, a **golden oriole** (including Dunmore East in May 1994, Brownstown in April 2005 and May 2010 and near Whiting Bay in May 2005), a **red-backed shrike** (Brownstown Head in October 1993–the first county record and Clonea in October 2004), **woodchat shrike** (near Tramore in June 1974, Clonea in March 1990, Brownstown in May 1993 and, in 2009, near Ballydowane in April and Westtown in July) while the **lesser grey shrike** has been seen just once, in Dungarvan in September 1991 (the third Irish record).

Corvids or crows are a widely distributed group of birds, highly successful and very adaptable. Six species occur along the Waterford coast, of which the **chough** is the most coastal. Choughs have distinctive red legs and bills, and their flight posture and habit is also characteristic. They are perhaps the most graceful of the corvids and the western European stronghold of the species is here in Ireland, and we therefore have a special responsibility to ensure that the specialised habitat it frequents (e.g. the coastal fringe), and the species itself, is maintained. It probes short vegetation and dung in the fields beside the coast and forages among rotting seaweed on the beaches for invertebrates and in stubble for spilt grain.

The bird nests in crevices in sea cliffs and dark caves along the Waterford coast, and the three or four pale-green, blotched-brown eggs are laid in April-May, which it incubates for 17-23 days. The young are helpless and downy on hatching and they fledge after around 38 days. Choughs are highly social

Choughs near *Faill an Staicín*, Helvick Head

birds and, although usually only pairs of birds are encountered, especially in the breeding season, flocks of up to 100 birds (occasionally even more) are possible, especially post breeding when adult birds, their young and non-breeders gather around communal roost sites, which generally offer shelter from adverse conditions, freedom from predation and disturbance, and access to good foraging habitat nearby. Recent surveys in Waterford found 191 birds in 1992 and 161 birds in 2002/03 (a 16% decline).

The biggest corvid to be seen in Waterford is the **raven,** which breeds in the coastal cliffs of the county. It is completely black, with a big head and a big, deep bill and is quite distinctive in flight with an equally distinctive call, a gruff 'kronk'. It is a highly territorial bird when breeding and it performs spectacular acrobatic displays, especially when courting in spring. It croaks loudly and when disturbed at the nest it becomes quite alarmed, calls incessantly and is very aggressive, at least towards any vegetation on which it lands, pulling out lumps repeatedly. It is an early breeder and is often sitting on up to six eggs in February, and the young are on the wing from May onwards, having being in the nest for five or

Hooded crow foraging on the shoreline

beaches throughout the year where it is a scavenger on beached birds, debris and any decaying matter it can find.

The other crow which breeds on the coastal cliffs is the **jackdaw**. It is the typical crow, all black and it is also the smallest species to be seen. They are a common bird in Waterford and can be a nuisance around cities, towns and villages as pairs breed in unprotected chimney pots of occupied houses, where vast accumulations of debris can collect down in the chimneys over time (and which is very difficult to remove if left for too long). They also build their nests in crevices and cracks in the cliffs, where their five or six eggs are carefully incubated for around 18 days. They are noisy birds when breeding, which usually identifies where their nests are located, but the nests themselves are normally well hidden and where the young are usually safe from predation for the month or so when they are in the nest.

six weeks, following hatching of the eggs after three weeks of incubation. The fledged young stay with the parent birds around the nest site for some weeks after leaving the nest. The young of the year and other non-breeding birds come together to form flocks during the late summer, but such congregations are more common in the Comeragh Mountains, where the bird also breeds in the coums.

The **hooded crow** is possibly the least appealing of the corvids, but it is easily distinguished from the other species by its distinctive black and grey plumage. It is widely distributed in Waterford and breeds in trees usually, though on the coast it builds its wool-lined stick nest on cliff ledges where it incubates its clutch of up to six eggs for almost three weeks. The adult birds are then busy feeding the young for another four weeks or so before they fledge; It is a much maligned bird and is generally not liked, largely because it is a predator of the nests of other birds and it will also attack disabled animals, especially sheep. It forages around farmland, dunes and cliff tops but it is a wary bird and keeps well clear of people, and for good reason, as it is widely persecuted, poisoned and shot. Small flocks of birds can also be seen on the coastal mudflats and

The other corvids don't actually breed on the cliffs but they may do so in the adjoining farmland and they may be found foraging along the coast at all times of the year. **Rooks** are noisy birds that nest colonially in the tree tops throughout the county, most prominently in shelter belts around farmhouses, and their raucous cawing resonates around the countryside from spring onwards and especially when the young (up to five) are present. Rookeries are busy places with birds constantly squabbling as they interact high in the treetops. There are rookeries close to many of the coastal areas of the county and birds from these rookeries regularly pass over the cliff tops, the beaches, the wetland areas and the salt marshes as they move between feeding areas and their nests. **Magpies** are also well known, extrovert and noisy. Their preferred habitat is farmland with a good supply of trees in which they can safely build their large stick nests, and so they are likely on the coast anywhere there are trees. While they are rarely encountered on the beaches, they are regularly seen near the cliff tops. The least likely corvid to be seen on the coast is the **jay**. They are largely woodland birds that are shy and wary and are often heard before they are seen. They have been recorded at Cheekpoint, Woodstown and in wooded areas on the lower Blackwater and once at Brownstown.

The **snow bunting** is a rare winter visitor, and has been seen on several occasions around Tramore Backstrand, and other records include at the Cunnigar in November 2006, at Bunmahon in November 2005, at Whiting Bay in February 2005 and at Helvick Head in October 2004. The **lapland bunting** was first seen in the county at Dunmore East in December 1975 and was seen again there in October 1993 (5 birds) and December 1993 (up to six birds), at Brownstown Head in September 1998 (one bird) and most recently at Brownstown Head in September and November 2010 and Clonea in October 2010. **Waxwings** are also rare winter visitors and occasional irruptions occur, which is related to weather conditions elsewhere; several birds may then arrive in the county and these are frequently seen in gardens. One was seen at Tramore in March 2009 (previously around 30 birds were there in February 1996) and one was at Abbeyside and Ballynacourty in Dungarvan in December 2010 (four were there at Abbeyside in December 2004). **Bramblings** are rare along the coast but flocks of up to 40 birds have been seen at Tramore with others at Ballymacaw, Brownstown Head, Stradbally and Dungarvan (Abbeyside, Barnawee, Clonea and Ballyneety).

The two main coastal headlands, Brownstown Head and Helvick Head, have received excellent coverage over many years, but particularly since the mid-1970s, and many interesting and rare birds have been seen. These include **blackpoll warbler**, **icterine warbler**, **melodious warbler**, **barred warbler**, **lesser whitethroat, garden warbler**, **greenish warbler**, **yellow-browed warbler**, **western Bonelli's warbler**, **common rosefinch**, **yellow warbler**, **Pallas's warbler**, **subalpine warbler**, **wood warbler**, **Radde's warbler**, **firecrest**, **northern parula**, **hawfinch**, **red-eyed vireo** and, in 2010, an **Iberian chiffchaff**, which will be a first for Ireland if confirmed. Large numbers of more common species and birds such as **lesser redpoll**, **crossbills** and **siskins**, that are less frequently recorded elsewhere on the coast, have also been noted. Both headlands have been very productive during seawatches and significant movements of seabirds offshore in either direction has been observed, especially in spring and autumn. Other areas like the Cunnigar have also been fruitful and the first Waterford record of a **booted warbler** was seen here in August 2006.

Land mammals

The Waterford coast is exposed, open and, for the most part, lacks cover where animals, especially the larger ones, can hide. Moreover, many of the coastal cliffs are sheer and dangerous and are avoided by most mammals. Consequently the mammal fauna of the coast is somewhat restricted in terms of species richness and numbers. Mammals are infrequently seen on the beaches, even by regular visitors, and animal tracks and signs may have to be relied on to establish occupancy by a particular species, though occasionally a live animal may be seen or a carcass found. However, the surrounding farmland beside the cliff tops offers better opportunities for mammals, and close to freshwater, though sightings of them are also likely to be fleeting and infrequent. The dune areas too are inhospitable places and conditions there are often harsh: limited food availability and little or no freshwater; limited cover in which to avoid detection by predators; and searing heat at times in summer. Mammals on the coast are more

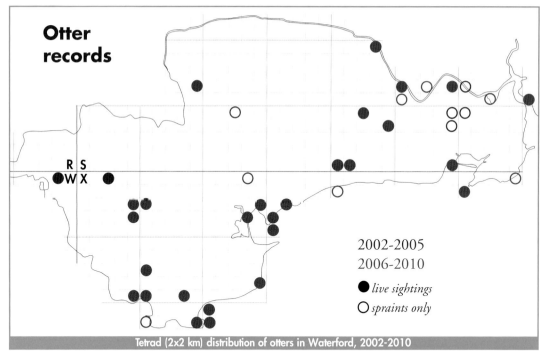

Otter records

2002-2005
2006-2010

● *live sightings*
○ *spraints only*

Tetrad (2x2 km) distribution of otters in Waterford, 2002-2010

likely to be active at night, when there are few people around to see them.

The **otter** is the only land mammal that forages in the sea along the Waterford coast and it also occurs along rocky shorelines and in the intertidal zone where shore crabs are likely to be looked for. However, the otter is often nocturnal and is only rarely seen by day anywhere. It has been recorded on the coast at Rincrew on the Blackwater (and at several inland locations along this river), East Point, Ardmore (and once about one kilometre from the shore), Ram Head, Mine Head, Ballinamona, on the Cunnigar (out at the tip), in Dungarvan (Abbeyside, Barnawee Bridge, Davitt's quay, Ballinard and Ballynacourty), Ballyvoyle, Ballydowane, Tramore boating lake, Saleen, Brownstown Head, Dunmore East and Passage East. Some of these records relate not to seeing otters themselves but rather signs of them. Otters regularly deposit their droppings, better known as spraints, on prominent features such as mid-stream rocks or tideline boulders. Spraints have a distinctive shape and smell and usually contain fish fragments, so they are a useful indication of the presence of this beautiful animal, that otherwise is largely unseen. However, the wave-washed coast isn't the best habitat to search for spraints as the diurnal coming and going of the sea usually washes away this valuable evidence.

The otter is a large land mammal and males may weigh up to 16 kilogrammes (females up to nine kilogrammes). They are sleek and muscular with a long, distinctive tail and they are ideally shaped and adapted to the watery environment in which they forage and feed. Breeding takes place in spring and summer and adult pairs are most likely to be seen together around this time. The young, numbering from two to five, are born after around 60 days but they may not leave the dens until around eight weeks old and they may not swim for another three or four weeks. It may be from six to 12 months later before the young otters finally leave the mother. Groups of otters seen together are more likely to be the female and her cubs, as otters are normally solitary animals. Otters need to maintain their fur in good condition to preserve its waterproofing and insulating properties, so access to fresh water is vital, and it is likely that otters move from the sea into the many watercourses on the coast, where they, or signs of them, are also likely to be found. All the indications are that otters occur all along the Waterford coast.

The **mink** is a voracious non-native species that has had a significant impact on wild bird populations, particularly ground nesting species, since its escape from mink farms in the 1950s. They are semi-aquatic and are good swimmers, though they are more abundant inland along waterways where the thick vegetation offers better cover than is available on the coast.

Brown rats are occasionally seen in the dune areas, where they live off seeds, invertebrates, birds and their eggs and they are always present around coastal towns, villages and farms and formerly at the county dumps, where food was plentiful. They also occur sparingly on the shore where they forage along tideline litter. Rats are not liked or encouraged, largely because of their contamination of foodstuffs and living areas by droppings and because they are considered a vector of some human diseases such as Weil's disease. They are a significant threat to nesting seabirds and they do untold damage at accessible colonies, where they destroy eggs and kill nestlings. At the Dunmore East kittiwake colonies they have wreaked havoc on occasions, though with active management and less waste lying around, they are less of a threat now than previously.

The **pygmy shrew** weighs no more than three to six grammes and is very definitely the smallest land mammal in the country. It is almost impossible to spot or to find in tall grass and even the signs they leave are so small as to be almost invisible. They issue high-pitched noises which are often just outside the auditory range of adult humans (though children may hear them) and so are difficult to monitor. The pygmy shrew was the only shrew species we had in Ireland until the **white-toothed shrew** was found in Tipperary in 2007. It may be some time before this addition to the mammal fauna of Ireland reaches the coast so the diminutive pygmy shrew is the only likely species.

Pygmy shrews are present all along the coast (near the beach at Bunmahon, for example) and in the dune areas (in the sandhills at Tramore, for example) but without an active trapping programme, they are hard to confirm in an area unless one is found dead. But they are forever active among the tall vegetation, feeding almost incessantly, and usually unseen, on beetles, flies, spiders, woodlice and any other insects that they encounter. They are a short-lived species and are usually lucky to survive for a year. Mortality is highest in the early months and they are preyed on by foxes, kestrels and owls. Short-eared owls are occasionally recorded in coastal dunes in Waterford, and they probably take a share of them.

Badgers are powerfully built animals that spend much of their lives in underground setts where an extensive network of interconnected tunnels and chambers is excavated. In constructing these underground setts, badgers leave signs such as a large mound of earth, entrance holes and a well-defined system of paths and these are usually obvious at active sets. These are the signs to look for since badger activity is primarily nocturnal and they are rarely seen, especially along the coast, where night visitors are few and far between. Badgers are found sparingly on cliff top turf and dunes along the Waterford coast. However, life on the coast is not easy for badgers despite the relative lack of disturbance and the non-availability of cover. Food may be a limiting factor as badgers are essentially foragers who feed on a variety of animal and plant food, and they vary their intake depending on time of year and location. Earthworms are the favoured food around farms and on the fringes of woodland, and these earthworms are absent in dunes and in short supply along the cliff tops, so on the coast they are likely to feed on insects, beetles, snails, slugs, small mammals, berries and fungi in season, birds and even carrion. Sand is a very friable substrate, and although easy to dig and excavate, it is also very prone to collapse and this factor further limits opportunities for living in sand dunes by an animal like the badger so dependent on underground structures. Coastal cliffs tops too are hard, stony and difficult to work so not all coastal areas are suitable for this highly social animal. Badgers are more widespread inland on farmland and around woods, though here too the animals, as on the coast, may remain elusive.

Foxes are primarily nocturnal though they can be seen about in the late evening or early morning, especially in summer, if the female fox, the vixen, is feeding cubs. They are resourceful, versatile and adaptable animals and are present in all habitats throughout the country. They are found all along the Waterford coast and are likely to be seen anywhere, including the cliff tops, the dunes and the adjacent farmland. However, foxes are wary animals, and tend to avoid humans, but on the coast where there is little cover, they may be seen scurrying across the fields after they have spotted the human intruder, but they usually stop after a while so this is a

good time to obtain good views of them. Signs of them are usually everywhere along the coast and feathers cropped close to the base–so characteristic of fox–are most common. Occupied dens are usually untidy, especially when the four or five cubs are present in summer; they are less careful than the vixen and outside of the den is usually littered with food remains. Foxes also leave a distinctive smell which is another indication of recent presence in an area.

Foxes have been seen in the coastal dunes, and, besides rabbits, which aren't present in the Tramore dunes, they are likely to take whatever is available, from snails and slugs early in the year to dewberries and blackberries in the autumn, and birds throughout the year, if they can catch them. Injured birds or those suffering from disease (usually gulls) are common and are readily available along the coast. Tideline litter in the form of bird and animal corpses are usually plentiful along the beaches and the small animal fauna of the coast will also be availed of, though rabbit is always likely to be the preferred prey for this wily predator.

The **Irish** (or **mountain**) **hare** is thinly distributed around the county and they are regularly seen on farmland adjoining the coast, and occasionally in the dune areas. The canter of a hare across the fields is very distinctive and they can move at speed when necessary. The female is slightly heavier than

Rabbits can be seen on the Cunnigar, where domestic animals also help to maintain an open sward

the male but they are otherwise difficult to tell apart. They are more noticeable in spring when involved in mating rituals, and sometimes more than one may be seen around the headlands or in the fields nearby. Breeding begins early in the year and boisterous gatherings may occur as males vie for females, and there is constant squabbling between the pair and the bevy of competing males and subordinate males also vying for the attention of the female. The young leverets, up to five in number, are born after around 50 days, though the female may be pregnant again with a second litter, which will be born after the first litter is weaned (after three weeks or so). However, mortality of the young hares is high, due in part to predation by foxes and even stoats. The oldest dated hare in Ireland, at around 28,000 years old, was found in the Shandon cave near Dungarvan, confirming that the hare is one of the longest-established animals in Ireland.

The **rabbit** is much smaller than the hare and is much more abundant along the coast, particularly in some areas where many may be seen running into ditches when walking across fields. In these densely populated areas they are subject to much predation, though without any real impact on their numbers, probably because of the prodigious rate of breeding that rabbits are capable of. They may breed throughout the year and the female is capable of producing up to seven litters a year (each with five or more young). Moreover, young born early in the year can breed themselves in the same year. However mortality is high and the rabbit is taken by foxes, mink, badgers and stoats, and disease takes a toll when numbers are high; many are also shot. Nationally rabbits were decimated by myxomatosis in the 1950s, which wiped out 99% of infected rabbits. It still occurs but its effects are lees pronounced because of increased resistance to the virus, though other diseases, such as rabbit viral haemorrhagic disease, may also have an impact.

Rabbits were almost certainly introduced to Ireland in the twelfth century by the Normans, as there is little evidence of their occurrence prior to that. Rabbit warrens were established, probably with the intention of providing a regular supply of rabbit meat and fur and they established quickest in loose sandy soil, hence the popularity of sand dunes as warrens. Warrens were also widespread in parts of Ireland in the seventeenth century and they are enshrined in two prominent placenames in Waterford, Tramore Burrow and the Cunnigar (the sand spit in Dungarvan Bay), names that can still be seen on modern Ordnance Survey maps. The Cunnigar or *Coinigéar*, according to Canon Power's *The Place-Names of Decies* means "Rabbit Warren" though it has also been suggested that it derives from *Coney Garth*, *Coinin/Coney* being the old French word for an adult rabbit and *Garth* meaning enclosure. The word rabbit also appears in other Waterford placenames, such as *Faill na gCoiníní* or "Rabbits' Cliff" near Ballymacart in west Waterford and *Cloch na gCoiníní* or "Rabbit's Rock" in Dungarvan.

Naughten, writing in 1901, stated that in Tramore:

the Rabbit Burrow consists of a cluster of sand hills and is thickly populated with rodents, whence it is named.

but Downey in 1919 was of the opinion that:

years ago the dunes were 'thick' with rabbits but bunny has vanished from his once favoured haunt.

Rabbit grazing can have a pronounced effect on dune systems, rendering them unstable and liable to serious erosion as small areas of bare ground around burrows are usually exploited by wind and may eventually lead to blowouts. They also feed on the shoots of some plants in winter, notably sand couch, which impairs the ability of this grass to initiate embryo dune growth. Thankfully, rabbits are no longer present in the Tramore dunes (though they may be seen near the dunes at Bass Point) but they do occur on the Cunnigar. A herd of cows are also present on the Cunnigar, but it is some time since farm animals grazed the Tramore dunes. Dunes tend to become rank over time and some controlled grazing is often desirable, but this is hard to achieve with rabbits who may completely undermine the habitat.

The **stoat** is a daring little animal with a long slender body, a distinctive black tip on its tail and a creamy throat and underside. They usually occur around stone walls and scrub-covered areas, and individuals are occasionally seen in the coastal dunes. They are probably more widespread in farmland and woodland areas near the coast. The stoat is a predator with a preference for young rabbits where they are plentiful, but it will also prey on rats, mice and even shrews and birds are also at risk from them, especially nestlings. They can also supplement their diet with invertebrates, berries and fish in rockpools. Males usually opt for rabbit while the female favours smaller prey items.

Stoats are normally solitary animals but breeding from May to July brings males in search of females and aggression between males can be pronounced when they meet. When the business of mating is over, the

Coastal stone ditches offer ideal habitat for stoats

female actively chases the larger male from her territory to maintain a monopoly on the available food supply. While pregnancy may last up to 10 months, the actual development of the foetuses usually only takes around 30 days following implantation of the slightly developed fertilised eggs (the blastocysts) in March of the year following mating. Up to 10 kits are born in late April/May and they are weaned 12 weeks later (and female kits are sometimes mated before they are weaned) but, as with all mammals, especially the smaller species, mortality is highest among juveniles. Although they aren't easy to observe, the stoat is a delightful animal, and sightings are worth cherishing.

House mouse and **wood mouse** are valuable food items themselves for stoats, foxes and birds of prey like the kestrel and the nocturnal barn owl. These are small mammals and are rarely seen out in the open so they are not found that often on the coast, but they occur around the coastal towns, villages and farms and adjoining areas. The **bank vole** hasn't yet been recorded from the Waterford coast but if it isn't already present there, it soon could be, as its distribution has increased considerably since it was first recorded in west Waterford in the early 1990s at Ballyduff, (it was first recorded in Ireland in Listowel, Kerry in 1964). It was recently found (2007) in barn owl pellets not far from Waterford City. The **hedgehog** is never common along the coast as it favours deciduous woodland or farmland close to woods, though it is common around coastal towns and villages and has been seen at Great Newtown Head, Brownstown and Bunmahon. However, it is largely nocturnal and is rarely seen alive; road casualties form the bulk of the sightings, which indicate that it is widely distributed in the county. **Feral goats** graze the cliffs above Passage East in Waterford Harbour, and small herds were known from Creadan Head and near Kilmurrin cove but these have not been seen recently. The **red squirrel** is a declining woodland species and isn't typical of coastal areas but it can be seen in the woods at Stradbally cove, for example.

The dense and highly characteristic flora of the coastal fringe, the cliffs and the dunes supports a huge moth population in summer, which in turn attracts feeding bats. However, given the difficulty of access to these habitats, the potential dangers involved in the night visits that are required, and the specialised equipment needed to confirm bat presence, there is little firm evidence and there are few published accounts of bats along the Waterford coast. However, using a basic Batbox, bats have been 'heard' (and often seen) at Saleen, the Tramore sandhills, the coastal strip between Helvick and Ballynagaul, between the pier and Saint Declan's Well at Ardmore, along the Cunnigar (near the car park and down along the dunes) and they have also been recorded at Ballymacaw and Brownstown Head. These were thought to be mainly **pipistrelles** (both **soprano** and **common**), and possibly **brown long-eared bats** and **Leisler's bats**. It is likely, therefore, that bats are present all along the coastal strip in Waterford.

Although roosting opportunities on the coast might appear to be limited, there are many dwellings (old and new) close to the coast where bats can roost by day, and there are innumerable crevices and cracks in the cliffs, though it isn't known if bats avail of these and whether the friable cliffs along many parts of the Waterford coast are suitable. Dusk on balmy clear nights is the best time to watch for them along the beaches as they hunt moths emerging from vegetation. Cheap and reliable bat detectors are widely available, which allows bats to be easily 'heard', and probably even seen, as they bounce ultrasound off passing moths.

The **viviparous lizard** is the only reptile to be found around the coast though records are very scarce; this is not surprising as they rapidly vanish into the undergrowth long before they are spotted. However, they have been seen at Ardmore, Muggort's Bay, Helvick, Bunmahon, Annestown, Tramore and Brownstown Head. They are also likely in the coastal dunes given that a ready supply of insects (grasshoppers and spiders mainly) and good ground cover is available and, just as importantly, surface temperatures in summer are favourable for a cold-blooded animal whose behaviour is very much dependent on keeping warm. They leave few tracks in the sand though occasionally feet impressions and body drag marks may be seen on the dune slopes.

Lizard, ©P. M. Walsh

Cetaceans

Whales, dolphins and porpoises (collectively known as cetaceans) are the mammals of the oceans, living well offshore and migrating large distances throughout the year. The seas around Ireland are important for these ocean travellers but they are a difficult group to study and much remains to be learned about their basic biology and movements. Importantly, there has been a huge increase in interest in, and records of, cetaceans off the Irish coast, including county Waterford. This is in part due to the web-based recording scheme maintained by the very active and progressive Irish Whale and Dolphin Group (or IWDG), which provides instant online updates of cetacean records as they occur around our coasts (all records are validated and available at www.iwdg.ie). There are now many more people with the necessary skills to identify whales offshore (these records are known as sightings) and occurrences are not just based on individuals that wash up dead, and sometimes alive, on shorelines (these records are referred to as strandings).

Whale-watching at Ram Head, August 2010

Many of the whales that wash up on our shorelines probably die from natural causes, though collisions with passing ships and entanglement in nets are contributory factors in some instances. The live strandings are more difficult to explain: perhaps one or more are injured, suffering from parasitic infection or are impaired by a heavy load of pollutants or biotoxins and the social cohesion between pods results in the mass strandings of all; or maybe the animals come too close inshore, possibly in pursuit of shoaling fish such as herring or mackerel and, with a falling tide, are then unable to return to the open ocean. There is no definitive answer as to why whales come ashore in mass strandings. However, one positive outcome of strandings is the opportunity it provides to sample tissues and assess the general condition of the dead whale, as a means of monitoring the state of the marine environment, the mammals that live there and their ultimate conservation.

The IWDG recommend Ardmore/Ram Head and Helvick Head for whale watching off the Waterford coast, and both localities, especially Ardmore/Ram have provided the bulk of the recent cetacean sightings, and especially between 2004 and 2010. Charter boats are also available, mainly out of Dunmore East, for whalewatching offshore.

Strandings of the **common** or **harbour porpoise** are reported more often than any

other species and it is also frequently seen off the coast. The earliest recorded stranding was at Dungarvan in November 1919 and there were 58 strandings in the period 1982-2010, though the species was seen regularly close inshore around Brownstown Head in the 1960s and early 1970s. The harbour porpoise has been found stranded at Caliso Bay, Whiting Bay, Goat Island, Ardmore, Ram Head, the Cunnigar, Clonea, Bunmahon, Annestown, Garrarus strand, Tramore and Dunmore East and the most recent stranding was at Ardmore in October 2010.

Between 2004 and 2010, there were 186 recorded sightings of up to seven harbour porpoises off the Waterford coast (including one sighting of two individuals in the river Suir), and the majority of these were seen from Ram Head during whale watches. The other sightings were from Mine Head, Helvick, Ballyvooney, Bunmahon, Tramore Bay, Brownstown, Waterford Harbour and offshore. The harbour porpoise is one of the smallest marine mammals to be seen off our coasts and because of their small size they may be hard to see in choppy waters offshore. It is likely that they are even more abundant and widespread than the records suggest.

Dolphins are relatively common around our coasts, especially along the western seaboard and they are well known; unlike the harbour porpoise they are not shy and are frequently seen close to boats. Dolphins occur in schools, which may be quite large (up to 200 have been seen together off the Waterford coast) and they are rarely seen alone. There were 206 sightings of **common dolphins** off the Waterford coast in the period 1997-2010, most of which were seen off Ram/Ardmore Head. They were also seen in the Suir, at Passage East, Waterford Harbour, Dunmore East, Brownstown Head, Annestown, Dunabrattin, Bunmahon, Dungarvan Harbour, Helvick Head, Mine Head and well off the coast.

Records of common dolphin strandings begin in 1938 (at Dungarvan), and thereafter in 1941 (Ballynagaul) and more recently at Tramore (December 1980, July 1981, February 2003, March 2004 and 2006), Dungarvan (November 1985 and 1988, April 2004, September 2010), Kinsalebeg (August 1990), Ram Head/Ardmore (January 1991, March 2003 and February 2007), Whiting Bay (February 1992 and 2001), Bunmahon (February 1998 and 2001, and March 2003), Ballydowane (February 1998) and Annestown (March 2007).

Dolphins breach frequently and common dolphins have a buff patch on either flank, between the head and the dorsal fin, which, if clearly seen, helps to distinguish this species from **bottlenose dolphin**, which is almost entirely dark grey (and it has a shorter beak than the common dolphin). This species was washed up at Ballyquin in August 1987 and at Tramore in November 1992 (alive but it then died), December 2003 and Ballynagaul in June 2004. It was also sighted 26 times between July 2002 and December 2010 off the coast, but there were relatively few sightings (three) at Ram Head confirming the relative rarity of this species off the coast, given the hours of whale watching which are enjoyed here by IWDG members. Away from Ram Head, schools of between one and 20 bottlenose dolphins were seen at Waterford Harbour, Dunmore East, Tramore Bay, Ballyvooney, Clonea, Dungarvan Harbour, Helvick Head and Mine Head.

The other dolphin species to be seen off the coast are much rarer. A decayed **Risso's dolphin** (measuring 3.15 metres) was found at the Backstrand in Tramore in December 1980 with further strandings at Ferry Point in May 1996 and Ballyquin in February 1997 and again in March 2005. There was a much earlier record of one in Dungarvan Harbour in April 1940. The species has been seen four times off Ram Head: October 2005 (three individuals); November 2007 (one); October 2008 (one) and September 2010 (two) and, additionally, two were seen off Mine Head in October 2010. A badly decomposed **Atlantic white-sided dolphin** was found washed up in Tramore and another was seen at Annestown, both in October 1990; more recently, one was found at Tramore in April 2010. A **striped dolphin** beached at Tramore in March 1991, another beached and was successfully refloated in late July 2001, and there were further records there in December 2005, September 2007 and July 2009. One was also freshly dead but partly bird-eaten at Whiting Bay in October 1990 and another was found at Bunmahon in March 2006 and November 2010. There is only one reported stranding of the **white-beaked dolphin**, in August 1931, when one was found in Dungarvan. There were no sightings of white-beaked, white-sided or striped dolphin off the Waterford coast up to the end of December 2010.

Whales are much bigger than either porpoises or dolphins and are easier to see offshore, though they can be difficult to handle when they are washed ashore, especially on beaches. Seven whale species have occurred along the Waterford coast.

The biggest, and the second largest animal on the planet, the **fin whale**, was sighted 136 times between November 2003 and

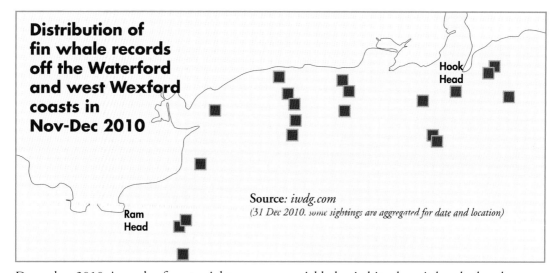

Distribution of fin whale records off the Waterford and west Wexford coasts in Nov-Dec 2010

Hook Head

Ram Head

Source: *iwdg.com*
(31 Dec 2010. some sightings are aggregated for date and location)

December 2010, in pods of up to eight individuals, mostly off Ram Head/Ardmore (61% of sightings) but also off Waterford Harbour, Dunmore East, Brownstown Head, Garrarus strand, Dunabrattin, Bunmahon, Clonea, Helvick Head, Mine Head and offshore. Interestingly, 29 of the 136 sightings were recorded in November and December 2010 all along the Waterford coast (and several more were off Hook Head). Up to six individuals were seen and even heard 'blowing' within 400 metres of the shoreline at Bunmahon, which is surprisingly close for such a large mammal (they can be up to 20 metres long). They were probably gathering to feast on the huge numbers of sprats and herring off the coast at the time.

There were five recorded fin whale strandings up to December 2010: one was washed up at the base of the cliffs at Knockmahon, near Bunmahon, in March 1983, one stranded at Paulsworth in March 1990 had probably been hit by a ship, and another washed up at Bass Point, Rinnashark on the 24th December 1997 was an impressive sight at 18 metres in length. The time of the year and the good weather ensured that this particular whale was seen by thousands of people, resulting in traffic jams around the narrow roads of Brownstown Head. Waterford County Council very

quickly buried it where it beached and, occasionally, its bones protrude from the sand here, following storms. The most recent strandings were at Ring in February 2001 and Whiting Bay in December 2001.

The **minke whale** at up to 10 metres in length is Ireland's smallest baleen whale and it has been stranded a number of times along the coast. The earliest known record is one in Dungarvan Harbour in October 1952. At Tramore one was washed up dead on the beach in July 1975, while one measuring 3.2 metres was seen in a mutilated condition at the Backstrand high up in Rinnashark channel in August 1979. An immature male beached at Woodstown in June 1976. The three strandings for the 1990s are: Caliso Bay (May 1990) and Whiting Bay (June 1990 and February 1995). At Coolum, east of Brownstown, one individual, thought to be this species, was found in October 2000. There have only been two strandings since: in December 2001 at Ballydowane and at Tramore in July 2010. The species was sighted 23 times between October 1992 and December 2010 off Ram Head and there were 19 other sightings at various locations along the Waterford coast (Waterford Harbour, Dunmore East, Tramore, Bunmahon, Ballyvoyle, Clonea, Helvick, Mine Head and offshore in the Celtic Sea).

Pilot whales are big and black, and five have been stranded on the Waterford coast up to the end of 2010: at Whiting Bay in March 1979; Ardmore Bay in October 1990; in Dungarvan Harbour in March 1994; in September 2009 in Tramore Bay; and most recently at Bunmahon in May 2010, when the skull only was found. The Whiting Bay individual was identified in 1983 from its skull found outside a house in Clashmore. The species has only been seen once off the Waterford coast, in September 2006, from the cliffs and beach at Rathmoylan, an unusual sighting so close inshore for this deep-water species.

There are no records of **humpback whale** strandings in Waterford though the species has been seen on 18 occasions, mostly involving one or two individuals, off Ram Head, Helvick Head, Mine Head, Tramore and offshore and most recently off Dunmore East in February 2010. There is only one record of **northern bottlenose whale**, a stranding, in Dungarvan way back in October 1938. The **killer whale** has stranded just once, when three individuals, (a male, a female and a young mammal) beached and died at Ballynagaul in July 1983. Two killer whales were seen off Helvick Head around the same time and two were off Brownstown Head in spring 1980. The rarest stranding in the county is the **pygmy sperm whale**, which washed up alive off the Cunnigar in December 2009 but later died. This is the first county record of the species and only the eight Irish record.

Turtles, seals & basking sharks
Turtles are reptiles and the **leathery** or **leatherback turtle** is the species most likely to be seen in Ireland, and accounts for around 80% of the turtle records. It is an open-ocean wanderer, and, unusually for a reptile, it can tolerate cold water, and even colder than that off the Irish coast in summer. It survives on a

Seal pup

diet of jellyfish mainly. There are 63 records of leather-back turtles off the Waterford coast, and all the sightings (e.g. live individuals offshore) involved animals that were heading west when seen. Nine of the 63 records were in the last 35 years or so, and all were of single individuals. One was caught in salmon nets near Woodstown in July 1976, another also became entangled in nets the following day near Ardmore, while one was taken near Ballydowane in September 1983. One found dead on Whiting Bay in August 1989 was around 2.13 metres (it was buried by Waterford County Council before it could be measured accurately), while in April 1997 at Ardmore, just the carapace was found on the beach. In the east of the county, at Clohernagh, one was washed up in September 2002, which was subsequently identified in October from photographs of the carapace. Other records since, all alive just offshore, include at Brownstown Head in July 2007, Ram Head in August 2007 and Ballyvooney in March 2008. There have only been three records of the **loggerhead turtle** off the Waterford coast, which is the second most recorded turtle in Irish waters.

Seals are regularly seen along the Waterford coast, and dead and even live animals (usually young or injured) are occasionally seen on the beaches. The majority of these are **grey seals** that sometimes breed in caves along the Waterford coast, though no direct evidence of breeding was recorded using ground surveys during the pupping season in October 2005. Sometimes they come in to the harbour at Dunmore East or Dungarvan. They have even ventured far up the river Suir beyond Waterford City, and there are records of them hauling out on the mud along the quay in Waterford; one was also captured in a canal beside the river Blackwater in January 1998.

The **common** or **harbour seal** is much rarer on the southeast Irish coast and there are few records for Waterford; it wasn't found at all during surveys in 1978 and 1993, though there are records for single individuals either seen just offshore (Ballynacourty pier in February 1985, Ballynacourty point in November 1986, Dungarvan quay and Ballyvooney cove in November 1993) or hauled out on rocks (Ballynacourty point in November 1993).

Basking sharks are recorded in the sea off the Waterford headlands from April through to November, though sightings are more likely between May and September. Water temperature influences the growth of their main food, plankton, and this seems to be critical to their appearance. There are sightings of individuals close inshore, probably because this is where the water is warmest. Although a shark, it is not an aggressive species and poses absolutely no threat to humans. As a filter feeder it lives off plankton, which it traps in comb like 'rakers' as it passes through the water column with its mouth wide open, allowing massive volumes of water to pass over its five gill-slits.

The basking shark is an impressive creature, and is the second largest fish in the world. It may reach a length of eight to 10 metres though most of those recorded are between four and six metres. When feeding on the surface, its large dorsal fin and tail fluke are immediately obvious in the water. In the eighteenth century, basking sharks were highly prized for their liver oil, which, in the absence of paraffin, was considered ideal for lighting lamps and the streets of Waterford were lit, apparently, by shark oil up until at least 1742.

There was an active fishery for basking shark off the Mayo coast from the early 1800s until 1880 but another fishery started on Achill Island, Mayo in 1947 and by the time it ceased in 1975, over 12,000 sharks had been captured and killed. The twin-lobe liver of the shark was the attraction as it makes up around one sixth of the total weight of the shark. Each liver could potentially realise 220 litres of oil or more, which, although it had no nutritive or medicinal value was used as an agent in manufacturing processes.

A fishery began on the southeast coast, mainly by Norwegian boats, around 1974. Three boats fishing out of Dunmore East that year caught 180 sharks and in 1975 four boats caught 350 between Mine Head and Castletownbere in Cork. Basking sharks were fished commercially off southeast Ireland up until 1986 when 2,465 sharks were killed, a decline from 4,442 in 1984. The species is no longer harvested but individuals continued to perish because of accidental entanglement in nets and some, washed up on the shore, probably also suffered the same fate. The cessation of coastal drift-netting for salmon off the Irish coast in 2006, has reduced, if not eliminated this cause of mortality (for example, between 1912 and 1915, around 10 became entangled in salmon nets at Ardmore and many more were seen offshore).

There were a number of sightings or strandings of basking sharks between 1980 and 1997, at Whiting Bay, Mine Head, Ardoginna Head, Ardmore and Coolum cove in east Waterford. Between March 2005 and June 2010, up to 35 at any one time were seen at various places along the coast, including Whiting Bay, Ram Head, Ardmore Bay, Ballymacart cove, Mine Head, Helvick Head, Dunabrattin and off Tramore. There were at least five sightings of 16 individuals off the Waterford coast in 2010.

Other fish

With a relatively long shoreline, several accessible beaches, a major Irish fishing harbour (Dunmore East) and several smaller

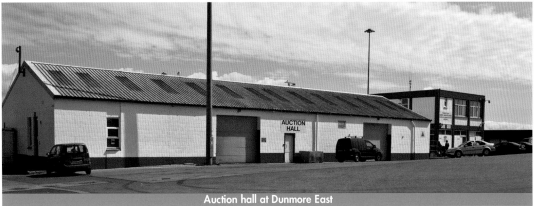

Auction hall at Dunmore East

harbours and piers, fishing (both recreational and commercial) is an important activity along the Waterford coast. The Gulf Stream off our coasts ensures relatively mild weather all year round and a diverse assemblage of marine species. Given our location in the far west of Europe, a large number of cold water species along with fish from sub-tropical areas occur off our coasts. Consequently fish of all shapes and sizes are landed on our shores, some incidentally while others are actively fished for commercially and by shore anglers.

Dungarvan was a once a thriving fishery port, and in the eighteenth century dried cod and hake were major export commodities from the town, though its large sailing fleet subsequently concentrated on coastal trade and to a lesser extent on summer hake and winter herring. The great Famine of 1845/46 caused considerable hardship in the region and many Dungarvan fishermen emigrated to America and never returned, leading to the decline of fishing in the town. On the west side of Dungarvan Bay, the construction in 1848 of the pier at Ballynagaul gave better protection to the many hookers and trammel boats that fished from there year round, and which supported a local curing industry. During the Famine, many fishermen sold or pawned their gear to buy food for themselves and their families, leading to some considerable destitution in Ring. However, a Quaker relief effort, spearheaded by the Reverend James Alcock, revitalised the

people, the area and the fishery. The opening in the early 1900s of a new pier at Helvick eventually allowed landing of fish at all stages of the tide (Ballynagaul was tide dependent). But changes in fishing methods (which many Dungarvan fishermen failed to embrace), the demise of the sailing boat and the political upheavals of the period resulted in a gradual decline in the fishery in west Waterford and many fishermen emigrated. Although a revival followed, the Second World War curtailed fishing activities, at least for a while. Helvick was an important fishery port in the 1950s and 1960s but declined thereafter. However, Dungarvan Bay is now important for shellfish, which are cultivated and harvested from Moat, on the west side of the Bay, and the long lines of trestles are visible from the surrounding countryside when the tide recedes off the Whitehouse Bank.

In the late nineteenth century, the herring spawning shoals moved eastwards from Mine Head along the Waterford coast leading to the development of Dunmore East as the major Irish herring fishing harbour to where boats from the east coast of Ireland and Great Britain gathered in winter. The early 1970s were particularly busy as boats fished out of Dunmore using paired mid-water trawls. The harbour was a hive of processing activities, with consequent benefits for the kittiwakes (and other seabirds) availing of the abundant fish offal available locally at a time of year when other food was scarce or only available far offshore. The first herring shoals usually appeared in mid-November on the spawning beds south of Hook Head, and the fleet followed the fish to Mine Head and beyond until the shoals disappeared in mid-February. In the 1970/71 season, just over 88,000 cran of herring were landed into Dunmore East, one of the best years for the fishery (one cran is around 169 litres or 37.5 gallons of fresh herring, which could contain from 700 to 2,500 herring, depending on size, and weigh around 178 kg or 28 stone).

Herring has always been an important commercial fish in the Celtic Sea off the Waterford coast. The herring catch from the Celtic Sea peaked at 44,000 tonnes in 1970. However, the stock collapsed in the late 1970s and the fishery was closed from 1977-82. Following the re-opening of the fishery in 1982, a quota (or Total Allowable Catch) of 20,000 tonnes per year applied. The market for herring changed considerably from providing salted fish for the European market, to one which became increasingly dependent on 'roe' herring for the Japanese market, which required mature fish about to spawn, and only the ovaries were processed. Consequently, the heavy exploitation of

mature fish on the spawning grounds could result in damage to the stock, and spawning ground closures were introduced on a rotational basis in 1988.

Hermaphrodite herring were caught at Dunmore East between 1989 and 1994. These are herring which have the reproductive organs of both male and female fish, which was established when the fish were processed for roe. It isn't known what causes the condition.

Mackerel are summer fish that arrive in large numbers off the Irish coast, though they were never exploited commercially off the Waterford coast to the same extent as the herring stock. Although frustratingly scarce at times, they are surprisingly easy to catch when the shoals come in close to shore in pursuit of sprats, usually in late July, August and September where anglers wait patiently for them, and the lines they cast from the rocks or harbour walls often return with all hooks festooned with fish. They are a fast growing fish and they may be up to 30 centimetres after three years but, once mature, growth usually slows; they are also a long-lived species, with some individuals reaching 15 years or even more. Mackerel harass and chase the sprats relentlessly and enclosed bays can literally fill up with both and what a sight it is to witness the dense shoals of sprats as they try to escape from the voracious predator. The shoals of mackerel themselves are prey for a host of other species, the most obvious of which are the gannets that spectacularly dive headlong from a height in an equally relentless pursuit of its energy-rich prey. They are also used as bait for catching other fish species.

Bass are voracious predatory fish that feed on a variety of other fish, sandeels, worms and crustaceans. In northern European waters they are slow-growing and, while individuals may reach eight kilogrammes, the average

Fishing for mackerel at Helvick pier, August

weight is usually around two kilogrammes. They mature when four to eight years old and they spawn from April to July, though May/June is probably the main spawning time. They favour strong currents for spawning which quickly carry the fertilised eggs and later the fry close to the shore. Young bass are invariably school fish, though they often become more solitary as they grow older. Bass were once abundant off the Waterford coast and large numbers were caught using nets and rods from the beaches and especially from and off the aptly named Bass Point at Rinneshark on the east side of Tramore Bay where boxes of bass were caught in nets shot among the breakers.

Over-exploitation severely depleted numbers locally and commercial fishing for bass is now banned, though illegal fishing still occurs occasionally. A ministerial bye-law has restricted angling for the species and a bag limit of two per angler per 24-hour period has been imposed, along with a size limit of 40 centimetres, in addition to a closed season from the 15th May to the 15th June. Shore fishing for bass is most rewarding from June to October, and in September–especially around the equinoctial tides–several anglers may line up along the beaches and out into the breakers. Night fishing is also rewarding and enjoyable, especially on balmy nights.

Mullet are very active fish who feed largely on marine plants, invertebrates and planktonic organisms. They congregate in shoals and are easily seen in inshore areas, especially at low tide, as they forage and frolic close to the surface. They constantly break the surface of the water as they zip about haphazardly but they are difficult to approach; they disperse to deeper water if disturbed and, unlike the mullet shoals, that sometimes forage up the estuaries, they are difficult to catch. Mullet are even more slow-growing than bass and a three kilogramme mullet may be 15 to 20 years

old. The thick-lipped grey mullet is the resident Irish species but the **thin-lipped grey mullet** and the **golden grey mullet** have also been recorded at Kinsalebeg, the latter being the first Irish record of the species.

Flatfish, principally **flounder**, are inshore fish that roam the sandy bottoms of estuaries and shallow bays; they also occur in fresh water, well above the tidal limit. They can bury themselves in the sand, which they mostly do during the day, as they feed at night on ragworm, prawns and even small fish. They are frequently caught from the beaches and summer is probably the best time for them. Anglers fishing for bass are often rewarded with a fluke, as the flounder is more commonly known, which is a worthwhile catch, especially when bass are scarce. **Plaice** and **turbot** are deepwater flatfish though occasionally immature individuals may be taken from the beaches.

Other common species are occasionally caught and these include **anglerfish**, **black sole**, **bream** (**gilthead** and **red**), **brill**, **coalfish**, **cod** (widely distributed and can be quite large), **conger eel**, **dab**, **gurnard** (**grey, red** and **tub**), **haddock**, **hake**, **halibut**, **John dory**, **ling** (eel-like member of the cod family, mostly caught off wrecks and reefs), **monkfish** (an ugly fish but beautiful to eat), **pollock** (similar to coalfish and found over areas of rough ground and wrecks), **pouting**, **ray** (several species), **rockling**, **shark** (**blue** and **porbeagle** mainly–one blue shark tagged off Dungarvan was recaught 360 days later in mid-Atlantic, 3,170 kilometres away), **skate** (**white**, **long-nose** and **common**; common skate is subject to catch and release), **wrasse** (**ballan** and the colourful **cuckoo**), **whiting** and **tope** (a shallow water shark common in summer). **Dogfish** are occasionally seen high up in the inlets, where they may be trapped by a falling tide but they are more likely to be underwater and unseen in any of the channels or just offshore.

Inshore, the rock pools and rocky platforms usually have smaller species, which are often marooned when the tide goes out. These dart away out of sight but they are often preyed on by cautious herons who stalk the shore at low tide. The well-camouflaged **shanny** has a clown-like appearance and it and the rarer **Montagu's blenny** feed on barnacles and other creatures of the shore. **Sea scorpion**, **sand gobies** and **rock gobies** are found in shallow waters, rock pools or in and around floating seaweed beds and the dark spots on the eel-like and slimy **butterfish**, a fairly common species, are distinctive. **Pipefish**, like the **seahorses**, can swim in an upright position, and their long, tube-like mouths are used to suck in seawater from which they ingest plankton and other marine organisms. Sometimes their shrivelled but readily identifiable remains (the **greater pipefish** is more likely) are occasionally washed up on the strand where the wind may move them further up the shore.

Many of these species aren't easily seen and they may have to be searched for in the shoreline pools or by snorkelling over rocky platforms, which on a good day, will reveal all the beauty of the shore and what lives there.

Sea trout are unusual in that part of their life cycle is spent in freshwater (initially and to where they return to breed) and the remainder in the sea where they shoal and feed close inshore on sprat, herring fry, crustaceans and small fish. This anadromous life cycle may be repeated several times. The **twaite shad**, like the sea trout, runs in from the sea through Waterford Harbour to spawn in the three sister rivers (Barrow, Nore and Suir). These are rarely, if ever, caught off the coast, though they are eagerly awaited at St. Mullins, on the Barrow in early summer.

Salmon, like the sea trout, are anadromous. They spend on average two years in the rivers before heading out to sea as smolts in the spring of the year. Most spend one year feeding voraciously at sea before returning as grilse (at a weight that is around three or four kilogrammes or less), usually in summer. Salmon that stay longer at sea usually enter the estuaries early in the year and it is these multi-sea winter spring fish that are particularly attractive to anglers on the major Irish rivers because of their potential size. However, they are the component of the Irish salmon resource that has suffered the most substantial declines in recent years and they are now subject to special conservation measures that apply in the rivers (either no fishing at all or catch and release). Offshore drift netting for salmon has ceased and only certain rivers are open for quota-based fishing (commercial and recreational), which is reviewed annually based on scientific advice. Nevertheless there is a considerable movement of salmon off the coast of Waterford each year as young move to the sea and mature fish arrive back later to the rivers where they were born.

Occasionally rare fishes are either washed up or are caught offshore, either accidentally in nets or are taken by sea anglers. Mr A. Neale of Newtown School wrote to Dr R. F. Scharff of the Natural History Museum in Dublin to inform him that a **skipper** was stranded on Tramore beach in late 1895, the first county record of the species. Another was taken from Tramore beach in November 1986 on a rod and line baited with ragworm. This fish weighed 59 grammes and measured 30.5 centimetres; it was the eighteenth record of the species from Irish inshore waters. The skipper (or saury pike) is an oceanic species that occasionally comes inshore in late summer in the temperate waters of the North Atlantic and in the Mediterranean.

A **painted ray** was caught off the Waterford coast in the early 1970s and other rare species encountered in the 1970s include a **blackfish** taken on feathers off Helvick

Head in July 1970 (another was caught off Hook Head in 1975 in a drift net), an **argentine** taken 18 kilometres due south of Dunmore East in 1979 and a **boarfish** caught in a lobster pot in May 1979 off Brownstown. There are three records of **skipjack tuna** (or oceanic bonito), the last of which was taken in a drift net two kilometres southeast of Helvick Head in July 1973 (the first record was off Ardmore in October 1958 and the second in Waterford Harbour in June 1960). Not a fish as such but large numbers of **sea snails** were caught in a fine-mesh trawl between Ballycotton in Cork and Dunmore East, also in 1979. An exceptionally large specimen (320-360 kg) of a **thresher shark**, which is uncommon in Irish waters, was taken off Helvick Head in late 1981, and was well above the weight normally recorded in European waters. A **moray eel** was captured in a beam trawl 32 kilometres off Mine Head in February 1997, the first Irish record of the species and the most northerly European record. In May 2003, a **bullet tuna**, a small and slender member of the tuna family, was caught in a salmon net off Cheekpoint, only the fourth Irish record. A **greater forkbeard** weighing two kilogrammes and measuring 60 centimetres was captured in a seine net off Dunmore East in April 1957.

There were four records of the **greater weever** up to 2004: October 1955 off Dunmore East; July 1957, again off Dunmore East; August 1960 in Waterford Harbour; and in July 2004, 11 kilometres off Mine Head (the 27th Irish record). Weaver fish are occurring increasingly on the Waterford beaches, where they bury themselves in the sand leaving only the dark dorsal fin exposed. If an unwary swimmer stands on this poisonous spine, pain is the immediate result, indeed an excruciating pain, which lingers unless the affected foot is bathed in hot water which helps to break down the poison. **Trigger fish** are found in the tropical waters of the Atlantic but appears to migrate into European waters in late summer and autumn. In some years relatively high numbers are recorded, usually having been caught on rod and line, though specimens are also taken in nets, weirs and lobster pots. Remarkably, eight trigger fish were caught by rod fishermen in September 1990 at Tramore beach, suggesting that more may have been moving around offshore. Two **purple sunstars** were caught off the Waterford coast in April 1994, the first on the south coast since the turn of that century.

Garfish are surface dwelling, predatory fish with elongate bodies and long beak-like jaws and they feed on crustaceans, worms and sandeels. Two species are encountered in Ireland, though up to 1984 only one species, the common garfish, was known to be present in northern European waters. Known locally as 'mackerel guides', they are occasionally caught when mackerel appear in late summer. They readily fall off the hook and are, apparently, quite tasty to eat, despite the green bones. One seen on the beach at Tramore in May 1996 was an early date for the species, and unlike many other creatures cast up on the shore at Tramore it was in reasonably good condition. There is only one record of the **opah**, and it was stranded on Tramore beach way back in October 1842.

A beached garfish

Sunfish, Garrarus strand, November 2008

Sunfish are the largest bony fish in the world and can grow up to 3.1 metres from tip (mouth) to tail fin, 4.3 metres from dorsal fin to anal fin tip, and weigh up to 2,235 kg. They spend large amounts of time on the sea surface with their large dorsal fin flipping from side to side. Females can produce up to 300 million eggs, the largest number of eggs ever recorded in any fish. Very little is known about the movements and behaviour of this unusual fish that is normally found in temperate waters but they are now occurring with increasing frequency in Ireland. One beached alive at Garrarus beach on the 2nd November 2008 was an unusual record since the majority of sunfish records off the Irish coast are in July and August when sea temperatures are more favourable. Sunfish spend most of their time in waters whose temperature is between 12 and 17 °C but when in cooler waters (around 12 °C) they normally have access to much warmer surface waters (15-17 °C), which obviously wasn't available off Garrarus in November (sea surface temperatures off Waterford were around 12.5 °C at the time). Perhaps the sunfish strayed too far north into cooler waters, became torpid, beached and perished.

Any of the coastal beaches are suitable for shore angling, especially east of Helvick Head or west of Ballyquin, though these may be more fruitful in early morning, late in the evening or even at night, especially in good summer weather when the beaches are thronged with people during the day. Other less popular areas, including rocky platforms and headlands, are also suitable, though these often require local knowledge, and an awareness of local conditions and tides. Crab, sandeel, strip mackerel and lugworm are good baits to use, and these are available locally, either in angling shops or they can be harvested on the mudflats. Fishing is possible at any stage of the tide, though high tide is often best. Float fishing, fly fishing with streamer flies or spinning with lures and plugs are some of the techniques that are used profitably to catch any of the species mentioned. Offshore sea fishing can also be exciting and charter boats and accommodation are available at Dunmore East, Tramore, Dungarvan and Ardmore or there are the many small coves, piers and harbours where small boats can be launched.

INVERTEBRATES

Invertebrates are small, often beautiful and abundant and they occur in all habitats, including along the coast. There are many thousands of species of invertebrates (animals without backbones) and many are referred to by their Latin names only. Some, like the butterflies, are well known and loved, though many others are almost unknown and some are even disliked.

Butterflies
Butterflies are usually big, bright and colourful and they are normally easy to observe as they flutter about the flower heads from spring through to autumn. Adult butterflies on the wing are either in search of a mate, or, in the case of the female, looking for a suitable plant on which to lay her eggs. Once the eggs are laid, sometimes singly or in large groups, they hatch very quickly and grow into caterpillars by feasting on the host

plant. As a caterpillar grows it moults occasionally, sometimes five or six times, before it stops feeding to form the chrysalis, from which the adult butterfly eventually emerges to begin the life cycle again.

Some adult butterflies may live for no more than a couple of weeks and in that time they need to find suitable flowers with an ample supply of nectar to stay alive while searching for a mate. They are most active on warm days in summer and this is the best time to watch them. Most species have one generation of offspring per year, though some species have two and there may even be three in a particularly warm year.

Butterflies are taken by a wide variety of predators throughout their life cycle, though they have specific adaptations to avoid predators such as giving off an unpleasant smell or taste, their bright vivid colours suggest danger or, when at rest with their wings closed, they are well camouflaged. Some species like the wall or the meadow brown have eye spots on the wings which are attacked first by birds, sparing the adult butterfly and perhaps giving it the opportunity to escape. Some species are natives and they rarely move too far from where they were hatched but others are migrants, occasionally arriving on the coast in thousands from southern Europe or Africa to brighten our summer days and breed.

The cliff top vegetation is usually good for butterflies, while the dune areas may be particularly attractive for some species and the woodland areas in the coastal glens will attract different species. The coastal lanes (around Brownstown, for example) and tracks (*Bóithrín a' Bhleaic* near Helvick, for example), with their ample and varied vegetation and surrounded by unimproved grassland are likely to be most productive in terms of species and numbers. These are the wild, semi-natural habitats where butterflies

are relatively common, and where they can be admired, photographed and studied in comfort, well away from the more sterile habitats where they are fewer in number and rarely stay for long.

Four 'whites' are likely on the Waterford coast, **small white**, **green-veined white**, **large white** and **orange-tip** but not in any numbers and they are more common inland. The large white is the biggest species, with a lot of black on the wing tips and bold spots. It is also a strong flyer and can be a bit of a pest, especially on cabbages, broccoli and other brassicas. But it appears every year and is a resilient species, despite the damage inflicted on it by gardeners. The small white is a smaller version of the large white but with less black on the wing tips. It may be confused with the green-veined white, which is similar in size, but which has more pronounced veins on the wings. Both species are less damaging than the large white, but since most gardeners don't distinguish between them, they, or their caterpillars, may suffer the same fate if found on or around garden plants in summer.

The orange tip is easily the most distinctive of the whites and has its name from the orange tips on the wings of the male only, which ensures that it usually isn't confused with any other species, though the female may easily be confused with green-veined white or small white, unless the distinctive underside pattern is seen. The species is on the wing in April and it is always nice to see one along laneways, verges or damp meadows. However, unlike many other species to be seen in Waterford, it is rare to see one beyond the end of June. Not particularly coastal, it is more likely to be seen near the coast or on a journey to a seaside beach than on the beach itself.

'Blue' butterflies are particularly at home in coastal dunes, where food plants such as

Female common blue

restharrow, kidney vetch and bird's foot-trefoil are abundant. The male **common blue** is largely all blue, though the variable female has a distinctive border pattern with orange margins on its wings, and is more brown than blue. It is widely distributed in summer and usually only one or two may be seen, but on the coast, and particularly in the dunes, large numbers may occur. On the Cunnigar or Ardmore dunes, for example, 60 or more may be seen in August, around the sea holly, ragwort or other dune plants. These could be adults from the second generation as the species is usually double-brooded and adults may be seen from May to September.

The common blue can be confused with the **holly blue**, which is rarer and smaller and more likely in wooded areas and urban gardens around coastal towns and villages, and inland. Both male and female are entirely blue and their undersides are lighter blue with black flecks. The **small blue** is the rarest of the blue butterflies to be seen in Ireland and it is also the smallest and probably the least conspicuous; it is very easy to miss with its unmarked brown wings (it is only blue on the undersides of the wing). But it is worth searching for from mid-May to the end of June in coastal dunes (two were seen in the Sandhills in 2001), especially where its food plant, kidney vetch, grows.

The **small copper** occupies a wide range of habitats and may be found anywhere from grassland, to roadside verges to sand dunes. A fast flier when on the wing, and therefore hard to follow, it is also fiercely territorial and very possessive of its home patch. In good warm summers, it may be out and about from May on, and even into November in particularly good years.

The brown **speckled wood** is a common species of woodland or shady tracks, where it flutters around between the dappled shadows, though it may be seen occasionally in coastal dunes and along the hedgerows fringing the beaches and coves. The male is territorial and he will defend his own sunny spot against intruding males by short, ritual dog fights that inevitably results in the intruder being chased away. The speckled wood is on the wing from April through to October, producing two and sometimes three generations and its distribution has, apparently, increased in recent decades, though it was probably always common here.

The 'browns' are somewhat drab compared with the more colourful butterflies of the coast. They usually close their wings when they land so they can be hard to identify and good views, especially of the wing markings, are needed to correctly identify them. The **wall** and the **meadow brown** occur in some abundance in the dunes, especially the meadow brown, the more common of the two. The wall likes warm places and can be seen basking in the sun on the coastal cliffs or embankments, areas that are also good for meadow browns. Both species lay their eggs on grasses, where the larvae feed on the leaves, usually at night.

Less conspicuous butterflies include **grayling**, **gatekeeper** and **ringlet**, all superficially similar brown butterflies that occur sparingly along the coast, though the ringlet is the more common species. All three species lay their eggs on grasses which hatch after two to four weeks. The **small heath** is a grassland species, that is more common inland than on the coast, though they can occur sparingly in dune areas and on the sea cliffs. It is a small, light brown butterfly but it may be hard to see when at rest and it only flies weakly when disturbed, and not for long, fading away into the vegetation.

The **peacock** is a big and handsome butterfly and the large and vivid 'eyes' on the wings are obvious when it alights. It may be seen anywhere, though inland areas near woodland are probably best. The **small tortoiseshell** can also be found in a wide variety of habitats and is widely distributed in the county and even sparingly on coastal embankments or cliffs. It hibernates in winter and many do so in houses where it may be found suspended on walls, curtains or in wardrobes, and from where they are easily disturbed. It is one of the earliest butterflies to appear on sunny days from March onwards and it may be seen into September. It travels widely in summer and may move several kilometres per day, unlike other species that are largely sedentary.

Migrant butterflies usually arrive first on the south coast having travelled hundreds or even thousands of miles from Africa or the Mediterranean and they usually appear every year, in variable numbers. All three migrant species have no particular habitat requirements and they are likely to be found anywhere, and they are more likely to be seen on the coast, at least initially, as they arrive on our shores and then disperse inland.

The **clouded yellow** is least likely to occur and several years may elapse before one or more appears. The clouded yellow is a fast-flying species and with its orange-yellow colour and black wing border it is unmistakable. 1998 and 2000 were good years for the species and in 2000 they were seen right into October all over Waterford. 2006 was another good year and 226 individuals were counted in the county,

mostly from June to September. The **pale clouded yellow** was reported along the Waterford coast in the late 1960s and early 1970s, though separating this species from pale forms of clouded yellow is extremely difficult, so this rare visitor, if it does occur, is likely to go unnoticed.

The other two migrants, the **red admiral** and the **painted lady**, arrive annually, though of the two, the red admiral is the most striking and also the most likely to be seen. It is big, beautiful and a fast-flier. Particularly dramatic are the red diagonal bars below the white patches on the black wings. Sometimes it offers good close views when it basks on willow leaves or butterfly-bush (buddleja) flowers in strong sunshine, and in some numbers at times, especially in the autumn. It arrives on the coast from late spring on, and it vigorously defends territories before moving on. It lays one egg at a time, usually on nettles, its favourite food plant, and these hatch after a week and the adults that result contribute to the large numbers that are often seen in late summer. The painted lady is slightly smaller than the red admiral and not as dazzling, though it too is an attractive butterfly. It is not nearly as conspicuous as the red admiral, and it is also more difficult to track as it flies between plants. It lays its eggs on a variety of plants, though thistles are preferred. Some years are more productive for painted ladies than others and 2009 was particularly good for the species when hundreds, even thousands, appeared in Waterford and other coastal counties and then dispersed all over Ireland.

Painted lady

Other rarer and less likely butterflies are seen occasionally, including **brimstone**, **dark green fritillary**, **silver-washed fritillary**, even **marsh fritillary** (now, alas, rarely recorded in the county), though these do not favour coastal habitats. Who knows either when the **comma**, seen probably for the first time in the county in Waterford City in August 2009, or the **Essex skipper** discovered in nearby Wexford in 2006, will spread their wings and advance towards coastal habitats in Waterford.

Moths

Most moths are nowhere near as colourful or as conspicuous as butterflies and, as many species are on the wing during the hours of darkness, specialised equipment is needed to trap and then identify them, which, although usually straightforward for the bigger moths (the macro moths) isn't easy for the smaller species (the micro moths). There are many suitable habitats for moths along the coast where these beautiful but mysterious creatures may occur in some abundance in the semi-natural vegetation. The dune areas, the coves and the cliffs are usually very productive, though trapping moths at these locations using electrically powered

Six-spot burnet

equipment can be logistically challenging. If moths are disturbed during the day, they very rapidly land on nearby vegetation, usually out of sight, so that only fleeting of views are obtained. However there are some day-flying moths, and these can be easily observed as they congregate on the flower heads in summer. Some of the day-flying moths, like the butterflies, are brightly coloured and they actively seek the sunshine.

The most obvious and the commonest of the day-flying moths is the **six-spot burnet**, a very attractive moth that occurs in some numbers on flowering sea holly and ragwort in the dune areas of the county, which provides a rich contrast in colour that enhances the dune vegetation in summer. The six-spot burnet is primarily a moth of the coastal fringe in Ireland and sand dunes are an important habitat for them. A distinctive species, it has six red blotches on the otherwise black forewing which blends nicely with the similarly red hindwing. The host plant is common bird's-foot-trefoil, a common plant of coastal embankments, headlands and dunes.

The **cinnabar** is superficially similar to the six-spot burnet; it also has red spots on the wing, two on either forewing with a long scarlet streak close to the front of the forewing. The eggs are laid in batches on ragwort and the emerging larva very soon devour and decimate the plant, leaving just the bare stem. The caterpillars are banded black and yellow and are easy to spot on ragwort in June or July; adults may be nearby but they are flighty, easily disturbed and therefore difficult to examine closely.

As with the butterflies, there are also migrant moths, the most obvious of which is probably the **silver Y**, a small brown moth with a distinctive metallic 'gamma' mark on either wing. It is easily flushed from coastal vegetation in summer, and, while it disappears like most other moths, it does so less readily and usually in a way that allows the conspicuous and characteristic silver Y mark to be seen. Like migrant butterflies, numbers appearing on the south coast are very variable; in some years, large numbers arrive from north Africa but in other years few, if any, may be seen. 2006 and 2009 were particularly good for the species and thousands were seen. It may produce up to three generations here in a good year and they are most abundant from May to September. The **beautiful golden Y** is rarer (but resident) and occurs in much smaller numbers; it has been seen occasionally along the Waterford coast.

Convolvulus hawkmoth. ©P. M. Walsh

Other migrant moths that occur, and are trapped at light boxes (mostly at Brownstown Head and Tramore), include **dark sword-grass** (a non-descript moth), **pearly underwing**, **small mottled willow**, **diamond-back moth** (thousands can occur), **rusty-dot pearl** (the rusty brown colour is distinctive), **rush veneer** (long and narrow and largely coastal), *Antigastra catalaunalis* (at Tramore in September 2006, the fourth Irish record), **dark mottled willow** (the 1st Irish record was from Brownstown Head in September 2008), **gem**, **vestal**, **nutmeg**, **delicate**, **white-speck**, **cosmopolitan**, **scarce-bordered straw**, **bordered straw** and **ni moth**, However, some of these are rare and may not occur every year.

Many of the hawkmoths are big, fast and maneuvrable and are almost certainly the most impressive moths that occur in Ireland. Some are day-fliers and one or two species hover conspicuously as they probe for nectar with their long tongues. Although they generally rest with the wings closed, they will occasionally flash their impressive and brightly coloured hindwings if threatened. Moreover, the caterpillars of most species are big, brightly coloured and impressive. The resident species are supplemented in summer by migrants that arrive from further south.

The **convolvulus hawkmoth** has a wing span of over 10 centimetres, so it is extremely large and is variously streaked. A migrant species, it is occasionally recorded on the coast, especially at Brownstown Head but it is never plentiful. The **hummingbird hawkmoth** is about half the size of the convolvulus hawkmoth but is more likely to be seen by day and anywhere from the coast to Waterford City. It has its name from the humming bird as it flies rapidly between plants, and hovers to feed on tubular flowers like red valerian and buddleja. It is a joy to watch as it moves about and it is probably the most recorded hawkmoth in Waterford because of the ease with which it is seen, by day and in gardens. As with any of the migrants moths it may be common one year and not seen at all in the following year or years. 2006 seems to have been a particularly good year for the species and 99 were recorded in Waterford. The **striped hawkmoth** also occurs (there are recent records for Brownstown Head and Tramore) but it is usually rare and, like many of the hawkmoths, it might not be recorded at all but for being attracted to light. Other resident hawkmoths include **eyed hawkmoth**, **elephant hawkmoth**, **small elephant hawkmoth** and **narrow-bordered bee hawkmoth**, while species like the **poplar hawkmoth**, although more common inland, are also occasionally found on the coast.

Moth trapping along the Waterford coast in recent years has revealed a wide variety of moth species including a few surprises or specialities. The rather non-descript **hoary footman**, although largely confined to southeast England (Dover and other places near the sea) and Wales (Pembrokeshire and formerly Anglesea), has been found on the Waterford coast, initially around 1866 and again in 1954. More recently it was trapped near Brownstown Head and Great Newtown Head and near Bunmahon in 2008. The first Irish or British specimens of the species were taken at Howth Head in Dublin in 1861, but there are no recent records from there so the Waterford area is possibly the only place in Ireland where this dull and elusive species is now known to occur. The **bordered gothic** (known only from the south coast in Ireland), **Barrett's marbled coronet** (known only from cliffs in Cork, Waterford and Dublin), **feathered brindle** and **silky wainscot** are localised cliff specialities.

In July 1997, a **rosy plume moth** was trapped in the Tramore dunes, that until then was known only from England and Wales, though it has since been discovered elsewhere in Ireland. Five species new to Ireland were also found at Tramore: in September 2006, *Bactra venosana*, a female **potato tuber moth** and an **old world webworm** were trapped along with other migrant moths; while in 2007, *Pediasia aridella* and *Epermenia aequidentellus* were found on the salt marsh and dunes in June and July, respectively. There has been a concerted effort since 2007 to assess the coastal occurrence of moths around Tramore Bay in particular, and other areas including Ram Head and Ballydowane have been monitored. Many species have been located including **fox moth, emperor moth, turnip moth, small blood-vein, rosy wave** (a rare species), **pod lover, gold spot, broom moth, Hebrew character, early thorn, August thorn, angle shades, early grey, shoulder stripe, shears** and various species of **rustics, carpets, waves, quakers, pugs** and **wainscots**. No doubt other species will be found along the coast by the dedicated band of enthusiasts now monitoring moths in the county, which will complement species found previously by equally committed entomologists.

Dragonflies

Dragonflies are dependent on aquatic habitats for breeding and the larval nymph stage is spent almost entirely under water, primarily in freshwater lakes, rivers, streams and ponds. Given the relative lack of freshwater along the coast, and the brackish nature of any waterbody near the sea, only a small number of species occur at just a few sites along the Waterford coast and never in any great abundance. That said, dragonflies are generally big and beautiful and some are relatively easy to watch, though others are more flighty and can be infuriatingly difficult to observe and identify, as they move constantly, erratically and rarely stay still long enough to give good views. However, they offer endless opportunities for enjoyment, if looked for in the right places. Fornaght bog is one such place, the pond on the landward side of the embankment on the northwestern corner of the Backstrand at Lisselan is another, and probably the new lake formed as part of the redevelopment of Lisselan for the new racecourse at Tramore (once the vegetation develops), and the brackish ponds at the Cunnigar in Dungarvan. However dragonflies may also occur along the drainage channels of any of the fields near the coast or around any of the rivers and streams in from the coast (the Anne valley, north of Annestown, for example).

The true dragonflies normally keep their wings outstretched when resting and the fore and hind wings have a different shape unlike the damselflies who have wings of the same shape and they hold their wings vertically or partly spread over the body when perched. Summer is the best time to see dragonflies, especially in warm sun, when these charming insects are most active around the aquatic habitats they favour. In dull weather, or in the early morning or late evening, they are usually inactive, preferring instead to rest in trees, shrubs or low vegetation until the weather improves.

Adult males are highly territorial around the breeding site and they will resolutely fend off other males. The males are conspicuous and brightly coloured whereas the females may be very different and sometimes drab. The breeding pond is like a powerful magnet and several species may be present with males constantly squabbling and females laying their eggs less conspicuously. However, newly emerged adults, not being sexually mature, may wander far from the breeding pond in search of flying insects, which may account for some of the dragonfly sightings along the coast away from aquatic habitats.

The **large red damselfly**, although not the biggest dragonfly, is strongly territorial and is also one of the most approachable. It is the only red-bodied damselfly we have in Ireland, and one of the earliest to appear in spring, though, conversely, they are rarely seen beyond August and sometimes earlier. Even the larvae are territorial as they forage in the pools and, not surprisingly, the most territorial larvae are bigger and more successful as adults. It is common in the county but it is probably more likely to be seen in bog pools at Coum Mahon in the Comeragh Mountains or at Fenor bog than it is on the coast, though it has been seen near Annestown, near Dunabrattin, north of Tramore Backstrand and near Kilmurrin and several other inland locations in the county.

The blue damselflies are, naturally enough, blue, and to separate them to species level requires good views of the abdominal segments. The **blue-tailed damselfly** is probably the easiest to identify as it is almost entirely black except that one segment near the tip is entirely blue. Like the large red it is tolerant of brackish conditions and is also more tolerant of pollution than any other damselfly. It has been recorded at Annestown, Ballynaharda and on the new racecourse at Lisselan, Tramore. A similar species is the **common blue damselfly**, the males of which

are the bluest of the blue damselflies. The females of both species are brownish but variable in colour, though the blue-tailed is more likely on the coast. The two other damselflies that may occur occasionally near the coast are the **emerald damselfly** and the **variable damselfly**. Both are on the wing from mid-May to August and neither are territorial. The **banded demoiselle** is a very graceful species and flits along, in butterfly fashion, over vegetation in slow-flowing, muddy streams. The dark blue-black wing bars are diagnostic and are obvious even from a distance; it has been seen near Kilmurrin cove and at Fornaght bog.

The true dragonflies are usually much bigger than the damselflies but are more flighty, and hence more difficult to identify, especially on warm days. The **common darter** is common in the county and moves around a lot so it may be seen anywhere; it has been seen near Ballymacart, Hacketstown (near Mine Head), the Cunnigar, the dunes at Tramore and Fornaght bog. It may be confused with the **ruddy darter** which has been seen near Ballynaharda and Fornaght bog; look for the all black legs and the club-shaped abdomen of the ruddy darter, which is always obvious if close views are obtained. The **four-spotted chaser** darts about aggressively and rapidly and is one of the few species to be found in brackish water; look

Common darter

for it along the Anne valley near Annestown or near Ballynaharda.

During a recent national survey of dragonflies (between 2000 and 2003), three species new to Ireland were found. The **migrant hawker** was first seen in Wexford in 2000 and gradually spread from there in subsequent years. It emerges late (late July) but it can still be seen in late October. It has been seen since at Hacketstown, Dungarvan, Ballymacaw, Rathmoylan and especially at Brownstown Head. It occasionally associates with the larger **common hawker** that has also been seen on the Waterford coast and with which it is easily confused. The migrant hawker is smaller and it has a yellow, golf-tee type marking on one of the upper body segments, which is diagnostic, and from August onwards is possibly the commonest large dragonfly along the Waterford coast.

The **emperor** is the largest dragonfly in Ireland; it was first recorded in 2000 in Wexford and it has since spread along the east and south coast. It is extremely territorial, a very fast flier, and it patrols its patch incessantly, chasing off any other dragonflies that appear. So it may be some time before it stops for a rest, and permit good views of what is, for Ireland, a large and impressive insect. It has been seen along the coast at Tramore Backstrand, Annestown bog and the Cunnigar. The third newcomer, the **lesser emperor**, first seen in Cork in 2000, is the rarest of the three, and breeding wasn't confirmed during the national survey of 2000-2003, though it was strongly suspected at Monaneea Lake, four kilometres north of the coast in west Waterford.

Other terrestrial insects

Insects are common everywhere along the coast, especially in summer when large numbers of many different species, of all shapes and sizes appear around the shores, on the cliffs, the dunes and elsewhere. Most insect species are usually ignored or only the brighter and more conspicuous ones such as butterflies are noticed. Fortunately they are generally small in size so their large numbers rarely cause a problem, though masses of flies around rotting seaweed are a nuisance on the beaches in summer. Most insects are almost impossible to identify on the wing and they are also hard to find when they land and disappear into the vegetation. Many of them are known only by Latin names which may be hard to pronounce let alone remember.

Relatively little is known about the insect fauna of the Waterford coast, though several interesting species have been found. Lionel Henry Bonaparte-Wyse (from Waterford) and Oliver Janson visited in 1922 and spent two weeks collecting insects in the county. They recorded two insects new to Ireland and 55 new to Waterford. The species new to Ireland, a ground beetle and a weevil, were found at Tramore beach and dunes respectively, and 17 of their new county records were collected around Tramore.

One of the most familiar insects is the bumblebee. They are big, noisy (you can hear them coming) and they are normally colourful and attractive; they are also less likely to sting than honey bees or wasps. They are important plant pollinators and the flowering plants of the coast provide useful nectar sources and where the dry and warm conditions may be an important refuge for them. Surprisingly, 102 bee species are known in Ireland, which seems a remarkable number, but this is less than half the number that occur in Britain. One species was only discovered in 2006, based on an analysis of specimens of two other species from whom it is difficult to separate. However most (81) of the species seen in Ireland are solitary bees and there are 20 bumblebee species and one honey bee. The true bumblebees, of which there are 14 species in Ireland, are social insects and the queen emerging in spring produces a colony of females whose sole function is to look after and supply the colony. Later on, the males, which have a different coat pattern to the females, and new queens are produced. At the end of the season all the females, males and old queens die off leaving only the new queens, and these hibernate for the winter.

Another group of bumblebees, the cuckoo bumblebees (six species in all), are parasitic on the true bumblebees to the extent that the more powerful female cuckoo bumblebee may kill off the hive queen and use her workers to raise her own offspring. So bumblebees can be very confusing to identify and before correct identification is possible the question must be asked: is it male or female, true or cuckoo and be careful of other species that mimic bumblebees (most of which are flies). That said, expect to find about 11 species of bumble bee along the Waterford coast, two of which are cuckoo bumblebees and the other nine are true bumblebees. Be aware, however, that other, rarer bumblebee species may be encountered as Waterford is poorly recorded, despite people's familiarity with these remarkable insects as a group, though generally not to individual species level.

There are really only half a dozen species that are common and likely to be seen anywhere, including the coast, and the best time to become familiar with these is in spring. This is the time when the emerging queens are on the wing (many will be social bumblebees), they are large and well-marked and there no workers (which can be very small) or males to confuse identification. The number and colour of banding on the thorax (below the head) and the abdomen (the rear end) is a useful feature in identifying the more common species. There are two common white-tailed bumblebees (*Bombus hortorum* and *B. lucorum*) which can be separated by the number of yellow bands on

Bumble bee on sea holly

the body (three for *B. hortorum*, two for *B. lucorum*), and one buff-tailed bumblebee (*B. terrestris*). The black-bodied red-tailed bumblebee (*B. lapidarius*) is, however, quite distinctive, with its rufous bum and otherwise black appearance but it can be confused with its host, the red-tailed cuckoo bee (*B. rupestris*), which has smoky brown wings. *B. pascuorum* is ginger-brown and doesn't have bands on the thorax. Other common species to look out for are *B. pratorum* (a short and compact species), *B. muscorum* (a ginger-brown, medium-sized species) and *B. magnus* (which is easily confused with *B. lucorum* and *B. terrestris*).

Other bees are more difficult to identify but some coastal areas in Waterford are important refuges for them. For example, three species that are declining nationally can still be found on the extensive coastal heath on the cliff top at Ardmore: *Andrena nigroaenea* (a mining bee), *Lasioglossum nitidiusculum* (a solitary bee) and *Nomada goodeniana* (a kleptoparasitic solitary bee).

The **honey bee**, like the bumble bee, feeds on pollen and nectar so the many colourful coastal flowers are attractive to them in summer. **Wasps** differ from bees in that they feed their young on meat, and, while they like pollen and sweet things, they are not as specialised as bees in exploiting such food resources. There are solitary wasps, social wasps, spider-hunting wasps, digger wasps and sand wasps and of course their lookalikes, the hoverflies, with which they are often mistaken but these do not sting. For many of these species the coast offers ideal conditions for nesting, basking in the sun or pouncing on passing insects.

Woodlice are important recyclers of nutrients and Ireland has 27 (possibly 28) species, though almost half of these have a restricted distribution or are rare. However, two or three species are common on the coast. The **common pill woodlouse** is widely distributed, and has the ability to curl up into a perfect closed sphere when disturbed or handled. The **common rough woodlouse** is equally common, but watch out for the many colour variations found in coastal areas. The **sea slater** is confined to the coast and the estuaries, usually along rocky sea shores, where it can vary its colour to suit that of the background. When fully grown it is the largest of all the woodlice and it is an impressive insect. It hides under stones by day only to appear at night to graze on seaweed and other algae nearby; if any of these stones are lifted, the sea slater rapidly disappears into nearby vegetation.

Hoverfly (*Helophilus pendulus*)

The **pill millipede** is more like a woodlouse than a millipede and it is easily mistaken for a woodlouse as it also rolls up into a ball when touched, though the shape so formed is more irregular than the spherical woodlice. The pill millipede has around 18 pairs of legs (a woodlouse has seven) and it is more likely to be found out in the open, often in some numbers. Other Myriapods (centipedes and millipedes) can be found under stones along with **common earwigs** and **ants** (whole colonies including grubs may be found under some of the larger stones), where they hide during the day, before emerging in darkness to hunt.

Beetles are widespread throughout Ireland, but their small size and mostly nocturnal habits ensure that they are often unseen or ignored. They are a very successful group of insects, occurring almost everywhere from the coast to the high mountain tops and they exploit a wide variety of food resources from vegetation to wood and even household carpets. Many species are nocturnal, preferring to avoid searing summer heat on the coast and these are best located at dusk, with the aid of a flashlight. Ground beetles are common in all habitats and none more so than the **bloody-nosed beetle**, which may be quite obvious at times in summer in the dunes, especially when mating. It may exude deep red blood from its mouth and other joints if disturbed, hence its very apt common name. The long **oil beetle** may be found on the embankments and headlands, though it is not numerous. The louse-like larvae that emerge from the many eggs laid by the female climb up onto spring flowers and wait for unsuspecting bees, to whom they attach and are then transported back to the nest where they eat eggs and nectar.

Many beetles fly, especially in warm weather, and these can be seen in high summer but they are usually impossible to identify on the wing. Species like the brilliant

Bloody-nosed beetle

green **rose chafer** are easily recognisable because of their size and vivid colouration but others, especially the smaller ones, are more obscure. **Weevils**, especially plant-feeding ones, may be found on the varied and abundant vegetation. Unlike other beetles, **ladybirds** are well known and liked because of their role in controlling aphids and greenfly. There are 15 species of ladybird in Ireland, which are easy to see and identify. Most are named on the basis of the number of spots on the body. The common species in Waterford are the 2-spot, 7-spot and 14-spot ladybird; their conspicuous red thorax with black spots is a warning to would-be predators to keep away. The orange ladybird also occurs and this smaller species is distinctive because of its colour.

A range of ground beetles have been recorded on or near the Waterford coast including *Amara apricaria, A. aenea, Agonum muelleri, A. afrum, A. marginatum, A. thoreyi, Bembidion lampros, B. tetracolum, Bradycellus verbasci, Calathus mollis, Cillenus lateralis, Dicheirotrichus gustavii, Harpalus affinis, Harpalus rufipes, Nebria brevicollis, Ocys harpaloides, Paradromius linearis, Pogonus chalceus, Pterostichus diligens, P. melanarius, P. niger, Trechus obtusus and T. quadristriatus.* In August 1990, Roy Anderson, a naturalist

from Belfast found three males and two females of *Curtonotus convexiuscula* near Tramore dump, along with some of those listed above. This ground beetle hadn't been found in Ireland since the late 1800s and was removed from the Irish list because there were no voucher specimens. It has since been found in Wexford and Wicklow. An investigation in May 1992 of the sandflats at Tramore confirmed the presence of three rove beetles (*Bledius subniger, Diglotta mersa* and *Diglotta sinuatoicollis*) and one ground beetle (*Cillenus lateralis*) in the top layers of sand on the Backstrand side of the dunes.

There are a vast number of beetles in the world and, while Ireland has around 2,000 species, more are surely waiting to be discovered here as was the case in 2008 when the first Irish record of *Ochthebius poweri*, (the **spindrift beetle**) was found at Ballydowane cove in secpages in the coastal cliffs there. Other beetle species (**water, diving, scavenger and soldier**) also occur along the Waterford coast, in the brackish ponds or in the vegetation, where they may be hard to locate and then identify.

The **common green grasshopper** is usually heard rather than seen and what an unmistakable chorus they provide on the coast, and dune areas in particular, in summer. Flies are usually ubiquitous in all habitats, from the tideline where large numbers of seaweed flies swarm over the tidal debris, to the dunes, the salt marshes and the nearby cliffs and farmland. All sorts of flies abound from hoverflies, predatory flies, robber flies, black flies to soldier flies, all of whom find a suitable niche along the coast.

Snails and slugs are probably the most obvious of the invertebrate fauna of the coastal dunes and they are least likely to disappear. The **common garden snail** occurs in some numbers, throughout the Tramore dunes, for example. In summer, following rain, large numbers may be seen in passionate embraces as they go about the business of reproducing, oblivious to the considerable risks to themselves from trampling, to predation and to being baked by the sun. Quite often, their shells are very faded presumably because of the effects of the sun, and in warm weather they grip the vegetation tightly to avoid drying out. But it must be warm inside in those shells in high summer and many may succumb to the heat. At any time of year, large accumulations of dead shells can be found within the dunes, and these offer temporary refuges to many spider species and other insects from predation and prevailing weather conditions.

The **black slug** doesn't have the protective shell of its near relation so it has to very careful, especially in summer. Consequently, fewer of these are seen, though they, and indeed all other slugs and snails, are more active at night or around dawn and dusk. Many slugs and snails avoid the worst of the scaring heat in summer by burrowing deep into the sand or by climbing high up the marram leaves to avail of cooling breezes.

Banded (or **grove**) **snails** are more attractive and they also occur in some numbers in the dunes. The banded shell is easily recognisable, even from a distance. Common species to be seen include **common chrysalis snail**, **strawberry snail**, **hairy snail**, the **wrinkled snail** and **striped snail**. Other non-marine molluscs should also be encountered, including the **heath snail**, that is declining nationally inland but populations are, apparently, stable on the coast. However, the **swollen spire snail**, which was formerly present at Tramore, no longer occurs there.

Over 100 spider species have been recorded in Waterford (of around 380 known to occur in Ireland) and many of these are found along the coast; some species might be easier to find near houses but a careful check of any of the coastal habitats should unearth a few species. However, identifying them might be a different matter.

Fauna of the mudflats, sandflats & salt marshes

Mudflats are extremely prolific and are one of the most productive habitats on earth. While the mudflats at Waterford Harbour, Tramore Backstrand, Dungarvan Bay and the Blackwater estuary might look barren simply because nothing obvious appears to grow there, they are highly productive places. Microscopic plants, especially unattached diatoms, grow in vast numbers on the surface film of water in summer and these organisms are consumed by invertebrate grazers who themselves are prey to wintering birds. Tides carry with them a large organic load, which spreads over the mudflats and when high tide recedes it removes a vast amount of organic material from the surrounding salt marsh and adjacent areas. All this detritus is food material and is readily available to the fauna that thrive on it, especially in the summer months, when productivity is maximised.

Intertidal sand and mud is a difficult environment in which to live as it is unstable, subject to regular inundation by tides and the occasional but severe disturbance by storms. There is also little refuge from predators like crabs and fish that arrive with the tide and, when the tide goes out, there are the seasonally varying atmospheric conditions of hot sun in summer, harsh winds and extreme cold in winter as well as the probing bills of birds. Consequently most animals that live in sand or mud do so below the surface.

Temperature, oxygen levels and salinity are the environmental factors that influence the abundance and distribution of mudflat animals. Offshore seawater is around 35‰ saline (35 parts per thousand) and there is little seasonal variation. However, in estuaries and lagoons subject to inputs of freshwater from local streams and from rain and also subject to evaporation, salinity may be quite variable. Excessive heat may bake an animal in summer and, conversely, low temperatures may freeze the body fluids in winter. Elevated temperatures also impact on oxygen levels, causing excess oxygen levels if there is high photosynthetic activity by algae in pools and creeks, or reduced oxygen levels, or even anaerobic conditions (no oxygen at all), if there is rapid bacterial growth on tideline litter or decaying seaweed. The sand particle size and its porosity is also of importance; if the particle size is too small and too finely packed then oxygen levels will be low resulting in conditions that few, if any, animals can survive in. Moreover the surrounding matrix has to allow burrowing animals to pass through and to retain the burrow shape once the animal is place; inevitably, for this reason, certain areas have a limited fauna while nearby areas are well populated. Fine sands (defined as having diameters in the range 0.125-0.25 millimetres) support the greatest concentrations of diatoms, bacteria and dependent animals. Sand is usually the most common substrate along the coast, though there are inshore areas in the estuaries and bays where finer material in the form of silt and clay predominates.

However, even within sites, distribution and abundance of marine animals may vary, depending on substrate and enrichment. For example, at Tramore Backstrand, the former dump and the Malcomson embankment, which divides the Backstrand into an inner and outer lagoon has influenced the species that occur and their numbers. Catworm, thin tellin and the **sand digger shrimp**, which prefer sandy sediments, dominate outside the Malcomson embankment in the outer lagoon, but they are practically absent inside the embankments. Around the dump, ragworm, **peppery furrow shell** and common cockle dominate, all of which prefer

Worm casts among the eelgrasses at Tramore

muddy sediments. Bristleworms and paddleworms are found away from the dump in the inner lagoon, and the gallery worm occurs in some numbers at the breach in the embankments, where they can withstand any residual leachate from the dump.

It is usually the topmost layer of sand that is so productive and below this layer oxygen may be a limiting factor. Here, bacteria survive without oxygen, breaking down organic matter by processes such as fermentation, and gases like the unpleasant-smelling hydrogen sulphide may be produced in such conditions. These lower levels are characterised by black sand and mud and the level at which this layer occurs depends on the oxygen content and the type of sand present; these areas support a fauna that may be very different to elsewhere. However in more sheltered areas, the accumulation of fine, well aerated and moist sand that is relatively undisturbed by wave action allows a vigorous growth of minute blue-green algae to develop which is exploited by a small number of salt-tolerant insects such as rove and ground beetles, who themselves may be prey to other insects.

The **lugworm** is probably one of the best-known worms of the mudflat areas of the county. It dislikes coarse sand and very fine mud as it cannot maintain a permanent burrow in this type of substrate. Highest densities occur in fine muddy sands and their presence is immediately obvious by the presence of untidy spaghetti-like casts on the surface of the mudflat. It builds a U-shaped burrow, that is maintained, enlarged and deepened as the worm grows. It lives at the bottom of the U, moving up the permanently open tail shaft to get rid of excess sand and waste matter. These faecal casts are very visible on the surface, especially in some areas where hundreds of them litter the surface. The lugworm feeds by ingesting sand from the other end of the U, into which a constant stream of sand falls by gravity from the surface above. The bait-digger can recognise these head shafts by the saucer shaped depressions on the surface; these are often partially blocked unlike the tail shaft, which

Honeycomb worm cases

allows a constant stream of water to enter thereby ventilating the burrow. The lugworm may be up to 20 centimetres long and there are 19 ringed segments at its thicker end. The swollen front end of the body is covered with bristles and the red gills, used for breathing, are at the narrow end. Colour varies depending on age, from pink when small to black when fully grown.

Lugworms are a valuable protein source and are preyed on by fish, especially plaice who will bite off the lugworm tail, which is regularly extended to expel waste. Birds like curlew, whose curved bills are used to good effect in finding and subsequently extracting them from their burrows, are also significant predators. In summer the juveniles leave the burrows of the female and move upshore. They overwinter in the top few centimetres of very fine sediment, where again they are preyed upon by the smaller wading birds such as dunlin and redshank. In the following spring, they move back down the shore to construct their first burrows. The lugworm is favoured by anglers as bait and, at low tide, there are always people out on the coastal mudflats with a buckets and spades digging holes in search of this worm.

The **ragworm** is smaller than the lugworm, though it can grow to around 12 centimetres. An active predator, fast and aggressive, it has powerful jaws to grab small worms. It feeds on the surface layers of sediment. Like the lugworm it lives in a permanent burrow which may be up to 30 centimetres deep, and it is more tolerant of freshwater than the lugworm. It may even be more numerous than the lugworm with several hundred or even thousands of individuals in a square metre of suitable mudflat. A conspicuous blood vessel runs the length of its body and there may be quite a variation in body colour. The two antennae on its head and a pair of tentacles at its rear end are also obvious.

The **sand mason** is a peculiar worm as it encases itself in a tube constructed with coarse grains of sand particles held together with mucus. It forms burrows of up to 30 centimetres deep but, when submerged, a mop of two or three centimetres of branched structures at the top of the tube project from the sand surface allowing the worm's tentacles to filter the passing seawater. It is also a surface deposit feeder and by combining these two modes of feeding it can exploit alternate food resources allowing populations to thrive and prosper. The best time too see this particular worm is at low spring tide close to the waters edge on stony ground.

Honeycomb worms live in colonies and are often attached to half buried rocks on coastal beaches, where they are subject to diurnal inundation by the tide. The worms themselves are quite small, around four centimetres, but they glue sand grains together to form masses of tubes which resemble honeycombs. The worms emerge at high tide to feed. Colonies of these can be seen at Ballyquin in the west of the county and near the pier on the west side of Tramore Bay. Other worms like the large and active **catworm** can be found on the coastal wetlands. It can burrow rapidly into muddy sand where it feeds on other worms like the small bristleworm whose rear ends are bitten off by the larger and more active predator.

The carnivorous **paddleworms** are long, thin and very active. They have many body segments, live under stones or in rock crevices. Some species like the **bloodworm** and the more fragile earthworm-like **gallery worm** can tolerate pollution more than many other worms and they may be found in some numbers close to the former dumps at Tramore and Dungarvan, where conditions are more anoxic (there is little or no oxygen).

The **coiled tube worms** and the **keel worm** are found on various coastal structures from where they emerge at high tide to feed and to where they can rapidly retreat if danger threatens or the tide goes out.

There are advantages for a soft-bodied animal to be enclosed in a shell; there is usually good protection from most predators and exposure to atmospheric conditions can be minimised. Many of the invertebrates of the mudflats are bivalve molluscs (examples are cockles and mussels) encased in shells of two halves which can be opened and closed when required. These molluscs live just under the surface but not quite as deep as the burrowing worms. Such animals have two extensible tubes or siphons, which can be raised to the surface when the shell opens on an incoming tide. One siphon is used either to draw down seawater (hence the mollusc is a suspension feeder) or sediment from above (hence it is a deposit feeder). Once the food and oxygen present is ingested the waste matter is expelled through the other siphon. A ligament holds the two shells together and these can instantly close the shells if the animal is disturbed. The characteristic rings on most seashells are the growth rings laid down as the animal inside ages.

Barnacles on limpets

The **cockle** is probably the best known bivalve of the coast. It is a suspension feeder with short, fused siphons and lives just below the surface. There are significant year-to-year variations in the numbers of cockles, which depends on how many adult cockles survive the previous winter and therefore the ability of the new spatfall to find space on the shore and grow. Cockles are subject to predation by shore crabs and fish like plaice but it is usually safe from these predators if it survives to two years of age. However, they are always at risk from wading birds like oystercatchers that have an uncanny knack of opening the shells to gain access to the rich food inside.

The **common mussel** is an economically important filter feeder that is widely cultured around our coasts. It also occurs naturally and small numbers are found in the coastal wetlands. It is unlike other bivalves in that it requires a strong support to which it attaches itself, and these take the form of stones, rocks, seaweed and even tidal debris and vertical posts. Pointed at one end, mussels are purple in colour and are a significant prey item for small wader species when young and especially for oystercatchers when older. Oystercatchers either stab their bills between the two shells to open it and then extract the living animal within or they hammer at the weakest part of the shell (usually that part which is exposed) until it breaks allowing them to feed on what is inside.

Limpets rely on just a single, low-profile conical shell in which to live and they are found on all rocky shores. A strong muscular sucker foot allows them to cling to flat rocks and stones. Once disturbed they maintain a vice-like grip and are almost impossible to remove; it also has the advantage of keeping the shell watertight and protecting it from strong waves lashing over the rocks. As the tide comes in they relax their grip, which

allows them to move around to feed on algae and seaweeds, and this is the time they are most vulnerable to avian predators.

Barnacles are superficially similar to limpets but splash them with seawater and immediately the difference between them is clear. Limpets are encrusted with a single, continuous shell without an apical aperture and are grazers whereas barnacles are filter feeders. Barnacles have plates, usually six in number, with an oval-shaped aperture at its apex, which opens, revealing a blue-orange valve from where the feathery legs emerge when the tide is in, allowing the barnacle to sieve nutrients from the seawater.

Periwinkles are grazers of algae, seaweeds and lichens growing on exposed shorelines. The shells are spiralled and the animal inside protects itself by means of the thick, nail-like cap or operculum it draws in closing the shell when the tide goes out or when threatened. The dark, grey-brown and edible **common periwinkle** is the largest and is found on brown seaweeds to which it clings when the tide goes out. **Flat** and **rough periwinkles** also occur; their colour varies but they are found from upper to middle to lower parts of the shore, where they graze on brown seaweeds and wracks. The **laver spire snail** or *Hydrobia ulva* is one of the most abundant snails on the shore and among the smallest at five to seven millimetres long. It has a pear-shaped aperture and six or seven whorls on the shell. A deposit feeder, it will float beneath a raft of mucus which it itself secretes once the tide comes in, and feeds either on algae and tidal litter on the surface mud or alternatively on its own bacteria-enriched mucus. In summer, many of these snails climb high on *Spartina* leaves to avail of cooling breezes. It is an important food item for wading birds.

Top shells and **dog whelks** favour rocky shores under seaweed. The gray-cream dog

Razor shell

whelk is a common sea snail of the lower shore or shallow water while the colourful top shells (two or three species occur) live on rocky shorelines. The tellin bivalves, especially the **thin tellin**, are characteristic of sandy substrates. They have easily-ruptured, wafer thin shells so they are mobile and usually live close to the surface. Occasionally long lines of them appear along the tideline of the coastal beaches, usually after storms disturb the underlying sands offshore.

Other shells are occasionally met with and the best known of these are probably the empty **razor shells** cast up on the strand. The two halves of the razor shell are held together by a strong ligament which can close the shell, leaving the ends open. It is a filter feeder so it has to remain close to the surface but, if disturbed, it can instantly pull itself into the sand using its strong muscular foot at the other end.

The commonest marine crustaceans of the coast vary in terms of size, numbers and habits. **Sandhoppers** are active amphipods who live under stones but especially around the seaweed along tideline litter. If approached or disturbed they can rapidly bury themselves in the sand or disappear under stones. The various species present are similar in appearance and critical examination may be necessary to identify them. Sometimes thousands of them may be seen at night along the high tide line of the beaches. The tail part is curved in under the animal and if it flexes this tail it can hop several centimetres, hence the name.

The commonest crab on the coast is the mottled **shore crab** and is found wherever there are rocks or other debris such as tyres or drums where they can hide when the tide is out. Young crabs also live under seaweed and algal mats in the salt marsh creeks and channels. They are both scavenger and predator, feeding on mussels, snails and other

Top shells

invertebrates as well as availing of dead animal matter found on the mud. They are in demand themselves from a variety of predators, and some great black-backed gulls are adept at locating them in the channels at low tide. They are also used as bait by shore anglers (hence the lines of tyres at low tide on some Waterford mudflats). In summer they are usually more abundant when food inshore is plentiful but are less conspicuous in winter when many move offshore to deeper water. Other crabs include the **porcelain crab**, the **hermit crab**, the **velvet crab** and the **edible crab** but some of these, and **prawns** and **lobster**, are lower-shore specialists or are sub-tidal where they are harder to see, unless snorkeling. The **common shrimp** is usually found in the sandy sediment offshore but the

Beadlet anemone

occasional straggler may be found in coastal pools or along the tideline.

The **bristletail** is so called because of its long bristly antennae and it also has a triple-forked tail. It is quite a distinctive species with a long tapering body and conspicuous black eyes. It scurries about the rocks on the upper shore and especially up the vertical cliff faces but it will rapidly disappear into crevices if alarmed or approached.

There are usually several species of anemones in pools on the shore or subtidally just offshore. The commonest of these is the **beadlet anemone**, a very simple animal related to jellyfish. They are normally red in colour and they are easily located in pools or at the base of damp rocks when the tide is out on rocky shores. They capture prey when submerged by means of tentacles waving about in the water. **Starfish** are predators of limpets, mussels and barnacles but they are mobile and usually found underwater, though occasionally one may become trapped in a pool or a dead one may appear on the beach. There are a number of species and they are more robust than the fragile looking **bristlestars** and **cushion stars** that also occur. Sea urchins usually stay underwater grazing on the algae and seaweeds as they are in danger from predators or waves once exposed. The empty shells of urchins are frequently washed up on the beaches. Expect to the see the **edible sea urchin** and the **green sea urchin**, which is harder to find.

Tideline litter along the coastal beaches is often a source of interesting marine material, that may be found scattered among the other debris of the shore. **Cuttlefish** 'bones' sometimes arrive in vast numbers. These are

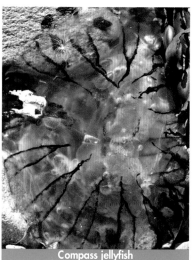
Compass jellyfish

the internal shells of the common cuttlefish, which assist in buoyancy when filled with gas and are collected for feeding to budgies, canaries and other cage-bound birds. **Mermaid's purses** are the empty brown egg cases of dogfish. The twisted tendrils on each corner attach to floating debris from where the young dogfish hatches and usually long before the hardened egg case washes up on the shore, empty. The brown, spongy, honeycomb egg mass of the **common whelk** occurs occasionally too.

Jellyfish are washed ashore annually, almost always in summer, and the **common moon jellyfish**, a free-floating blob that feeds on plankton, is probably the commonest. The distinctive purple horseshoe-shaped rings are the reproductive organs. Others species like the **compass jellyfish** are also likely; it has brown markings on the dome shaped body and a mass of trailing tentacles. The **by-the-wind-sailor**, a close relative of the jellyfish, is translucent blue and is kept afloat at sea by a float enclosed by a skeleton; this bears a fin-like sail which catches the wind. In some years large numbers of these wash up on coastal beaches, though they are harmless. Nastier however are the **lion's mane jellyfish**, the **blue jellyfish**, the **purple stinger**, the **barrel jellyfish** and the **Portuguese man o' war** (the most venomous), which are occasionally blown from the Gulf Stream into our coastal waters and hence our beaches by strong onshore summer winds. Some of these can give quite a serious sting and they are best avoided, even if they appear to be dead on the shore, as the primitive stinging cells may still be active. If stung, wash off the affected area with seawater and use vinegar to neutralise the venom.

Maritime Facilities on the Waterford Coast

A number of buildings and other facilities along the Waterford coast are associated with maritime activities in the county. Many of these were built in the 1800s, using highly skilled labour, often working in difficult conditions and the continued presence and use of these facilities attests to the craftsmanship and materials used in their construction. The most prominent are the lighthouses, which, because of their function, are located on coastal headlands and their vertical composition enhances the sites they occupy. There is a strong affinity locally with many of these maritime facilities, partly because of the vital services they offer to coastal communities but also because of the historical and familial associations, perhaps over many generations.

While the lighthouses may be the most prominent structures visually on the coast, there are other less imposing facilities, which serve equally useful purposes and which enhance the coastal setting in which they are placed because of their form and function. The harbours and piers, in particular, have many uses and are widely used for recreation and for commercial activities.

LIGHTHOUSES

Lighthouses are dotted around the coast of Ireland and are an essential component of a maritime safety system that ensures the safe passage of ships through and into our coastal waters. Each lighthouse has a characteristic colour pattern that uniquely identifies it during the day, and, at night, each light has a characteristic flashing sequence. Other navigational aids which may be present at the lighthouse include fog signalling equipment (though its use was discontinued in January 2011), a radar beacon (which emits a distinctive morse signature that can be recognised by incoming ships) and differential global positioning systems (which provides accurate positional information). While the original rationale for the network of lighthouses around Ireland (emitting powerful, long-range lights at night) has been superseded by modern technology, nevertheless, lighthouses are essential in identifying landfalls and safe channels, as hazard warnings and in providing position checks. Given the harsh conditions which these lighthouses endure, they need to be regularly maintained and fitted with modern

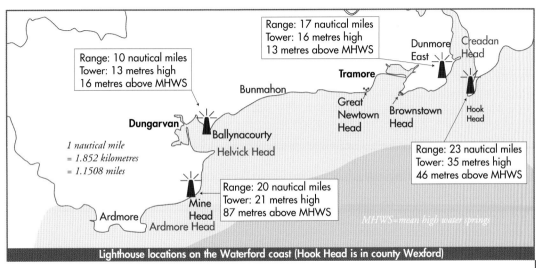

Lighthouse locations on the Waterford coast (Hook Head is in county Wexford)

Range: 17 nautical miles
Tower: 16 metres high
13 metres above MHWS

Range: 10 nautical miles
Tower: 13 metres high
16 metres above MHWS

Range: 23 nautical miles
Tower: 35 metres high
46 metres above MHWS

Range: 20 nautical miles
Tower: 21 metres high
87 metres above MHWS

1 nautical mile
= 1.852 kilometres
= 1.1508 miles

MHWS=mean high water springs

Dunmore East · Creadan Head · Tramore · Bunmahon · Great Newtown Head · Brownstown Head · Hook Head · Dungarvan · Ballynacourty · Helvick Head · Mine Head · Ardmore · Ardmore Head

Hook Head lighthouse and heritage centre, county Wexford

technology. These duties are undertaken by the Commissioners of Irish Lights, which is the statutory body responsible for management of lighthouses around Ireland.

Hook Head lighthouse

Hook Head is a prominent headland in county Wexford and it dominates the east side of the entrance to Waterford Harbour. At the tip of the headland is Hook lighthouse, a unique example of an almost intact medieval lighthouse. It is the oldest lighthouse in Ireland, and one of the four oldest operational lighthouses in the world. Hook Head lighthouse, while not in Waterford, is a distinctive coastal landmark in the southeast of Ireland and it has a clear attraction for many people living in the southeast and beyond. It defines the entrance to Waterford Harbour and has welcomed arriving mariners for centuries; it has also been a fine sentinel for those leaving our shores, some of whom never returned. More lately, it has enthralled those visitors who arrive by road to visit this enchanted headland, or for those who admire it from the nearby Waterford coastline.

In the fifth century a Welsh monk named Dubhán, established a monastery not far from Hook Head; the promontory thereafter became known as Rinn Dubhán, or the Point of Dubhán and from which it was

subsequently known as the Point of Hook (the Irish word *dubhán* means fishing hook). Saint Dubhán, it seems, established a beacon on Hook Point, which was probably a portable stove on top of a mound of stones burning timber or other locally obtained fuels. This proved to be a valuable navigational light for vessels entering Waterford Harbour. Around 1171, a Norman from Pembrokeshire, Raymond LeGros, husband of Strongbow's only sister, landed at Baginbun, and is reputed to have built the first tower of Hook around 1172, to replace the original beacon, and this acted as a castle to guard the entrance to Waterford Harbour. However, Hook tower has also been attributed to William Marshal, the Earl of Pembroke, who established the port of New Ross upriver. He, apparently, was responsible for the construction of a tower in 1245. The monks from the nearby monastery, who lived in the tower, continued to act as lightkeepers until around 1540 when they probably left the area and their lightkeeping duties ceased; they were certainly gone at the outbreak of Civil War in 1651.

By the middle of the seventeenth century, the lighthouse was no longer operational but during the reign of Charles II, Sir Robert Readinge was charged with establishing six lighthouses around Ireland, one of which was at Hook Head, and it was re-established by him around 1667. Queen Anne subsequently vested the operation of all Irish lighthouses to the Revenue Commissioners.

Henry Loftus, of nearby Loftus Hall, who acquired lands on the Hook peninsula following Oliver Cromwell's campaign in Ireland, assumed ownership of the lighthouse, which he then leased to the authorities. On his death ownership passed to his son Nicholas, who, in 1728, threatened to extinguish the light unless the Commissioners advanced a rent of £200; they eventually agreed to pay £120. In 1791 the Revenue Commissioners granted Thomas Rogers a contract to maintain and staff Hook Point and other lighthouses around the Irish coast. Rogers erected a new 3.65-metre diameter lantern at the Hook, abandoned the coal-operated light and installed twelve argand whale-oil lamps with reflectors. The apparatus was improved in 1812 and again in 1864. The Commissioners of Irish Lights assumed control of the light in 1867. Coal gas replaced oil lamps in 1871 and these lasted until 1910. On New Year's Day 1911, a revolving 500 millimetre focal length optic replaced the dioptric lens, and vapourised paraffin replaced coal gas as the source of light. In 1933 the colour of the tower was altered from white with three red bands to white with two black bands. The lighthouse was electrified in 1972 and the new light increased the range of the lighthouse to 25 nautical miles.

A fog signal bell was introduced in 1838 to be replaced by a gun in 1872 and in turn in 1905 by an explosive charge. The explosive fog signal was discontinued and replaced in 1975 by a compressed air-operated emitter, which gave one blast every 30 seconds. Finally, in 1995, this pneumatic fog signal was replaced by an electric horn with a character of two blasts every 45 seconds.

Hook tower was originally 18 metres high and approximately 8.5 metres in diameter. It was subsequently enlarged to 24 metres and is around 12 metres in diameter (it is not truly circular) with a spiral stone stairway between the outside of the old wall and the inside of the newer wall. The tower is constructed of local limestone and the original building survives almost intact at just under 36.6 metres high. It consists of two tiers linked by a mural stairway of 115 steps.

The station was automated in March 1996 and is now remotely controlled from Dun Laoghaire, Dublin where the headquarters of the Commissioners of Irish Lights is based. Some of the ancillary buildings attached to the lighthouse were converted to a heritage centre in 2000, where food, refreshments, books and other momentos of a visit to the Head can be purchased; regular guided tours of the lighthouse are also available,

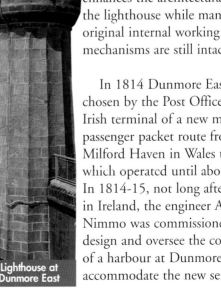

Lighthouse at Dunmore East

The Dunmore East lighthouse
The lighthouse at Dunmore East is an elegant and visually appealing structure at the end of the pier and is a prominent landmark in the harbour. The fluted detailing and the high quality stone masonry enhances the architectural value of the lighthouse while many of the original internal working mechanisms are still intact.

In 1814 Dunmore East was chosen by the Post Office to be the Irish terminal of a new mail and passenger packet route from Milford Haven in Wales to Ireland, which operated until about 1835. In 1814-15, not long after arriving in Ireland, the engineer Alexander Nimmo was commissioned to design and oversee the construction of a harbour at Dunmore East to accommodate the new service.

Alexander Nimmo was a remarkable engineer. Born in Kircaldy, Scotland in 1783, he moved to Ireland in 1811 where he was employed by a number of government bodies on various key projects throughout the country. He conducted surveys for the Bog Commission in Kerry and Galway and in 1820 he was employed by the Commission for Irish Fisheries, for whom he surveyed two-thirds of the Irish coastline. Some of his notable projects include the erection of over forty piers along the west coast, the founding of the village of Roundstone in Galway and the construction of two hundred and forty-three miles of road in the west of Ireland. He died at his home in Marlborough Street, Dublin, in January 1832.

The construction of the harbour at Dunmore East was a considerable feat of engineering at the time given the depth of water, the tidal conditions and the often harsh winter weather. His design included a freestanding single-bay, three-stage granite ashlar lighthouse with coursed cut-stone walls on a polygonal plan comprising a tapered fluted shaft with a moulded cornice, which has a single-bay, single-stage lantern and an ogee-domed capping.

In July 1818, a temporary light was placed on the end of the pier, in preparation for the arrival of the first mail packet. The lighthouse column was completed in October 1824, inspected in March 1825 and became operational in late 1825 once the required lighting mechanism had been installed and commissioned. The light was fixed, showing red to sea and white or clear to land, and the tower was initially painted white but by 1903 the natural stone colour prevailed. A four-bay single-storey flat-roofed store was added around 1875.

The oil lamps and reflectors were used

until 1922 when the light was converted to acetylene and the lightkeeper was replaced by an attendant. The 100-watt light was electrified in January 1964 using a 100 volt battery with a charger supplied by mains electricity. In August 1981 the optic lamp was switched to mains electricity with an emergency standby diesel generator cutting in automatically in the event of a power failure.

The east breakwater pier was extended by approximately 91 metres (300 feet) during the mid-1960s and two temporary red lights were erected towards the end of 1965/early 1966 to mark the end and mid-way point of the extension, which were replaced by permanent flashing lights in July 1971.

The Metal Man

Tramore Bay has always been a notorious graveyard for boats of all sizes, and particularly for sailing ships in the nineteenth century. In the period 1566-1911 at least 114 ships were wrecked in the Bay, 89 of them between 1816 and 1899, with the loss of 440 lives. The most tragic of these was *The Sea Horse*, which went down in bad weather in January 1816 and 363 people were drowned (of the 394 on board). This tragedy alerted the Admiralty to the dangers posed to ships by Tramore Bay and in June 1821 a newspaper notice appeared in the *Waterford Mirror* stating that it was intended to erect three towers on Great Newtown Head on the western side of Tramore Bay and two on the eastern side at Brownstown Head in an effort to direct ships away from the Bay. The five pillars were erected in 1823. These are freestanding rubble-stone, tapered shafts on a circular plan and constructed using high quality stone masonry, whose design is attributed to Alexander Nimmo.

On the center pillar of the three on Great Newtown Head, a

The Metal Man at Great Newtown Head

metal statue approximately 4.27 metres (14 feet) tall was positioned; it was probably carved by the Cork sculptor Thomas Kirk, who also carved Nelson's Pillar in Dublin (blown up in 1966). This figure points seawards informing incoming ships to stay clear and is more commonly known as The Metal Man; he has an identical twin on Perch Rock in Sligo Bay. Both figures are dressed in the uniform of a Royal Navy able seaman of the time–a short navy-blue coat, a pair of white trousers and a red coat. However, despite his dominating presence, the pillars proved to be ineffective in bad weather and at night. These impressive beacons are now a prominent feature of the Waterford coastline. The Metal Man, in particular, is enjoyed and appreciated by local people and is a tourist attraction, appearing in promotional brochures for Tramore and the southeast.

Ballynacourty Point lighthouse
The lighthouse at Ballynacourty was first established in July 1858 on its own grounds and is both visually appealing and picturesque, defining the northeastern side of Dungarvan Bay and is perhaps even more visually dominating because of the strong white emphasis of the seaward wall. It was built to designs prepared by George Halpin (1779-1854), a prominent civil engineer who was Inspector of Works for the Dublin Ballast Board (the predecessor to the present Commissioners of Irish Lights). He was responsible for the establishment of 53 new lighthouses around the Irish coast, in addition to many of the important civil and mechanical works around Dublin port.

It is a freestanding single-bay, two-stage lighthouse on a circular plan with a single-bay, single-stage domed lantern and it retains its original form and character. The light was converted to acetylene operation in 1929 and electrification took place in February 1964. The present light source comprises a cluster of four 35-watt halogen

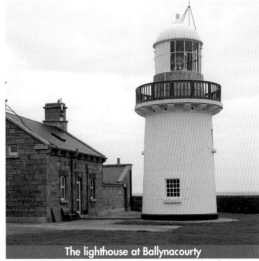

The lighthouse at Ballynacourty

lamps, installed during the overhaul of the station in 2005/06. Adjacent to the lighthouse is a detached three-bay, single-storey keepers house, which was built around 1860. It has coursed squared limestone walls and a dormer attic and is a fine complement to the nearby lighthouse, and both together form a self-contained cluster of attractive buildings in this scenic location.

Mine Head lighthouse
Mine Head lighthouse is located on the high cliffs of Mine Head, in *An Sean Phobal* (Old Parish), a Gaeltacht or Irish-speaking area of west Waterford and it is a dramatic landmark on the Head. Designed by George Halpin, the lighthouse towers 87 metres or almost 290 feet above sea level, reputedly the highest above sea level of any of the Irish lighthouses. It is a freestanding single-bay, four-stage lighthouse on a circular plan and retains its original aspect with a tapered shaft and a single-bay, single-stage glazed lantern. The construction of the shaft demonstrates high quality stone masonry and fine-tooled detailing and the lantern and its operation is of technical interest. The lighthouse here has been very well maintained over the years, and it largely retains its original form and fabric. There is a collection of related outbuildings, including the low-profile lightkeepers house, which enhances the

Mine Head lighthouse

overall aesthetic, visual and architectural value of the site. Established in June 1851, it was electrified in September 1964. The beacon flashes white and red every 2.5 seconds and it has a range of almost 40 kilometres due to its height above sea level. One of the last keepers here was Matt Crowley, who retired in the 1980s. The lighthouse is now fully automated, it is not accessible, may be hard to find and is not open to the public.

To the east is Ballynamona court cairn, a good example of one of the earliest megalithic tombs in Ireland, more commonly known as court tombs and is dated to around 2000 B.C. It is known locally as *Cailleach Bheara* ("The old Hag from Beara"). It was excavated in May 1938 by the Office of Public Works in collaboration with the National Museum. The excavators discovered small fragments of decorated pottery, as well as numerous flint flakes, which allowed the team to ascertain if there was human activity nearby. The beliefs of the people who built the tomb are unknown, though it is thought they were sun worshippers as this was common around the island at the time.

OTHER MARITIME BUILDINGS

A network of 54 Coast Guard units and their stationhouses are based at strategic locations around the Irish coast, and are largely operated by volunteers, both male and female. The units have a strategic maritime capability with a range of equipment depending on location, which includes air support, cliff equipment, rescue boats and vehicles. Many of these units are housed in buildings originally built by HM Coastguard, which were taken over by *Saorstát Éireann* on the formation of the State. The service was subsequently renamed the Coast and Cliff Rescue Service (CCRS), and later became the Irish Marine Rescue Service (IMES) before being renamed the Irish Coast Guard (IRCG) in 2001. The IRCG is overseen by the Department of Transport and is responsible for search and rescue, pollution and salvage response, communications and safety in the marine area around Ireland.

There are old coastguard stations at Dunmore East, Tramore, Helvick and Ardmore and these also have attractive coastguard houses nearby (now largely in private ownership). At Dunmore East there are well-composed, modest-scale houses in the Classic style, originally built as accommodation for the coastguard station workers (now in use by the Irish Coast Guard Service), and these are important and elegant buildings in the village.

At Tramore a detached nine-bay, two-storey over part-basement coastguard station, built in 1875, is set back from the road in its own grounds on an elevated site on the west side of Tramore Bay. It remained in use until 1922, when it was occupied by the *Garda Síochána* until 1988. Thereafter it remained unoccupied, was gradually vandalised and eventually burned in early 2000 but was rebuilt in 2003. It is an attractive building and is a prominent landmark in the townscape of Tramore. There are a number of other associated coastguard houses and boathouses at Tramore, now in residential use or unused, each with characteristic features and styles which typify the craftsmanship that was used in their construction.

A unit of the Irish Coast Guard is based in a modest building just outside the village of Bunmahon, and it covers a wide search area stretching from Annestown to the east all the way along the coast to Clonea to the west. This area contains some of the highest and most spectacular cliffs in the county and the unit has full cliff rescue status. There are also coastguard stations at Helvick Head and Ardmore; the old one at Ardmore, constructed on the Odell Estate in 1867, is particularly prominent on an elevated site on the headland, which, apart from offering a panoramic view of the coast, also provides excellent radio coverage. A previous coastguard station down near the strand fell victim to coastal erosion. The new three-

Pilot station, Shanooan, Dunmore East (now closed)

storey stationhouse adjoins the old coastguard station, which is now an apartment complex.

Watchtowers can be seen along the Waterford coast at Brownstown, Dunabrattin and Ardmore (one at Helvick Head was demolished). The bland appearance of these buildings belies their significance during 'The Emergency' (1939-1945), when very valuable intelligence was gathered at them for later analysis in Dublin. Most are now abandoned and derelict. However there is an attractive freestanding single-bay, two-stage Gothic-style watchtower on the cliff top at Ardmore Head, which may have had a defense purpose but, despite its abandoned state, it is an attractive feature here and visually appealing for the many visitors who follow the coastal path nearby. The abandoned pilot station at Shanooan, Dunmore East is a freestanding single-bay, two-storey flat-roofed building constructed around 1940 on the cliff top and was formerly used for directing portal traffic through Waterford Harbour. Small, compact and exposed, it is still a prominent but deteriorating feature in the area.

HARBOURS AND PIERS

There are many small but attractive piers along the Waterford coast, which were originally built to support an active fishing industry or to provide work and employment for famine-stricken communities in the nineteenth century. An indication of the importance of these piers for local fishing communities is the number of boats and

NUMBER OF BOATS AND FISHERMEN IN WATERFORD IN 1836				
Area	Hookers no., men	Yawls no., men	Rowing Boats no., men	Fishermen
Ardmore	-, -	-, -	43, 252	252
Helvick	94, 564	7, 35	80, 400	999
Bunmahon	-, -	9, 54	39, 166	220
Islandikane	-, -	-, -	18, 72	72
Ballymacaw	4, 16	2, 8	60, 240	264
Dunmore East	3, 15	34, 204	-, -	219

[Helvick probably included Ballynagaul, and Ballymacaw probably included Portally]

source: Report of the Commissioners on Irish Fisheries, 1836

fishermen which used them in the 1800s. The piers and harbours of the county are still in constant use today, but nowhere near the same numbers use them, though they can be busy in summer when the recreational users join the commercial fishermen.

Dunmore East harbour

In the mid-eighteenth century, Dunmore East was frequented by boats but few people lived there. It appears that a successful

Pier at Dunmore East

herring fishery commenced soon after, though the area was bypassed by shipping, which continued up Waterford Harbour to Passage East and even to Cheekpoint. The Post Office decided that a new packet station at the mouth of Waterford Harbour was preferable to the packet ships sailing upriver to Waterford City, which was subject to considerable delays, depending on tidal conditions and weather. Work began on building the pier, which was designed by Alexander Nimmo, at Portcullin cove, Dunmore East in 1814 and was substantially completed by 1822 when the passenger and mail service to Milford Haven in Wales began. Interestingly, Nimmo designed a diving bell for use in constructing the harbour foundations, which weighed around five tons and was sufficiently large to provide air for one person for 24 hours (though the bell had room for up to 6 people). It also allowed work in deeper waters than was common elsewhere. As the packet steamers became more powerful, it was less challenging to reach Waterford City, which had more extensive quays and better facilities than those available at Dunmore East, so eventually Dunmore was bypassed completely and the service transferred to Waterford.

The harbour was renovated in 1969 and a new pier added on the western side. There are impressive coursed cut-stone walls on the

Monument at Dunmore East to those lost at sea

original pier wall but some sections were replaced with mass-concrete in 1969.

The population of the village was 1547 people in 2006, which, surprisingly, had declined by around 12% in the previous five years, despite an increase in house building activity in the area.

Dunmore East is one of six designated fishery centres in Ireland. Fishing activity is centered in the harbour area, and there are three quays: the west wharf (which includes the ice berth, is 160 metres long), the Auction Hall landing berth (south pier, 60 metres long) and the east picr (270 metres long), which services the local fleet of trawlers and half-deckers, and boats of all sizes arrive from Cork and Wexford mainly. The harbour is usually very busy and crowded during the autumn herring and spring fishing seasons, when a number of foreign vessels also arrive, though the harbour is only accessible for the larger vessels about two hours before and after high tide. Berthing during onshore southeast winds is always difficult and, if

CATCH LANDINGS (IN TONNES) AT DUNMORE EAST					
	2003	*2004*	*2005*	*2006*	*2007*
Deepwater	12	32	14	100	0
Demersal	3,273	4,196	5,458	3,820	5,653
Pelagic	2,211	6,682	3,575	1,508	865
Shellfish	776	966	2,326	1,295	2,073
Total	6,272	11,876	11,373	6,723	8,591

source: Sea Fisheries Protection Authority

severe, may damage berthed vessels. The average water depth is around three metres and reducing because of silting. In summer, the usage of the harbour increases dramatically when yachts and pleasure craft arrive but most of this activity takes place in the outer harbour near the yacht club and the adventure centre, which is serviced by a concrete slipway. A synchro lift caters for vessels with a maximum draft of around nine metres. The local auction hall is managed by the Dunmore East Fishermen's Co-Op but shellfish is the only local processing activity. The harbour and its related industries are an important source of employment in the area.

Dunmore East is also a developing cruise destination, though these usually anchor offshore and passengers are ferried onshore where they are taken to beauty spots around the southeast and to Waterford City.

There are plans for the development of a new breakwater and an outer pier for commercial activity which will provide a

Cut-stone mooring bollard and stone cobbling at Ballynacourty pier

water depth of up to seven metres. The existing inner pier will be developed for amenity uses. However the inner harbour sediments are heavily contaminated with TBT, which makes dredging difficult and costly and with a risk of undermining the east pier wall, a protected structure. If and when this new outer pier is developed it will alleviate many of the deficiencies identified at Dunmore East (lack of marina facilities, exposure to inclement weather, conflict between leisure craft and commercial boats, insufficient water depth due to siltation and parking difficulties, especially in summer).

Tramore pier

The pier on the west side of Tramore Bay at Lady's cove was opened in 1907, two years after construction began. It replaced an earlier structure that was destroyed by a succession of storms in 1883. To the south of the Pier are two attractive bathing areas, the Guillamene and Newtown cove, the construction of which was facilitated by the opening of cliff road in 1872 on the site of an old coastguard path. The Guillamene was maintained as a bathing area by the Christian Brothers for their congregation in the 1880s, and it was declared to be a 'men only' area. The sign proclaiming this remains, though purely for nostalgic reasons.

Boatstrand

The small harbour here was built in July 1883, and was used by many boats carrying cargoes of coal and fertiliser for local supply. It was also an important harbour for local fishermen and is still in use by small fishing boats and pleasure craft.

Ballynacourty pier

The pier was constructed in 1832 on a cranked L-shaped plan and is an appealing focal point on the north side of Dungarvan Bay, near the Gold Coast Hotel. There are impressive coursed squared limestone walls with a swept batter to the south, a cut-stone date-stone plaque, flights of cut-stone steps to the water level, cut-stone mooring bollards and sections of rubble stone cobbling, all constructed using high quality masonry techniques. The pier was formerly the hub of maritime activities that once supported the local economy of Ballynacourty and Dungarvan; its use now is tide-dependent.

Strandside South and Davitt's Quay, Dungarvan

A section of random rubble limestone quay wall was built around 1820 at Strandside South, which encloses a strand to the east of Dungarvan Bay. It was extended to the south/southeast in the 1940s. In Dungarvan a long section of quay wall, again built around 1820, has square coursed limestone walls with a slight batter, along with flights of cut-stone steps down to water level. These constructed maritime features are an important reminder of the historical importance of the area in once supporting commercial activity locally, particularly a thriving fishing industry in the Dungarvan area. While there is less of this activity now, these facilities are important recreational assets which are much used for sailing, fishing and other marine activities.

Ballynagaul pier

Alexander Nimmo, the prominent engineer (1783-1832), designed a fishing pier at Ballynagaul in 1815, which included a village with over 100 buildings, including fishermen's houses, stores and a roofed market house on the wharf. Streets were to be parallel to the shore, and one of them was named Stuart Street, in honour of Lord Villiers-Stuart, who owned much of the surrounding land. The village was never built and the pier at Ballynagaul was constructed later, in late 1848, on an L-shaped plan, and roughly similar to the one designed earlier by Nimmo. There are irregular coursed squared rubble limestone walls with batter, rendered mooring bollards, and an irregular coursed

Helvick pier

squared rubble limestone parapet. Small but attractive, the pier was extensively used for fishery related activities in the 1800s and 1900s, and supported a thriving community locally. It is still in use today, though to a much lesser extent than previously.

Helvick pier

The pier at Helvick was constructed in the early 1900s, on a curved L-shaped plan using more modern elements than in other piers in the county. There are mass-concrete walls with batter and concrete steps down to the water level with concrete coping on the parapet but a section of random rubble stone wall is in place to the southeast and there are wrought iron railings on the western side.

The pier continues to support an important though declining fishing industry

Rescue helicopter in Dungarvan Bay

Lifeboat at Dunmore East

locally but is increasingly important for recreational activities; it is also an attractive focal point at Helvick Head. The scenic Comeragh Mountains form an impressive backdrop to the north.

Ardmore pier

Ardmore pier was built around 1920 with mass-concrete walls and is an important element of the architectural heritage of Ardmore, apart from its use locally to support fishing-related activities and, increasingly, marine leisure sports.

RNLI

The Royal National Lifeboats Institution, better known as the RNLI, is a charity that provides a continuous lifesaving service around the coasts of Ireland, England, Scotland and Wales using locally based volunteers on permanent standby in case of marine emergencies anywhere in coastal waters. Three lifeboats are based in Waterford with onshore stations and ancillary facilities needed to support the service.

A lifeboat station, including a boathouse and slipway was first constructed by the RNLI at Dunmore East in 1884. Dunmore

now has a 25-knot Trent class lifeboat, called the *Elizabeth and Ronald*, with a range of 250 nautical miles and a crew of six. It is permanently moored near the Auction Hall in the harbour. Nearby, a modern two-story building provides all the support services required for this important local service.

At Tramore a lifeboat station was first established in 1858 and an inshore lifeboat station was established at the pier in 1964, which now houses a D-class lifeboat (the D-643 *Trá Mhór*). Dungarvan has had a lifeboat presence since 1859, first on the north side of the Bay, then at Ballynacourty before it was moved to Crow Point (near Helvick) in 1899 and then to Helvick harbour in 1930. However the all-weather lifeboat was withdrawn in 1969 and the station closed. In 1997 the service was reinstated and an Atlantic 75 inshore lifeboat, the B-760 *Alice and Charles*, was placed in service in 1999. A lifeboat was first placed at Ardmore by the RNLI in 1857 and the attractive boathouse down in the village was built in 1876 (the beautiful stonework of the boathouse there can still be admired). However, in January 1895 the RNLI decided that the lifeboats at Youghal and Ballycotton would adequately serve the coastal area here.

Archaeological Sites on the Waterford Coast

With a long coastline close to a wealth of nearby opportunities for food, social interaction, ritual, ceremonial and religious activities and defence, there are many archaeological features still visible on the coastal landscape in Waterford. Some of these features define the area where they occur, such as the round tower at Ardmore, which is an important national monument, while others are scarcely visible or cannot be seen at all. Some are very accessible and easily seen while others are less obvious and some searching may be required to find them. They are, however, worth the effort involved in locating them, as a potent reminder of the use to which the land has been put by our ancestors and the almost timelessness of the landscape that we are so fortunate to enjoy and live in. By visiting these sites we can claim a shared experience with our ancestors who have lived in the county before us.

The extracts below are largely taken from *The Archaeological Inventory of County Waterford*. The features are described alphabetically and then from the east to the west of the county (from Creadan Head near Dunmore East to East Point at the mouth of the river Blackwater). Site number (as given in the *Archaeological Inventory*), site name and eight-figure grid references are given (where the site location is known), which may help in seeking further information and assisting in locating these ancient monuments.

Ardmore ecclesiastical remains
at Ardocheasty/Monea
The Déisi were an ancient tribe of native Irish people some of whom ruled over much of the land that is now defined by the Roman Catholic Diocese of Waterford and Lismore (which includes some parts outside of county Waterford). Saint Declan converted the

people of the Decies to Christianity and he founded an early Christian settlement at Ardmore in the fifth century, possibly prior to the arrival of Saint Patrick, so he was a contemporary of Saint Patrick, though he was, apparently, also a contemporary of Saint David (the bishop of a Déisi colony in Wales). Whatever about this conflict of religious history, what remains at Ardmore is a remarkable group of ancient ecclesiastical remains [1312], which are a fine testimony to the influence and ability of Saint Declan in defining the religious importance of Ardmore at that time. There is quite a remarkable round tower (which dominates the hinterland at Ardmore), the remains of a particularly interesting church more commonly referred to as a cathedral, a rudimentary oratory, a

Sculpture at Ardmore depicting Saint Declan

The round tower at Ardmore.
The round tower and the cathedral nearby are two of
Ireland's most important Romanesque monuments and
extraordinary architectural detail is apparent in both

second church close to a holy well and a series of other artifacts (ogham inscribed pillar stones, for example), all of which attest to the religious significance of Ardmore during the life of Saint Declan and in the following centuries.

The spectacular round tower [**1312**: *18917736*], built in the twelfth century, is the most striking of all the monuments at Ardmore. Perfectly formed using very even sandstone blocks and extremely well preserved, it is almost 30 metres (100 feet) high, in a prominent position in the village with commanding views of Ardmore Bay and the surrounding countryside. It is five metres in diameter at the base and because of the pronounced batter (the inclination of the wall inwards) the external diameter at the top windows is just over three metres. There are four windows in all on the top floor, each equidistant from the other, with one at each

of the cardinal points of the compass; a number of simpler openings on the other floors also provide light, while the entrance doorway is around four metres from the ground, which assisted in the defensive purpose of the tower at times of attack. The most obvious external features, apart from the projecting form and its conical stone cap, are the projecting stone rims, which divide the tower into four storeys; less obvious are the sculptured corbels, sixteen in all, between floors internally. The capstone was damaged by musket balls in the 1860s and was replaced in 1875-6. This rock cone, with its distinctive cross, adds around 3.5 metres to the height of the tower.

Nearby and to the north, the cathedral [**1312**: *18877738*], although not as dominant, is equally interesting for the varied ecclesiastical architectural styles that are visible in the structure. There are a wonderful series of arcades and panels on the entire western external gable, remarkable for their detail and clarity. The arcading consists of a row of thirteen panels on a chamfered string course, nine of which contain Romanesque figure sculptures. Some of these have been determined as The Last Judgement, Majestas and a number of bishops. Below these panels are two lunettes (originally there were three), with the left one depicting Adam and Eve, and the right one The Judgement of Solomon over the Adoration of the Magi.

The cathedral was built in the twelfth century and consists of a nave and chancel. Three ogham stones were found at the site and two of these are now located in the chancel; one was originally built into the east wall of Saint Declan's Oratory while the other, which has a small incised cross, was located beside a grave; a third, found built into a low wall of the cathedral, is in the safe keeping of the National Museum of Ireland. There are also eight medieval sandstone grave slabs in the nave while an octagonal font was

The west wall of the church near the round tower at Ardmore

moved to the nearby Church of Ireland in the early nineteenth century.

The oratory [**1312**: *18917736*] to the east of the cathedral, sometimes referred to as Saint Declan's Grave, is a primitive sixth century type church with high-pitched gables, a square-headed doorway with inclining jambs and prolonged side-walls. This little church may have been erected in the century following the death of Saint Declan and the site is popularly presumed to be where his ashes once reposed. In 1716 a slate roof was added by Bishop Thomas Mills of Waterford. On a rocky ledge beneath the beach, a glacial boulder of conglomerate known as Saint Declan's Stone [**1725**: *19337752*], is supported by projecting points of the underlying rock and was a focal point on the feast of the Saint on the 24th July annually, when people crawled with difficulty beneath the stone three times to avail of the apparent healing ability of the boulder. A second, though much smaller Saint Declan's Stone, also, apparently, with healing powers, disappeared in the nineteenth century. Saint Declan's Well [**1354**: *19847729*] is at the beginning of the spectacular cliff walk just beyond the Cliff House Hotel and is beside the remains of a twelfth century church,

Dysert Church, which may have been the parish church of Ardmore.

Ardoginna house
There is an impressive Georgian gothic house, Ardoginna House [not listed in *The Archaeological Inventory of County Waterford*], to the west of Ardmore. It is a detached, three-bay, two-storey, castellated structure set in its own grounds and close to the cliffs. There is a mention of Ardoginna House in the Civil Survey of 1654-1656, when it was owned by James FitzGerald, but the present house and the four-bay, two-storey coach house, both now in ruins, date from around 1775. The freestanding single-bay, four-stage tower was added in 1847, while the freestanding single-bay single-storey mausoleum, was added around 1875. It has an impressive life-size carved statue and is the burial place of Sir Stephen McKenna, probably its most famous owner. He was both chairman and managing director of the National Bank of Ireland and he purchased the property in 1865, the same year he was elected MP for Youghal in 1865 (he was knighted in 1867). He died at Ardoginna, in 1906, aged 89. Other owners include the Costen family (early seventeenth century), Sir Francis Prendergast (later seventeenth

Saint Declan's well at Ardmore

century), the Coghlans (eighteenth century), Lawlors (early nineteenth century), the de Castries family and Marshall McMahon (President and Marshal of France in 1873). It was abandoned around 1918 or soon afterwards, and, once left untended, it was looted and plundered, and eventually became derelict. However, it is an imposing edifice, despite the overgrown state of the building and the dilapidated nature of the site close to a dramatic coastal setting.

Church

1390: *Kilmacleague West, 63370203*
Parish church of Kilmacleague, dedicated to Saint Michael the Archangel comprising a nave and later chancel. A possible bullaun stone and stoup are missing, as are earthworks north of the church which were mentioned by Canon Power or the deserted graveyard which were described around 1840.

Church site

Early ritual sites were abandoned following the arrival of Saint Patrick in the fifth century and the adoption of Christianity. Many were

adapted for Christian purposes, though hardly anything is known about some early ecclesiastical sites, probably because of their general antiquity.

1. 1325: *Ballynarrid, 42039752*
On a sea stack. The name 'Templeobrick' indicates the site of a church. Apparently the foundations of a building were still evident here in 1840. Inaccessible.

2. 1362: *Island, 35609583*
An early ecclesiastical site. It is a large grass-covered circular area defined by an earthen overgrown bank with internal and external stone-facing. The entrance at the western end is possibly modern. There is an ogham stone in the interior [**1490**] and a bullaun stone has also been found here (a saddle quern).

Court cairn

A court cairn is a type of megalithic tomb, which has a gallery of one or more oblong chambers connected by projecting stones and the gallery opens on to a court. They are more common in the north of Ireland.

4: *Ballynamona Upper, 28768358*

In rough pasture on top of the headland. There is a gallery of two chambers with two portal-stones and a septal-stone opening to the west where there is a court represented by four stones. This site was excavated in 1938. The chambers had been disturbed but fragments of cremated bone, two pottery vessels, one of which was decorated, and flint flakes were recovered during the dig (see also p. 164).

Crannóg

A crannóg is an artificial or man-made island, usually circular in construction, in a lake, river, marshland or estuarine waters, with a base of stones and tree-trunks layered with wood and peat to form a platform, which was above the water level. It may have been surrounded with a palisade fence of closely-set wooden stakes to act as a defensive barrier. The stumps of the stakes may be visible when preserved by the waterlogged conditions in which they were placed, which also preserved other artifacts. They were usually inhabited and they served the same purpose as ringforts, which were in use around the same period. With so few lakes in Waterford, only two crannógs sites are known (around 2,000 are known nationally).

1280: *Duffcarrick, 19247768*

There are no visible remains of the crannóg, which was discovered on the beach at Ardmore in 1879 by Richard John Ussher (the famous ornithologist), when the sea eroded a shingle bank. It consisted of a double row of oak piles, pointed at the base and embedded in peat. The interior was composed of peat. Metal and wooden artifacts and animal bones were also recorded.

Enclosure

These are probably ringforts, whose exact identification is difficult because many have been removed to ground level during ground clearance works, though below surface remnants may remain. Ringforts are the commonest visible monuments in the Irish landscape; they were constructed as protected enclosures around habitation sites during the early Christian Period (500-1100 AD).

1. 802: *Ballynamona Lower, 28388264*

On high ground 300 metres from the sea cliffs. It is a D-shaped, grass-covered area with straight sides at the southwest and northwest ends, defined by an earth and stone bank. Two upright stones on the bank on the northwest may represent a

Ardoginna house

blocked entrance. No internal features are visible in this enclosure.

2. 798: *Ballykilmurry, 25878102*

On a small shelf or subcircular platform, above the sea cliffs, overgrown with bracken and known locally as 'Clancy's Garden'. Defined by a drystone wall at the south and west and enclosed by a natural cliff which rises over it to the north and east. Inaccessible.

Fulacht fiadh

These are burnt stone mounds and are primitive cooking or washing sites, usually close to or on wet, marshy sites so the stone or wood-lined trough naturally filled with water. The water in the trough was heated by adding hot stones warmed in a nearby fire. The stones eventually cracked because of the constant heating and these were discarded around the edges of the trough, forming the U-shaped mounds that are dotted all over the Irish landscape, though they may not necessarily stand out as ancient features.

415: *Woodstown (Annestown), 50509901*

In agricultural pasture on a northwest-facing slope. It is a circular mound of burnt and broken stone.

Holy well

Holy wells have always been associated with Christianity and are usually near to churches, but they may also be isolated and far removed from ecclesiastical sites.

1530: *Monatray East, 14097728*

On a severe east-facing slope overlooking the panoramic Whiting Bay. Known as 'Saint Uchta's or Saint Ita's Well', which was formerly venerated. Opens under a rock outcrop as a recess defined by a masonry wall. Still maintained but a pattern is no longer held here.

Midden

A midden is simply a collection of layered organic material, usually only found on the sea shore, where mesolithic hunter gatherers disposed of inedible material over time.

The court cairn at Ballynamona

1734: *Tramore Burrow, 60221197*
At the 'neck' in the sand dunes at
Tramore. A spread of broken and burnt
shells in a black matrix.

Ogham stones
Ogham is one of the earliest written forms of
Irish, which is based on Latin but the letters
are inscribed using strokes and notches, read
from bottom to top. Waterford has a
remarkable collection of ogham stones,
usually at church sites.

1496: *Knockmahon, 44269856*
A stone fragment was found in the 1980s
and another complete stone was found in
the 1990s.

Prehistoric mines
482: *Ballynarrid, 41759767*
Thirteen mine openings are visible on the
headland of Dane's Island beneath a
promontory fort. These may be Bronze
Age copper mines but they may also be
eighteenth century silver and lead mines.

Promontory forts
These are coastal defence systems on
promontories or cliff headlands, comprising a
bank and fosse, which had to be dug down to
the bedrock. Sometimes more than one line
of defence was used, usually close together,
though a berm separates them at Ballyvooney.
The defences were built at the narrowest part
of the promontory. Many of the coastal
promontories in county Waterford have
defensive forts associated with them. They
probably date from the Iron Age to the
beginning of Christianity.

1. 502: *Shanooan, Dunmore East,
69109977*
Defences leveled and the topsoil was
removed in the 1970s to create a carpark.

2. 508: *Rathmoylan, 66129846*
A triangular promontory, defended by a
grass-covered earthen bank and outer
fosse. An outer berm separates the fosse
from a modern field bank.

3. 499: *Coolum, 62999843*
Triangular and grass-covered, it is
defended by three earthen banks with two
intervening fosses.

4. 509: *Westtown, 55879829*
Rectangular, grass-covered and cut off at
the northern end by an earthen bank with
an outer flat-bottomed fosse.

5. 503: *Garrarus, 54959832*
Grass-covered area of around one hectare,
defended at the narrowest point by two
eroded banks and fosses.

6. 505: *Islandikane, 53479808*
Lying partly on Sheep Island which is
being eroded by the sea into two distinct
islands. The island is now inaccessible but
it has an oval hut site within a
grass-covered enclosure.

Canon Power, in *The Place-Names of
Decies*, states that:

> on the islets, as well as on the
> mainland immediate adjoining, are
> some foundations of cloghâns, or
> primitive stone houses of the beehive
> type–the only remains of the kind so
> far discovered in Waterford–and the
> site of the cloghâns is surrounded by
> a strong earthen fence of the lios type.

The 6" Ordnance Survey map of the area
indicates "ancient Irish dwelling" here,
though it is no longer identifiable as a
feature on the ground.

7. 506: *Kilfarrasy, 51839821*
On a coastal promontory jutting south,
and defended on the landward side by a
fosse with a central causeway.

The midden at the 'neck', Tramore dunes

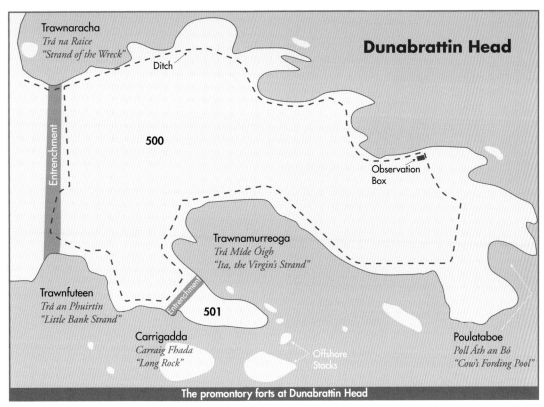

Trawnaracha	
Trá na Raice	
"Strand of the Wreck"	**Dunabrattin Head**

Ditch

Entrenchment

500

Observation Box

Trawnamurreoga
Trá Míde Óigh
"Ita, the Virgin's Strand"

Trawnfuteen
Trá an Phuirtín
"Little Bank Strand"

Entrenchment

501

Carrigadda
Carraig Fhada
"Long Rock"

Offshore Stacks

Poulataboe
Poll Áth an Bó
"Cow's Fording Pool"

The promontory forts at Dunabrattin Head

8. **510**: *Woodstown (Annestown),*
50049867
A sea promontory jutting south, cut off
on the landward side by a grass-covered
bank and outer fosse. Brown's Island may
once have been part of this fort.

9. **492**: *Annestown, 49249883*
Inaccessible due to coastal erosion but
some remnants of both the fosse and the
bank survive.

10. **500** & **501**, & **868**: *Dunabrattin,*
47549822
Site number **500** is a large (around six
hectares or 14.8 acres), grass-covered
headland cut off from the mainland by an
east-west fosse. There is evidence of hut
sites within the bank. **501** is within **500**.

868, although not visible on the ground,
appears as a crop mark on aerial
photographs. It is outside the fosse of the
promontory fort **500**.

11. **507**: *Knockmahon, 44269856*
A grass-covered coastal promontory, cut
off on the landward side by an eroded
earthen bank. Two offshore stacks may
have been part of the fort originally.
Ogham stones were found in the fosse in
1980s and again in 1990s.

12. **495**: *Ballynarrid, 42259783*
A narrow isthmus defended by a slight
inner bank. Labelled 'Slippery Island' on
Ordnance Survey maps.

13. **496**: *Ballynarrid, 41739770*
Dane's Island is on a sea stack now
connected to the mainland by an eroded
and impassable rock isthmus. The interior
is reputed to have a number of hut sites
and the headland has mine workings (see
482 above).

14. **497**: *Ballyvooney, 38899745*
Cut off at northern end by a grass-covered
bank and fosse. The interior is flat.

Dunhill castle

1. **153**: *Ballymacaw, 65339879*
On top of vertical sea cliff, known locally as the 'White Lady'. Made from conglomerate, the top has been damaged by frost action.

2. **217**: *Islandikane East, 53839836*
Possible site at the top of a sea cliff, rectangular and oriented north-south.

3. **266** (*& 267 further N*), *Woodstown (Annestown)*: 50069891 (*& 50429923*)
Both are Old Red Sandstone.

4. **252** *& 253*: *Rathnamaneenagh, 28448605 & 28678598*
Both are on gentle east-facing slopes close to the sea cliffs. The second one is damaged at the top. They are only possible standing stones.

15. **504**: *Islandhubbock, 35009511*
Grass-covered, defended by a fosse, a central bank and an outer fosse. Within the defences are two possible hut sites.

16. **494**: *Ballynamona Lower, 28658281*
Defended on its western side by a section of rock outcrop surmounted by a grass-covered earthen bank with an outer flat bottomed fosse. The interior is rectangular in plan.

17. **493**: *28658281, Ballynaharda*
Defended at the west end by a section of rock outcrop surmounted by a grass-covered earthen bank with an outer flat-bottomed fosse. The interior is rectangular in plan.

Standing stones
The precise prehistoric symbolic significance of standing stones cannot now be precisely determined. They were probably erected in the Bronze Age. Burial sites from the Bronze and Iron Age have been found close to them but they may also have been placed to mark boundaries, significant routes or the conquest of mountain passes.

Tower house
1609: *Dunhill castle, 25072268*
This is an imposing tower house built on a rocky outcrop with commanding views of the coast and the Anne valley and stream (which flows into the sea just to the east of Annestown). It was built by the la Poer family in the early 1200s but there is evidence of an earlier Celtic fort here; *Dun Aill*, "Fort of the Rock", apparently, derives its name from an ancient fortress or stronghold of an unnamed Irish chief, which was situated on the rock where the ruined castle now stands. It remained in the control of the la Poer family (the Powers) until the Cromwellian attack on Dunhill and its capture in December 1649. It is a rectangular tower with cut-stone quoins surviving to the first floor, flat-arched doorways, mural stairs and embrasures (doorways with slanting sides). The castle is now in ruins, having been abandoned in the 1700s and subject since to the ravages of weather and decay. There are ruins of a church and an eighteenth century graveyard within the site. Although delapidated, the site is accessible.

Beaches, Coves and Cliff Walks

*B*eaches are the most accessible parts of the coast, where public access is guaranteed, and where many of us visit for a variety of activities, at all times of the year and in all weather conditions. We are irresistibly drawn to the coastal beaches, for inspiration, meditation and recreation and we usually leave with a heavy heart but sure in the knowledge that beaches are eternal and will always be there when we return.

We are lucky here in Waterford that the long coastline is dotted with coves and beaches, which offer ample opportunities for enjoyment for the visitor. Some are small and confined while others are large, extensive and well served with facilities. But all are exposed to the sea and offer ample fresh air in scenic surroundings. There are relatively few coastal cliff walks but some of the beaches provide stunning views of the dramatic coastal cliffs and offshore stacks adjacent to them.

The purpose of this chapter is to describe all the beaches, coves and cliff walks in the county, which the visitor might like to enjoy. The journey begins in the extreme west of the county and follows the coastline eastwards to Woodstown. Grid references are provided for accessible carparking areas and notable features are described as they occur.

Ferry Point to East Point
Carparking near X17:115780

There is a small brackish lake near the carparking area, which has no obvious interest, though rock sea lavender and sea aster can be seen growing near the road end. The vegetation here is grassy and high in places; flocks of linnets may be seen at any time of year and swallows too flying low over the ground in summer and early autumn. Northeast of the road is the large expanse of either open water or mudflat (depending on the state of the tide); low tide might offer

Youghal from the rocks near Ferry Point

Youghal harbour from the shingle beach at Ferry Point (sea-kale in the foreground)

better birdwatching opportunities. Large flocks of gulls regularly roost and forage over the mud, and while these might be mostly black-headed gulls, some great-black backed gulls, herring gulls and common gulls should also be present and are likely to be mostly immature birds in summer. Large flocks of cormorants occasionally roost on the mud here; their size, colour and the spread wings (held out to dry in the wind) should distinguish these from other nearby birds. Herons and little egrets should also be scattered about, eagerly looking for fish in the meandering channels. But wading birds are likely to be most abundant over the mudflats, especially in winter. Oystercatcher and curlew should be present throughout the year (occasionally joined by whimbrel at migration time in spring and autumn), but the smaller wading birds, apart from being less obvious on the mud, are usually only present in winter. In summer, these mudflats are covered in gutweed, the green alga that takes over when temperatures rise. Bird interest in that season is likely to be limited to gulls and a few oystercatcher on the shore.

The walk out along the road to Ferry Point is short and scenic; the top of the wall nearby has sea mayweed, sea beet, sea mouse-ear, rue-leaved saxifrage, bird's-foot-trefoil and sea plantain along with large rosettes of the white lichen, *Ochrolechia parella*. Sea beet grows extensively at the top of the shoreline on the far side of the wall, with sea purslane further back but look out too for knapweed, sow-thistle, eyebrights, lesser hawkbit, pyramidal orchid, yellow-rattle and even common broomrape. The rocky tip might have oystercatcher and turnstone foraging among the stones or the seaweed while further south, more oystercatchers and gulls might be feeding around the mussel beds just offshore if the tide is out or receding. In autumn terns may be feeding offshore but it is more likely that their distinctive call will be heard before the birds themselves are seen. Sea rocket, oraches and sea sandwort are the obvious tideline plants but dove's-foot cranesbill and rock sea-spurrey grow more sparingly. The tall and gangly ragwort should be present further back from the saline influence of the sea.

While resting at the Point, take a minute to survey the surroundings. Capel Island is obvious in the distance, just off the Cork coast, while East Point is the projecting headland to the left. The dominant aspect of the view, however, is the town of Youghal on the far side of the Blackwater estuary. There are long lines of variously coloured buildings, whose different levels command superb views eastwards. This attractive townscape is the most appealing element of the view and draws the eye to the shapes and form of the houses on the headland.

The walk back eastwards over the shingle is straightforward, though walking over shingle is never easy. Do stop to check for sea-kale on the upper shingle; in some years this large and gangly plant grows here and rock samphire should occur annually. If the tide is out, it is possible to walk along the shoreline to East Point without any danger (though do take care over slippery rocks). The shoreline here is very rocky and these are covered with brown and green seaweeds (*Ascophyllum nodosum*, wracks and gutweed dominate) and limpets. On a receding tide (the best time to walk here), the tideline will be dotted with gulls, oystercatcher and curlew as they forage around the rocks; in summer common sandpipers may be seen (or heard as they fly away in alarm), while landbirds such as hooded crow, rock pipit, wheatear (a summer migrant to our shores) and pied wagtail may also occur. Keep a look out offshore for cormorants, gulls and other seabirds. A chough or two may pass by calling distinctively and if you are observant enough you might see otter tracks on the mud or other evidence of them such as spraints deposited on elevated rocks or ridges.

Elevated rocks higher up should have thrift though golden samphire is rarer and more likely in late summer into autumn. The low and vegetated cliffs here are unsuitable for breeding seabirds or other cliff-nesting birds, though the more common passerines nest in the dense vegetation. The base of the cliffs is usually littered with seaweed, especially in late summer and, at times, the smell of decaying seaweed may be overpowering, though the flies attracted to the rotting mess provide food for pipits and wagtails and family parties may gather for the feast in autumn. Especially obvious is the long line of sea mayweed that flowers spectacularly here in summer; in places silverweed is equally abundant but isn't anyway near as beautiful when in flower. Higher up and close to the road, willowherbs and common fleabane offer contrasting colours when in flower in late summer.

The mudflats to the northeast of Ferry Point, better know as Kinsalebeg, are used as a high-tide roost and feeding area by many of the birds that winter in and around the Blackwater estuary. Most of the species present at Kinsalebeg can be seen with little effort and at reasonable viewing distances, either from the main road on the Waterford side of Youghal bridge (though traffic volumes are often high on the N25) or, preferably, from Ferry Point, where the birds can be seen and admired in comfort. In addition to the main species, there may be small wintering numbers of gadwall, pintail, shoveler, scaup, goldeneye, knot and sanderling. Scarcer waders seen at Kinsalebeg include little stint, ruff and curlew sandpiper in the autumn, with odd records of spotted redshank and green sandpiper even in winter; a baird's sandpiper, a first for the county, was seen here in September 1982 while a ring-billed gull in January 1985 was also a first county record. Ferry Point and Kinsalebeg, at the western extremity of the county, receive relatively little coverage and with more sustained coverage it is likely that, over time, other rarities might be recorded. For example, a first-winter caspian gull seen at Kinsalebeg in February 2007, was the first county record of this Asian species.

Shoreline at Caliso Bay

consequently there is occasional dumping; the burnt out factory near the carparking area is another deteriorating eyesore.

The grassy vegetation near the car park is weedy with scarlet pimpernel, knapweed, pineappleweed, silverweed, clover, plantains, dandelion and thistles dominating, though coastal plants like bird's-foot-trefoil, sea mayweed, rock samphire and wild carrot can also be seen along with more unusual species like common mallow, montbretia and ladies bedstraw, while the upper shoreline shingle has ragwort and oraches. Perhaps the greatest concentration of yellow-horned poppy in Waterford can be seen on the shoreline at Caliso Bay; some of these plants are very small and will in time (the following year) become the large and attractive flowering plant that this poppy is. The vegetated cliffs at Caliso Bay are not particularly impressive; the sheer cliffs are at the western end of the Bay here. Ravens occasionally breed on these cliffs and their stick nest should be visible on a lofty ledge; whitewashing, if present in autumn, will confirm the use of the nest in the breeding season just gone, but the birds themselves are unlikely to be about then. If young are present, the adults will be agitated, demonstrative and noisy.

The walk around Ferry Point to East Point and back is no more than four kilometres.

Caliso Bay

Carparking at X17: 135766

Caliso Bay is relatively remote and difficult to reach with a winding and narrow road down to it. It is undeveloped, even neglected and

Whiting Bay, beach and shoreline

There is very little exposed rock on the sloping, shingly beach and so little for wading birds and gulls to forage over. Nevertheless, rotting seaweed on the shoreline may attract pied wagtails, rooks even and there will always be a few oystercatcher about along with gulls; passing gannets offshore are another attraction. Sedge warbler and whitethroats have been seen in the dense vegetation on the landward side of the beach. This is a short shoreline and ambling around up and down the beach is a distance of no more than two kilometres.

Whiting Bay

Carparking at X17: 156778

Common fleabane grows in abundance inside the fence on the western side of the carpark, along with silverweed, amphibious bistort and sea mayweed. On the west side of the stream a dense aggregation of sea rocket grows in summer. To the west, along the upper beach, oraches (including Babington's and frosted) and some sea sandwort may be seen near the sleepers; look out too in late summer for common fleabane on the vegetated bank above the beach. This bank has little of botanical interest and the usual weedy species are present (winter heliotrope, thistle, bindweed, great horsetail, perennial sow-thistle, ragwort and some willowherb). Further west again, the sloping earth banks are slumping suggesting undercutting by the sea and ongoing erosion; off these banks masses of seaweed cover the beach.

The most important natural interest here is the sand martin colony; anywhere between 100 and 200 holes may be counted in the upper areas of the more vertical sandy faces. These may not all be in use in any one year but it is always worthwhile to watch the birds coming and going as they tend their young in summer and to await their return in spring, following the bleak winter months when the cliffs here are deserted. Apart from the sand martins, pied wagtails will be about the

Sea-kale near the east carpark at Whiting Bay

seaweed along with gulls and oystercatchers dotted around the shoreline; little gulls have also been seen and, in autumn, sanderling, dunlin and ringed plover may gather along the tideline, scurrying around and probing the sands in search of invertebrates. This is probably the best time to see them as the adults may still be in breeding colours and the fresh plumage of the juvenile birds is instantly recognisable. These small wader flocks should be checked for curlew sandpiper. Rarer species seen at Whiting Bay include long-tailed duck, red-throated and great northern diver, golden oriole, snow bunting and hoopoe. Small flocks of tree sparrows can be seen at Ballysallagh (over 50 were seen here in March 2007, probably the largest flock ever recorded in Waterford). Up to 40 choughs have also been seen.

The upper shore is constantly lashed by raging seas in winter and there is much evidence of erosion with shattered concrete structures randomly scattered about the eastern beach and the occasional breach in the bank above. There is therefore very little

The view towards Ardmore Head

beautiful beach with a nice aspect and interesting formations in the cliffs. A coastal drive to Goat Island from Ardmore, some 3.2 kilometres distant, is also possible, though the last part of the road to it is narrow.

Whiting Bay is a gently sloping, sandy beach, which is safe for swimming and excellent for families; for this reason it can be popular in good summer weather. Whiting Bay is an interesting spot at any time of year and it may provide an invigorating walk of up to five kilometres, depending on how much is wandered over.

Ardmore cliff walk

Carparking: anywhere around X17: 192776

Ardmore beach is due north and what an impressive beach it is. Long, sandy and safe, there are always people about there, either walking, swimming or just sitting on the sands admiring the view. Continue on east uphill, past *An Straoillean* (there are steps here down to a rocky beach) and continue past *Port na mBád*. You might hear Sandwich terns calling in spring or early autumn and the rocks below may have oystercatcher. The walls have ivy-leaved toadflax and pellitory-of-the-wall and the walls down to the small

shoreline vegetation. However, sea-kale grows in some years though sea beet is surprisingly scarce; around the car park on the eastern side of the beach lesser sea-spurrey may be seen and mallow grows on the bank of the stream flowing onto the beach here. It is possible to visit Goat Island from the eastern end of the beach, where there is a small but

The approach to Saint Declan's well

boat harbour have polypody, wallflower and fuschia. The walk uphill offers good coastal views and nearby distractions include craft shops and small, dainty houses; the Cliff House Hotel is on the left and this popular hotel is sensitively stitched into the cliff face and offers guests panoramic views of the coastline here; however, carparking opposite is private to the hotel but do note the *sedum* roof on parts of the hotel as you begin the cliff walk proper. The gardens and areas of scrub and sycamores near the hotel provide the best habitat for migrant passerines, and have produced a range of scarce or rare species in autumn (including red-eyed vireo). The whole area from the Round Tower out to Ardmore Head is worth checking in the right conditions (northeast to southeast winds in spring or autumn, and potentially any time in late September or October). Species of interest which have been seen include turtle dove, hoopoe, tawny pipit, black redstart, icterine warbler, lesser whitethroat, yellow-browed warbler, firecrest, pied flycatcher and crossbill. Offshore eider, red-necked phalarope, black tern and diver species have been recorded; an adult bonaparte's gull was noteworthy in October 2007.

The old walls near Saint Declan's Church have Hart's-tongue and soft-shield fern while the walls of the church have pellitory-of-the-wall, ladies bedstraw, polypody and bracken. In spring the ground just before the church is a mass of three-cornered leek and the aroma may be overpowering; cowslip grows in the grassy areas above the path and the hybrid between Japanese and burnet rose may be seen near Saint Declan's Church. This is a nice, peaceful place to linger in for a few restful moments; beautifully cared for, it is easy to see how Saint Declan was drawn to this coastal haven.

There is a well-trodden path out beyond the Hermitage; the ground on either side is very overgrown with bracken, ivy, bramble,

The wreck of the Samson near Ardmore Head

gorse, docks and grasses but more attractive plants like scabious, goldenrod and clover may be seen here as well. The track may be muddy in places following rain but it is always passable. There are excellent views to the northeast of Ardmore Bay and the cliffs eastwards to Ballymacart; the top of Mine Head lighthouse is just visible. Further out towards Ardmore Head, exposure is greater so the vegetation is less vigorous, more grassy and coastal plants are more frequent. These include thrift, sea campion, burnet rose, sea plantain, devil's bit scabious, hawkbits, bird's-foot-trefoil and knapweed. There is some coastal heath with abundant autumn gorse and heather. Hare's-foot clover grows on the cliffs but this attractive plant is unlikely to be seen from the cliff walk. With care shags and fulmar may be seen around the rocks and on ledges in the cliffs below.

Wooden steps have been incorporated into more awkward parts of the walk and a bench or two here and there provides a resting place from where the view can be admired. If the

Ardmore beach

wind isn't too strong several butterfly species may be seen here in summer, including tortoiseshell, red admirals, painted ladies and large whites. These might be about the heath on the cliff side of the track. This coastal heath is practically impenetrable though there are one or two faint tracks leading down to the sheer cliffs below. You should also see house martins flying about the cliffs, where they breed, and watch out for black guillemots, small numbers of which breed out of sight in cliff crevices near here. The large and impressive gannet will almost certainly be passing offshore, probably diving on occasions in search of fish but the auks (razorbills and guillemots), if present offshore, may be harder to see.

The rusting wreck of the crane ship, *The Samson*, dominates the view; it ran aground

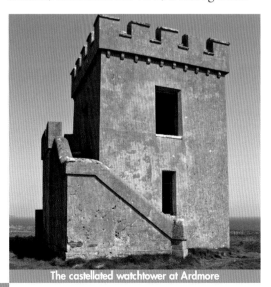
The castellated watchtower at Ardmore

here in December 1987, while being towed from Liverpool to Malta. An unsightly mess it is firmly set in the cliffs. It does offer roosting perches for gulls and pigeons and photo opportunities for passing visitors who, inevitably, stop and stare and probably wonder why it was left to despoil the coastal scenery. Further on (around 1.75 kilometres from the carpark) is the empty lookout post, built, apparently, in a day in 1940 by the Government of the time to facilitate monitoring of ships and aircraft that passed the headland. It must have been comfortable too, with its windows and a fireplace; a cosy vantage point to watch the comings and goings in such a scenic but exposed location. More interesting nearby is the castellated watchtower or signal station built around the time the coastguard station was constructed in 1867. It still has presence though it has long been abandoned (since 1921).

The headland around Ram Head is largely heath but sea mayweed, sea campion, wild carrot and sea beet all occur and add a varied colour in season to the purples and yellows of the heather and autumn gorse, which is the dominant vegetation here; there is also some rock sea-spurrey, ladies bedstraw, thyme and sheep's bit, and linnets too might be scattered among the grasses in search of seeds. The main seabird cliffs are at Ram Head and westwards to just before Father O'Donnell's well; kittiwakes outnumber other species, with smaller numbers of fulmars, large gulls and, in some years, small numbers of shags, guillemots and razorbills. A cliff near Ram Head is known as *Leac na gCánóg* – "Flagstone of the Puffins", which suggests that puffins (or possibly Manx shearwaters, the literal translation of *Cánóg*) formerly bred on these cliffs (Manx shearwaters have been heard here close inshore at night on several occasions during storm petrel ringing sessions and thousands have been seen passing off the Head by day). A treat too in April 2007 was a red-backed shrike, the fourth county record of this attractive species.

Once around Ram Head, Capel Island is the obvious island in the distance but the adjacent Cork cliffs are low and unspectacular. However the near cliffs are dramatic with striking folds and formations; these same cliffs come alive in spring and summer with the noisy activities of seabirds (kittiwakes and fulmar mainly), that breed in ledges on these cliffs. Rock pigeons arc ever-present, choughs might be ambling lazily overhead and scolding as they go, ravens occasionally appear and you might be lucky to see a hunting bird of prey, perhaps a kestrel, a sparrowhawk or even a peregrine. Father O'Donnell's well is the last structure almost at the end of the walk proper (2.3 kilometres from the starting point). It is thought that a Father O'Donnell came to the area, prayed and read his office at the well here but it seems that T. P. Rahilly, who came to Ardmore to recuperate from illness, built the present structure with local help because of the restorative properties associated with the waters from the well. There is a seat nearby, which offers an opportunity to relax and admire the coastal scenery here.

Thereafter, the coastal walk veers inland back into Ardmore. The track is well defined all the way and meanders through fields, some in grass and others in cultivation (barley and root crops like carrot); some of the fields here are heavily invaded by sea mayweed, which, although they look

Common fleabane at Ballyquin

attractive, must be a nuisance for the farmer. At the end of the walk it is possible to veer right back towards the coastguard station or continue left and then right along New Line, the high road at Ardmore, which offers excellent views of the beach, Ardmore Bay, the Round Tower and the house styles of the area. Halfway along this road, concrete steps lead back down into the village through narrow streets lined with attractive and well-kept houses. The overall distance involved is around four kilometres.

Ballyquin, northeast of Ardmore
Carparking X27: 204799

A plaque near the car park states that Ballyquin beach won a Green Coast Award in 2007. The Green Coast Award is conferred on beaches which meet European Union bathing water quality standards, and which are prized for their natural, unspoilt environment. The programme operates in Ireland, Wales and Northern Ireland. Public toilets are available at the carpark.

Ballyquin has a nice, gently-sloping beach, is safe and expansive (especially when the tide

Looking west along Ballyquin beach

is out), with good, clear views of coastal cliffs off to the east and Ardmore to the west. Close to the access pathway onto the beach, a low vegetated bank is fronted by protecting boulders. The shore near here is rocky but offers excellent rock-pooling opportunities for children. Further east the beach is more open and sandy and ideal for walking.

There is extensive water seepage running off the land through the vegetated bank so horsetail grows in abundance in the damp conditions. All the usual weedy species are present (ragwort, coarse grasses, willowherbs, hogweed, clover, field bindweed, winter heliotrope, some sea mayweed and thistle) which probably reflects the origin of this vegetated bank. Despite all the weeds here, the bank is worth checking for common fleabane which grows in abundance and which flowers beautifully in late summer. However, few coastal plants grow at the base of the low cliffs here, due to ongoing scouring of the area by wind, waves and high seas throughout the year. Also worth looking out for in summer are the sand martins that frequent and breed in the upper parts of the sandy cliffs here; up to 60 or so breeding holes occur, though not all of these are occupied every year. Pied wagtails, wheatears, stonechats and rock pipits should be about

the beach with flocks of gulls (these are more likely to be black-headed gulls), oystercatcher and probably curlew foraging along the tideline or on the rocky shoreline; shelduck have also been seen.

It is possible to walk comfortably eastwards for around one kilometre as far as a stream (where grey wagtail may be seen). There is an access road down to a small carpark on the far side of the stream but the ground is much rockier here and further east, and isn't easy to walk over.

Heading southwestwards from Ballyquin carpark leads eventually to Ardmore, a distance of around 2.5 kilometres and is easy walking all the way. If the tide is in, initially a scramble across limestone rocks is required (a change from the more usual Old Red Sandstone rocks of most of the Waterford coast). These rocks are covered in lichens, *Verrucarias* (black species), *Caloplacas* (orange) and some *Xanthoria parietina*. Flowering plants include sea plantain, rock samphire, thrift, a little common fleabane, sea mayweed, bird's-foot-trefoil and restharrow along with wild carrot, buck's-horn plantain, some orache, ragwort, a little sea beet and docks. Beyond the rocks, there is a nice sandy beach backed by shingle and a vegetated earthen bank. Yellow-wort grows in one particular spot and common fleabane grows among the weedier species. The shallow waters offshore are good for Sandwich terns in late summer into autumn as they prepare for their long migration south. Where the earthen cliffs are more vertical, sand martins may be seen flying about and the many holes confirm that they breed here.

Near the outflow stream (at 199793) there is limited carparking for a couple of cars. The substantial, low-profile private house almost on the beach is worth a glance and the extensive rock armouring around it confers some protection from the winter storms and confirms the potential damaging effects of these storms on coastal buildings located so near the coastal zone. The buddleja growing on the cliff just west of the house might have migrant butterflies, particularly red admiral and painted lady; sea buckthorn also grows here, obviously planted. Further west the banks are low and degraded but sea radish and sea aster may be seen. Limited carparking is available at 199790 (essentially in a field). A rocky headland here can be walked across or veer around it, though the masses of

colourful field bindweed here in summer and the common blue butterflies they attract might be worth a look. Common mallow grows on the west side of the headland and the jagged rocks on the shoreline may have turnstones and common sandpipers and inland birds like starlings, rock pipits and even linnets and greenfinch. It is possible to continue southwestwards on the cliff top (it is really only an earthen embankment) but parts of it either cross or are close to private property so it may be preferable to stroll carefully over the limestone platform below it which affords an excellent opportunity to examine the nooks and crannies for wild flowers. Thrift is abundant in season but watch out too for autumn hawkbit, golden samphire and yellow-rattle as you walk west. Choughs may be frolicking about overhead and the flashing white rump of a wheatear may be seen as it flies off ahead, stopping occasionally to watch for danger.

Ardmore beach proper begins at 195786 at the Curragh end. Of interest here, just inland is the small Curragh pond. This is largely a reedbed, with little or no open water, but in summer it may have breeding

Ardmore beach from the east (near the Curragh end)

moorhens, sedge warblers and other reedbed species. The bay outside can be good for terns, particularly Sandwich terns, in autumn and whimbrel in spring. Other waders are regular, and ringed plover breed. In winter and spring, Ardmore Bay is worth watching for red-throated and great northern divers, and black-throated diver has occurred, while a yellow-legged gull was seen in October 2009. There is a busy caravan park nearby so the beach here is popular in summer. At the eastern end of Ardmore beach just off the caravan park an amount of seaweed accumulates which attracts wagtails and pipits. There is extensive rock armouring protecting the caravan park where sea rocket, common poppy, frosted orache, sea mayweed, sea beet and common mallow may be found growing in and around the boulders. There is also carparking at 194385 from where the beach and surrounding area may be explored.

Ardmore Bay is large and extensive. The Cliff House Hotel and the old coastguard station dominate on the headland to west and the Round Tower is a dominant feature of the view. The long beach at Ardmore is sandy, shallow and safe and is ideal for swimming, walking and boating. The sea offshore is always worth scanning for cormorant, shag, gannet and other seabirds that breed on the cliffs nearby. A line of vertical railway sleepers protect the low vegetated embankment all the way from the rock armour at the east end of the beach to Ardmore itself. Some of these have, however, either rotted away or have been removed over the years by the constant action of wind and waves and the relentless power of the sea bombarding the area, especially in winter. The exposed dunes here are at constant risk from erosion by the sea. The dunes closer to Ardmore (fronting the caravan park) are more substantial but are not particularly impressive, given that they are corralled and therefore not subject to the natural processes that result in dynamic dune systems. By and large the vegetation is grassy and weedy but there are some interesting and attractive species like sea mayweed, bird's-foot-trefoil, common fleabane and some montbretia; bee orchid has been recorded here in some years. These and other

The rocky shore at Ballymacart cove

flowering plants like selfheal, clover, knapweed, tufted vetch and silverweed attract butterflies and moths and several common blue butterflies and six-spot burnets may roam these dunes in search of nectar and mating opportunities. Look out too for red admiral, painted lady and the rarer clouded yellow which have been seen here in summer.

The car park at the beach (191778) or indeed anywhere in the village at Ardmore is an ideal starting point if the beach is to be walked from the village itself. The beach to the rock armouring at the Curragh is only around one kilometre long but the attractive village, its narrow streets, shops and local amenities are always worth investigating. The cliff walk too is invigorating.

Ballymacart

Carparking X28: 252810

The 'main' road at 248817 is 1.35 kilometres from the car park at the cove. A long and narrow road leads down to the cove, which tends to become overgrown as the summer progresses; moreover, there are two hairpin bends and it can be very difficult, if not impossible, to pass another car en route to the cove. There is no signpost pointing the way to the cove at Ballymacart, which is probably the remotest cove in Waterford, but notwithstanding the remoteness of the area, the area is well worth a visit.

Ballymacart has a small, rocky beach backed by high, vegetated cliffs that are particularly impressive off to the east when viewed from the west side of the cove. There are many jagged rocks projecting from the beach and there is a wildness and ruggedness about the area that isn't found elsewhere in the county. There may be masses of seaweed washed up on the beach, especially after storms, and in the autumn these rotting accumulations may be home to wagtails and pipits feeding on the flies that feast among the debris. Choughs are almost certain to be

Hare's-foot clover at Ballymacart

seen or heard and the larger gulls (great black-backed and herring) should be about too. Wading birds include oystercatcher and common sandpiper in summer and gannets plunge-diving offshore may be an added attraction. Keep an eye out overhead for kestrel and sparrowhawk; these breed in the nearby cliffs and woods and they might be seen hunting over the slopes, or with kills in summer as they supply growing broods.

The cliff bank to the west of the beach has bracken, gorse, ivy, bramble and ragwort as weedy species but look out for heather on the slopes while the deep ravine in the cliffs has a dense stand of common valerian (especially low down on the banks) and willow. The exposed lower area of the cliff bank is more interesting botanically with bird's-foot-trefoil, rock samphire, sea mayweed, sea campion, common orache, thrift, a few sea aster plants and rock sea-spurrey in some of the lower ledges and on rock shelves.

Old Red Sandstone boulders litter the beach and many of these display the characteristic red colour of the rock, as does the shingle near the car park. With such an abundance of fragmented rock and projecting boulders the lower shore at Ballymacart is ideal for rock-pooling and sea-fishing (for mackerel or pollock, perhaps), though the outer boulders, from where fishing is more likely to be successful, may be difficult to reach and a wet suit might be useful. With the tide out, it is possible to walk eastwards to a sandier beach. However, those in search of breeding seabirds will be disappointed. Although the cliffs are high, they are not sheer, and are generally sloping and vegetated so there are no suitable breeding ledges. The cliffs are also wave-lashed so flowering plants are restricted to the more vegetated and uneroded parts of the lower cliffs. Higher up on these cliffs, the vegetation is generally rank and grassy though there are some opportunities for the more attractive flowering plants around rocky knolls.

The Ballymacart river, which drains much of the Drum Hills, enters the cove near the carpark. This may be worth checking for grey wagtails and perhaps even dipper. There is a defined walkway which meanders upslope on the east side of the cove. If walking, or even cycling, this might be an alternative route back out. If so listen carefully for songbirds singing in the under-watched woods in the valley above. Good numbers of commoner passerine migrants occur on occasion, with species like blackcap, chiffchaff and goldcrest regular in late autumn. Rarer species have

included a honey buzzard, while firecrest, yellow-browed warbler and other scarce species have occurred, though the woods here are difficult to monitor, given the large amount of woodland present.

Also worth looking for on the way back up the road is hare's-foot clover, a transitory species which grows on the wall top near the upper hairpin bend. It is possible to spend an hour or two rambling around Ballymacart cove, and while long walks here are not possible (less than 1.5 kilometres would be typical distance covered in wandering around), the remoteness and ruggedness are the redeeming features of the area.

Ballynagaul pier east to Helvick pier
Carparking X28: 298887

The pier and surrounding area is always worth checking for birds, especially if the tide is low or at migration times when flocks, some in breeding plumage, may be present. Small numbers of waders can be seen here too, sometimes at very close range, and, being far out in Dungarvan Bay, there are sure to be seabirds offshore. Greenshank, oystercatcher, turnstone and redshank are the more usual species in winter but you may also find small numbers of brent geese, mostly on the shoreline left (or west) of Ballynagaul pier. The pier here is one of the best locations from which to check Dungarvan Bay for

Ballynagaul pier

Ballynagaul beach

slavonian and great crested grebes and for divers (including black-throated diver on occasion). Black redstart can occur in late autumn and winter here and elsewhere around Dungarvan, and a hobby was a surprise in June 2007.

Flocks of curlew may be about, if nothing else, scattered over the mudflats in the autumn, which is always a magical time to visit. The pier itself has a long line of sea mayweed growing in cracks in the mortared walls along with rock samphire; both species are more obvious in the summer months. There is a small but well-used beach just east of the wall (especially if students from *Coláiste na Rinne* are around for a swim in good summer weather). Further east the sand is less extensive and so is less attractive to visitors and is less popular.

The lower shore is stony and rockier; carpets of seaweed (mostly *Ascophyllum nodosum*, brown wracks and some green *Enteromorpha)*. Above the tide is where the flowering plants flourish and are at their most attractive in summer. Along the tideline here look out for sea mayweed, sea rocket and the oraches while the vegetated slope above may have ragwort, bracken, thistles, docks, willow, buddleja, bindweed, winter heliotrope, willowherbs, ivy and Japanese knotweed, fuschia and montbretia. Discarded plants that

grow include roses, nasturtium and solanum while an outflow stream further east has an extensive growth of water-cress. Watch out too for rock pipits and hooded crows along the shore, probably feeding among the litter cast up by the tide. Small numbers of oystercatchers, curlew, turnstone and whimbrel in season may also be seen and common sandpipers and Sandwich terns just offshore might be about in late summer. A heron or two might also be foraging and, in summer, a red admiral or painted lady, both migrant butterflies, may be among the flower heads in search of nectar. The bushes above should have resident robins, tits, blackbirds, thrushes and wood pigeons and these might be joined by chiffchaffs, willow warblers and other migrants in summer; all these birds are likely to be more active and audible in spring and early summer but less so as the breeding season wanes and the ongoing demands of reproduction decline.

In places too at the top of the embankment, projecting timber stakes dangling freely attest to the ongoing erosion that continues along this shoreline. A more obvious manifestation of this erosion is the rock armouring and concrete rampart further down along the shoreline. If the tide prevents walking along the base of the rampart, it is possible, with great care (and by holding onto the railing), to walk along a wide ramp at the

Helvick pier

top of the wall. Look out for the attractive common fleabane inside the railing.

At the end of the ramp, climb over the railing and ascend the short but steep slope to the road above. Otherwise continue walking along the shoreline past the rock armouring and ascend the boulders just beyond the sewage plant. There might be linnets and stonechats in the vegetation around the entrance gate to the sewage plant. It is difficult, if not impossible, to continue walking along the shoreline to Helvick pier just a short distance away. An easier option is to walk the road above to the pier, a short but revealing stroll, which offers excellent views of distant landscapes (the Comeragh Mountains and the Waterford coast are especially appealing) and the attractive pier itself. There are always gulls about the pier, whose numbers and species vary according to season. The smaller landbirds should be obvious about the landward vegetation; these include stonechats and linnets, while house sparrows should be chattering higher up around the cottages above the pier, and swallows and house martins should be about in numbers in summer (and lining the

The stacks off Helvick Head

Dungarvan Bay from above Murray's pub, near Helvick (Comeragh Mountains in the distance)

overhead wires in early autumn as they prepare to migrate southwards).

There is a fine terrace of cottages above the pier which show simple traditional design elements (such as vertically sliding slash windows, strongly coloured front doors emphasising the traditional porches behind large battered gate posts and black/blue slate on steeply pitched roofs); note too the larger unit at the end of the terrace and how it effectively marks the road junction. Compare these visually appealing features and the symmetrical detail with those on more recent residences in the general area. Regardless of wildlife, Helvick pier is well worth a visit. There is always activity here usually related to fishing, nets, pots or boats whether by the full-time fishermen who earn their livelihoods from the rich waters offshore, or by the recreational anglers who fish off the wall in summer and in some numbers when the mackerel are running in late summer.

Helvick Head

Helvick Head holds an important seabird colony (mainly kittiwakes, guillemots, razorbills and fulmars), in addition to being a good site for seawatching and landbird

migrants. Outside the pier and off Helvick Head itself, particularly in rough weather, good numbers of seabirds are often present, feeding, roosting or on passage. Some of the diver species may be about, and cory's, great, sooty and Balearic shearwaters have been seen here more often than elsewhere in Waterford, in addition to impressive sea-passages of Manx shearwaters, mainly in autumn. Both great and arctic skuas occur regularly, and a black tern or two could be with the tern flocks (mainly Sandwich) that feed or pass offshore. Keep an eye out too for osprey, which occasionally pass by, probably on their way north to breeding areas in Scotland.

Ideal seawatching conditions are during strong southerly winds, and good views can usually be had from the pier carpark (from the car-window if necessary!), or the nearby cove or, for the best views, from the clifftop further south. Helvick pier often has some of the rarer gulls present, especially in winter, with occasional records of glaucous, Iceland and Mediterranean gulls.

There is a well-worn track from the pier out towards the Head, which is surrounded on both sides by dense growths of bracken and montbretia with rampant bindweed and a few sycamore trees, surprisingly healthy despite the coastal exposure. Stonechats, linnets and wrens may be present among this vegetation and further out among the pine trees keep a careful eye out for migrant birds in spring and late summer (goldcrests, willow warblers and chiffchaffs) and for vagrants. Several rare species have been seen at Helvick Head including turtle dove, short-eared owl, hoopoe, ring ouzel, redstart, reed warbler, radde's warbler (seen in October 2009, the second county record), melodious warbler, icterine warbler, lesser whitethroat, garden warbler, yellow-browed warbler, firecrest, red-breasted flycatcher, red-backed shrike, brambling and snow bunting. One of the more recent additions to the county list was a red-rumped swallow seen here in late October 2009. Apart from the birds, keep an eye out for common porpoises and basking sharks offshore; even killer whales have been recorded just off the Head.

There is a sheltered cove (though not if the wind is blowing from the north or northeast) out near the Head. The small beach here is safe for swimming but is probably more appealing in the morning before the sun swings around the headland. The projecting rocks are always good for sea angling but the cliffs are subject to erosion (warning signs have been erected by Waterford County Council). There are excellent views of the Waterford coast from here and on clear days the three pillars at Great Newtown Head (near Tramore Bay) should be visible. Views off south and west are restricted by Helvick Head though the vegetated islands off the Head are just visible; these have a small number of breeding herring gulls in summer and larger flocks of gulls (all species), cormorants and shags at other times of the year; black guillemots breed just west of these offshore islands but these are less likely to be seen. The stacks are shown, erroneously, on the Ordnance Survey maps as 'The Gainers'. Older names for these are *An tOileán Glas* or *Oileán Heilbhic* or *An tOileán* or *Carraig an Oileáin*; *Carraig na Fuinneoige*; and *Na hOileáin Bheaga* or *Clocha an Oileáin*, though it isn't possible, with any certainty, to assign any of these names to a particular island or stack. The meaning of the word Helvick isn't known; Canon Power considered that it wasn't Irish and was almost certainly Scandinavian. Vallancey's 1785 map of Ireland uses Helwick Head. Other Irish names used here include *Ceann an Bhathla*, *Ceann an Bhatlaigh*, *Ceann an Bhatlach* or *An Fatlach*, *An Mathlach* and *An Bathlach* (all very similar names which mean 'Clown's

Muggort's Bay with Mine Head in the distance

Ballynagaul from the east

Head'). Helvick Head proper is difficult to access as it requires crossing private property and the Head above the cove is overgrown with dense gorse thickets and is practically inaccessible (though less so now, for a while at least, as much of this was burned in 2008).

Choughs breed in the cliffs around the Head and it is likely that these attractive birds will be seen (or heard); ravens are also possible overhead. House martins breed in the cliffs and these should be seen flying about, while rock pipits should be around the lower rocks chasing flies. However, the impressive seabird colonies are on the sheer and vertical cliffs south of the Head but these vegetated cliffs are dangerous and not for the faint-hearted. Moreover, the seabird colonies cannot be seen from the cliff-top and so the vertical precipices on which they breed are best left to the birds themselves.

The walk back to Ballynagaul pier along the main road is the easiest option. There are two possibilities:

1. not far beyond Murray's Pub go left uphill along a narrow, twisty road. This is a very rural and unspoilt area of a kind that is

hard to find now anywhere in Ireland. Agriculturally the land is still in use but not intensively and there is hardly any recent housing development (planning applications for housing have been refused because of the sensitivity of the area and the deficient road infrastructure with poor sightlines) and there are clear, uninterrupted views. The ditches are well vegetated and overgrown with bramble, hawthorn, gorse, sycamore and elder but look out too for ragwort, agrimony, silverweed, sheep's bit, wild carrot, meadow vetchling, blackthorn, knapweed, thistle, herb-Robert, cow parsley, nettle, tufted vetch, bird's-foot-trefoil, ground-ivy and hedge woundwort while privet, fuschia and some montbretia are plentiful near houses. Blue tits, starlings, rooks and swallows in season are the main bird species to be seen.

Some 1.2 kilometres from the main road, a lay-by offers excellent views of the coastal cliffs west to the dominating Mine Head in the distance, views that are at their best in the morning in good weather. The sea offshore should have gulls, gannets and auks and you might be lucky to see a passing whale. The sloping cliffs nearby are dominated by western gorse and heathers. This fine area of coastal heath extends well beyond Muggort's Bay and provides nesting opportunities for robins, stonechats and wrens and there are sure to be choughs about too. Continue along this coastal road and after 2.2 kilometres (at 303886) either veer left to the crossroads at Ballynagaul (go straight through, down to the next cross roads and right there to Ballynagaul pier) or veer right downhill to the main Helvick road, turn left there to the next crossroads (turn right there, continue down to the next cross roads, turn right and continue down to Ballynagaul pier);

2. otherwise continue walking west which offers excellent views of Dungarvan Bay, the Comeraghs to the north and the Knockmealdowns to the northeast. An interesting variation is to veer off right at 301887 and continue down to the end of this narrow road. Then veer left downslope and exit opposite *Tig an Cheoil* public house. The entire walk is around 4.5 kilometres and should take no more than two hours (or even less if stopping to admire the attractive views and watching the wildlife is not a priority).

Ballynagaul pier west to Moat

Walk along the shoreline close to the earthen bank where there is sycamore, ash, willow, bracken, hogweed, ivy and bindweed, which should be alive with calling songbirds in spring and early summer. Along the base it should be possible to see ragwort, sow-thistle, docks and thistles, tufted vetch, herb-Robert, montbretia, yellow vetchling, some purple-loosestrife, meadowsweet, great horsetail, great willowherb, winter heliotrope, cleavers, oxeye daisy and Japanese knotweed, while the more maritime species include oraches, thrift, sea mayweed and sea beet. A low tide exposes extensive rocky areas, dominated by brown wracks and *Ascophyllum nodosum*. Flocks of oystercatchers may be foraging among the seaweeds while gulls and Sandwich terns (in early autumn) may be feeding just offshore. Decaying seaweeds along the shore always attract flies and the resident rock pipits are forever active chasing them.

This is a fine coastal area and there is an impressive backdrop of mountains, hills and sea in the distance while across the Bay, Ballynacourty lighthouse stands out visually because of its painted white walls. Nearer the shore are the houses and cottages of the peninsula and if the tide is well out, men in their yellow leggings and coats may be seen harvesting the shellfish beds on the Whitehouse Bank off the Cunnigar. As you walk west you may come across oyster trestles, now unused, nearer the shore and there are always oystercatchers around these; greenshank, common sandpipers, whimbrel, little egrets and curlew may also occur as indeed may any of the other species that overwinter or pass though Dungarvan Bay. It is possible to walk this shoreline at almost any stage of the tide though care may be needed on spring high waters (which occur around eight o'clock, when walking is least likely). The slipway at Moat is 1.25 kilometres from Ballynagaul pier and it is around the same again to continue west to the Cunnigar. However, apart from a longer walk back by road, the shoreline walk here isn't as impressive as it cuts inland and away from the superb coastal views here. Before leaving the slipway look out for grey wagtails

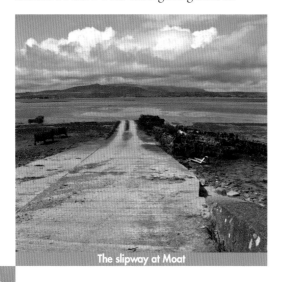

The slipway at Moat

Sharp rush on the Cunnigar (Helvick Head in the distance)

that breed along the outflow stream. Continue back by road and in spring or early summer the rookeries in the high trees before Mooney's pub are always a hive of activity. 1.25 kilometres from the slipway at Moat, turn left and continue on down to the cross roads and from there turn left down to Ballynagaul pier, a satisfying walk of no more than 3-3.5 kilometres in lovely surroundings.

Cunnigar

Carparking at X28: 274896

The Cunnigar is probably the best winter birdwatching location around Dungarvan Bay, or even in Waterford, and is well worth a visit. It is one of the main high-tide roosts in the Dungarvan area and a winter walk here (anytime between late August and March/April), which coincides with high tide or within an hour on either side of it, is ideal for seeing large numbers of birds. September is a particularly good month as many of the birds may still be in summer plumage and, with luck, weather may be favourable with relatively long daylight hours and good light. The early autumn is probably the best time for roosting oystercatcher, with up to 2,000 birds recorded. At the right time of year, in excess of 30 species of birds should be seen

here. The dwarf cherry growing on the higher ground above the carpark is also worth looking for before setting off.

In harsh winter weather, the Cunnigar is impressive, particularly on crisp, bright days in December or January. The sand nearest the carpark may well be alive with dunlin, ringed plover and sanderling; these smaller waders are especially flighty, so with large numbers present, spectacular views may be obtained of the birds wheeling and carting over the sands. In the autumn, the wader flocks are well worth checking for little stint and curlew sandpiper, or rarer species such as the wood sandpiper seen in August 2009. A lesser yellowlegs, the fourth county record of this species, was seen here in November 2009 and a long-billed dowitcher lingered for a while in October 2010 (the first county record).

Walk off left across the stream at the entrance to the carpark. The tall and stately plants ahead are sharp rush and there are several of them beside the walkway. There is a small wet area nearby; you may hear moorhen calling from the vegetation here and in summer look out for dragonflies, the most spectacular of which is the flighty emperor,

The view north from the southern end of the Cunnigar

but common darter and large red damselfly may also be seen flitting between the irises and sea club-rush in search of passing insects. The bushes above are usually home to house sparrows who constantly chatter and scold and they may be joined by flocks of starlings, which can be quite large in late summer and autumn, when the young of the year join their parents in search of food.

Further on, the mudflats and salt marsh west of the Cunnigar should have several interesting species. Small flocks of little egret may be about nearby, either in the creeks or on the salt marsh, while curlew and shelduck may be foraging over the mudflats at any time of year. Knot, grey plover and bar-tailed godwit may be roosting with more dunlin, turnstone and several hundred oystercatcher out near Cunnigar point. Large numbers of oystercatchers also roost on the west side of the spit and the marshy areas can be good for teal and snipe. Massive wader flocks are possible at times, which may depend on the tide or the severity of the prevailing conditions, and these pack densely on the salt marsh when the tide is high. In winter, brent geese are usually always present while closer

to shore, pied wagtails, hooded crows and flocks of rooks may be foraging around tidal debris and you might hear or see a stonechat on the tops of bushes. Black-headed gulls are usually to be seen too. In summer, a fledged brood of wheatears may be flitting about awkwardly while their agitated parents fly from rock to rock calling in alarm; hoopoe has also been seen here and the fourth Irish record of a booted warbler, a rare migrant from Russia and China, was found on the Cunnigar in August 2006.

The dunes nearby are littered with tall ragwort plants and these colourful plants are irresistible to large numbers of 6-spot burnet moths that gather on the flower heads to feed and breed; later the caterpillars of the cinnabar moth may be seen devouring the leaves. If you see one common blue butterfly you are likely to encounter several as you walk north beside the dunes. With luck red admiral, painted lady and, at times, large numbers of silver Y moths can be seen; the other migrant, the clouded yellow, is more sporadic in occurrence and none may be seen for several years only for hordes of them to arrive the following year.

While the dunes initially are fenced off there are breaches here and there on the eastern side and at the northern end where it is totally open. A notable plant to be seen growing abundantly in these dunes is sea-holly, a most attractive plant when in its prime in summer. The tall and stately common valerian also occurs among the marram and slender thistle grows in more open areas. Common spotted orchid may sometimes be seen in the grassy vegetation in summer while sea mouse-ear, a low-profile plant, should be also be present on the more open areas of the sandy turf.

As you walk on or close to the rocky shoreline on the east side, it should be possible, with care, to see ringed plover, dunlin and turnstone foraging around the rocks or seaweed while large flocks of the bigger and more colourful oystercatcher should be obvious, even from a distance. Groups of cormorants may be perched along the tideline or on the sandflats off the shore if the tide is out; these are obvious even from a distance and one or more may have their wings outstretched, drying them in the breeze. In late summer Sandwich terns congregate here and these form spectacular flocks as they wheel overhead if disturbed. They may also constantly fly by overhead as they move between the inner and outer Bay. Landbirds to be seen include linnets and maybe another pair or two of stonechat. Out almost at the tip of Cunnigar point, up to 20 herons and sometimes more can often be seen roosting on the salt marsh or on the elevated stony ditch and shingle bar.

The lower shore here is covered in brown and green seaweed and large amounts washed up on the stones will give off an unpleasant smell as it decays. The upper shoreline on the west side of the spit has annual sea-blite, sea purslane, rock sea-lavender, sea sandwort, a little sea aster, thrift and some sea campion. Further in, the ground is wet and soggy and

Herons near the tip of the Cunnigar

is dominated by rushes with gorse and marram on higher ground nearer the dunes. Out near the tip, around where the herons roost, some cord-grass may be seen and there is a forest of glassworts along with sea-blite and lavender and more giant rush plants. Weedy species here include scarlet pimpernel and low-growing knotgrasses.

The tip of the Cunnigar is around 3.6 kilometres from the carpark if meandering on the west side. It is always a nice place to sit and rest as it is almost always quiet and peaceful. The busy town of Dungarvan is opposite and the boats in the harbour can be seen, some of which might be coming and going in the channel, depending on the tide. Be careful where you sit though, as the odd prickly saltwort plant can be painful if sat on. Also here are sea beet, sea-holly, groundsel, docks and, surprisingly, the occasional tomato plant; several more may be seen along the edge of the dunes, all remarkably healthy given the coastal exposure; later in the year these may provide a tasty tomato or two.

On the way back look out for yellow-horned poppies between the two

Dungarvan from Abbeyside

Cunnigar. Sea mayweed, sea beet and some mallow grow along the base of the sea wall here. There should be birds about the shore somewhere, depending on the state of the tide. These should include gulls (a number of species), oystercatcher, a heron or two and usually a little egret. The slipway near here offers access to the channel for boats but it is probably too rocky for casual walking.

The preferred option for accessing the strand area is close to the seaward side of the church where steps lead down onto the beach. The attractive beach is accessible to Dungarvan and offers a short and pleasant walk over the shoreline here. Underfoot is largely shingly sand with sandflats and wrack-covered stones. When the tide is out you may see people collecting shellfish on the shore and further out, and there are sure to be a boat or two navigating the channel, especially in good weather. You might hear the cackling of brent geese that feed on green algae on the shoreline or the evocative calls of curlew or redshank as they probe the mudflats in search of invertebrates.

The big glossy leaves of sea beet are conspicuous on the upper shore initially with grassy/weedy vegetation on the rock embankment and then near the roadway. Further along a sandier beach is backed by a concrete rampart, which is being undercut by the sea; this has groundsel growing along its base but little else. When the tide is in, it may not be possible to walk beyond the end of the prom but it is possible to do so using the road above. Behind it is a wet field with little interest; the main attraction here is offshore. There should be flocks of brent geese around somewhere from autumn on, gulls, waders, several little egrets and maybe cormorants either roosting on the sandbars or foraging in the channels. When the tide is out the sandflats off the Cunnigar on the Whitehouse Bank is usually a hive of activity as people harvest the shellfish trestles.

boulder fields (surprisingly not elsewhere), some large and some small; the larger ones may be in flower and the yellow petals are distinctive. Opium poppy is also likely along the edge of the dunes (around 26 plants were there in 2009). Prickly saltwort grows in some numbers between the boulder fields and the edges of the dunes here should have sea-holly, always an attractive plant, especially when in flower; Ray's knotgrass might also be seen. The rocky shoreline along the way may have turnstone, ringed plover and oystercatcher scattered about. The walk back along the east side of the dunes is around 3.25 kilometres giving a total distance of around 6.8 kilometres, which is a good walk in pleasant surroundings with lots to see.

Abbeyside beach and prom, Dungarvan
Parking at X29: 266928
There is a large grassy area close to Saint Augustine's church, which offers commanding views of the Cunnigar to the south just across the narrow channel and the inner harbour area on either side of Dungarvan and the vast expanse of Dungarvan Bay on the seaward side of the

Beyond the wall you should find sea rocket growing on the narrow dune area along with sea mayweed, silverweed and a little sea sandwort. Otherwise the vegetation on the low and grassy upper bank is weedy with gorse, bramble and bindweed predominating. After around 870 metres the underfoot conditions change dramatically and the rough, stony ground is then awkward to walk over and, although it is possible to walk further east, it isn't comfortable to do so.

Before turning back, it might be a good time to admire the view here. Helvick Head peninsula is very striking and its bulbous head even more so, though a late morning sun and a possible glare off wet sand might diminish views of it to some extent. There is a vast area of sandflat in Dungarvan Bay, which is at its most extensive when the tide is out. There is also a massive area of mudflat between Strandside and the Gold Coast further north along the near shore; the Gold Coast hotel is most prominent there. The tide sweeps in under Kilminnin bridge and, on an incoming tide, the entire area is covered very quickly.

THIS ABBEY OF THE HERMITS OF ST. AUGUSTINE WAS FOUNDED C.1290. THE SURVIVING BUILDINGS CONSIST OF THE 13TH CENTURY CHANCEL AND THE 15TH CENTURY TOWER. AFTER THE SUPPRESSION OF THE MONASTERIES IN THE 16TH CENTURY THE FRIARS WERE DRIVEN FROM THE ABBEY AND LANDS. AND BY 1654 THE BUILDING WAS RUINED AND DESTROYED. THE PRESENT CHURCH WAS BUILT C.1820 AND THE CHANCEL WAS REPAIRED IN 1923. THE RUIN IS KNOWN LOCALLY AS THE 'CLOGGHAS'.

ERECTED BY THE AUGUSTINIAN 700 COMMITTEE 1990.

Wall-plate on Saint Augustine's church

On the way back, Saint Augustine's church is worth a look. The limestone walls have rock samphire and pellitory-of-the-wall but the main interest is the church, both the original church founded in 1290 by the hermits of Saint Augustine, the shell of which (just the chancel and the fifteenth century tower) adjoins the newer church built in 1820.

The walk is only around two kilometres but it can be extended by walking up along the sea wall, which offers excellent views of the inner harbour at Dungarvan and the many boats that lie marooned there when the tide is out. The wall itself has sea fern-grass, rock samphire, pellitory-of-the-wall and buck's-horn plantain. You could also go right around and into Dungarvan along the Quay and perhaps visit the prominent thirteenth century King John's castle, which stands out, even from this side.

Dungarvan town offers good opportunities for birdwatching and the walk right around the quays to the sports centre past the old swimming baths can be rewarding in terms of birds seen. Many of the diving species that

Dungarvan Bay from the beach near Abbeyside prom

The view south from Clonea beach

winter in Dungarvan Bay will be present in small numbers in the channel offshore, and at very close range at times. Great crested grebes, red-breasted mergansers and goldeneye are the most regular, but occasionally, the much rarer slavonian or red-necked grebes are seen. Great northern divers, usually single birds, may also be present. Brent geese will almost always be present, feeding around the seaweed near the swimming baths or on the playing fields by the sports centre (where tight flocks of several hundred can occur at times). Keep a look out for colour-ringed birds and for 'black brant' and 'dark-bellied' brent that have been seen here. Mediterranean or little gulls can occur among the gull flocks inside the tip of the Cunnigar, and sabine's gull and little auk have been seen. A citrine wagtail (the first county record) was seen near Abbeyside promenade in September 2009 and a hobby was present in September 2006. Cattle egrets stayed around Killongford in December 2007 (one had earlier been seen at Garrarus, probably the first county record for the species, and a flock of eight were present near Clashmore in January 2008) and an alpine swift was seen in April on three occasions over the town (in 2005, 2006 and 2008).

Clonea south

Carparking at X39: 309929

This is at the southern end of Clonea beach, and while it is more awkward to get to, it may be less crowded in good weather than the main access point for Clonea beach around the Clonea Strand Hotel, which can be very busy in good summer weather, not just for carparking but also for the number of people that gather here to enjoy the considerable amenities of the area.

From the carpark, it is possible to walk south or northeast. The walk south over the narrow band of sloping shingle is awkward and the enclosed area here may have masses of rotting seaweed. At low tide the wrack-covered rocky shoreline should have scattered oystercatcher, turnstone curlew, gulls, perhaps a heron or two, grey crows, possibly whimbrel (several hundred may be seen in spring) and Sandwich terns in autumn while purple sandpiper are regularly seen. Rarities have included a buff-bellied pipit (first county record) in October 2010 as well as semipalmated sandpiper and lesser yellowlegs. The southern end towards Ballynacourty point is also worth checking for passerines. There may be dozens of rock pipits feeding among the seaweed and other debris strewn on the shore, and good numbers of white wagtails among them in September especially; pied wagtails should also be seen, catching flies around the seaweed. A few black redstarts usually winter, especially at Ballinard, and large numbers of migrant wheatears have been seen in early spring.

The trees and bushes at Ballinard and behind Ballinclamper provide good cover for warblers and other night-migrants, and are worth checking, particularly after south-easterly winds; both red-backed and woodchat shrike have occurred and wryneck has also been seen (in April 2007). Winter finch flocks occasionally include a few bramblings or tree sparrows among all the more usual species.

There is very little vegetation along the narrow, wave-washed shore with sea mayweed, sea beet and oraches the only prominent species to be seen. Tree-mallow grows here and, further on, while the ground is more vegetated, the plants are largely weedy species (docks, thistles, bindweed and sow-thistle). Further on again, where it is more exposed, there is thrift, bird's-foot-trefoil, silverweed and sea plantain on the limestone rocks of the shore. Flocks of linnets may be feeding on the seeds of the flower heads in autumn and there are sure to be butterflies about, most likely large whites and green-veined whites, though some of the migrants are possible too.

The views of Helvick Head from here are superb on a good day, as are the coastal views of Ballyvoyle Head to the east, especially those at Island. It is a short walk (less than one kilometre) west but the walk could be extended if walking further on towards Ballynacourty lighthouse.

The walk to the northeast is longer, more impressive and popular. The vegetation on the narrow shingle band and the low grassy bank above it is uninspiring, though sea mayweed, oraches, sea beet, silverweed, sow-thistle and sea sandwort may be seen; there are also occasional plants of sea radish, with their big jagged leaves, and look out too for field and hedge bindweed, tufted vetch and the reddish-pink Babington's orache. It is only around 800 metres to the Strand Hotel.

Carparking at X39: 312936
(around Clonea Strand Hotel)

It is possible to walk east along the grassy embankment which later reverts to shingle. There is little additional botanical interest

Clonea beach looking towards Ballyvoyle from near the Clonea Strand Hotel

The northeastern end of Clonea beach, close to Ballyvoyle

though common mallow may be seen in places. There is an extensive reedbed behind the beach with a dense conifer forest nearby. The reedbed might have sedge warbler, which are worth listening for. Yellow-horned poppy grows on the embankment in some areas and many teasel plants can be seen near the dark-blue cottage. Further east there are several willow plants, more sea radish and stonecrop hugging the shingle on the relatively protected landward side of the embankment.

The walk to here is around 1.5 kilometres and a brisk walk back over the beach is around the same distance. Clonea beach, a Blue Flag beach, is very sandy and safe and is ideal for swimming, walking and sunbathing. At times large breakers roll in offering excellent surfing for younger children, though the waves are rarely large enough or sustained to attract more able surfers. And of course the coastal views from anywhere on the beach are impressive and likely to leave a long-lasting impression on anyone who spends time on Clonea beach.

Clonea–a Blue Flag beach

Brent geese regularly feed along the shoreline at Clonea. Other wildfowl include eider or long-tailed duck among the more frequent red-breasted mergansers or common scoter on the sea. Red-throated and great northern divers are regular (the latter often in tight flocks), with smaller numbers of great crested grebes and black guillemots. Rarer visitors include black-throated diver, red-necked grebe and little auk. Good numbers of gulls are usually present, and Mediterranean gulls are regular. This is probably the best location for viewing terns in Waterford, with good numbers of Sandwich and common tern, especially in autumn, both feeding and resting on the beach. Roseate, arctic and black terns occur in smaller numbers, and white-winged black tern has been seen; even rarer species may occur such as the American golden plover seen in September 2009. Arctic skuas regularly harass the terns along the beach and in Dungarvan Bay. Rare waders here include a buff-breasted sandpiper seen in September 2006 and a white-rumped sandpiper (the second county record) in October 2010.

Clonea east

Carparking at X39: 317942

The eastern end of Clonea beach is less popular than further west (nearer the Hotel) but can be busy in good summer weather and carparking can be a problem, though people usually park on the road, which may require quite a walk to the beach at very busy times.

Walking east from the carpark, there is a low embankment fronted by a rocky shoreline. Expect to see silverweed, rock samphire, bird's-foot-trefoil, sea mayweed, wild carrot, rock sea-spurrey, buck's-horn plantain, kidney vetch, sea beet and oraches on the upper shoreline and rock pipits are sure to be about too. After about 0.5 kilometre the shoreline is even rockier and, while there is no problem walking here at low tide, it might not be as easy when the tide is in. Once beyond the rocks, there is a big expanse of shallow beach, backed by shingle and a low earthen embankment. Some of the protective concrete walls on the upper shoreline have been fractured, displaced and washed away over the years.

There isn't a sandy beach as such (so the area might not be good for prolonged sunbathing) but it is an excellent area for walking. Further east, a long concrete rampart supports a high sloping bank and the road above, to protect the area from the ravages of the sea. Beyond this are the vertical, free-standing timber posts from an earlier, but ultimately unsuccessful attempt to shore up the bank here. Flocks of gulls and oystercatchers may be scattered along the beach, especially further east. There is a stand of Japanese knotweed and a single spruce tree just above the shingle (which is extensive here). Less welcome is the large amount of seaweed washed up on the shingle near the concrete rampart, at least when it is rotting, and the smell is none too pleasant. This may deter a walk further east, which is more difficult because of rocky ground. The walk to here is around 1.8 kilometres and, overall, the walk is about 3.5 kilometres. On the way there are excellent views of Ballyvoyle Head (to the east) and Helvick Head off in the distance, more or less due south.

Ballyvoyle

Car parking (for one car) at X39: 336950

Ballyvoyle isn't really a beach as such and opportunities for walking or bathing here are very restricted; there is limited carparking at Ballyvoyle bridge (one car) and further west up the road (maybe one or two more cars).

The view to the west from the vegetated slopes near Ballyvoyle cove

Several sea radish plants grow on the shingle on the west side of the stream that enters the cove; also here are sea mayweed, oraches, some rock samphire, herb-Robert, sea beet and ragwort. There is a more grassy/weedy flora near the road along with a big stand of Japanese knotweed, some montbretia and a stunted sycamore. Ballyvoyle bridge has a few additional species such as maidenhair spleenwort and sea spleenwort growing in the mortared limestone walls. East of the stream, there is another stand of Japanese knotweed and some sea aster may be seen growing on the low cliffs nearby.

Ballyvoyle is very rocky and stony with no beach and swimming would be difficult here. Flocks of gulls should be foraging among the rocks, where oystercatcher and curlew should also be seen. The bridge at Ballyvoyle is, however, attractive and the stream here might be worth checking for dipper and grey wagtail, both of which breed nearby. There are also excellent views of Helvick Head and the coastline west towards Clonea, though the low grassy cliffs restrict the view to the east. These vegetated slopes are good for songbirds in season and should resonate with the sounds of chiffchaff, willow warbler, tits and the other passerines that breed. Choughs are regular too and, as ravens occasionally breed in the cliffs out towards Ballyvoyle Head, they will also be coming and going if present in spring and early summer.

Stradbally

Carparking at X39: 370970

The entrance to Stradbally cove at the very picturesque Cove Lodge is narrow and a sharp turn off the road is required; hence care is needed if driving.

The Tay river flows to the sea under Stradbally bridge and there is always a chance of seeing dippers here and grey wagtails are almost always present. A tree-lined roadway

to the beach has alder, sycamore, ash, apple, elm, hawthorn and beech growing beside the river. There is an understorey of ferns, cow parsley, montbretia, bramble, buttercup, bindweed, bracken, herb-bennet and winter heliotrope, while a big stand of Japanese knotweed dominates further down. A tiny dune area at the top of the beach (near the carparking zone), is degraded by the constant movement of people and cars and species diversity is low. Dandelions grow abundantly here but there is some sea sandwort in and around the small area of marram grass where a few oraches also grow.

The river Tay flows seawards on the east side where it is constrained by a long meandering line of boulders. Otherwise the beach is surprisingly flat, sandy and extensive, especially when the tide is out. The eastern side of the cove is densely vegetated with oak mostly, though ash, holly, ivy and blackthorn may also be seen. These are, however, stunted and formed in the direction of the prevailing wind (southwest) and, closer to the sea, the exposure is too much for the trees and gorse and bracken then dominate initially before the lower-growing autumn gorse and heather take over out near the headland where exposure from salt-laden winds is greatest. In late summer and autumn, the yellows and purples on the headland are an attractive feature. The cliffs nearby have rock samphire, sea aster and sea mayweed while the boulders are covered in bladder wrack.

Interpretative sign at Stradbally

The beach, the Tay and the wooded slopes at Stradbally cove

If the tide is out, flocks of gulls and oystercatcher may be foraging among the seaweed. Offshore is always worth checking. On the east side, small numbers of black guillemot may be seen in spring bobbing up and down on the waves. On the offshore stacks on the west side, cormorants breed in some years and they may also do so on the mainland cliffs opposite. The very same cliffs are good for fulmars and these like nothing better than to glide back and forth along the cliffs or hang into the updraughts. Choughs and ravens breed in the cliffs on either side of the cove and the choughs occasionally fly into the cove and feed around the decaying seaweed. Gannets from the nearest breeding colony on the Great Saltee Island pass by regularly and dive spectacularly into the waters off the beach, as do Sandwich terns when they arrive from wintering quarters in spring and again in early autumn before they depart our shores for southern Africa.

In strong winds, big waves pound the shore here and following prolonged heavy rains, the waves are dark brown in colour such is the volume of water entering the cove. The area is used for schooling horses and there are always people rambling about the beach. In good summer weather Stradbally cove is a popular bathing area. There is enough room for everyone, though when the tide is full, the area is a little more congested as people congregate on the upper beach.

The west side of the cove is more spectacular with its high and heavily indented jagged cliffs. These cliffs are good for rock doves, and rock pipits should be about the lower rocks. Rock samphire, sea aster and sea mayweed are prominent plants low down on the cliffs while one wet face has many stunted royal fern plants, an unusual site for the species. Higher up, the vegetation is largely gorse with bracken, ash, blackthorn and willow. A walkway, accessible from near the limekilns, meanders through this vegetation and is worth walking to obtain spectacular views of the cove, the cliffs and the sea beyond. However, it does end abruptly at the cliff-top, on private land.

The limekiln at the entrance to the cove is an interesting feature and a reminder of the former activities that occurred here. The walls of the limekiln have Hart's-tongue and pellitory-of-the-wall along with ivy, bramble and a stunted willowherb or two. A number of interpretative signs near here are worth reading for the interesting information they provide on the area and its attractions. A mature forest of trees dominate the western side of the cove near the carparking area, which provides good shelter in summer and a safe haven for a variety of plants and animals. In 1742, the local landowner, Maurice Uniake, planted the lower three kilometres of the Tay valley with over 152,000 trees. A good variety of trees grow here: oak, ash, hazel and alder (natives) and beech, sycamore, Scot's pine and Norway spruce (all exotics). Both species of oak occur along with hybrids between the two. The woods are usually good for butterflies, among them speckled wood and small tortoiseshell, and in spring the woods resonate with songbirds; red squirrels have also been recorded and the carpets of bluebells are an added attraction in spring and early summer.

The walk around Stradbally cove, the river Tay and the woods is no more than two kilometres in length so time can be passed ambling about and enjoying the considerable coastal attractions here. The short walk up to Stradbally village is also worthwhile.

Ballyvooney

Carparking at X39: 382974

Ballyvooney cove is rugged, rocky and inspiring at any time of the year and there is a small carparking area from where the beauty of the cove can be admired. A small, unworked quarry just above the carparking area has autumn gorse and heather species, which flower beautifully in the early autumn. The limestone seating area is equally attractive and the interpretative sign nearby explains the natural features of Ballyvooney. Other signs on the cliffs explain the geological aspects of the area.

The attractive bridge has pellitory-of-the-wall and sea spleenwort; sea mayweed, bindweed, purple-loosestrife, docks, meadowsweet, bramble and nettle also grow on the shingle nearby. The stream gushes seawards through the shingle, the volume of which depends on recent rainfall amounts. In dry weather barely a trickle filters through but following heavy rains, at any time of the year, a strong flow enters the cove, which may be difficult to cross without getting wet. There is a vast amount of shingle at Ballyvooney and the lack of vegetation

The rocky shoreline and shingle beach at Ballyvooney

confirms that the rocks and stones are constantly being reworked by the waves, which crash violently on the shore here in windy weather. The cliffs too are sheer and eroding and there is little vegetation to be seen other than sea mayweed and sea aster, which occur in places. Where the cliffs are more sheltered on the west side, rock samphire, burnet rose, scabious, thrift and sea campion may be seen.

If the tide is out it is possible to scramble about over the boulders and walk west to obtain better views of Gull Island, just offshore in the distance. In the breeding season cormorants, herring gulls and great black-backed gulls breed here. Nearby a heron may be seen standing over the pools waiting for fish to appear and pied wagtails and rock pipits should be about the upper shoreline; whinchat and redstart have also been seen here. With such a rocky shoreline, oystercatchers are sure to be foraging among the seaweed. Offshore gannets, gulls and other seabirds may be seen. In some winters scoters occur here in small numbers, notably surf and common scoters. Divers (especially red-throated) can also be seen regularly in winter and spring and great skuas and puffins have also been seen offshore. Sand martins sometimes nest in clay banks just below the cliff top to the west. The scrubby vegetation on the sides of the stream on the landward side of the bridge is also worth checking for resident breeding bird species and for interesting migrants in spring and autumn.

On the east side the cliffs are sheer, friable and daunting. The rocky shoreline offshore should be investigated if the tide is out but take care as the rocks may be wet and slippy. Look out too for the remains of a ship, the *SS Cirilo Amoros*, that beached here in February 1925 on its way from Spain to Liverpool with a food cargo. You could walk off eastwards but be aware of the tide, which fills rapidly here. The mass concrete wall at the

mouth of the cove not only protects the cove from erosion, it also offers a resting place where it is possible to relax and admire the view if the sun is shining. The occasional rock samphire plant grows in the wall.

Ballyvooney cove doesn't offer long walks or safe bathing but it is an ideal place to potter about the rocks or relax on the shingle or even enjoy lunch on the limestone table.

Ballydowane

Carparking at X49: 406979

The walk down to the narrow entrance on to the beach is enlivened by the sea mayweed, sea aster and montbretia flowering on the vegetated slopes in spring and autumn. Take some time to read the plaque mounted on a limestone plinth, which describes graphically the geological features of the area. There is a fair amount of shingle at the base of the cliffs at the cove entrance but, to the east, the initial cliffs are sloping and grassy. Prominent here among the vegetation is sea mayweed; less obvious is great horsetail, some rock samphire, sea plantain, kidney vetch, thrift and some rock sea-spurrey. Beyond these sloping cliffs are the high and daunting, even dangerous-looking sandstone cliffs, which

Columnar stack on the east side of Ballydowane cove

look ready to collapse. These are almost bare of vegetation though there is gorse and mayweed. Fulmar occupy some of the ledges and jackdaws breed in the cracks and crevices. Choughs could be flying about and rock pipits may chase each other over the faces, depending on the season.

The east side of Ballydowane cove is rocky and there are sure to be oystercatcher about. The aptly named *Faill Dearg* ("Red Cliff") projecting seawards usually has several fulmar scattered on breeding ledges across the face of the cliff. Saint John's Island, just offshore at the tip of the cliff, may have roosting gulls and maybe more fulmar. The rock projection close to the shore is covered with rock samphire and yellow lichen; look out too for an entrance hole near the top on the landward side: an air shaft for former silver mine workings here, now filled with sand.

The base of the cliffs off to the west of the entrance is usually well scoured by wind, waves and rain and, following heavy rainfall, several rivulets and streams run off the slopes and into the sea. Occasionally too the constant wetting from above and scouring at the base results in slumping of the earth banks. The constant dampness also encourages horsetails to grow in some abundance in places on the western cliffs.

There are many crags and boulders around the tideline on the west side, which can be easily explored when the tide is low. Sea aster and tree-mallow are conspicuous on one of the high stacks and grey wagtails may be about the shoreline. The waves constantly crash on the shore here and the effect is therapeutic as the breakers form, break and dissipate up the shore in a noisy cascade of moving sand and water. Offshore is good for passing gannets and, at times in winter, large numbers of red-throated divers may be seen; the occasional great northern diver comes in close allowing good views to be had. Oystercatcher and the occasional common sandpiper gather around the rocks or shoreline to feed.

Menacing looking cliffs at Ballydowane

The beach at Bunmahon from the west side

Ballydowane is one of the more appealing beaches on the mid-Waterford coast, despite the dangerous looking cliffs but be mindful too of rip-tides, which this enclosed bay is noted for. There isn't much walking available here (around one kilometre or so) but the coastal scenery is appealing.

Bunmahon

Carparking at X49: 431986

The carpark and slipway onto the beach are on the west side of the bay. Sea beet, sea radish, bird's-foot-trefoil, kidney vetch, sea mayweed, thrift, oraches, red clover, plantains and docks are abundant on the fringes of the carpark and mugwort can be seen to the east on the floor of the derelict shed. Further west on the cliffs, sea campion can be seen high on the vegetated slopes along with some rock samphire and one or two sea aster plants, which flower later in summer.

Hooded crows, linnets, rock pipits and pied wagtails may be about the shore or base of the cliffs somewhere and oystercatcher might be foraging along the shoreline or on the rocks, while offshore, gannets and terns (in season) should be flying by or feeding; flocks of gulls are usually either scattered along the shoreline or perched on the rocks at either end of the beach. Common scoters have also been seen off the beach in winter and two black terns were there in September 2008. You might be lucky to see butterflies flying around the flower heads and peacock, small tortoiseshell and a migrant species or two are most likely.

There is only a short beach to the right of the slipway but a decent walk can be had by walking off east. The dunes are protected by protective boulders which are fronted initially by a line of shingle, where common and Babington's orache can be seen, though the odd sea rocket and sea radish also grow. Further east the shingly sand has no vegetation and the easternmost section of the upper beach is higher and sandier and the soft sand is difficult to walk over. The lack of vegetation here suggests that the sea and the waves meet the boulders at high tide, and the constant movement of the mobile sands prevents plants from germinating. Masses of seaweed are also likely to be deposited on the shore here but these are usually mechanically removed, leaving high ridges and mounds on the strand. Natural debris is also thrown up in some quantity at times on the shore at the eastern end of the dunes where the river Mahon enters the sea. Large accumulations of sand obscure the stone boulders at the end of the dunes, unlike the western end, where they are freestanding and prominent.

The Mahon river is deep where it enters the sea and usually too deep to wade across. It is tidal here and a small salt marsh area can be seen along its banks where sea aster and sea purslane grow. Around the edge of the landward side of the dunes, where the sands are not impacted by waves, sea sandwort may be seen. Marram dominates the dunes themselves but other plants grow in the more open areas; these include sea-holly, bird's-foot-trefoil, sea campion, ragwort, wild carrot, gorse, knapweed, thrift, autumn hawkbit, carline thistle, sea mayweed, plantains and, in places on the seaward side, rock samphire, spurge (abundant in some areas), burnet rose, devil's-bit scabious and wild thyme. Tree-mallow grows at the western end of the dunes along with sea beet, and a low-growing alder is the only tree species on the landward side of the dunes, away from harsh winds. Such a collection of plants attracts moths and butterflies and at times several silver Y moths may be seen along with red admirals, small tortoiseshells and speckled

woods; you might even be lucky to see a humming-bird hawkmoth sucking nectar from the many flower heads.

The walk around Bunmahon is short and pleasant and is not more than two kilometres.

Stage cove

Limited carparking at X49: 443986

This small but attractive cove can be easily reached by walking down a narrow lane bordered by a dry stone wall on one side and a mortared wall on the other. Look for thrift, polypody, plantains, sea campion, sea spleenwort, pellitory-of-the wall, wall rue, buck's-horn plantain and the occasional sea mayweed plant growing on these walls.

The beach is shingly, small and views from it are restricted because of projecting headlands. The slipway is probably the easiest part to walk over and is a good way of entering the sea here for a swim, or maybe just to paddle about in the water. The usual rock pipits and pied wagtails should be about the shoreline, with gannets offshore and Sandwich terns in the autumn calling as they fly by or dive into the clear waters chasing sandeels. Old mine shafts can be seen on the eastern cliffs here, dating from the 1800s,

Knockmahon (Stage cove) from the east

when the area around Bunmahon and Tankardstown was extensively used for copper mining. Interpretative signs on the wall describe the geology of the area and the mining industry that once thrived here. Near the signs, a blue/green leachate oozing off the grassy slopes confirm the presence of copper ore in the cliffs and underlying rocks.

Staining at Stage cove

Stage cove is one of the smaller of the Waterford beaches, and while it may not have the dramatic scenery of other coastal areas of the county, it is steeped in history and industrial heritage. It is possible to sit on the slipway here and imagine the hive of activity when copper was shipped from this very cove (over 7,000 tons of ore were exported per annum from the area in the late 1830s, requiring around 75 annual shipments).

Kilmurrin

Carparking at X49: 466987

Kilmurrin cove is an enclosed, circular bay with two scenic headlands (the western headland is the more dramatic of the two),

though the vegetated cliffs aren't sheer or high. The upper beach is topped by an elevated shingle bank and a small stream flows into the west side of the cove. Behind the beach, the backlands are wet and heavily vegetated and, on the landward side of the road beyond, is a dense belt of plantcd trees.

The signs here confirm that there are strong currents, though the sea is usually inviting, especially when the tide is out and the walk over the exposed sands is easy. The vegetated embankment around the carpark is largely dominated by weedy species like buttercup, clover, dandelion, docks, nettle and grasses, though there is usually one or two sea radish plants and a single tree-mallow. The east side has a high concrete wall (recently constructed) to help protect the fragile earthen cliffs here from ongoing erosion by the sea. A line of boulders nearby completes the coastal protection works.

There is some sea beet and oraches on the western end of the shingle embankment and

Kilmurrin cove

a mass of horsetail on its landward side, along with some bindweed, but little else. The backlands are impenetrable. Land birds to be seen here include pied wagtails and rock pipits and watch out for redstarts and black redstarts in the autumn. The shoreline might have flocks of gulls, the odd oystercatcher and occasionally a cormorant; more rarely, a great northern diver might be seen on the sea. Choughs too are regular visitors, possibly flying by overhead to nearby breeding sites, or foraging about the cliffs or shore in search of insects and invertebrates.

Boatstrand

Carparking at X49: 476985 (top of road)
or X49: 478985 (at the pier)

Steps lead all the way down to the beach at Boatstrand from the road above. You can also drive down the cobbled roadway to the pier where there may be limited carparking (but bear in mind that Boatstrand is a working pier so do not cause an obstruction). The high bank beside the steps on the way down has common mallow, common valerian, elder, ivy, nettle, bramble, purple-loosestrife, sea mayweed, horsetail, gorse and silverweed and the drainage channel at the base has a mass of water-cress along its length. Big iron bollards are in position at the top of the beach; these were manufactured in 1892 by Grahams of Waterford.

If the tide is out it is possible to walk off left (northeastwards) along the shore where you are sure to encounter flocks of gulls (mostly great black-backed gulls and herring gulls) roosting on the shore; these might be worth checking for unusual species as Iceland gulls have been seen here. This is a very sheltered area and there are excellent views off to the east as far as the stacks off Kilfarrasy. High up on the vegetated cliffs, you should see montbretia and fuschia among the dense ivy. The base of the cliffs here are scoured by the sea so little or no vegetation grows. The walk eastwards is generally safe but is rocky in places and take care of an incoming tide.

There is a small sandy beach enclosed between the pier walls, which can be popular in summer. At the top of the beach sea radish, sea mayweed, dandelion and bird's-foot-trefoil grow and common valerian may be seen at the very top. An anchor prominently displayed on the pier is from the schooner, *Morning Star*, which foundered on rocks outside the pier during a storm in October 1915 with the loss of four lives. Above it, a mass of hedge veronica overhangs

Boatstrand

Benvoy beach

the cliffs which attracts small tortoiseshells and white butterflies when in flower.

The walk back up the road offers excellent views offshore and to the east along the coast. Sea mayweed, sea aster, hedge veronica and rock samphire dominate the cliff bank on the landward side, while golden samphire grows abundantly on the lichen-covered rocks over the wall on the seaward side, along with sea aster and rock samphire; some hedge veronica and rock samphire even grow on the tops and vertical faces of the wall. This sun-lit vegetation might have red admirals, painted ladies butterflies and silver Y moths in summer, and other common species.

Benvoy

Carparking at X49: 489989

A short but narrow road leads down to a surprisingly spacious carpark at Benvoy. A large mass concrete plinth has a concrete stairway down onto the beach. Although constructed relatively recently to replace an earlier barrier washed away by the sea, even this large concrete mass is beginning to suffer from the relentless impact of the sea and large cracks and gaps are beginning to appear between the steps in the access stairway.

The cliffs off to the east are low, sloping and grassy with few flowering plants and the cliff base is littered with shingle. Seaweed cast up on the shore should have rock pipits and pied wagtails feeding off the hordes of flies that feast on the rotting debris. The most impressive cliff here is the big high cliff at the easternmost end of the beach on the seaward side where rock samphire and some sea aster can be seen on rock ledges.

The beach is flat and sandy and there are always gulls (black-headed gulls are most likely, though a few great black-backed gulls and herring gulls are also possible) and oystercatcher about, either along the tideline or on the rocky platforms that punctuate the beach. The cliffs to the west are somewhat higher but are even less vegetated. The base of these cliffs are boulder strewn and the rocky configuration here is awkward to walk over but on a good day, with the tide out, it is possible to walk all the way to Boatstrand and maybe walk back along the road, which would be an excellent walk with superb views of this part of the Waterford coast. Otherwise stroll about the beach and take the stairway back to the car. Be careful if exiting out onto the main coastal road by car as there are

The west-facing cliff on the east side of Benvoy

limited sightlines at what can at times be a busy road, especially in summer (which might explain why Benvoy isn't signposted).

Annestown

Carparking at X49: 499988

There is ample carparking at the popular beach at Annestown, though bars at the entrance prevents anything higher than a car from entering. The prominent limekiln at the carpark is worth looking at before walking onto the beach proper. A long concrete wall defines the beach area, and it protects the landward side from the ravages of the sea. In front of the wall a vast accumulation of shingle has been piled up over time by the relentless rise and fall of the sea, and is at its highest at the wall; it then slopes down to a flat beach, which in turn has some rocky platforms that are exposed at low tide. The area is framed by projecting headlands but the eastern headland is breached so it can be walked through safely at low tide.

There is some stunted vegetation near the entrance to the beach: sea mayweed, sea beet, buck's-horn plantain, field bindweed and oraches, all heavily trampled on by people coming and going. There is little or no vegetation along the base of the wall because of the mobile shingle. At the western end a raised concrete platform is often in demand in summer for sunbathing. A well used walkway continues west along the cliff top, where sea campion and thrift flower heavily in summer along with silverweed, sow-thistle and ribwort plantain. However the walkway veers right into private property and becomes less defined further west where it is closer to the cliffs and hence more dangerous. The walkway does provide excellent views to the east of Annestown beach and beyond. It might be best to walk back eastwards inside the wall where a long line of sea mayweed and sea beet at the base of the wall is impressive in summer. Also growing here is rock sea-spurrey and plantains while the face of the wall is covered with yellow (*Caloplacas*) and black (*Verrucaria*) lichens. There are also good views of the Anne valley from the walkway, which might also be worth a detour to see; the Anne river flows into Annestown and there are excellent opportunities for watching wildlife along its length, including dipper, mute swan and little egret. The bog is also worth investigating in summer for orchids (marsh orchids and both species of spotted orchids grow among the yellow iris, cottongrass and other vegetation).

It is possible to walk eastwards through the breach in the headland, but **only** on a falling tide. Initially there are large boulders to be negotiated (these may be slippy so be careful when walking over them), and beyond these there is an extensive area of large stones and shingle. However it does become easier further east on finer shingle, though walking on shingle is never easy and can be tiring and energy-sapping. Little or no vegetation grows on the base of the cliffs because of the

The beach at Annestown from the west side

constant reworking of the shingle by the sea and the huge waves that often impact violently on the shore here. Similarly the lower part of the sloping cliffs are unvegetated because of wave action. There is an amount of rock samphire on the cliffs initially but many of the cliffs are grassy and uninteresting. However, some sea radish and a little sea aster may be seen along with sea mayweed, plantains, gorse and bramble. The shoreline off the cliffs is rocky and covered in seaweed and there are sure to be flocks of gulls, curlew and a scattering of oystercatcher about, depending on the state of the tide and a heron or two might be seen standing patiently over large rock pools. With luck a seal or two may be seen just offshore along with gannets, gulls and the odd cormorant. The appropriately named *Faill an tSeabhaic* ("Hawk's Cliff") is high, sheer and daunting (it is surely the most impressive cliff in the area) and you might see a kestrel hovering over it or a pair of choughs calling as they land on ledges. Fulmars breed in these cliffs and one or two of these might hang in the wind on a breezy day or fly back and forth effortlessly on the updraughts. Very little vegetation grows on this fractured cliff and clumps of it regularly fall to the base below.

Kilfarrasy Island (though not an island) is the dominating headland to the east and there is an opening in the cliff just before it, which offers an alternative route back to the carpark at Annestown but it could be a dangerous option because of the fragile nature of the cliff top. It is preferable to walk back along the base of the cliffs, provided tidal conditions are suitable. It has to be emphasised that a knowledge of the tide times is absolutely essential when undertaking this walk. This is a high energy coast and the tide turns rapidly on spring tides and fills the area quickly so it is possible to be cut off, and, if this happens, an upward ascent is neither possible or advised because of the sheer nature of the cliffs. There have been incidents here so make sure you undertake this walk only if the tide is going out giving enough time to savour the rugged coastal environment here and return safely. Overall an hour or two can be enjoyed at Annestown and an invigorating walk of four or five kilometres is possible.

Kilfarrasy

Carparking at X59: 526983

The walk down from the carpark onto the beach shows marked evidence of the erosive

221

power of the sea with the shattered remnants of the fragmented path littered about. On the landward side of the bridge near the carpark there is some sea beet, sea mayweed and bindweed and what a beautiful view is available to the residents of the dominating two-storey house that overlooks the beach.

The cliffs just to the west are earthen and eroding. There is some sea aster and sea mayweed in places on the more stable part of the cliffs and sand martin breeding holes may be seen in the clay tops. In season, the birds themselves should be about, entering and leaving the holes and possibly tending young. It isn't possible to go further west along the base of the cliffs but the stacks offshore are dramatic, as are the western cliffs along the rugged coastline. A stream enters under the carpark and exits at an attractive bridge, which can be admired from the beach.

The beach at Kilfarrasy is gently sloping and is generally shingly sand, and, with little coarse shingle, the area is popular for walking at any time of year and for swimming in summer. Heading east, the cliffs are

Kilfarrasy beach

wave-washed and crumbly, and little or no vegetation grows, apart from a few sea rocket plants and oraches. Further east the cliffs are more sloping and vegetated with other coastal plants such as sea mayweed and bird's-foot-trefoil. Occasionally kestrels hover overhead in search of small mammals, insects and birds. At the eastern end of the beach, a large boulder field litters the shore from fragmentation of the cliffs above. These rocks and boulders are difficult to walk over and the tide needs to be going out or low to do so safely. But it is definitely worth venturing beyond this rocky part of the beach. The shore beyond, although awkward to walk on, is framed by substantial cliffs on the landward side and there are rocky platforms covered in seaweed just off the beach with a few large stacks and at times a raging sea with thundering waves impacting on the shore.

Masses of kelp are usually washed up on the sand here, which attracts wagtails and pipits. If the sea is rough—as it often is—it may be difficult to see birds on the water, though gannets may be diving offshore and, further east, a black guillemot or two may be seen. Gulls breed on the offshore stacks and cormorants do so in some years on any one of the low stacks. A heron or two might also be foraging in the rock pools. The cliffs beyond the boulders are high and impressive and walking along the shingly base isn't difficult. Rock samphire grows abundantly on the ledges and cracks along with gorse, sea mayweed and sea aster. The cliffs are heavily eroded, especially on the lower parts, and plant cover is sparse. Rockfalls regularly occur where the sea cuts away at the cliffs and, in time, the rock debris is worked, reworked and moved by the sea, so within a few years all evidence of the rockfall disappears.

Further east (beyond Sheep Island) the coast is less exposed and more sheltered. The cliffs are even more dramatic and the beach sandier, though it is still coarse. This is an

The coastline west of Sheep Island

important area for choughs and there are always birds about somewhere. A few pairs breed in the cliffs but roosting flocks of anything up to 100 birds occur, and sometimes more, especially in autumn, when young of the year join the adult birds. These are substantial numbers and the area is clearly attractive to the birds for the safe roosting that is possible on the cliffs and the good feeding habitat available on the land above. A wheatear or two may be about and ravens sometimes breed in the high cliffs. Oystercatcher are almost always on the shore, fulmars and gulls breed on the cliffs and on the stacks, and seabirds on the sea or passing by offshore are easier to see because of the relatively sheltered conditions. A ravine in the cliffs has common valerian, purple-loosestrife, wild carrot and sea mayweed, and ivy dominates the cliffs further east.

This part of the coast is seldom visited, usually only by a handful of people who know the area well. On a good day, several hours can be spent here, often in total isolation, and after the breeding season–say in early autumn–the area can be strangely quiet without the raucous chattering of the gulls and ravens. At this time of year, only the

waves dissipating on the shore disturb the peace and tranquility, but the waves themselves are usually tame, having been attenuated by the shallow waters offshore.

After around 1.9 kilometres, the end of the beach terminates in a high cliff and substantial boulders hamper progress further east. These can be surmounted but to walk further east to a small cove framed by high cliffs depends on the tide being well out and, if in doubt, don't venture; if it is possible to walk further make sure that your return is not cut off by an incoming tide. The walk back is just as interesting and many of the species encountered on the way may be seen again and others too are possible. Overall, the walk is around 3.3 kilometres and should take less than two hours.

Garrarus

Carparking at X59: 547984

The stream which flows along the east side of the densely vegetated glen beside the carpark is worth a look before venturing down onto the beach. Montbretia grows here as does monkeyflower just over the wall (it has quite a colourful flower when in bloom). The dense scrub in the valley is good for

Garrarus beach from the west

songbirds in spring and autumn and you might see a whitethroat or hear chiffchaffs, willow warblers or other birds singing melodiously in the undergrowth.

The small memorial sign fixed into the wall near the access ramp onto the beach commemorates Mickey Mac who died in 2002. He lived in the farmhouse just up the road and was regularly seen beachcombing on Garrarus strand. He was widely known, especially by all those who used the beach throughout the year.

Sea aster grows on the cliffs and near the end of the concrete slip. Off on the east side, accumulations of seaweed and kelp occur throughout the year but especially in autumn. Natural debris, including seaweed, gathers on the high tideline along the beach at times and the flies can be a nuisance, and elsewhere on coastal beaches in the county. The flies attract rock pipits and wagtails and several of these may be seen, especially from late summer on when family parties chase each other and the flies. The easternmost cliffs have thrift, bird's-foot-trefoil, sea mayweed, plantains and, up on the clifftop, an expanding mass of hottentot-fig may be seen, which is quite spectacular when in flower in summer.

The cliffs just to the west of the entrance are sloping, earthy, indented and eroding. Part of these clay cliffs collapsed in late 2009, following prolonged rain and they are under constant threat from the sea. Further on, the cliffs are more substantial but, even though some look crumbly and fragile they are usually safe. However, cliffs such as these are liable to partially collapse at any time, or, at the very least, shed a few rocks or loose earth, though these occasional events are more likely to happen in winter when few people are about. There is a prominent buttress in the middle of the beach, which cuts off access further west if the tide is full in. There is also a marked change in ground conditions on either side of the buttress. East of it, the beach is usually soft and sandy, though winter storms may cause significant upheavals and scour the beach of its fine sediment. West of the buttress, the beach is mostly shingle, and large accumulations are thrown up high on the shore, which may be augmented by fragmentation from above, and then capped by debris of all descriptions brought in by the sea. While the buttress is responsible for these varying beach profiles because it prevents longshore movement eastwards, an inadvertent effect is that very few people use the shingly ground west of the buttress. In high summer, the sandy beach east of the buttress is favoured and it may become very busy in good weather.

The cliffs beyond the buttress are high, somewhat sloping and vegetated with fragile-looking earthen tops. The flora on these cliffs is limited because of their exposure and ongoing erosion but thrift, sea mayweed, bird's-foot-trefoil, sea campion, a little ragwort, sea plantain, hawkbits and gorse all add colour and variety to the sheer faces. Look out too for yellow-horned poppy, a few plants of which flower on the cliffs here in summer, and for rock samphire, sea aster and a little orache in places. The low rocks near the outflow stream at the end of the beach have a good covering of lichens, particularly *Ochrolechia parella*, *Ramalina siliquosa*, and *Xanthoria parietina*.

Usually a handful of gulls may be seen on the rocks and oystercatcher on the rocky shoreline. Choughs are regularly seen here, sometimes in pairs and, at other times, larger flocks occur. These may stop and forage on the clifftop or they may tumble and frolic overhead as they pass by. Ravens have breeding territories on either side of Garrarus and they too regularly pass, calling loudly as they do, and in spring they may perform aerial acrobatics as they display and interact. Kestrels are regular, usually single birds, and they may hover overhead in search of prey in the cliff vegetation. Offshore, shags and cormorants may be seen on the rock pinnacles; of the two the cormorant is the more conspicuous, especially if it spreads its wings when perched, allowing the drying wind to flow through the feathers. Hundreds of Manx shearwaters have also been seen just offshore (in May) and the occasional great northern diver appears.

Garrarus is very picturesque and scenic. There is an ambience here which is captivating, especially in good weather, when the projecting headlands and offshore stacks confer an almost exotic Mediterranean character to the scene. The beach is short (only around 0.7 kilometre) and swimming is safe, though is less attractive at low tide, when a large area of rocky platform is exposed (ideal for rockpooling and winkle picking) and the available swimming area is compromised to some extent by forests of kelp below the waterline. At such times, it might be better just to sit and wait for the tide to fill, admire the view and marvel at the coastal scenery which is so attractive here.

Garrarus can be difficult to access in warm summer weather give its popularity locally. When open, the carpark fills rapidly and arriving visitors then park up along the narrow access road; if any of these cars are inappropriately parked, difficulties may arise.

Tramore

Carparking at S50: 595010

It is possible to park anywhere along the Prom at Tramore (though there is a parking charge in summer) or further east beyond the entrance to the old dump, which is awkward

The view to the east from Garrarus beach on a bright day

to reach given the undulations and hollows in the rather rough road surface. The general area around this particular parking area is also degraded and the former dump is now a massive grassy mound and is unnaturally elevated on the otherwise flat landscape. A series of vertical pipes in the vicinity discharge methane gas from the many tonnes of rubbish decaying under the earthen layers. However, strawberry clover has been recorded between the carparking area and the dump. The embankment nearby is also unattractive, and although it obscures views of the sea, it has a vital function in protecting the landward side from inundation by the sea during frequent storms that lash the area, especially in winter. Off to the west, the town of Tramore dominates the distant view, and the many painted buildings stand out on sunny days. To the north and northwest, the mudflats and salt marsh are rather more bland but these are enlivened by the regular calls of wading birds foraging in the creeks, channels and on the salt marsh.

Once up on the well-walked embankment, the scene changes for the better and there are excellent views of the two headlands,

Brownstown Head from Tramore beach

Brownstown Head to the east and Great Newtown Head to the west, which frame the wide and expansive Tramore Bay. Nearby the beach is particularly impressive, because of its length and scenic character. There are always people walking on the beach, regardless of weather and season, though good summer weather draws people from all over southeast Ireland, and the beach off to the west will be thronged with people.

The upper part of the beach, in all directions, is largely shingle and below that is gently sloping and sandy all the way to the tideline. There is little soft dry sand but sometimes sand accumulates on the upper parts of the beach at the western end, only for it to be washed away and redistributed by high waves and winter storms.

Waves constantly impact on the shore at Tramore but their character depends on the wind and tidal conditions. During severe weather events, high, crashing waves pound the shoreline with a ferocity that can be both spectacular and dangerous as they eat away at the shore and the enclosing embankments and seawalls. At other times, they are much more gentle, and they scarcely disturb the sediment, as they dissipate quietly up the shore. The energy and sounds associated with breaking waves is a constant companion when walking on Tramore, and can be uplifting and invigorating.

In summer the sanderlings will be gone from the beach but feeding gannets offshore often provide a spectacular display in that season as they dive-bomb into the Bay. Closer to the dunes, a ringed plover or two may call in alarm or behave erratically if someone passes by, indicating the presence of eggs or young. One or two pairs attempt to breed somewhere along the upper beach every year but they suffer terribly from passing dogs and walkers and they are constantly off their nests. Nevertheless they persevere and

Tracks within Tramore burrow

occasionally raise young, despite the disturbance. Near Rinnashark, Sandwich terns are obvious in spring when the adults arrive from their wintering haunts and particularly in the autumn when the adults are joined by young of the year on their return migration. The productive waters of the Bay and Rinnashark are favoured and the sandbars provide good roosting sites for these majestic birds between feeding bouts.

The embankment is as good a route eastwards towards the Sandhills, initially at least. On the seaward side there is marram, sea-holly, dandelion, some spurge, sea beet, sea sandwort, sow-thistle, wild carrot, buck's-horn plantain, hawkbits and sea mayweed, all stunted and squashed because of the constant trampling. In places further east, common stork's-bill may be encountered, which usually flowers until the autumn. The salt marsh off to the left in the distance is largely dominated by the invasive cord-grass (or *Spartina*) and the breached Malcomson embankments are obvious out in the Backstrand. The embankment on which

you walk is also partially breached in places, revealing the vertical sleepers that assist in holding the embankment together. In places also, more recent efforts at maintaining the integrity of the embankment in the face of the impact of the relentless storms, are visible in the exposed, stone-filled wire mesh enclosures. Dog dirt is another nuisance to be dodged and ducked but the views, seaward especially, are compelling from this elevated embankment. Occasionally horses are schooled on the beach and in the waves, which adds an extra visual element to the view and, overhead, incoming planes or the red Coast Guard helicopter may overfly the beach or dunes as they arrive at Waterford airport just inland at Killowen. Flocks of meadow pipits, a skylark or two and maybe a stonechat might be among the vegetation, and, in winter, sanderlings with a few ringed plover or dunlin, may be seen scurrying along the tideline, picking off invertebrates disturbed by the incoming waves.

The embankment narrows considerably further east, and becomes less defined. It terminates close to the rock armouring at the 'neck' of the dunes, whose purpose is to protect this fragile area, the narrowest part of the extensive dune system, from frontal attack by the waves. Close to the boulders there is a large patch of rock samphire and a few sea radish plants may also be seen here. The dune area on the north side of the boulders is fenced off to prevent people walking over the very fragile dune system here but a timber walkway has been incorporated to allow people to continue to move between the Backstrand and beach side of the Sandhills, without compromising the integrity of the dunes. The enclosed area is also of interest archaeologically for the kitchen midden that can be easily seen from anywhere outside the fenced enclosure. The masses of shells are the leftovers of our Mesolithic ancestors, all hunter gatherers who feasted here on locally available shellfish.

It is around 1.5 kilometres from the carpark to the boulders and once these are reached, it is best to go out onto the beach and continue eastwards from there on the seaward side of the high dunes. There is one big blowout on the front face of the dunes, caused by wind, waves and raging seas over many years, which recent remedial work has attempted to reverse. The area is fenced off and large hessian sheets have been incorporated into the dunes in an attempt to trap sand. There is some regeneration and the main dune building agent, marram grass, is growing strongly. However there are also bare slopes, suggesting ongoing erosion and limited regeneration in places.

Debris, mostly plastic and wood, is always scattered about the upper shore at the base of the dunes. Occasionally, civic-minded citizens gather all this unsightly rubbish and accumulations are placed at intervals along the edge of the dunes, for later collection.

A simple white cross on the edge of the dunes marks the location where the Irish Air Corps Dauphin helicopter crashed on a dreadfully foggy night in July 1999. A defined track into the dunes, another cross and a handrail leads to the actual spot where the helicopter came down. A more substantial cross here with an inscribed plaque commemorates the four gallant men on active duty who lost their lives here and wreaths and flowers suggest that the area is regularly visited by friends, families and colleagues and that they are not forgotten.

The dynamic nature of dune systems is one of erosion and rehabilitation as natural coastal processes exert considerable changes over time. Any regular walker here can see the changing profile of the dunes, even over just one year of activity. The natural order is one of dune building in summer, when weather conditions are less severe and plants are actively growing and trapping sand; conversely in winter, regular storms, violent

Memorial crosses within the dunes

waves and high tides may strip the foredunes and lash the main dunes, leaving vertical sand faces and exposed roots and debris. Sloping dune faces with a good amount of vegetation indicates that the dunes are recovering from a number of years of erosion, but vertical sand cliffs show ongoing erosion by the sea.

At certain times, the sea offshore may be very quiet and few birds may be seen, possibly just a few gulls or oystercatchers on the shoreline or Sandwich terns just offshore in autumn. But at other times, several species may be seen and in some numbers too, especially in winter when large rafts of seabirds may appear to feed on fish shoals congregating offshore. The occasional little gull has been seen around the breakers among the black-headed gulls, whose numbers have declined since the sewage outfall pipe close to the shore is no longer functional. If conditions aren't too rough, red-throated and great northern diver may be seen offshore.

The tideline is worth checking for beached birds and marine mammals, as rarely a week goes by without dead gannets, auks or gulls appearing somewhere along the shore. These should be checked for leg rings, and the details posted off, which eventually will

realise details of the origin of the bird. Porpoises and dolphins are less frequent and when they do appear, they are always an attraction initially but when the smell becomes unbearable they are usually given a wide berth and they become battered and bruised as they roll around in the waves. At least they don't create the major problem that beached whales cause when they occasionally wash up on Tramore beach.

It is around 3.2 kilometres to the tip of the dunes and a good option then is to continue up along Rinnashark channel and walk back along the perimeter of the dunes on its northern side. Water flows through Rinnashark are always strong, especially on spring tides, and the strong current will quickly move any birds that may be feeding in the channel. These are likely to be shags or cormorants, and, occasionally, great northern or red-throated diver in winter. Flocks of brent geese may fly by or they may be foraging on the far shore or even drinking the freshwater flowing into the channel near the grotto, provided people aren't around. A scattering of waders might be about too, usually oystercatcher, and you might be lucky to see a heron or two and little egrets or, exceptionally, cattle egret. The far shore is

The north side of the Tramore dunes in the late 1990s. The 'island' in foreground has since disappeared

North side of the dunes in the late 1990s

popular for walking and, at times (late summer and early autumn), for fishing. A more recent and unwelcome development are the scrambler bikes that drive down the shore to access the dunes, where they race up and down and destroy the vegetation.

The dunes nearby are dominated by marram grass but along the edges you should find sea beet, sea-holly, oraches and sea rocket and there are areas of sea purslane in places. Tramore Burrow is where spring vetch grows, its only site on the south coast; notable species also include wild asparagus, dune fescue, heath dog-violet, dewberry, sand couch and, very occasionally, bee orchid.

The dunes are heavily indented initially around the north side and the sand is usually soft and damp so walking may be awkward. But there are always things to see, more brent geese close to the shore perhaps or red-breasted mergansers frolicking in the channels. In winter, when the tide is out the ducks and waders will be scattered about the Backstrand and might be hard to see, and, when the tide is in, they roost on the northern side in big flocks but, alas, too far away for comfortable views of what can be

quite considerable and spectacular gatherings. Tramore is internationally important for the numbers of pale-bellied brent geese that winter annually in the area. Nationally important numbers of golden plover, grey plover, lapwing, dunlin and black-tailed godwit also winter, and red-throated diver numbers in the outer bay can be high.

The high dunes on this side of the Sandhills are steep and impressive. However, the highest one is fenced off, to protect it from walkers, runners and skateboarders. Otherwise the Backstrand is flat and featureless with massive sandbanks where flocks of gulls and cormorants occasionally roost, while waiting for the tide to rise. The channels between the sandbanks could be buzzing with birdlife in winter and watch out for long-tailed duck near the Malcomson embankments, while the mudflats nearest the 'neck' of the dunes may have ringed plover, sanderling and curlew. If the tide is in, and the wind is strong, big waves may be generated and birds resting on the choppy waters might then be difficult to see.

The stony shoreline is covered with brown algae and on very low tides, the tube-like

North side of the dunes and the Backstrand, from near the 'neck'

sand mason can be seen. The high point of the dunes (Knockaunriark) is prominent on this side and obvious too are the unvegetated channels that run up its sides. The walk westwards along the northern edge of the dunes can be cold and damp during northerly winds in winter but provides good shelter when southerly winds blow.

All the dunes on the north side are slumping and the edges vertical, with little vegetation to consolidate the sand. There is also a big blowout near the 'neck' which seems to widen every year, despite efforts to halt the erosion that is eating into the dunes here. The entrance to the blowout is fenced off, which may keep people out, but is ineffective at keeping the sea at bay; seaweed and other debris hanging from the wire mesh confirms the ingress of the sea here and the ongoing threat to the integrity of the dune system. Nearby, vertical and decaying railway sleepers are detached from the dunes they were erected to protect in an earlier attempt to stabilise the system here.

The walk back from the western end of the dunes is unspectacular. The embankment on the left is grassy and weedy and the salt marsh on the right is flat and featureless. Underfoot the path is degraded and many of the coastal plants are damaged by the constant feet of passing walkers, though certain prostrate species like buck's-horn plantain and daisy seem to thrive in this environment. There is, however, good salt marsh habitat between the southern embankment and the carpark and, in summer, a distinctive flora is present from the top of the marsh right down to the mudflats. A carpet of pinks and purples bloom here and several other less conspicuous plants grow among the thrift and sea lavender, the most widespread of which is sea purslane. At other times of the year curlew and redshank forage in the channels while grey crows and rooks amble about on the salt marsh.

Blowout near the 'neck'

A walk out along the southern Malcomson embankment is worthwhile, and offers extensive views of the Backstrand. At high tide the embankments are roost sites for flocks of waders, though they tend to be restless and flighty if approached too closely. Even the surfaces of the stones here are home to conspicuous lichens (mostly white and orange in colour) and very mobile sand hoppers and sea slaters scurry away if any of these rocks are lifted.

The entire walk from the carpark, around the dunes and back is around seven kilometres and will take around two hours at a leisurely stroll, which means an occasional stop to admire the view and the natural attractions on offer. The walk can be extended to include the entire beach to the west, the magnificent Prom, the boating lake and the very different amusements. Outside of the holiday season, the boating lake regularly holds good numbers of feeding black-tailed godwits and smaller numbers of other waders (occasionally ruff or common sandpiper). Several dozen mute swans are often present along with mallard, and brent geese are also frequent. A few diving ducks occur in most winters, including gadwall and scaup recently. The main attraction here in many recent winters is ring-billed gull, with two or more birds present on occasions. Mediterranean gull has also occurred, and other rare gulls are possible. A final option is to continue walking on the west side of the Bay, perhaps along the Doneraile to the pier, or even further south along cliff road, which offers great views of the Bay.

Saleen

Carparking at S60: 628005

A grassy, earthen mound at the front of the carpark restricts views of the Backstrand and towards Kilmacleague from a car, unless you are very close to it. When the tide is out, the Backstrand is a flat expanse of featureless sandflats, through which a number of channels meander. The extent and direction of these channels varies with the season and the changes brought to the mobile sands by tides and climatic conditions. However, the narrow channel at low tide close to the carpark, which flows from Clohernagh and Kilmacleague inlets, maintains a more or less constant profile throughout the year. Birds are always foraging along its length, and their numbers are greatest in autumn and winter, when their constant calling may be heard. You should see oystercatchers, brent geese, redshanks and black-headed gulls and there is sure to be a heron or two along with little egrets, which might be more numerous

The beautiful Tramore beach from the west (Gallway's hill)

further up along the creek. Cormorants may be fishing in the main channel and, in winter, a great northern diver or two might appear. Further out one or more pairs of red-breasted mergansers might be fluttering about in the water, either chasing each other or diving in search of fish. Great crested grebe are likely too and flocks of gulls, cormorants, waders and brent geese may be roosting on the sandbars or strolling around the fringes, foraging on the tideline. When the tide is in, there may be fewer birds about, as many of them—the waders in particular—are then probably at their high tide roosts on the northern side or around the old dump and the Malcomson embankments.

The trees and bushes around the car park and down along the access road to Saleen are worth checking for passerines, especially the commoner ones such as robin, dunnock and finches, but you never know what might be about here and they might be productive for warblers, newly arrived on the coast in the spring; hoopoe has also occurred here.

The walk down along the shore is always possible regardless of tidal conditions. Saltmarsh rush grows at the top of the shore with occasional patches of sea milkwort, and colt's-foot grows in the sloping earthen bank early in the year. From autumn on, if the tide is out, brent geese are likely to be on the shoreline or up some way along it, drinking the fresh water flowing from the land near the small grotto. If present these might be worth checking for colour-rings and with good light and patience, these can be easily read. Look out too for young birds (these have barring or obvious white stripes along the upper-wing coverts) and then for the family parties that the young belong to.

The earthen embankment on the left as you walk down the shore is largely marram and grassy, though there is some sea beet, sea mayweed, sea rocket, oraches, autumn

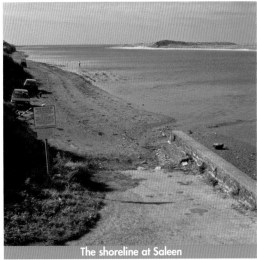
The shoreline at Saleen

hawkbit, sea-holly and spurge. The shoreline initially is accessible to vehicles but thereafter the sand on the upper shore is soft, deep and dry and risky for vehicles to drive through. The shore here is sloping and shingly lower down. The tide races through the channel, especially after the tide turns on spring tides and swimming is definitely **not** recommended because of the strong currents.

Although its profile changes through the year and between years, Bass Point always has actively growing foredunes. This is probably the best place in the area for sea rocket, and several plants may be seen, which have masses of flowers varying from white to pink to mauve or purple. Further south on the shoreline, brent geese may be seen foraging on the rocky shoreline or feeding on the *Enteromorpha*. The brent regularly move between this site and the other feeding areas around the Backstrand, so keep an eye out for flocks flying over the channel in characteristic V-formations.

Further south the land rises and the sandy cliffs are higher. In places these have been undercut by the sea and are sheer and unvegetated. There may be sand martin holes in the upper parts of the sandy cliffs as they exploit new breeding opportunities when they arrive in spring from their wintering

233

Tramore Bay from the fields above Saleen

grounds in Africa. A rock pipit or two may be about the rocks and stonechats may be in the vegetation above. The tideline should have the odd redshank or greenshank, a little egret or two and black-headed gulls and cormorants may be roosting on any of the sandbars, either on this shore or on the far side of the channel. In the autumn, large numbers of terns appear, mainly Sandwich terns but occasionally little terns and common/arctic terns are seen.

Once the long and extensive beach at Tramore comes into view, on balmy days the shimmering shapes of people walking on the strand will be seen; there are always walkers on Tramore beach, though relatively few complete the entire walk around the dunes. There may be an angler or two (usually more in autumn) around the breakers rolling into Rinnashark. At times these very breakers are spectacular and pound the shoreline with a ferocity that is awe-inspiring. Likewise the breakers along Tramore beach are ever-present, rolling in relentlessly regardless of tide and season. When disturbed and high, these cloak the beach in a mist of sea spray, which at times may almost obscure the beach. There are times, however, when the waves impacting on the shores here are gentle and benign and, on such occasions, the true

tranquility of the area can be appreciated. However such conditions rarely last and at other times, big breakers crashing violently on the shore at high tide can move mountains of sand and inflict untold damage on the dunes, the embankments and the man-made features at Tramore.

As you near the end of Rinnashark, Tramore Bay should be carefully scanned, particularly in autumn or winter after storms and onshore winds. Red-throated and great northern divers, gannets, common scoters, arctic skuas and, on occasions, large numbers of kittiwakes are possible.

The three massive pillars at Great Newtown Head stand out conspicuously at the tip of the headland to the west, especially on sunny days when their vivid white colours make them especially prominent. The many houses on the headland around Newtown cove and the pier are also obvious, but are not anywhere near as dramatic.

There is much outcropping rock further south along the walk, projecting up from the sand. Low down on the shore these are covered with seaweeds and barnacles, while at the top of the shore they are covered in lichens that are white (*Ochrolechia parella*), orange (*Xanthoria parietina*) and black (*Verrucaria* species). Mid-shore, where waves constantly scour the rocks, they are bare and the characteristic colour of the parent rock material, Old Red Sandstone, is apparent in the conglomerate. Where the cliffs nearby are washed by incoming tides, they are largely rock lower down and distinct layering is apparent in the cliff profile. The lowest beds are fine sedimentary sands while just above is pebbly conglomerate. The tops are vegetated with gorse, ivy, bracken and willow in the grassy vegetation; thrift should also show nicely in summer at the cliff edge.

You can walk safely for around two kilometres from the carpark, a little more if the tide is out and you don't mind hopping over rocks. Before turning back, look west to just beyond the pillars at Great Newtown Head, where the islands off Kilfarrasy may be seen on the distant coastline.

The dunes at Saleen are small and unremarkable, and certainly so compared with the quite spectacular dunes on the far side of the channel. However, you should see rabbits (which are not present in the Sandhills on the opposite shore) and perhaps flocks of linnets, greenfinches and maybe a stonechat or two; a bluethroat (the second county record) stayed here for a while in April 2008. These dunes are very weedy in places with masses of nettles, thistles and bracken but more characteristic coastal plants are also present, including meadowsweet and the rare meadow fescue. The area is occasionally grazed by cattle, and their constant poaching and manuring has altered the vegetation and many flowering plants are much reduced in occurrence and abundance. There are also wide, unvegetated paths through these dunes, caused by scramblers and quad bikes that race noisily around the area, which, apart from the damage to the vegetation detracts from the ambience of the area and degrades this pristine coastal area.

Foredunes at Saleen (sea rocket in the foreground)

The overall walk is around 4.5 kilometres and should take no more than two hours, and a lot less if time is short and a fast pace is set. Saleen, however, shouldn't be rushed as there is much to see and appreciate.

The walk northwards from the carpark is less interesting and very few people choose to walk over the stony surface. At low tide, waders will be scattered all across the mudflats, while tighter flocks can be viewed (rather distantly) on a rising or falling tide, along the sandbank west from Kilmacleague and Clohernagh. Whimbrel are regular at migration periods and Kilmacleague inlet, at the north end of Saleen strand, is worth scanning for common sandpipers, though these are unlikely to be seen from the carpark. Gull flocks are worth checking from Saleen (especially with a telescope)–these are mainly lesser black-backed gulls–but rarer species have included yellow-legged, ring-billed, Mediterranean and glaucous gulls.

On land, the most obvious migrants are usually swallows, skylarks and meadow pipits, which can be seen passing east or west overhead, especially in September and October, sometimes several hundred in a few hours. These are often accompanied by smaller numbers of sand martins, and occasionally by a turtle dove, yellow wagtail or tree pipit (a tawny pipit has also been seen). Finch movements (chaffinch, redpoll and siskin) also occur, in late autumn.

Nocturnal migrants are usually fewer in number and less obvious, and may require patient and careful searching of suitable cover, especially around the gardens and hedgerows. Optimum conditions are after southeasterly winds from late March to early June and from late July to mid-November, when commoner migrants and the odd rarity pass through. A good place to start looking is along the edge of the gardens at the south end of the access road to Brownstown, just before the lane which leads down to the Head proper. These provide good shelter and feeding for species attracted to trees and willow scrub. Over the years, several scarce or rare species have been recorded here in spring or autumn including redstart, bluethroat, tree pipit, lesser whitethroat, reed, icterine, melodious, barred, wood, western Bonelli's, Pallas's and yellow-browed warbler, firecrest, red-breasted and pied flycatcher, and, from North America, red-eyed vireo, yellow warbler and northern parula. An Iberian chiffchaff, the first record for Ireland, was a surprise in June 2010.

Brownstown Head

Brownstown Head
Limited carparking at X69: 620985

Brownstown Head doesn't have a beach or a defined walk but it is an attractive, if remote, area of east Waterford that is accessible from Waterford City, Tramore or Dunmore East and is one of the best birdwatching sites in county Waterford. The walk down the lane eventually leads out to the Head, from where the sea offshore can be surveyed and passing seabirds noted.

Brownstown is an excellent site for observing good numbers of both seabird and landbird migrants on the Waterford coast and is equalled only by Helvick Head, further west. Situated at the southeast corner of Tramore Bay, Brownstown projects almost as far south as Hook Head in county Wexford to the east, and compares well in the range and numbers of migrants recorded over the last few decades. Most notably, the site has produced records of a number of North American passerine species.

Coverage along the lane towards the tip of the Head, with occasional binocular scans along the hedges of adjacent fields, will usually reveal some common migrants in spring or autumn, including whitethroat (which also breed in good numbers). Whinchats are most likely to be seen here. Rough tracks can be followed across several of the fields bordering the boreen, and by keeping to the extreme margins of the fields it is possible to systematically search the hedgerows for birds. In this part of Brownstown, small migrants often flit ahead of the observer along the hedgerows (or bury themselves deep in cover!), but a careful or sit-and-wait approach can be rewarding. Black redstart, blackcap, and garden warbler are the most frequent 'scarcities' here, but firecrest, lesser whitethroat, reed, icterine, melodious, barred and yellow-browed warbler have all occurred, with blackpoll warbler the highlight; a rosy starling (in October 2006) and little bittern (April 2008) were other notable species.

At the east margin of Brownstown Head, a stream down to Coolum cove flows through an impressive, densely vegetated, steep-sided glen, which can be viewed from above in places. Towards its north end, the glen closes in and the stream is bordered by dense, but more accessible willow and thorn scrub. Access is by a rather long walk along the cliff-top west of Brazen Head, or, more easily, along a track running east from the 'main road' further back along the Head. Species recorded include wryneck, ring ouzel, lesser whitethroat, reed, yellow-browed and greenish warbler, and firecrest.

Field-margins and scrub back along the 'main road' from the Head (woodchat shrike has occurred here in spring) and gardens and scrub at the northwest side of the Head, overlooking the northeast corner of Tramore Bay, are also worth checking if time allows. Apart from migrant species, locally-breeding passerines include chough, stonechat, reed bunting, and cliff-nesting house martins. Good numbers of thrushes may occur in winter, along with various wader species in the fields. Birds of prey are regular, including fairly frequent sightings of merlin in autumn and, more rarely, hen harrier and short-eared owl. Very occasionally geese feed in the fields near the Head in winter.

Striped hawkmoth at Brownstown Head (June 2009)

©P. M. Walsh

The western cliffs at the Head also provide a good vantage point, in calm conditions in winter, from which to scan Tramore Bay for divers and common scoters.

Ideal conditions for seawatching at Brownstown are onshore winds, from between a southeasterly and a southwesterly direction, especially with reduced visibility in mist or rain. Some shelter from the elements is available inside or behind the observation hut on the tip. From spring to autumn, Manx shearwaters, gannets, kittiwakes, guillemots and razorbills are the most abundant species, with a thousand or more passing per hour on occasions. Even in mid-winter, large passages of kittiwakes and auks are occasionally recorded. Other species including divers, common scoters, sooty shearwaters and skuas are fairly regular at the appropriate seasons. Common porpoises too have often been seen offshore during seawatches and there have been records of whales and Risso's dolphin.

Brownstown Head has also proved to be an important area for moths and recent

Ballymacaw cove

trapping has been fruitful for a number of interesting species including fox moth, emperor moth, the magpie, clouded border, brimstone moth, scalloped hazel, muslin moth and mother shipton, hawkmoths (convolvulus, eyed, poplar, hummingbird, striped and elephant), hoary footman and feathered brindle and the migrants delicate, vestal, dark sword-grass, pearly underwing, silver Y and rusty-dot pearl. Most of these moths remain hidden by day (though the silver Y will take flight when disturbed) but all the resident butterflies are likely to be seen, as well as migrant red admirals and painted ladies, and clouded yellows in some years. Many of these butterflies warm themselves on willow leaves there in summer.

Ballymacaw

Carparking at X69: 647990

Ballymacaw is a small sheltered cove with low, vegetated, sloping cliffs which enclose a rocky beach. Two streams flow into the cove; the main stream does so under an attractive central bridge. There is room for five or six cars near the beach and occasionally larger vehicles park on the beach itself.

There is a gravelly cliff beside the carpark and the small shingly beach nearby has

orache, sea beet and sea mayweed with water-cress and winter heliotrope growing around the smaller inflow stream on the west side. Gorse is the main plant on the cliff above while the bank on the far side of the stream has wind-shaped blackthorn with sea mayweed, thrift, bird's-foot-trefoil and plantains lower down.

The underlying geology is Old Red Sandstone, which is visible in the cliffs, in the outcropping rock on the west side and in the shingle underfoot. The enclosing headlands restrict views of the coast on either side of the entrance. The east side is heavily vegetated but there is a small projecting pier. Choughs might be about overhead, common sandpipers might be on the rocks at the mouth of the cove and you might see gannets passing by offshore. The main bird interest is likely to be the songbirds and migrants that frequent the densely vegetated and impenetrable sides of the valley on the landward side of the bridge. Breeding species here include willow warbler, chiffchaff and occasionally blackcap in addition to commoner species like robin, dunnock, blackbird and wren. Small passerines find plenty of shelter and feeding here at migration times, but because there is so much

Rathmoylan cove

dense, tall cover, they can be difficult to see. However, the easternmost glen can be viewed from the roadside above and flitting shapes in the branches can be gradually picked out. Most will be tits, willow warblers, chiffchaffs or goldcrests, but yellow-browed, garden and melodious warblers, firecrests and pied flycatchers have all occurred.

Rathmoylan
Limited carparking at X69: 657988
Rathmoylan is a small but sheltered cove and has an outflow stream entering the beach on the eastern side. Beside the stream is a degraded shingly/sandy area which has sea rocket, orache, sea mayweed and sea beet. The rotting seaweed and other debris cast up on the shore attracts flies and wagtails but the smell can be overpowering at times and the mess awkward to walk over. There might be a handful of gulls on the shoreline but the cove is too enclosed to attract seabirds in any numbers, though you might hear and see Sandwich terns offshore in autumn.

The cliffs on the west side are more impressive but even these are unspectacular compared with other coastal cliffs in the county. A feature of the cliffs is how obvious the parent rock, Old Red Sandstone, is here and in the shoreline rocks; the sandstone layering is especially obvious in the western cliffs. The botanical interest is limited but sea aster and sea mayweed grow in the cliffs. If the tide is out, it is possible to see Falskirt Rock just off Swines Head to the east; a walk out along a vegetated walkway to the eastern headland offers better views of the coastal cliffs outside the cove.

At the top of the beach, the western side is heavily fortified with rock armouring to protect the shore. Tree-mallow grows on the top of these boulders and some rock sea-spurrey grows on the wall. You might see choughs about the cove and stonechats, wagtails and rock pipits are almost always present; black redstarts have also been recorded in autumn. The extensive low scrub along the stream running down to Rathmoylan cove, and on the adjacent hillside, provides excellent migrant habitat, although the site is under-watched. Nocturnal migrants are frequent in spring and autumn, usually goldcrests, willow warblers and chiffchaffs but occasionally rarer species like melodious warbler or firecrest may occur. Breeding species include sedge warbler and yellowhammer, and sand martins occasionally in the cliff top. Small numbers of herring gulls and fulmars breed along the cliffs east and west of the cove.

In summer, butterflies to look out for include small tortoiseshells, common blues, red admirals and painted ladies.

Portally

Limited carparking (one car) at X69: 671991
Portally is one of the least accessible of the Waterford beaches. There isn't any car park and if you go down to the end of the access road, turning is restricted and you could end up in a private driveway.

The walk down the road offers excellent views of the Hook Head peninsula and Hook lighthouse. Once at the end of the road, the steep track (beyond the last house) down to the cove is often overgrown and may be wet, slippery and even muddy following heavy rain. There is little botanical interest but montbretia grows on the way down and golden samphire down near the end. This sheltered track does attract speckled wood butterflies and small tortoiseshells might also be seen. There are also good views of the far side of the cove from the track and that

headland is a fine example of coastal heath dominated by heathers and autumn gorse, and is particularly attractive when these flower in late summer and autumn.

The beach is small, shingly and enclosed and reasonably sheltered. Pied wagtails and rock pipits forage about the seaweed and there might be an oystercatcher or two on the shore. A kestrel might appear overhead but views offshore are restricted by the enclosing headlands. The top of the beach has silverweed, sea sandwort, sea beet, orache, bindweed and a little winter heliotrope. Sea spleenwort grows in some of the cracks and crevices low down in the cliffs on the east side, which can be safely examined if the tide is out. Masses of thrift grow higher up on the cliff along with sea mayweed. There are small outflow streams on either side of the cove and common reed grows near the western stream.

A walkway from the east side of Portally all the way to Dunmore East was improved in 2009, and is now safe and secure, with stiles, access ramps and protective fences where the track is close to the cliffs. From the eastern clifftop at Portally to Dunmore is

Portally cove from the east side

Main strand at Dunmore East

only around two kilometres. A walk back by road would be an invigorating experience, given the coastal location. Even if the entire walk is not followed, it is worth walking out along the track on the east side of cove at Portally. The coastal heath is attractive with several interesting plant species, the most important of which is sea carrot, which, for some reason, is the dominant subspecies at Portally (and not wild carrot, which is much more common in Waterford).

Around 40-50 pairs of kittiwakes breed on the cliffs at the mouth of the cove on the east side, though these do so on sheer faces and aren't easy to see safely. Fulmars, shags and herring gulls also nest and black guillemots have been seen (in 2009) and they may breed. Birds, though relatively scarce, are the main attraction on the cliff walk between Dunmore East and Portally with herring gulls, pigeons, choughs and breeding fulmars at Red Head, nearest Dunmore. The glen at Portally, and the small broad-leaved plantation leading down to the small beach can be productive for common passerine migrants, and there is potential for rarities with more regular coverage.

The walk back up is steep; however the entire walk down to the beach and back is no more than one kilometre.

Dunmore East

Carparking at S60: 689008
(beside the Strand Hotel)

The beach under the Strand Hotel is small and sandy and is backed by a high and heavily pointed sandstone wall that is devoid of vegetation. A stream flows onto the beach through an attractive arch in the wall beside the access ramp to the beach. This stream has been the source of contamination, thought to be of agricultural origin further upstream, thus denying the beach Blue Flag status in some years. The cliffs off to the left are high and natural but there is limited vegetation; nevertheless sea beet, sea aster, plantains, hedge veronica, gorse, ivy and thrift can be seen on ledges or near the top. Fulmars breed here in summer and may be seen gliding around back and forth. You might see rock pipits and flocks of gulls might be roosting on the beach or just offshore.

If the tide is in, it is not possible to walk to Counsellor's strand nearby. Both these beaches can be busy in summer when throngs of people arrive to enjoy the pleasant village of Dunmore East. If the tide is out the walk across to that beach is short. You could continue up the ramp and walk back the short distance by road, which offers good views of the area, especially if the day is warm and sunny. You could also hop over the boulders out to Cathedral Rocks near the Foilakipeen headland.

The views from the beach are nicely framed by the low headlands. Hook peninsula is obvious in the distant view with Hook lighthouse prominent at its tip. Nearby the lighthouse in the harbour at Dunmore East is much less imposing by comparison but is attractive all the same. The woodlands behind the strand are high and there is an excellent walk through these woods if time allows. The church spire is also a prominent feature as are the attractive houses around the harbour here, especially the thatched cottages just above the strand.

The beach is small and not amenable to long walks. Nevertheless the area is very scenic with many of the natural features of coastal areas along with all the amenities to

ensure a pleasant stay in majestic surroundings. A longer walk can be enjoyed by walking through Dunmore East and by visiting the coves and harbour along the way. The Haven Hotel enjoys a parkland setting with commanding views of Waterford Harbour in the distance. The park opposite can be visited and from there two attractive coves can be reached. Mens (or badgers) cove is probably more accessible and is sometimes used as a deep water swimming area. It has a bustling kittiwake colony in summer which is boisterous and noisy because the birds constantly squabble and fight as they rear their young on the sheer sandstone cliffs here. There is a steep stairway down to the next cove, which is fine going down but is tiring coming back up. Kittiwakes also breed here and the area is in constant use by clients of the adventure centre opposite for rock-climbing, canoeing and other water sports.

There are many thatched cottages in the village of Dunmore East and these attractive dwellings can be admired on the way down to the usually busy harbour. This is primarily a fishing harbour, which has all the facilities for handling fishing boats and their catches (an ice plant, auction hall, synchro lifts) but

Picturesque thatched cottages at Dunmore East

Roof-nesting herring gull at Dunmore East

All the colonies are at their noisiest from May to July when the birds are breeding.

The other prominent breeding species in Dunmore is the herring gull, which nests on rooftops of many buildings, including hotels, factories and private houses in the town. Fulmars breed in the cliffs on either side of Counsellor's strand and anyone carefully watching the inner harbour kittiwakes will also find blackbird, dunnock, wren, collared dove and pied wagtail breeding in the dense vegetation (hedge veronica is prolific here).

yachts and sailing boats also use the harbour so there are always boats of some description coming and going. In summer the area around the boat club is a hive of activity for sailing and adventure activities. The inner harbour area is also home to a kittiwake colony, famous for its proximity to man. There are two other main colonies at outer harbour (the largest colony) and Black Knob. The outer harbour birds can be viewed safely from a number of vantage points at badger's cove and men's cove. Black Knob is the most dangerous of the three and caution is required if kittiwakes are viewed from above.

Dunmore East in winter is ideal for both common and scarce gulls. Despite recent declines in breeding numbers, herring gulls are usually the most abundant species, but good numbers of black-headed, common and great black-backed gulls also occur. Glaucous and Iceland gulls, scarce 'northern' species, were formerly regular in winter but are less frequent nowadays. Little gulls are occasional from September to April, and sabine's and Mediterranean gulls have occurred.

The sea wall at inner harbour offers a nice walk which overlooks Waterford Harbour and the seas offshore. The rocks below the

The inner harbour at Dunmore East

wall usually have turnstone, purple sandpiper (the best site in Waterford for the species) and oystercatcher foraging among the seaweed and gulls roost here all year round. Shanooan, the headland above these cliffs can also be visited from where there are even better views of Waterford Harbour, Hook Head and the waters off to the west. This is a good site for some seawatching and, apart from the usual species such as gannet, gull and kittiwake (large flocks of which can occur in winter), you might see skuas, terns, auks, Manx shearwaters and storm petrels in autumn in the productive waters offshore. Occasionally great northern divers or common scoters can be seen, and Balearic shearwater and velvet scoter have occurred.

Dunmore East is potentially a good site for landbird migrants and the best birds to date have been a wryneck near Dunmore East in 1877 (first Irish record), a golden oriole in 1994, and an Indian house crow in the 1970s; better coverage would almost certainly produce an increase in notable records.

From Shanooan you could walk back to the Strand Hotel, through the village. A longer alternative is to continue westwards uphill and either walk through the woods or continue by road back to the hotel.

Fornaght

Limited carparking at S70: 700037
The flat, sandy lane down to the beach is lined with bramble, nettle, bindweed, bracken, dock, thistle, hedge woundwort, various grasses and wild carrot and there are sure to be stonechats and other passerines in the ditches that will have a hungry brood to feed in summer. Butterflies dancing about the ditches might include peacock, the 'whites', speckled wood and common blues and migrant species like red admiral and painted lady might also be seen.

There is a large, expansive estuarine environment off the beach, which is best appreciated when the tide is out. Large numbers of birds may be about, scattered over the shore. These include three or four species of gull (herring gull, great black-backed gull, black-headed gull and lesser black-backed gull), oystercatcher and curlew with little egret and herons also possible. In winter these may be joined by small numbers of wading birds like redshank, godwits and occasionally even brent geese.

Creadan Head from Fornaght beach

Knockavelish Head with the Wexford shoreline in the background

When the tide is out, the shellfish trestles on Woodstown beach off east of Knockavelish Head are exposed and this is the time when tractors and trailers appear and workers in their yellow leggins work the trestles in a frenzy of processing activity before the tide turns. Even off Fornaght beach, there are usually always people stooped over harvesting shellfish or bait by hand in a much less intensive way. There are excellent cockle beds on these mudflats and masses of periwinkle and mussel shells are cast up on the beach at Fornaght, another reason perhaps why people gather here to collect shellfish.

The beach is gently sloping with the characteristic profile of many coastal beaches, which is pronounced here because it is less exposed than beaches along the more open coastline further west: low down on the beach shingle dominates, then there are crinkly carpets of cockle shells, followed by lines of seaweed along the high tideline and ultimately, at the top of the beach, soft sands. There is a limited flora at the top of the beach but there is some sea beet, sea sandwort, sea rocket, oraches and sea plantain but it is mostly grassy vegetation with encroaching marram and sand sedge. There is also some alder and wild carrot and the

landward side of the beach is a marshy area where common reed dominates along with willows, bulrush, sea and grey club-rush. Flowering plants include the prominent spikes of purple-loosestrife and there is also a little common mallow. However, the 'dunes' are relatively poor and grassy with a lot of clover and docks though there is bird's-foot-trefoil, yarrow and some ragwort to brighten the view. The most prominent plant is giant rush (though these are not as impressive or as plentiful as those on the Cunnigar, near Dungarvan) and royal fern grows deep in the marsh in several places.

The bog west of the strand at Fornaght can be a good site for migrant landbirds, although it is less productive now than in the past because of improved drainage. Nevertheless, water rails can often be heard squealing in the dense vegetation of the bog and they undoubtedly breed here and sedge warblers and other passerines also occur.

An outflow stream enters on the south side of the beach and it is possible to walk inland a small distance along the banks of the stream. This might be worth it to check for dragonflies that frequent the marshy but normally impenetrable bog behind the beach. There are a limited number of species here

Woodstown dunes and beach

because of the coastal conditions but large red damselflies should be obvious in spring and early summer and the emperor, a recent arrival in Ireland, might be seen later in the year. Rock pipits might be around the breached and battered storm wall at the Creadan Head end of the beach and linnets should be around the grassy vegetation at the top of the beach.

Of interest too, lower down on the beach below the shingle, is a band of what looks like compacted earth, which has an amount of decaying tree trunks and roots ingrained in the compacted matrix. It is likely that these are the remnants of what was once a low wooded bank, either here or nearby, long since eroded by the sea. Also of interest on the shore if the tide is out are the lines of tyres on the mud, strategically placed to trap crabs that enter the tyres when the tide is going out for shelter and protection from predatory gulls only to be cropped later when the mud is exposed. The ongoing erosion here is also obvious in the headland at Knockavelish, where a bare, high earthen bank (though it does have some gorse) is heavily fortified at its base on the landward side by rock armouring. There is some great

willowherb and montbretia around the armouring and a narrow walkway inland passes the cottages and meanders eventually to Woodstown beach. This is an enchanting walk up the narrow lane, and never more so in summer in fine weather; ivy broomrape has been recorded here and there should be many other plants of interest.

If the tide is either out or going out, it is possible to walk around the headland at Knockavelish along the rocky shoreline to Woodstown and then walk back by road. There are many large pools on the Woodstown side and these attract herons, little egrets, gulls and waders while on the cliffs nearby you should see sea aster, sea plantain and thrift on the higher parts of the cliffs at the headland. Further back is dominated by ivy, blackthorn, ash, alder and sycamore while the pines on the southern side of the headland are very prominent. However, be careful of the advancing tide, which fills quickly here.

Unlike other beaches in Waterford, Fornaght beach has an impressive distant view on the far side of the estuary in county Wexford. There is a long, relatively low coastline, cliffed in places and on a good day some of the beaches on that shore may be obvious (Booley Bay and Dollar Bay) and Duncannon beach off to the left will always stand out conspicuously. Fornaght beach is nicely framed by the wooded Knockavelish Head on the left, and more dominantly by Creadan Head on the right. The parent rock material of the area, Old Red Sandstone, is obvious in the exposed soil, the cliffs and in the shoreline rocks.

It is possible to spend an hour or two, or even more, pottering about either headlands, or the beaches and there are ample opportunities for walks around the roads in pleasant and scenic surroundings. The basic walk around the beach and back is only around 2.5 kilometres.

Woodstown

carparking at S60: 696048

Woodstown is a very popular beach, especially for walking throughout the year, but perhaps more so in winter when many people enjoy the relatively sheltered conditions, especially at weekends. Horses are regularly brought to the beach and the sight of groups of these cantering over the sands is inspiring, though inevitably their presence is unwelcome for some. The beach is also popular in summer, but if the tide is out, swimming off the beach isn't all that appealing because of the extensive mudflats exposed at low tide and the distance which has to be walked before the shallow offshore waters are reached. Carpets of green algae along the entire shoreline in summer are also disconcerting and can make walking difficult, especially over the stony north end.

There are a number of places where carparking is available, but the best carpark is at the southern end of the beach, which allows for walking the full length of the beach, if required. If you are lucky here you might see mugwort at the base of the low wall fronting the carpark but less welcome is the stand of Japanese knotweed at the northern end near the stream. Rooks breed in the trees beside the carpark, and the constant calling and squabbling is pronounced from late spring on, when the young are in the nests high in the canopy, and always demanding food from the parent birds.

Woodstown beach is relatively short (a little over 2 kilometres) and yet it is long enough, back and forward, for an invigorating walk in a coastal environment, which is always more sheltered than other beaches, whatever the prevailing conditions. The walk along the length of Woodstown beach is without difficulty and should take no more than an hour. The relatively flat Wexford shore is on the far side of the estuary where Duncannon is the most obvious feature. You might see small boats, yachts and even container ships moving through the estuary on their way out or up to the ports of New Ross or Waterford.

There is a long strip of sand dune nearby, which usually has an interesting flora in summer, but these dunes are small and so relatively few species grow. Bracken is the dominant plant species, especially to the back of the dunes. Common species like purple-loosestrife, knapweed, yellow vetchling, willowherbs, ladies bedstraw, ragwort and hawkbits flourish on the grassy embankments at the northern end. Large clumps of red bistort grow at the southern end of the car park while the open dune areas have restharrow and sea bindweed; bear's breech is also well established at the back of the dunes. Hoary cress can be seen as you cross the stream on your walk north along the beach. Wallflower (red and white varieties) have invaded the dunes and these offer a varied blaze of colour. You might also hear or see stonechats in the vegetation or grey crows calling in the pine trees, where they often build their nests. A colony of sand martins nest in the cliff tops near the north end of the beach, and these can be seen entering and leaving their nests in summer.

At low tide a massive area of mudflat is exposed and is used for feeding by wintering shorebirds that usually roost elsewhere. Oystercatcher can be numerous, and there are often good numbers of bar-tailed godwits and smaller numbers of sanderling and knot present. Great crested grebes can occur immediately offshore, but given the distance, these are likely to be just specks, and possibly hard to identify without a telescope. Woodstown also holds a large night-time gull roost, with up to 4,000 black-headed gulls and 3,000 common gulls recorded. Species such as Mediterranean or Iceland gull also occur on occasions. In recent years, brent geese have taken to feeding on the shoreline and, when the tide is in, these may be seen close inshore. Apart from birds, the mudflats offshore are usually a hive of activity at low tide as the shellfish processors busy themselves harvesting their crop.

The walk back along the beach is usually the preferred option but a variation might be to walk back along the road. Traffic is rarely an issue and Woodstown bog is always worth a look; you might see a grey heron or two and hear water rails that breed in the extensive reedbeds. Sedge warblers breed here too (reed warbler has also been heard singing), and chiffchaffs occasionally winter.

Once back at the carpark, it is possible to continue south up the road and through the woods. This is a lovely walk, and, if desired and the weather is good, it can be followed all the way to Fornaght, a delightful beach nearby. Woodland dominates the walk initially, and among the oaks (sessile, pedunculate and turkey oaks mainly) you might see sweet violet, wood-sedge, wood avens, sanicle and burnet rose while the shaded conditions are good for ferns (soft-shield fern and maidenhair spleenwort in particular) but perhaps less welcome is the invasive winter heliotrope in the woods and along the verges. The damper areas have water-cress and fool's-water-cress and the tall great horsetail plants should be obvious from spring onwards.

The woods resonate in spring with the sound of songbirds calling from the tree tops. This beautiful cacophony of sound is probably best in the morning when willow warblers, chiffchaffs, robins, wrens, thrushes, blackcaps, goldcrests, chaffinches, greenfinches, blackbirds and tits (blue, great and coal) enliven the area with their vibrant, melodious songs.

The sun going down near Sheep Island, between Garrarus and Kilfarrasy

Changes to the Waterford Coast

We in Waterford are fortunate to have such a varied coastal zone nearby. Most people in the county value the health of our coasts and seas as they are probably the places we visit most often for recreation and tranquility, and for the better quality of life they provide. However, despite initiatives and legislative safeguards aimed at either maintaining or improving coastal areas, the quality of our coasts and seas continue to decline. Despite reductions in 'point source' discharges of sewage and industrial effluents at the major coastal towns in the county (Tramore and Dungarvan), with the commissioning of new sewage treatment plants and the closure of dumps, other areas are not as well served and water quality is compromised. The key issues affecting the Waterford coast are erosion, coastal development, water quality and lately, climate change, all of which affect and change the coast and the marine areas around us. Sustainable coastal management, better planning and the use of science to improve decision-making are crucial themes in maintaining the quality of the marine areas and the surrounding coasts, and are of even greater relevance now given the possible effects of climate change and sea-level rise, which may have profound implications for many parts of the Waterford coast, especially for the beaches and other 'soft' areas.

EROSION

The county surveyor for Waterford, W. L'Estrange Duffin, wrote in 1884 that, on being appointed to the position, his attention was drawn to:

the encroachment of the sea, which is very marked at every point on the coast where the margin is formed of soft materials.

Richard Ussher, writing in the journal of the *Waterford & South-East of Ireland Archaeological Society* (Vol 1, 1894-5), of his discovery of a crannóg near the beach at Ardmore, stated the following:

it fell to my lot to discover, in 1879, a crannoge under very peculiar circumstances, its site being now covered by every tide. To the north of Ardmore village in this county the beach forty years ago ran approximately straight in a direction a little to the east of north, and the road to Dungarvan ran parallel to it. On leaving the village by this road one first crossed a small stream, beneath whose basin was an extensive bed of peat that ran out to low-water mark or beyond it. The road here traversed a great bank of shingle that had been piled by the sea upon the peat. Farther on the road rose upon a high bank of till, or boulder clay, which presented to the sea a high escarpment. Between the road and the escarpment stood a large school house, and on the landward side of the road were a range of coastguard houses. Within my memory the sea has devoured the land here so rapidly that, first the school house, then the road, and then the coastguard houses have been successively washed away. The great accumulation of shingle between the coastguard houses and Ardmore was also removed, its vestiges being now much further inland...

..and considering the rapid inroads that the sea has made within my own memory, it is reasonable to conclude that centuries ago Ardmore Bay was filled up to a much greater extent than recently, and a protecting sand bank may have enclosed its mouth, like the warren at Tramore or

Rock armouring on the seaward face of the Cunnigar

the Cunnigar at Dungarvan Bay, leaving
inside a spacious lagoon or morass.

He also wrote, in his seminal work, *The Birds
of Ireland*, of:

the incursions that the sea has made
along the Waterford coast, removing two
successive school-houses within my
memory, may well have washed away
any low flat island that existed in
Tramore Bay.

Coastal erosion is an ongoing and natural
geomorphological activity on all coasts,
caused primarily by wind and waves (ice is
less of a threat now on the Waterford coast).
Waves impact on all shorelines and the
constant buffeting over time releases vast
quantities of rock fragments, which are
eventually whittled down to smaller grains.
Once these grains are small enough, the wind
does the rest, moving large amounts in the
direction of the wind. The impact of wind
and waves are most pronounced and obvious
on 'soft' shores likes beaches, dunes and
mudflats, where large amounts of material
can be reworked in short time periods,
particularly during storm surges, when wind
speeds and wave heights have the greatest
potential for doing damage. Hard surfaces
like the coastal cliffs are constantly
undermined by crashing waves and while the
effects are usually less obvious, over centuries

vast amounts of rock debris is removed from
the cliffs. Erosion rates on rocky shores and
cliffs may be quite small (usually less than
0.01 metres per century) but over geological
time this constant erosion has given us the
arches, stacks and caves that are dotted along
the Waterford coastline. Wave action
constantly whittles away the base of glacial
cliffs leading to collapse of the material above
and, where there are clay cliffs, the effect is
usually worse as the unstable cliffs tend to
slide along joints created by rainwater ingress
from above. Occasionally, when the
undercutting is severe, significant rockfalls are
possible, which may cause disruption close to
coastal towns and villages and houses locally.

The Waterford coastline is around 170
kilometres long. Rock outcrops and cliffs
make up 48% or 82 kilometres of this
dramatic coastline, hard structures (piers,
harbours and sea walls) are around 5% or 8
kilometres, clay cliffs and banks are 27% or
46 kilometres and the remainder, 20% or 34
kilometres, are the other 'soft' coasts (shingle,
dunes and beaches). These various categories
are subject to different rates of change over
time because of their structure and
composition. The soft coastline areas of the
county are most at risk from attack by the
sea, which includes glacial cliffs, shingle
embankments, dune areas and beaches. The
clay cliffs of the coastline are at the west end
of Tramore beach, Benvoy, Ballyvoyle and

Whiting Bay. The sandy beaches backed by protective dunes are at Woodstown, Tramore, Bunmahon and the Cunnigar. Coastal areas where there are shingle embankments are the centre section of Tramore beach and the eastern section of Clonea beach. Other areas that have been impacted on by the sea include Passage East, Dunmore East, Rathmoylan, Clohernagh, Garrarus, Kilfarrasy, Annestown, Abbeyside, Ballynagaul, Ballymacart, Glencorran, Ballyquin and Ardmore.

Passage East

Passage East is an attractive village on the west side of Waterford Harbour and it has a car ferry linking Waterford to Wexford, which runs continuously in daylight hours throughout the year. A sandy, stony beach is popular with local people, though isn't widely used otherwise, perhaps because of the estuarine nature of the area and the shallow waters. The beach is protected by Waterford Harbour and isn't subject to the same degree of erosion as other coastal areas in Waterford. Nevertheless, it is vulnerable to high winds blowing from the east and southeast, which, if accompanied by high tides, may result in beach material being deposited into the village, particularly those properties facing due east. Rock armouring is in place here which protects the most vulnerable areas.

Woodstown

The beach at Woodstown is around 2.1 kilometres long and is widely used by walkers throughout the year. Woodstown is further south on the west side of Waterford Harbour and, like Passage East, is relatively sheltered from severe coastal conditions, though storms from the east or southeast occasionally cause considerable damage. There are clay cliffs at the northern end, which are prone to erosion. A linear strip of dunes in the central part of the beach are occasionally stripped vertically by the sea and the grassy embankment at the southern end of the beach, near the main

Shattered seawall at Fornaght/Creadan

carpark (and now protected by rock armouring), is also prone to overtopping by high tides and high waves, usually in winter. Planning permission was granted in October 2010 to allow a resident to reinforce eroding cliffs at Knockavelish using rock armouring.

Creadan/Fornaght

Fornaght faces east but it is more sheltered than either Passage or Woodstown because of the protective influence of Creadan headland, whose southern flank attenuates high waves coming in off the sea. Nevertheless, Fornaght beach has suffered from coastal erosion, particularly the hard structures at the southern end, which have been undermined, fractured and scattered over the beach. The presence of tree roots in the beach (visible at low tide) attests to the amount of beach which has been lost here over the centuries.

Dunmore East

The picturesque village of Dunmore East sits on Old Red Sandstone rock, and there are impressive cliffs in and around the village, with small but popular beaches between some of them. Cliff instability and the occasional collapse are an ongoing threat in the village, its amenities and properties (some on which are built on the clifftop), as happened in

Coastal protection works at Dunmore East, May 2008

1977 and again in early 2010. In places the undermining by the sea of soft mudstones at the base of the sandstone cliffs weakens their support of the overlying harder conglomerate, which is compounded by the ongoing opening of joints from above by water, ice, vegetation and vibration due to passing traffic, particularly heavy vehicles. Cliff stabilisation works have been required in recent years at Counsellors strand, Dock road, the inner harbour and Shanooan.

Portally/Ballymacaw/Rathmoylan
These are three sheltered coves between Dunmore East and Tramore Bay, which are protected by enclosing sandstone cliffs. There are small beaches at the top of each cove, but given their enclosed nature, coastal erosion isn't as much of a problem here as elsewhere along the Waterford coast, though they are lashed by storms in winter.

Clohernagh/Saleen/Tramore
The coastal system at Tramore is one of the most impressive in Waterford. There is a rectangular Bay, framed by dominating headlands (Brownstown Head to the east and Great Newtown Head to the west), a long and spectacular sandy beach, an impressive dune system at the end of a

sand spit that isolates the beach from a very productive Backstrand area, which is import for the wintering birds it supports. However, the area receives the full brunt of high waves, onshore winds and high tides and no area of the system has been spared the damaging effects of coastal erosion. Given the popularity of Tramore as a tourist attraction and the value of the natural environment there as a recreational resource along with its ecological importance and the ongoing threat to this environment from the sea, major efforts have been made to protect the system at Tramore. Consequently the area is better described than any other area in the county and has been the subject of many reports, investigations and academic studies over the years. A report published in May 2006 (commissioned by the Heritage Office of Waterford County Council to review coastal protection at Tramore strand) included a comprehensive list of the historical material available in relation to coastal damage and protection works at Tramore, and the summaries provide chronological detail of efforts over the years to maintain the amenities at Tramore in the face of the relentless onslaught from the sea.

In his report to the Institute of Engineers in Ireland in 1884, L'Estrange Duffin described efforts to deal with encroachment by the sea and damage to the fragile sea walls fronting Tramore beach. J. P. Quigley wrote a paper for the December 1946 Bulletin of the Institute of Civil Engineers of Ireland. He referred to the large turf area beneath the strand, which confirmed the sinking of the area in post glacial times and suggested that the process is continuing. Based on differences in beach lines between cartographic surveys of 1841 and 1922, direct measurements from foundations covered by sand, the inward step between seawalls

Annual rates of erosion (-) and accretion (+) (in metres) along the Waterford coast

Period 1841-1990
(based on cartographic evidence)
Source: J. O'Flynn, Institute of Engineers, 1991

Waterford City

Woodstown -0.1

Tramore
-0.14 west
+0.6 east

Bunmahon
Stradbally
Clonea
Dungarvan
-0.42
-1 to -1.4
-0.2 to -0.3
-0.1 to -0.2

Ballyquin
Ardmore
-0.2 to -0.45
Whiting Bay -0.5 to -1.8
-0.78 to -0.8

Erosion rates on Waterford beaches

and local knowledge of the former position of the beach line, Quigley concluded that the rate of erosion varied from one foot (30.5 centimetres) at the western end of the beach to three feet (almost one metre) at the centre and decreased from there to zero at the sandhills, but that, apart from natural loss caused by wind, waves and currents, some of the loss was due to the ongoing removal of beach material.

Quigley also concisely summarised the history of the sea defences at Tramore: the Doneraile Estate built the first seawall around 1820. In 1884 it was taken over by the Grand Jury who spent £400 on remediation works. The Grand Jury piled the beach to the east of this seawall in 1867 and there were further works and repairs in 1871 and 1877 respectively (costing £520) before piling was abandoned in 1879 due to excessive costs. Groynes were placed in the same area in 1881. Sea buckthorn was planted in 1910 on the shingle embankment but these were vandalised and, due to a lack of funds, a suggested extension of the groynes did not take place. A second seawall built in 1896 at

a cost of £5,000 was damaged in 1897 which required repairs costing £300 but it too was subject to ongoing storm damage. The main Promenade was built over two years between 1913-15 but scouring at the base removed up to four feet of the protecting sand blanket revealing the masonry apron. The third seawall was built in 1930, and despite being stepped inland, was also being outflanked by the sea along its eastern end towards the shingle embankment. Efforts were also made to stabilise the top of the embankment using stakes and brushwood but were compromised by people gathering the material for firewood. Natural methods such as planting of marram grass, lyme grass, tamarisk and shrubby sea-blite were also attempted.

Quigley considered that the sandhills were still forming due to the accumulation of blown sand from the beach but that vegetation in the dunes was suffering as a result of grazing by rabbits (which, even after five years of trapping and ferreting, were still present), cattle (*"which are turned out for free.. and are surprisingly fond of the marram shoot"*) and fires started by people having picnics. The presence of lichens, mosses and shrubs in

Rock armouring at the 'neck', Tramore beach.
Reflective scour can occur around rock revetments resulting in further erosion of the frontal beach and areas adjacent to the ends of the boulder fields. Moreover, they are not considered suitable in areas subject to longshore drift

the low, stable areas between the dunes (the dune slacks) suggested that trees like Corsican pine, Austrian pine and maritime pine could be planted though he doesn't say whether any planting was carried out.

Quigley further addressed the Backstrand and salt marsh areas and outlined the building of three seabanks by Dutch engineers on the instructions of Mr. Malcomson and Mr. Power in 1857, which enclosed 202 hectares of the west side of the Backstrand, where the racecourse and golf links were established. However, the seawalls were finally breached in 1912 and the area was lost to the sea. Quigley himself planted *Spartina* in June 1944 on sections of the inner bay, as he was impressed by its establishment elsewhere and its ability to reclaim land [the planting of *Spartina* is no longer considered to be best practice]. He said that it had the added advantage that it could be used as feed by livestock (but not

cows as, apparently, milk was tainted by it). He was of the opinion that if this particular area of Tramore could be meadowed:

> *the unhealthy and unsightly slob land would be eliminated and replaced by firm, productive land over which passage would be possible.*

He concluded by saying that, due to limited financial resources, coastal defences would have to rely increasingly on the cultivation of plants which would bind the areas together.

An Foras Forbartha (the National Institute for Physical Planning and Construction Research) were asked by Waterford County Council in October 1976 to advise on the possible implications of erosion occurring on the north side of the 'neck' of the Tramore dune system. In his report of February 1977, David Cabot estimated that high water mark varied between 12.87 metres to 25.74 metres

The breach in the Malcomson embankment, Tramore Backstrand

along the line of the dunes there, which represented an annual erosion rate of 0.21-0.43 metres per annum for the 60-year period over which the assessment was based (by comparing the 1905 Ordnance Survey map with an aerial survey carried out in 1965). He recommended that a protective barrier (gabions) should be erected to prevent further erosion, which, if it continued, would eventually result in Tramore Burrow being breached (this protective barrier was never erected). He further recommended that the 'neck' area of the dunes be fenced off to allow marram regeneration and prevent further damage by trampling.

John O'Flynn, the Waterford County Engineer at the time, wrote a paper for a seminar on Coastal Protection organised by the Institute of Engineers in February 1991, which provides a comprehensive account of coastal erosion in county Waterford, and the impacts of a succession of storms that devastated the Waterford coast in the winter of 1989/90. This report gives additional information for Tramore and provides details of the sleeper wall that was erected at the base of the clay cliff at the western end of Tramore beach in the early 1960s. This proved reasonably successful until it was badly damaged by the big storm of December 1989, which required the construction of a rock armour revetment at the base of the cliff. Part of this clay cliff subsided again in 1997, requiring further rock armouring for additional protection against undercutting by the sea, which is ongoing, given that the sea laps the base of the cliff.

Sleeper walls were erected along the shingle embankment in the centre of the beach which, in 1974, were said to have helped in stabilising the beach there. This embankment was further strengthened in 1997, with the burying of rock gabions enclosed in wire mesh baskets, the tops of which are occasionally visible.

A consultants report on protecting the coastline at Tramore was commissioned by Waterford County Council in 1996, which outlined the consequences of a breach occurring along the vulnerable shingle embankment and the need for further stabilisation works in the area to protect the material assets to the north of the embankment. The report also stated that the dunes appeared stable but that blowouts in the system appeared to be growing and that remediation works would be required. The same consultants subsequently reported on the condition of the main Prom at Tramore and the works that would be required to strengthen the structure of this important

The north side of the dunes at the 'neck', Tramore beach, showing the older method of dune protection (railway sleepers), newer methods (fence, gabion, hessian), a blowout and the extent of the loss of dune material

WIDTHS, IN METRES, OF THE BLOWOUTS NEAR THE 'NECK' OF THE TRAMORE DUNES			
	north side	*seaward east*	*seaward west*
GPS reading	*60900053*	*61040036*	*60990039*
February 1996	4.78	7.93	14.02
May 1997	8.23	27.43	28.35
November 2000	19.5-23.46	30.58	36.27
January 2010	51.84	40.3	44.8

seawall. These works were carried out, at considerable cost, in 2001. The remediated Tramore dump was also given protective rock armouring on its south-facing side to prevent undermining of the dump, which had been occurring, and releasing dump contents (mostly plastic) to the area.

During the 1989 storm a breach of 15 metres occurred in the dunes near the 'neck', allowing seawater to pass directly into the Backstrand and a further 30 metres were seriously damaged. There was also serious overtopping of the top of the beach, more or less along its length. Temporary banking of beach material near the 'neck' stabilised the breach and a 77-metre length of rock armour was positioned on the beach side of the dunes in 1990. A management scheme was implemented around the 'neck' of the dunes in 1997, which included planting of marram, fencing to limit access and hessian sheeting with brushwood fencing to trap sand and aid dune regeneration, signage to explain the purpose of the scheme (these were subsequently vandalised) and the emplacement of rock gabion baskets within two dune blowouts. Further brushwood fencing was positioned in 2003 and an access ramp across the fragile 'neck' was added later.

Finally the Coastal & Marine Resources Centre at UCC compiled a dedicated Geographical Information System (GIS) for Tramore as outlined in the May 2006 report, based on the collation of all the data available for the area, which it was hoped would assist in management of the coastal zone at Tramore. A subsequent report, again commissioned by the Heritage Office of Waterford County Council, was published by the CMRC in October 2008, which is intended to support the preparation of a coastal zone plan for Tramore Bay and the development of an integrated management plan for the area.

Other areas around Tramore have also suffered ongoing damage due to the impact of the sea. Saleen, on the east side of Tramore Bay, has clay cliffs which periodically collapse due to undermining of the soft basal beds. The small but important dune area there is constantly being reworked by the sea and the savage currents that regularly flow in Rinnashark Channel. Further north at Clohernagh, clay cliffs subside and sea walls crumble during storms and the heavily embanked polder lands at Kilmacleague west and Lisselan need constant reinforcement to withstand the impact of high seas. The embankment at Kilmacleague has been breached on occasions leading to significant flooding on the sloblands nearby. It was proposed (in late 2009) to permanently breach this embankment to create a compensatory wetland on foot of a ruling by the European Court of Justice (C-494/01) in relation to the operation of the Tramore dump which adversely affected Tramore Dunes and Backstrand, a candidate Special Area of Conservation. New embankments will be constructed on the north and west side of the new wetland area, using material from Castletown and Ballygunnercastle, which are also subject to a ruling by the ECJ.

Garrarus

Garrarus has prominent clay cliffs just at the entrance to this attractive beach, which have been heavily eroded over the years. The cliff-top above has the remnants of an old road, more of which was washed away in 1955, indicating the extent of the loss that has taken place here. The very wet and cold winter of 2009/2010 saturated these clay cliffs, leading to considerable slippage and a split appeared in the road nearby, resulting in closure of the road as a precaution (though people could still walk down the road and access the beach). Further west along the beach, higher clay cliffs have also receded and the nearby rocky cliffs have also fractured and suffered from the constant pounding of the high-energy waves that bombard the shoreline here. The constant scouring by the sea has, however, kept the cliffs free of vegetation allowing the complex and fascinating geology of the rocks to be seen.

H. C. Hart, the Donegal botanist, in his walk along the Wexford and Waterford coastline in July 1883, kept a careful watch out for purple spurge. This rare plant was found in Garrarus in 1837 by Miss Trench, the only site where it has been recorded in Ireland. She deposited a voucher specimen in TCD so there is no doubt about the veracity of the record. Hart followed the base of the cliffs in search of the species and he checked all the beaches between Tramore and Youghal, and especially those between Tramore and Dungarvan, but without success. He met a woman at Garrarus cove who said:

> she knew it [purple spurge], *but that like everything else along the shore it was "tore out of it" by the terrible storms of September and October 1881. Perhaps she was right, since the plant grows along the margin of the tide.*

Coastal erosion can, therefore, impact on the natural environment and is an ongoing threat to rare plants like purple spurge and sea kale, which have a tentative niche on the exposed parts of beaches.

Kilfarrasy

Like the eroding cliffs at Garrarus, the clay cliffs close to the access point to the beach are suffering most from coastal erosion, and rock armouring is in place to protect the fragile cliff here and the seawall supporting the carpark. Further east along the beach, the substantial rockfalls attest to the ongoing erosion of even the hardest structures here; cliff subsidence occasionally occurs but the remnants of such events are quickly dispersed by the sea. The offshore stacks and islands around Sheep Island were almost certainly connected to the mainland, until time (a lot of it) and the sea eroded away the more fragile parts, leaving what is now part of a dramatic and still evolving coastline.

Annestown

A seawall protects the main beach at Annestown and large accumulations of shingle have been heaped up by the sea along its length, which otherwise would be dispersed inland and across the main coast road. The fragile cliffs at the west end of the

Rockfall, east of Annestown, 2009

Access ramp at Benvoy

are clearly eroding because of the impact of the sea on this high-energy coast. The rocky platform offshore seems to generate waves with an awe-inspiring intensity, which ravages the cliffs. The softer cliffs regularly subside and the base of all the cliffs here are littered with accumulations of rocks and large shingle, which are constantly reworked by the sea and are especially awkward to walk over.

Benvoy

The soft cliffs at Benvoy, especially those to the east of the access ramp, have been heavily eroded by the sea and significant recession has taken place. The access area itself has suffered greatly over the years and was most recently replaced with a fairly substantial mass of reinforced concrete which supports the steep access steps. This rampart is also protected by rock armouring. Much of the previous rubble masonry and concrete wall, which was later proved to have badly withered joints, collapsed during the severe storm of December 1989, thereby exposing the clay cliff behind it to wave erosion. The damage inflicted was such that the access road to the popular cove had to be closed off. However, the new construction is beginning

beach have also been fortified and the concrete massing all along the upper beach confers a foreign but necessary element to this appealing coastal area. When the tide is falling, it is possible to walk east along the base of the high and spectacular cliffs, which

Rock armouring at Bunmahon

to show signs of deterioration and widening gaps have appeared in the steps, which shows how severe and damaging coastal conditions here will eventually undermine any structure, regardless of the quality and strength of its construction. Further west, and closer to Dunabrattin, the curved coastline has receded due to the long-term erosion of the relatively low clay cliffs by the sea.

Bunmahon

The beach at Bunmahon is around 600 metres long and it, and the backing dunes, have been subject to ongoing erosion. A rate of erosion of greater than one metre per annum has been measured at Bunmahon, leading to a recession of the beach area of 140 metres, with a consequent loss of around eight hectares of shore. Protection was achieved using railway sleepers in the 1970s, but this was destroyed in the storms of the winter of 1989/90, which also overtopped and breached the dunes in two places, leading to a recession of around 15 metres and serious damage to the caravan park and surrounding area. The dunes at Bunmahon are only a remnant of a more extensive dune system that was in place here, which was

removed in the late 1960s/early 1970s to make way for the caravan park.

Stradbally

The cove at Stradbally is shallow and is well protected by the headlands on either side. Moreover, the cliffs within the cove are rocky and largely perpendicular to the waves, so that rock falls are few and incidences of coastal erosion are rare, so the area has been spared from damage that has afflicted other areas along the coast. Nevertheless, high tides, strong winds and lashing waves impact on the shallow beach and the upper parts of the cove, where a remnant dune system is frequently disturbed and battered with debris brought in by the sea.

Clonea/Ballyvoyle

The low-lying area from Ballyvoyle to Ballynacourty has been ravaged by the sea and by storms over the centuries and a recession of 70 metres of coastline has been estimated for the period 1841-1990. Several coastal structures have been lost here, including the remains of Clonea Castle, which fell into the sea in 1989, soon after the big storm of that year. All sections of the

Coastal protection at Clonea

Ongoing erosion at the east end of Ballyvoyle beach: note the bank of earth on the boulder, the redundant railway sleepers and the earthen bank (2010)

coastline here have suffered but the impacts have been severe at the eastern end near Ballyvoyle and all attempts at protecting the coast road here have, to some extent, been undermined by the sea, usually on either side of the defences, creating further problems nearby. Give the urgency of the situation at Ballyvoyle, Waterford County Council, in 1966, sought a preliminary investigation and a report on the feasibility of a coastal protection scheme for Clonea/Ballyvoyle, as required by the Coast Protection Act of 1963. However it wasn't possible to advance the scheme beyond the third step of a 23-step procedure in the following 26 years, while the area continued to suffer from coastal erosion, which supports the contention that the 1963 Act is inflexible and clearly unsuitable for the purpose for which it was drafted. The seafront at Ballyvoyle/Clonea is the area most under threat from coastal erosion in the county and erodes further each year.

Ballinard/Abbeyside

Dungarvan is well served by coastal amenities, all within easy walking distance of the town. However the low-lying nature of many of these amenities and the continuous impact of the sea ensure that they are at risk from coastal erosion and flooding is an ongoing problem during storm events. One of the areas most at risk is the section of coastline between the Abbey (Saint Augustine's Church) and Lands End and around Pinewood where erosion and undermining of the hard surfaces is ongoing, which has to be monitored and remedial action implemented when necessary. Areas such as Abbeyside and Ballinard regularly require focussed coastal protection works to protect property and maintain amenities but, given the popularity of these areas, their proximity to a large urban population and their scenic attractiveness, environmental constraints have also to be considered. To alleviate flooding, a number of proposals have been made, including new storm sewers at Shandon, a large retention pond near the Sallybrook housing estate and changes to the existing drainage infrastructure for the Duckspool and Burgery areas.

Cunnigar

The Cunnigar is a valuable protective barrier in Dungarvan Bay and attenuates the erosive power of the incoming sea and thereby affords considerable protection to Dungarvan town itself, the inner bay and the surrounding low-lying areas. However, it has suffered badly from constant bombardment by high waves and the sea crashing around its edges. In the early 1920s, Dungarvan Golf Club laid out a 9-hole links course on the Cunnigar but coastal erosion and the inaccessibility of the course (it had to be reached by boat from Dungarvan) led to its eventual abandonment. It was breached in places in 1963 and in 1989, requiring ongoing protection works (tyres, railway sleepers and rock armouring) and it was also damaged by storms in October 2005. The Cunnigar is an important amenity and is used extensively for walking amidst the exceptional scenery of the hinterland. There

Coastal protection east of Ballynagaul, near Helvick

is some evidence that recreational activities are impacting on the fragile dunes and part of the dune system is fenced off, to allow the marram to regenerate (though this barrier is now breached in places). However, it is the sea ultimately that will determine the fate of the Cunnigar and the implications of its loss due to coastal erosion are profound with severe consequences likely for surrounding farmland, the N25 (the national route) and even Dungarvan itself.

Ballynagaul

The soft cliffs on the south side of Dungarvan Bay from the Cunnigar out to Helvick Head are constantly being whittled away by the sea and remedial action has been required in several areas, particularly between Ballynagaul and close to Helvick pier, where a concrete rampart, supplemented more recently by rock armouring, protects the shoreline and the coastal road above. A walk along the shoreline between the Cunnigar and almost to Helvick pier, reveals the loss of land to the sea. There is ongoing slumping, particularly of the soft clays, usually as a result of wet and saturated slopes, already weakened along the base by the sea and unable to support the extra weight above.

Glencorran/Ballyquin/Ardmore

Unusually for Waterford beaches, Ardmore faces due east, and despite some protection from Ardmore Head on its south side and the cliffed coast on its northern flank, the area has experienced severe erosion, leading to the loss of a coastal road, buildings (coastguard station, lifeboat station and schoolhouse). In the early 1800s an erosion rate of up to 3 metres per annum was estimated. More recent estimates of erosion are 0.8 metre per annum and a recession of 120 metres. Ballyquin beach, to the north of Ardmore beach, and backed by clay cliffs, has been badly eroded requiring ongoing protection using railway sleepers and, more lately, rock armouring in places.

Whiting Bay

Erosion has been severe at Whiting Bay due to the presence of clay cliffs and annual rates of erosion of up to 1.8 metres have been calculated, mostly at the western end. It is estimated that up to 160 metres of the beach at Whiting Bay has been lost since 1841, amounting to around 26 hectares. A county road parallel to the shore and which linked two of the existing approaches to the beach has been washed away (elements of which can still be seen on the beach, some distance seaward of the top of the shore).

Notable storm events

While much of this erosion goes largely unnoticed, the occasional spectacular storm or weather event focusses minds on the potential threat and the devastating power of the sea. It is these events that prompt remedial action where coastal structures have been damaged or revealed, and the reports that are written provide a comprehensive chronological account of the events themselves, their impacts and the long-term loss of coastline to the sea.

While many storm events have had an impact on the Waterford coast, the most devastating in recent times, and the most comprehensively recorded, was on the night of December 16th 1989. Stormy seas, heavy rain and high spring tides contributed to the severe damage caused by a deep depression (941 hPa) that lashed the Irish coastline that particular night. The storm originated in the south Atlantic and the long fetch over which it travelled generated very high seas, which, along with the higher than predicted high tide (by around 0.6 metres), due to the

exceptionally low pressure, and the unfavourable southeasterly direction of the wind, created a storm surge which impacted severely on 23 defined areas of the Waterford coast, mostly the 'soft' coastal areas, the coastal defences and facilities nearby.

Further storms through late January and February 1990 exacerbated the extent and scale of the initial damage and before emergency repairs could be completed. For example, at Woodstown, which is probably the least exposed part of the Waterford coast, protective grassy banks at the southern end of the beach were overtopped and large quantities of beach material and flood waters were deposited on roads and carpark. At Tramore an initial breach of 10 metres in the rubble seawall (the wall east of the Prom) caused by the December storm progressively worsened and eventually a 50 metre section had to be replaced. The entire seafront at Tramore and private property nearby was damaged to varying degrees, which was compounded by severe flooding caused by weakened coastal defences. At Benvoy a large section of the retaining seawall collapsed, which exposed the clay cliffs nearby, previously protected by the concrete ramps,

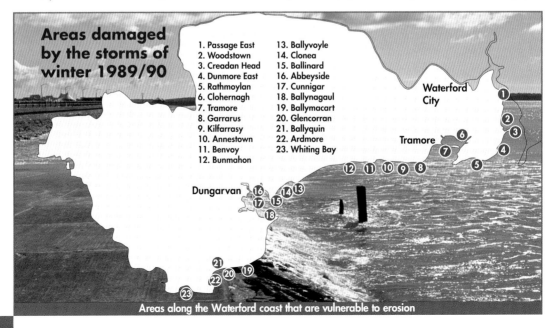

Areas damaged by the storms of winter 1989/90

1. Passage East
2. Woodstown
3. Creadan Head
4. Dunmore East
5. Rathmoylan
6. Clohernagh
7. Tramore
8. Garrarus
9. Kilfarrasy
10. Annestown
11. Benvoy
12. Bunmahon

13. Ballyvoyle
14. Clonea
15. Ballinard
16. Abbeyside
17. Cunnigar
18. Ballynagaul
19. Ballymacart
20. Glencorran
21. Ballyquin
22. Ardmore
23. Whiting Bay

Waterford City

Tramore

Dungarvan

Areas along the Waterford coast that are vulnerable to erosion

Warning sign at Ballyvooney

to further erosion and subsequent slippage. Bunmahon suffered extensive damage when the dunes were breached resulting in widespread flooding and extensive damage to the caravan park behind the dunes; moreover the recently refurbished sleeper wall was demolished and 15 metres of the dunes was washed away. At Clonea the retaining wall behind the shingle embankment was breached, which resulted in widespread flooding, the deposition of large quantities of sand and shingle inland and damage to property. At the Cunnigar, a section of the sleeper wall and rock armouring protecting the seaward face of the spit was demolished and scattered about the beach.

Conclusions
It is clear that the Waterford coastline, and particularly the 'soft' areas of the coast, which comprise almost half of its length, will continue to erode due to ongoing attack by the sea and that costly repairs will be required after each storm event. Given the predictions for increased storminess due to climate change, decisions will have to be made in respect of what areas can be reasonably protected, which may mean that some areas will have to be abandoned to the sea, and that other areas may have to be prioritised for protection. Given the scenic attractiveness of

the Waterford coastline, and particularly the popularity of those areas most at risk, these decisions will not be easy, and may depend as much on economic conditions prevailing at the time of the damage event as any other factor (for example, no money was allocated to coastal protection in Waterford in 2011). However, one thing is clear: the ongoing, even annual maintenance of coastal protection works in the county should be prioritised, which may reduce the ultimate cost and difficulties that arise when future damaging storms impact on the coast.

COASTAL DEVELOPMENTS

High levels of economic activity generate large amounts of wealth which may be used to transform the land we live in for the benefit of all, as happened during the boom years of the Celtic Tiger in Ireland. Every county in Ireland benefitted from the unprecedented levels of growth, development and wealth generation. Every city and county council in the country, whose function by law is to regulate and control development in their jurisdiction, benefitted from the surge in building and development in terms of

Cliffed dune profile—a sure sign of winter erosion

increased income from development activity and the resulting enhanced local infrastructure. The wide range of activities that take place along Ireland's coastline in boom times include coastal protection structures, the construction of marinas, port facilities and other buildings and developments linked with increasing urbanisation and the promotion of tourism, particularly the building of holiday or second homes within or outwith coastal tourism complexes. However, the most scenic areas are subject to the greatest level of development pressure, which, if not strictly regulated and controlled (and even forbidden, if necessary) can potentially damage these areas. Further activities, such as the often necessary dredging of ports and harbours and land reclamation around wetlands, may also damage fragile coastal ecosystems.

Heritage, and all it encompasses, is however an important feature of our lives and the land we live in, and especially those scenic landscapes which we cherish so much. It is these very landscapes that are viewed by some as prime areas for development, which may suffer if subject to uncontrolled and excessive development. Conflict is the inevitable end result between those keen to protect our heritage and those keen to exploit heritage areas for development. Proper planning and development and sustainability are key to the preservation and maintenance of our heritage for future generations to enjoy. The most important heritage areas are usually protected by national legislation such as the Wildlife Act or the National Monuments Act or by EU legislation such as the Birds Directive or the Habitats Directive, and most of these Acts list the areas or monuments they protect, why they need to be protected and the actions required if any changes are proposed.

Waterford County Council, as the planning authority for Waterford county (there is a separate planning authority for Waterford City), is required to prepare a development plan for its functional area and to review it every six years, following public consultation. The development plan outlines the overall strategy for the proper planning and sustainable development of the county. The Planning Acts clearly specifies those matters that must be included in a county development plan and the plan has to be consistent, so far as possible, with national plans, policies and strategies which relate to proper planning and sustainable development. The plan has to include objectives for defined provisions, which include the conservation and protection of the environment including the natural heritage; the conservation and protection of European sites and the preservation of the character of the landscape including the preservation of views and prospects and the amenities of places and features of natural beauty or interest.

The legal basis for formulating and enacting development plans is contained in the Planning and Development Act 2000-2002 and the development plan is, in effect, the bible by which all development is assessed, regulated and ultimately controlled. Protected areas and structures, landscapes and monuments and the legislative acts and directives that relate to them are listed in the plan (usually in appendices) as is the process to be followed where development is proposed that might impact on designated areas or structures.

The Planning Acts allow for public participation and submissions and observations on proposed developments are allowed, subject to time constraints and the payment of a fee, which are taken into consideration when the development is being assessed by the local authority. Once a decision is made, the applicant or appellants may appeal the decision to an independent planning appeals board, An Bord Pleanála, who reassess the application *de novo*, and all relevant documents relating to the development, including all appeal documentation, are critically examined by an Inspector from An Bord Pleanála. Following consideration of the development and the appeal documentation, which normally includes a site visit, the Inspector compiles a report with a recommendation which is then assessed by An Bord Pleanála who make the final decision. This decision is usually binding on all parties.

In respect of landscape protection (Section 8.3), the Waterford County Development Plan (2005-2011) is clear:

in keeping with the Sustainable Rural Housing Guidelines for Planning Authorities 2004, under this plan there will be a presumption against the granting of planning permission for development in coastal and upland areas, which are located outside of settlements, in areas liable to flooding, and in water supply catchment areas. This restriction will also apply to development in those

areas adjacent to Scenic Routes or in Visually Vulnerable, and Visually Sensitive Areas. Developments in the above areas will be considered in the context of their impact on the amenity of the area, and in accordance with the Scenic Landscape Evaluation in Appendix 4. The coastal areas may generally be regarded as being those areas within the first seaward watershed (see Coastal Zone Map) areas of high visibility as viewed from the coastal road.

and the policy with respect to habitat protection (8.7) is equally unequivocal:

designated areas (candidate and proposed NHAs, SACs and SPAs) require protection as: they contain valuable habitats where organisms (some rare) live in a relatively natural state; they are, in most cases, proposed Natural Heritage Areas and other categories (Special Protection Areas or proposed Candidate Special Areas of Conservation), which are or will be protected under national legislation; they often contain aquifers of regional importance that are vulnerable

The view from the Gold Coast Hotel, Ballynacourty

to groundwater pollution; and development in such areas has the potential to cause major visual change in the landscape.

Developmental pressure on coastal areas is immense, and can be particularly acute during economic growth periods when there is strong demand for the building of retirement and second homes, urban expansion and tourism infrastructure leading to a large increase in the numbers of marinas, hotels, golf courses and houses near the coast. These developments further increase the number of people (currently around 60 percent of the population) living in coastal areas and there is always the risk of over-development with its potential impacts on seascapes, landscapes, protected habitats and species and ultimately the right of the general public to freely access the coastal zone. The County Development Plan, in relation to the coastal zone, states (p.117):

in general, development within the entire Coastal Zone (i.e between Youghal and Cheekpoint) will be encouraged into the existing settlements. In particular development will be restricted where such development will interfere with views and prospects over the coastline. Development on the seaward side of the Coastal Route will not be permitted where views from the road are obscured or impeded. New development in the coastal zone must be in accordance with the Scenic Landscape Evaluation.

The success of the Waterford County Development Plan in protecting the coastal zone and the seascapes, landscapes, protected habitats and species therein can only be assessed in the context of developments that have been proposed and considered by the planning process and how they adhere to the principles outlined in the plan, and, perhaps more importantly, how the plan provisions

are interpreted and applied. A number of developments have recently been proposed for the Waterford coast, which allows for such an assessment.

Clonea has a superb beach and is a very appealing recreational area at all times of the year but especially in summer when good weather attracts large numbers of people from all over the southeast of Ireland and even beyond. As it is on the coastline it is considered to be 'vulnerable' according to the Scenic Landscape Evaluation and the policy in relation to such areas is:

these areas or features designated as vulnerable represent the principal features which create and sustain the character and distinctiveness of the surrounding landscape. To be considered for permission, development in the environs of these vulnerable areas must be shown not to impinge in any significant way upon its character, integrity or uniformity when viewed from the surroundings. Particular attention should be given to the preservation of the character and distinctiveness of these areas as viewed from scenic routes and the environs of archaeological and historic sites.

A number of developments have been proposed for the Clonea area since 2000 in areas that are zoned for rural, agricultural and tourism uses: planning application number 03/659 was for 166 holiday homes and a three-storey hotel at Kilgrovan and permission was granted by Waterford County Council in July 2004, despite the planner who dealt with the application considering that the development was excessive in density, even though the site was zoned for intensive tourist uses. There were seven appeals to An Bord Pleanála, who overturned the decision of Waterford County Council and refused the application for four reasons (PL24.207809), the first one of which was:

having regard to the visually vulnerable nature of the site and its location in a coastal zone where stringent development control standards apply, and having regard to the location, scale, massing, design and layout of the proposed development, it is considered that the proposed development would have an adverse visual impact on the landscape quality and character of the area and would hence be contrary to development plan provisions with respect to protecting same. It is considered therefore that the proposed development would not be in accordance with the proper planning and development of the area.

There were other issues (absence of a readily potable water supply, deficiencies in sewerage facilities and a substandard local road network), which also influenced the decision of An Bord Pleanála.

07/614 was for a mixed-use development, including a hotel, 98 houses, 33 apartments and a village centre, also at Kilgrovan, and permission was granted in May 2008, but there were five appeals to An Bord Pleanála. The Planning Inspector who dealt with the file (PL24.229386) considered that:

the proposed development would materially contravene development plan policies relating to the environment, coastal zones and the location of development....the locational characteristics of the site do not lend themselves to such an intensive form of development. The landscape in the locality does not have the capacity to absorb this scale and intensity of development which would be wholly detrimental to its character and appearance...

Refusal was recommended for one reason which encompassed these concerns. However,

the Board decided not to accept the recommendation of the Inspector:

having had regard to the zoning objective of the site and considered that the visual impact of the proposed development on the beach could be dealt with by way of condition.

and permission was granted.

08/455 was for the demolition of two agricultural structures, the construction of an integrated tourism facility including an equestrian arena, stables and 20 detached holiday houses at Ballynacourty. Permission was granted by Waterford County Council (in June 2008) subject to 24 conditions. However, there was one appeal to An Bord Pleanála (PL24.230021) on a number of grounds, which included a poor road network nearby and that the proposal didn't meet the minimum requirements to qualify as an Integrated Rural Tourism and Recreational Complex (IRTRC), which was facilitated by a variation in the 2005-2011 Development Plan. The Planning Inspector reviewed the Development Plan policy and quoted extracts from the Plan:

tourism development: Section 6.7 provides policies and guidance on tourism. "It is recognised that the growth of the tourism industry is critical to the economy of the county. This is particularly true in rural areas where employment levels in agriculture are in decline. While seeking to ensure that most tourism development with associated accommodation facilities is located on or close to towns or villages or on tourism zoned lands, the council recognises that, by its nature, some tourism developments may require other locations. In this regard consideration will be given to the provision of Integrated Rural Tourism and

Recreational Complexes at appropriate locations throughout the county.

Under Objective ED7 of the Waterford County Development Plan 2005 it is policy "to support the development of appropriately scaled holiday home/second home development within existing settlements or on tourism zoned lands or in association with IRTRC or integrated into medium sized tourism developments in accordance with the Settlement Strategy set out in chapter 3 or the Rural Tourism policy". The majority of the site is located within an area zoned for tourism.

Waterford County Council in its response explained the rationale for the adopted IRTRC variation:

The IRTRC policy was adopted as a variation to the CDP to allow low density residential developments for permanent accommodation or holiday home use removed from designated settlements. It is considered that the development of tourist developments in rural areas justify limited on-site residential development.

The Bord Pleanála Inspector, having considered the application decided to recommend refusal for one reason:

having regard to the excessive level of residential development proposed in a location remote from established settlements with services and facilities, the suburban layout of the proposed development, the high concentration of dwellings/holiday homes in the area and the substandard road network serving the area, the proposed development would be contrary to development plan policy, would set an undesirable precedent for other such inappropriately scaled developments in locations that are not within or adjacent to existing settlement nodes and would be detrimental to the

Coastal views from Dunmore East (looking north)

*rural character of the area. The proposed
development would, therefore, be contrary
to the proper planning and sustainable
development of the area.*

However, the Board declined to accept this
recommendation and granted permission:

*in deciding not to accept the Inspector's
recommendation to refuse permission, the
Board had regard to the zoning of the site
and the policy in the development plan to
support the development of appropriately
scaled holiday home development in
certain areas and decided, subject to the
limitations imposed by conditions, to
grant permission for the development.*

There are no nature conservation
designations in the Clonea area so this aspect
didn't feature in planning decisions, though
other Development Plan policies did apply.

Applications have also been submitted for
designated coastal areas, which adds an extra
dimension to the consideration of
development proposals. For example,
07/1318 was an application to build a house
(125 m²) in a field, 250 metres away from
the coast near Bunmahon. The temporary
Student Planner who dealt with the file, in a
report to the Senior Planning Officer, noted:

*the NHA Ballyvoyle Head to Tramore
coastal area is located to the south of the
proposed site, while the site is located
within the mid-Waterford Special
Preservation [sic] Area.*

The site designation wasn't raised again on
file documents or in the further information
request or in the clarification of the further
information received. There was one
objection to the application, the grounds of
which were that the area was unsuitable
because of the presence of mine shafts in the
area. Permission was recommended by an

Assistant Planner subject to 10 standard
conditions and was granted in April 2008.

However, the permission was appealed to
An Bord Pleanála (PL24.229119) but the
grounds of the appeal didn't include the SPA
designation of the site. The Inspector who
assessed the appeal noted that the application
site was located within a coastal strip
considered to be 'visually vulnerable' on the
Scenic Evaluation map (Figure 8) of the
Waterford County Development Plan and
that it was also within the designated 'coastal
zone'. The Inspector further considered that
development within these areas must be in
accordance with the provisions of appendix 4
of the plan which states that all proposals
must satisfy a list of general site suitability
and technical considerations that are similar
to the general criteria included in chapter 9
of the Plan. Section 6.1(a) states that
development within vulnerable areas:

*must be shown not to impinge in any
significant way upon its character,
integrity or uniformity when viewed from
the surroundings.*

The Inspector noted too that figure six of
the plan indicated that the strip of coast
adjacent to the site was part of the Ballyvoyle
Head to Tramore proposed Natural Heritage
Area (e.g. 23 kilometres of coast with cliffs
and coastal dry heaths that are important for
breeding birds including cormorants,
choughs, peregrine falcons and guillemots)
and that the site was also within the Mid-
Waterford Special Protection Area (SPA), and
that policy E8 seeks to protect, conserve and
enhance wildlife habitats and designated sites.
A further consideration was that appendix 2
stated that the county has a particularly rich
geological heritage with a long heritage of
mining activity and that it was Council
policy to protect from damage/inappropriate
development a number of sites including the
area known as the Copper Coast (Tramore to

Ballyvoyle Head). It was also stated in the appendix that UNESCO has recognised the south coast of the county between Garrarus and Ballyvoyle Head as a Geopark (and it is promoted as such in interpretative material describing the area). In the assessment, the Inspector considered the impact on the natural heritage:

> *although the current planning application is further away from the coast than the previous application that was refused (07/649), the current application site is within the boundary of the Mid-Waterford Coast SPA that extends 300 metres inland from the cliff edge. The special conservation interest relates to the following species, namely chough, peregrine, cormorant and herring gull. The application site is also adjacent to a pNHA and part of the Copper Coast. Accordingly, I consider that the proposed location for this poorly designed bungalow is totally inappropriate in terms of its potential impact on the natural heritage.*

The Planning Inspector noted that the planning report on the previous application in the same field (07/649) rightly referred to the proposal as being unacceptable, as it would '*appear visually obtrusive when viewed from the public road interrupting attractive views of the coast*' (though other than stating that the site was within a Special Preservation [sic] Area, the temporary Assistant Planner who dealt with that application, didn't mention the designation in the recommended grounds for refusal). The current application was closer to the road and would be even more visible than the previous proposal, not less visible, according to the Inspector and considered that the bungalow would be visually intrusive within this landscape (i.e. due to its siting, scale, design and window proportions). The Inspector further suggested that the proposal conflicted with the national guidelines that require new houses in rural

areas to be sited and designed so as to integrate well with their physical surroundings, and with the Development Plan criteria for development in such visually vulnerable areas.

Following consideration of the issues, the appeal documents and the Development Plan provisions, An Bord Pleanála subsequently refused the application for three reasons, the first two of which were:

> *1. the site is located in an area that is designated as visually vulnerable in the current Waterford county development plan, where it is the policy of the planning authority to control development to ensure that it does not impinge in any significant way upon the character, integrity or uniformity of the landscape when viewed from the surroundings. This designation and policy are considered reasonable. The proposed bungalow would detract to an undue degree from the rural character and scenic amenities of the area due to its location and design. It is considered, therefore, that the proposed development would contravene this policy and be contrary to the proper planning and sustainable development of the area.*
>
> *2. the site is located within the Mid-Waterford Coast Special Protection Area. The development plan seeks to protect, conserve and enhance wildlife habitats and designated sites. It is considered that the construction of a house on this site would contravene this policy, be detrimental to the protection and conservation of these special conservation interests, and therefore be contrary to proper planning and sustainable development of the area.*

A planning application (08/24) was submitted to Waterford County Council in

January 2008 for the renovation of an existing single storey dwelling close to the cliffs at Tankardstown, near Bunmahon, which included a single-storey extension to provide for an artist's retreat complete with studio and a new site entrance, three single-storey artist's retreats complete with studio, accommodation and access roads, a two-storey building to provide for workshop studios, art gallery, cafe and owner-occupied accommodation, sculpture/art park including open air amphitheatre, underpass to public road complete with safety barriers, proprietary wastewater treatment plant with pumped raised bed polishing filter and the upgrading of an existing agricultural entrance to provide for a new site entrance. Further information was requested on the 12th March 2008 (received on 25th May 2008). Over thirty submissions were received (including one from Birdwatch Ireland on the possible impacts on the SPA, and the Department of the Environment, Heritage and Local Government on archaeological aspects).

The Assistant Planner in a report to the Senior Executive Planner, pointed out that

the site was located along a scenic route as designated in the Scenic Landscape Evaluation section of the Development Plan and in a request for further information asked that more information be supplied on bird usage of the area, impacts of the development on birds in the area and proposed mitigation measures to avoid adverse impacts on the SPA.

Waterford County Council issued their decision on the 24th June 2008, which was to refuse the development for two reasons, (which didn't include any reference to the nature conservation status of the site):

1. the site is located along a scenic route as designated in the Waterford county Development Plan 2005-2011 and having regard to the exposed nature of the site and to the scale and bulk of the development it is considered that the proposal would be at odds with the rural character of the areas, create an incongruous element in the landscape, which will dominate and detract from the rural character and visual amenities of

Looking east towards Garrarus from Sheep Island

the area. The proposed development would be contrary to the proper planning and development of the area.

2. traffic movements arising from the proposed development would endanger public safety by reason of traffic hazard because of inadequate visibility available at the location of the proposed entrance and local road.

The decision was not appealed but an application was made on the 11th June 2009 for a much-reduced development (09/325) to include the restoration of the existing single storey cottage dwelling, the construction of a grass roof covered single storey extension to the existing single storey cottage, the provision of a proprietary domestic wastewater treatment plant with an associated percolation area and site works. Following a request for further information (received 10th August 2009) Waterford County Council granted permission on 3rd September 2009. The decision was appealed to An Bord Pleanála (PL24.234829) by the applicant and three appellants. An Bord Pleanála issued its decision on the 19th February 2010, which allowed the development to proceed as the concerns of the Inspector could be overcome by way of condition (the Inspector had recommended a refusal because of the potential impact of the extension on a nearby well and the underlying aquifer).

A planning application (08/55) was submitted to Waterford County Council on the 25th January 2008 for a 10-year permission for the demolition of farmyard buildings, including a former habitable house, and the construction of a hotel complex consisting of 142 suites, including a clubhouse, bar, restaurant, function room, spa and leisure centre, 18-hole golf course, 51 golfing lodges associated with the hotel, 28 permanent executive houses, gate lodge, servicing area, landscaping, underground storage tank, carpark and associated site and development works. The 90 hectare (222 acres) irregularly-shaped development site is located along the southern coastline of county Waterford and two kilometres of the southern site boundary consists of a cliff-face. The site is approximately three kilometres west of Tramore in the townlands of Caher, Islandikane South and Islandikane East at Garrarus strand, which is currently used as farmland. Further information was requested from the developer by Waterford County Council on the 19th March 2008, which was received on the 18th December 2008. Over 300 written submissions were received in respect of the development, the majority of them against the proposed development (including ones from Birdwatch Ireland and the Department of the Environment, Heritage and Local Government on the possible impacts on the SPA). Permission was granted for the proposed development on the 10th February 2009, subject to 24 conditions. The planning permission was appealed to An Bord Pleanála (PL24.232989) by 14 appellants (including Birdwatch Ireland and the Department of the Environment, Heritage and Local Government on the possible impacts on the SPA) and several observers also submitted their views.

This proposal was the first tourism-related development to be considered under the Integrated Rural Tourism and Recreational Complex (IRTRC) variation to the County Development Plan 2005-2011, adopted five weeks earlier by Waterford County Council on the 18th December 2007, the purpose of which was to facilitate the development of golf courses, hotels, racecourses and other tourist facilities located in rural unzoned areas, which provide an important local/national amenity while also allowing limited on-site residential development (which was previously contrary to Development Plan policies). Developments considered under the IRTRC policy are subject to certain criteria and they must comply with the Scenic Landscape Evaluation and coastal development and landscape policies of the County Development Plan and also that they do not have a significant adverse impact on sites of nature conservation value or archaeological importance.

This was quite a massive development proposed for a greenfield site away from designated settlement areas and in an area designated as an SPA and a pNHA, nature conservation designations which reflect the importance of the site for one species in particular, the red-legged chough. It was a substantial application and several issues were raised by the proposal, each of which was dealt with by the developers, Waterford County Council and the appellants though, inevitably, each party emphasised the various issues differently and it was ultimately left to An Bord Pleanála to decide the outcome, following the granting of permission. The Planning Inspector carefully and comprehensively considered all the issues relating to the development and identified the potential impact of the proposal on choughs and the integrity of a designated site as the crux of the appeal. However, her assessment of the development was unusually frank in respect of certain aspects of the proposal and the decisions of Waterford County Council, which related to its ultimate granting of permission. Relevant extracts from the Planning Inspectors report are as follows (critical comments are in bold type):

*7.3 In terms of national planning policy, the **proposal flies in the face of the National Spatial Strategy and the Sustainable Rural Housing Guidelines**…*

This proposal, albeit tourism related, is in my view urban sprawl on a sensitive green-field site along the unspoilt coastline of west Waterford. The development is a

stand-alone project, which has no physical links to the wider area, Tramore or the surrounding villages…

The Spatial Strategy does not in fact advocate building on or into the south-east's attractive landscapes, as proposed under the current scheme.

7.4 The planning authority adopted variation No. 7 of the county development plan in December 2007, which very conveniently appears to suit the proposed scheme. I would question whether the variation as adopted is in line with the National Spatial Strategy or the Department's Guidelines on Sustainable Rural Housing…

*Overall, based on basic national planning principles and guidelines, and local development plan policies, **it is incomprehensible how the nature and scale of the dwellings could be included and permitted on the subject site given it's European status, national and local planning policy and given the sensitivity of the ecology and the superior quality of the amenities at the location.** I would recommend the Board refuse the proposal on these grounds amongst other matters arising...*

7.7 There has been serious opposition to the proposal from third parties, the Department of the Environment, Heritage and Local Government and Birdwatch Ireland regarding the potential impact of the proposal on choughs and the integrity of the designated site. This issue is the crux of the appeal…

Under European Law the planning authority has a duty to ensure the protection of the habitat and the birds as they are listed under Annex 1 if the EU Birds Directive.

"West of Tramore there is 20 miles of almost unbroken cliff and precipitous slopes tenanted by seabirds and a wealth of wildflowers, with small villages nestling in gaps of the rocky wall, where streams enter the sea"
Robert Lloyd Praeger, 1937

"The site itself is breathtakingly beautiful and as it unfolds from east to west, it exhibits an astounding untamed coastal countryside, which is an unspoiled wilderness worth protecting as part of our national heritage. In my opinion, the Development Plan policies should seek to preserve such landscapes for future generations to enjoy and experience as these areas are diminishing rapidly along our national coastline"
An Bord Pleanála Inspector, 2010

The beach east of Sheep Island, Islandikane

*7.9 **The planning authority's justification for granting the proposal in the context of chough conservation, is in my view, irresponsible**.*

*7.10 ….. The Director of Services (Planning) supported the planning authority's technical reports recommending a grant of permission and stated the potential economic benefits of the proposal to Tramore and the surrounding area has not been included in the planner's assessment but are a material consideration in trying to achieve sustainable development in the area. **I would strongly oppose this philosophy**. Having regard to the above assessment, I can find no justifiable socio-economic benefits that substantiate the loss or destruction of an internationally important habitat and a protected species, both of which under European legislation the planning authority has a statutory obligation to protect.*

7.11 The proposed development should be refused because it is considered the development will have a significant adverse impact on the SPA and the protected bird species in the area. The proposal conflicts with paragraph 8.7 of the county development plan regarding habitat protection…

this site is of international significance in it's own right, and therefore it is in [the] interests of the wider community and the common good that it should be preserved and not developed to the financial benefit of a small minority.

7.14 I consider this coastal [site?] to be of special amenity value regardless of its SPA and NHA designations. It contains a fragile landscape and habitat. Nationally coastal areas are under continual development pressure from residential and tourism developments. The site has limited capacity to absorb development and the focus of any proposal should be to ensure any form of development on the site does not damage or detract from the basic qualities and attractions of this coastal location…

***Given the remote and sensitive layout, the entire design is obnoxious, obtrusive and overbearing on this unspoiled and pristine coastline**. One only has to examine the photomontages of the proposal from the eastern beach to understand the impact this proposal will have in visual terms. The same beach during my site inspection was significantly populated with tourists and families. It is unacceptable that the proposal could detract from the visual and recreational amenities of Garrarus beach, a natural amenity which the local community cherish and enjoy, and is also a tourist attraction for the area. The beach has strong visual qualities in terms of the cliffs, the curved sandy beach, the caves and Burke's Rock. To insert a large development within clear view of the beach would destroy the natural dramatic setting of the beach. The individual houses which are visible from the beach are large bulky dwellings which have been insensitively positioned…*

The proposal is monolithic creating an overwhelming, disproportionate and an inappropriate form of development on the open countryside and coastal location.

*7.15 Based on my knowledge of the proposal and the site, it is my opinion that **this proposal is wholly inappropriate for this scenic coastal location**. Given the scale, design, massing, height and layout of the scheme, I consider it to be urban and suburban in*

Sheep Island off Islandikane

character and totally unsuitable for this visually sensitive location which has a high amenity value. The site itself is breathtakingly beautiful and as it unfolds from east to west, it exhibits an astounding untamed coastal countryside, which is an unspoiled wilderness worth protecting as part of our national heritage. In my opinion, the development plan policies should seek to preserve such landscapes for future generations to enjoy and experience as these areas are diminishing rapidly along our national coastline. To encourage and permit the proposed scheme given its scale, design, location and impact, **is a travesty in planning and environmental terms** and I would advise the Board to refuse the development on these grounds also.

8.0 RECOMMENDATION

*8.1 Having examined the planning file, the site and the appeal documentation, **I cannot comprehend the planning authority's assessment or decision***

relating to the proposed development based on the European legal status of the site, *European Case law, Ministerial advice and guidance, and national and local planning policy governing the area. The irreversible loss of an internationally important habitat and the uniquely adapted bird species along the Mid-Waterford coastline is a high and unnecessary price to pay for this poorly substantiated economic development, **which is unjustifiable in planning and environmental policy grounds**. I recommend the Board overturn the planning authority's decision, and REFUSE the proposed development.*

Following a lengthy consideration of the appeal, the Board accepted the recommendation of the Planning Inspector and overturned the decision of Waterford County Council. They refused the development for three reasons:

1. It is considered that the proposed development, by reason of its monolithic scale, design, height, bulk and layout on an elevated coastal site, which is highly visible from the eastern coastline and the adjoining road network, would constitute a development out of character with the existing relatively unsettled and unspoilt coastal area, would seriously injure the visual and recreational amenities of the area, would adversely impact on the coastal landscape and would contravene the policies of the planning authority, as expressed in the Waterford county development plan, 2005-2011, on development proposals on rural landscapes. The proposed development would, therefore, be contrary to the proper planning and sustainable development of the area.

2. Having regard to the National Spatial Strategy for Ireland 2002-2020, to the Sustainable Rural Housing Guidelines for Planning Authorities issued by the Department of the Environment, Heritage and Local Government in April, 2005 and to the current Waterford county development plan, the proposed development would be located in a rural area considered to be strong in terms of population growth whereby the principle planning response is to strengthen the town and village settlements and reduce urban sprawl. Having regard to the permanent homes proposed under the scheme, the proposed development is considered to be sporadic suburban-like development on the open countryside within a highly scenic and protected coastal landscape and would, therefore, be contrary to the settlement strategy contained in the current development plan for the area and contrary to the policy of the planning authority to permit genuine rural housing need at suitable locations on a scale and a pace which will not diminish county Waterford's high quality rural environment. The proposed

development would, therefore, be contrary to the proper planning and sustainable development of the area.

3. The site is located within the Ballyvoyle Head to Tramore (Natural Heritage Area Site Number 1694) and mid Waterford Coast (Special Protection Area Site Number 4194), a site which has been selected under the EU Birds Directive as being of conservation interest for a number of listed bird species, in particular the chough which is listed on Annex 1 of the E.U. Birds Directive. It is considered that the likely significant effects of the proposed development on priority heath habitats within the site, including habitat loss and fragmentation, human interference and untested management of the habitat, would result in an unacceptable degradation of the protected habitat, and would also result in an unacceptable risk to the chough, which is of high conservation value. It is considered, therefore, that the proposed development would have a significant adverse effect on the integrity of the Annex 1 Bird Species and would be contrary to the proper planning and sustainable development of the area.

The Board also had concerns with regard to the proposals for the treatment of wastewater but decided not to pursue this issue further having regard to the substantive reasons for refusal.

What was surprising in the planning report accompanying the An Bord Pleanála decision was the forcefulness of the assessments presented by the Planning Inspector (see the passages in bold type), which was presumably endorsed by the Board, in respect of not just elements of the development but the entire proposal and the Council's assessment of the proposal. It is unusual for the same development, assessed by two different and highly competent planning authorities, to arrive at staggeringly different conclusions, rather than different interpretations leading to contrary conclusions, as is usual when planning decisions are reversed.

The Planning Inspector referred to the procedural issue raised by some of the appellants in respect of the lack of public knowledge and poor advertising of variation number 7 to the Development Plan (the IRTRC policy document) and the rapid submission of the planning application so soon after the adoption of the variation by Waterford County Council but correctly stated that this aspect was beyond the remit of An Bord Pleanála and its functions and so was unable to comment further on the issue. However, the Inspector did state:

I would comment that given the extensive number of settlements included in the Settlement Strategy for Waterford county, the amount of zoned land within three kilometres of the site and the fact the general coastline of Waterford is under constant development pressure, I could find no reasonable and sustainable justification to insert such a radical and contradictory planning policy into the development plan.

Clearly, the IRTRC policy document had created planning issues where tourist developments were proposed for scenic areas and protected habitats outside the settlement areas, which the Development Plan had always attempted to protect.

Planning application 09/469 was for a substantial development (dwelling and outbuildings, 500.12 sq. metres gross floor area) at Brownstown, close to the cliff and overlooking Tramore Bay. The development was refused by Waterford County Council, for two reasons, the first of which was that:

the site was in a visually vulnerable area as designated in the Scenic Landscape Evaluation of the County Development Plan 2005-2011.

Another application (10/10) for the same site and the same substantial property, but set back away from the cliff, was also refused for the same reasons. The decision was appealed to An Bord Pleanála (236459) but they decided, in December 2010, to uphold the decision and the development was refused for just one reason:

the site is located on Brownstown Headland, a generally unspoilt headland overlooking Tramore Bay, which is a primary tourist asset and local amenity in county Waterford, and designated as 'visually vulnerable' under the current Waterford County Development Plan. It is considered that the proposed development, notwithstanding the design

Coastal cliffs near Red Head, Dunmore East. The 588 sq metre house (07/1415) near the cliff was moved approximately 30 metres to the south of the site, with the agreement of Waterford County Council following a written request in March 2006, from that permitted under the original application (02/631)

and landscaping of the site, would be a visually obtrusive feature in this exposed landscape and would seriously injure the visual amenities of the area and would be contrary to Development Plan policy in relation to such visually vulnerable landscapes. The proposed development would, therefore, be contrary to the proper planning and sustainable development of the area.

By and large, the Waterford coast is free of man-made structures, other than one-off houses, some of which blend inauspiciously into the landscape, perhaps because of their low profile and architectural character but other houses are more dominant and often make an unwanted statement close to the cliff top. There are no offshore structures, and none are planned, so only the stacks, islets and rocks dominate and enhance the view as the sea swells around them. It is hard to predict the future with any certainty, but declining oil resources may increase the dependency on wind or wave generated energy, which could yet see energy-generating structures off our coast as the technology for construction in inhospitable environments develops. Likewise, a surge in oil price could see hitherto uneconomic offshore oil fields in production, though most of these are too far offshore for any material structures to be noticeable. Moreover, energy generation is likely to be nationally driven by Governments, and may be outside the provisions of county development plans.

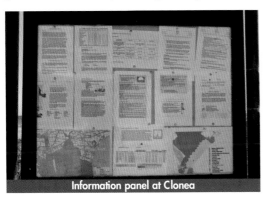

Information panel at Clonea

Maximum EU Directive values		
	Guide	Mandatory
Total coliforms (/100 ml)	500	10,000
Faecal coliforms (/100 ml)	100	2,000
Faecal streptococci (/100 ml)	100	
Mineral oils (mg/l)	0.3	no visible film
Surfactants (mg/l)	0.3	no lasting foam
Phenols (mg/l)	0.005	0.05, no odour

Water Quality

Waterford is surrounded by water, with the Suir bordering its northern flank, Waterford Harbour and the Blackwater estuary bounding it to the east and west respectively, and by a large expanse of sea on its southern side. It is the coastal waters off the Waterford coast that attract many people for a wide variety of activities, all of which enhance peoples lives. The maintenance of this pristine environment is of paramount importance and the quality of the seawater off the coast is absolutely critical to the enjoyment of it. While the waters off the coast may look in good condition, it is important to have measurable parameters by which the quality of the water may be assessed objectively. EU regulations require that these parameters are measured wherever people swim in coastal waters or where the sea is used to cultivate material for eventual human consumption. It is also important to measure the overall water quality outside of these areas, so seawater is sampled at regular intervals to assess the overall state of the Irish marine environment.

Bathing areas

The legislation governing the quality of bathing waters in Irish coastal waters is set out in the Quality of Bathing Waters Regulations, 1992 (S.I. 155 of 1992) and amendments, which transposed the EU Directive 76/160/EEC concerning the quality of bathing water, the purpose of which is to ensure that bathing water quality is

WATER QUALITY PERFORMANCE FOR ARDMORE AND DUNMORE EAST (MAIN STRAND), 2004-2010								
	2004	2005	2006	2007	2008	2009	2010	failures
Ardmore	G	P	S	S	P	S	G	2
Dunmore East	P	G	P	S	G	P	G	3

G = good, S = sufficient, P = poor

monitored, maintained and, where necessary, improved. The 1992 regulations will eventually be superseded by a new Directive on bathing water (Directive 2006/7/EC), which came into force in March 2006 and will replace the 1976 Directive when fully implemented from 2015 on.

Specified standards are set, which the bathing waters are assessed by, and these standards are aimed at protecting human health and the coastal environment. Responsibility for monitoring the quality of the bathing waters rests with the local authorities, which in Waterford, is Waterford County Council, in whose area the bathing waters are located. They are obliged to sample every two weeks from 1ᵗ June (sampling usually begins in May) to the end of August and a minimum of seven samples must be collected, unless the bathing water quality is consistently good, in which case four samples is acceptable. The parameters to be sampled for are total coliforms, faecal coliforms, mineral oils, surface active substances and phenols, and the levels recorded are then used

to classify the bathing waters as **good** (if the levels are compliant with both guide and mandatory values), **sufficient** (if compliant with mandatory values only) and **poor** (if non-compliant with mandatory values). A new category, **excellent**, with very stringent values, will apply when the new Bathing Directive is fully implemented in 2015.

Local authorities are obliged to publish the results of testing and information boards giving up-to-date information on the water quality are strategically located at the designated beaches of county Waterford. They also submit all the years' data to the Environmental Protection Agency who publish an annual report, which gives the results for the entire country as well as comparing the information from previous years for each site. The Office of Environmental Enforcement of the EPA can investigate sites where the water quality fails to reach the minimum mandatory standards.

The presence of coliforms, and especially *Escherichia coli*, in bathing water confirms recent faecal contamination by humans or animals who excrete these bacteria in vast numbers. Hence bathing waters are sampled for faecal coliforms, which may indicate the presence of disease-causing pathogens. However not all coliforms are of faecal origin so waters are also sampled for total coliforms, as some forms can occur in the soil; the results for total coliforms give an indication of the general microbiological contamination of the receiving waters. Bathing waters are visually assessed by beach users who perceive a colour in the water to indicate pollution. However, a high colour in seawater rarely

RANGE OF VALUES RECORDED, 20ᵗʰ MAY-26ᵗʰ AUGUST 2008, AT ARDMORE

In water samples at the centre of the bathing area. Sampled by the Health Service Executive (11 samples).

Parameter	range
Faecal coliforms (/100ml)	13-3,100
Faecal streptococci	7-2,900
Colour	none
Surfactants	none
Oils	none
Phenols	none
Transparency (m/depth)	>1
Floating residues	none

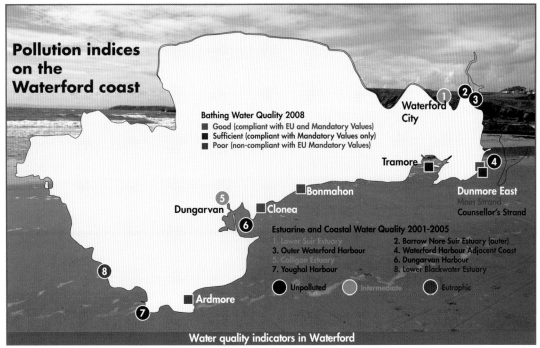

Pollution indices on the Waterford coast

Bathing Water Quality 2008
- ■ Good (compliant with EU and Mandatory Values)
- ■ Sufficient (compliant with Mandatory Values only)
- ■ Poor (non-compliant with EU Mandatory Values)

Waterford City

Tramore

Bonmahon

Dunmore East
Main Strand
Counsellor's Strand

Dungarvan

Clonea

Estuarine and Coastal Water Quality 2001-2005
1. Lower Suir Estuary
2. Barrow Nore Suir Estuary (outer)
3. Outer Waterford Harbour
4. Waterford Harbour Adjacent Coast
5. Colligan Estuary
6. Dungarvan Harbour
7. Youghal Harbour
8. Lower Blackwater Estuary

● Unpolluted   ○ Intermediate   ◐ Eutrophic

Ardmore

Water quality indicators in Waterford

poses a health hazard and is likely to indicate the presence of sediment or other natural debris in the water. Colour is measured on aesthetic grounds only. The presence of phenols indicate contamination of the bathing waters from industrial sources or runoff from roads or roadworks.

There are six designated bathing areas in county Waterford (main strand and Counsellor's strand at Dunmore East, main strand at Tramore, Bunmahon strand, Clonea and Ardmore) and these are regularly monitored in summer; all other beaches and coves are not sampled. In 2008, Ardmore was deemed to have poor water quality and was non-compliant with EU mandatory and guide values for faecal coliforms and total coliforms, while Counsellor's strand and the strand at Tramore were non-compliant with EU Guide values for faecal coliforms but were deemed to have sufficient water quality. The summer of 2008 was particularly wet, leading to excess runoff from the land and sewer overflows, which may have contributed to the values recorded and the deterioration in status of Ardmore (which had a sufficient

water quality status in 2007) and Counsellor's strand and Tramore strand (both of which had a good water quality status in 2007) between 2007 and 2008. However the water quality status at Bunmahon improved from sufficient in 2007 to good from 2008-2010. The water quality at Ardmore also improved from poor (2008) to sufficient (2009) to good (2010), while Tramore changed from sufficient to good between 2008 and 2010. Disappointingly, Ardmore and the main strand at Dunmore has rather variable water quality between years and failed the EU mandatory and guide values in some years in the period 2004-2010.

EU Directive regulations require that, where a bathing area has poor water quality status for five consecutive years, a permanent prohibition on bathing or advice against bathing in the area concerned should be issued by the local authority (Waterford County Council).

Ardmore experienced significant house construction in recent years and the beach is also subject to a stream inflow from the rural

Disused shellfish trestles near Ballynagaul

catchment area. In June 2000 Waterford County Council erected a public notice at the entrance to Ardmore beach advising people not to paddle or bathe in the waters of the stream until further notice on the direction of the South Eastern Health Board but no reason was given (apparently, raw sewage was being discharged into this stream on the ebb tide). Similarly, the variable water quality recorded at Dunmore East has been explained by contaminated runoff which inflows onto the beach near the Strand Hotel. Both Ardmore and Dunmore East are included in a proposed Grouped Villages Sewerage Scheme and when these wastewater treatment facilities are fully operational, a significant improvement in bathing water quality is expected.

Blue Flag beaches

The International Blue Flag Programme is owned and run by the Foundation for Environmental Education (FEE), an independent, non-profit organisation consisting of members representing 37 countries within Europe, North and South America, Africa and Oceania. An Taisce (the National Trust for Ireland), coordinates the Blue Flag scheme in Ireland on behalf of the FEE with support from the Department of the Environment, Heritage and Local Government. The Blue Flag Programme monitors beaches (and marinas) and 27 strict criteria dealing with water quality, environmental education and information, environmental management, safety and other services have to be met to achieve a Blue Flag. Each year local authorities nominate beaches and marinas for a Blue Flag award and must prove compliance with defined criteria. They must also nominate an official to deal with the Blue Flag Programme and nominated beaches must be accessible for unannounced inspections. Only bathing areas designated by the Irish Government are eligible for the Blue Flag Award.

A Blue Flag is awarded for one bathing season (June 1st to August 31st) at a time and a team of assessors inspects all Blue Flag beaches and marinas to ensure compliance with the criteria. If some of the criteria are breached during the season or the conditions change, local authorities are contacted and asked to act to ensure compliance; a Blue Flag can be withdrawn from the bathing area for non-compliance. Waterford usually has six designated Blue Flag beaches for which applications are submitted annually by Waterford County Council. These are:

Sewage treatment plant near Helvick Head

Ardmore, Bunmahon, Clonea East, Dunmore East (Counsellor's strand and main strand) and Tramore (main strand).

A Blue Flag beach is a cherished designation and is widely accepted by all those who use a Blue Flag beach as an indicator of good water quality and environmental services in the area. Moreover, it is an important Flag for tourists to see when they visit our shores, given the international status of the Blue Flag award. The overall quality of Irish bathing waters is high and, in 2008, 93% (122 of 131 areas) were compliant with the minimum EU mandatory values and achieved sufficient water quality status. Only six seawater areas failed to achieve this level of compliance (which included Ardmore). In 2010, An Taisce awarded 76 Blue Flags for Irish beaches and marinas, and two were awarded for Waterford: Clonea and Bunmahon (which also received awards in 2009).

Coastal areas are also assessed by the Clean Coasts Programme and the Green Coast Awards, which were established to improve the coastal environment in Ireland and Wales. It is coordinated and run in Ireland by An Taisce. The Green Coast Award can be awarded to beaches that have good water quality but because of a lack of local infrastructure do not qualify for Blue Flag status. There is a strong emphasis on community involvement in management, through Coast Care Groups. Beaches which obtained Green Coast Awards in 2010 in Waterford were the Guillamene, Annestown, Boatstrand beach, Ballyquin and Goat Island.

Shellfish areas
Article 5 of the Shellfish Directive (2006/113/EC) and section 6 of the Quality of Shellfish Waters Regulations (S.I. No. 268 of 2006) require the preparation of pollution reduction plans (PRPs) for designated shellfish areas to enable shellfish to survive in unpolluted waters and hence generate high quality edible shellfish products. These PRPs relate to oysters, mussels, cockles, scallops and clams but do not cover crabs, crayfish and lobsters. To comply with the Shellfish Directive, waters where shellfish are cultivated have to satisfy several water quality parameters such as pH (how acid or alkaline the water is on a scale from 1 to 14: pure water has a pH of 7), temperature, colour, suspended solids, salinity, dissolved oxygen, trace contaminants and faecal coliforms (which gives an indication of contamination

by sewage) and there are imperative values (which must be fully achieved) and more stringent guideline values (which should be aimed for). Two shellfish areas are designated in Waterford: Waterford Harbour (designated in 2009) and Dungarvan Harbour (also designated in 2009).

A classification scheme is in place, which requires treatment options depending on the level of faecal contamination (*E. coli*) in 100 grammes of shellfish flesh and intra-valvular liquid. Where levels are low (<230), the shellfish may be eaten directly (class A), higher levels (<4,600) require purification or relaying to achieve class A status, while the highest levels (<46,000) require that the shellfish are relayed for at least two months prior to sale. Contaminated shellfish can cause outbreaks of Paralytic Shellfish Poison (PST), Diarrhetic Shellfish Poisoning (DSP), Amnesic Shellfish Poisoning (ASP) and Azaspiracid Shellfish Poisoning (AZP), caused by naturally occurring marine organisms. When these organisms are detected (usually in summer), the production area is closed and harvesting ceases. Such algal blooms are more common on the west coast of Ireland, and probably originate offshore rather than inshore due to human agents of enrichment.

Dungarvan Harbour: The designated shellfish area at Dungarvan is located to the east side of the Cunnigar within Dungarvan Harbour cSAC and SPA and the catchment area includes Helvick Head, which is also an SPA. It is 6.9 square kilometres in area and is delineated by straight lines from the tip of the Cunnigar to the slip pier at Ballynacourty to Ballynagaul pier and by the Cunnigar and the Ring peninsula. The surrounding catchment area is almost 222.64 square kilometres. Fifty five areas are designated for oysters (comprising 2.9 square kilometres or around 42% of the area) and one area is designated for periwinkles (0.008 square kilometres or 0.1%).

Water quality measurements in some parts of the shellfish catchment area indicate that the mandatory and guideline values of the Directive were not breached but the guideline values for faecal coliforms in shellfish samples was breached in late 2008 and 2009, which indicates faecal contamination in the shellfish area. There are also water quality issues with dissolved inorganic nitrogen and dissolved oxygen. The largest urban wastewater treatment facility in the shellfish catchment area is at Dungarvan, where the secondary treatment plant is designed to serve a population equivalent (PE) of 25,000 people, which is adequate to service current and projected future populations. The Ring/Helvick/Ballynagaul treatment plant also incorporates secondary treatment and is an element of the Dungarvan and Environs Sewerage Scheme. Diffuse sources of contaminants may also arise from the large number of private wastewater treatment systems and the intensive agricultural activity in the catchment area.

Waterford Harbour: The designated shellfish area, which lies within the Waterford Harbour cSAC, is 30 square kilometres in area and extends from the confluence of the Suir and Barrow rivers downwards to a line from Ardnamult Head across to Broomhill in Wexford. It has a catchment area of 9,232 square kilometres and is fed by the Barrow, Nore and Suir rivers, a system that is the second largest in the country after the Shannon. Mussels and oysters are the main shellfish that are cultivated, with 26 areas designated for mussels (8.5 square kilometres or 28% of the area) and seven areas designated for oysters (2.7 square kilometres or 9% of the area). Monitoring of the waters and the biota in the shellfish area indicate that there are water quality issues and that there is also faecal contamination in some of the shellfish waters. The Waterford Harbour shellfish area has an early season class B classification which stipulates that shellfish destined for human consumption requires either treatment in a purification centre or relaying and it has a class C classification between 1st of August and 31st of December which requires a longer purification time. These classifications are necessary so that the harvested shellfish comply with the health standards for live bivalve molluscs as laid down in the EC Regulation on Food Safety (Regulation (EC) No. 853/2004).

There are 14 urban wastewater treatment plants within the catchment area and these include the plants at Waterford City (which also treats discharges from Abbey Park and Giles Quay), Dunmore East, Duncannon, Arthurstown, Ballyhack, Campile, Passage East, Crooke and Cheekpoint (though five of these have insufficient plant capacities to deal with the areas they serve). Waterford City is the largest with a design capacity of 180,000 PE and incorporates secondary treatment. The plants at Dunmore East, Duncannon, Arthurstown, Ballyhack and Cheekpoint are scheduled for improvement while the recently installed plant at Crooke incorporates secondary treatment. There are also a large number of private treatment systems in the catchment, many of them located in hydrologically unsuitable conditions, which, along with the intensive agricultural activity in the region, may be contributing to the faecal contamination and elevated nutrient levels found in the shellfish area.

Estuarine and coastal areas
The two main estuaries in county Waterford, are fed by substantial river systems, which deposit a large load of nutrients, organic matter and other debris that arise from the many cities, towns, villages and other sources along their length. Urban wastewater treatment plants, although designed to treat human waste to a much greater degree than is possible by natural assimilation alone, often discharge into estuaries or the coastal zone and large municipal dumps also have the potential to pollute through leachate (though none of the dumps in the county are now operational). Ultimately, these discharges end up in the sea, with potential adverse impacts on the coastal zone if the quantity arising exceeds the capacity of the system to assimilate and disperse the discharges. The sea itself is also a dumping ground for various materials and there is always the risk of oil pollution incidents from passing ships, who either deliberately discharge the contents of tanks or they do so accidentally when they break up during storms.

It is important that the inputs of all these discharges into the estuarine and coastal environment is monitored through objective parameters, which provide not just an ongoing assessment of the state of the marine environment, but also as to the effectiveness of legislation and pollution control measures, and more importantly, the likely impacts on the people who use the coastal areas where these discharges end up. Various organisations are involved in monitoring the water quality status of coastal and estuarine waters in Ireland, each with their own perspective and areas of interest. The main parameters that are monitored are dissolved oxygen (oxygen

Part of the sewage treatment works at Ballynacourty, Dungarvan

The remediated town dump at Dungarvan (May 2010)

having the ability to support fish life) and inorganic nitrogen and phosphate (these cause enrichment and the growth of algae). Various criteria are set for these parameters and depending on the levels found, the sampled waters are considered to be eutrophic, potentially eutrophic and intermediate if they exceed the thresholds set for these categories or they are unpolluted (none of the thresholds are reached). In Waterford, various sites in the Blackwater estuary, Dungarvan Harbour and Waterford Harbour have been sampled.

The tidal limit of the three sisters river catchment (the rivers Barrow, Nore and Suir) extends far inland (to St. Mullins, Inistioge and Carrick-on-Suir, respectively) and there is a high tidal range, varying from 2.2 metres at Dunmore East to 3.8 metres at New Ross, which results in good mixing of the receiving waters, at least lower down in the estuary, which have a large assimilative capacity, despite the large nutrient inputs from the municipal areas and the intensively farmed catchment areas around the rivers and tributary streams flowing into them.

Elevated levels of nitrogen have been recorded in the upper reaches of all three rivers and high levels of chlorophyll and low dissolved oxygen levels have been noted for the Barrow and upper Nore, and were classed as potentially eutrophic. Problem areas in the past on the lower Suir have included the Clodiagh catchment (due to enrichment from

an old tannery), Waterford City (organic inputs) and the St. Johns river (also in Waterford City, due to industrial discharges mainly), though because of the capacity of the Suir to absorb these inputs and the strong tidal flows, the inputs are quickly dispersed and there is rarely a persistent problem. The recent commissioning of the wastewater treatment plant at Belview to treat urban waste from Waterford City will reduce the impact on organic inputs to the system. The Barrow has had higher levels of nitrogen and phosphates than the Suir but the seaward section of the combined estuaries (e.g. below Cheekpoint) have been found to be unpolluted during most recent surveys.

A new wastewater treatment plant has recently (2007) become operational at Tramore, which discharges into Tramore Bay through a long two-kilometre sea outfall pipe. The town dump is closed, capped over and has been remediated. Consequently, the water quality around Tramore has almost certainly improved, though leachate from the dump may continue to locally contaminate the sediments in the inner Backstrand area for some time to come.

Dungarvan Bay is large (around 20 square kilometres in area) and is subject to high tidal flushing (around 65% of the area is uncovered at low tide). The Colligan and the Brickey discharge into the Bay and the principal inputs are urban (from Dungarvan town), industrial and the decommissioned town dump at the head of the Colligan estuary. Two new wastewater treatment plants, at Ballynacourty (for Dungarvan, with a design capability of 25,000 person equivalents) and Ballynagaul (on the west side of Dungarvan Bay for 1,600 person equivalents) were operating at full capacity in July 2007. The Ballynacourty plant discharges the treated effluent 750 metres offshore into Dungarvan Bay and the Ballynagaul plant discharges to the sea nearby. The effluent from both plants meets EU standards for urban wastewater as outlined in the EU Urban Wastewater Directive (1991) and water quality in Dungarvan Bay is, apparently, considerably improved as a result.

The Colligan estuary upstream of Dungarvan has always been in an unsatisfactory condition, which has been attributed to leachate from the town dump in the upper estuary (the dump is now closed) and to tannery discharges, mainly chromium compounds, around the town itself (the tannery closed in 1996). The remediation of the dump has probably reduced leachate entering the Colligan estuary and ultimately Dungarvan Bay. Nevertheless, despite all these improvements, Dungarvan Harbour moved from an unpolluted status between 1999-2003 to intermediate status following the most recent assessment in 2002-2006.

The Blackwater in the west of the county is a large, though relatively narrow river, with a long tidal influence of around 38 kilometres from its mouth at Youghal to Lismore, a high tidal flow rate (around 80 cubic metres per second) and a high tidal range (around 3.5 metres) generating strong currents in the estuary. The main tributaries are the Lickey, Finnisk and Bride. The three towns in Waterford along its length are Lismore, Cappoquin and Youghal, which contribute generally small nutrient loads to the river. The estuary itself is well mixed.

While there have been problems with phosphates and oxidised nitrogen in the past, and the discharge of untreated sewage from Youghal, recent assessments indicate that Youghal Harbour is unpolluted, although biochemical oxygen demand (BOD) has been found to be above recommended limits; this problem may be ameliorated when a new urban wastewater treatment is operational in Youghal in 2011/2012.

The Water Framework Directive is a relatively new EU Directive (2000), the purpose of which is the protection and improvement of water resources and aquatic ecosystems all across Europe, including groundwater, rivers, lakes, estuaries, coastal waters and wetlands. One of the objectives of the Water Framework Directive is ensuring that the chemical and ecological status of all water bodies will be good or high by 2015, and that there will be no deterioration in the current status of each waterbody. The eight river basin districts in Ireland are the management units with the relevant local authorities for each river basin district and the Environmental Protection Agency (EPA) responsible for implementing the Directive. Carlow is the responsible local authority for the southeastern region.

An ecological classification systems is being developed by the EPA which will assign surface-water bodies to one of the five status classes: 'high', 'good', 'moderate', 'poor' and 'bad' based on ecological and chemical status using standards and targets, which must be achieved by 2015.

Trace metals (mercury, lead, cadmium) and chlorinated hydrocarbons are also routinely monitored in fish samples from Dunmore East and all complied with EU maximum levels for such contaminants. Low levels of organochlorines were found in kittiwake eggs sampled from the Dunmore East colonies in 1998, which themselves were an order of magnitude lower than levels found a decade earlier. Similarly, radioactivity levels in shellfish monitored in the period 2001-2006 were low overall, and the levels from human sources (Sellafield, for example) were small compared with the natural background levels. There have been no recent oil pollution incidents along the Waterford coast, though the occasional oiled seabird washes up on Waterford beaches, which could have been contaminated far offshore.

CLIMATE CHANGE

Ireland has become warmer in recent decades (mean annual temperature increased by 0.5 °C in the twentieth century; globally temperatures are expected to rise by between 1.4 °C and 5.8 °C by 2100), largely due to increasing levels of carbon dioxide in the atmosphere arising from land use change and the burning of fossil fuels. Rising sea levels (currently at around one millimetre per year in Ireland, are expected to increase by up to six millimetres per year by 2100), increasing sea temperatures, ocean acidification and changes in coastal and oceanic currents are the main consequences arising from climate change that will have an impact on the marine environment off our shores.

Increasing ocean temperatures causes thermal expansion of seawater, which is probably the main agent of the observed sea level rise, that may swamp low-lying areas and particularly those along the coast.

It has been predicted that sea level will rise by an average of 50 to 60 centimetres by the end of the present century, leading to inundation and eventual loss of low-lying coastal land, including the estuarine sandflats, mudflats and wetland areas in Waterford, some of which are cSACs. This rise in sea level threatens all the areas along the Waterford coast that have been subject to flooding and erosion in the past, especially

those areas protected by hard structures, which may be swamped by rising sea levels, and dune areas and soft cliffs, in particular, are at greatest risk. Moreover, there will almost certainly be an increase in winter wave heights off our shores, perhaps by up to 30 centimetres; an increase in frequency of high waves is another factor, through this may be more pronounced off the west coast.

Increasing sea temperatures will almost certainly alter the functioning of marine ecosystems, with consequent changes in the abundance and distribution of marine organisms; some species, unable to tolerate warmer waters will move elsewhere, while other species will advance and these changes will be exacerbated, at least for some species, unable to withstand the increased ocean acidity as seawater absorbs the higher levels of carbon dioxide in the atmosphere. There may be changes in timing and intensity of algal blooms, which might cause more of a problem than has been observed up to now. Changes in abundance, variety and growth of commercially valuable species will occur; some species will undoubtedly be lost but opportunities for exploiting new species may arise, that are attracted by the warmer waters around our shore. Aquacultural activities could suffer from changes in near-shore salinities and greater sediment loads arising from increased riverine flows and there may be higher levels of mortality from higher temperatures, which may affect production, and if algal blooms occur then shellfish-induced illnesses in humans may also result in a cessation in commercial production.

The following assumptions have been widely used in predicting the climate-induced changes that may occur by 2055:

- carbon dioxide levels will continue to increase in the atmosphere;

- average summer temperatures will

increase by 2 °C and winter temperatures will increase by 1.5 °C;

- summer rainfall will decrease by up to 40% in summer (which will be most pronounced here in the southeast) and increase by 10% in winter;

- Extreme weather events (increased storminess in winter and more sustained heatwaves in summer) will increase in frequency and intensity.

A complicating factor is the behaviour of the Gulf Stream, the warm surface current that flows northeast across the Atlantic from the Gulf of Mexico, and keeps Irish coastal waters around 7 °C warmer than sea temperatures elsewhere at the same latitude, which maintains our mild oceanic climate. There is a return current of colder, deeper and heavier water from the cooler northern regions, which perpetuates the ocean circulation system. If this circulation system were to slow down, or worse, stop, temperatures around our coast could reduce by up to 5 °C, leading to significant climate change and very cold conditions with consequences that could be quite severe and equally, if not more so, than those that will arise if global warming persists.

All the predictions and likely outcomes of global warming and sea-level rise, have an element of uncertainty about them, and we are reliant on existing and historical data to generate the complex mathematical models which try and predict what may happen in the future. Obviously these data need to be comprehensive and robust and there is a clear need to measure all the parameters necessary to more accurately predict what may happen. Whether this qualitative data set is being gathered in Waterford isn't clear, but what is clear is that if predictions are in any way correct, then county Waterford will suffer, perhaps disproportionately, from sea level rise

and all its likely effects, and the impacts are likely to be greatest and most severe in the low-lying coastal areas of the county.

Waterford County Council published its Climate Change Strategy 2008-2012 in March 2008 but there was no mention of the Waterford coast or likely coastal erosion in this document. Moreover, the county Development Plan 2005-2011 did not include any reference to climate change or sea level rise in the county. There is almost certainly a need for a dedicated plan with a clear set of strategies on the potential impacts of global warming along the Waterford coast, which would gather and analyse long-term data, create inventories of coastal structures, and monitor events as they unfold (storm frequencies and their impacts, for example) and outline key marine policy areas and coastal management priorities. The County Development Plan is one document where all these considerations might be enshrined.

The Manager's Report for the draft Plan 2011-2017, published in July 2010, recommended the inclusion of the following section, which is incorporated in the County Development Plan 2011-2017:

Coastal Zone Management
Waterford's coastline is a valuable natural resource providing a buffer for extreme weathers, an important wildlife area for a range of protected habitats and species and a scenic landscape asset of tourism value. The coastal zone is generally taken as the area between Mean High Water Mark (MHWM) and the nearest continuous road. A growing body of evidence illustrates that rising sea levels, increasing storm frequency and wave energy will increase the rate of erosion, loss of habitats and incidence of flood-related events in vulnerable areas of the Waterford coast. The impacts of climate change may have wide reaching

The Cunnigar in Dungarvan Bay: will it adapt to the predicted sea-level rise?

implications for the heritage and tourism value of the coastline. It is necessary that future management and development of coastal areas is carried out in a manner that protects coastal functions and values including natural coastal defence, habitat value and landscape/seascape character. Integrated Coastal Zone Management seeks to achieve a more effective and sustainable use of coastal resources by involving all coastal users in planning for appropriate management of the coast. Waterford County Council has carried out some baseline work on the principle of ICZM in the east of the county and seeks to apply the process on a county basis with the support of all the relevant agencies and organisations.

Objectives for Coastal Protection
CP1 To explore the process of ICZM in the future management and sustainable development of the Waterford coastline;

CP2 To include seascape assessment as part of a Landscape Character Assessment of the county to be prepared during the lifetime of the plan;

CP3 To recognise the value of the county's natural coastal defences including estuaries, dunes and sand dunes and ensure their protection;

CP4 To protect the scenic value of the coastal zone from Cheekpoint to Youghal including landward and seaward views and continuous views along the coastline and manage development so it will not detract materially from the visual amenity of the coast;

CP5 To facilitate public access to the coast and development of coastal walkways including recognition of public rights of way;

CP6 To protect the designated shellfish waters in Waterford Harbour and Dungarvan Bay.

The Importance & Future of the Waterford Coast

*A*s an island nation, surrounded by water, we are fortunate in having a dramatic and generally pristine coastal landscape. The Irish coastline has been largely shaped by natural processes and is constantly evolving with time to provide us with superb features that present generations admire and revere. However the coast is subject to constant human influence and to impacts from developments that coastal regions offer for commerce and trade. The Waterford coast is relatively long, indented in places and spectacular and has a range of habitats that are important for a wide variety of species. The importance of these habitats and the species that live in them has been recognised nationally and internationally and our membership of the European Union (EU) obliges us to enact various directives and designations to protect and preserve important habitats and species for which we in Ireland have a special responsibility.

Environmental designations apply to areas or features that have a natural, landscape or cultural significance and these areas are normally either different to or they stand out from the other areas that surround them.

Nationally, responsibility for designated areas lies with the Government (mainly through the National Parks & Wildlife Service of the Department of the Environment, Heritage & Local Government), local responsibility rests with local authorities while the European Union (EU) has responsibility for EU Directives, which apply to all Member States. The EU Habitats Directive (94/43/EEC) was enacted by all Member States and each Member State is obliged to designate Special Areas of Conservation (or SACs) to protect these special habitats and the species occurring therein, which are listed in annexes of the Habitats Directive.

NATIONAL/EUROPEAN DESIGNATIONS

The National Parks & Wildlife Service has designated parts of the Waterford coast for their nature conservation value. This is a statutory requirement under European and national laws as a means by which the best examples of natural and semi-natural habitats and various species of flora and fauna can be protected throughout the EU. There are three main types of nature conservation designations: Natural Heritage Areas, which

Coastal heath west of Ram Head at Ardmore: a priority habitat under Annex I of the EU Habitats Directive

are national designations; Special Areas of Conservation and Special Protection Areas, which are European designations. These designations apply to defined areas, and the reasons for the designations are described in detail, and all the important species found in the designated site are listed. In Waterford there are nine Special Areas of Conservation (SACs), five of which are on or near the coast: Helvick Head SAC, Tramore Dunes and Backstrand SAC, Ardmore Head SAC, Lower river Suir SAC, Blackwater river (Cork/Waterford) SAC. There are six coastal Special Protection Areas (SPAs) in Waterford: Tramore Backstrand SPA, Blackwater Estuary SPA, Dungarvan Harbour SPA, Helvick Head Coast SPA, Helvick Head to Ballyquin SPA and Mid-Waterford Coast SPA.

The EU Habitats Directive and the EU Birds Directive are the legal instruments under which SACs and SPAs are chosen and designated, respectively. Under the National Wildlife Amendment Act (2000), Natural Heritage Areas (NHAs) are legally protected, though only a small number (75) have so far been designated. The majority (630) are proposed NHAs (pNHAs) and have not, as of yet, been statutorily proposed or designated; all the Waterford sites are proposed NHAs (December 2010).

LOCAL PLANS

Waterford County Council has a statutory responsibility for the protection of the natural environment locally. They have enacted various plans, usually following extensive consultations, to fulfil these functions and have commissioned reports on issues relating to its responsibilities. Many of these Plans and reports are available on the County Council website. The important ones in relation to the Waterford coast are:

County Development Plan
The Waterford County Development Plan 2005-2011 was adopted in July 2005 and remained in force until 2011, when it was replaced by the Waterford County Development Plan 2011-2017, following a prolonged and thorough consultation process, as required by the Planning and Development Acts 2000-2007 and Development Plan Guidelines issued by the Department of the Environment, Heritage and Local Government (DoEHLG).

The Development Plan sets out an overall strategy for the proper planning and sustainable development of the county and it includes objectives for the zoning of land, the provision or facilitation of the provision of

---

COASTAL NATURAL HERITAGE AREAS IN COUNTY WATERFORD (AS LISTED IN THE 2011-2017 PLAN)

1693 Ballyvoyle Head to Tramore X4598: 23 kilometres of coast with cliffs and coastal dry heaths. Important for breeding birds including cormorants, choughs, peregrine falcons and guillemots.

0072 Blackwater river & estuary (contains pNHA and cSAC) X0890: Drowned river valley with wet woodland and good floodplain marshes. Good for wintering birds at Kinsalebeg and Youghal.

2116 Creadan Head S7203: Coastal heath in good condition.

664 Dunmore East Cliffs S6900: Large kittiwake (gull) colonies on several cliffs, well studied.

663 Dungarvan Harbour (contains an SPA) X2791: Large estuarine bay, which dries out considerably at low tide giving mudflats. Some marginal salt marshes and sandy beaches but birdlife is the main interest, with major wintering flocks.

infrastructure, conservation and protection of the environment, including natural heritage, and the conservation and protection of European sites and the preservation of the character of the landscape, including the preservation of views and prospects and the amenities of places and features of natural beauty or interest.

The designations for the Waterford coast are specifically listed in the Development Plan and these are essentially brief summaries of the published National Parks & Wildlife Service site synopses. Section 8.19 and 8.21 of the 2011-2017 Plan describes and lists the protected areas in the county:

8.19 SPAs and SACs
The Habitats Directive places an obligation on member states of the European Union to establish an EU-wide network of special conservation sites including Special Protection Areas (SPAs) and Special Areas of Conservation (SACs). This network is known as Natura 2000. SPAs and candidate SACs are designated by the National Parks &

Wildlife Service of the DoEHLG. These sites must be managed to ensure maintenance or restoration of their favourable conservation status. There are nine SACs and six SPAs designated in county Waterford;

8.21 Natural Heritage Areas (NHAs) and Nature Reserves
There are 28 NHAs in Waterford proposed for designation by the National Parks & Wildlife Service under the provisions of the Wildlife (Amendment) Act 2000 in recognition of nationally important habitats, species and sites of geological interest. [The only Nature Reserve in the county is Fenor Bog].

The Planning and Development (Amendment) Act 2010 requires that any proposed draft land use plan must be screened for any potential impacts that may arise on designated Natura 2000 sites. Moreover, planning authorities, when considering an application for a development that is likely to have a significant effect on a SAC/SPA, must ensure that an Appropriate

Coastal heath near Muggort's Bay

COASTAL NATURA 2000 SITES WITHIN COUNTY WATERFORD (AS LISTED IN THE 2011-2017 PLAN)

SACs

002123 Ardmore Head: Dry coastal heath and vegetated sea cliffs.
Conservation Objectives: To maintain the Annex I habitats and Annex II species for which the cSAC has been selected at favourable conservation status. To maintain the extent, species richness and biodiversity of the entire site. To establish effective liaison and co-operation with landowners, legal users and relevant authorities. [A Management Plan has been published for Ardmore Head cSAC]
Threats: Amenity use, residential and other development in adjacent areas, encroachment of scrub.

000072 Blackwater river (Cork/Waterford): Estuary, mudflats, shingle banks, salt meadows, floating river vegetation, old oak woods, alluvial woodland, yew woodland, freshwater pearl mussel, white clawed crayfish, shad, lampreys, salmon, otter, Killarney fern.
Conservation Objectives: To maintain the Annex I habitats and Annex II species for which the cSAC has been selected at favourable conservation status. To maintain the extent, species richness and biodiversity of the entire site. To establish effective liaison and co-operation with landowners, legal users and relevant authorities.
Threats: Professional fishing, taking of flora, fauna, water pollution, climate change, change in species composition, aquaculture, bait digging, aggregate extraction, industrialisation, port/marina, communications networks, water pollution, reclamation of land, coastal protection works, invasion by a species, erosion and accretion, overgrazing, infilling and reclamation, inappropriate grazing levels, clearance for agriculture or felling for timber, increased development. Obstructions, impassable weirs, channel maintenance, barriers, eutrophication, leisure fishing, drift-netting, use of pesticides, fertilisation, removal of hedges and copses, removal of scrub, felling of native or mixed woodland, professional fishing (including lobster pots and fyke nets), hunting, trapping, poisoning, poaching, sand and gravel extraction, mechanical removal of peat, urbanised areas, human habitation, continuous urbanisation, industrial or commercial areas, discharges, disposal of household waste, industrial waste, inert materials, other discharges, routes, autoroutes, bridge, viaduct, water pollution, other forms of pollution, infilling of ditches, dykes, pods, pools, marshes or pits, drainage, management of aquatic and bank vegetation for drainage purposes, removal of sediments, canalisation or modifying structures of inland water course. Collection of samples, outdoor recreation, woodland clearance, overgrazing, hydrocarbons, global warming, climate change, modifications to the hydrology of sites through afforestation, road development or hydro-electric engineering. Air pollution.

0671 Tramore Dunes and Backstrand: Mudflats and sandflats, shingle banks, salt meadows, embryonic, white and fixed dunes.
Conservation Objectives: To maintain the Annex I habitats and Annex II species for which the cSAC has been selected at favourable conservation status. To maintain the extent, species richness and biodiversity of the entire site. To establish effective liaison and co-operation with landowners, legal users and relevant authorities.
Threats: Erosion, walking, horse riding and non-motorised vehicles, trampling, overuse, sea defence or coastal protection works, undergrazing, invasion by a species, camping and caravans, agricultural improvement, stock feeding, overgrazing, paths, tracks, cycle routes, golf courses, restructured agricultural land holding, disposal of household waste, sand and gravel extraction, other pollution or

human activities, aquaculture, professional fishing, bait digging, removal of fauna, aggregate extraction, removal of beach material, industrialisation, port/marina, communication networks, water pollution, reclamation of land.

000665 Helvick Head: Vegetated sea cliffs and dry heath.
Conservation Objectives: To maintain the Annex I habitats and Annex II species for which the cSAC has been selected at favourable conservation status. To maintain the extent, species richness and biodiversity of the entire site. To establish effective liaison and co-operation with landowners, legal users and relevant authorities.
Threats: Agriculture, burning, sand and gravel extraction, urbanisation, industrialisation, acidification, tropospheric ozone and nitrogen enrichment caused by atmospheric deposition.

SPAs

Tramore Backstrand: brent geese, golden plover, grey plover, black-tailed godwit, bar-tailed godwit, lapwing, dunlin, sanderling. Nationally important numbers of shelduck, wigeon, red-breasted merganser, grey plover, golden plover, lapwing, knot, sanderling, dunlin, redshank and turnstone.
Conservation Objectives: To maintain the bird species of special conservation interest for which this SPA has been listed at favourable conservation status.
Threats: Disturbance, water quality, invasive species.

Dungarvan Bay: brent goose, black-tailed godwit, bar-tailed godwit, of international importance.
Conservation Objectives: To maintain the bird species of special conservation interest for which this SPA has been listed at favourable conservation status.
Threats: Disturbance, water pollution, climate change, change in species composition, aquaculture, bait digging, aggregate extraction, industrialisation, port/marina, communications networks, water pollution.

Blackwater Estuary: little egret, golden plover, bar-tailed godwit, Sandwich tern, roseate tern, common tern.
Conservation Objectives: To maintain the bird species of special conservation interest for which this SPA has been listed at favourable conservation status.
Threats: Disturbance, water pollution.

Helvick Head Coast: peregrine, chough, kittiwake and guillemot.
Conservation Objectives: To maintain the bird species of special conservation interest for which this SPA has been listed at favourable conservation status.
Threats: Development, change in agricultural practices, agricultural abandonment, encroachment of scrub, loss of close-sward grazing.

Mid-Waterford Coast: peregrine, chough.
Conservation Objectives: To maintain the bird species of special conservation interest for which this SPA has been listed at favourable conservation status.
Threats: Development, change in agricultural practices, agricultural abandonment, encroachment of scrub, loss of close-sward grazing.

Assessment is undertaken to assess the implications of the development for the conservation status of the site. The 2011-2017 Plan contains such a screening assessment, which includes a description of the Natura 2000 sites in the county and the potential threats they are under (summaries of these sites are also given in Chapter 8 and in Appendix 10 of the Plan).

County geological sites

County geological sites have no statutory protection but are considered within the planning system. The Geological Survey of Ireland established the Irish Geological Heritage (IGH) programme in 1998 with the objective of identifying and selecting sites that best represent the geological heritage of Ireland for designation as Natural Heritage Areas. The IGH identified 37 geological sites of interest in county Waterford. Some of these sites may eventually be designated as Natural Heritage Areas. The various coastal geological sites are listed in the County Development Plan and these are given for both the 2005-2011 Plan and the 2011-2017 Plan. Policy NH27 of the 2011-2017 Plan aims to protect from inappropriate development the scheduled list of geological heritage sites detailed in Appendix A14 of the 2011-2017 Development Plan.

Unesco Geopark

The United Nations Economic Social and Cultural Organisation (UNESCO) has recognised the south coast of the county between Garrarus and Ballyvoyle Head as a Geopark, one of only two in Ireland; it is one of a network of European sites of geological interest with management plans which address economic, social, cultural and sustainability issues. Policy NH28 of the 2011-2017 Plan aims to promote the geological heritage of the Copper Coast Geopark and provide for the sustainable management of this coastal amenity.

Scenic Landscape Evaluation

Appendix 9 in the 2011-2017 Plan (appendix 4 in the 2005-2011 Plan) includes a Scenic Landscape Evaluation and areas within the county are zoned as vulnerable, sensitive, robust, normal and degraded. These categories and the areas they designate are shown on maps accompanying the Plan, and reflect the capacity of the zoned areas to absorb new development as well as the potential of developments to create disproportionate visual impacts.

6.1(b) **Areas Designated as Vulnerable:**
The coastline;
All headlands and promontories;

Salt marsh at Barnawee bridge. An accessible hight tide roost at Dungarvan

The inner harbour kittiwake colony at Dunmore East: a proposed pNHA

All beaches and strands, including headlands and promontories, from Waterford Harbour to East Point.

6.2(b) Areas Designated as Sensitive:
Intertidal flats (at Clohernagh along the northern side of the Backstrand, Dungarvan Harbour ([north] Abbeyside to Kilminnin to Ballynacourty point and [south] Cunnigar point to Ballynagaul) and Kinsalebeg to Ardsallagh. Coastal Lagoons. Tramore Bay. Beaches, dunes and sands. Salt marshes.

Both Development Plans have defined policies in relation to the scenic routes of the county, which are shown on accompanying maps. Scenic routes are defined as public roads from which views and prospects of areas of natural beauty and interest can be enjoyed and it is incumbent on any application for development along these routes to clearly show that there will be no obstruction or degradation of the views towards visually vulnerable features nor significant alterations to the appearance or character of sensitive areas.

6.6(b) Coastal Scenic Routes
5. From Youghal Bridge east along the N25 to Dungarvan;
7. East from Gorteen along third class route via Monamraher to the R674. East to Helvick (Heilbhic) Head, west to N25.

14. From Ballyvoyle Head east on the R675 to the junction with the R677. Continuing south along the R675 to Bunmahon, east via Kilmurrin and Annestown and north-east to Fenor. East onto Tramore and north to Waterford City.

15. South-east from Waterford City on the R683 to Mount Druid. South along the R684 to Belle Lake and east on third class road via Woodstown to Waterford Harbour. North to Passage East along the Harbour, continuing north towards Cheekpoint. South at junction to R683 and west to Waterford City.

A number of amendments to the draft Development Plan 2011-2017 were proposed following public consultation, which were

GEOLOGICAL HERITAGE SITES LISTED IN THE COUNTY DEVELOPMENT PLANS

2005-2011 Plan

County Waterford has a particularly rich geological heritage with a long heritage of mining activity. It is a policy of the Council to protect from damage or inappropriate development, the sites listed: these are recommended for designation by the Geological Survey of Ireland:

1. X17:199773. Ardmore lead mine. An early Irish lead mine probably dating from the seventh-ninth century;

2. X17:195774. Ardmore pier. Sedimentary rocks exposed, marking the Devonian/Carboniferous transition;

3. X28:212803. Ballyquin. Good sequence of the local rock type is exposed on the beach;

4. X49:4598. Ballyvoyle-Tramore coast. Coastal section of complex geology (volcanic and sedimentary);

5. X27:200798. Black Rock. Shale-rich limestones exposed on beach;

6. X49:435984. Knockmahon Bridge. Pillow lavas exposed in roadside outcrops;

7. S50:580008. Lady Doneraile's cove, Tramore. Mixed shales and limestones showing a complex history in the local rocks: the upper rocks are partly fossiliferous;

8. X59:568993. Newtown cove. Rock sequences related to those at Lady Doneraile's cove to the north;

9. X17:162773. Whiting Bay. Rock section exposed on beach includes varied sandstones with ripple marks and limestones, some rich in chert, others in iron;

10. Ardmore-Whiting Bay-Goat Island. Representative section of Devonian-Carboniferous stratigraphy. Link between South Munster Basin and the Carboniferous geological era;

11. X29:218950. Ballynacourty Point-Clonea strand. A selection of Tournaisian crinoids and other shelly fauna;

12. S60:612036. Quillia. An exposure of the Tramore Limestone formation;

13. S70:704078. Raheen-Newtown Head (in Waterford Harbour). Fossil-rich, Ordovician sequence, and Andesitic tuffs, breccias, etc. Caradoc trilobite and brachiopod fossil fauna;

14. Tramore-Ballyvoyle Head (Copper Coast). The whole coast displays a series of geologically important volcanic and sedimentary phenomena illustrating Caledonide development from Island Arc to Active Continental Margin volcanism during the Upper Ordovician. The Duncannon Group Campile Formation succession comprises the products of two volcanic centres, both mainly submarine. Copper minerals and mineworkings occur in several places. Diverse shelly fossil faunas in carbonates of the Tramore Limestone Formation, and graptolite fossils in a black shale horizon.

2011-2017 Plan

1. X17:193780. At Ardmore, a shore platform has been cut across steeply dipping grey Carboniferous sandstones and shales, and perched on it is Saint Declan's Stone, allegedly carried miraculously by waves from Wales, but is in fact a glacial erratic left on the shore: the nearby beach of sub-rounded gravel of varied types is also of glacial origin;

2. X17:170770. Ardmore-Whiting Bay-Goat Island. Link between South Munster Basin and Carboniferous;

3. X17:170765. At Ardoginna a monoclinal fold and synclinal dell are prominent in the cliffs. A deep branching geo has been cut out along faults, near Father O'Donnell's well;

4. X28:252816. Ballymacart river. Incision of river, from road bridge to coast;

5. X19:180950. Ballynacourty. Tournaisian crinoids and other shelly fauna;

6. X27:200790. Ballyquin beach. Behind Ballyquin beach, bluffs cut in glacial drift show slumping caused by seepage, fronted by a shore platform that has been cut across steeply southward-dipping strata fronting grassy bluffs in glacial drift: the platform has been exhumed from the drift, and was originally of Pleistocene age;

7. X28:206806. Ballyquin (north side of Ardmore Bay). Transition to Carboniferous;

8. X39:349950. Ballyvoyle (coastal section). Thinner development of upper part;

9. S61:693137. Cheekpoint to Ballyhack. Gorge. river Suir: one side of channel is rock cut cliff;

10. X39:313935. Clonea strand. Base of Waulsortian;

11. X59:512984. Copper Coast. Rhyolitic intrusions at locations along the coast west of Tramore;

12. X49:456985. Copper Coast. Old Red Sandstone outcrops in the high cliffs backing Ballydowane cove, where the rocks are red and green, and behind the cove is a prominent conical stack of conglomeratic Old Red Sandstone overlain by glacial drift deposits. The Kilfarrasy Volcanics outcrop along a coast of small headlands and coves, some related to transverse faults, and a tall stack juts up from the rocky shore. Behind Knockmahon strand are black mudstones over banded pale grey and buff limestones. The Pipes of Baidhb are a colonnade of pale grey rhyolite columns which rise and fall in the cliffs along the contact with mudstones, and the pebbly beach includes grey-green andesite and pale rhyolites, as well as waste material from mine workings along the cliffs;

13. X49:478988. Copper Coast (Tramore-Stradbally), The whole coast displays a series of geologically important volcanic and sedimentary phenomena illustrating Caledonide development from Island Arc to Active Continental Margin volcanism during the Upper Ordovician. The Duncannon Group Campile Formation succession is the products of two volcanic centres, both mainly submarine;

14. X49:478988. Copper Coast, copper minerals. (Tramore-Stradbally). Brochantite/ Langite, 'Azurite, Malachite' (underground);

15. S71:710030. Dunmore East. Coastal section from Brownstown Head to Templetown;

16. X17:164769. Goat Island cove. Fault/vein mineralisation in basal Carb (beach exposures);

17. S70:703065. Newtown. A complex site with an interglacial (Gortian) exposure overlain by a suite of tills and solifluded deposits. Gortian is only 10 cm thick;

18. S61:612103. Quillia, Tramore. Limestone locality;

19. S70:701070. Raheen shore. Sequence of andesitic tuffs, breccias, etc. and rhyolitic tuffs, agglomerates, perlitic and flow banded lavas, with sediments containing a very fine shelly fauna;

20. S70:701070. Raheen Shore. Caradoc trilobite and brachiopod fauna;

21. X49:429988. Bunmahon. Vein systems, gossans, spectacular secondary copper minerals. Mined extensively in the nineteenth century. Cliff exposures and underground workings. Significant inactive copper mine in quartz veins minor lead and cobalt;

22. X59:568986. Tramore. Caradoc diverse faunas in carbonates;

23. S60:607004. Tramore spit. Sand spit, salt marsh, cobble beach with dunes. The Tramore spit, at the western end narrow, backed by salt marsh, with low dunes fronted by a protective cobble beach, and large boulders had been dumped in a sector where a breach was possible. East of the boulders the spit widens, with high grassy dune hills (Tramore Burrows). The tide falls to expose a wide sandy beach with scattered pebbles, backed by uncut grassy dunes with dark-green marram grass On the point are parallel foredunes and Rinnashark Harbour, the entrance to the tidal marine Backstrand interrupts the beach, with dunes resuming on Bass Point to the east.

Waterford Harbour between Passage East and Cheekpoint: part of the coastal scenic route

then made available for public comment, prior to their adoption in the final Plan. Those in respect of the coast, or protected habitats along the coast include:

The strategic nature of many of the policies and objectives contained in this plan will require an Appropriate Assessment screening to be carried out at individual plan and project level to ensure there is no negative impact on the integrity and conservation objectives of Natura 2000 sites and that the requirements of Articles 6(3) and 6(4) of the EU Habitats Directive are fully satisfied. Support of policies contained in other policy/strategy and guidelines documents shall be subject to AA screening where required, prior to implementation by the local authority.

Sections on the coastal zone are presented in both Development Plans, which are:

2005-2011 Plan
In general, development within the entire

Coastal Zone (i.e between Youghal and Cheekpoint) will be encouraged into the existing settlements, In particular development will be restricted where such development will interfere with views and prospects over the coastline. Development on the seaward side of the Coastal Route will not be permitted where views from the road are obscured or impeded. New development in the coastal zone must be in accordance with the Scenic Landscape Evaluation (see Appendix 4);

2011-2017 Plan
Policy ENV5: Development in areas outside of settlements, along the coast road (from Youghal to Cheekpoint) and in upland areas, will only be considered where such proposals do not have an adverse impact on the landscape and where they satisfy the criteria set out under the settlement strategy policy.

The 2011-2017 Waterford County Development Plan includes a new section on Marine Leisure:

6.15 Marine leisure

Marine recreation relates to leisure activities in and on the sea, inshore and offshore and along the seashore. County Waterford boasts an extensive coastline and is well positioned to further develop its marine leisure product. County Waterford boasts a magnificent coastline from Woodstown in the east to Ardmore in the west of the county. Long sandy beaches at Tramore, Bunmahon, Clonea and Ardmore are key attractions in the county and host a range of activities such as surfing, sea kayaking and kite surfing. Sailing is popular in Dunmore East and Dungarvan and the Copper Coast offers one of the most scenic coastal drives in Ireland with dramatic cliff faces. The Council shall encourage and promote integrated clusters of water-based tourism with associated land-based activities on appropriately zoned land, which would serve to attract local, national and international visitors and further contribute to the economy of the region;

Policy ECD25

To develop the marine leisure sector in a coherent and sustainable manner, including the development of marinas, improvement of quays and slipways and enhanced interpretation and safety.

The 2011-2017 County Development Plan refers to the water quality regulations and the twin objectives (ENV2 and ENV7) of achieving the bathing water standards of the EU Bathing Water Directive, and increasing the number of Blue Flag beaches in the county.

The Strategic Environmental Assessment prepared for the draft Plan 2011-2017 refers to the estuarine and coastal waters (4.4.5), the shellfish growing areas (4.4.6), the bathing waters (4.4.7, which lists the Blue Flag beaches and the years in which awards were achieved) and the Water Framework Directive (4.4.8, which includes a register of protected areas, considered to require greater protection either because they have sensitive habitats or wildlife species, they contain drinking water sources, bathing areas or shellfish growing areas, all of which are listed, or there is a clear need to protect human health). There is also a comprehensive section on coastal flooding (2.3), which outlines the issues and the work done to date, but doesn't indicate what actions will be taken during the lifetime of the Development Plan to address the problem:

2.3 Coastal flooding

The coastline of county Waterford is experiencing both erosion and deposition and some flooding through normal coastal processes and is also at risk in the future from increased storm activity and sea level rise. Parts of the coast in Waterford are low-lying and vulnerable to flooding in the long-term from sea level rise and it is essential that current and future plans and development do not create significant problems in the future. Continued investment needs to be made in research on long-term options for the protection of coastal towns from long-term sea level rise and increased storm activity.

Coastal flooding and coastal erosion are issues with serious economic and social impact. In 2002 the Department of the Marine initiated a National Coastal Protection Strategy Study to review coastal protection generally, examine policy options and set out a basis for effective decision making in regard to resource allocation. Information is being assembled on the current and historic position of the coastline, the nature of the coast, its vulnerability to erosion and flooding and the nature of the hinterland in terms of its economic, heritage and environmental assets.

Walkers near the end of the dunes at Tramore close to Rinnashark channel

The OPW is in the process of producing a national set of maps of areas prone to coastal flooding and erosion. These maps are available in draft form. A strategic level flood risk assessment for the coastline study has been completed and predictive floodplain maps prepared showing both the extreme flood outline representing the 0.1% AEP and the indicative floodplain representing the 0.5% AEP (AEP=Annual Exceedance Probability). *A review of the predictive floodplain maps shows coastal flooding occurring in or near coastal settlements such as, Cheekpoint, Waterford City, Tramore and Dungarvan. A strategic level erosion risk assessment for the coastline has also been completed and predictive erosion maps prepared for the years 2030 and 2050. A review of the erosion risk maps shows that primary erosion risk areas identified included Tramore. In contrast to the assessment of coastal flood risk, the coastal erosion risk assessment along the south coast has indicated that there is generally little risk from erosion in the larger urbanised areas. This is primarily due to the fact that the urbanised coastline is mostly either naturally resilient or protected by man-made defences.*

Tramore Local Area Plan, 2007-2013
The Tramore Local Area Plan sets out an overall development strategy and framework for the proper and sustainable development of Tramore for the period 2007-2013. The purpose of this Plan is to establish physical

development policies for Tramore up to the year 2013 and to identify specific objectives for the achievement of those policies.

A number of sections in the Plan, mainly in Chapter 10, relate to the nearby coast:

10.1 Coastal zone management
The National Development Plan highlights that coastal erosion is a serious threat to public infrastructure, tourist amenities and areas of ecological importance.

The National Plan indicates that a strategic approach will be adopted to addressing these problems in the context of a national coastal protection strategy. The emphasis is on the adoption of environmental friendly approaches to coastal protection. The Council recognises the need for a strategic approach to coastal protection. It is considered that management of the coastal resource in the form of coastal zone management policies and strategies is necessary to ensure that future development does not adversely impact on the coastal area, and that protection measures are undertaken in a structured way that ensure that they are environmentally friendly and do not produce knock-on effects further down the coastline. Research has shown that engineering solutions have not always been successful and management or 'soft' environmental options require an integrated management strategy.

10.1.1 Protection of the Sand Dunes

Tramore possess a varied and attractive landscape with one of the major attractions being the beach and sand dunes. Tramore Dunes and Backstrand lie at the head of Tramore Bay, east of Tramore. This area is designated a proposed Natural Heritage Area (pNHA), a candidate Special Area of Conservation (cSAC) and a Special Protection Area (SPA). The dunes are well developed and contain several habitats as listed on Annex I of the Habitats Directive, including the priority habitat fixed dune with herbaceous vegetation. The Backstrand is an area of some importance for shore birds on the south coast. The site regularly supports internationally important numbers of brent geese and nationally important numbers of golden plover.

The main threats to the Tramore dunes and the Backstrand area are listed as follows:

threats from recreational purposes including horse riding, bike scrambling and casual walkers; proximity to Tramore town leading to high usage and trampling; erosion.

It is the clearly stated aim (p.69) of Waterford County Council to protect the sand dunes in so far as possible, using sand fencing and sand ladders, subject to successful applications for funding for carrying out the necessary work. There are policy objectives outlined in the Plan in relation to the dunes at Tramore:

CZM1

It is the aim of the Council to protect where possible the sand dunes in Tramore and to implement any findings that may arises from the Centre for Marine and Coastal Resources Report (2006);

Policy OP2

Integrate heritage management with the protection and enhancement of Tramore Dunes and Backstrand.

Dungarvan Town Development Plan, 2006-2012

A Development Plan for Dungarvan and its environs was adopted by Dungarvan Town Council in November 2006. There are a number of sections in the Plan, mainly in Chapter 10, in relation to the nearby coast.

10.3 Habitat protection

The Plan clearly recognises the need to protect the diversity of the natural environment, and the need to conserve habitats. Designated areas (pNHAs, cSACs and SPAs) in particular require protection as:

they contain valuable habitats where organisms (some rare) live in a relatively natural state;

Tramore is surrounded by superb coastal facilities, all of which are subject to ongoing change by the sea

there are, in most cases, proposed Natural Heritage Areas and other categories (Special Protection Areas or proposed candidate Special Areas of Conservation), which are or will be protected under national legislation;

development in such areas has the potential to cause major visual change in the landscape.

Full details of these areas and details of the relevant legislation are presented in Appendix C of the Development Plan.

10.3.1 Estuarine habitat protection

The Plan states that Dungarvan Bay is a Special Protection Area (SPA), and is important for over 20,000 wintering waterfowl. The SPA was designated for a range of wildbird species using this area, including the light-bellied brent goose. The SPA designation is below the high water mark and does not take in the salt marshes or the Cunnigar. Both of these are included in a much larger area proposed for designation as a Natural Heritage Area (pNHA). Dungarvan Harbour, including the river Colligan

upstream as far as Ballyneety Bridge is also designated as a Special Protection Area, as well as a proposed Natural Heritage Area. The Colligan river is also important for salmonids. Specific policy objectives are included in the Plan:

OP6
Support the implementation of the Heritage Plan for county Waterford.

OP7
No development shall be permitted which would have an adverse impact on the habitats and species associated with the SPA and the pNHA unless it can be demonstrated to the satisfaction of the Council and the Department of the Environment, Heritage and Local Government that compensatory mitigation is to be undertaken. The Council will fully take into account the advice and recommendations of the Department of the Environment, Heritage and Local Government, both in respect of whether or not to grant permission for a development in the vicinity of the SPA/pNHA and in respect

Crohaun at the southern end of the Comeragh/Monavullagh Mountains as seen from the Gold Coast

of the conditions which are to be attached, if granted.

OP8
The Council shall have regard to any future management plans prepared for the SPA and the pNHA.

OPO3
Prepare an overall habitat map for the Dungarvan Town Plan area to record habitat and biodiversity resources.

10.3.2 Protected species
The Plan recognises that, where new development is proposed, the potential for occurrence of protected species (as set out in the 1976 Wildlife Act, as amended by the 2000 Wildlife Act, the Flora Protection Order 1999, Annex 1 of the Birds Directive 1979 and Annex 2 of the EU Habitats Directive 1992) should be determined and if protected species are found, that the Department of Environment, Heritage and Local Government shall be consulted, though there are no specific policy objectives within the Plan in relation to protected species.

10.4 Coastal zone management
In view of the serious threat that coastal erosion poses to public infrastructure, tourist amenities and areas of ecological importance (as outlined in the The National Development Plan 2000-2006), Dungarvan Town Council recognises the need for a strategic approach to coastal protection. It considers that management of the coastal resource in the form of coastal zone management policies and strategies is necessary to ensure that future development does not adversely impact on the coastal area. The Plan states that coastal erosion is an issue in the vicinity of Pinewood and along the stretch of coast between the Abbey and Lands End. A number of policy objectives are outlined:

OP9
Restrict development in areas zoned 'Coastal Amenity' to provide for and improve coastal and riverside amenity including the conservation of areas of scientific interest, flora and fauna and protected species.

OP10
Assess, on an ongoing basis, the need for additional coastal protection works within the Dungarvan area.

OPO4
Seek funding to implement recommendations of the Coastal Erosion Study undertaken at Lands End.

OPO5
Liaise with Waterford County Council in the preparation of a joint Coastal Zone Management Strategy.

County Waterford Heritage Plan, 2006-2010
This Plan was published in 2006 and it outlines various actions aimed at increasing public awareness of heritage in county Waterford. The 1995 Heritage Act defines heritage under 13 headings, namely monuments, archaeological objects, heritage objects, architectural heritage, flora, fauna, wildlife habitats, landscapes, seascapes, wrecks, geology, heritage gardens and parks, and waterways; the Waterford Heritage Forum added three more headings to the national list: archives, traditional skills and cultural heritage.

Objective 1.1
Establish and publish baseline information on heritage in county Waterford.

1.1.20 Protect the geological sites listed in the County Development Plan and review the list where appropriate.

Oystercatchers over the Cunnigar

Objective 2.3
*Promote heritage in county Waterford's
education sector.*

*2.3.6 Continue the Copper Coast
Geopark education work for schools.*

Aim 4.0
*Promote best practice with regard to our
heritage.*

*4.1.24 Integrate heritage management
with the protection and enhancement of
Tramore Dunes and Backstrand.*

**County Waterford Local Biodiversity
Action Plan, 2008-2013**
A Biodiversity Action Plan for county
Waterford was published in 2008 with the
support of the Heritage Council, following
the establishment of the Biodiversity Working
Group of the county Waterford Heritage
Forum. In relation to biodiversity the Plan
explains in some detail what it is, what
policies and legislation are in place to protect
biodiversity, what is known and documented
about it in county Waterford and what
threats there are. Three specific objectives are
outlined in the Plan, each of which has a
number of actions, identifying further steps
to be taken.

The Waterford coast is
mentioned in the Plan, as follows:

P11
*Coastal heath and sea cliffs of
international importance are found at
Ardmore Head and Helvick Head where
notable seabird colonies also occur. The
Tramore Backstrand and dunes*

*ecosystem is a good example of the
transition from strandline vegetation to
fixed dune habitats;*

*The salt marsh found here is of the lagoon
type, which is the rarest in Ireland. As
well as its significance for internationally-
important numbers of brent geese, this
area supports seven other wetland birds in
nationally-important numbers: golden
plover, grey plover, lapwing, dunlin,
sanderling, black-tailed godwit and
bar-tailed godwit. The intertidal
mudflats and sandflats have an
interesting fauna including molluscs,
lugworms and ragworms, with eelgrass
beds used by feeding wildfowl;*

*Helvick Head SPA has a nationally-
important flock of kittiwakes and a
regionally-important population of
guillemots, as well as breeding chough
and peregrine.*

P14
*The 2003 harbour (common) seal
population assessment found a notable
gap in seal populations on the south coast.
Only one record, with a total of one seal,
was recorded from Waterford, and this
was at Dungarvan. Older records show
this species occurring at Creadan Head,
Dunmore East, Waterford Harbour,
Ardmore and Ballynacourty. Though
no grey seals were recorded for
Waterford during the harbour
seal survey, they have previously
been recorded for almost all of the
county's coastline and the Irish Whale and
Dolphin Group have recorded groups of
this species including during 2007.*

All Irish coastal waters within the economic exclusive zone (out to the 200-mile limit) were declared a sanctuary for whales and dolphins in 1991. Whales and dolphins are regularly seen off the Waterford coast, and sometimes are found stranded on the shoreline. At least fourteen species are known to occur in the area, including Bottle-nosed and Common Dolphins, and Minke, Fin and Humpback Whale. All whales and dolphins are protected.

The Actions in the Plan are designed to identify and address information gaps, increase understanding and raise awareness of biodiversity issues and maintain and enhance biodiversity through management.

Objective 2
Raising awareness:
These actions are designed to raise awareness of what biodiversity is and why it is important, particularly in critical sectors.

Action 2.6
Install information signage for special habitats at access points e.g. Ardmore Head, Tramore and other appropriate locations.

Objective 3
Maintaining biodiversity:
These are priority actions for active management of critical biodiversity features of the county.

Action 3.1
Introduce measures to protect and enhance coastal biodiversity as part of Integrated Coastal Zone Management at Tramore (Action 4.1.24 of the Heritage Plan).

Appendix 1 of the Plan lists the nature conservation areas in county Waterford (these

are brief summaries of cSACs, SPAs and pNHAs site synopses).

Waterford County Council Wind Energy Strategy
Future energy requirements are a pressing concern for governments and their agencies. Waterford County Council have committed to the promotion and facilitation of the use of wind energy in the county and have published a wind energy strategy to advance these aims, in response to both national and EU policies with regard to renewable energies, which have defined renewable energy targets.

The wind energy map for Waterford and related policies was adopted as a variation to the 2005-2011 Waterford County Development Plan on the 18th of December 2007 and was enshrined in the new Plan 2011-2017, with minor amendments, which included a requirement for screening for Appropriate Assessment to ensure that there would be no negative impact on the integrity of any Natura 2000 site located at or adjacent to a proposed site for wind energy development and that the requirements of Articles 6(3) and 6(4) of the EU Habitats Directive 92/43/EEC would be fully satisfied.

A wind energy map was also published and is to be used in the assessment of all wind energy applications in county Waterford. The county has been categorized into four classes

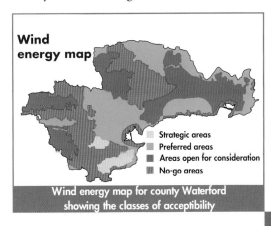

Wind energy map

Strategic areas
Preferred areas
Areas open for consideration
No-go areas

Wind energy map for county Waterford showing the classes of acceptibility and these are shown on the wind energy map. The classes are:

Strategic areas (yellow)
These key areas are deemed eminently suitable for wind farm development and should be reserved for such purposes.

Preferred areas (blue)
These areas are suitable for wind farm development and should normally be granted planning permission unless specific local planning circumstances would support a decision to refuse permission in the context of the development plan.

Areas open for consideration (green)
Applications for planning permission will be treated on their merits with the developer having a clear responsibility to demonstrate as to why the development should be granted permission.

No-go areas (red)
These are areas that are particularly unsuitable for wind farm development. While these areas are considered primarily unsuitable for wind farm development, there may be pockets of land within these 'no-go areas' which, due to specific criteria such as significantly high wind speeds, distance from populated areas and screening by natural topography from scenic views and prospects, may be considered for wind farm developments subject to applicants providing appropriate submissions including wire frame analysis, zones of visual influence and digital terrain models.

The strategic areas are mainly in the west of the county and on the Drum Hills, within sight of the coast. The 'no-go' areas include most of the coastal strip. However parts of the coast are included in areas that are open to consideration for wind energy developments (these areas are Muggort's Bay to south of Mine Head in the west of the county and from Coolum cove to near Passage East in the east).

Integrated Rural Tourism and Recreational Complexes and associated Residential Developments

Waterford County Council is tasked with promoting and enhancing the tourism potential of the county and have enshrined policy statements in the County Development Plan to this effect:

Policy ECD21
It is the policy of the Council to facilitate the expansion of tourist activities in appropriate locations where they can be supported by, and provide support for, existing communities. In all cases, development will be required to comply with key sustainable tourism principles and the development management standards as set out in Chapter 10.

Proposals to develop low-density residential developments for permanent accommodation or holiday home use removed from designated settlement centres were previously contrary to the policies of the 2005-2011 County Development Plan as set out in Chapter 3 (Settlement Strategy), Chapter 6 (Economic Development) and Chapter 9 (Development Standards). However it was considered that the development of golf courses, hotels, race courses and other tourist developments and leisure facilities located in rural unzoned areas, which provide an important amenity, may form the basis for justifying limited on-site residential development. Hence the Integrated Rural Tourism and Recreational Complexes (IRTRC) policy was adopted on the 18th of December 2007 as a variation to the 2005-2011 Waterford County Development Plan. The process of drafting the new Development Plan 2011-2017 began in 2009

Ballyquin beach

and 112 pre-draft submissions were received, six of which suggested that the IRTRC policy be amended or abolished and one suggested that it be retained. The County Manager, having considered all the submissions, made recommendations on policies to be included in the draft plan, one of which, in respect of tourism (5.7.3), was:

> *to retain the IRTRC policy as per the County Development Plan.*

The draft Plan, when published, retained the IRTRC policy and there were no changes to the various criteria by which developments proposed under it would be considered. Further public submissions were invited on the draft Plan and the Manager's Report for the draft County Development Plan 2011-2017 listed all the issues raised during the public consultation period and his recommendations in respect of each submission received. It was decided to retain the IRTRC policy but with a number of amendments and the policy is now included in the new Development Plan 2011-2017.

IRTRC developments have to comply with certain criteria, some of which relate to the coast, the countryside or sites of nature conservation value. These criteria require that IRTRC developments:

> *must comply with the Scenic Landscape Evaluation and coastal development and landscape policies;*

> *will not have a significant adverse affect on the character or appearance of the county's countryside and will generally retain the open nature of the land;*

> *will not have a significant adverse impact on sites of nature conservation value.*

One substantial development earmarked for the Waterford coast and in part of the Mid-Waterford Coast SPA was assessed under the IRTRC policy variation of the 2005-2011 Plan. The development was endorsed by Waterford County Council but emphatically rejected by an Bord Pleanála on appeal. An amendment was proposed to the 2011-2017 Plan, to take account of the An Bord Pleanála decision and submissions received during the consultation process for the new Development Plan 2011-2017:

> *screening for Appropriate Assessment will be carried out where required to ensure that there is no negative impact on the integrity (defined by the structure and function and conservation objectives) of any Natura 2000 site located at or adjacent to a proposed site for an IRTRC*

The Anne valley north of Annestown: will it eventually be lost to the sea?

development and that the requirements of Articles 6 (3) and (4) of the EU Habitats Directive 92/43/EEC are fully satisfied.

A further amendment was proposed for the 2011-2017 Plan, which may restrict areas along the coast where IRTRC developments might be proposed:

there shall be a general presumption against development on the seaward side of the nearest road to the coastline except in designated settlements as set out in the Plan or in exceptional circumstances where the Planning Authority is satisfied that the proposed development shall not have a significant adverse effect on the surrounding landscape and amenity of the area. There shall also be a presumption against development on/or adjacent to areas protected under the Habitats Directive and Natural Heritage Areas.

Summary: It is clear from the plethora of directives, legislation, policies and actions, that the Waterford coast is of some considerable importance for the variety of habitats and species that occur there, and that there is a genuine commitment to maintain and enhance the pristine coastal environment that we have in Waterford, notwithstanding the considerable development pressure that

prevails in coastal areas, and despite the occasional lapse. However, there are conflicting demands on regulatory authorities and Waterford County Council, with its wide remit of responsibilities, is no exception. Moreover, not all of the policies and objectives it adopts (and enshrines in successive County Development Plans) are compatible with nature conservation and the protection and enhancement of the designated sites. It is incumbent on us all, therefore, to be vigilant and then proactive in maintaining the integrity of the coastal areas we know and love so well.

THE FUTURE

What does the future hold for the Waterford coast? Over the millennia the coast of county Waterford has been subject to all sorts of changes, big and small, natural and man-made. Natural changes are brought about by geological activity and weather, which we can do very little about, and man-made changes include the necessary sea defence works required to consolidate existing coastal facilities and structures. Ongoing sea-level rise and increased storm surges will require that these works must continue, perhaps on a scale not seen up to now, and someone at some stage in the future may be faced with the dilemma of continuing these expensive works or abandoning them in the face of the relentless rise of the sea that may swamp parts of the coastline. The sea will inevitably win the battle in the low-lying and less developed areas, which may include the dunes and salt marshes, though the loss of these natural elements of the coastal zone will have consequences for some coastal habitats, many of which are designated sites, and the species that live in them. Their loss will also increase the pressure on adjoining areas also subject to continuing sea level rise. Climate change will have an impact on the species that live in the coastal zone, both on and offshore; some species, unable to withstand drier summers, will be lost but new species will arrive, especially offshore as warm-water species migrate northwards. Nature will adapt quickly and new habitats that are created will be readily colonised by coastal species availing of new opportunities presented by the impact of climate change. People too will adapt as the long time scale over which these changes are likely to occur will outstrip peoples' memory of existing species and habitats.

Carbon dioxide levels in the atmosphere have been increasing since the beginning of the industrial revolution and it is estimated that levels in the atmosphere are now 30% higher than previously; around a third of atmospheric carbon dioxide has been absorbed by the oceans, which have become more acid as a result (by around 30% since the industrial revolution) and the process is ongoing at a rate never previously recorded in the earths' history. Moreover it has been projected that the acidity of seawater will increase irreversibly by a further 120% by 2100. The ramifications of these changes in coastal chemistry are difficult to predict but increasing acidity will impact severely on marine organisms that form shells (e.g. corals, cockles, mussels, oysters, clams, star fish, sea urchins) and could, in extreme circumstances, lead to mass extinctions of certain organisms. Other indirect effects are also likely, which

may be compounded by climate change and the marine ecosystem around our coasts may change irrevocably with direct impacts on shellfish production and the life cycles of many fish species, for which Irish waters–the Celtic Sea, for example–are critically important (especially for certain migratory pelagic species). While the changes arising from increasing ocean acidity are unlikely to be noticed by a casual walker on any of the Waterford beaches, nevertheless, the marine waters off the Waterford coast will change and may be less productive, with fewer species and socio-economic consequences for coastal communities in the county.

So far the Waterford coast has been spared large complexes outside of the existing settlements but there are ongoing demands for these developments, which come in many forms, such as tourist and recreational facilities. These may become more attractive in warmer summers, and as people elsewhere on the planet flock to our coasts to avoid unbearable temperatures in their own countries. Maintaining the pristine coastal environment of county Waterford, the protected habitats and the species that live there, while at the same time promoting tourism, which often requires an extensive infrastructure close to the resource is an onerous responsibility, and one that is not easily resolved. Clearly, hard decisions will have to be made to avoid conflicts.

There may also be a proliferation of structures associated with oil and gas exploration offshore, and, increasingly into the future, wind farms. An oil field was discovered at around 80 metres depth some 40 kilometres off the Waterford coast in 1983. A minimal facilities unmanned buoy development was proposed in May 2010 to assess the development feasibility of this highly productive Helvick Head oil field, using modern technology instead of the more expensive manned platforms. It remains to be seen what the outcome of these, and future feasibility developments will be, where the extracted oil and gas will be landed and processed and what the impacts, if any, will be for the Waterford coast.

The quest for alternative energy sources may involve the marine areas around our coasts and the scale of the renewable energy facilities necessary to harness the power of the wind and the waves and on a scale necessary to satisfy future energy needs will surely have a significant visual impact on the coast. Developments undertaken to harness wind energy onshore are visually dominant, regardless of mitigation efforts, and the visual integrity of coasts close to areas earmarked for wind energy developments (e.g. the Drum Hills area of west Waterford), will be compromised by the imposition of dominant visual structures. Offshore facilities are more difficult to hide, particularly when they have to be constructed close to the coastline for ease of harnessing the energy produced.

There have been numerous requests over the years for the replacement of the existing Foreshore Act and Coastal Protection Act with a single act, which would consolidate all aspects relating to the coastal zone and its management. The primary emphasis of the new act and the new agency implementing it, would be the management of the national coastal resource through the formulation and implementation—in association with the local authorities—of Coastal Zone Management Plans for each coastal county. The new agency would be responsible for regulation of development in the coastal zone and policies

would be proactive rather than reactive, as is the case currently. However successive governments have not implemented these long-standing recommendations and control of the coastal zone remains with the local authorities, with all the competing demands on them for their limited and diminishing resources. Local authorities rarely gather the long-term data required to underpin critical decisions and the formulation of management plans in their coastal areas; rather they respond to emergencies as they arise, and these invariably relate to coastal protection after severe storms wreak havoc on the coast. Usually there isn't any long-term vision or plan for the coastal zone, but the changes that are inevitable as a consequence of climate change and all the perturbations that will occur in the coastal zone as sea level rises will require more focussed and management-led discussions and eventual decisions based on sound research and quality data collection, which, unfortunately, isn't currently a priority. Integrated coastal zone management has been discussed at length in recent years in Ireland but there has been little progress in advancing the concept beyond discussions by various committees and the production of costly reports.

Conclusion
Change is on the way; of that there is no doubt. The real issue is how we, and future generations, will adapt and manage this change and still maintain the beauty, landscape integrity and scenic character of the Waterford coast. In the meantime, the Waterford coast is there to enjoy so get out there and do so while you can.

Brent geese foraging on the tideline at Tramore Backstrand

Useful Information

WEATHER & CLOTHING

Weather is rarely an issue in coastal areas, where the mild oceanic climate ensures that conditions are usually favourable. The only weather conditions to be aware of are strong winds and gusts, which may create very turbulent seas and catch out the unwary. Weather updates are available on www.met.ie or on local radio station websites. Use clothing that is suitable for the prevailing conditions, and a good rucksack is great for storing wind cheaters and extra layers when necessary. Windproof clothing (jumpers, fleece jackets, gore-tex raincoats or similar) is an essential requirement when strong winds whip in off the sea. Tracksuit bottoms are ideal for walking along the coast and allow much freer movement than jeans, which are very uncomfortable if they get wet. Any type of shoe is acceptable for walking on the beaches but for cliff walking or rambling over rocky shores, good leather boots with vibram soles (or equivalent) are essential for both comfort and safety, though they are usually expensive. Wellington boots are fine for the wetland areas of the coast but they can be very dangerous on wet rocks.

EQUIPMENT

Coastal areas can be quite hot in summer so bottles of clean water should always be carried to quench the thirst. Some food (sandwiches, chocolate, fruit) is essential during long coastal walks, and while food is usually available in any of the coastal villages nearby, what better way to relax and enjoy the surroundings than by eating lunch on a beach or coastal rock in warm weather.

Binoculars are useful on the coast, where there is always something to see and they are essential for watching wildlife. Usually 7 to 10 (the magnification factor) by 40 or 50 (the diameter of the front lens in millimetres) are used but bigger figures mean heavier binoculars, which may be awkward to carry and also difficult to hold steady in coastal breezes, despite the good magnification they provide. The better quality binoculars are more expensive but are often worth it for the crisper images they offer and there is less eye strain after prolonged use.

Telescopes are more specialised and magnification powers of 15 to 60 with a big lens diameter of 60 or 70 millimetres are available, though a tripod is essential to keep the telescope steady, regardless of magnification power. The combination is also much heavier than binoculars so be prepared for tiredness after lugging one around for a while, but they are essential for any type of serious wildlife watching or counts of species.

A notebook is useful for sketching, recording counts or just noting details of species seen. Pens and pencils are needed too.

Handheld GPS (Global Positioning System) devices are now commonplace, cheap and light and are essential for the more serious recorder. They allow accurate grid references to within 10 metres or less to be

Shore angling at Kilfarrasy beach

obtained, if required, without having to fumble with a map. Some models have high sensitivity receivers and are less likely to lose the satellite signal. Make sure you are familiar with all the functions of the unit and spare batteries are as essential as the unit itself.

Mobile phones are a standard personal item and some even have maps included (though these are usually expensive). Make sure the unit is fully charged before going out but be aware that the mobile phone signal is usually poor or even unavailable along many parts of the Waterford coast, and especially the beaches.

SAFETY

Many of the cliffs along the Waterford coast are high, loose, friable and dangerous. The base of cliffs can be treacherous at any time if covered with slime or seaweeds but they are especially so when wet so do take care when scrambling over coastal rocks. There are very few safe cliff walks and where there are, they may be dangerously close to the edge in places, so great care is required when walking along cliff tops, and particularly in windy or wet conditions (which are inappropriate anyway, as very little can be seen).

A knowledge of tide times is particularly important for anyone walking over the

NOTICE RE LIFEGUARDS

The following code applies to the flying of flags by lifeguards

RED BAND OVER YELLOW	LIFEGUARD ON DUTY
RED FLAG	DANGER BATHING UNSAFE
NO FLAG FLYING	NO LIFEGUARD ON DUTY

The flag codes on beaches in summer

coastal wetlands or walking along the base of cliffs, because of the danger of being cut-off by an incoming tide, especially during spring tides which fill rapidly. Therefore it is absolutely critical to know the tide times; these are given in the daily national newspapers and tide tables are available locally.

Almost all of the coastal beaches are very safe for swimming provided the usual precautions are adhered to: don't swim after a heavy meal or with drink taken and never swim alone; keep close to the shore and be careful of incoming waves. Lifeguards are on duty in the summer months at only some of the Waterford beaches (Dunmore East, Tramore, Bunmahon, Clonea, Ardmore) and it is advisable to obey their instructions (remember a red flag means that prevailing conditions are not suitable for swimming). It might be best to seek advice if swimming off any of the other beaches, and, if in doubt, don't swim at all. At some beaches (Saleen and Kilmurrin, for example), Waterford County Council have erected notices warning of strong currents. It is best to take heed of the signs and not to swim in these areas.

Be extra careful if swimming in deep water or at the deep water swimming coves (such as those at Newtown cove and the Guillamene, on the west side of Tramore Bay).

Jet skis are noisy and fast and they usually disturb the birds and the tranquility of coastal areas

Sailing out of Dungarvan Harbour

Boating in any of the coastal areas can be an enjoyable experience, particularly in calm weather in summer. However it is important to observe routine safety precautions when venturing out into what might become hazardous and unsafe sea conditions. Life jackets are essential but are useless unless worn; the weather forecast should always be obtained; and inform someone on land of the activity planned, the route to be taken and the expected time of return.

Surfing and allied activities are increasingly popular. Make sure you are aware of local conditions and it is usually best to contact the local surf centre or local surfers for advice on prevailing conditions. Tramore is the most popular area for surfing and there are several surf schools near the beach. Sailing is an important leisure activity in summer and is concentrated at Dunmore East and Dungarvan, though Tramore and Ardmore also offer more limited possibilities for smaller boats.

There are lifeboat stations at Dunmore East and Helvick Head and smaller inshore lifeboats at Tramore and Boatstrand. The Tramore Cliff Rescue team can be contacted by ringing 999 or 112 or through Tramore Gardaí at 051381333.

GUILLAMENE
SWIMMING COVE
MEN ONLY

THE "MEN ONLY" SIGN
HAS BEEN DISPLAYED
IN THE GUILLAMENE
FOR MANY YEARS
AND IS RETAINED MERELY AS
A RELIC OF TIMES PAST

The Guillamene is on the west side of Tramore Bay

ANIMAL WELFARE

Exhausted, oiled or injured seabirds are regularly seen alive along the coastal beaches. Badly injured birds have little or no chance of survival and are best put down humanely. Exhausted birds may appear after storms and should be kept in a warm place in a darkened box and given some food and water (which they may not take). They may revive after a few hours and should be released, preferably where they were found, and in the evening, to avoid them having to contend with marauding gulls. Efforts can be made to rehabilitate oiled birds by using detergent-soaked sponges on the affected feathers; the survival of the birds after release depends to some extent on the degree of oiling. Oiled birds tend to preen their contaminated plumage and oil may be toxic if ingested. Gulls are prone to botulism, especially in summer, though less so now that the dumps at Waterford City, Tramore and Dungarvan are closed. These contaminated birds may be moribund and easily captured but be careful and only handle birds using rubber gloves, as botulism is easily transferred to humans and always wash your hands after handling birds, alive or dead. Bird carcasses should be disposed of by burial where found. Local vets or

315

the ISPCA will advise on the merits of treating injured or oiled birds.

Cetaceans are regularly washed up on the Waterford coast and there are occasional live strandings. Porpoises, dolphins and seals are more frequent than whales and their rotting carcases soon disappear from the beaches. However, the bigger whales are more of a problem when they appear, and Waterford County Council usually bury them if on accessible beaches. They also attract huge numbers of people. Live strandings also draw people, many of whom are genuinely concerned for the welfare of the distressed animals. However, any marine mammal is very difficult to handle on land and is best left to the experts. Ring the local Wildlife Ranger (or the Gardaí who will contact the Ranger), to mobilise a trained team. Keeping the mammal moist is the best that anyone can do while awaiting help but

be very careful as a beached mammal, while outwardly appearing calm and placid, may be distressed and can very easily become agitated putting those around it at risk. The Irish Whale and Dolphin Group coordinate movements of cetaceans around our shores and they welcome observations, which can be entered online on their very informative website (www.iwdg.ie).

Seals are occasionally seen on beaches, and these are usually pups that become separated from their mother who may be just offshore. Pups are best left alone if they look healthy as the cow may abandon the young seal if there is too much human disturbance. Do not force the seal back into the water and if the animal looks injured or diseased it may have to be rescued. However seals can be quite aggressive and may also give quite a nasty bite which can cause disease. If you are not prepared to attempt a rescue contact the Irish Seal Sanctuary, based in Courtown Harbour, Gorey, Co. Wexford (053 9424980), who will be able to offer advice on stranded seals and how best to handle them safely.

The 1976 Wildlife Act is the legislative instrument protecting native wildlife. Any suspected breaches should be reported to the Wildlife Conservation Ranger for Waterford at 0878541961 or the local Gardaí at Tramore or Dungarvan. Avoid unnecessary disturbance to wintering or breeding birds, replace stones or debris if searching for insects and do not gather wild flowers. Instead take photographs of any species of bird, animal or flower, which will last longer than the species themselves.

Maps
The 1:50,000 Ordnance Survey maps (Discovery Series) for the county are recommended, and are much more

Be careful on cliff tops, which are liable to collapse at any time, as here near Coolabeg, Ardmore in 2010

informative than the old one inch and six inch Ordnance Survey maps, which should be available for consultation in the local libraries along with Sites and Monuments Record maps. The Ordnance Survey of Ireland produced their first metric map in 1988 using digital methods at a scale of 2 centimetres to one kilometre or 1:50,000, with each map covering an area of 40 km x 30 km. Three 1:50,000 maps are needed to cover the Waterford coast: sheets 76, 81 and 82 (sheet 75 encompasses a small area around Tramore, also covered by 76). Other maps are also available from the Ordnance Survey Office, Phoenix Park, Dublin, which might be appropriate for specialised survey work. Many of these maps can be purchased online, in digital form if required, from www.osi.ie.

ACCESS
Generally there are no restrictions on walking along the Waterford beaches but most of the land around the beaches is privately owned and permission may be needed if crossing the clifftops or passing through coastal fields.

You are reminded of the following:
Be especially careful when around walls,

REMOVAL OF BEACH MATERIAL PROHIBITED
Please do not remove sand or shingle from beaches

fences and gates (which should always be closed if opened). If a stone wall or a fence is accidently damaged then it should be repaired immediately. The goodwill of coastal landowners is important so please do nothing that will antagonise local people. There are strict bye-laws governing dogs on beaches in summer. Dog fouling is the main issue, which can be a health hazard for other beach users so to avoid a hefty fine, obey the beach bye-laws and leave the dog at home, but never leave the dog in a car in stiffling weather. The other bye-laws, which are usually posted near the beach entrance, should also be obeyed. Make sure you bring litter home. The best advice for fires is not to light them as, in dry weather and particularly near dunes, large areas may be torched when a fire goes out of control. Moreover, when the fire is quenched, an unsightly mess remains which isn't pleasant for other beach users.

ACCOMMODATION
Fáilte Ireland is the national body that promotes Ireland as a high quality tourist destination. The regional Fáilte Ireland tourist information office is based in Waterford City (051 875823), and is open all year round. Other offices open in summer

Newtown cove on the west side of Tramore Bay

are: Ardmore (024 94444), Dungarvan (058 41741) and Tramore (051 381572). All the tourist offices maintain an up-to-date database of B & Bs and guesthouses and will offer advice and documentation on what is available locally.

FURTHER READING
Books on flora, fauna & geology
The Flora of County Waterford.
P. R. Green, National Botanic Gardens, Dublin, 2008.

The Botanist in Ireland.
R. L. Praeger, Hodges Figgis, Dublin, 1934.

Exploring Irish Mammals. T. Hayden, R. Harrington, Town & Country House, Dublin, 2000.

The Handbook of British Mammals.
G. B. Corbet, S. Harris, Blackwell, London, 1991.

The Lichens of Great Britain and Ireland.
C. W. Smith, A. Aptroot, B. J. Coppins, A. Fletcher, O. L. Gilbert, P. W. James, Richmond Publishing Co. Ltd, 2009.

Mosses and Liverworts of Britain and Ireland, a Field Guide. I. Atherton, S. Bosanquet, M. Lawley, British Bryological Society, 2010.

Grasses, Ferns, Mosses & Lichens of Britain and Ireland. R. Philips, Pan Books, 1980.

Mushrooms–a comprehensive guide. R. Philips, Macmillan, London, 2006.

New Atlas of the British and Irish Flora. C. D. Preston, D. A. Pearman, T. D. Dines, Oxford University Press, Oxford, 2002.

An Irish Flora. D. A. Webb, Dundalgan Press Ltd., Dundalk, 1967.

Collins Flower Guide. D. Streeter, C. Hart-Davies, A. Hardcastle, HarperCollins Publishers, London, 2010.

New Flora of the British Isles. C. Stace, Cambridge University Press, 2010.

The Wild Flowers of the British Isles. I. Gerard, D. Streeter, Midsummer Books, London, 1998.

The Butterflies of Great Britain and Ireland. A. Maitland Emmet, J. Heath, Harley Books, Colchester, 1990.

The Millenium Atlas of Butterflies in Britain and Ireland. J. Asher, M. Warren. R. Fox, P. Harding, G. Jeffcoate, S. Jeffcoate, Oxford University Press, Oxford, 2001.

The Orchids of Ireland. T. Curtis, R. Thompson. National Museums Northern Ireland, 2009.

The Dragonflies of Great Britain and Ireland. C. O. Hammond, Harley Books, Colchester, 1985.

The Natural History of Ireland's Dragonflies. B. Nelson, R. Thompson, Ulster Museum, Belfast, 2004.

The Butterflies and Moths of Northern Ireland. R. Thompson, B. Nelson, Ulster Museum, Belfast, 2006.

Colour Identification Guide to Moths of the British Isles. B. Skinner, Harley Books, 2009.

The Atlas of Breeding Birds in Britain and Ireland. J. T. R. Sharrock, Poyser, Calton, 1976.

A robber fly

Flora of County Waterford

Paul Green

A Field Guide to the Moths of Great Britain and Europe. P. Waring, M. Townsend, R. Lewington, British Wildlife Publishing, 2009.

A Field Guide to the Birds of Britain and Europe. R. Peterson, G. Mountford, P. A. D. Hollom, HarperCollins, 1993.

The Atlas of Wintering Birds in Britain and Ireland. P. Lack, Poyser, Calton, 1986.

The New Atlas of Breeding Birds in Britain and Ireland: 1988-1991. D. W. Gibbons, J. B. Reid, R. A. Chapman, Poyser, 1993.

Bird Guide. K. Mullarney, L. Svensson, D. Zwetterstrom, P. J. Grant, HarperCollins Publishers, London, 1999.

A Beginners Guide to Ireland's Seashore. H. Challinor, S. Murphy Wickens, J. Clark, A. Murphy, Sherkin Island Marine Station, Cork, 1999.

Sea Shore of Britain & Northern Europe. P. Hayward, T. Nelson-Smith, C. Shields, HarperCollins Publishers, London, 1996.

Handbook of the Marine Fauna of North-West Europe. P. J. Hayward, J. S. Ryland, Oxford University Press, Oxford, 1995.

Environmentally Friendly Coastal Protection (ECOPRO), Code of Practice. Government Publications, Dublin, 1996.

Local books, papers & journals
By Cliff and Shore, Walking the Waterford Coast. Michael Fewer, Anna Livia Press, 1992.

Report on the Flora of the Wexford and Waterford coasts. H. C. Hart, *Scientific Proceedings of the Royal Dublin Society,* Vol. IV (N.S.), Part 3, 117-146, 1883.

Zostera in Co. Waterford. M. J. P Scannell, I. K. Ferguson, *Irish Naturalists' Journal,* 16 (6): 176-177, 1969.

Polygonum maritimum L. New to Ireland. I. K. Ferguson, L.F. Ferguson, *Irish Naturalists' Journal,* 18 (3): 95, 1974.

The Plume Moth *Marasmarcha lunaedactyla* (Haworth), new to Ireland, in Cos. Waterford and Wexford. K. G. M. Bond, *Irish Naturalists' Journal,* 26 (3/4): 128, 1998.

The Birds of Ireland. R. J. Ussher, R. Warren, Gurney & Jackson, London, 1900.

Waterford Bird Report, 1976-1986. P. M. Walsh, D. McGrath, City of Waterford Vocational Educational Committee, Waterford, 1988.

Where to Watch Birds in Waterford. D. McGrath, P. M. Walsh, Irish Wildbird Conservancy, Waterford, 1990.

The Lepidoptera of Waterford City & County. M. O'Meara, Waterford, *2000.*

A Bibliography of the Flora & Fauna of County Waterford. M. O'Meara, Waterford, 2001.

The Dragonflies of Waterford City & County. M. O'Meara, Waterford, 2001.

The Spiders of County Waterford. M. O'Meara, Waterford, 2002.

A Revised List of the Birds of Waterford. M. O'Mcara, Watcrford, 2002.

The Woodlice of Waterford City & County. M. O'Meara, Waterford, 2002.

The Beetles of Waterford City & County. M. O'Meara, Waterford, 2008.

The Amphibians, Reptiles & Mammals of Waterford City & County. M. O'Meara, Waterford, 2001.

The Snails & Slugs of Waterford. M. O'Meara, Waterford, 2008.

The Mayflies of Waterford. M. O'Meara, Waterford, 2008.

South-east county Waterford and south Tipperary: Ordovician Volcanics and Sedimentary Rocks and Silurian Turbidites. C. J. Stillman in: *The Caledonian & Pre-Caledonian Rocks of South-east Ireland, Geological Survey of Ireland.* Guide Series No. 2, 41-60, Dublin, 1978.

Geology of South Wexford. D. Tietzsch-Tyler, A. G. Sleeman, Geological Survey of Ireland, Dublin, 1994.

The Copper Coast. J. H. Morris. Geological Survey of Ireland, "Landscapes from Stone" Series, 1999.

Other
Archaeological Inventory of County Waterford. M. Moore, Dúchas, The Heritage Service, Dublin, 1999.

Log-Ainmneacha na nDéise. The Place-Names of Decies. Rev. P. Canon Power, Cork University Press, 1952.

Liostaí Logainmneacha Contae Phort Láirge. Stationary Office, Dublin, 1991.

Logainmneacha as Paróiste na Rinne Co. Phort Láirge. An Cumann Logainmneacha, Baile Átha Cliath, 1975.

Water Quality Management Plan for the Suir Barrow Nore Estuary. Carlow, Kilkenny, Tipperary SR, Waterford, Wexford County Councils & Waterford Corporation, 1990.

Waterford County Development Plans, 2005-2011 & 2011-2017. Waterford County Council, Waterford.

An Illustrated Guide to Tramore and its Neighbourhood. Naughten 1901.

A Guide to Tramore and its Neighbourhood. E. Downey 1919.

An Linn Bhuí, Iris Ghaeltacht na nDéise. Uimhir 4. Pádraig Ó Macháin, Aoibheann Nic Dhonnchadha, 2000.

The mine buildings at Tankardstown, on the Copper Coast

Placenames of the Waterford Coast

*C*anon Power's *The Place-Names of Decies*, supplemented by *Liostaí Logainmneacha Phort Láirge* are invaluable sources of placenames for county Waterford. However, relatively few of the placenames presented here can be associated with cliffs or features along the coast. Canon Power, in listing the subdenominations, usually presents the placenames from east to west along the coast (though west to east is used occasionally). Generally the placenames are listed from east to west here or follows the sequence used by Canon Power. However some names may not be in the correct order as their precise location isn't known. Likewise for Helvick Head, where some placenames in the text are taken from *Logainmneacha as Paróiste na Rinne, Co. Phort Láirge*, which maps all known placenames from the towlands in the parish of Ring, though cliff and coastal names are not as accurately delineated. It is likely that some of the placenames associated with coastal features are lost forever. For example, R. J. Ussher, in his notes, refers to File na Gower (*Faill na nGabhar* – "Cliff of the Goats"?) and Quosh an Imme (*Cuas an Ime* – "Butter Cove"?) between Mine Head and Ballycurreen, File na Moint (*Faill na Móint* ?), File na Dreameragh (*Faill na Dreameragh*?) at Glencorran, Splaincannoor (*Splainc an Úr*?) at Ballycurreen, Cooneen Tawn (*An Cuanín Táin?*) at Stradbally and *An Poll Dubh* at Island. None of these particular placenames are listed in *The Place-Names of Decies* for these areas, though Ussher may have mis-spelled or mis-interpreted what he heard. Placenames are presented as the townland name (in small capitals) followed by the subdenominations, their Irish equivalent where known (in italics) and the meaning in English (in inverted commas, if appropriate); names shown in bold are those given on the 6" Ordnance Survey maps, and those in semibold in square brackets are from the Ordnance Survey Discovery maps (1:50,000 scale).

Oonarontia (*Uaimh na Róinte* – "Cave of the Seals") near Portally cove

DROMINA: *Drom Eidhne* – "Ivy Ridge"
[**Newtown Head** – *Ceann an Bhaile Nua*]; **Carrickvara**: *Carraig an Bharraigh* – "Barry's Rock"; "The Pollock Rock".

KNOCKAVELISH or KNOCKAVEELISH: *Cnoc Mhílis* – "Myles' Hill"
Woodstown Strand (*Trá Mhílis*); "The Short Head" (as opposed to Creadan or the Long Head); *An Ché Frainnceach* – "The French Quay".

FORNAGHT: *Fórnacht* – "Completely Bare (Hill)"
Cúilín na Trá – "Garden of the Strand".

CREADAN: *Ceann Chníodáin* or *Ceann Chríodáin* (meaning unknown)
Forty Steps; **The Packs**; **Clashrory**: *Clais Ruairí* – "Rory's Trench"; **Creadan Cove**; **Green Cove**; **Ardnamult**: *Ard na Molt* – "High Place of the Wethers"; *Tobar Pocáide* – "Ulcer Well".

DUNMORE: *Dún Mór* – "Great Fort"
Foilakipeen: *Faill an Chipín* – "Cliff of the Broken Piece of Stick"; **Laweesh**: *Láimhís*; **Cathedral Rocks**; *Poll Dubh* – "Black Hole"; **Counsellor's Strand**; **Dunmore Strand**; **Carrickea** (or Carriglea) or "Goosey's Rock"; **Ladies' Cove**; **Poulnaleenta**: *Poll na Líonta* – "Hole of the Nets"; **Badger's Cove**; **Stony Cove**; **Shanooan** (or Shanoon): *Sean Uaimh* – "Old Cave"; **Black Knob**; **Oonagollum**: *Uaimh na gColm* – "Pigeons' Cave"; **Oonagh**: *Uaimh an Eich* – "The Horse's Cave"; **Flat Rocks**.

COXTOWN: *Coilleach* – "Woody Place" or *Coileach* – "Cock"
Uaimh Ráithe – "Cave of the Rath"; "Aby's Folly" (a path down the cliff); *Uaimh na Scadán* – "Cave of the Herrings"; *Port Sruthán* – "Haven of the Little Stream";

Old ship's rock & old ship's cove, west of Dunmore East

Robin Red Breast Rock; **Red Head**; *Uaimh an Ghaibhlín* – "Cave of the Little Estuary"; **Portnasrughaun**: *Port Sruthán* – "Haven of the Stream"; **Pusnahooan**: *Pus na hUamha* – "Lip of the Cave"; **Bishop's Cave**; **Oonarontia**: *Uaimh na Rónta* – "Cave of the Seals"; **Polladurrish**: *Poll an Dorais* – "Hole (or Pool) of the Door".

PORTALLY: Port Fhalla [*Port Ailigh*] – "Haven of the Parapet all" *Poll a' tSéine* – "Hole of the Seine Net"; *Cuan Phort-Fhalla* – "Portally Cove"; *Poll Uí Cheagadáin* – "O'Ceagadan's (Cadogan's) Pool"; *Faill na gCaorach* – "Cliff of the Sheep"; *Leac na bhFear* – "Flagstone of the Men"; *Uaimh Dhubh* – "Black Cave".

RATHMOYLAN: *Ráth Mhaoláin* – "Maolan's Fort"
Stony Cove; *Poll an Ghuail* – "Coal Hole"; *Faillscirt* – "Cloven (?) Cliff";

Carraig Fhaillscirte – "Rock of the Cloven Cliff"; *Port Seiche* – "Haven of the Hide"; *Uaimh Mhionnáin* – "Cave of the Crown"; *Gearr Uaimh* – "Short Cave"; **Green Cave**; *Glas Uamha* – "Green Caves"; **Rathmoylan Cave**; **Old Ship's Cove & Rock**; *Sean Long* – "Old Ship"; **Swines Head**; **Falskirt Rock**; *Port Ghreanaí* – "Gravel Haven"; Uaimh an Róin – "Seal Cave"; *Uaimh na Méighleach* – "Cave of the Bleating"; *Uaimh Dhubh* – "Black Cave"; **Rathmoylan Cove**.

BALLYMACAW: *Baile Mhic Dháith* – "MacDavid's Town (or Homestead)"
Portaclea: *Port an Chlaí* – "Haven of the Earthen Fence"; **Ouremma**; **Portavodda**: *Port an Mhaide* – "Haven of the Stick (Piece of Timber)"; **Flat Rock**; *Cuan Bhaile Mhic Dháith* – "**Ballymacaw Cove**"; *Carraig na mBád* – "Boats' Rock"; *An Seomra* – "The Chamber"; *Faill Fhada* – "Long Cliff"; *Uaimh an Iarainn* – "Cave of the Iron"; **Portnagowna**: *Port na Gowna* – "Haven of the Goats"; **Goats Cove**.

CORBALLY: *Corr an Bhaile* – "Point (Peak) of the Homestead"
Uaimh an Chasáin – "Cave of the Pathway"; "Palm Oil Hole"; "Flour Hole"; **Beenlea Head** (or Benlea Head): *Beann Liath* – "Grey Headland"; **Cloonliamgowel**: *Cuan Liam Gallda* – "Harbour of William the Foreigner"; **Coolum**: *Cúl Lom* – "Bare Ridge Back".

BROWNSTOWN: *Baile an Bhrúnaigh* – "Brown's Homestead"
Portalaun: *Port Oileáin* – "Island Haven"; **Beengarvoge**: *Binn Garbhóige* – "Wild Mustard Headland"; **Brazen Head**; **Foilnagurk**: *Faill na gCorc* – "Cliff of the Corks"; *Poll na gCorc* –

"Pool of the Corks"; **Poulhoulen**; Poll Howlett; **Sruhnaleam**: *Sruth na Léim* – "Stream of the Waterfalls"; **Carrigaunboy**: *Carraigín Buí* – "Little Yellow Rock"; *Scoilt an Chinn Aird* – "Cleft of the High Head" (the extreme point underneath the southwest tower); **Foilnaracka**: *Faill na Raice* – "Cliff of the Wreck"; **Portoonaka**: *Port Uaithne* – "Green Haven"; **Pouljoe** and Poulhardy (from the men named who lost their lives there?); **Portoonakabeg**: *Port Uaithne Beag* – "Little Green Haven"; **Clashlacky**: *Clais Leacaí* – "Flaggy Trench"; **Portteige**: *Pointe Thaidhg* – "Taidhg's Point"; **Cooneenclogher**: *Cuainín Cluthair* – "Little Cosy Cove"; **Bar Rock**; **Rinnashark**: *Rinn na Searc* – "Headland of the Sharks"; **Muscle Bank**; **Bass Point**: *Pointe na mBairs* – "Point of the Bass"; **Rabbit Burrow**; **Saleen Strand**; *An Rúisc*; *Glugar* – "A Gurgling Sound"; *Faill a' Mhadra* – "Cliff of the Wolf (or Dog)"; *Poll Suingean* – "St. John's Hollow"; *Sean Tuinne* – "Blow Hole"; *Trá Bheag* – "Little Strand"; *Cloch Liath* – "Grey Rock"; *Cuainín an Fhíona* – "Little Cove of the Wine"; *Faill na Scean* – "Cliff of the Knives"; Fouhnalium; *Leac an Éisc* – "Flagstone of the Fish"; *Poll Faoite* – "White's Pool"; *Cionn Liath Buí* – "Yellow Grey Head"; *Scoilt an Duilisc* – "Cleft of the Duileasc".

TRAMORE BURROW: *An Dhaibhche* – "The Sandhill"
 The Cush: *An Chois* – "The Place Lying-adjacent-to (the Sandhill)";
 Slate Point: *Pointe na Slinne* – "Point of the Slates"; **Knockaunriark**: *Cnocán an Radhairc* – "Little Hill of the View or Lookout"; **Tramore Burrow**; **Rabbit Warren**; *Garraí an Gormógaigh* "Gormog's Garden" (Gormog, or Gormogach, is a spirit which reputedly lives in the Sandhills at Tramore); **Windgap** – *Bearna na Gaoithe*.

TRAMORE: *Trá Mór* – "Great Strand"
 An Splinneín – "The High Projecting Cliff".

NEWTOWN: *Baile Nua*
 Lady Doneraile's Cove; **Lady Elizabeth's Cove**; **Carrigaghalia**: *Carraigín Liath* – "Little Grey Rock"; **Fish Cove**: *Uaimh an Éisc* – "Fish Cove"; **Newtown Cove**: *Gleann na mBád* – "Boat Glen"; **Oodonagha**: *Uaimh Dhonnchaidh* – "Denis's Cave"; *Uaimh an Phoill* – "Cave of the Hole"; Oonacomalee: *Uaimh na nGammal* – "The Simpletons' Cave"; Tranaparkeen: *Trá na mBáircíní* – "Strand of the Boats"; **Lady's Cove**: *Gleann a' Chuain* – "Glen of the Haven".

WESTTOWN
 Faill Chlaí na Teorann – "Cliff of the Boundary Fence"; **Oonagappul**: *Uaimh na gCapall* – "Cave of the Horses"; **Chair Cove**; **The Chair** – *An Chathaoir*; **Oyen Rock**; *Ceann an Róin* – "Seal's Head" (the point on which the three pillars stand including the Metal Man, beneath which is a cave with two arched entrances, called *Uaimh an tSolais* & *Uaimh na nÉan* – "Cave of the Light" & "Cave of the Birds"); **The Stags**; **Ronan's Bay**: *Trá Rónáin* – "Ronayne's Strand"; **Little Island**; **Twelve Birds**; **Hanrahan's Rock** (from the man killed by a fall there while gathering seabird's eggs); **Illaunglas**: *Oileán Glas* – "Gray-Green Island"; *An Gáirdín* – "The Garden"; **Great Island**; *Muirbheach na nGamhan* – "Sandy Beach of the Calves"; *Trá an Ghaibhlín* – "Strand of the Little Inlet"; "Waterspout"; *Trá na nÉadála* – "Strand of the Treasure Trove (from Wrecks)"; *Port* – "Embankment"; *Poll na Circe* – "Deep Place of the Hen"; *Poll an Róin* – "Cave of the Seal"; *Poll na Raice* – "Hole of the Wreck"; *Faill an Tairbh Mhóir* – "Great Bull Cliff" & *Faill an Tairbh Bhig* – "Little Bull Cliff".

GARRARUS: *Garbh Ros* – "Rough Shrubbery" *Carraig an Bharraigh* – "Barry's Rock" (on the east side of Garrarus Strand); **Illaunacoltia**: *Oileán an Choite* – "Island of the Skiff"; *Cuan na mBan nUasal* – "**Ladies' Cove**"; *Rinn Chaol* – "Narrow Headland"; *Cuainín an Mhúin* – "Little Haven of the Putrid Water". [**Burke's Rock**].

ISLANDIKANE: *Oileán Uí Chéin* – "O'Kane's Island" **Boat Strand**: *Trá na mBád*; **Carrickanine**; **Sheep Island**: (there are two islands: the innermost is *Oileán na gCaorach* – "Island of the Sheep" and the outer is *Oileán na bhFranncach* – "Island of the Frenchmen" or "of the Rats"); **Eagle Rock**: *Carraig an Iolair;* **Black Door**: *Doras Dubh*; *Poll an Tobac* – "Tobacco Hole"; *Trá an Chomhartha* – "Strand of the Mark"; *Oileán de Búrca* – "Burke's Island".

KILFARRASY: *Cill Fhearghusa* – "Church of Fergus" **Yellow Rock**: *Carraig Bhuí*; *Gleann Liath* – "Grey Glen"; **Kilfarrasy Island**.

WHITEFIELD: *Bán na bhFaoiteach* – "Field of the Whites" **Hawk's Cliff**: *Faill an tSeabhaic*; *Sean Shráid* – "Old Village"; *Faill na Muc* – "Cliff of the Pigs"; *Trá Larry an Ghabhar* – "Strand of Larry-the-Goat".

ANNESTOWN: *Bun Abha* – "River Mouth" **Green Island; Carrickadurrish**: *Carraig an Dorais* – "Rock of the Door". [**Corcoran's Island; Carriginnyamos Rocks**].

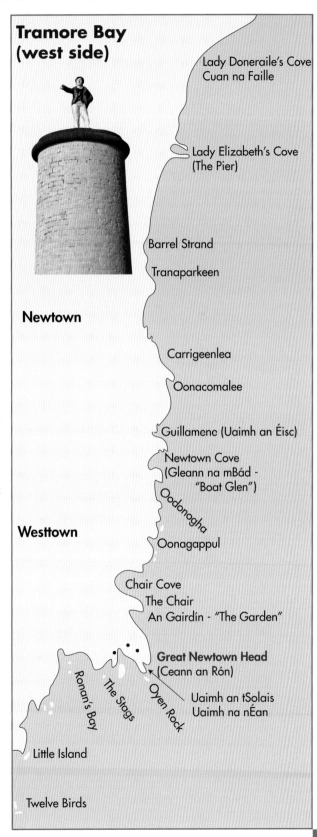

Tramore Bay (west side)

Lady Doneraile's Cove
Cuan na Faille

Lady Elizabeth's Cove
(The Pier)

Barrel Strand

Tranaparkeen

Newtown

Carrigeenlea

Oonacomalee

Guillamene (Uaimh an Éisc)

Newtown Cove
(Gleann na mBád - "Boat Glen")

Oodonogha

Westtown

Oonagappul

Chair Cove
The Chair
An Gairdín - "The Garden"

Great Newtown Head
(Ceann an Rón)

Ronan's Bay

The Stags

Oyen Rock

Uaimh an tSolais
Uaimh na nÉan

Little Island

Twelve Birds

Yellow rock (*Carraig Bhuí*) west of Kilfarrasy, from the yellow lichens that grow on it

BENVOY: *Beinn Bhuí* – "Yellow Peak", also known as *Cnocán Rua* – "Little Red Hill"
Morageeha: *Móradh Gaoithe* – "Increasing (rising) of Wind?"; **Carricknamusty** (or
Carrignanusly) **Rocks**: *Carraig na Murailí* – "Rock of the Mussels"; *Carraig Fhada* – **Long
Rock**; *An Rinn* – "The Headland"; *Faill an Aitinn* – "Cliff of the Furze"; *Trá Leathan* –
"Wide Strand".

KNOCKANE: *Cnocán* – "Little Hill"
Stookeen Rock: *Carraig an Stuaicín* – "Rock of the Stook (Pyramid)"; *Trá an Chnoicín* –
Knockane Strand.

DUNABRATTIN: *Dún na mBreatan* – "Fort of the Britons" (the 'Fort' is the entrenched headland).
[**Carrigaseeach**]; **Carrickyready Rocks**: *Carraig Uí Riada* – "O'Reidy's Rock"; [**Illaunglass**];
[**Carrigaddas**]; *An Príosún* – "The Prison"; "Boatstrand" – *Trá an Bháid*; *Trá an Phoirtín* –
"Little Bank Strand"; *Trá Míde Óigh* – "Ita, the Virgin's Strand"; *Cnocán Ó gCeallach* –
"O'Kelly's Little Hill"; *Bán na Spioraide* – "Field of the Ghost"; **The Goul Cave**.

KILMURRIN: *Cill Mhuirín* – "Muirne's Church"
Reiligeach – "Early Church Site"; *Gort an
tSagairt* – "Priest's Garden"; **Foilnacartan**: *Faill
na Ceárta* – "The Forge Cliff"; *Poll an Róin* –
"Seal Hole"; "Na Cribbies" (?); *Faill an Chuain*
– "Cliff of the Haven"; St. Muirne's Cave.

TANKARDSTOWN: *Bóithrín na Muice* – "Little
Road of the Pig"
[**Captain's Rock**]; **Carrickadda Rock**: *Carraig
Fhada* – "Long Rock"; **Foilboy**: *Faill Bhuí* –
"Yellow Cliff"; **Foilaneena Cashel** (*& **Cove**):

High cliffs near Ballyvoyle Head

326

St. John's Island, just east of Ballydowane cove

Caisleán Faille an Fhíona – "Wine Cliff Castle"; *Carraig na Coiscéime* – "Stepping Rock";
Drumcappul: *Drom Capaill* – "Horse Ridge"; **Drumboe**: *Drom Bó* – "Cow Ridge"; *An Ceallachán* (?); *Tobar na gCat* – "The Cats' Well".

KNOCKMAHON: *Cnoc Machan* – "Hill of the Mahon"
    Casaunnagreana: *Casán na Gréine* – "Sunny Path"; *Sáilín* – "Remnant (of land)";
Cúilín –"Little Corner"; Mt. Eyre Strand and Stage Strand; *Faill na Lice* – "Cliff of the Flagstone"; *Faichín na nUan* – "Little Green of the Lambs".

TEMPLEYVRICK: *Teampall Uí Bhric* – "O'Bric's Church"
    Bunmahon: *Bun Machan* – "Mouth of the River Mahon". **Trawnamoe**: *Trá na mBó* – "The Cows' Strand"; **Trawnastrella**: *Trá na Streille* – "Strand of the Wailing" or "of the Splash"; **Gull Island**; **Shag Island**: *Oileán na Seagaí*.

BALLYNARRID: *Baile Nairid* – "Norwood's Homestead"
    Slippery Island: Oileán Sleamhain; **Foilnaglogh**: *Faill na gCloch* – "Cliff of the Stones"; **Wine Cliff**: *Faill an Fhíona*; **Templeobrick**; **Drumcappul**: *Drom Capaill* – "Horse's Ridge"; **Dane's Island** or **Illaunabrick**: *Oileán Uí Bhric* – "O'Bric's Island"; **Rinnamoe**: *Rinn na mBó* – "Headland of the Cows".

BALLYDOWANE: *Baile Uí Dhubháin* – "Duane's Homestead"
    Cooneenacarton: *Cuainín na Ceárta* – "Little Cove of the Forge"; **St. John's Island**: *Oileán Sheáin* – "John's Island"; **Poulatunish**; *Faill an Phlúir* – "Cliff of the Flour"; *Stalca* – "Something Stiff and Solid".

BALLYVOONEY: *Baile Uí Mhúimhnigh* – "O'Mooney's Homestead"
    Lady's Cove; *Cuainín Dhonnchaidh* – "Denis' Little Harbour"; *Faill na Croiche* – "Cliff of the Crane"; *Faill an tSagairt* – "Priest's Cliff"; *Faill na Raice* – "Wreck Cliff";

Cúilín na Hogiséad – "Little Corner of the Hogsheads"; **Boat Harbour**; **Gull Island**: *Oileán na bhFaoileán*.

STRADBALLY: *An Sráid Bhaile* – "The Street Town"
   Plateen: *Plaitín* – "The Scalp"?; **Blind Cove** – *An Cuan Caoch*; *Faill an Airgid* – "Cliff of the Silver"; *Faill na Smuite* – "Cliff of the Snout"; *Faill na dTéad* – "Cliff of the Ropes"; *Faill an Chaca* – "Cliff of the Ordure"; *Faill na Lice* – "Cliff of the Flagstone"; *Srón Seons* – "Jones' Nose"; *Carraig an Chomhartha* – "Rock of the Mark (or Sign)"; *Faill an Sconnsa* – "Earthwork Crowned Cliff"; **Gulls Island**.

ISLAND: *Sean Oileán* – "Old Island"

ISLAND HUBBOCK: *Oileán hObuc* – "Hobuck's Island"
   Faill Ghairid – "Short Cliff"; *Stuaic na bPocán* – "Rock Cone of the He-Goats"; *Bord an Rí* – "The King's Table".

BALLYVOYLE: *Baile Uí Bhaoill* – "O'Boyle's Homestead"

Murdoch Mackenzie's 1764 survey uses Ballinawith Head while Vallancey's 1785 map uses Ballynahinch Head for Ballyvoyle Head

   Poll na 'madán – "Fool's Hole"; *Carraig an Dorais* – "Rock of the Door"; *Buille Chlaíomh* – "Sword Cut"; *Poll an Tobac* – "Tobacco Hole"; *Faill an Tobair* – "Well Cliff".

CLONEA: *Cluain Fhia* – "Meadow of the Deer"

BALLYNACOURTY: *Baile na Cúirte* – "Homestead of the Court (Mansion)"
   Carrignamoan; **Carricknagaddy**; [**Wyse's Point**]; *Carraig Stronng* – "Strong's Rock"; *Cuan na mBan* – "Women's Cove"; *Pointe na Rannaidí* or *Pointe na Reanna Duibhe*; *Carraig an tSúsa* – "Rock of the Blanket"; *Carraig na bhFranncach* – "Rock of the Frenchmen"; *Clocha Liatha* – "Grey Rocks"; *Sean Thine Aoil* – "Old Limekiln"; *Cuan na Scartóige* – "Haven of the Little Waterspout"; *Carraig Bhreach* – "Speckled Rock"; *Carraig Fhada* – "Long Rock"; *Carraig Mhór* – "Great Rock"; *Carraig an Chaipín* – "Little Cap Rock"; *Carraig na dTurcach* – "Rock of the Turks"; *Baile an Aird* – "Homestead of the Height"; *Baile an Chlampair* – "Homestead of the Dispute" (or "of the Quarrel"); *Baile an Chuaichín* – "Little Cuckoo Homestead"; *An Cnoicín* – "The Little Hill"; [**Deadman's Sand**].

CARRIGEEN: *Carraigín* – "Little Rock"

CUNNIGAR: *Coinigéar* – "Rabbit Warren", also called "*An Cois*"
   [**Whitehouse Bank** – *Banc an Tí Ghil*].

BALLYNAGOUL: *Baile na nGall* – "Homestead of the Foreigners"; [the Ordnance Survey maps use Ballynagaul]
   Carraig Áilis nó Carraig Áil Lois (?) – "The Rock of the Baby Foxes"; *Carraig Shéarlais* – "Charles' Rock"; *Cúil an Ché* – "The Quay Nook"; *Trá* – "Strand".

BALLYREILLY: *Baile Uí Raghallaigh* – "O'Reilly's Homestead"
   Na Ráithíní – "The Flint Rocks"; [**The Gaynors**]: *Na Gaibhnthe* – "The Smiths (?)"; *Gaibhlín an tSolais* – "Sea Pool of the (phosphorescent) Light"; *Carraig an Mhadra* – "The Dog's (Wolf's) Rock".

An Chabha, Ceann Heilbhic

HELVICK: *Heilbhic* – meaning unknown (Scandinavian?)

> *Pointe an Phréacháin* – "**Crow's Point**"; *Carraig an Oileáin* – "The Island Rock"; *An Sonnta* – "Sound"?; *Carraig Chlúmháin* – "Plumage Rock"; *Poll Tí an Chabha* – "Cave House Hole"; *An Cabha* – "The Cove"; *Faill an Phíobaire* – "**Piper's Cliff**"; *Faill an Ghunna Mhóir* – "Great Gun Cliff"; *Gualainn an Weatherach*; *Faill an Chairéil* – "The Quarry Cliff"; *Faill an Draighnín* – "Cliff of the Blackthorn"; *An Strapa* – "The Stile"; *Faill an tSaighdiúra* – "The Soldier's Cliff"; *Faill an Chlára* – "Flat Faced Cliff"; *Cuan na gCorrán* – "Haven of the Reaping Hooks"; *Cuan Reidhrí* – "Rory's Haven"; *Ceann an Bhathlaigh* – "Clown's Head"(?); *Na Corráin* – "Sharp-pointed Rocks"; *Cúilín Antoine* – "Antony's Little Nook"; *Carraig an Tabhair (nó tSabhair)*?; *Carraig Dhubh* – "Black Rock"; *Carraig Bhalldair*; *Carraig an Scamaill* – "Rock of the Shadow"; *Carraig na bPotaí* – "Rock of the (Lobster) Pots"; *Carraig an Díle* – "Rock of the Water-Drip"?; *Carraig an Draighnín* – "Blackthorn Rock"; *Carraig Bhréan* – "Stinking Rock"; *Carraig Ghéar* – "Sharp Rock"; *Carraig Fhada* – "Long Rock"; *Carraig Eibhlín Chríona* – "Old Ellen's Rock"; *Carraig Sheáin Uí Chorráin* – "John O'Carey's Rock"; *Carraig an Choiscéim* – "Stepping Rock"; *Carraig na nEascon* – "Rock of the Eels"; *Na Bioránaigh* – "Sharp-pointed Rocks"; *Na Crainn* – "The Trees"; *Faill an Úachair (or Uchaire* – "Spawn"?); *Carraig na mBioránach* – "Rock of the Spratts"; *Carraig na mBan* – "Rock of the Women"; *Carraig na nGadaí* – "Rock of the Robbers"; **Muggort's Bay** – *An Mheadh.*

KILLINOORIN: *Cill an Fhuarthainn* – "The Cold Spring"

> *Linn Bhuí* – "Yellow Pool"; *Faill na gCaorach* – "Sheep Cliff"; *Faill an Uisce* – "Water Cliff"; *Faill an Stáicín* – "Little Stack Cliff".

Other Ring cliff names: *Poll an Tobac* – "Tobacco Hole"; *An Poll Dorcha* – "The Dark Hole"; *Carraig an Chrúibín*; *Gualainn an Phríorsúin*; *Faill an Iomair*; *Gaibhlín na Brúine* – "Browne's Sea Inlet"; *Poll an tSéideáin* – "Hole of the Blowing (Wind)"; *Cloch an tSasanaigh* – "Stone of the Englishman"; *Carraig na Seagaithe* – "Rock of the Cormorants"; *Géim an*

Cliffs on the south side of Helvick Head.
Helvick, although its precise meaning isn't known, is probably old Norse [vik = bay]; it, and
possibly Baile na nGall, offers good placename evidence for a Viking presence on the Waterford coast

Chapaill; An Gearrán Dubh; Leac an Áir – "Flagstone of the Storm"; *Drom an Chapaill nó Drom Capaill* – "Horse's Ridge"; *Faill an Ghlais; Séipéal Charraig an Mhadra; Faill Ifrinn.*

RATHNAMENEENAGH: *Ráth na mBiríneach* (now *Miníneach*) – "Rath of the Coarse Grass (or Sedge)"
Carrickbrean: *Carraig Bhréan* – "Stinking Rock".

BALLYCURREEN: *Baile Uí Churraoin* – "Curran's Homestead"
Faill na Bó – "Cliff of the Cow"; *Faill na Muc* – "The Pigs' Cliff"; *Faill na Luinge* – "Cliff of the Ship"; *An Gleann* – "The Glen"; *Faill na Buinní* – "Cliff of the Water Gush".

BALLYNAMONA: *Baile na Móna* – "Homestead of the Bog"
Poll Rua – "Red Hole (Cavern)"; *Páirc na dTurcach* – "Field of the Turks (or Turkeys)"; *Tigh Chaille Bhéara* – "Caille Beara's House" (the court cairn at Ballynamona); *Faill an Ghlíntín* – "Cliff of the Streamlet". [**Carraignanean**: *Carraig na nÉan* – "Rock of the Birds"]; [*An Ghróig* – **The Rogue**].

MONAGOUSH: *Móin an Ghiúis* – "Bog of the Fir"
Mine Head: *Mian Ard* – "High Mine", (from mines formerly worked by the Earl of Cork).

BALLYNAHARDA: *Baile na hArda* – "Homestead of the Height (Ridge)"
Boat Harbour; *Faill an Chnoic Rua* – "Cliff of the Red Hill"; *Cabhar an Ime* – "The Butter Causeway"; *Rinn an Oileáin* – "The Island Point"; *Faill an Ghabhair* – "The Goat's Cliff"; *Faill an Ghlíntín* – "Cliff of the Streamlet".

BALLYKILMURRY: *Baile Mhic Giolla Mhuire* – "MacGillemory's Homestead"
Faill an Uisce – "The Water Cliff"; *Faill na gCaorach* – "Cliff of the Sheep"; *An Bruachán* – "The Little Bank (or Border)"; *Carraig na Rónta* – "The Seals Rock"; [**Longship Rock**].

Cliffs near Ballynamona and *Carraig na nÉan*

BALLYMACART: *Baile Mhac Airt* – "MacArt's Homestead"
  Gleann Anna – "Anne's Glen" and *Gleann an Aifrinn* – "Mass Glen"; *An Tulach* – "The Eminence"; *Cuan (agus Faill) Bhaile Mhac Airt* – "Harbour (and Cliff) of Ballymacart"; *Soc Dubh* – "Black Ploughshare"; *Faill na gCaorach* – "Sheep Cliff"; *Cumar* – "Confluence (of Streams)"; *Faill na gCoiníní* – "The Rabbits' Cliff"; *Faill na mBuíochán* – "Cliff of the Primroses"; *An Bhréanlach (Breaccach)* – "Cliff of the Fetid Seaweed".

CROBALLY: *Crua Bhaile* – "Stiff-soiled Townland"
  Faill Dhearg – "Red Cliff"; *Cois Druide* – "Foot of the Starling"; *Carraig an Deargáin* – "Rock of the Bream"; *Gaibhlín Bréan* – "Stinking Narrow Sea Inlet"; *Faill an Fhíona* – "The Wine Cliff"; *Cois an Oileáin* – "(place) Beside the Island"; *An Cumar* – "The Confluence (or 'Valley')"; *Carraig na Seagaí* – "Rock of the Cormorants"; *An Cúlaim* – "A Haven?"; *Béal an Chuain* – "Mouth of the Haven"; *Faill an Aitinn* – "The Furze Cliff"; *Faill Dhúngarbhán* – "Dungarvan's Cliff"; *Faill Ifrinn* – "Hell's Cliff"; *Faill na mBreallán* – "Cliff of the Shellfish"; *Cúil Bhréan* – "Stinking Corner".

BALLYEELINAN: *Baile Uí Iarnáin* – "O'Hiarnan's Homestead"
  Faill an Mhadra Rua – "The Fox's Cliff"; *Léim Bheag agus Léim Mhór* – "Little Leap" and "Great Leap"; *Faill Sheáin Mháire* – "Cliff of John (son) of Mary"; *An Cuainín* – "The Little Haven"; *Gaibhlín an Bhlaincéid* – "Little Creek of the Blanket"; *Faill an Uisce* – "The Water Cliff"; *Cuas na Lárach Báine* – "The White Mare's Cave"; **Glencorran**.

DYSERT: *Díseart* – "Hermitage"
  Black Rock; **Portnamaud**: *Port na mBád* – "Boat Haven"; **Ardmore Head**; **Ram Head**: *Carraig* (also *Ceann*) *an Ráma* (meaning unknown); **Coolabeg**: *Cúlaim Beag* – "A Little Haven?" and **Coolamore**: *Cúlaim Mór* – "A Big Haven?"; *Leac na gCánóg* – "Flagstone of the Puffins"; *Faill na Daraí* – "Cliff of the Oak Tree"; *Faiche Mhór* – "Great Plain" (or *Fathach*

Mór? – "Great Giant", a huge cliff); **Tea Flag**: *Leac an Té* – "Flagstone of the Tea"; *Droichidín* – "Little Bridge"; *Cúil an Chaisleáin* – "Castle Corner"; *Carraig Liath* – "Grey Rock"; *Lónáin* – "Lonan's Flagstone"; *Faill na Slinneacha* – "Cliff of the Slaty Places"; *Pointe Mhic Raghallaigh* – "Mac Raghailigh's Point"; *Faill na Méaróg* – "Cliff of the Pebbles" or "Finger-post".

ARDOCHEASTY: *Ard Uí Shéasta* – "O'Cheasty's Height"
Poulnagat: *Poll (agus Faill) na gCat* – "Cave (and "Cliff") of the Wild Cats"; *Leaca Dhóite* – "Burned Glen Slope"; *Páirc na Scolb* – "Field of the Splinters (or skewers for thatching)"; *Faill an Duilisc* – "Cliff of the Edible Seaweed".

ARDOGINNA: *Ard Ó gCionáith* – "O'Kinny's or Kenna's Height"
Gleann Phiarais – "Pierce's Glen"; *Faill na nGairdíní* – "Cliff of the Gardens"; *Gaibhlín an Phuith (?)* – "Narrow Sea Inlet of the Wind Gust"; *Carraig Fhada* – "Long Rock"; *Gaibhlín an Chubhair* – "Sea Inlet of the Froth"; *Faill an Mhadra Rua* – "The Fox's Cliff"; *Cois Céim* – "Stepping Stone"; *Cúil an Ghearráin* – "The Old Horse's Corner"; *Falla Bán* – "White Wall"; *Faill na bPréachán* – "Crows' Cliff"; *Pointe an tSeaga* – "The Cormorant's Point"; *Faill na Bó* – "The Cow's Cliff"; *Poll na Gaoithe* – "Windy Cavern"; *Gaibhlín na Mealbhóg* – "Narrow Sea Inlet of the Pouches"; *Faill an Iarrainn* – "Iron Cliff"; *Faill na gCaorach* – "Sheeps' Cliff"; *Gleann Beag* – "Little Glen"; *Gabhlín an tSeaga* – "Narrow Sea Inlet of the Cormorant"; *Cloch (nó Croch) an Oidhre* – "The Heir's (or Gallows) Rock"; *Faill Fhada* – "Long Cliff"; *Carraig an tSasanaigh* – "The Englishman's Rock"; *Clais na mBolamán* – "Trench of the Shad (Horse Mackerel)"; *Oileán na nGabhar* – **Goat Island**; *Gaibhlín an tSagairt* – "The Priest's Little Sea Inlet"; *Gort an Dúinín* – "Garden of the Little Fort"; *Carraig Uí Bhric* – "O'Bric's Rock"; *Carraig Bhuí* – "Yellow Rock"; *Carraig an Mhadra* – "Rock of the Dog (Wolf)"; *An Lochtaigh* – "Cliff of the Ledges"; *Carraig Philib* – "Philip's Rock"; *Faill an Leanmhanaigh* – "Cliff of the Pursuer"; *Faill na Cuaille Seasaimh* – "Cliff of the Standing Pole"; *Faill an Reithe* – "Cliff of the Ram"; *Faill na mBioránach* – "Cliff of the Sprats" or "Sharp-pointed Rocks".

Whiting Bay (not an Irish name).
Canon Power states that *Béal Abha* ("River Mouth") is the local name for the strand at Whiting Bay and the land inland from it; he also states that locals believed that the river Blackwater once flowed into the sea here

332

BALLYSALLAGH: *Baile Saileach* – "Willow Abounding Homestead"
  Whiting Bay; *An Charraigín* – "The Little Rock"; *Cloch Laith* – "Grey Rock"; *Carraig Dhubh* – "Black Rock"; *Faill Bhuí* – "Yellow Cliff"; *Gaibhlín na Leathóg* – "Sea Inlet of the Plaice".

MONATRAY: *Móin Oitreach* – "Rough or Uneven Bogs" or "Otter's Bog"
  [**Cabin Point; Caliso Bay; Blackball Head**]; **East Point**; *Cuainín* – "Little Cove"; Gleann Beag – "Little Glen"; *Gaibhlín na mBollaí* – "Creek of the Bowls"; *Cuainín Roibeáird* – "Robert's Cove"; *Carraig na Pollóige* – "Pollock Rock"; *Faill an Chapaill* – "The Horse's Cliff"; *Geal Trá* – "Bright (White) Strand"; *Gaibhlín hArtaigh* – "Harty's Sea Inlet"; Gheárd – "Yard"; *Tobhar an Chuaille* – "Well of the Pole"; *Gaibhlín Glan* – "Clean Sea Inlet"; *Nead an Naoi* – "The Babe's Resting Place (Nest)"; *Carraig an Stolla* – "Standing Rock"; *Carraig Láir na Trá* – "Middle Rock of the Strand"; *Inse Uí Fhlaithbheartaigh* – "O'Flaherty's Island" ("Calasoe Bay"); *Poll Bréan* – "Stinking Hole"; *Tráighín Bheag* – "Little Strand"; *Poll na gCág* – "Cave of the Choughs"; *Barra na Rinne* – "The Headland Summit"; *Béardí na Rinne*(?); Casán an Mhadra – "The Dog's Path"; *Poll an Ghuail* – "Coal Hole"; *An Gaibhlín* – "The Sea Inlet"; *Gaibhlín Buí* – "Yellow Sea Inlet" ("Carty's Cove"); *Tobar Udhachta* – "Well of Will (Penance)". **Ferry Point**.

Additional coastal placenames from *Logainmneacha as Paróiste na Rinne*

Na Pointí Jake – "Jakes's Point"; *Poill Ghort na Daibhche* – "Hole of the Garden of the Cauldron (or Hogshead)"; *An Sciorlóg*; *Banc na Gibiní (nGiminí)* – "Gibbons's Bank"; *Poinnte na Coise* – "Point of the Cush"; *Cloch an Diúic* – "The Duke's Stone"; *Gaibhlín an Diúic* – "The Duke's Sea Inlet"; *Teampall Réamainn* – "Reamon's Temple"; *Cloch an Freak* – "Freak's Stone"; *Clocha Chineá* – "Kenny's Stones"; *Faill na Scoinne*; *An Com (Cam?)* – "The Curve (Hollow?)"; *Poll an Phúca* – "The Pooka's Hole"; *An Chora* – "The Weir"; *An C(h)omair*; *Róidín Dheain*; *Róidín na Binne* – "Little Road of the Point"; *Gualainn na Binne* – "Shoulder of the Point"; *Róidín na gCapall* – "Little Road of the Horses"; *An Scarbhach* – "Overgrown or Hard, Tough Place?"; *Cé Bhaile na nGall* – "Ballynagaul Quay"; *Trá Bhaile na nGall* – "Ballynagaul Strand"; *An Chlais* – "The Trench"; *Cúil an Fhíodóra* – "The Weaver's Corner"; *An Cloch Liath* – "The Grey Rock"; *Cúl Corráin* – "Corner of the Sharp-Pointed Rocks"; *An Cé Nua agus Cé Heilbhic* – "Helvick (New) Pier"; *Cúl an Choicís* – "Corner of the Fortnight"; *Poll an Óir* – "Hole of the Gold"; *Poll an Phúdair* – "Hole of the Powder"; *Ballán Tigh Chaba* – "Round Green Space of the Cove House"; *Tigh Cabha* – "Cove House"; *Carraigín Tigh Chabha* – "Little Rock of the Cove House"; *Carraig Chlúmháin* – "Plumage Rock"; *An Stáisiún* – "The Station"; *Ceann Helbhic nó An Ceann* – "Helvick Head", (also *Gob Heilbhic, Gob Talamh Heilbhic, Gob an Chinn, An Gob, Faill an Chinn, Ceann an Bhatla*); *Gualainn Heilbhic nó Gualainn an Chinn nó Gualainn an Bhatla* – "Helvick's Shoulder??"; *Tighín an Chinn* – "Little House at the Head"; *An tOileán Glas, Oileán Heilbhic, An tOileán, Carraig an Oileáin, Carraig na Fuinneoige, Na hOileáin Bheaga, Clocha an Oileáin* – [rocks and islands off Helvick Head, none of which are "The Gainers" as shown on the Ordnance Survey maps]; *Gualainn an Phríosúin* – "Prison Shoulder"; *Léim an Chapaill* – "The Horse's Leap"; *Faill an Ghunna Mhóir* – "Great Gun Cliff"; *An tOileán Briste* – "The Broken Island"; *An Cairéal* – "The Quarry"; *Poll na mBó* – "Hole of the Cows"; *Trá na mBó* – "The Cow's Strand"; *Oitir na Shrimps* – "Bank of the Shrimps"; *Carraig an Scamaill* – "Rock of the Shadow", (also *Gob Charraig an Scamaill, Sunnta Charraig an Scamaill*); *An Bhearna Dearg* – "The Red Gap"; *Séipéal Carraig an Mhadra*; *Carraig na Rón* – "Seal's Rock"; *Faill an Duine* –

"The Man's Cliff"; *Gaibhlín an tSolas* – "Sea Inlet of the Light"; *Faill agus Carraig na gCaoireach*; *An Poll Cam* – "Crooked Hole"; *An Cairéal Briste* – "The Broken Quarry"; *Carraig nó Carraigín nó Cloichín Shéarlais* – "Charles's (Little) Rock"; *Faill an Uisce* – "Water Cliff", *Cloichín Faill an Usice* – "Little Rock of the Water Cliff", *Trá Faill an Usice* – "Water Cliff Strand"; *Carraig na Croise* – "Rock of the Cross"; *Faill an Chrúibín* – "The Trotter's Cliff"; *Poll an Chapaill* – "Hole of the Horse"; *An (t)Umar* – "The Vessel or Trough", *Faill an Umair, Caipín an Umair, Cathaoir an Umair*; *Clais an Fhéir* – "Trench of the Grass"; *Léim Mhaitia(i)s* – "Matthew's Leap"; *An Charraig Caol* – "The Narrow Rock"; *An Staicín* – "The Little Stack", *Faill an Staicín*; *Carraig na Mairt* – "Rock of the Beef Cattle"; *Faill na Croise* – "Cliff of the Cross"; *Loistín Buí* – "Yellow Lodgings"; *Na Clocha Ramhra* – "Fat-lamb Rocks?"; *Binn an Chornáin* – "Peak of the Hemlock", *Carraig an Chomhra*; *Carraig an Draighnín* – "Rock of the Blackthorn"; *Cloch Mháire Éamainn* – "Mary Eamon's Stone"; *Gaibhlín na bPrataí* – "Sea Inlet of the Potatoes"; *Gaibhlín na nOrlach?* – "Sea Inlet of the Inch"; *An Carraig Fhada* –"The Long Rock"; *An Cúltrá* – "The Back Beach"; *An Charraig Ghéar* – "The Sharp Rock"; *Gaibhlín an Churraigh* – "Sea Inlet of the Wet Place"; *Binn nó Faill Shúilleabháin* – "Sullivan's Point or Cliff", *Binn na mBrón* – "Point of the Handmill or Mourning?", *Clocha Bhinn na mBrón*"; *Faill an Chailín* – "The Girl's Cliff"; *Tobair na gCailiní* – "The Girl's Well"; *Gaibhlín, Faill agus Poll na mBó* – "Sea Inlet, Cliff and Hole of the Cows"; *Léim Bheibhil* – "Beverley's Leap"; *Faill Briste* – "Broken Cliff"; *Gleann Bhúinne* – "Glen of the Torrent"; *Na Gaibhne* – "The Gaynors" are offshore rocks exposed at low tide, about 0.8 kilometres north of Helvick Head.

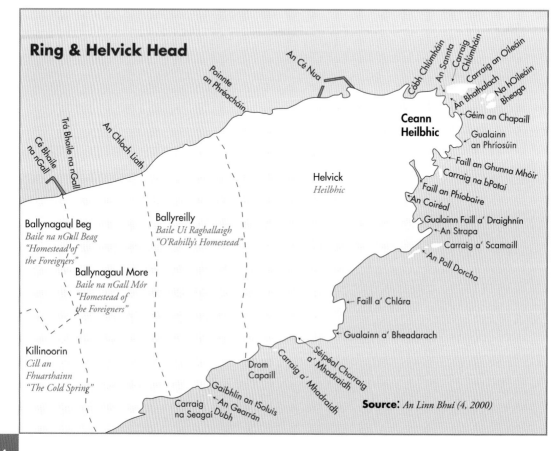

Ring & Helvick Head

Poinnte an Phréacháin
An Cé Nua
Cóbh Chlúmháin
An Sannta
Carraig Chlúmháin
Carraig an Oileáin
An Bhathalach
Na hOileáin Bheaga
Géim an Chapaill

Ceann Heilbhic

Gualainn an Phríosúin
Faill an Ghunna Mhóir
Carraig na bPotaí
Faill an Phíobaire
An Coiréal
Gualainn Faill a' Draighnín
An Strapa
Carraig a' Scamaill
An Poll Dorcha

Helvick
Heilbhic

An Chloch Liath

Trá Bhaile na nGall
Cé Bhaile na nGall

Ballyreilly
Baile Uí Raghallaigh
"O'Rahilly's Homestead"

Ballynagaul Beg
Baile na nGall Beag
"Homestead of the Foreigners"

Ballynagaul More
Baile na nGall Mór
"Homestead of the Foreigners"

Killinoorin
Cill an Fhuarthainn
"The Cold Spring"

Faill a' Chlára

Gualainn a' Bheadarach

Drom Capaill
Carraig a' Mhadraidh
Séipéal Charraig a' Mhadraidh
Gaibhlín an tSoluis
An Gearrán Dubh
Carraig na Seagaí

Source: *An Linn Bhuí (4, 2000)*

List of Species

Common mallow

Rock samphire at Ballyquin

Sea aster

Parmotrema perlata

Black-tailed godwit

Jackdaw

Starlings

Mammals, seals, turtles & basking sharks

Turnstone

Bordered gothic, Ballydowane
©P. M. Walsh

Worms

Bivalves & shells

Tree-mallow at Helvick

Ballydowane